PRENTICE HALL

INTRODUCTION TO
Culinary Arts

THE CULINARY INSTITUTE OF AMERICA®

Prentice Hall Staff

Editorial: Lois Ann Freier, Gary Schwartz

Design: Marianne Frasco, Linda Punskovsky

The text has been prepared with the assistance of Gleason Group, Inc. Norwalk, CT.

Project Manager: Gerald Gleason

Art Director/Developmental Editing: Pamela Ross

Writers: Mary Donovan, Kathy Baruffi,
   Stephen Eglinski, Julia Della Croce,
   Michael Buchman, Emily Kelting

CIA Reviewer: Chef David Kamen

Marketing: Patricia Schmid

Production: Ted Kechris

Photo Researcher: Margaret Otterstrum

Associate Editor: Marilyn Young

Copyeditor: Malinda McCain

Composition: PDS Associates; The Format Group, LLc

Additional Interior Design: Alicia Sullivan

DISCLAIMER AND SAFETY NOTICE

The user is expressly advised to consider and use all safety precautions described in this book or that might be indicated by undertaking the activities described in this book. Common sense must also be used to avoid all potential hazards and, in particular, to take relevant safety precautions concerning likely or known hazards involving food preparation, or in the use of the procedures described in this book. In addition, while many rules and safety precautions have been noted throughout the book, users should always have adult supervision and assistance when working in a kitchen or lab.

Any use of or reliance upon this book is at the user's own risk. While the information contained in this book has been compiled from sources believed to be reliable and correct at the time of original publication, neither the publisher nor the author makes any warranty, express or implied, with respect to the use of any techniques, suggestions, and ideas disclosed in this book. The publisher and author disclaim any and all liability for any damages of any kind or character, including without limitation any compensatory, incidental, direct or indirect, special, punitive, or consequential damages, loss of income or profit, loss of or damage to property or person, claims of third parties, or other losses of any kind or character arising out of or in connection with the use of this book or the accuracy of the information contained herein, even if the publisher or author has been advised of the possibility of such damages or losses.

Information in this book, including URL and other Internet Web site references, is subject to change without notice.

ISBN 0-13-117140-2

2 3 4 5 6 7 8 9 10   09 08 07 06

Foreword

The Culinary Institute of America has a strong commitment to culinary education. We have been in the forefront of culinary education since we first opened our doors in 1946. It is precisely because we feel so strongly about the benefits of a great education that we have partnered with Pearson/Prentice-Hall to prepare the textbook you hold in your hands.

A culinary education offers you a clear path to a career—it does not just include culinary theory, it also provides practical knowledge and skills you can apply to your first job and throughout your professional life. As the food-service and hospitality industry becomes more competitive, you need to have appropriate skills. This book reflects the areas we concentrate on in our Associate's and Bachelor's programs: product knowledge, sanitation and safety, nutrition and food science, and of course, culinary and baking techniques.

There are many reasons to join the ranks of those who work with food for a living. Most people enter the culinary arts because they love food and cooking and because they want to make people happy. However, throughout your culinary career, you will find that what you offer to the industry, and what you can expect from it, will change. That is what a career is all about.

Keep your interest alive, and your love for food and cooking fresh, by trying new foods and new restaurants, taking classes or attending workshops, and perhaps even trying new types of work. Remember the spark that first urged you toward a culinary education. Do your best to nurture it, feed it, and keep it alive and growing. The rewards from this industry are among the greatest you could ever hope to achieve.

Dr. Tim Ryan
President
The Culinary Institute of America

Teacher Advisory Panel

The Culinary Institute of America and Pearson Prentice Hall thank the following educators for their important contributions as this text was developed.

Guy "Skip" Ailstock, CSM
Chef Instructor/Program Director Culinary Arts
Virginia Beach Technical and Career Education Center
Virginia Beach, Virginia

Jennifer Barksdale, FMP
Culinary Arts Instructor/Program Coordinator
Franklin Technology Center
Joplin, Missouri

Mary Anne Birt
Culinary Instructor
Area 30 Career Center
Greencastle, Indiana

Beverly G. Bonebrake
Culinary Arts Instructor
Washington County Technical High School
Hagerstown, Maryland

Vincent Calandra, CCE
Department Chair, Culinary Arts
Pinellas Technical Education Center
Clearwater, Florida

Kathleen M. Cole
Culinary Technology Instructor
Warren County Career Center
Lebanon, Ohio

Barbara Colleary
Director
Arizona Careers through Culinary Arts Program (C-CAP)
Tempe, Arizona

Rusty Furdell, CCE, CWPC
Chef Instructor
Lake Shore/Carrier Career and Technical Academy
Angola, New York

Dianthia Lee
Culinary Arts Instructor
Gary Area Career Center
Gary, Indiana

Toni Morucci
Home Economics Careers and Technology Instructor
Oroville High School/Butte County Regional Occupational Program
Oroville, California

Jan Rattazzi
Family and Consumer Science Teacher
Crown Point High School
Crown Point, Indiana

Dean Ritter, CEC, CCE, AAC
Culinary Arts Instructor
Lehigh Career and Technical Institute
Schnecksville, Pennsylvania

Warren R. Schueler
Former Culinary Arts Instructor/Consultant
Tottenville High School
Staten Island, New York

Douglas G. Weih
Instructor of Culinary Arts, Baking, & Pastry
Myers Park Senior High School
Charlotte, North Carolina

Introduction to Culinary Arts
Table of Contents

UNIT 3 **Culinary Applications** **240**

UNIT 4 Breads & Desserts 532

Feature Lists

CULINARY SCIENCE

CULINARY HISTORY

Feature Lists

CULINARY MATH

CULINARY DIVERSITY

BASIC CULINARY SKILLS

Continued on next page

Feature Lists

Your Recipe for Success

Introduction to Culinary Arts teaches you:

- **Kitchen Basics** such as sanitation, safety, food service equipment, knives, and smallware.
- **Culinary Basics** such as using standardized recipes, seasonings and flavorings, mise en place, and cooking methods.
- **Culinary Applications** from breakfast cookery to desserts.
- **Culinary Management** including service, menu planning, nutrition, and the business of running a restaurant.

Key Concepts and *Vocabulary* are highlighted at the beginning of every section.

13.2 Beans & Other Legumes

READING PREVIEW

Key Concepts
- Identifying legumes
- Selecting and storing legumes
- Preparing legumes
- Presenting legumes

Vocabulary
- aflatoxin
- beans
- hummus
- legume
- lentils
- peas

The cooked grains are then combined with a dressing or other sauce along with additional ingredients such as vegetables, fruits, or meats. Serve grain salads on chilled plates. Cold grain salads are typically served as a side dish or as an appetizer.

Reading Checkpoint *What is the correct way to serve a hot grain dish?*

FIGURE 13-4 ▶
Tabouli
A cold Middle Eastern salad that consists of bulgur, chopped tomatoes, parsley, mint, and scallions.
Classifying *Is this a warm-weather presentation or a cold-weather presentation?*

13.1 ASSESSMENT

Reviewing Concepts
1. What are the four common parts of a single seed of grain?
2. What are the three major types of grain?
3. What are the basic steps involved in boiling or steaming grains?
4. Why are grains regarded as being versatile?

Critical Thinking
5. Comparing/Contrasting What is the difference between masa harina, polenta, and hominy grits?
6. Applying Concepts Why do wheat berries take longer to cook than bulgur?
7. Comparing/Contrasting What is the difference between rolled oats and instant oats?

Test Kitchen
Prepare steel-cut oats, rolled oats, and instant oats. Time the preparation of each. Taste each finished cereal for taste and texture. Evaluate the results in terms of preparation time, taste, and texture.

SCIENCE

Parts of Grains
Research the individual seeds of rice, wheat, corn, oats, barley, rye, and quinoa. Draw and label the parts of each seed. For each grain, describe which component parts of the grain are removed by various types of processing.

❝Whether served as a simply flavored dish or made into complex stews or casseroles, beans have a place of importance, though not always of honor, in nearly every great cuisine. **❞**
— Bill Phillips

Legumes

A **legume** (LEG-yoom) is a plant with a double-seamed pod containing a single row of seeds. Depending on the variety of legume, people eat the seeds or the seeds together with the pods. As you know from Chapter 12, legumes such as green beans, where the seeds are eaten with the pods, are treated as vegetables. This chapter deals with legume seeds that are removed from the pod and dried. After they are dried, the seeds can be stored for long periods and then cooked by boiling them in water until tender enough to chew and digest easily.

There are three types of legumes. Dried legumes that are longer than they are round are labeled **beans**. Examples are navy beans, kidney beans, and fava beans. Legumes that are round are called **peas**. Examples of peas are black-eyed peas, green peas, and chickpeas, which are also known as garbanzo (gar-BAHN-zoh) beans or ceci (cheh-chee).

Bill Phillips
The Culinary Institute of America

Learn first hand from renowned chefs and culinary professionals.

Assessment questions at the end of sections help prepare you for chapter exams.

Step-by-step procedures teach basic culinary skills.

BASIC CULINARY SKILLS

Cooking Crêpes

1. **Combine** the eggs, cream, milk, and oil and beat until just blended.
2. **Sift** together the flour, sugar, and salt and place in a mixing bowl.
3. **Add** wet ingredients and mix until smooth, scraping down the bowl as you go.
4. **Add** flavoring ingredients and stir until blended and the batter is smooth.
5. **Rest** batter under refrigeration for up to 12 hours; strain if necessary.
6. **Preheat** and butter a crêpe pan over moderate to high heat.

7. **Add** batter to the pan, swirling the pan to coat it evenly with the crêpe batter.

8. **Cook** over moderate heat. When set, turn over and finish the other side.

9. **Cool** crêpes, if desired. Place on parchment paper and hold cold.

Visualize it! Many high-quality photos show culinary activities.

✓ Reading Checkpoint *What are the basic ingredients of a pancake or waffle batter?*

Breakfast Breads and Cereals

A variety of breads are served at breakfast. They can be served as an accompaniment to eggs for a hearty breakfast or with coffee, tea, and juice as a **continental breakfast**. Baking bread is discussed in Chapters 17

Reading Checkpoints offer a quick review of key concepts in the text.

and 18. Food-service establishments often use ready-made breakfast breads, including:

- Toasted bread, such as rye, white, or whole wheat bread
- English muffins
- Bagels, made plain or with sesame seeds, raisins, or other ingredients
- **Croissants** (kwah-SAHNTs), which are buttery-rich, crescent-shaped yeast rolls
- Pastries, which are often filled with almond paste, fruit, or cream
- Donuts, which are deep-fried and often ring-shaped
- Muffins, such as corn, blueberry, or bran muffins
- Loaf-style breads, such as banana bread and cranberry nut bread
- Biscuits, which are light and flakey. A **scone** is a rich biscuit that sometimes contains raisins and is served with butter, jam, or thick cream.

Easy-to-understand text highlights vocabulary and pronunciations.

▲ *Continental breakfast with croissant*

CULINARY HISTORY

French Toast

No one knows who first made French toast. A recipe for white bread, soaked in milk and beaten eggs, fried in oil, and covered with honey, dates back to Ancient Rome. Another recipe, from Medieval Italy, calls for sugar and rose-water instead of honey.

Many European countries have similar recipes but different names for the dish we know as French toast. In Spain it is called torriga; in England, it is "Poor Knights of Windsor." In this country, it has been called German toast and nun's toast. One theory for how it was named French toast starts with tavern owner Joseph French in Albany, New York, in 1724. He put the dish on his menu as French toast instead of the grammatically correct "French's toast," leading people, generations later, to believe it was a French dish.

One thing is certain. If you go to France, you won't find French toast on the menu. The French call it pain perdu, meaning "lost bread," based on the tradition of reviving day-old bread with milk and eggs and then cooking it on a hot griddle.

Research

Use the Internet to research some of the historic French toast recipes. How do the recipes compare with today's version of the dish?

Learn about the history, math, and science behind culinary arts.

Culinary Careers

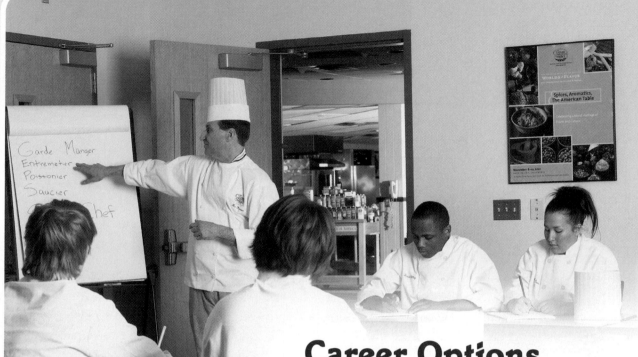

Career Options

What do people with culinary training do? The answer is that they do just about anything you can think of—so long as it has something to do with food. The food-service industry has an almost endless number of job possibilities. To make it easier to focus, you will look at six general categories of culinary careers:

- **Chefs and cooks**
- **Banquets & Institutions**
- **Caterers & Private Chefs**
- **Research & Development**
- **Managers**
- **Food Communications**

READING PREVIEW

Key Concepts

- Learning about career options
- Understanding the types of culinary education and training
- Learning what to expect on the job

You will learn about the types of jobs available within each type of culinary career. You will learn about the types of education required by the jobs. And you will be introduced to people who have made their living within that culinary profession.

Your dream job in the culinary profession is out there for you—you just need the skills to do the job and the ambition to find it!

Chefs & Cooks

Chefs and cooks can determine the reputation and success of a restaurant. Chefs typically supervise cooks. Both must work independently and as a team, often under a great deal of pressure in tight quarters, but always with the aim of pleasing the customer. There are three management positions in the kitchen:

Executive chefs are in charge of large kitchens, even chains of kitchens. They must have a diploma or certificate from a school or organization that can grant the title "Certified Executive Chef" (indicated by the initials "C.E.C" following the chef's name).

Head chefs are chefs with professional cooks working for them. In kitchens without an executive chef, the head chef is in charge.

Sous-chefs are second in command, reporting to the chef who in is charge of the kitchen. This is the lowest administrative position in the kitchen.

The next level of work in the kitchen is done by cooks working on specific types of food. Some examples are:

Sauté cooks are responsible for sautéed items and their sauces. This is often considered the most glamorous of the various cooks' jobs. This job demands experience, stamina, split-second timing, an excellent memory, and the ability to multi-task.

Grill cooks are responsible for the preparation of all grilled or broiled items. Grill cooks have the same job requirements as sauté cooks.

Fish cooks must know the various types of fish and shellfish and understand their anatomy.

At the lower level of the kitchen staff, employees often start with an apprentice or intern program.

Apprentices or **prep cooks** are where most people begin their culinary careers. The work is not highly skilled, but it is very important. Apprentices generally clean, trim, and prepare vegetables for stocks, soups, and salads. They also may be responsible for preparing the salads, salad dressings, and other simple menu items.

Melissa Perello

"I knew I wanted to be a chef since I was a little kid," says Melissa Perello, "and I did everything I could to make it happen."

Melissa graduated from the Culinary Institute of America in 1996. As part of her CIA education, she worked at Aqua, a restaurant in San Francisco. After graduation, she returned to Aqua, where she polished her skills under the guidance of Michael Mina (a 1989 CIA graduate).

Melissa rose through the ranks at Aqua and then took the position of line chef at Charles Nob Hill, a sister restaurant of Aqua. In 1999, Melissa was appointed sous-chef, and then in 2001 she became executive chef. This was just five years after graduating from the Culinary Institute!

Today Melissa's talent is getting national attention. In 2004 she was named a James Beard Award nominee as "Rising Star, Chef of the Year." That year *Food & Wine* magazine named her one of its ten Best New Chefs. Her culinary visions have also helped catapult Charles Nob Hill into the *Nation's Restaurant News* "Fine Dining Hall of Fame," and she received exceptional reviews from the *San Francisco Chronicle* Magazine section. To any culinary student, her success is a dream come true.

Melissa has an A.O.S. degree (Associate in Occupational Studies) and a major in Culinary Arts.

CAREER PROFILE

Requirements

Culinary degree for upper-level positions; food-service experience for entry-level positions.

Helpful to Have: Knowledge of nutrition, accounting, and business management for upper-level positions.

Salary Ranges

Executive Chef: $35,000–$90,000+

Chef: $27,000–$60,000+

Sous-Chef: $26,000–$45,000+

Cook: $14,000–$27,000+

Salaries can be higher depending on region.

Scott Holtzhouser

Scott Holtzhouser was asked to be a member of a team of chefs who supervised the food service for thousands of people during the opening and dedication of the Clinton Presidential Library in Little Rock, Arkansas. The team was responsible for overseeing 25 bakers, 50 cooks, and 120 servers.

Although high-volume food service doesn't always sound glamorous, one of the high points of the opening ceremonies for Scott was the opportunity to prepare a private lunch for former President Clinton, Senator Hillary Clinton, and 12 members of the Clinton family.

A 2000 graduate of the Culinary Institute of America, Scott has three restaurants in New York. His ability to move comfortably between being a restaurant chef and being a high-volume chef, while unusual, is something that every individual entering the culinary profession should note. This profession often affords unusual opportunities for those who have the skill and desire to take advantage of them.

Scott has an A.O.S. degree (Associate in Occupational Studies) and a major in Culinary Arts.

Banquet managers and chefs at hotels, convention centers, and banquet halls serve large numbers of diners, using their own kitchens and dining rooms. Many operations count on conventions, meetings, and special events such as weddings, bar mitzvahs, and receptions to generate a large part of their revenue. The banquet chef is crucial to the success or failure of this part of the operation.

Banquet managers and chefs are responsible for developing menus that can be adjusted to meet the guests' requirements. Menus must be carefully priced so customers perceive them as a value yet the business generates the greatest possible profit. It is generally easier to make a specific profit margin when you know in advance how many people will be dining, at exactly what time, and on exactly which evening.

In a large hotel, several events may take place on the same day, even at the same time. Banquet managers and chefs must be able to organize an incredible number of details. The advance preparation, cooking, and service require concentration, endurance, and skill. Banquet managers and chefs work in public view, which presents its own set of physical and emotional demands. They are often perfectionists who find great reward in their ability to bring off an event perfectly.

An institutional chef cooks meals for schools, hospitals, businesses, and nursing homes.

Institutional chefs (also called high-volume chefs) are responsible for cooking appropriate food for a specific institutional setting. Sometimes institutions use cafeteria style, with multiple choices available for each course, as in a school cafeteria. In other cases, they prepare meals for individuals with special dietary needs, as in a nursing home or hospital. Management and organizational skills are critical for this position, but there is little contact with the public.

CAREER PROFILE

Requirements

Culinary degree for both banquet chef and high-volume chef, in addition to foodservice experience.

Helpful to Have: Accounting and business management (banquet manager/chef). Knowledge of nutrition (high-volume chef).

Salary Ranges

Banquet Manager/Chef: $26,000–$48,000+

Institutional Chef: $20,000–$34,000+

Salaries can be higher depending on region.

Caterers & Private Chefs

A caterer's job is similar to the job of a banquet manager or chef. They both develop menus, manage support staff, and organize details. The biggest difference between the two is that a caterer must often cook and serve the event in an unfamiliar location.

Caterers must be creative chefs with people skills who can plan and price a pleasing menu. They must be experts in foodservice, determining how to execute the menu—how much can they prepare in their own kitchen and how much will they need to prepare onsite?

To ensure a successful event, caterers must be able to visualize the entire affair from beginning to end. A caterer must provide everything needed for the event. This includes not only the raw ingredients for the dishes but also cooking supplies, tableware, and paper supplies. A caterer might need to order everything from portable refrigerators and stoves to rented chairs, tables, tents, linen, and china. People who choose catering as their vocation must be extremely organized.

Some individuals, families, and businesses employ private chefs. Usually the private chef works alone, buying the food, cooking it, and serving the dishes.

Private chefs oversee the operation of their employer's kitchen. Private chefs must be easygoing, versatile, and creative, developing menus that avoid repetition. They may need to develop meals for a special diet or prescribed nutritional program. They may also be responsible for dinner parties, which could be a small dinner for eight or a large reception for one hundred. For such events, they would need to hire and manage additional staff. Private chefs often must be willing to have flexible schedules. The job is not for everyone, but it can be incredibly fulfilling.

Stacey Slichta

Stacey Slichta knows what's cooking in the lives of some celebrities. That's because she has worked as a private chef in the Los Angeles, California, area almost since graduation. It's a career choice she loves, but also one she never expected to make when she was a student at the CIA.

Stacey's culinary education began early, cooking alongside her father as a child. She arrived at the CIA with a background in foodservice management and a bachelor's degree in English and philosophy. She had no plans to work in a kitchen after graduating in 1997 with her associate degree in culinary arts. But a student job in the college's Career Services Office led to a summer position as a private chef, and that launched Stacey's career in the field.

Stacey's client list features several celebrities, including comedian Don Rickles and his wife. Her duties include buying the food, beverages, and other supplies used by the household as well as preparing daily meals and food for dinner parties and receptions. Additionally, Stacey does catering and teaches at Chefmakers, a new culinary school for home cooks and children in Pacific Palisades, California. She is also involved in children's cooking programs on cable TV.

Stacey has an A.O.S. degree (Associate in Occupational Studies) and a major in Culinary Arts.

CAREER PROFILE

Requirements

Foodservice experience, ability to work independently, organizational ability, supervisory skills. Culinary degree a plus.

Helpful to Have: Knowledge of accounting and business management (caterer). Knowledge of nutrition (private chef).

Salary Ranges

Caterer:
$19,000–$65,000+

Private Chef:
$25,000–$60,000+

Salaries can be higher depending on region.

Research & Development

John Kirkpatrick

John Kirkpatrick graduated from the Culinary Institute of America in 1988 and then worked with the Minnesota Vikings Foodservice in his hometown of Minneapolis. After a position as executive chef, he became corporate chef at the training facility of the Vikings football team.

From there he moved to Birmingham, Alabama, and the test kitchens of *Cooking Light* magazine, where he has been for seven years. John tests and edits recipes that come in from developers. He also does product reviews. His crowning achievement so far is the issue for which he wrote and developed the cover story "One Great Grill Dinner" and did the food styling for the cover.

A highlight of his culinary career occurred a few years back when he dined with a handful of writers, editors, and guest-of-honor Julia Child. It was a memorable occasion and a flawless meal.

He enjoys working at *Cooking Light* because of its relaxed environment in one of the most beautiful corporate campuses in the nation. The work in the test kitchen is always interesting, and it provides opportunities to meet and work with world-renowned chefs such as Rick Bayless, Graham Kerr, and Emeril Lagasse.

John has an A.O.S. degree (Associate in Occupational Studies) and a major in Culinary Arts.

Companies that produce food products are constantly looking for new items that will capture the interest of the buying public. Before a new product is introduced, it must undergo exhaustive evaluation and research.

Test kitchen researchers help major food companies, restaurant chains, and specialty food producers develop new products. Using their culinary skills in professional test kitchens, researchers analyze how the product acts when it is heated, refrigerated, stored on a shelf, or frozen. Test kitchen professionals must be organized, methodical, and scientific in their approach to their work.

Test kitchen recipe developers work at food magazines. They must be able to develop recipes that will showcase the flavor, texture, color, or nutritional characteristic of a particular food. Recipe developers must research the food and write about it in a way that will be useful for the home or professional cook. This work may also offer an opportunity to break into the world of food styling and even food photography.

Another area of culinary research is recipe testing for cookbooks. A huge number of cookbooks are published each year, and their recipes must be checked by independent testers for accuracy.

Recipe testers are hired by cookbook authors to check recipes before publication. An author needs to know if a recipe is easily understood and if the measurements produce a dish that is appealing, tasty, and attractive.

To break into this work, you can write to publishing houses that have produced cookbooks you admire. Or, you can read trade journals that might have information about who is working on a cookbook, and then write directly to the author to find out if he or she is looking for help testing recipes.

Recipe testers are paid a flat fee per recipe, and are reimbursed for the food items purchased to prepare the recipes.

CAREER PROFILE

Requirements

Culinary degree and organizational skills (test kitchen researchers), culinary and writing skills (test kitchen recipe developers), culinary skills (recipe testers).

Helpful to Have: Knowledge of marketing (test kitchen researchers).

Salary Ranges

Test Kitchen Professionals:
$20,000–$55,000+

Recipe Testers:
Compensation per recipe varies

Salaries can be higher depending on region.

Managers

There are many managers in the culinary profession. An executive chef, for instance is a manager. So is a banquet manager or a caterer. Lower-level managers are also needed for specific areas within a food-service business.

Managers in a foodservice business usually serve in a specific function. For example, a large hotel restaurant might employ a purchasing agent or a storeroom supervisor. These managers must have a strong background in math and accounting. They also typically need strong computer skills and some specific management training (often related to safety and sanitation) for their position.

A manager must be able to organize work that is done by others. The ability to communicate effectively, including providing positive and negative feedback to workers, is a critical job skill. In some situations, being multilingual is an advantage if employees speak languages other than English.

Management is sometimes required to work long hours to accomplish tasks specified by upper-level management. Managers need to be very competent in their particular area. The general thought is that a manager should be able to perform any job function performed by their subordinates.

Small business owners are actually managers, as well. They must make all of their own decisions, and the success or failure of their businesses depends on their decisions.

Small business owners need to have a full complement of skills that will allow them to both perform specific tasks and to manage others who may be performing those tasks. As a small business owner, whether you own a deli, a bakery, a pizzeria, or a bed-and-breakfast, you must be able to perform any and all tasks that need to be accomplished by your business. If you aren't able to do them, who else will?

Matthew Schmid

Matthew Schmid has realized a twenty-year-old dream. He and his wife purchased a bed and breakfast in Spring Lake, New Jersey, just a few blocks from the boardwalk. Matthew says "Looking back on my career since graduation, it is amazing how often I refer to what I learned in my culinary education. The knowledge I gained, is something that is constant too—not something that goes away. It's a part of my daily life!"

As an owner and manager of a bed and breakfast, Matthew feels that every experience that he's had has prepared him for his current life. Matthew worked as a restaurant manager, but realized he needed to know more about the business so he enrolled in the Culinary Institute of America. After graduating in 1985, he cooked for a while, but decided to return to the CIA for its four-year program. Matthew said, "After receiving my bachelor's degree in 1995, I became the banquet manager at the Rainbow Room in New York City, and then joined W Hotels working in Manhattan, setting up the company's banquet operations around the country." He later became director of banquets at the Waldorf Astoria in Manhattan.

Degree: A.O.S (Associate in Occupational Studies), B.P.S. (Bachelor of Professional Studies). Major: Culinary Arts.

CAREER PROFILE

Requirements

While a Culinary degree may be helpful, it is more important tounderstand the specific aspects of the area that you are managing.

Helpful to Have: Business management, supervision, accounting, safety, and sanitation courses.

Salary Ranges
Managers:
$26,000–$48,000+

Small business owner:
$12,000–$84,000+

Salaries can be higher depending on region.

Food Communications

Nick Tolbert

Nick Tolbert began his culinary career at the age of 16, when he worked part-time as floor chef in various hotels in his native city of Cincinnati. He honed his skills at the CIA, graduating in 1977. For 15 years after graduation, Nick was head chef at several major gourmet restaurants, pastry shops, hotels, and country clubs on the East Coast, developing management skills at the same time that he improved his culinary and baking abilities.

Nick built a reputation for his effective management skills and was asked to take a position in TAP (Transfer Achievement Program), which focuses on providing opportunities for disadvantaged individuals. He traveled throughout the Midwest to promote the program.

In recent years, Nick has been dedicated to teaching others the art of cooking. He was a featured writer for several magazines and newspapers. In 1998, he launched "Denova"—a company that created a popular local cable television program called "The Midnight Gourmet." In 2001, the program was picked up by BET (Black Entertainment Television) to be broadcast nationally and internationally. Denova has also debuted a popular radio show, "Recipes for Romance."

Nick has an A.O.S. degree (Associate in Occupational Studies) and a major in Culinary Arts.

Food communication is the coverage of culinary topics in newspapers, magazines, and books, and on radio, television, and the Internet. People in this field have found careers that range from food writer to TV chef.

Food writers are communicators with a good basic knowledge of food and cooking. Some food writers edit or write books. There is a huge market for food books on every imaginable subject.

Food writers also submit articles to magazines and newspapers. To write these articles, you need to be well read in the culinary arts and proficient in the kitchen. Articles could range from a simple discussion of how to brew a pot of tea to an informational piece on nutritional cooking.

A food writer with good presentation skills might be featured on a local radio program or might even become part of a television food show.

Restaurant critics are food writers who understand what good food, good cooking, and good service is all about. They are able to discuss the style of a restaurant and trends in the restaurant business. Restaurant critics are very important to restaurants, especially when their good reviews increase business.

Have you ever picked up a magazine or a book simply because the food on the front cover looked so appealing that you wanted to eat it? This is the work of food photographers and stylists.

Food photographers have the talent of making food look visually appealing in print. You see their work in ad campaigns, magazines and book jackets. Their challenge is to photograph food so the viewer can almost taste it. What's required is an understanding of photography and lighting.

Food stylists work with food photographers. They are responsible for preparing and placing the food just right on the plate. Their culinary knowledge is critical—how to select the best product, apply the right technique, cut the item expertly. It is up to the stylist to make sure that the lettuce leaves are perfect, with not a single blemish, and the entire presentation is picture-perfect.

CAREER PROFILE

Requirements

Culinary and writing skills (food writers and critics), culinary skills and knowledge of photography and design (food photographers and stylists).

Helpful to Have: Broad knowledge of the food industry and all food media outlets.

Salary Ranges

Food Writers, Photographers, Stylists:
$20,000–$55,000+
Many jobs are freelance, paid on a per project basis.

Salaries can be higher depending on region.

Culinary Education & Training

The path toward achieving professional status involves:

- Formal education
- Certification
- Continuing education
- Professional development
- Establishment of a professional network

Formal Education. A sound and thorough culinary education is a logical first step in the development of your culinary career. Increasingly, employers are looking for job applicants who have culinary degrees. There are more than 800 schools in the United States alone that offer some form of post-secondary culinary education. Some schools are dedicated to the culinary arts; others are part of a community college or university. Schools may offer programs that result in an associate or bachelor's degree. Master's programs with a strong emphasis on food, as well as degrees in related areas such as nutrition and food science, are also important to professional chefs. The best culinary schools incorporate plenty of hands-on application in their curriculum.

An apprenticeship is a way to achieve a formal education without attending culinary school. The apprenticeship program sponsored by the American Culinary Federation (ACF) combines on-the-job training with technical classroom instruction.

Certification. Certification provides a way to prove that you have met certain standards in the culinary field. A certification is recognition of your skill level. Typically a certification program involves a specific level of experience in the field, course work, and passing of a written and practical cooking examination. To maintain your certification, you will need to refresh your knowledge and provide documentation of continuing education and professional development.

▲ Becoming a chef involves both formal education and hands-on training.

Continuing Education. Once you have achieved your initial training, you need to keep your skills current. The culinary profession is constantly evolving, and you will need to attend classes, workshops, and seminars to hone your skills in specialized areas and to keep up with new methods and styles of cooking.

Professional Development. As your career progresses, you should join professional organizations; read professional magazines, newsletters, and books; and participate in culinary competitions.

Establishing a Professional Network. You will want to network with other professionals to gain insight, recommendations, or guidance. Perhaps you can find a mentor or coach to help you reach a new level in your career. You can also mentor others when appropriate.

Working In Restaurants

The staff in a restaurant's kitchen must be ready to prepare, at any moment, a great variety of dishes. This can only be accomplished if they all organize their work properly and complete tasks efficiently. They know the importance of doing all the backup work, taking as much care with it as with the final stages of cooking. Here's a preview of a day in the life of a large restaurant that serves only dinner on a Saturday night.

3-4:00 a.m. The baker is the first to arrive in the kitchen, to make the breads and baked desserts for the day. After everything is baked, the baker finishes by scrubbing down all the work surfaces, tools, and equipment in the work area. Often the last thing the baker does is sweep the floor.

11:00 a.m. Just as the baker finishes and tosses the morning's apron into the laundry bag, the pantry cook and prep cooks arrive. After checking the existing stock, the pantry chef reviews the list left by the chef from the night before and writes a list of tasks to accomplish. The pantry chef and the prep cooks check off the tasks and, before they leave, they wipe down the cutting boards and work tables and hone the knives.

3:00 p.m. Line cooks, the sous-chef, and the chef arrive. They immediately want to know how many reservations there are. The line cooks

prepare for the dishes they will be making. The sous-chef decides on the nightly specials.

5:00 p.m. One of the line chefs prepares the "family dinner," the meal served to the staff before service begins.

6:00 p.m. Dinner service starts slowly, but begins to build rapidly as more guests arrive..

8:00 p.m. Dinner service has built to a frenzied pitch. The chef is acting as an expediter to make sure the kitchen stays organized. The sous-chef has jumped in on the grill line to help. All the orders are coming in at the same time and all the line chefs are cooking dishes rapidly, but also with an eye to maintaining quality.

10:00 p.m. The official closing time finally arrives. Things begin to slow down gradually. The staff is still working hard, but now their attention turns to cooling, wrapping, and storing food. Some of them begin to prepare for the next day. They all are responsible for cleaning their stations. The chef talks to the dining room manager to get feedback on the night. The sous-chef prepares an order for supplies the restaurant needs.

11:30 p.m. Once the final counter is cleaned and polished and the last pots and pans are stored, it's time to turn out the lights and go home.

Restaurant Industry Overview

- There are more than 900,000 restaurant locations in the United States, serving more than 70 billion meals and snacks.

- The restaurant industry employs an estimated 12.2 million people, making it the nation's largest employer outside of government.

- Latest restaurant sales forecasts show sales rising by nearly 5% annually.

- The restaurant industry provides work for more than 9% of those employed in the United States.

- More than 7 out of 10 food and beverage businesses are single-unit ("mom-and-pop") operations.

- In a recent year, average sales were $730,000 at full-service restaurants and $619,000 at limited-service restaurants.

Source: National Restaurant Association, www.restaurant.org.

PRENTICE HALL

INTRODUCTION TO

Culinary Arts

THE **C**ULINARY **I**NSTITUTE **OF A**MERICA®

Kitchen Basics

1.1 Sanitary Food Handling

READING PREVIEW

Key Concepts

- Learning the importance of food safety
- Developing good grooming and personal hygiene habits
- Cleaning and sanitizing
- Disposing of waste and recycling
- Controlling pests

Vocabulary

- bacteria
- biological hazards
- chemical hazards
- cross-contamination
- direct contamination
- foodborne illness
- fungi (fungus)
- parasites
- pathogen
- pest management
- physical hazards
- potentially hazardous foods
- safe foods
- sanitizing
- sanitizing solution
- temperature danger zone
- viruses
- water activity (Aw)

> **"F**ood safety has become a global concern. Every individual working in the foodservice profession needs to take it seriously, every working minute. **"**
>
> – Richard Vergili
> The Culinary Institute of America

Importance of Food Safety

Safe foods are foods that won't make you sick or hurt you when you eat them. Unsafe foods, or foods that have been contaminated by various hazardous materials, can make you sick or injure you. An illness that results from eating contaminated foods is referred to as a **foodborne illness**.

Guests expect safe food when they come to a restaurant. They typically don't think about food safety. However, if a restaurant serves unsafe food and someone gets sick or hurt, the consequences can be enormous. Both the restaurant's profits and reputation can be hurt.

If someone can prove they got sick from eating unsafe food in a restaurant, they might sue. The incident could become public and the restaurant might be named in an unflattering news report.

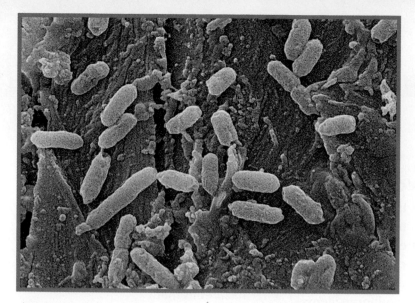

Figure 1-1
Bacteria
Magnified view of bacteria (rod shapes) on a cutting board.
Drawing Conclusions *What would happen to food cut on this cutting board?*

Figure 1-2
Roundworms (Parasite)
Pork is the most common vehicle for the foodborne roundworm Trichinella spiralis.
Applying Concepts *Why would you make certain there are no signs of pink color in cooked pork?*

If a restaurant is found to have served unsafe food, it might be charged more for insurance. When people feel your food is unsafe, they talk about it. They may stop coming and the restaurant will lose customers. Eventually, the business could fail.

Food-service establishments of all sorts, whether they are fine dining restaurants, diners, or cafeterias, have a responsibility to their customers and to themselves to serve safe foods. Cooks and chefs play a critical part in making sure the foods their customers get are as safe and wholesome as can be. Taking a course in food safety, such as the "ServSafe Essentials" program from the Educational Foundation of the National Restaurant Association, teaches food handlers safe practices. Getting a certificate in food safety is an important part of your culinary education.

There are three potential hazards that can contaminate food and produce foodborne illnesses:

- Biological hazards
- Physical hazards
- Chemical hazards

Biological Hazards **Biological hazards** are the living organisms found in or on foods that can make us sick. There are four basic types of biological hazards:

- Bacteria
- Viruses
- Parasites
- Fungi (including molds)

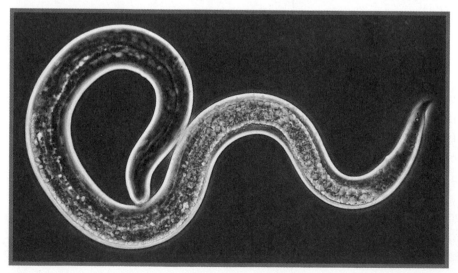

Bacteria are single-celled organisms that can live in food or water and also on our skin or clothing. Not all bacteria make you sick. If there is only a very small amount of bacteria in or on food, the bacteria may not make you sick. However, a contaminated food contains a great many bacteria. It is the volume of bacteria in a contaminated food that makes us sick.

Viruses invade living cells, including those in foods. Once a virus invades a cell, it tricks the host into making another virus and the process continues. The living cell is known as the host for the virus. A virus needs a host in order to reproduce.

Parasites are multi-celled organisms that are far larger than either bacteria or viruses. Some are actually large enough to see without a microscope. Similar to bacteria, they reproduce on their own. But similar to a virus, they need a host to provide a home and nourishment. Parasites include roundworms, tapeworms, and various insects. When we eat foods that contain parasites, the eggs or larvae take up residence in our bodies.

Fungi can be single-celled or multi-celled organisms. ("Fungi" is the plural of "fungus.") A mold is an example of a fungus you can find in foods. Yeast is another example. We rely on some molds and yeasts to produce foods such as cheese or bread. However, harmful molds can contaminate foods. As a fungus grows and reproduces, it creates byproducts, including various toxins, alcohol, and gases that can cause foodborne illness or foodborne intoxication.

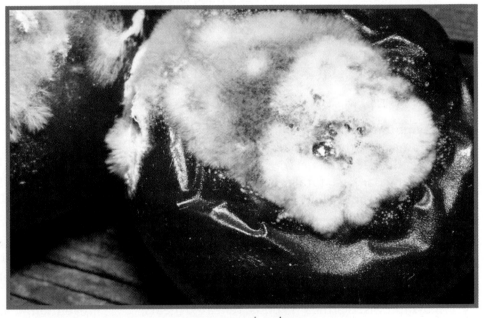

FIGURE 1-3
Moldy Tomato
Mold is a type of fungus found in spoiled food.
Drawing Conclusions *Some kitchens cut off the moldy parts of food and use the remainder. Would you want to eat food from such a kitchen?*

Physical Hazards If you find a hair, a piece of a food's packaging, a bandage, or a piece of metal or glass in your food, you've found a physical hazard. **Physical hazards** are foreign objects, usually large enough to see or feel while you are eating. They are often responsible for injuries such as chipped teeth or cuts.

Chemical Hazards Cleaning compounds, bug sprays, food additives, and fertilizer are all examples of man-made **chemical hazards**. Any of these products, if not used properly, can contaminate food. Symptoms from eating chemically contaminated food can often be felt immediately and might include hives; swelling of the lips, tongue, and mouth; difficulty breathing or wheezing; and vomiting, diarrhea, and cramps.

Another chemical hazard involves toxic metals. Mercury and cadmium are toxic metals that have found their way into our food and water, often as a result of industrial pollution. The effects of these toxic metals can range from subtle symptoms to serious diseases.

Biological Hazards

BACTERIA	Bacillus cereus	**Found in:** soil, foods **Incubation*:** 8 to 16 hours
Symptoms: cramps, diarrhea, nausea, vomiting	**Foods:** cereal products, cornstarch, rice, custards, sauces, meat loaf	**Prevention:** Cool hot foods quickly. Reheat foods evenly to 165°F. Don't store precooked foods in refrigerator for too long.

BACTERIA	Campylobacter jejuni	**Found in:** animals **Incubation*:** 3 to 5 days
Symptoms: diarrhea, fever, nausea, abdominal pain, headache	**Foods:** unpasteurized milk and dairy products, poultry, beef, pork, lamb	**Prevention:** Thoroughly cook food. Avoid cross-contamination.

BACTERIA	Clostridium botulinum	**Found in:** animals, water, soil **Incubation*:** 12 to 36 hours
Disease: Botulism **Symptoms:** blurred vision, cramps, diarrhea, difficulty breathing, central nervous system damage; fatality rate up to 70%	**Foods:** refrigerated or improperly canned foods; low-acid foods (spinach, tuna, green beans, beets, fermented foods), smoked products	**Prevention:** Maintain a high temperature while canning food. Boil 20 minutes before serving. Don't use food from swollen cans. Don't use home-canned food commercially.

BACTERIA	Clostridium perfringens	**Found in:** soil, dust, animals **Incubation*:** 9 to 15 hours
Symptoms: diarrhea, nausea, cramps, fever, vomiting	**Foods:** reheated meats, raw meat, raw vegetables, soups, gravies, stews	**Prevention:** Cool meat quickly. Reheat to 165°F. Avoid cross-contamination of raw meat and cooked meat.

BACTERIA	Escherichia coli (E. coli)	**Found in:** animals, humans **Incubation*:** 12 to 72 hours
Symptoms: nausea, vomiting, diarrhea	**Foods:** raw and undercooked ground beef and other meats, imported cheeses, unpasteurized milk	**Prevention:** Thoroughly cook ground beef. Avoid cross-contamination and fecal contamination. Practice strict personal hygiene.

* "Incubation" refers to the period between infection and onset of symptoms.

BACTERIA	Listeria monocytogenes	Found in: soil, water, humans, animals Incubation*: 1 day to 3 weeks
Disease: Listeriosis **Symptoms:** nausea, vomiting, headache, fever, chills, backache, meningitis, miscarriage	**Foods:** unpasteurized milk and cheese, vegetables, poultry, meats, seafood, chilled ready-to-eat foods	**Prevention:** Use only pasteurized dairy products. Cook foods thoroughly. Avoid cross-contamination. Clean and disinfect surfaces. Avoid pooling of water.

BACTERIA	Salmonella	Found in: humans, animals, birds, insects Incubation*: 6 to 48 hours
Disease: Salmonellosis **Symptoms:** headache, diarrhea, cramps, fever. Can lead to arthritis, meningitis, typhoid. May be fatal.	**Foods:** eggs, poultry, shellfish, meat, soup, sauces, gravies, milk products, warmed-over food	**Prevention:** Cook to proper temperatures and reheat leftovers to 165°F. Eliminate rodents and flies. Practice strict personal hygiene. Avoid cross-contamination.

BACTERIA	Shigella	Found in: humans, food, water Incubation*: 12 to 48 hours
Disease: Shigellosis **Symptoms:** diarrhea, fever, cramps, dehydration	**Foods:** beans; contaminated milk; tuna, turkey, macaroni salads; apple cider; mixed moist foods	**Prevention:** Use safe water sources. Control insects and rodents. Practice strict personal hygiene.

BACTERIA	Staphylococcus aureus (Staph)	Found in: humans Incubation*: 2 to 4 hours
Symptoms: vomiting, nausea, diarrhea, cramps	**Foods:** foods high in protein, moist, handled much, left too warm (milk, egg custards, turkey stuffing, chicken/tuna/potato salads, gravies, reheated foods)	**Prevention:** Store foods below 41°F and reheat thoroughly to 165°F. People with infected cuts, burns, or respiratory illnesses shouldn't handle food.

BACTERIA	Streptococcus pyogenes	Found in: animals, humans Incubation*: 1 to 4 days
Symptoms: nausea, vomiting, diarrhea	**Foods:** milk, pudding, ice cream, eggs, meat pie, egg and potato salads, poultry	**Prevention:** Cook foods thoroughly and cool quickly. Practice strict personal hygiene. Use pasteurized dairy products.

* "Incubation" refers to the period between infection and onset of symptoms.

Biological Hazards

VIRUS Hepatitis A	**Found in:** humans, water **Incubation*:** 10 to 50 days	
Symptoms: jaundice, fever, cramps, nausea, lethargy	**Foods:** shellfish from polluted water, milk, whipped cream, cold cuts, potato salad	**Prevention:** Cook shellfish thoroughly, to over 150°F. Heat-treat or otherwise disinfect suspected water and milk. Practice strict personal hygiene.

VIRUS Norwalk virus	**Found in:** humans **Incubation*:** 24 to 48 hours	
Symptoms: nausea, vomiting, diarrhea, abdominal pain, headache, low-grade fever	**Foods:** raw shellfish, raw vegetable salads, prepared salads, water with fecal contamination	**Prevention:** Obtain shellfish from approved certified sources. Practice strict personal hygiene. Thoroughly cook foods. Use chlorinated water.

PARASITE Anisakidae (roundworms)	**Found in:** fish **Incubation*:** 1 hour to 2 weeks	
Disease: Anisakiasis **Symptoms:** nausea, cramps, fever, abscesses	**Foods:** raw or undercooked seafood	**Prevention:** Cook fish to a minimum of 140°F. Freeze fish for 24 hours. Purchase fish from reliable supplier.

PARASITE Giardia lamblia (protozoa)	**Found in:** humans, animals, soil, water **Incubation*:** 7 to 14 days	
Disease: Girardiasis **Symptoms:** diarrhea, cramps, nausea, weight loss	**Foods:** uncooked food, contaminated water or ice	**Prevention:** Practice strict personal hygiene. Use safe water sources. Wash raw fruits and vegetables well.

PARASITE Trichinella spiralis (roundworm)	**Found in:** swine, wild game, rats **Incubation*:** 4 to 28 days	
Disease: Trichinosis **Symptoms:** fever, diarrhea, sweating, muscle pain, vomiting, skin lesions	**Foods:** improperly cooked pork	**Prevention:** Cook pork to 150°F. Avoid cross-contamination of raw meats. If frying, cook to 170°F.

FUNGUS Mycotoxins	**From:** molds and yeasts **Incubation*:** Time varies	
Symptoms: hemorrhage, fluid buildup, cancer	**Foods:** moldy grains, corn, corn products, peanuts, pecans, walnuts, milk	**Prevention:** Keep grains and nuts dry.

* "Incubation" refers to the period between infection and onset of symptoms.

FAT TOM Some foods offer a friendly environment for **pathogens**, disease-producing organisms. These foods are referred to as **potentially hazardous foods**. If these foods become contaminated, the pathogen will grow easily. When you know what a pathogen needs to grow, you can take steps to keep foods safe. "FAT TOM" stands for each of the conditions that pathogens need for growth.

Pathogens first need a food source in order to grow and reproduce. Meats, dairy products, fish, and eggs are rich in protein. Cooked beans, grains, pasta, and starchy vegetables are a food source for pathogens. They contain some protein as well as carbohydrates. Sweet foods, such as fruits, are also a good food source for pathogens.

Pathogens grow rapidly when conditions are right. The length of time they are permitted to grow is a major factor in determining whether there are enough pathogens to make you sick.

FAT TOM

Food
Acidity
Temperature
Time
Oxygen
Moisture

***FOCUS ON* SAFETY**

Food Allergies

People have allergies to a wide array of foods. Some have mild reactions; others can have severe, even fatal, reactions to certain foods. The following foods account for nearly 90 percent of allergic reactions:

- Milk
- Eggs
- Wheat
- Peanuts
- Soy
- Other nuts
- Fish/Shellfish

CULINARY SCIENCE

The pH Scale

Some foods, such as vinegar or citrus juice, are highly acidic. Others, such as baking soda, are alkaline. The acidity or alkalinity of a food is measured on the pH scale. On that scale, 0 to 7 is acidic and 7 to 14 is alkaline. A pH of 7 is neutral; this is the pH of distilled water. The most favorable pH range for pathogens to grow is between 4.6 and 7.5, a range into which most foods fall. To measure the pH of a substance, scientists used strips of specially treated paper that change color depending on the acidity or alkalinity of the substance.

Research

1. Research the pH of various common foods and condiments.

2. Research the development of the pH scale.

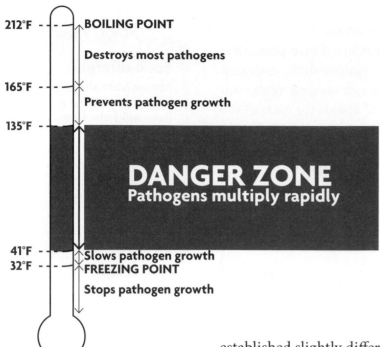

FIGURE 1-4
Temperature Danger Zone
Pathogens thrive and reproduce between 41°F and 135°F.
Predicting *Why do you think chefs rapidly cool food to below 41°F as a preparation for storing the food?*

Bacteria reproduce by dividing in two once the cell becomes large enough. One bacterium becomes two, two become four, and four become eight, and so on. A single bacterium can become nearly ten billion bacteria in just ten hours.

Pathogens also prefer to live in conditions that are warm, very similar to the conditions humans need to survive. They need foods that are at the right temperature. For most pathogens, a temperature close to our own body temperature of 98.6°F is desirable. However, pathogens can grow in temperatures from 41°F to 135°F. This range is known as the **temperature danger zone**. (Some states have established slightly different ranges for the temperature danger zone.

Specific types of pathogens have specific oxygen requirements. Some pathogens need oxygen to stay alive, others do not, and others can live with or without oxygen.

Water activity (abbreviated as Aw) is a measurement of the amount of moisture available in a food. The scale runs from 0 to 1.0, with water having an Aw measurement of 1.0. Potentially hazardous foods have a measurement of .85 Aw or higher.

Sources of Contamination A food can become unsafe in two ways, by direct contamination or by cross-contamination. With **direct contamination**, when food is received by the restaurant it already contains enough bacteria, fungi, viruses, or parasites to make you sick.

Storing foods properly, cooking them to safe temperatures, and serving them properly are all important ways to control the contamination in food.

Cross-contamination occurs when a food that is safe comes in contact with biological, physical, or chemical contaminants while it is being prepared, cooked, or served.

FIGURE 1-5
Cross-Contamination
Raw meat and raw vegetables on the same work surface.
🚫 **Drawing Conclusions** *What's wrong with this picture?*

In this book, the symbol 🚫 means something is wrong with the picture.

One of the most common causes of cross-contamination occurs when pathogens from raw foods are transferred to cooked or ready-to-eat foods through a chef's contaminated hands, equipment, or utensils. For example, bacteria from a raw chicken can be transferred to a ready-to-eat food such as lettuce or a tomato when the same cutting board is used without being washed and sanitized between foods.

 **Reading Checkpoint** *What are the three types of hazards that can contaminate foods?*

FOCUS ON SAFETY

Fingernails
Many food-service businesses do not allow fake fingernails or painted fingernails.

Grooming and Hygiene

Everyone who works with food needs to make an effort to avoid cross-contaminating food. Keeping yourself clean, well-groomed, and healthy is a vital part of keeping foods safe from contamination.

Hand Washing Washing your hands conscientiously and frequently is one of the most important elements in keeping foods safe. Every kitchen must have a proper hand-washing station, outfitted with hot and cold running water, soap, a nailbrush, and single-use paper towels.

BASIC CULINARY SKILLS

Proper Hand Washing

1. **Wet hands**, using hot running water.
2. **Apply soap** and work it into a lather.

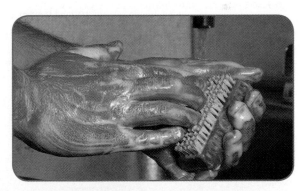

3. **Scrub hands**, between fingers, and forearms for at least 20 seconds.
4. **Scrub under your fingernails** with a brush.

5. **Rinse hands** and forearms under warm running water.
6. **Dry hands** with clean single-use paper towels.
7. **Turn off water**, using towel.
8. **Open door**, using towel if necessary.
9. **Discard towel** in waste container.

Sanitation ▲ **13**

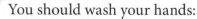

CHEF'S TIP

FITS LIKE A GLOVE
Disposable gloves are available in various sizes. Choose a size that fits snugly, but without pinching.

FOCUS ON SANITATION

Latex Allergy
Some people are allergic to the latex used in most disposable gloves.

FIGURE 1-6
Disposable Gloves
Gloves act as a barrier between your hands and ready-to-eat foods.
Applying Concepts *Why is it still important to wash your hands before putting on gloves?*

▼

You should wash your hands:
- ☑ When arriving at work or returning to the kitchen
- ☑ After using the bathroom
- ☑ After sneezing
- ☑ After touching your hair, face, or clothing
- ☑ After eating, drinking, or smoking
- ☑ After taking off, and before putting on, a new pair of gloves
- ☑ Before handling food that will not be cooked again or ready-to-eat food, such as salads and sandwiches
- ☑ After handling garbage
- ☑ After handling dirty equipment, dishes, or utensils
- ☑ After touching raw meats, poultry, and fish
- ☑ After caring for or touching animals
- ☑ Anytime you change from one task to another

Disposable Gloves In addition to washing your hands frequently, you should wear disposable gloves to prevent your bare hands from coming in contact with ready-to-serve foods. For instance, if you are cutting up an onion to cook in a stew, you don't need to wear gloves, because the onion will be cooked before being served to a guest. However, if you are slicing scallions to serve raw on a salad, you need to wear gloves.

Gloves act as a barrier to keep any microorganism on your hand from getting into the food. But, gloves can become contaminated if they touch other foods or a dirty surface. If your hands aren't clean when you put the gloves on, contamination from your hands can get on the gloves. Once your gloves are contaminated, they can contaminate the foods you are preparing.

Wash your hands thoroughly before putting on gloves. Change your gloves whenever they become ripped or dirty. If you are handling raw meats, fish, poultry, or eggs, change your gloves after you are finished handling them and before you start working with cooked or ready-to-eat foods. Never handle money with gloved hands unless you immediately remove and discard the gloves. Money is highly contaminated from handling,

Treat disposable gloves as a second skin. Whatever can contaminate a human hand can also contaminate your gloves. Whenever your hands should be washed, you should put on a new pair of disposable gloves. Never reuse or wash disposable gloves.

Grooming Your uniform is a potential source of pathogens that can get into foods and cause foodborne illness. Start each shift in a clean uniform. Whenever possible, put your uniform on at work, rather than wearing it from your home to the workplace. Do not use aprons or towels hung on the apron string to dry or wipe down hands, tools, or equipment.

Control your hair (this includes beards) by wearing hairnets, hats, or beard restraints. Otherwise, your hair could fall into the food. Hairnets also reduce the need to touch your hair while on the job.

If jewelry falls into the food you are preparing or serving, it can be a physical hazard in the kitchen. It can also be a source of cross-contamination. Pathogens can contaminate jewelry and be transferred from the jewelry to food. In many kitchens, the only piece of jewelry that is allowed is a plain wedding band. Even watches are a potential source of contamination.

Personal Hygiene If you are sick with a contagious cold or disease, you should not come to work until the chance that you might infect others has passed. Keep your fingernails trimmed and do not wear polish. Keep makeup to a minimum, if you wear any at all.

Wear a bandage to cover any cuts or burns on your skin. Change bandages frequently so they don't become a breeding ground for bacteria. Wear gloves to prevent bandages on your hands from falling into food.

 **Reading Checkpoint** *What are the steps in proper hand washing?*

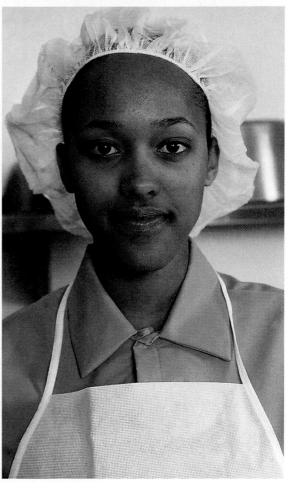

▲
FIGURE 1-7
Good Grooming
Hairnets are required by most food establishments.
Predicting *How would you feel if you were in a restaurant and saw a kitchen worker without a hairnet?*

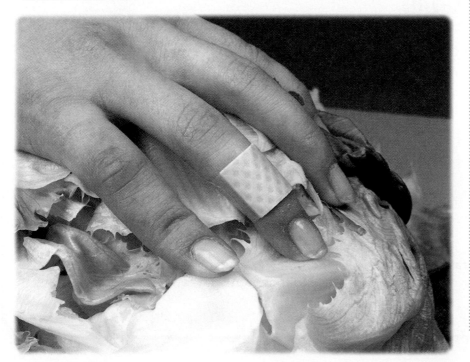

◄
FIGURE 1-8
Bandaged Finger
You should wear gloves to prevent bandages from falling into the food.
 Classifying *What two types of hazards does this picture represent?*

CHEF'S TIP

FILL IT UP
Some kitchens have "fill-to" lines in their three-compartment sinks. If your sink has fill-to lines, use them.

Cleaning and Sanitizing

In a professional kitchen, you must both clean and sanitize anything that comes in contact with foods. Cleaning and sanitizing your tools and work area is one of the most important ways to prevent cross-contamination. It is actually a three-step process. First, clean the surface by washing it. Then, rinse it thoroughly. Once it is rinsed, sanitize the surface.

Cleaning involves removing soil or food particles from surfaces such as cutting boards, knives, pots, pans, and other preparation and cooking equipment and utensils. It also involves sweeping the floor and removing grease and dirt from the stove's ventilation hoods, the walls, and the refrigerator doors.

Once an object is cleaned, it can be sanitized. In a professional kitchen, **sanitizing** means that you have used either heat or chemicals to reduce the number of pathogens on a surface to a safe level.

You can sanitize surfaces by using hot water (180°F) or a chemical sanitizer. Small tools and dishes can be submerged in hot water or a mixture of water and a sanitizer. Larger surfaces and appliances, such as meat slicers, can be sanitized after they are cleaned by wiping or spraying them with a **sanitizing solution**, a solution made by mixing water and a chemical sanitizer.

Sanitizing can be done manually. Small tools, containers, pots, and pans can be washed by hand, or manually, in a three-compartment sink. The first compartment is filled with hot water and a detergent. The detergent helps to loosen food particles or grease so they can be rinsed away. The second compartment contains clean water to rinse away the dirt as well as the detergent. The third compartment

Types of Cleansing Agents

Type of Cleaner	Description
Detergent	Penetrates quickly and softens soil so the soil can be scrubbed and rinsed away.
Degreaser	Special type of detergent that contains a grease-dissolving agent. Also known as solvent cleaners.
Acid cleaner	Used to remove mineral buildup in coffee makers, steam tables, and dishwashing machines. Not for use on aluminum.
Abrasive cleaner	Used carefully to scour dirt or grease that has baked or burned onto pots and pans.

Types of Sanitizers

Sanitizer	Advantages	Disadvantages
Chlorine	Inexpensive; good for most sanitizing needs	Corrodes metal; irritates skin
Iodine	Moderate cost; less corrosive and irritating than chlorine	Can stain
Quaternary ammonium compounds	Stable at high temperatures (such as dishwashing machines)	Expensive; can leave a film when used with hard water

contains either very hot water (at least 180°F) or a mixture of water and a chemical sanitizer.

The amount of sanitizer you add to the water depends on the type of sanitizer you are using. Leave the item you are sanitizing in the sanitizing sink long enough for the sanitizer to work. Be sure to read and follow the sanitizer's directions.

Dishwashing machines can be used to clean and sanitize tools and containers. Dishwashing machines use special detergents for cleaning.

FIGURE 1-9
Three-Compartment Sink
Use cleansers and sanitizers properly.
Predicting *How might switching from one sanitizer to another change the amount of sanitizer you need to add to the third compartment of the sink?*

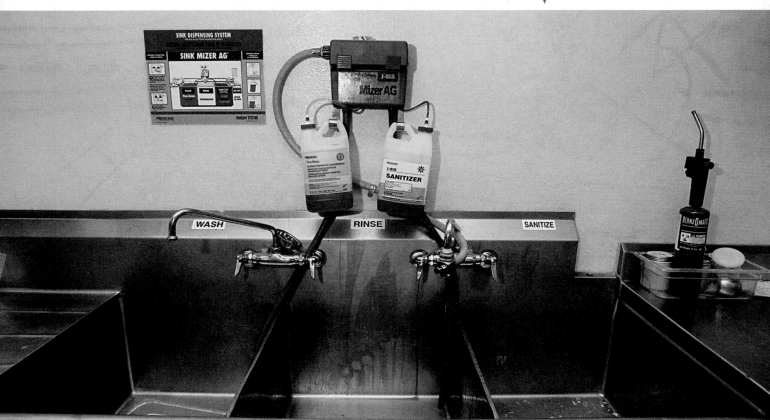

Some use very hot water to rinse and sanitize items, while others use chemical sanitizers. To keep these machines operating properly, be sure to scrape items before you put them into the machine.

Once tools and equipment are properly cleaned and sanitized, let them air dry before putting them away. Towels should not be used. They might be a source of cross-contamination.

Reading Checkpoint *What is the difference between cleaning and sanitizing?*

Waste Disposal and Recycling

The garbage that accumulates as you work in the kitchen is not only unsightly. It is also a potential source of food contamination.

CULINARY SCIENCE

Chemical Hazard: Mercury in Fish

Mercury is released in the air through industrial pollution. Eventually it falls to earth, accumulating in streams and oceans. Bacteria in the water cause a chemical change that turns mercury into methylmercury (meth-ul-mer-cur-ee). This type of mercury is a potent toxin that can damage the brain and nervous system, causing learning disabilities and other developmental problems in babies and children.

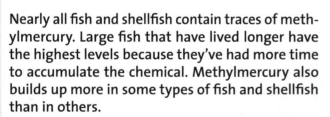

Nearly all fish and shellfish contain traces of methylmercury. Large fish that have lived longer have the highest levels because they've had more time to accumulate the chemical. Methylmercury also builds up more in some types of fish and shellfish than in others.

Forty states have issued advisories warning residents to restrict their consumption of some types of fish because of this chemical hazard. Government findings show that 8% of all woman of childbearing age in the United States have unsafe mercury levels. This translates to over 300,000 babies who are born at risk each year.

The Food and Drug Administration (FDA) and the Environmental Protection Agency (EPA) have issued the following recommendations for young children, nursing mothers, pregnant women, and women who may become pregnant:

• Do not eat shark, swordfish, king mackerel, or tilefish because they contain high levels of mercury.

• Eat up to 12 ounces (two average meals) a week of a variety of fish and shellfish that are lower in mercury, such as small ocean fish, shrimp, canned light tuna, salmon, pollock, and catfish. Be aware that albacore ("white") tuna has more mercury than canned light tuna.

• Check local advisories about the safety of fish caught by family and friends in your local lakes, rivers, and coastal areas.

Research

Find out what the safe amount of mercury is for a 6-ounce portion of fish. Make a list of the fish you eat, both fresh and canned. For fresh fish caught locally, contact your local health department to find out the mercury levels of your local waters. For store-bought fresh and canned fish, go to the FDA food-safety website and the EPA fish advisory website to find out what the mercury levels are for them.

Waste Disposal   As you are cooking, you create a good deal of waste. Wrappers, packaging, bones, cans, and paper towels are all examples of the trash that you need to remove from the kitchen. Put all trash into a container as soon as possible so it can't get mixed with the food you are preparing.

Cover garbage cans and empty them every four hours or whenever they are full. Rinse out the container before you bring it back into your work area, and line it with a clean plastic liner.

Recycling   Getting rid of garbage is expensive. Many restaurants use recycling to try to cut down on the amount of waste they produce. Depending on the community or state you live in, you may be able to recycle a variety of containers: cardboard boxes, glass jars or bottles, metal cans, and plastic containers. Notice the recycling symbol on recycling receptacles and some recyclable materials.

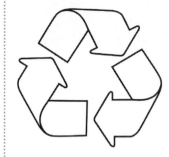

 **Reading Checkpoint**   *Typically, how often should garbage cans be emptied?*

Pest Control

Plenty of pests can come into a kitchen—mice, flies, cockroaches, and mosquitoes are just a few examples. No one likes to see pests, and for good reason. They can be the source of foodborne illness by carrying a pathogen. The pathogen may be found on the pest's skin or hair. Their droppings may also carry a potentially dangerous virus or bacteria.

Keeping pests out of the kitchen is an important part of keeping the kitchen sanitary. Most pests reproduce quickly. It takes only a short time for a couple of flies to go from being a nuisance to becoming a hazard.

Keeping Pests out of the Kitchen   To keep pests out of the kitchen, you have to make it hard for them to get into the kitchen in the first place. They can arrive through any holes or gaps around doors or windows. They can come through almost any opening, including the roof or drains. All windows and doors need to shut tightly. Screens covering doors or windows should be free from rips or holes. Blocking any gaps along the foundation or in the roof also keeps pests out of the kitchen.

Pests look for food, so clean all areas and surfaces thoroughly. Wipe up spills immediately and sweep up crumbs. Storing foods properly also helps keep pests out of the kitchen. Keep foods covered or refrigerated.

FIGURE 1-10
Recycling Cardboard
Take boxes apart and fold them flat.
Applying Concepts *How does properly recycling cardboard boxes help manage waste and cut down on pests?*

Never store foods on the floor or touching the wall. Garbage cans should be lifted off the ground and must have tight-fitting lids. Don't pile bags of garbage over the rim of garbage cans or dumpsters. Cover recycling containers. Make sure cans and bottles for recycling are rinsed. Check all boxes and packaging for pests. Get rid of boxes as soon as you unpack the food. Some pests can hide in the packaging.

Pest Management Sometimes, no matter how careful you have been, pests can invade the kitchen and become a real problem. Then you may need to rely on pesticides to control them. Pesticides are dangerous materials that must be stored well away from foods. They need to be applied properly to be effective. Local, county, and state regulations regarding the use of pesticides may differ, so many restaurants use a special service to control pests.

Ultimately **pest management** involves three steps:
- Maintaining the kitchen so pests can't get in it.
- Taking care of all waste properly, so pests can't find food.
- Using pesticides to eliminate any pests.

Reading Checkpoint *What is meant by pest management?*

1.1 ASSESSMENT

Reviewing Concepts

1. What is a foodborne illness?
2. What are the nine steps in proper handwashing?
3. What is the difference between cleaning and sanitizing?
4. Why is trash a problem in a kitchen?
5. What are the three steps involved in pest management?

Critical Thinking

6. **Predicting** Which do you think would have a higher Aw (water activity): a watermelon or a walnut?
7. **Inferring** Based on your knowledge of FAT TOM, why do chefs cool food quickly? (Explain your answer in terms of the conditions specified by FAT TOM.)
8. **Comparing/Contrasting** What is the difference between direct contamination and cross-contamination of food?

TEST KITCHEN

Gather food from the kitchen. Predict whether each item is acidic or alkaline, and then predict the pH of the items. Test the actual pH (for solid food, grind the food and mix with distilled water).

SCIENCE

Outbreaks of Foodborne Illness

1. Describe a recent outbreak of a foodborne illness at a food establishment. Describe the specific cause, how many people were affected, and their symptoms. Discuss how the establishment could have avoided the outbreak.
2. Research how the Department of Health recommends food establishments respond to an outbreak of a foodborne illness. Create a step-by-step procedure for a restaurant in the event of an outbreak.

The Flow of Food

READING PREVIEW

Key Concepts

- Describing the flow of food
- Purchasing and receiving foods safely
- Cooking foods safely
- Serving foods safely

Vocabulary

- dry goods
- flow of food
- holding
- one-stage cooling method
- perishable goods
- time-temperature abused food
- two-stage cooling method

> **"T**he expression 'from farm to table' has as much to do with food quality as it does with food safety. **"**
>
> – Howard "Corky" Clark

The Flow of Food

Food-service establishments of all sorts, whether they are fine dining restaurants, delis, or cafeterias, have a responsibility to their customers to serve safe foods. Cooks and chefs play a critical role in making sure the food the customer eats is as safe and wholesome as it can be.

Food can become contaminated between the time it arrives at the kitchen and the time it is served to customers. The **flow of food** is the route food takes from the time a kitchen receives it to the time it is served to the customer. Learning about the flow of food through a restaurant helps you to learn not only when foods might become contaminated, but can also how to reduce or eliminate the risk of contamination.

Howard "Corky" Clark (left)
The Culinary Institute of America

Purchasing, Receiving, and Storing Foods

Purchasing The foods that are purchased by a restaurant must come from a reputable source. The restaurant is responsible for being certain that the companies or individuals from whom it buys food meet all the necessary requirements for supplying and delivering safe foods. The source is responsible for providing the food in good condition.

Receiving The first step in the flow of food is receiving. When you receive food, there's a handoff of responsibility. You are now taking responsibility for the food your restaurant receives. You must always inspect any food you receive for damage. Different types of food have different potential problems.

Perishable goods, for example, are foods that must be properly wrapped and kept cold until they arrive at your restaurant. There are two types of perishable goods—those stored in the refrigerator and those stored in the freezer. Examples of perishable goods requiring refrigerator storage are meats and milk. You are responsible for checking deliveries to be sure perishable goods are at safe temperatures when you receive them.

Perishable goods that require storage in the freezer should be completely frozen when you get them. The packaging should not have any rips or tears. If you see large ice crystals or drips, the food has started to thaw while it was on its way to you.

Foods such as flour, tea, sugar, rice, or pasta are known as **dry goods**. These foods should arrive at your restaurant well wrapped. Any packaging should be free from tears or rips. Canned goods should never have bulges, dents, signs of rust, or leaks.

You should reject any food that does not have clean, intact packaging or that is not at the appropriate temperature.

FIGURE 1-11
Receiving Foods Safely
Meat must be received at the proper temperature.
Solving Problems *What would you do if you received meat that was too warm?*

▼

Storing Once you are certain food you just received is safe, make sure it is stored correctly. This is the second step in the flow of food. You need to avoid cross-contamination and spoilage, while storing foods efficiently. Store freshly delivered food behind food you already have on hand so the oldest food gets used first. This is referred to as a "first in, first out" (FIFO) system. Many food establishments write the date they received a food on the packaging, using an indelible marker.

All perishable goods requiring refrigeration must be transferred immediately to the refrigerator. If possible, store raw ingredients and prepared food separately. If raw ingredients and prepared food must be stored together, always store the raw food below any cooked or ready-to-eat foods to avoid cross-contamination. Foods that might drip or leak should be placed in clean, sanitized containers. Check the temperature of the refrigerator frequently with an appliance thermometer. Refrigerators should be kept between 36°F and 40°F. However, the ideal storage temperature for specific food items may require lower or higher temperatures than normally available in a refrigerator.

Frozen food must immediately be transferred to the freezer. Never place hot food directly into the freezer. It will raise the freezer's temperature and could cause other frozen foods to thaw. Freezers should be kept between –10°F and 0°F.

Put dry goods away in a dry, clean, cool storage area well away from cleaning supplies or chemicals. If you need to transfer food from its original container, be sure the containers you use are clean, sanitized, and have tight-fitting lids. Dry goods should be at least six inches off the floor and six inches away from the wall. Dry storage areas should be kept between 50°F and 70°F.

CHEF'S TIP

FIFO

"First in, first out" is abbreviated FIFO. It means you use up the stock you have on hand (if it is still safe to use) before using new deliveries.

FOCUS ON SAFETY

The Ideal
The ideal storage temperature is the temperature that is both safe and insures that the food item is at its optimal quality. It may be necessary to store food on ice in the refrigerator, for example, to achieve the ideal storage temperature.

Ideal Storage Temperatures

Food Item	Ideal Storage Temperatures
Meat and poultry	32° to 36°F
Fish and shellfish	30° to 34°F
Eggs	33° to 38°F
Dairy products	36° to 41°F
Produce (Refrigerated)	32° to 50°F

 **Reading Checkpoint** *Name the first two steps in the flow of food.*

Cooking Foods Safely

When you cook foods, it is important to protect them from cross-contamination. Clean and sanitary work habits and proper food-storage procedures are important parts of keeping foods safe from cross-contamination.

CHEF'S TIP

THERMOMETERS

Clean and sanitize thermometers after every use.

Preparing Foods Safely Store perishable foods in the refrigerator until you are ready to prepare them. Work with only what you need for about an hour. Don't let food sit on the counter. Return any unused portion to the refrigerator.

One of the biggest concerns when you are preparing food is cross-contamination. Be sure your hands, tools, and any surface the food might touch are clean and sanitized. Prepare different types of food on separate cutting boards or in different areas.

Keep a container of sanitizing solution nearby. (It's very important to use the correct proportion of sanitizer and water.) Also keep plenty of single-use towels on hand. Dip a single-use towel into the sanitizing solution and wring it out before you use it to wipe down cleaned cutting boards or knives. Spray the solution on tools that are difficult to wipe. You should also keep your hand tools (spoons, ladles, and whisks, for instance) in a container of sanitizing solution between uses. Replace the solution when it gets dirty. Dirt in the sanitizing solution keeps it from working properly.

Monitoring Food Temperature You should expect raw foods, especially meats, fish, and poultry, to contain harmful microorganisms. Hazardous foods need to come to temperatures high enough to kill these pathogens.

Once you begin to cook, it is important to bring food to safe temperatures as quickly as possible. Since most foods are served at temperatures that fall within the temperature danger zone (between 41°F and 135°F), you need to minimize how long foods stay in that range.

You need to bring food up to a safe temperature and then hold the food at that temperature for an appropriate amount of time before it is served. The exact temperature varies according to the type of food you are preparing. Make sure your thermometers are accurate when checking temperatures.

FIGURE 1-12
Colored Cutting Boards
Colored cutting boards are used for preparing specific types of food (yellow is used for poultry, red for raw meat, and so on).
Relating Concepts ***How would colored cutting boards reduce cross-contamination?***

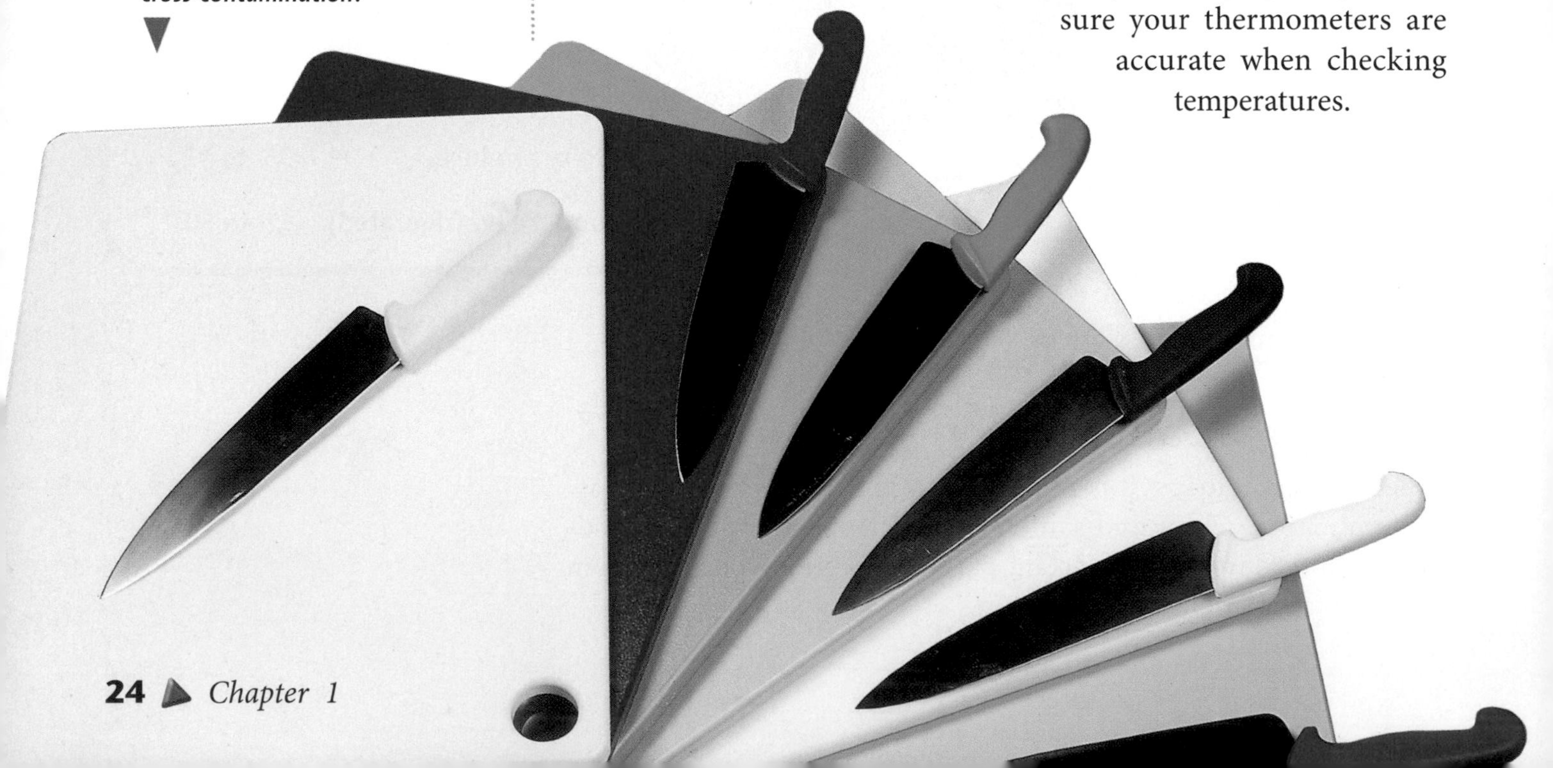

◄

FIGURE 1-13
Checking the Temperature of Cooked Food
A thermometer indicates when the food comes to a safe temperature.
Drawing Conclusions *The thermometer reads 145.7°F. Is this rotisserie chicken safe to serve?*

Fully cook meats before adding them to other dishes. Casseroles and other foods that contain a combination of raw ingredients such as meat and poultry must be cooked to the final temperature of the food requiring the highest internal temperature. Don't mix leftover food with newly prepared food.

The distribution of heat in a microwave oven is often uneven. To distribute heat more evenly, stir and rotate the food frequently.

Safe Food Temperatures

Food Type	Minimum Internal Temperature	Minimum Time at Safe Temperature before Serving
Beef roasts (rare)	130°F 140°F	112 minutes 12 minutes
Roasts (medium beef, pork), lamb, veal	145°F	4 minutes
Ham	155°F	4 minutes
Fish, pork, and beef (other than roasts)	145°F	15 seconds
Ground meats (beef, pork, and game), ham steak	155°F	15 seconds
Poultry, stuffed meats	165°F	15 seconds

▲

Figure 1-14
Special Equipment for Cooling Cooked Foods
Using a chill wand to cool stock (left) and a blast chiller to cool pork (right).
Solving Problems *What cooling methods would you use if this equipment was not available?*

Cooling Foods Safely One of the leading causes of foodborne illness is improperly cooled foods. Cooked foods you plan to store for later use need to be cooled down to below 41°F as quickly as possible. There are two methods for cooling foods. Always depend on a thermometer reading to determine that the appropriate degree of coolness has been reached.

- **The One-Stage Cooling Method.** Using the **one-stage cooling method**, food should be cooled to below 41°F within four hours.
- **The Two-Stage Cooling Method.** The **two-stage cooling method** was approved by the Food and Drug Administration in its 1999 Model Food Code. In the first stage of this method, foods must be cooled down to 70°F within two hours. In the second stage, foods must cool down below 41°F within an additional four hours. The total amount of time elapsed during cooling the food is six hours.

Refrigerators are designed to keep foods cold, not to cool hot foods. They cool too slowly and food is at the temperature danger zone for too long a period. For example, it can take 72 hours or more for the center of a five-gallon stockpot of steamed rice to cool down to below 41°F when taken directly from the stove and placed in a refrigerator. You need to cool food much more rapidly to ensure it is safe.

Thawing Foods Safely Never thaw food by simply leaving it out at room temperature. Frozen food may be safely thawed in several ways:

- **In the Refrigerator.** The best—though slowest—method of thawing food is to allow the food to thaw under refrigeration. Place still-wrapped food in a shallow container on a bottom shelf of the refrigerator to prevent any drips from

Tips for Cooling Food Safely

Liquid Food

- Pour liquid into a stainless steel container before you begin cooling it.
- Place container holding liquid in an ice-water bath. The bath should reach the same level as the liquid inside the container.
- Stir liquid frequently.
- In a water bath, set bricks or a rack under the container to allow cold water to circulate.
- In a water bath, use an overflow pipe to allow water to run continuously as the food cools.
- Add ice directly to condensed food (this both cools it and dilutes the food).
- Use a chill wand.

Solid or Semi-Solid Food

- Place food in a stainless steel container before you begin cooling it.
- Cut food into smaller portions (true especially for meat).
- Spread food in a single layer in a shallow container.
- Leave food unwrapped until after it cools.
- Stir food, if possible.
- Put the container of hot food in an ice bath (a larger container filled with ice).
- Use a blast chiller.
- Wrap all cooled food before refrigerating.

contaminating other items stored nearby or below. The time it takes to thaw a food in the refrigerator varies depending on the thickness and texture of the food.

- **Under Running Water.** Place covered or wrapped food in a container under running water of approximately 70°F or below. Use a stream of water strong enough to wash loose particles off the food, but do not allow the water to splash on other foods or surfaces. Clean and sanitize the sink before and after thawing foods under running water.
- **In the Microwave.** You can use a microwave oven to thaw some foods. This method is recommended primarily for individual portions that will be cooked immediately after thawing.

Once thawed, food should be used as soon as possible. For optimal quality and flavor, thawed food should not be refrozen.

Reading Checkpoint *What is the two-stage cooling method?*

FOCUS ON SAFETY

Single Portions
Single portions of frozen food may be cooked from the frozen state, so long as the cooked item is at a safe temperature when served (examples: hamburger patties, french fries).

Serving Foods Safely

Keeping food safe from the time you receive it and throughout the time you cook it is a good way to control most of the hazards that can cause illness or injury. Serving foods safely is the final step in making sure everything you serve your guests is not only delicious and attractive, but also safe.

Holding Some food is served as soon as it is cooked. Other food is prepared ahead of time and then kept hot in steam tables or cold in the refrigerator until you are ready to serve it. This is referred to as **holding** food. Holding food at the right temperature is an important part of keeping the flow of food safe.

Set the temperature controls on all food-holding equipment to the correct temperatures for food safety. Hold hot foods above 135°F. Hold cold foods below 41°F.

Use a sanitized instant-read thermometer to check the temperature of the food you are holding. Discard food that has been in the danger zone longer than two hours. This type of food is referred to as **time-temperature abused food**.

CULINARY HISTORY

Before the Refrigerator

Before the refrigerator, people had to find other ways to store and preserve their food. In some cases, people used ice that was cut from ponds in the winter and stored in sawdust for use in the summer. But people also preserved food in many other ways.

Foods were often pickled—stored in salty water or vinegar with a mix of herbs and spices. Cucumbers, onions, green beans, tomatoes, cauliflower, broccoli, and many other vegetables were pickled so they could be enjoyed long after they were harvested. These pickled vegetables are still an important component of the Italian appetizer, antipasto (ahn-tee-PAHS-toe). In other cuisines, nuts, fish, meat, and even eggs are sometimes pickled.

Green cabbage was pickled in a different way. In Germany, it was shredded, salted heavily, and then kept in a cool, dry place. The salt caused the cabbage to ferment and become sauerkraut. In Korea, cabbage is the major ingredient in kimchi (kimchee). In this spicy condiment, the cabbage is seasoned with garlic, chilies, onions, ginger, and other spices. It is stored in sealed jars in underground

Pickled vegetables ▶

cellars or sheds for a month while it ferments.

Cod fish were salted heavily as a way of preserving them. This caused the cod to lose all its moisture, becoming as hard as a board. In this state it could be preserved almost indefinitely. To use the cod, which was called bacalao (bah-kah-LAH-oh) in Spanish and South American cuisines, it was necessary to soak it in water for a day, replacing the water three or four times as it dissolved the salt.

Research

Research any of the types of preserved food described here. Describe how the food was preserved and how it is used in the cuisine. Provide a recipe that uses the preserved food.

Reheating Improperly reheated food is a frequent culprit in food-borne illness. When food is prepared ahead and then reheated, it should move through the danger zone as rapidly as possible and be reheated to at least 165°F for at least 15 seconds within a two-hour time period.

A steam table will maintain re-heated foods above 135°F but will not bring foods out of the danger zone quickly enough. Bring food to the proper temperature over a source of direct heat such as a burner, flattop, grill, or oven. You may also use a microwave oven to reheat small batches of food or individual portions.

The greater the surface area of the food and the shallower the layer, the more rapidly the food will heat. Use a clean and sanitized instant-read thermometer to check temperature. Clean and sanitize the thermometer after you use it.

FIGURE 1-15
Holding Food Safely
Check the temperature of chilled foods during service.
Applying Concepts *Why is it important to check the temperature of this potato salad?*

 **Reading Checkpoint** *What is the temperature for holding hot foods? Cold foods?*

1.2 ASSESSMENT

Reviewing Concepts

1. What is meant by the "flow of food"?
2. What are the first two steps in the flow of food?
3. Cooked foods you plan to store for later use need to be cooled below what temperature?
4. What is the temperature for holding hot foods? Cold foods?

Critical Thinking

5. **Comparing/Contrasting** What is the difference between the one-stage cooling method and the two-stage cooling method?
6. **Relating Concepts** Some restaurant owners serve time-temperature abused food, arguing that it is wasteful to discard food if it has been held for only an additional half hour. How would you respond?
7. **Inferring** Why is it a good idea to "expect raw foods, especially meat, fish, and poultry, to contain harmful microorganisms?"

TEST KITCHEN

Use two cans of commercially prepared soups. Empty each can in a separate pot and heat quickly to 145°F. Empty each pot in identical stainless steel storage containers. Place both containers into a separate ice-water bath. Stir the soup in one container constantly, but don't stir the other. Record the temperature of the soups every five minutes. Evaluate the results over an hour's time.

SCIENCE

Thermometers

Prepare a report comparing five thermometers (including instant-read digital thermometers). Focus on their stated accuracy, features, and ease of use. Indicate if some are better suited for some types of cooking situations than others. Include your final recommendation.

The HACCP System

READING PREVIEW

Key Concepts

- Defining a food-safety system
- Using the seven steps of HACCP

Vocabulary

- corrective action
- critical control point
- critical limits
- FDA Food Code
- food-safety audit
- food-safety system
- HACCP
- hazard analysis

"**F**ood can be pleasurable, but food improperly prepared can kill. Using HACCP, with validated controls, while monitoring critical limits is the only way to assure that meals are safe. "

– O. Peter Snyder, Jr., Ph.D.
Hospitality Institute of Technology and Management, St. Paul, MN

Food-Safety System

A **food-safety system** is a system of precautionary steps that take into account all the ways foods can be exposed to biological, chemical, or physical hazards. A food-safety system's goal is to reduce or eliminate risks from those hazards.

Standards and Inspections The Food and Drug Admininistration (FDA) has established sanitation standards that apply throughout the country. These standards are part of the **FDA Food Code**, a document that is updated frequently to reflect new findings about keeping foods safe. The FDA Food Code is not a federal law or regulation. It is simply a set of recommendations. It is up to state and local governments to establish their own laws and regulations. They can do this by adopting some or all of the FDA Food Code. They can also establish their own standards. However, the standards they

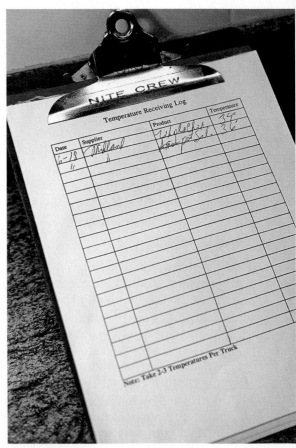

PARSIPPANY DEPARTMENT OF HEALTH
SANITARY INSPECTION REPORT

Emily's   2026 Maple Avenue
NAME OF ESTABLISHMENT   STREET ADDRESS OF ESTABLISHMENT

SATISFACTORY

DETAILED SUPPORTING DATA SHEETS ARE AVAILABLE UPON REQUEST
ON THESE PREMISES AND AT THE LOCAL DEPARTMENT OF HEALTH

develop must meet the national standards. Often, local standards call for more careful controls than the national standard.

Every food-service establishment must be inspected by a representative of the local health department. The inspection is known as a **food-safety audit** (also called a health inspection). The number of times the establishment has to be inspected depends on a number of factors such as the number of meals served, the types of food on the menu, and the number of past violations. It is a good idea for a food-service establishment to conduct self-inspections periodically to prepare for an official audit. That way, it can identify and correct any problems it may find.

When it is time for your establishment to be inspected, you should cooperate with the inspector. Whenever you can, you should accompany the inspector during the audit. You can learn a great deal during this inspection. The inspector will be looking carefully at foods and supplies, the grooming and hygiene of the staff, the temperatures for holding and serving foods, your procedures for cleaning and sanitizing, and your water supply, waste disposal, and pest control.

Once an inspection is complete, the food-service establishment receives the results. If there are any violations, it must correct the situation. If it does not correct them, it may have to pay fines.

▲

FIGURE 1-16
Health Inspection Report
The city health department gave this restaurant a satisfactory inspection.
Drawing Conclusions *Do you think there is a connection between a restaurant's cleanliness and the quality of its food?*

Serious violations that remain uncorrected could mean the establishment is closed.

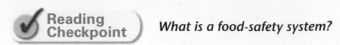

Reading Checkpoint *What is a food-safety system?*

The Seven Steps of HACCP

HACCP is a system for maintaining food safety. The letters stand for "Hazard Analysis Critical Control Point" and the term is often pronounced "HAS-sup." HACCP is a scientific, state-of-the-art food-safety system originally developed for astronauts. It takes a systematic approach to controlling conditions that are responsible for most foodborne illnesses. It attempts to anticipate how and when food safety problems are likely to occur and takes steps to prevent them.

The HACCP system has been adopted by both food processors and restaurants, as well as by the FDA and USDA (the U.S. Department of Agriculture). Although a food-service establishment will need to make an initial investment of time and people to create a good HACCP plan, the system can ultimately save money and time, as well as improve the quality of food served to customers.

The heart of HACCP is contained in the following seven steps (each step is examined in more detail later in this section):

1. Conduct a hazard analysis.

2. Determine Critical Control Points (CCP).

3. Establish critical limits.

4. Establish monitoring procedures.

5. Identify corrective actions.

6. Establish procedures for record-keeping and documentation.

7. Verify that the system works.

1. Conduct a Hazard Analysis. A **hazard analysis** examines the flow of food from the moment you receive it until you serve it. As you know, there are two ways in which hazards are introduced into food: by direct contamination and by cross-contamination. You need to be aware of the points in that flow when conditions are most likely to encourage the growth of pathogens in a food. You also need to be aware of points when foods might be exposed to pathogens or other contaminants from other sources. Of particular concern are potentially hazardous foods: meats, fish, poultry, milk, eggs, and fresh produce.

2. Determine Critical Control Points A **critical control point** is a specific point in the process of food handling where you can prevent, eliminate, or reduce a hazard. To quote the 1999 FDA Food Code, a critical control point is "a point or procedure in a specific food system where loss of control may result in an unacceptable health risk."

The cooking step in the flow of food is an example of a critical control point. By meeting safe temperatures for storing, holding, cooking, and serving foods, you can control hazards at various critical control points in the flow of food. Another way to do this would be to focus on how long a food is kept at a given temperature.

3. Establish Critical Limits **Critical limits** indicate when foods are at unsafe temperatures. Critical limits also indicate how long food can be held at an unsafe temperature. These limits are established by local health departments and are typically based on the FDA's Food Code.

Your food-service establishment may have even stricter limits in place, especially if you are cooking for people with special needs, such as elderly people, young children, or people who are sick. When you know the critical limits, you can make decisions about how to handle the food properly as you cook, serve, or store it.

4. Establish Monitoring Procedures Entering accurate measurements of time and temperature in a log book gives a food-service establishment a record of how foods were handled. This record also alerts the establishment to any corrective steps they may need to take.

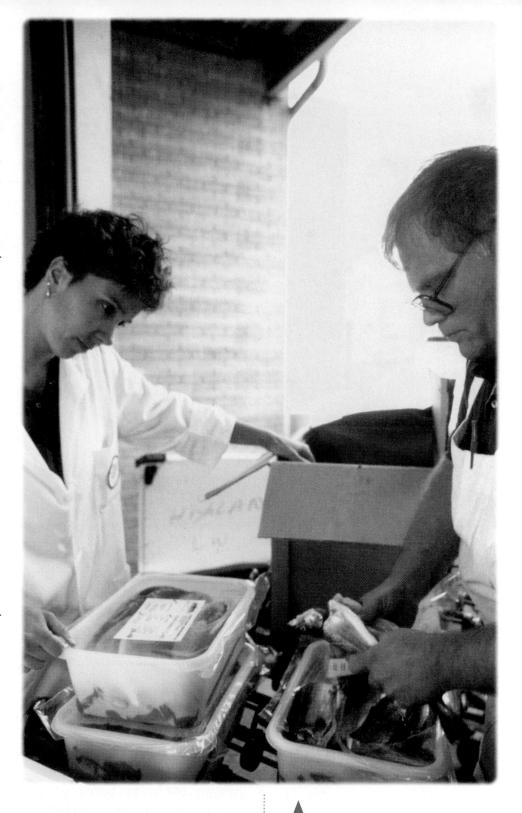

▲
FIGURE 1-17
Inspecting Food
Check the condition of all foods when they arrive.
Applying Concepts *Why is it important to check the condition of food as it arrives?*

▲
FIGURE 1-18
Monitoring
Monitor the temperature of
foods held in a steam table.
Inferring *How do critical limits
and monitoring procedures make
the job of a food-service worker
easier?*

A good HACCP plan describes what measurements should be taken by a food-service establishment and how often. The plan also indicates the person responsible for taking and recording specific measurements.

5. Identify Corrective Actions Whenever a measurement indicates that food is not at the right temperature or has been held in the danger zone for too long, a food-service establishment must do something about it. This action is known as a **corrective action**.

For example, if food is held at an unsafe temperature for too long (such as 120°F for more than 2 hours), the corrective action would be to discard that food. If the food has fallen below the appropriate temperature, but has not been at an unsafe temperature for too long a time, the corrective action would be to heat the food to a safe temperature.

6. Establish Procedures for Record-Keeping and Documentation Documentation for HACCP typically consists of time and temperature logs, checklists, and forms. It is important to record enough information so a food-service establishment can be sure standards are being met. However, it is not a good idea to try to record so much information that food-service workers can't keep up with it. Forms need be easy to understand and fill out.

7. Develop a Verification System To be sure the system is working and the information being recorded is accurate, a food-service establishment needs a system to double-check, or verify, the information recorded in the forms.

A supervisor, executive chef, or outside party should take time and temperature measurements to double-check the information. If their measurements don't match the measurements recorded in the log, it is likely that proper procedures are not being followed.

When the food-service establishment looks into the situation, it may find there are not enough thermometers or the thermometers are not working properly. It may find that the forms are too difficult to fill out and are untrustworthy. Or it may find that the person responsible for keeping the record is not doing the job correctly. If the establishment doesn't verify the system, however, it will never know it isn't working and, therefore, it will not be able to make the changes necessary to fix the problems.

 **Reading Checkpoint**   *What are the seven steps of HACCP?*

1.3 ASSESSMENT

Reviewing Concepts

1. What is a food-safety system?

2. What are the seven steps of HACCP?

Critical Thinking

3. **Applying Concepts** Why would the types of food on the menu be a factor in the number of times a food establishment is given a formal food-safety audit?

4. **Comparing/Contrasting** What are some advantages and disadvantages of food-safety systems such as HACCP for a food-service establishment?

5. **Inferring** Why is it important for a food-service establishment to develop its own verification system?

TEST KITCHEN

If your school has a cafeteria, research its HACCP program. Ask about each step in the program. If possible, watch a food-service worker who is responsible for monitoring a critical control point. Pay attention to the worker's monitoring procedures and ask to review the logs for that particular critical control point for the previous week. Report on your findings.

SCIENCE

Lessons from the Space Program
Research the background of the HACCP program as it relates to the space program. Describe why the system was developed and how it was implemented in space. What relevance does its use in space have for earth-bound food establishments?

Review and Assessment

Reviewing Content

Choose the letter that best answers the question or completes the statement.

1. Botulism is caused by
   a. bacteria
   b. a virus
   c. a parasite
   d. fungi

2. Freezers should be kept between
   a. 36°F to 41°F
   b. 30°F to 32°F
   c. 0°F to 10°F
   d. –10°F to 0°F

3. The first step in the HACCP system is to
   a. establish critical limits
   b. establish monitoring procedures
   c. conduct a hazard analysis
   d. determine critical control points

4. Hepatitis A is caused by
   a. bacteria
   b. a virus
   c. a parasite
   d. fungi

5. The ideal storage temperature for meat and poultry is
   a. 32°F and 36°F
   b. 30°F and 34°F
   c. 38°F and 41°F
   d. 41°F and 45°F

6. A pathogen is a (an)
   a. type of sanitizer
   b. organism that causes disease
   c. type of cleansing agent
   d. virus that causes salmonella poisoning

7. The second compartment in a three-compartment sink is used for
   a. cleaning dirt
   b. sanitizing
   c. rinsing dirt and detergent
   d. sterilizing

Understanding Concepts

8. What is a foodborne illness?

9. What are the three types of potential hazards that can contaminate food and produce foodborne illnesses?

10. What is meant by the term "flow of food"?

11. What are the seven steps of the HACCP system?

12. What is FAT TOM? What does each letter stand for?

13. What is meant by the term "temperature danger zone"? What are the actual temperature limits for this danger zone?

14. What is the best, but slowest, method for thawing foods safely?

Critical Thinking

15. **Comparing/Contrasting** What is the difference between direct contamination and cross-contamination?

16. **Communicating** Explain why the seventh step of the HACCP system is necessary?

Culinary Math

17. **Applying Concepts** Is a food that has a pH of 8.5 a potentially hazardous food?

18. **Applying Concepts** Is a food that has an Aw of .85 a potentially hazardous food?

On the Job

19. **Applying Concepts** A customer asks for the chef to cook a piece of beef very rare. Is the customer at risk? Is the restaurant at risk? Explain your answer.

20. **Drawing Conclusions** How does the identification of corrective actions (the fifth HACCP procedure) make the job of the food-service staff easier?

LAB ACTIVITY

Project 1: HACCP Procedures

Answer these questions when your class works through Project 1.

- What are your school's critical control points?
- What types of critical limits does your school use?
- What would it be like to monitor HACCP procedures at your school?
- What sorts of HACCP logs are kept by your school?
- What were the results of your school's last food-safety audit?
- How would it feel to participate in a food-safety audit at your school?

TEST PRACTICE

Choose the letter that best answers the question or completes the statement.

1. What is anisakidae?
   A   a type of bacteria
   B   a type of virus
   C   a type of parasite
   D   a type of fungi

2. What is the minimum internal temperature for a medium beef roast?
   A   130°F
   B   135°F
   C   140°F
   D   145°F

3. What is the minimum internal temperature for poultry?
   A   135°F
   B   145°F
   C   150°F
   D   165°F

4. What is the recommended storage temperature for produce?
   A   32°F to 36°F
   B   36°F to 41°F
   C   41°F to 45°F
   D   45°F to 50°F

5. Cooked foods you plan to store for later use need to be cooled down below what temperature as quickly as possible?
   A   45°F
   B   41°F
   C   36°F
   D   32°F

6. Using the one-stage cooling method, how quickly should food be brought down to the appropriate temperature?
   A   within 1 hour
   B   within 4 hours
   C   within 6 hours
   D   within 8 hours

7. The cause of listeriosis is a
   A   bacteria
   B   virus
   C   parasite
   D   fungi

8. Food that has been in the temperature danger zone for longer than two hours is referred to as
   A   a pathogen
   B   a time-temperature abused food
   C   a perishable food
   D   a biological hazard

9. A piece of metal or glass in food is referred to as
   A   a pathogen
   B   a chemical hazard
   C   a physical hazard
   D   a potentially hazardous food

10. Food that has a pH of 4.6 to 7 is
    A   a potentially dangerous food
    B   an acidic food
    C   an alkaline food
    D   A and B

KITCHEN SAFETY

READING PREVIEW

Key Concepts

- Identifying fire hazards
- Controlling fires by using alarms and extinguishers
- Using a fire emergency plan

Vocabulary

- arson
- assembly points
- automatic systems
- evacuation routes
- fire detectors
- fire emergency plan
- fire extinguishers
- hood systems

> **"I**t's a nightmare to have the hood system set off in the middle of a busy night. You have to throw out all the food that's doused in the chemicals they release. **"**
>
> **– David Bruno**
> The Culinary Institute of America

Fire Hazards

If there was no intention to start a fire, then it is an accidental fire. An accidental fire can start in a kitchen for a variety of reasons. Open flames might set paper or cloth aflame, or a buildup of grease might ignite when it gets too hot. Water might splash into an outlet and create a spark that causes a fire. Even though an accidental fire might result from someone's carelessness, it is not caused by someone intentionally starting a fire.

Arson is the opposite of an accidental fire. Arson is the act of deliberately setting a fire. The best defense against arson is having a good fire-safety plan and keeping your building as secure as possible.

To avoid fires in the first place, you need to be aware of fire hazards. Some common types of fire hazards are open flames and heat, grease, electrical wiring, and unsafe storage areas.

Open Flames and Heat Fires can start in a kitchen for a number of reasons. Open flames, such as gas burners or wood fires, can set paper, food, grease, clothing, and even metal on fire.

Even things that are no longer flaming can be hot enough to catch something on fire. Metal cookware and wiring can get hot enough to start a fire if an easy-to-burn material gets close to them.

Items commonly found in the kitchen or the dining room may also produce a flame: matches, candles, or cigarettes and cigars. Throwing matches that are still glowing or hot into a wastebasket filled with papers might lead to a basket filled with flames.

The motors that run appliances and equipment—including mixers, grinders, refrigerators, and freezers—can get hot enough to start a fire.

Grease Grease fires are another common type of fire. A layer of dirt or grease is often the cause of a flare-up or fire in the kitchen. When equipment is kept clean, the kitchen is safer.

Follow a regular cleaning schedule for walls and work surfaces. Cooking appliances such as ranges, oven hoods, fryers, broilers, and ovens must also be kept clean. Heating, air conditioning, and ventilation units, including hoods and filters, must also be kept clean to avoid the risk of a grease fire.

Electrical Wiring More than thirty percent of all accidental fires in restaurants are caused by faulty electrical wiring, by electrical equipment, or by the improper use of electrical equipment.

Electrical plugs and outlets should always be used carefully. Never pull a plug from an outlet by the cord. If a cord looks frayed or if a plug appears to be damaged, it should be replaced. The plugs on equipment may be either grounded (plugs with three prongs) or ungrounded (plugs with two prongs). Use the right kind of outlet for the plug you have. A grounded outlet has three holes to accommodate each of the prongs on a grounded plug. An ungrounded outlet has only two holes.

Overloaded outlets are a common cause of electrical fires. Be sure you don't have too many items plugged into a single outlet. The plate covering the outlet should be securely attached without any cracks or holes. Keep all outlets and plugs dry.

Unsafe Storage Areas Space for storage is limited in any kitchen. It is important that your storage areas are designed for fire safety. Store flammable items, such as paper supplies and linens, away from open flames or heating units. Keep cleaners or bleaches separated from flammable items as well. The combination can cause fires.

 **Reading Checkpoint** *What are four common types of fire hazards?*

Fire Control

In case a fire starts in the kitchen or dining room, every food-service establishment must have certain systems in place. Fire detectors, automatic hood and sprinkler systems, and portable fire extinguishers are necessary for fire safety.

Fire Detectors **Fire detectors** are devices that warn you about a fire so you can get out of the building safely. There are two basic types of fire detectors: smoke detectors and heat detectors.

- **Smoke detectors.** To detect the presence of smoke, smoke detectors work best when there is good air flow. If there is no way for the air to move—for example, at the end of a hall-way—the smoke detector cannot function properly.
- **Heat detectors.** Activated by a sudden rise in temperature, heat detectors can sense a fire even when there is no smoke.

Fire detectors must be well maintained. If they are battery-operated, it is important to replace the batteries on a regular schedule. Fire detectors must be installed and maintained by a fire-safety expert.

Automatic Hood and Sprinkler Systems **Automatic systems** include extinguishers, sprinklers, and alarms triggered by the heat of a fire. These systems work whether or not the building is occupied. Sprinkler systems release water to put out a fire. They are used in areas such as the dining room or the bathroom, but not in areas where food is prepared.

The National Fire Protection Association (NFPA) requires that special systems be installed in areas over ranges, griddles, broilers, and deep fat fryers. These systems, sometimes known as **hood systems** (or as ansul systems), are located in the ventilation hood above the equipment. Instead of water, they release chemicals (either in a liquid or powder form), carbon dioxide, or gases (known as inert gases) that can smother a fire and put it out.

FOCUS ON SAFETY

Smothering Flames
If flames erupt in a pan, put a lid on the pan to smother the flames. Pull the pan off the heat until the fire is extinguished.

FIGURE 2-2
Hood Ventilation System
Hood systems release chemicals that blanket the fire.
Predicting *If a restaurant's hood system went off during service and the food being cooked was all discarded, would you re-cook all the food and continue or refund customers' money and close for the night?*

Sprayers

Fire Extinguishers Fire extinguishers are handheld devices you can use to put out a small fire.

A small fire is described as being no more than three feet wide or three feet tall. If the fire is larger than that, you should call the fire department immediately. If it is small enough to handle with a fire extinguisher, be sure to choose the right type of extinguisher.

Specific types of fire extinguishers are designed to handle specific types of fires. Fires are grouped into five classes, depending on the material involved in the fire.

Every fire extinguisher is marked with the class of fire it is meant to handle. Some fire extinguishers can be used for more than one class of fire, so there may be more than one letter on the extinguisher's label.

- Water-based extinguishers work by dousing the fire with water. They are recharged with a clean water source. They can be used only on Class A fires.

Fire Extinguishers & Classes of Fires

Class of Fire	Type of Flammable Material	Type of Fire Extinguisher to Use	
Class A	Paper, cloth, wood, plastic	Class A	Class A:B
Class B	Gas, grease, oil, liquid stored under pressure (spray cans)	Class A:B	Class A:B:C
Class C	Electrical equipment, cords, outlets, circuits, motors, switches, or wiring	Class A:C	Class B:C
Class D	Combustible switches, wiring, as well as metals, including iron or copper	Class D	
Class K	Fires caused by deep fat fryers and other appliances that cook foods with combustible oils or fats	Class K	

◄

FIGURE 2-3
Fire Extinguishers
The fire extinguisher on the left is a water-based extinguisher. The one on the right is a dry-chemical extinguisher.
Applying Concepts *On which types of flammable materials should each fire extinguisher be used?*

- Foam extinguishers work by cooling the fire down and covering it in a blanket of foam that keeps air from getting to the fire. These extinguishers will not work if they freeze. Use foam extinguishers for Class A or Class B fires only.
- Dry-chemical extinguishers interrupt the chemical reactions that keep a fire burning. These extinguishers may be approved for use on Classes A, B, and C (A/B/C) or for Classes B and C (B/C) only.

You should know where extinguishers are located in the kitchen and what types of extinguishers they are. It is also important to learn how to use portable fire extinguishers safely—before you actually need to use one. A simple way to remember how to use a fire extinguisher is to use the PASS system.

PASS System for Using Fire Extinguishers

Pull the pin.

Aim low, at the base of the fire (stand 6 to 8 feet away from the fire).

Squeeze the trigger.

Sweep from side to side.

Flames of Different Colors

The color of a flame depends on two things: the amount of air that can get to the flame and the type of material that is burning.

Fire needs oxygen to keep burning. The less oxygen that mixes with the flame, the more yellow the flame looks. A candle or a campfire burns yellow because particles of the candle or wood are not being burnt. These tiny unburned particles are carbon, left over from burning the candle or wood. Carbon glows a very bright yellow when it gets hot. Soot and smoke are nothing more than these unburned carbon particles.

If you look closely at a candle flame, you'll see that some of the flame is a different color. The center of the flame is blue, while the areas farther from the wick are yellow. That's because the area closest to the candle's wick burns at a much higher temperature; there are fewer unburned carbon particles in the blue area.

The flame on a gas stove is mainly blue because air is blended with the gas for a very hot flame that doesn't contain much unburned carbon. A blue flame burns at around 1,700°C, while a yellow flame burns at only about 1,000°C.

The color of a flame also depends on the material being burned. Lots of fuels produce blue flames when burned. The most commonly available fuels used in the household are natural gas and propane. Both burn with blue flames. Butane, found in lighters, also has blue flames. Other chemicals make flames of other colors. For instance, a mixture of copper and chlorine makes a greenish, turquoise, or bright blue flame. Lithium burns brilliant red. Carbon powder from graphite or charcoal dust burns bright yellow-orange, like a candle flame.

Natural gas burns with a blue flame.

Experiment

Compare the efficiency of various fuels by evaluating the amount of unburned carbon produced by the fuel over an identical period. Use four fuel sources: a candle, sterno (or alcohol lamp), propane, and natural gas. Light each fuel's source and hold a small pan in the upper part of the flame for 10 seconds (making sure to hold the pan's handle with a pot holder or other appropriate heat protection). Compare the residue left on the knife. How would you rank the various fuels in terms of their efficiency in completely burning their available carbon? Does this have implications for cooking, holding, and serving food?

All portable fire extinguishers need to be recharged on a regular basis as part of their maintenance. Recharging is done only by an approved fire extinguisher service company.

 **Reading Checkpoint** *What are the five classes of fires and what types of flammable materials does each type include?*

Fire Emergency Plans

A well-designed **fire emergency plan** means you have an established plan of action in case of a fire. Such a plan requires that you post the numbers for the fire department and emergency rescue teams on every phone. It also requires that you post a diagram of the floor plan showing escape routes, fire exits, and assembly points.

Escape Routes Escape routes, or **evacuation routes**, give everyone in the building at least two ways to get out of the building. Fire exit doors need to be clearly marked and kept clear at all times. Fire doors open outward by pushing on the door; they do not need to be opened with a key when you are exiting the building.

FIGURE 2-4
Evacuation Route
An evacuation route gives everyone in the building at least two ways to escape.
Inferring *Why is it important to have more than one evacuation route out of a building?*

Having two routes means you can still get out even if a hall, stairwell, or fire door is impossible to get through because of smoke or fire. Exit routes and fire doors should have some type of battery-powered lighting.

Assembly Points Assembly **points**, or meeting points, are predetermined spots at a safe distance from the building. Everyone who has exited the building must come to one of the assembly points so it can be determined that everyone has left the building.

Fire Drills Drills give you a chance to practice escape routes. They also give you the opportunity to practice safe behaviors that might save lives during a real fire. Whether you are practicing in a fire drill or the fire is real, remember the following:

☑ Call the fire department immediately.
☑ Stay calm.
☑ Shut off any gas valves if you can.
☑ Start to get people out of the building as soon as possible. If there are guests or customers in the building, show them the best escape route. Tell them where to meet when they have come out of the building.
☑ Meet at the assembly point.
☑ Let a firefighter know immediately if someone is missing.

FIGURE 2-5
Exit Sign
An escape route is marked by an illuminated exit sign.
Inferring *Why do you think exit signs and emergency lighting are often battery-powered?*

 **Reading Checkpoint** *Why should there be two escape routes as part of a good fire emergency plan?*

2.1 ASSESSMENT

Reviewing Concepts

1. What are some common types of fire hazards?
2. What are the four steps in the PASS system for using fire extinguishers?
3. What is a fire emergency plan?

Critical Thinking

4. **Drawing Conclusions** How would a regular cleaning schedule minimize the risk of a fire?
5. **Analyzing Information** Which class(es) of fire extinguisher(s) is/are best suited for a fire involving electrical equipment?
6. **Applying Concepts** Which type of fire extinguisher (water-based, foam, or dry-chemical) would be best used for a fire involving a deep fat fryer?

TEST KITCHEN

Examine the fire detectors, hood systems, sprinkler systems, and fire extinguishers in your school's kitchen and dining area. Determine the class of fire for which each extinguisher is intended. Talk to the person at your school about its fire emergency plan.

SCIENCE

Types of Fire Extinguishers

Research the way each of the most common types of fire extinguishers works (water-based, foam, and dry-chemical). Why are different types of extinguishers needed for different types of fires? How does each type put out a specific type of fire? Report on your findings.

READING PREVIEW

Key Concepts

- Identifying common accidents and injuries
- Using basic safety guidelines to prevent accidents and injuries
- Learning first aid and emergency procedures
- Understanding safety as an ongoing process

Vocabulary

- accident report
- automated external defibrillator (AED)
- carcinogenic
- cardiopulmonary resuscitation (CPR)
- corrosive
- Environmental Protection Agency (EPA)
- general safety audit
- Hazard Communication Program
- Hazard Communication Standard (HCS)
- Heimlich maneuver
- Material Safety Data Sheet (MSDS)
- obstructed airway maneuver
- Occupation Safety and Health Administration (OSHA)
- worker's compensation

Todd Knaster
The Culinary Institute of America

> "**A**ccidents do happen, even in the best-run kitchens and bakeshops, but you can avoid most of them simply by keeping your mind on your work."
> – Todd Knaster

Types of Accidents and Injuries

An accident is any unplanned event that hurts someone or damages someone's property. Accidents and injuries are a constant concern in any work environment. When you know the most common types of injuries or accidents and how they happen, you can take steps to avoid or prevent them. The most common types of accidents in food-service establishments are:

- Burns
- Cuts
- Sprains, strains, and falls

Burns Some burns are more serious than others, but all burns require immediate care. Burns are described as being first, second, or third degree. Degree refers to how severe the burn is.

Burns

Degree	Description	Treatment
First-Degree Burn	Skin turns red, feels sensitive, and may become swollen.	Treat with cool running water or by covering with towels soaked in cool water. Do not apply ice.
Second-Degree Burn	Burn is deeper and more painful than in first degree. Blisters form. Blisters may ooze and are quite painful.	Cool the skin as directed for first degree burns. Do not apply ointments or bandages. Seek medical attention.
Third-Degree Burn	Skin may turn white and become soft, or it may turn black and feel leathery or hard. Burned area does not have feeling because the burn has damaged the nerves.	Cover burn with cool, moist, sterile gauze or a clean cloth. Do not apply ointments, a cold compress, or cold water. Seek immediate medical attention.

Cuts It comes as no surprise that cuts are one of the most common injuries for cooks. You can get a cut from a knife or any sharp edge. Cleaning up broken glass can cause a cut, as can handling paper. There are different types of cuts.

- **Abrasions.** A minor cut, such as a rug burn, caused by rubbing the skin against something else.
- **Lacerations.** A cut or tear in the skin, such as a knife cut. Lacerations can be quite deep. Deep lacerations or those in a place on the body that can open easily, such as your forehead, may require stitches.

FOCUS ON SAFETY

Dull Knives
The worst cuts come from dull knives because they cut unevenly and require more force.

Figure 2-6
Cutting with a Knife
Never underestimate the sharpness of a kitchen knife.
Drawing Conclusions *Why is it important for a new chef to focus immediately on learning appropriate knife skills?*

- **Avulsions.** A cut that removes a piece of skin or even a part of the body, such as a fingertip. Depending on severity, an avulsion may require immediate medical attention.
- **Punctures.** A wound resulting from a sharp object that pierces the skin and makes a deep hole in the skin. Depending on depth and location, a puncture wound may also require immediate medical attention.

Strains, Sprains, and Falls Sprains and strains are the result of twisting or wrenching your body out of its normal position. They are often caused by tripping or falling over something. If you step into a hole or onto something slippery, it is very easy to sprain an ankle.

When you fall, you might try to stop yourself by grabbing something or putting your hands behind or in front of you. A sprained wrist or shoulder might then result.

You might suffer from strained muscles when you stand in the same position for too long, hold yourself in an awkward position (such as when you stretch or bend over to work), or make the same motion over and over again.

One of the most common types of strain is a back strain caused by lifting heavy things improperly.

 **Reading Checkpoint** *What are the most common types of accidents in food-service establishments?*

Preventing Accidents and Injuries

Preventing accidents and injuries is your responsibility. You can make yourself safer at work by observing safe work habits as described in this chapter. When you work safely, you help to create and maintain a safe environment for everyone.

Dressing for Safety You can protect your safety when you work in the kitchen by wearing the right kind of clothing, using the right tools and equipment, and learning to use all the tools and equipment in the kitchen properly and safely.

Large or dangling jewelry such as necklaces, earrings, bracelets, and rings can get caught in machinery. Take such items off before you start work.

The toque (TOKE) prevents hair from falling into the food. It also is open at the top for coolness.

Never wear loose or baggy clothing that could get caught on something or tangled in machinery or equipment. A chef's double-breasted jacket protects against burns and scalding on the arms. Be sure to keep your arms covered.

FIGURE 2-7
Uniform and Kitchen Safety
A complete uniform offers protection.
Forming a Model *What parts of the uniform protect you from injury?*

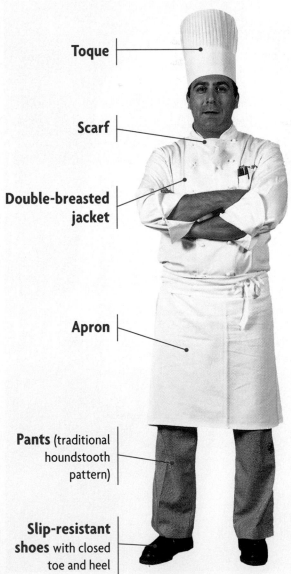

Toque

Scarf

Double-breasted jacket

Apron

Pants (traditional houndstooth pattern)

Slip-resistant shoes with closed toe and heel

You can re-button a double-breasted jacket on the alternate side if one side becomes dirty.

The chef's apron adds another layer of protection. You can also change it easily if it becomes unduly soiled. The houndstooth pattern of the traditional chef's pants does not show dirt.

Wear slip-, grease-, and heat-resistant shoes to protect your feet. They should either lace up tightly or they should have no laces at all. Closed toes (and even steel-reinforced toes) in your shoes can protect you from being cut if a knife should fall. Closed toes also can help prevent bruises if something heavy falls on your feet and can protect against stubbed toes. The shoes' heels should be low to avoid twisted or sprained ankles.

Wear additional protective gear when appropriate, especially when you are working with chemicals such as those in cleaning compounds. You may need to wear goggles, a mask, and rubber gloves to protect yourself from chemicals or from the particles that might fly out of a meat grinder or mixer. Wear heavy leather gloves when you are opening crates or lifting heavy objects.

Handling Knives and Other Cutting Tools Safely To avoid cutting yourself, keep your knives sharp as you work and keep your hands and your knives clean and dry. Keep your knives organized and safely stored at your work station. Don't let your work area become so cluttered that it is difficult for you to work safely. If a knife falls, do not grab for it—just try to get out of its way.

To avoid cutting someone else with your knife, pass it to someone else safely by laying it down on a flat surface with the handle extending to the person receiving the knife. Let them pick the knife up from the table, rather than passing it in midair.

If you must carry a knife through a crowded kitchen, walk carefully with the blade pointed down and the knife held close to your side. Put the knife in a shield if possible.

Wear mesh cutting gloves to protect your hands, especially when you must exert pressure on the blade. Opening oysters and slicing meats are good examples of situations when a mesh cutting glove would help avoid accidents.

◀ **FIGURE 2-8**
Carrying a Knife
Hold the knife properly to avoid hurting others.
Drawing Conclusions *Why is this the best way to carry a knife in a crowded kitchen?*

Take special precautions when you are working with machines or appliances that cut food (slicers, grinders, mandolines, graters, and so on). Most of these machines have guards that are meant to keep your fingers or hands away from the blade. Be sure you always use these guards properly. When you are cleaning any motorized equipment, be sure it is turned off and unplugged before you begin cleaning.

Other common sources of cuts in the kitchen are can openers, open metal cans, and the cutting bars on rolls of aluminum or plastic wrap. Keep your hands away from sharp and jagged edges.

Broken glass can cut an unwary person easily. Clean up broken glass right away with a broom. Ask people near the area to simply stay where they are until you finish cleaning up. Many establishments have a separate container to hold broken glass. It would be easy for broken glass to break through a plastic trash-can liner and cut you when you empty the can.

Preventing Burns An open flame, the handle of a hot pan, sputtering grease, and chemicals can all cause burns. The best way to prevent burns is to keep your skin away from hot or caustic materials.

Your uniform is one way you can protect yourself from burns. Wear long sleeves and keep them rolled down. When you need to move or carry a hot pot or pan, use oven mitts or dry side towels to protect your hands. Tell other workers that a hot pan or tray has been left to cool.

If you must walk through the kitchen with something hot, let people know you are walking near them. If possible, let them know before you start walking.

Putting hot pans or dishes into a sinkful of water is not good for the utensils. It could cause them to buckle or even break. It is also dangerous for anyone who might unknowingly reach into the sink. Let hot pots and pans cool before washing them or putting them in the sink. Always keep a dry side towel on the handle of a hot pan to let other workers know the pan and handle are hot.

The steam that is released when you lift the lid on a pot or pan can cause serious burns. To prevent steam burns, lift the lid so the side farthest from you opens up first. This directs the steam away from your face.

FIGURE 2-9
Preventing Burns
The chef's uniform and towel protect him from burns.
Predicting *How might a restaurant cope when a chef cannot work because of a serious burn?*

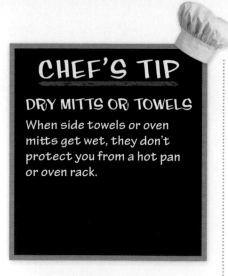

CHEF'S TIP

DRY MITTS OR TOWELS

When side towels or oven mitts get wet, they don't protect you from a hot pan or oven rack.

FIGURE 2-10
Prevent Slipping
Let others know that the floor is wet or slippery.
Applying Concepts *Why is using both a sign and a verbal warning the safest way to alert others that the floor is wet?*

▼

FIGURE 2-11 ▶
Prevent Back Strain
Lift a heavy object safely.
Inferring *If a chef strained his or her back badly and was unable to cook, what would the consequences be for the restaurant?*

A hot blast from an oven could be enough to cause burns on your face. If you wear glasses, the hot air could cause the lenses to fog up, temporarily obscuring your vision. Open oven doors carefully by opening them just enough for some of the hot air to escape before you open the door the rest of the way and then bend to look into the oven.

Hot oil and grease sputters when water is added to it. Moist food, frozen food, batter, and other liquids all contain enough water to cause oil to fly out of the pan or deep fryer. You should dry food as much as possible before adding it to hot oil. When you are adding food to the pan or the fryer, lower the food carefully into the oil. If possible, place food so the edge closest to you is placed in the hot oil first.

Avoiding Slips and Falls When you are walking, look where you are going. Be conscious of potential problems. Wet floors, uneven carpeting, broken pavement, loose steps, and objects that stick out into your path all can trip you. Keep floors and walkways clean, dry, and free from obstructions. Tell others about any hazards that might make them fall.

Walking in the dark makes it impossible to see hazards clearly, so turn on a light or use a flashlight. Replace light bulbs or use a flashlight so you can see more easily.

Cleaning Up Spills Even a little spill on the floor can be enough to make someone slip and fall. Whenever you see liquid on the floor, clean it up immediately. Water is easy to lift up, but grease is more difficult to clean. Use mops or absorbent toweling to soak up the liquid. You may also need to scatter an absorbent material such as cornmeal on spills, especially grease spills, before scooping it up.

No matter what type of material is spilled on the floor, the first thing you should do is let the people in the immediate area know. Direct them to walk around the spill, or put up signs to indicate that the floor is wet or slippery.

Lifting and Moving Heavy Objects Safely You may need to move heavy or bulky objects into or out of storage, take a large pot off the stove, or lift a pan of food out of the oven. Moving heavy objects improperly can easily result in a strained or aching back.

Before you start to lift a heavy object on your own, take a minute to consider each of the following questions:

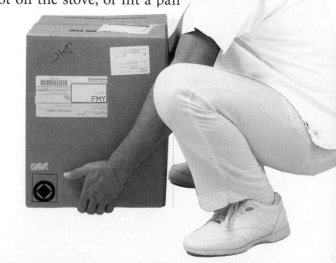

- Can you lift the weight on your own or should you get some help?
- Is the load balanced?
- Could the contents splash or spill as you walk?
- Is your path clear of all obstacles?
- Is there somewhere for you to put the item down safely once you reach your destination?

When you have the help you need and have made sure the path is clear, you are ready to begin. To lift heavy items safely, use your legs and not your back. To do this, squat down, keeping your back straight, rather than bending over. Get a secure grip on the item you need to move. While you are holding the item firmly, lift yourself up with your legs.

Using Ladders Safely Your storage area may have shelves that are above your head. To safely store or retrieve items higher than you can easily reach, you must use a ladder.

There are three basic types of ladders:
- Step stool
- Step ladder
- Straight ladder

A ladder is usually labeled with information about how much weight it can safely carry. Each part of the ladder should be in good condition. All of the steps (or rungs) should be intact. Ladders should have nonskid feet to keep them in place when you are using them. If your ladder is made of metal, make sure it is not touching anything electrical, such as wires, motors, or outlets.

The ladder you choose should be tall enough so you don't need to step on the top of step stools or the top two rungs of a straight ladder. Make sure the ladder won't slip or move when you get on it. Step stools and folding ladders may have a brace that holds the legs of the ladder open. Be sure the braces are completely locked in place.

If you are using a straight ladder, you need to lean it at an angle, with the bottom of the ladder about two or three feet away from the shelf or wall. Lean the top of the ladder against the shelf or wall. Check the ladder to make sure it won't slide or slip. If something you are trying to reach is not close enough to reach without leaning, get down from the ladder and move the ladder closer to the item. You should never lean to one side.

Get help if you need it. You should always have someone hold the bottom of a straight ladder steady as you climb it. If you can't carry the item you need to move with one hand, get someone to stand by who can hand you things or hold the things you've retrieved.

After you finish using a ladder, be sure to put it away properly. Tall ladders can easily fall, so be sure they are secured.

▲
FIGURE 2-12
Step Ladder
A ladder is typically labeled with information about how much weight it can safely carry.
Communicating *If you needed help retrieving an object from a high storage shelf, but everyone seemed busy, what would you do?*

Driving You may be called on to drive for a work-related activity. It is important that you observe all safe-driving procedures. Your license must be up-to-date. Employers may want you to complete a defensive driving program. They may also check your driving record.

The vehicle you are driving should be safe to drive. The brakes should work. All lights, including turn signals and brake lights, must work properly. Tires need to have enough tread for traction on the road. If a vehicle supplied by your employer is not safe, bring it to your employer's attention immediately.

Wet, windy, snowy, icy, and dark conditions all make driving more difficult. Take extra care when you must drive at these times and leave plenty of room between yourself and other cars so you can react to other drivers and stop safely.

Avoid distractions while you are driving. Anything that takes your attention away from traffic, such as changing the station on the radio, talking on a cell phone, eating or drinking, could easily cause an accident.

Follow safe-driving procedures. Always observe the posted speed limit and other traffic signs. Never pass a stopped school bus, and wear your seatbelt at all times.

 **Reading Checkpoint** *What is the right way to lift something heavy?*

First Aid and Emergency Procedures

First aid is the care you give in response to an accident. It is important to assist the injured person as quickly as possible. Every kitchen should

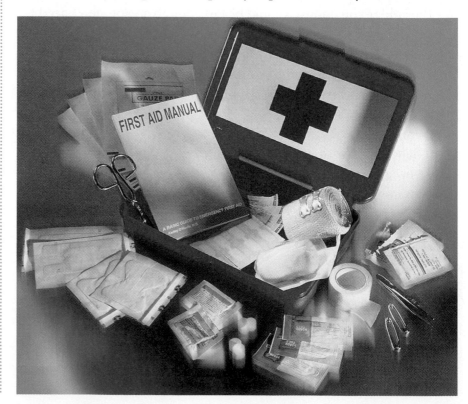

FIGURE 2-13 ▶
First Aid Kit
This first aid kit includes bandages, ointments, tweezers, and aspirin, along with a first aid manual.
Predicting *Which supplies do you think will need to be replaced most frequently?*

have properly stocked first aid kits that can be used for a variety of injuries including cuts, burns, and sprains. If your establishment offers delivery service or if they use trucks for catering, first aid kits should be placed in these vehicles as well.

The kit should include materials and supplies such as bandages, ointments, tweezers, scissors, and some medications, such as aspirin. It should also include a first aid manual with information about how to treat various injuries. Whenever there is an accident and someone gets hurt, follow these guidelines:

- Check the scene of the accident.
- Stay calm and keep the victim calm.
- Ask anyone who is not directly assisting the victim to stand back.
- Call for medical help, if appropriate, or ask someone to call for you.
- Administer first aid, using the information in your first aid manual.
- Stay with the victim until medical help arrives.
- Complete an accident report.

The American Red Cross offers courses that teach the correct procedures in case of workplace accidents. You can contact your local office to find out when these courses are offered, and you could even take a course in first aid to become certified.

Burns Whenever someone is burned, the first step is to remove the heat source. This may involve removing clothing that is soaked with hot water or grease and moving the victim to a safe place. Keep the victim calm and still so he or she can rest while first aid is administered or until medical help arrives. Soak the burned area in cool water. If you can't easily get the burned area into a basin of cool water, soak some cloth in cool water and drape the cloth over the burn.

Cuts Clean the area well with soap and warm water. If the cut is bleeding heavily, cover the wound with sterile gauze pads and apply pressure until the flow stops. Cover the wound with a sterile dressing or bandage. The bandage should be changed frequently to keep it from becoming a potential site for cross-contamination. Anyone helping someone with a cut should wear disposable gloves and avoid coming in contact with blood.

Sprains, Strains, and Broken Bones Rest the injured part of the body. If possible, elevate the injured part so it is higher than the person's heart. This will help keep the swelling down. Apply ice to the injured area during the first 24 hours. Leave the ice in place for about 15 minutes each hour. Wrap or bandage the injured area to give it support. Serious sprains should be kept as still as possible. Some falls are strong enough to break, or fracture, a bone. Then, an x-ray and a visit to the emergency room or a medical professional is required.

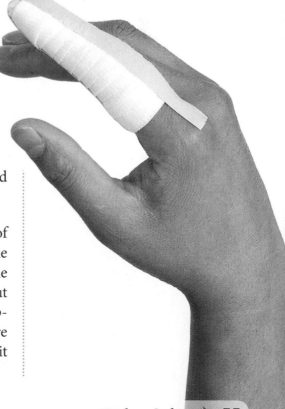

Choking A guest or co-worker can easily choke on a piece of food. When something gets lodged in a person's airway, that person is not able to talk or breathe. The **obstructed airway maneuver**, or **Heimlich** (HIME-lick) **maneuver**, is performed to remove the obstruction. Food-service establishments should have posters that show how to perform this maneuver.

Obstructed Airway Maneuver (Heimlich Maneuver)

1. Make a fist and place the fist just above the victim's navel, with the thumb facing in.

2. Use a quick, upward thrust. Repeat this thrusting motion until the obstruction is coughed up.

CPR **Cardiopulmonary resuscitation (CPR)** (card-ee-OH-PULL-mohn-ayr-ee ree-suss-ih-TAY-shun) is a technique used to restore a person's breathing and heartbeat. CPR is called for if someone stops breathing because of shock, drowning, or other serious injury. It involves breathing into the mouth of the victim at regular intervals. You also compress the chest at regular intervals by pressing down on the chest with your hands. To become certified in CPR techniques, you need to complete a training program. Both the training and certification need to be renewed every year. Do not try CPR without appropriate training.

AED An **automated external defibrillator (AED)** (AUT-oh-may-ted eks-TURN-uhl dee-FIB-rill-a-tor) is a device that shocks the heart into starting again. Using this device properly and quickly often means the difference between life and death when someone has a heart attack. If your establishment has an external defibrillator, learn its location. If you are not trained to use it, find out who on the staff does have the appropriate training so no time is lost when a real emergency occurs. Do not try to use an AED without appropriate training.

Preparing for Emergencies There is no way to guarantee safety in every single situation. Natural disasters, including floods, earthquakes, blizzards, wind storms, and forest fires, are almost impossible to predict accurately. Losing power, no matter what the reason, is a serious safety concern as well. If someone shows up at your restaurant armed with a gun or explosives intent on either harming someone or robbing the establishment, more than one life could be put at risk.

The only way to protect yourself, your coworkers, and your guests against these situations is to use sensible safety precautions and to be prepared.

Different parts of the country experience different types of natural disasters. Blizzards are a danger in some parts of the country, hurricanes in others, and tornadoes and lightning strikes in others. To prepare for these situations, you should have bottled water, blankets, flashlights, and a battery-operated radio on hand. Make certain that all battery-powered devices have working batteries. Learn the best safety procedures for situations you are likely to encounter.

To protect your establishment from intruders, keep doors secured. Try to have at least two people on hand whenever you must open or close the establishment. Turn on lights in parking lots and alleys when it is dark. Make sure alarms and other security devices are turned on to warn of a break-in.

✓ Reading Checkpoint *How do you perform the obstructed airway maneuver (the Heimlich maneuver)?*

FIGURE 2-14
Emergency Preparedness
Some basic emergency items: first-aid poster for choking, emergency phone numbers, first-aid kit, and fire extinguisher.
Forming a Model *What other emergency items might you include for your part of the country?*

▼

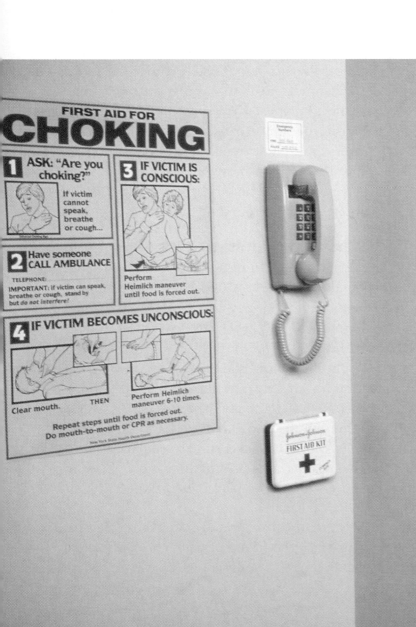

Safety As an Ongoing Process

Keeping yourself and your establishment safe from fire, accidents, and injuries is a job that is never complete. Safety is the result of staying alert, using safe procedures, and monitoring safety procedures on a daily basis to be sure they are being followed. Because safety is such an important concern, there are several federal regulations all employers and managers must know about and follow carefully.

Occupational Safety and Health Administration (OSHA) Workers have the right to a safe working environment free from hazards. The **Occupation Safety and Health Administration (OSHA)** is a federal agency that is charged with keeping the workplace safe. OSHA regulations require the employer to post safety and health information in the workplace. OSHA also requires that all employees follow the regulations for workplace safety.

The safety of every employee and every customer is the legal responsibility of the food-service establishment. Any food-service establishment that does not meet this responsibility is legally responsible for any accidents, injuries, illnesses, or deaths that might result. This responsibility extends through the entire premises, including the kitchen, dining room, bathroom, parking lot, or any area in or surrounding the building.

Hazard Communication Standard Chemicals, such as cleaning agents, dishwashing compounds, sanitizers, or bleach, are often found in the kitchen. You may also find pesticides, metal polishes, and materials to control mildew and fungus.

The **Environmental Protection Agency (EPA)** plays a part in regulating workplace safety along with OSHA by requiring food-service operations to track any chemicals that pose a risk to health. The **Hazard Communication Standard (HCS)**, also known as "Right-to-Know" or "HAZCOM," makes sure the employer tells all employees about the chemical hazards present on the job. This standard also requires employers to train employees in the safe use of any products containing chemical hazards.

Chemicals that are a hazard to your safety are those that can irritate or eat away your skin, the lining of your nose and throat, or (if they are ingested) damage your entire digestive system.

The Red Cross

You've seen the symbol of a red cross on first aid kits, boxes of bandages, and other first aid supplies. That symbol stands for an important international organization, the Red Cross, with a long history.

In 1862, a young Swiss businessman named Henry Dunant wrote a book called *A Memory of Solferino*. He described what he had seen on a battlefield in northern Italy in 1859. Nearly 40,000 soldiers had been killed or wounded. They were simply left on the battlefield, without any help. After his book was published, his concern and that of many others resulted in the birth of the International Committee of the Red Cross.

While the idea of an organization dedicated to providing help to those fighting in wars was spreading throughout Europe, the American Civil War was being fought in the United States. Clara Barton, a former schoolteacher and government worker from North Oxford, Massachusetts, went into the battlefields to help care for the wounded. She was given the nickname "Angel of the Battlefield." When the Civil War ended, she traveled to Europe, where she first learned about the Red Cross Movement. She joined in the work of bringing aid and relief to civilians during the Franco-Prussian War of 1870–71.

Today the Red Cross has many goals, including programs that send nurses into areas where communicable diseases are a problem. The Red Cross has also started first aid and industrial safety campaigns as well as water safety campaigns to help prevent drownings.

You may have heard about the Red Cross's training courses in CPR, first aid, water safety, and health-care training. These programs have saved many lives. Learning how to care for victims of accidents and people who need help in an emergency is one of the ways you show your professionalism as a member of the culinary profession.

This 1917 American Red Cross poster incorporates a quote from President Woodrow Wilson.

Research

Find the number and address of your local chapter of the Red Cross. Find out what training programs they offer. How often are the courses offered? Can you get a certificate from the program? How often do you need to renew your training to keep your certification current?

DANGER

HAZARDOUS CHEMICALS

These irritating substances are referred to as **corrosive** (core-OH-siv) materials. The most common type of hazard associated with chemicals is burns, either from direct contact between the material and your unprotected skin or from a fire caused by the chemicals. Some chemicals can burst into flame easily, and some can ignite if exposed to air, moisture, or other chemicals.

The chemicals that pose a risk to your health are those that are toxic, poisonous, or cancer-causing, or **carcinogenic** (car-sin-oh-JEN-ik). Health hazards from chemicals include long- and short-term injuries or illnesses. Short-term illnesses may be relatively minor and last only a few days or weeks. However, long-term illnesses can last for months, years, or your entire life. Cancers that result from chemical exposure in the workplace can be life-threatening.

Material Safety Data Sheets (MSDS) A **Material Safety Data Sheet (MSDS)** describes the specific hazards posed by a chemical. There must be an MSDS for each product that contains chemicals. These sheets are usually supplied by the chemical manufacturer or supplier. Everyone working in the establishment must have access to this information. Every MSDS is divided into ten sections.

Hazard Communication Program A **Hazard Communication Program** is part of an effective safety program. It includes several important documents that can be used as evidence that reasonable care was taken if someone is injured. It includes the following:

- A written policy, stating that the establishment has the intention of complying with OSHA requirements for job safety.

- An up-to-date list, known as a hazardous chemical inventory, of every hazardous chemical product used or stored in the establishment, including the name, the amount on hand, and where it can be found in the establishment.

- A Material Safety Data Safety Sheet (MSDS) for every hazardous chemical included on the inventory. These sheets must be stored in a central location that is always accessible to every employee.

- Labels for each chemical-containing product, including its name, its hazards, and the name and address of the manufacturer.

- A written copy of the training program for employees.

- A written copy of the Hazard Communication plan.

Accident/Illness Reports and Records Accidents can cause injuries and illness that may result in time lost from work. Too many accidents indicate that proper safety practices are not being followed.

Material Safety Data Sheets (MSDS)

Name and contact information for the manufacturer

1: Product identification

Both the chemical and the common name of the product

2: Hazardous Components

The chemical and common name of the ingredients that pose either a physical or a chemical hazard

3: Physical Data

A physical description of the product, including its appearance, odor, boiling point, pH, and any other characteristics that might help identify it

4: Fire and Explosion Data

Information about any explosive or fire hazards, including whether or not the chemical is flammable

The type of fire extinguisher or special firefighting procedures necessary to put out a fire caused by the product

5: Reactivity Data

Information concerning other substances or conditions that should be avoided in relation to the product (for instance, some chemicals should never be mixed with water)

6: Spill or Leak Procedures

How to store and handle the product, clean up spills safely, and dispose of used product and its container properly

7: Health Hazard Data

How the product can enter the body (for example, by breathing it in or through direct contact with the skin)

Effects of being exposed to the product

Information about any cancer-causing effects of the product

8: First Aid

The emergency procedures you should follow if you are exposed to the product

9: Special Protection Information

Information about protective gear such as masks, gloves, or goggles

Appropriate procedure for keeping the area ventilated as you work

Any specific hygiene procedures you should follow before or after working with the product

10: Additional Information

Information or instruction that does not fall into any of the other sections on the sheet

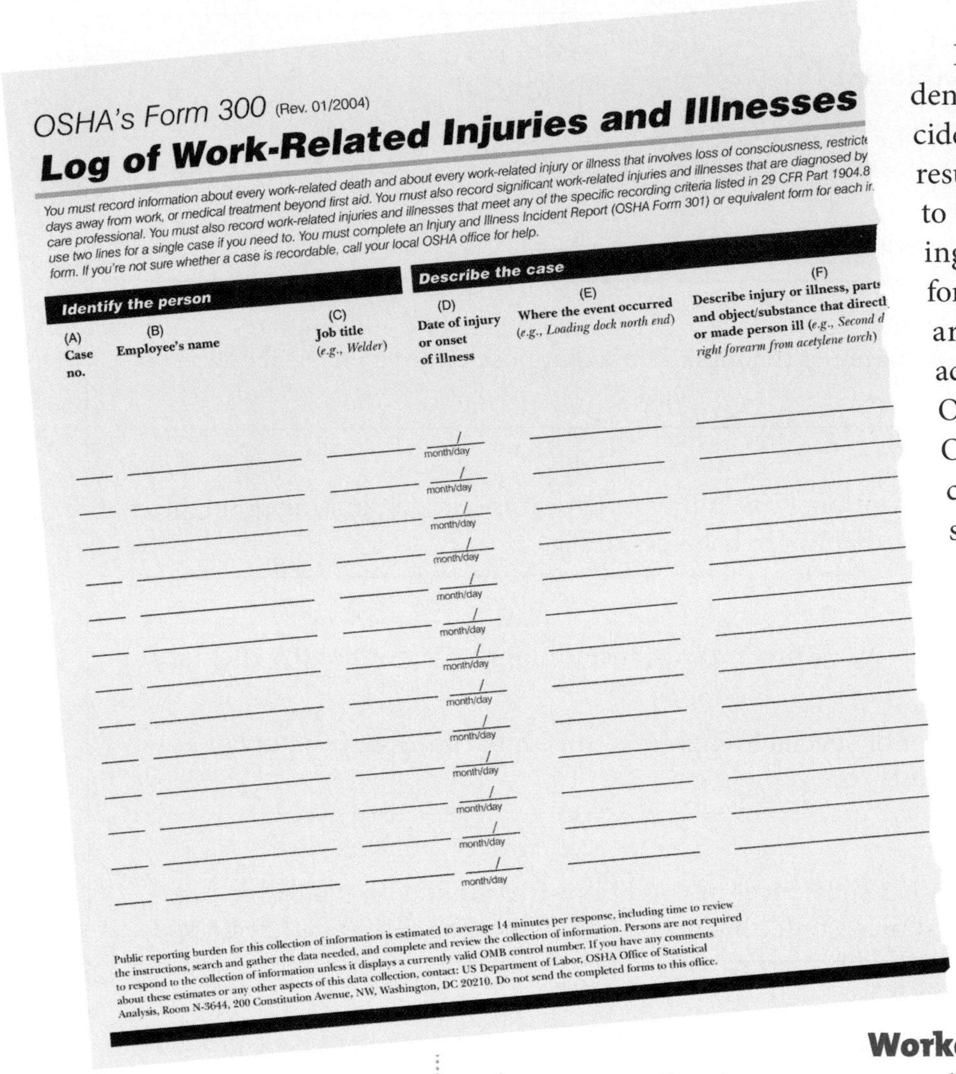
OSHA's Form 300 (Rev. 01/2004)

Log of Work-Related Injuries and Illnesses

You must record information about every work-related death and about every work-related injury or illness that involves loss of consciousness, restrict days away from work, or medical treatment beyond first aid. You must also record significant work-related injuries and illnesses that are diagnosed by care professional. You must also record work-related injuries and illnesses that meet any of the specific recording criteria listed in 29 CFR Part 1904.8 use two lines for a single case if you need to. You must complete an Injury and Illness Incident Report (OSHA Form 301) or equivalent form for each ir form. If you're not sure whether a case is recordable, call your local OSHA office for help.

Identify the person			Describe the case		
(A) Case no.	(B) Employee's name	(C) Job title (*e.g., Welder*)	(D) Date of injury or onset of illness	(E) Where the event occurred (*e.g., Loading dock north end*)	(F) Describe injury or illness, parts and object/substance that directl or made person ill (*e.g., Second d right forearm from acetylene torch*)
			/ month/day		
			/ month/day		
			/ month/day		
			/ month/day		
			/ month/day		
			/ month/day		
			/ month/day		
			/ month/day		
			/ month/day		
			/ month/day		
			/ month/day		
			/ month/day		
			/ month/day		

Public reporting burden for this collection of information is estimated to average 14 minutes per response, including time to review the instructions, search and gather the data needed, and complete and review the collection of information. Persons are not required to respond to the collection of information unless it displays a currently valid OMB control number. If you have any comments about these estimates or any other aspects of this data collection, contact: US Department of Labor, OSHA Office of Statistical Analysis, Room N-3644, 200 Constitution Avenue, NW, Washington, DC 20210. Do not send the completed forms to this office.

It is important to report accidents properly. If there is an accident at your establishment that results in a death, you must report to OSHA within eight hours, using a standard **accident report** form. If three or more employees are hospitalized because of an accident, you must report that to OSHA within eight hours as well. Other employee injuries and accidents must be reported within six working days.

All establishments are also required to keep a log of accidents and injuries that happen on the workplace for one year. A specific form is filled in with the information from that log. The report must be posted where all employees can read it throughout the month of February of the following year.

Worker's Compensation **Worker's compensation** is a program run by each state that provides help for employees who are hurt or who become sick because of an accident on the job. It supplies money to replace earnings that the employee loses because he or she can't come to work and also pays for medical treatments, rehabilitation programs, and, if necessary, retraining for the employee.

General Safety Audit A **general safety audit** is a review of the level of safety in an establishment. Generally, audits are set up like a checklist, with a checkbox for yes or no. Any items that are checked "no" must be taken care of as soon as possible to keep the restaurant, its employees, and its guests safe.

The four areas of review include:

- The building
- The equipment
- Employee practices
- Management practices

The audit reviews the condition of interior and exterior walls and floors, the roof, the foundation, the electrical wiring, and the plumbing.

Parking lots, storage areas, and outside seating are also reviewed. Depending on the location of the restaurant, the audit may include such items as flood-water drainage, snow and ice removal, and meeting any necessary standards to withstand earthquakes, tornadoes, or hurricanes.

Equipment has to be kept in working condition, whether it is a delivery truck or a refrigerator. The audit reviews the condition of the furniture and rugs. Fixtures, including lighting and bathroom fixtures, must function safely and properly. Fire extinguishers must be installed and maintained properly.

Employees are also part of the general safety audit. They are responsible for being trained in safe procedures. Once trained, they are responsible for following those procedures.

The review is also concerned with the employer's Hazard Communication Program, including its training program for employees and proper record-keeping procedures for accidents and illnesses.

 **Reading Checkpoint** *What is included on an MSDS?*

2.2 ASSESSMENT

Reviewing Concepts

1. What are the three classes of burns? Describe each and indicate its treatment.
2. What is the right way to lift something heavy?
3. How do you perform the obstructed airway maneuver (the Heimlich maneuver)?
4. What is included on a Material Safety Data Sheet (MSDS)?

Critical Thinking

5. **Drawing Conclusions** Why should an employee review the MSDS for any products which that employee may be required to use?
6. **Predicting** What does a food-service establishment's annual log of accidents and injuries tell you about that establishment?
7. **Comparing/Contrasting** For whom do you think the Hazard Communication Program is more important: employers or employees? Why?

Test Kitchen

Check your school's Hazard Communication Program. Review the MSDS for three common kitchen cleaners (such as oven cleaners, grease cleaners, or floor wax). Evaluate how you would deal with the variety of emergencies each product could cause.

SOCIAL STUDIES

OSHA

Research the history of OSHA in the United States. Find out what rights workers had before OSHA. Why was OSHA created? How have OSHA regulations changed over time? Create a time chart that shows your findings.

Review and Assessment

Reviewing Content

Choose the letter that best answers the question or completes the statement.

1. A Class B fire extinguisher is used for which type of flammable material?

    a. paper, cloth, wood, and plastic
    b. electrical equipment, cords, and outlets
    c. deep fat fryers
    d. grease, oil, liquid stored under pressure

2. The best way to put out a stovetop grease fire is

    a. to spray it with water
    b. to sprinkle it with baking soda
    c. to sprinkle it with salt
    d. to smother it with a damp cloth

3. The best way to carry a knife in a kitchen is

    a. to hold the blade pointing outward and close to your side
    b. to hold the blade pointing upward and above your head
    c. to hold the blade pointing downward and close to your side
    d. to hold the blade pointing inward and above your head

4. A carcinogenic material

    a. causes cancer
    b. irritates or eats away other materials
    c. causes burns
    d. causes blindness

5. A toque is

    a. the name for a chef's jacket
    b. the name for a chef's hat
    c. a hot object from the oven
    d. a dry mitt used to handle a hot object

6. Foam extinguishers are used for

    a. Class A fires
    b. Class B fires
    c. Class A and B fires
    d. Class B and C fires

7. In the Heimlich maneuver, the fist is placed

    a. just below the victim's throat
    b. high on the victim's chest
    c. at the midpoint of the victim's chest
    d. just above the victim's navel

Understanding Concepts

8. What are the five classes of fires?

9. What are the four steps for the PASS system?

10. What are the steps in the Heimlich maneuver?

11. What is an automated external defibrillator?

12. What information is included on a Material Safety Data Sheet (MSDS)?

13. What is included in a Hazard Communication Program?

14. What is the best way to lift heavy objects?

Critical Thinking

15. **Analyzing Information** What information contained in a Material Safety Data Sheet would you consider most important as an employee?

16. **Comparing/Contrasting** Compare the responsibilities of employees and management in relation to a general safety audit.

Culinary Math

17. **Applying Concepts** If more than 30% of all accidental fires in restaurants are caused by faulty electrical wiring, and a restaurant needs 15 fire extinguishers, about how many Class C fire extinguishers should the restaurant have?

18. **Analyzing Data** A large restaurant/catering establishment has 317 employees. Last year 63 separate employees were injured on the job. What percent of employees were injured last year?

On the Job

19. **Communicating** You work at a restaurant that offers voluntary safety training classes. However, employees are not paid for attending these classes. Would you attend? Explain your answer.

20. **Communicating** Why is the ability to deal with health emergencies part of a culinary professional's job

LAB ACTIVITY

Project 2: Hazard Communication Program

Answer these questions when your class works through Project 2.

- Does your school have a Hazard Communication Program?
- What products are listed on the hazardous chemical inventory?
- What types of potential health hazards are represented by the products listed in the hazardous chemical inventory?
- Would you be equipped to provide the first aid shown as required by the MSDS?
- What kind of employee training is offered by your school?
- Has there been a recent general safety audit? If so, what were the results?

TEST PRACTICE

Choose the letter that best answers the question or completes the statement.

1. An ungrounded plug has how many prongs?
   A one prong
   B two prongs
   C three prongs
   D either two or three prongs

2. Hood systems are required over what kitchen equipment?
   A deep fat fryers
   B refrigerators
   C A and B
   D Neither A nor B

3. What is a cordon?
   A an electrical device used with grounded plugs
   B a negative general safety audit
   C the scarf worn by chefs under their jacket
   D another name for a Class K fire extinguisher

4. What can you use to extinguish a small grease fire?
   A water
   B baking powder
   C cornmeal
   D baking soda

5. What absorbent materials can you scatter on a spill, especially a grease spill?
   A cornmeal
   B salt
   C A and B
   D neither A nor B

6. What is an automated external defibrillator?
   A a technique for removing an obstruction from a choking person
   B a device that shocks the heart into starting again
   C a technique use to restore a person's breathing
   D a battery-powered lighting system used for emergencies

7. What is the sixth item in an MSDS?
   A the hazardous chemical inventory
   B an accident report
   C spill or leak procedures
   D health hazard data

8. If three or more employees are hospitalized because of an accident, how soon must the food-service establishment submit a report to OSHA?
   A eight hours
   B twenty-four hours
   C forty-eight hours
   D three days

9. Who runs the Worker's Compensation program?
   A the employer
   B the city
   C the state
   D the federal government

FOOD SERVICE EQUIPMENT

3.1 Work Flow in the Kitchen

READING PREVIEW

Key Concepts

- Understanding workstations and work lines
- Understanding kitchen work flow

Vocabulary

- mise en place
- work flow
- work lines
- work sections
- workstation

"**A** good workflow helps you get the most work done with the least effort. Even small details, like an outlet where you need one, have a big effect."

— Elaine Bell
Elaine Bell Catering Company
Sonoma & Rutherford, CA

Workstations and Work Lines

A restaurant or banquet hall is a business that serves the public. Its kitchen is like a factory that converts raw materials into products. The kitchen is organized for efficiency, turning raw ingredients into satisfying and nourishing meals.

Workstations One of the most important ways a commercial kitchen increases its efficiency is by using workstations. A **workstation** is a work area containing equipment and tools needed for accomplishing a specific set of culinary tasks. Chefs often refer to workstations as simply "stations." This means a chef might talk about the "fry station" or the "grill station." The fry station, for example, prepares all the fried food for the entire kitchen. The grill station prepares all the grilled items for the entire kitchen.

Each station includes the necessary equipment for the function performed at that workstation (either frying or grilling). Each also might include an appropriate work surface. Each station would ideally include some type of small cold storage or freezer that might contain only enough ingredients for one night's service. Each station would also be equipped with the necessary tools to do the grilling or the frying. Carts might be parked nearby so a chef could use them to transfer raw ingredients from the kitchen's main cold storage or freezers. Trash bins would also be necessary for efficient waste disposal. The workstation would have everything within easy reach. For efficiency, the staff at a particular workstation should not have to leave their workstation to accomplish their tasks.

Work Sections and Work Lines Workstations are the building blocks of a kitchen. Workstations are combined into larger work areas called **work sections**. For example, the fry workstation might be combined with the grill workstation.

To create work sections, workstations are positioned in different **work lines**, or geometric arrangements of equipment. Work lines are designed to fit the available space and to improve the efficiency of staff. Work lines determine how equipment, cooking, preparation, and storage areas are placed. There are five common arrangements of work lines:

- **Straight-Line**
  The straight-line arrangement is usually considered the most efficient work-line .

- **L-Shaped**
  The L-shaped arrangement uses a limited amount of space, but is still able to provide a large amount of work space.

- **Back-to-Back**
  The back-to-back arrangement is very efficient but requires a large amount of space.

- **U-Shaped**
  The U-shaped arrangement offers the maximum of work surface.

- **Parallel** (or **Face-to-Face**)
  In this arrangement, two work lines are arranged face-to-face, with one common work aisle.

 **Reading Checkpoint** *What are workstations and work lines?*

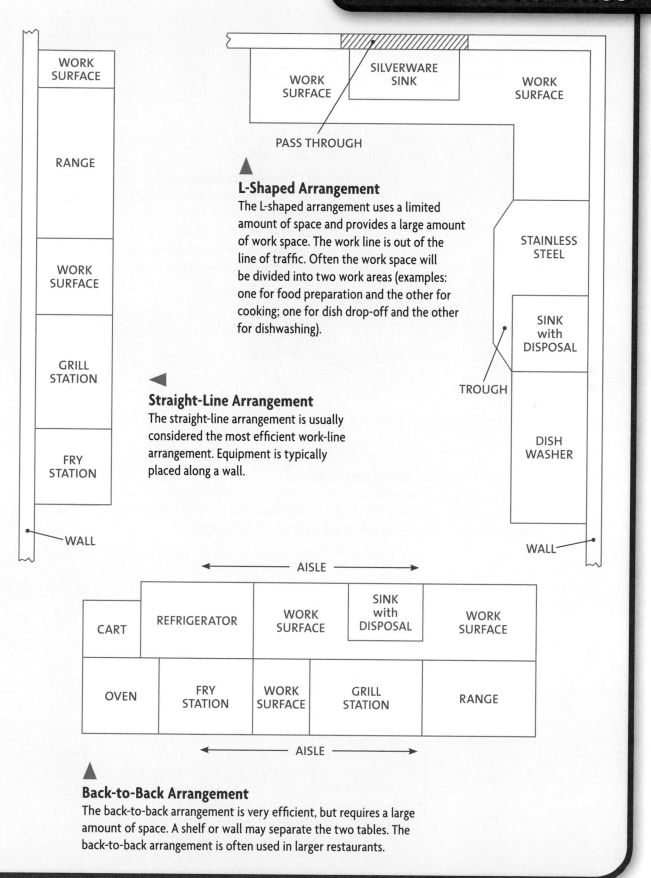

L-Shaped Arrangement

The L-shaped arrangement uses a limited amount of space and provides a large amount of work space. The work line is out of the line of traffic. Often the work space will be divided into two work areas (examples: one for food preparation and the other for cooking; one for dish drop-off and the other for dishwashing).

Straight-Line Arrangement

The straight-line arrangement is usually considered the most efficient work-line arrangement. Equipment is typically placed along a wall.

Back-to-Back Arrangement

The back-to-back arrangement is very efficient, but requires a large amount of space. A shelf or wall may separate the two tables. The back-to-back arrangement is often used in larger restaurants.

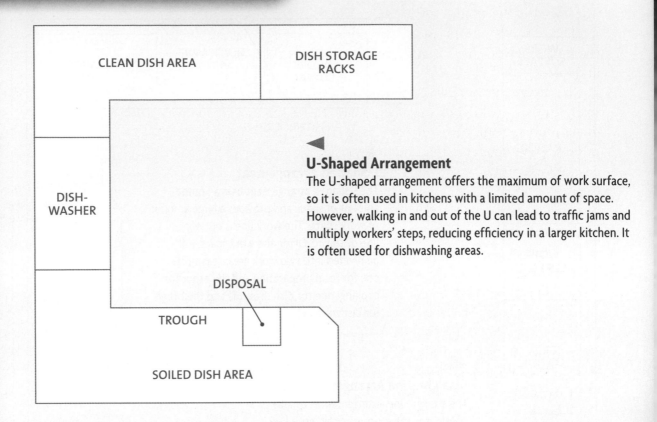

U-Shaped Arrangement

The U-shaped arrangement offers the maximum of work surface, so it is often used in kitchens with a limited amount of space. However, walking in and out of the U can lead to traffic jams and multiply workers' steps, reducing efficiency in a larger kitchen. It is often used for dishwashing areas.

Parallel (or Face-to-Face) Arrangement ▼

In this arrangement, two work lines are arranged face-to-face, with one common work aisle. The parallel arrangement also requires a large amount of space but is quite efficient (particularly when communication between workstations is required).

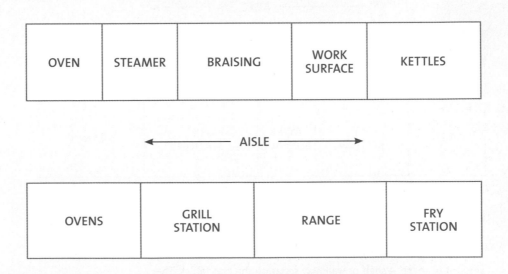

Work Flow

The layout of the kitchen, including the types of work lines within the kitchen, directly contributes to the efficiency of the kitchen. So does the kitchen's work flow. **Work flow** is the planned movement of food and kitchen staff as food is prepared.

To assure customer satisfaction and restaurant profitability, the work flow in the kitchen must be efficient. An efficient kitchen produces higher-quality food at a lower cost and in less time. Diners do not become impatient. The restaurant is able to sell more meals. The cost of food and labor is controllable. Good work flow reduces worker fatigue, while also reducing the risk of accidents or food poisoning that can threaten the restaurant's existence. A good work flow in the kitchen requires:

- Planning
- Timing
- Communication

Planning One of the most important aspects of any workstation's work flow is the concept of **mise en place** (MEEZ uhn PLAHS). This French term means "to put in place." Mise en place includes gathering all the raw materials required for your station (doing whatever is necessary to make them ready to be used) and making sure you have all the equipment and tools required for your culinary operation. For efficient work flow, you don't want to stop what you are doing to prepare more raw ingredients or locate a missing tool or piece of equipment.

Other important types of planning that could apply to each workstation would be estimating the number of individual dishes that will be required by that workstation on a particular night or knowing each dish for which the workstation is responsible so you can prepare it consistently.

Timing The staff of every workstation needs to be aware of the role they play in making each diner's experience a pleasant one. That is why timing is a critical component of the culinary work flow.

FIGURE 3-1
Importance of Timing
All the food for a large group must be ready at the same time.
🚫 **Drawing Conclusions** *What's wrong with this picture?*

One of the most important aspects of a diner's eating experience has to do with the timing of the various dishes. In a restaurant, diners typically move through successive courses and order different items, each of which can take different times to prepare. A group of diners would have an unpleasant dining experience if everyone did not receive appetizers at the same time or if one diner's main meal was delayed until the other diners were eating their desserts.

Communication In most food service establishments, communication between workstations is critically important. Additionally, as you will learn in later chapters, there is typically an individual who is in charge of making sure that each workstation does its job when it is needed. For example, preparing a dish too early can sometimes be just as much a problem as preparing it too late. In other cases, creating a dish requires the direct assistance of another workstation. The only way to make sure everything is prepared when it should be, and as it should be, is through communication.

✓ Reading Checkpoint *What is mise en place?*

3.1 ASSESSMENT

Reviewing Concepts

1. What is a workstation?
2. What does the term mise en place mean?

Critical Thinking

3. **Inferring** Why could a U-shaped work line be inefficient?
4. **Comparing/Contrasting** What is the difference between a workstation, a work section, and a work line?
5. **Predicting** Suppose the mise en place for a workstation was not completed before a restaurant began serving dinner. What would the person working at that station be required to do?

Test Kitchen

Working in teams, roughly sketch your school's kitchen. Identify workstations, work sections, and work lines. Point out the most efficient and least efficient aspects of your kitchen's workflow.

CULINARY MATH

Using a Scale Drawing

Convert the sketch of your school's kitchen from the "Test Kitchen" (above) to a scale drawing. Measure the actual work area and equipment. Use grid paper with ¼-inch grids. Use a scale of ¼ inch to 1 foot (1 square represents 1 square foot).

Receiving & Storage Equipment

READING PREVIEW

Key Concepts

- Understanding receiving equipment
- Understanding refrigeration equipment
- Understanding storage equipment

Vocabulary

- cold storage area
- counter scale
- dry storage area
- floor scale
- hanging scale
- infrared thermometer
- low boy
- platform scale
- portable refrigeration cart
- reach-in
- refrigerated drawer
- undercounter reach-in
- walk-in

> **"I**t is easy to take your refrigerator for granted. It's smart to treat it like one of your most valuable assets when it comes to the quality of your service and the success of your business. **"**
>
> **– James Smith**, Director of Purchasing
> New York Marriot Marquis, New York, NY

Receiving Equipment

As you know from Chapter 1, the flow of food starts in the receiving area. The receiving staff is responsible for the inspection and acceptance of incoming food, equipment, and supplies. They make sure the food service establishment gets what it ordered, that ingredients are safe, at the proper temperature, and not damaged or contaminated. After the food has been received and checked, it is stored.

A food service establishment typically inspects incoming goods in the receiving area at a receiving counter. This counter may have a low surface for inspecting packages and a high surface for paperwork. The receiving area is equipped with box cutters, scales, and a thermometer. Hand trucks and dollies are also stored at the receiving area for moving accepted goods from the receiving area to a storage area.

CHEF'S TIP

RECEIVING EQUIPMENT

A pen or pencil and a pocket calculator are important pieces of equipment for the receiving staff.

To check pre-packed goods, such as cases of canned goods or bottles, the receiving staff can just count items and read labels. For other items, they must check quantity and quality. They check the look and smell of fresh produce, meat, and fish. They weigh bulk items. They also check the temperature of hot and cold items.

The receiving staff often uses an **infrared thermometer** to scan the temperature of foods without actually touching the food. These thermometers read surface temperatures instantly by measuring invisible infrared radiation. Infrared thermometers come in several styles. They are also used in kitchens to check the temperatures of foods that are being held.

Receiving areas may have several kinds of scales: counter scales, platform scales, floor scales, and hanging scales. Modern scales show weights electronically. A **counter scale** sits on a counter and weighs moderate sized packages. In some food-service businesses, a **platform scale** on the receiving platform weighs bulky or heavy packages. Other businesses use a **floor scale** inside, in the receiving area, for such purposes. Both platform scales and floor scales may be equipped with rollers and are typically installed flush with the floor. A **hanging scale** weighs large items that can be lifted on a hook, like a side of beef.

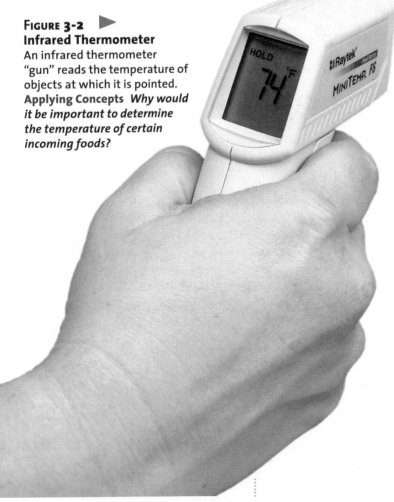

FIGURE 3-2
Infrared Thermometer
An infrared thermometer "gun" reads the temperature of objects at which it is pointed. **Applying Concepts** *Why would it be important to determine the temperature of certain incoming foods?*

✓ **Reading Checkpoint** *How do you check temperature without actually touching food?*

Refrigeration Equipment

Proper refrigeration keeps foods fresh and assures food safety. This improves quality and reduces costs caused by spoilage. Well-planned refrigeration also reduces labor costs by improving the work flow. Refrigerated storage is often referred to as cold storage.

Types of Refrigeration Equipment Large kitchens often have a few different types of refrigeration units. Kitchens keep the majority of the stored food in large units, transferring only enough food for a few hours to smaller units located at specific workstations.

- **Walk-Ins.** The largest refrigeration or freezing unit is called a **walk-in**. These units usually have shelves that are arranged around the walls and a plastic air curtain to keep the cold air in the walk-in. Walk-in units may be in the kitchen or even outside the building with an indoor entrance. Large walk-in refrigeration units allow for storage on the shelves as well as storage of refrigerated items on carts.

- **Reach-Ins.** Similar to the refrigerators we are all used to, a **reach-in** may be a single unit or part of a bank of units. Reach-ins come in many sizes. Some reach-ins have pass-through doors that allow both wait staff and kitchen staff to access them. Reach-ins with glass doors let staff see items without opening the doors. This saves time finding ingredients. It also reduces electrical costs, because opening doors lets warm air in.
- **Refrigerated Drawers and Undercounter Reach-Ins**. At individual workstations, a **refrigerated drawer** or an **undercounter reach-in** (often called a **low boy**) lets kitchen staff store a small amount of ingredients (typically enough for a few hours or a single night) within easy reach, thus increasing efficiency. This eliminates trips to the larger reach-ins or walk-ins during busy service hours. Typically, a drawer holds less than an undercounter unit, but drawers are often more efficient.
- **Portable Refrigeration Carts.** When a food service establishment needs temporary refrigeration units or does off-site catering, it uses a **portable refrigeration cart**.

▲
FIGURE 3-3
Reach-In Refrigerator
Kitchens often have a bank of reach-in refrigerators.
Inferring *Why is it important to store food correctly in a reach-in refrigerator?*

Cleaning Refrigerators and Freezers As you learned in Chapter 1, it is important to keep food service equipment clean and sanitary. Maintain a regular cleaning and sanitation schedule. Before beginning any cleaning process, consult the person responsible for cleaning your establishment's equipment.

Follow these general guidelines for cleaning reach-in and portable refrigerators and freezers (clean walk-in refrigerators as instructed by your supervisor). Clean refrigerators every day. Freezers can be cleaned less often.

1. Turn off the unit, if instructed to do so by your supervisor.

2. Remove the food. Place it in a cold storage area.

▲
FIGURE 3-4
Shelves
These stainless steel shelves are made of rods so food or dirt will fall through the shelves to the floor.
Drawing Conclusions *Why is stainless steel typically used for kitchen shelves?*
▼

3. Wash the interior with warm soapy water.

4. Rinse the interior with a clean damp cloth.

5. Sanitize the interior with a sanitizing solution.

6. Dry the interior with a single-use paper towel.

7. Turn on the unit and refill it with food.

8. On a daily basis, wash, rinse, and sanitize the outside.

 **Reading Checkpoint** *How do small versions of refrigeration equipment improve a kitchen's performance?*

Storage Equipment

Storage equipment should have four important qualities. It should be strong, durable, easily cleaned, and easily accessed. These qualities apply equally to storage containers and to shelves and shelving units.

Shelves Goods such as flour, dry pasta, canned goods, and supplies can be stored safely on shelves at room temperature in what is commonly called the **dry storage area**. Goods are also stored on shelves in walk-in refrigeration units in a **cold storage area**.

Stored goods must be easy to reach. The storage area may open to the kitchen or be in a separate room. Aisles in storage areas are usually 3 to 4 feet wide to accommodate carts. Shelves come in many sizes, but

the maximum height is usually 6 feet, the maximum depth is usually 24 inches, and they stand at least 6 inches off the ground. With these dimensions, almost all staff can store and access goods without strain.

Kitchen shelves are generally made of stainless steel, galvanized steel, aluminum, or high-impact plastic. Wooden shelves are less common because they are harder to keep clean. Some departments of health prohibit wooden shelving.

Solid shelves have easy-to-clean rounded edges. Shelves made of mesh, wire, rods, or tubes are more common, though. These shelves hold goods securely but let dirt fall through to the floor and allow air to circulate. Shelving units usually stand at least six inches from the floor, on legs. This makes cleaning floors easy and keeps food dry and away from dirt and pests.

Shelves are also used in work areas to hold pots, plates, and spices. Dishes and silverware are often stored on specially designed carts for easy movement to serving areas.

Storage Containers Storage containers hold food and protect it from contamination. They also help staff move food between storage, preparation, and service areas. Foods in the kitchen may be stored raw, partially prepared, or cooked. Storage containers include insulated containers, bins, and a variety of bowls, pans, and canisters. Stainless steel, glass, and plastic containers are easiest to clean. Using glass containers can be a problem in the kitchen. If they break, they can cause physical contamination. Insulated containers can keep foods hot or cold. They are used for extra storage or for carrying meals off-site. Liquids can be served in insulated containers with spigots.

Before placing any foods in a storage container, clean and sanitize the container. Bring hot foods to the right temperature before refrigerating them. Always cover containers with tight-fitting lids or with heavy plastic wrap or foil. Finally, label and date the container, and indicate its contents. That way you can identify the contents at a glance and know what is too old to use. (Remember to use the FIFO system with all stored food.)

CHEF'S TIP

ORDER, ORDER
Most kitchens specify where different types of ingredients (vegetables, dairy, meat, and so on) go in the walk-in.

FIGURE 3-5
Storage Containers
It is important to label and date each storage container.
Applying Concepts *If you were a chef and you saw a stored item in the refrigerator that wasn't dated, would you serve it?*

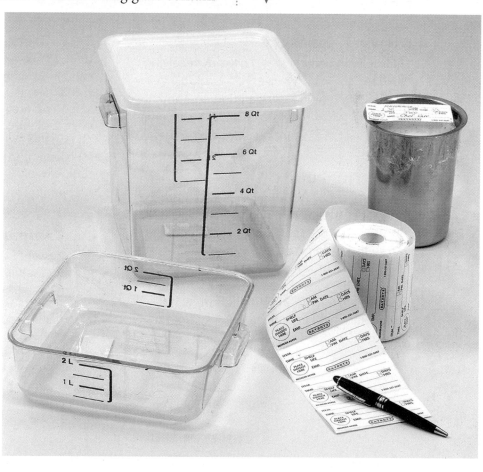

Wire bins are often used to hold packaged items. Plastic bins can hold dry goods such as rice, beans, and flour. Bins with wheels are easy to move to and from work areas.

Cleaning Shelves and Storage Containers Follow these general guidelines to clean shelves and storage containers:

1. Remove all food from shelves and storage containers.

2. Clean dry storage shelves and storage containers with hot, soapy water.

3. Rinse with a clean damp cloth or clean water.

4. Sanitize the shelves and storage containers.

5. Dry the shelves with a single-use paper towel. Let storage containers air dry.

6. Refill the shelves and storage containers with food. (Remember to use the FIFO system, "First In, First Out.")

 **Reading Checkpoint** *How does refrigeration equipment improve kitchen performance?*

3.2 ASSESSMENT

Reviewing Concepts

1. Name four kinds of scales used by receiving staff.

2. Name five types of refrigeration equipment you might find in a kitchen.

3. Name four important qualities of storage equipment.

Critical Thinking

4. **Inferring** Why would receiving staff need to weigh incoming goods and check their temperature?

5. **Drawing Conclusions** Why should the aisle in a walk-in be wide enough to allow a cart?

6. **Comparing/Contrasting** Why are some foods held in walk-in refrigeration, while others are held in undercounter refrigerated drawers?

Test Kitchen

Work in teams to fill three different kinds of containers with water. Close and label the containers, testing the closed containers to make sure there are no leaks. Store in a refrigerator for two days. Describe each container based on the ease of (a) transferring water into the container, (b) sealing, (c) labeling, (d) storing/stacking, and (e) taste after refrigeration.

LANGUAGE ARTS

Compare/Contrast
Research three different types of refrigeration equipment. Write a description of each type (including prices), pointing out their similarities and differences. Focus on details you think would be appreciated by chefs and food preparation staff.

READING PREVIEW

Key Concepts

- Understanding food-preparation equipment
- Understanding cooking equipment

Vocabulary

- blender
- blending
- broiler
- buffalo chopper
- combination steamer oven
- convection oven
- convection steamer
- countertop blender
- countertop mixer
- deck oven
- deep-fat fryer
- flattop range
- food chopper
- food processor
- freestanding mixer
- griddle
- immersion blender
- meat grinder
- meat slicer
- mixer
- mixing
- open-burner range
- planetary mixer
- pressure steamer
- range
- ring-top range
- salamander
- smoker
- spiral mixer
- steam-jacketed kettle
- Swiss brasier
- vertical chopping machine (VCM)

> **"C**hefs and musicians both perform for the public. The stove is where chefs perform. In Europe, we even call the stove a piano. **"**
>
> – Xavier LeRoux
> Escoffier Restaurant
> The Culinary Institute of America

Food-Preparation Equipment

Food-preparation equipment is potentially the most dangerous equipment in the kitchen. When working with equipment for chopping, slicing, and grinding:

- ☑ **Learn to use a machine safely**. Ask an experienced operator to show you how to use the machine. Read the manufacturer's instructions. Do not use the machine if you haven't been trained in its use.

- ☑ **Use all safety features**. Always use blade guards, food plungers, and food holders. Wear wire mesh gloves or eye protection whenever appropriate.

- ☑ **Maintain and clean equipment properly.** Keep large equipment in good working order. Clean and sanitize the equipment thoroughly after each use.

Cutting Safely

Most cutting equipment is designed with safety features. Always use blade guards and food holders as you pass food across a cutting tool. Always secure lids and covers. Whenever appropriate, wear eye protection.

▲ *Food Processor*

▲ *Food Chopper*

▲ *Meat Slicer*

☑ **Turn off and unplug the machine for cleaning.** Remember to turn off and unplug electrical equipment before cleaning and before you take it apart or put it back together. Leave equipment unplugged between uses.

☑ **Be sure equipment is complete and stable.** All pieces of equipment must be properly reassembled. Lids should be secure. The machine should be on a firm surface and not tilted.

☑ **Promptly report any problems.** Your manager should be told about any problems or malfunctions regarding the equipment. Also be sure to alert co-workers about any problem.

Chopping, Slicing, and Grinding Equipment With specialized cutting, blending, and mixing equipment, large volumes of food can be prepared rapidly. You may need this equipment to be efficient, but remember that this equipment can be extremely dangerous if it is used incorrectly or without appropriate attention. Make sure to review the guidelines in the previous section concerning safe and proper use of equipment. A typical kitchen includes many of the chopping, slicing, and grinding pieces of equipment described in this chapter.

- **Food Processor.** The motor in a **food processor** is separate from the bowl, blades, and lid. With different attachments, a food processor can slice, grind, mix, blend, and crush foods.
- **Vertical Chopping Machine (VCM).** A motor at the base of a **vertical chopping machine (VCM)** is attached to blades in a permanently attached bowl. The VCM (also referred to as a vertical cutter/mixer) is used to grind, whip, blend, purée, or crush large quantities of foods. As a safety precaution, the hinged lid must be locked in place before the unit will operate.
- **Food Chopper.** Available in floor and tabletop models, a **food chopper** (also called a **buffalo chopper**) is obviously used to chop food. The food is placed in a rotating bowl that passes under a hood, where blades chop the food. Some units have hoppers or feed tubes and interchangeable disks for slicing and grating.
- **Meat Slicer.** Used to slice foods to even thicknesses, a **meat slicer** is especially useful for slicing cooked meats and cheeses. A carrier moves the food back and forth against a circular blade, which is generally high carbon stainless steel.
- **Meat Grinder.** A meat grinder grinds various cuts of meat. Restaurants can use either a dedicated machine or a meat-grinder attachment for a mixer or a food chopper. Meat is dropped through a tube and pushed through the machine, where it is cut by a blade, and the meat is then forced out. Sausage casings can be attached to some meat grinders so the

meat is pushed into the casing as the meat is ground. A meat grinder typically has disks of varying sizes to create a range of textures.

Mixing and Blending Equipment Although they are very similar, chefs don't usually use the terms mixing and blending in exactly the same way. **Mixing** is the process of combining ingredients so they are evenly spread throughout the mixture. **Blending** is a type of mixing in which the ingredients are chopped so the overall mixture has a uniform consistency. In addition to combining ingredients, blenders and mixers introduce air into the food.

Here's an example that illustrates the difference between mixing and blending: When chocolate-chip cookie dough is mixed, the chocolate chips are mixed evenly throughout the dough, without being broken up. If the cookie dough were blended, the chocolate chips would all be chopped up and the dough would turn into chocolate cookie dough (without any chocolate chips).

A **mixer** is a machine consisting of a bowl and mixing tool for combining ingredients, primarily for batter and dough. Compared to blenders, mixers operate more gently and slowly. They are used primarily by bakers. Some mixers are used only for bread dough. Others can create several types of mixtures.

There are two sizes of mixers: countertop mixers and the larger freestanding mixers. **Countertop mixers** are typically used when the kitchen is not a commercial bakery. Larger countertop models stand about 2 feet high and can weigh over 100 pounds. Countertop mixers come in sizes ranging from five quarts to twenty quarts. **Freestanding mixers** sit on the floor and are typically used in commercial bakeries.

FIGURE 3-6
Meat Grinders
A dedicated meat grinder (left) produces large quantities of ground meat. A planetary mixer with a meat grinder attachment (right) produces smaller quantities of ground meat.
Predicting *What would influence a restaurant's choice between using a dedicated machine or a mixer attachment?*

▲
FIGURE 3-7
Countertop Planetary Mixer
This mixer is using a whisk attachment. Most kitchens require the use of a safety cage when a mixer is in operation.
Predicting *Why might a small restaurant have many attachments for its planetary mixer?*

These large mixers stand about 5 feet high and weigh 3,000 pounds (the weight of a minivan). They can process more than 500 pounds of dough in one batch. There are two basic types of mixers:

- **Planetary Mixer.** The mixing bowl doesn't move in a **planetary mixer**. The mixing tool moves within the bowl, like a planet orbiting the sun. These mixers can use bowls in various capacities (7-quart, 10-quart, 20-quart, 40-quart, and so on). Planetary mixers (also known as vertical mixers) typically have three standard attachments for different uses: a paddle, a whip, and a dough hook. However, multipurpose attachments can transform a planetary mixer into a food processor. You can add a vegetable slicer, a shredder/grater, or a meat grinder. A large restaurant that does a lot of baking can get several uses from its investment in a planetary mixer.

- **Spiral Mixer.** On a **spiral mixer**, the bowl turns instead of the mixing tool (which is typically a spiral-shaped hook). Spiral mixers are used for mixing bread dough because they work gently. A special type of spiral mixer called a French fork spiral mixer or oblique mixer is used to make French-style bread dough. It has a fork-like attachment.

A **blender** can make coarse or fine mixtures and frozen drinks by using a rotating blade. Blenders operate at relatively high speeds and typically chop ingredients so they are all the same size. There are two basic types of blenders:

- **Countertop Blender.** A motor at the base of a **countertop blender** (or bar blender) turns a propeller-like blade in its bottom. A removable glass, plastic, or metal container on top holds ingredients. The container has a removable lid. Speed settings for the motor are in the base.

- **Immersion Blender.** Also known as a hand blender, stick blender, or burr mixer, an **immersion** (ih-MER-zhuhn) **blender** is a

◄
FIGURE 3-8
Blenders
One of the countertop blenders has a glass container, and the other has a stainless steel container. An immersion blender is lying on the counter in front of the two countertop blenders.
Applying Concepts *Which type of blender do you think you would find most useful for your home cooking?*

long, stick-shaped machine that houses a motor on one end and a blade on the other end. Its advantage is that foods can be blended directly in the cooking vessel. Most kitchens use hand-held immersion blenders.

Cleaning Food-Preparation Equipment Always follow safety precautions when using electric food-preparation equipment such as chopping, slicing, and grinding equipment or mixers and blenders. Water conducts electricity, so make sure to turn off and unplug equipment to avoid shocks. Sharp blades can easily cut you. Use special caution when cleaning sharp blades and wear wire mesh gloves..

The following procedures do not replace instruction manuals or your supervisor's directions. They offer general guidelines for safe and effective cleaning of all electric food-preparation equipment.

1. Turn off and unplug the equipment.

2. Remove any attachments or bowls. Use blade guards, if necessary.

3. If necessary, take apart any processing assemblies to reach the parts that touch food. Lay out parts on a counter for easy reassembly.

4. Wash each part with hot, soapy water. Wash blades by using motions that avoid the sharp edge.

5. Dry with a clean cloth.

6. Sanitize.

7. Wipe the equipment base and frame with a soapy cloth and then rinse with a damp cloth. Dry with a clean cloth and then sanitize.

8. Reassemble the cleaned, dry, sanitized parts.

9. Immediately replace any blade guards.

10. Lubricate with oil as specified by the manufacturer.

 **Reading Checkpoint** *What are five pieces of equipment that are used for slicing, chopping, or grinding food?*

Cooking Equipment

Large restaurants and hotels often require specialized types of cooking equipment.

FOCUS ON SAFETY

Locked and Tagged

To prevent industrial accidents, OSHA requires procedures for isolating energy sources from equipment during cleaning and repair. Always turn off and unplug equipment before cleaning. Notify your supervisor of broken equipment so it can be locked and tagged until it is repaired.

Kettles and Steamers With kettles and steamers, chefs can prepare large amounts of food efficiently. Covered kettles and steamers use moist heat that is applied over a much larger area than is possible by using a single burner.

- **Steam-Jacketed Kettle.** Available in both freestanding and tabletop models, a **steam-jacketed kettle** is a kettle that provides an even heat by circulating steam through its walls. Units may tilt and may have spigots or lids. Available in a range of sizes, these kettles are excellent for producing stocks, soups, and sauces.

- **Swiss Brasier.** Large, relatively shallow, and freestanding, the **Swiss brasier** (also known as a tilting skillet or tilting fry pan) is used to cook large quantities of meats or vegetables at one time. Swiss brasiers are very versatile. They can be used to perform many types of cooking.

- **Pressure Steamer.** In a **pressure steamer,** water is heated under pressure in a sealed compartment, allowing it to reach temperatures above the boiling point, 212°F. The cooking time is controlled by automatic timers, which open the exhaust valves after a specified amount of time. This releases steam pressure so the unit can be opened safely.

- **Convection Steamer.** Pressure does not build up in a **convection steamer.** The steam is generated in a boiler and then piped to the cooking chamber, where it is vented over the food. It is continuously exhausted. This means the door may be opened at any time. However, you need to wait for the steam to clear away before reaching into the convection oven. Otherwise, you could receive a serious burn.

Figure 3-10
Swiss Brasier
A chef can prepare large amounts of meats or vegetables quickly and efficiently by using a Swiss brasier.
Analyzing Information *Would a small restaurant be likely to use a Swiss brasier?*

Ranges, Ovens, Broilers, Fryers, and Grills Stoves with which you are familiar probably have a stovetop (typically called a **range**) and an oven. The oven is often below the range. However, in a professional kitchen, there are many variations on this standard arrangement. Gas or electric ranges are available in many sizes and with various combinations of heating surfaces. Most ovens cook foods by surrounding them with hot air. This is a gentler and more even source of heat than the direct heat from the range.

- **Open-Burner Range.** Using electric elements or a gas burners, an **open-burner range** lets you quickly adjust the heat level. Each element or burner has individual controls. Pots and pans are set directly on an electric element. Gas burners have a grid to hold the pot slightly above the flame.

- **Flattop and Ring-Top Range.** Consisting of a thick solid plate of cast iron or steel set over the heat source, the plate on a **flattop range** takes a while to be heated. After that, it provides an indirect, less intense heat than an open burner. The heat cannot be quickly adjusted. Pots and pans are set directly on a flattop. Flattop ranges (also called French-top ranges) are ideal for items that require long, slow cooking. A **ring-top range** is similar to a flattop range but has concentric plates, or rings, that can be lifted from the surface to provide more intense direct heat.

FOCUS ON SAFETY

Finding the Fire Extinguisher
Any heat source can get out of control. Know where the nearest fire extinguisher is in the kitchen and in the service area.

FIGURE 3-11
Restaurant Kitchen
Many common pieces of equipment are used in this kitchen.
Interpreting Illustrations *Would you classify this kitchen's work flow as a straight-line arrangement or a parallel one?*

Salamander

Planetary Mixer with Safety Cage

Open-Burner Range

Grill

Deep-Fat Fryer

Oven

- **Conventional Oven.** The heat source in a conventional oven is under the bottom of the inside of the oven, which is also called its deck. Heat is conducted through the deck to the cooking space. Conventional ovens can be located below a range top. Food is generally placed in pans on wire racks.

- **Deck Oven.** Ovens can be stacked like shelves, one above another, like pizza ovens. These are called **deck ovens**, and the food is placed directly on the deck rather than on a wire racks. Deck ovens normally consist of two to four decks, although single-deck models are available.

- **Convection Oven.** Fans force hot air to circulate around the food in a **convection oven**, cooking the food evenly and quickly. Some convection ovens have the capacity to introduce moisture. Special features may include infrared and a convection-microwave combination.

- **Combination Steamer/Oven.** Capable of using a combination of cooking methods, the **combination steamer/oven** (also referred to as a combi oven) can be powered by either gas or electricity. It can be used in steam mode, hot-air convection mode, or heat/steam (combi) mode.

- **Broiler.** With an intense radiant heat source directly located above the food, a **broiler** cooks food quickly. Some units have adjustable racks that can be raised or lowered to control cooking speed. **Salamanders** are small broilers, used primarily for browning or melting foods.

- **Smoker.** Used for smoking and slow-cooking foods, a true **smoker** treats foods with smoke and can be operated at either cool or hot temperatures. Smokers generally have racks or hooks, allowing foods to smoke evenly.

- **Microwave Oven.** By using electricity to generate microwave radiation, a microwave oven is able to cook, reheat, or thaw foods very quickly. Microwave ovens do not brown foods effectively, however. This is why some models offer convection heating as well.

- **Deep-Fat Fryer.** Floor and countertop **deep-fat fryers** hold frying oil in a stainless-steel reservoir. A heating element, controlled by a thermostat, raises the oil to the desired temperature and maintains it at that temperature. Stainless-steel wire baskets are used to lower foods into the hot oil and lift them out.

- **Grill.** Grills have a radiant heat source below a rack on which food is cooked. Some grills may burn wood or charcoal; however, their fires require tending and special ventilation. Units

FOCUS ON NUTRITION

Keep Oil Fresh

Clean deep-fat fryers on a regular schedule, and filter and replace the oil. Cooking causes oil to change into unhealthy saturated and trans fats. Also, old and dirty oil cannot fry as hot. This means foods absorb more oil and become soggy, fatty, and unappetizing.

in restaurants usually use gas or electric sources of heat.

- **Griddle.** Similar to a flattop range, a **griddle** has a heat source located beneath a thick plate of metal. Foods are cooked directly on this surface, which is usually designed with edges to contain the foods and a drain to collect used oil and waste.

Cleaning Cooking Equipment

Open-Burner Ranges

1. Turn off range and allow to cool. Remove the grids (and the drip pan, if necessary).

2. Soak grids (and drip pan) in hot, soapy water.

3. Wash the rest of the range with hot, soapy water.

4. Rinse and dry range.

5. Wash, rinse, and dry the grids (and drip pan).

6. Replace grids (and drip pan).

Flattop and Ring-Top Ranges

1. Turn off range and allow to cool. Loosen burned food with a scraper.

2. Clean with hot, soapy water.

3. Rinse and dry.

Microwave, Conventional, and Convection Ovens

1. Turn off oven and allow to cool. Unplug microwaves when possible.

2. Remove racks (shelves and turntables).

3. Clean racks in hot soapy water. Rinse.

4. Dry turntables. Air-dry shelves.

5. Clean inside and out with warm soapy cloth.

6. Rinse with clean wet cloth and dry.

7. Polish the outside with a clean cloth.

▲
FIGURE 3-12
Griddle
Griddles are often used to make hot sandwiches.
Predicting *What would happen in a busy lunch hour if you ran out of space on a griddle for hot sandwiches?*

Broilers

1. Turn off broiler and allow to cool. Let the unit cool completely.

2. Take out the rack.

3. Soak rack in hot, soapy water, removing caked-on food with a scraper or wire brush.

4. Rinse with a clean, wet cloth.

5. Dry with a clean cloth.

6. Scrape caked-on food from the inside of the broiler.

7. Remove the drip pan.

8. Wash the drip pan with hot, soapy water.

9. Rinse the drip pan with a clean, wet cloth.

10. Dry the drip pan with a clean, dry cloth.

11. Replace the drip pan and racks.

Deep-Fat Fryers (Daily)

1. Turn off fryer and allow to cool.

2. Wash all removable parts with hot, soapy water.

3. Clean all exterior surfaces of the fryer with hot, soapy water. Do not use cleansers, steel wool, or any other abrasives on the stainless steel.

4. Follow manufacturer's directions to filter the cooking oil, and replace if necessary. Filter oil more often under heavy conditions.

FOCUS ON SAFETY

Deep-Fat Fryers
Deep-fat fryers are dangerous. Hot oil can cause serious burns. A trained staff member should perform filtering and weekly maintenance.

Deep-Fat Fryers (Weekly)

1. Turn off fryer and allow to cool. Completely drain the fryer vessel into either the filter or a steel container. Do not use a plastic bucket or glass container.

2. Clean the vessel with a good grade of cleaner or with hot water and a strong detergent.

3. Close the drain valve and refill with either the cleaning solution or water and detergent.

4. Using protective gloves and a brush, scrub the interior above the oil line until gummy deposits and carbon spots are eliminated.

5. Drain the vessel and rinse several times with clear water.

6. Rinse with a vinegar and water solution.

7. Rinse again with clear water to eliminate the vinegar and water solution.

8. Dry thoroughly with a single-use paper towel, paying close attention to drain area and heating elements.

CULINARY SCIENCE

The Microwave Oven

Radar, which uses short-wavelength signals to locate objects, helped win World War II. In 1946, Percy Spencer, a famed inventor at the Raytheon Company, stopped in front of a magnetron, the power tube that drives a radar set. To his surprise, Spencer noticed that the chocolate bar in his pocket was melting.

Spencer was curious and asked for some popping corn. Holding the bag of corn next to the magnetron, Spencer watched as the kernels exploded. Later Spencer put the magnetron tube near an egg. Spencer and a curious colleague watched as the egg began to tremble and shake. When the egg exploded, Spencer reasoned, if an egg can be cooked by microwaves, why not other foods?

Spencer and Raytheon went on to develop the microwave oven. In 1947, the first microwave oven weighed 750 pounds and was 5½ feet high. The first ones were used to cook large quantities of food quickly—in restaurants, railroad cars, and ocean liners.

The early microwave oven had some shortcomings. Meat would not brown, and French fries turned white and limp. To make matters worse, the cook for Raytheon's chairman quit because the chairman demanded that all his food should be prepared with a microwave oven.

The home microwave oven appeared in 1967 when Amana, a division of Raytheon, introduced its domestic Radarange. Other companies joined the countertop microwave oven market. By the end

▲ A model demonstrates an early version of Raytheon's Raydarange.

of 1971, the price of countertop units began to fall and their abilities grew. By 1975, sales of microwave ovens exceeded those of gas ranges.

Research

Use the library or the Internet to research the history of stoves. Describe how stoves have changed over time.

Polishing a Griddle
Avoid circular polishing. This scratches the griddle's surface.

Griddles

1. Turn off griddle. (Unplug electric units.) Let griddle cool completely.

2. Polish the top with a special griddle stone or griddle cloth. Work in the direction of the grain of the metal.

3. Recondition the top by coating it lightly with oil as specified by the manufacturer.

4. Heat the griddle to 400°F and wipe clean.

5. Repeat if necessary. The clean griddle should shine.

6. Wash the rest of the griddle with warm soapy water. Rinse and dry.

Grills

1. Turn off grill and allow to cool.

2. Clean the rack thoroughly with a wire brush and scraper, removing any burnt food particles.

3. Oil the rack as specified by the manufacturer.

 **Reading Checkpoint**   *What is the difference between an open-burner range and a flattop range?*

3.3 ASSESSMENT

Reviewing Concepts

1. Name 5 kinds of slicing, chopping, and grinding equipment used for food preparation.

2. Name 2 types of blenders and 2 types of mixers.

3. Name at least 12 types of large cooking equipment.

Critical Thinking

4. **Comparing/Contrasting** What is the difference between a pressure steamer and a convection steamer?

5. **Predicting** Which do you think would heat up faster: an open-burner range or a flattop range?

6. **Inferring** Why might a food-service business want to use a single piece of equipment in several ways? Why might a food-service business want to use specialized equipment?

Test Kitchen

List the equipment in your school kitchen in the categories used in this section: (1) Chopping, Slicing, & Grinding Equipment; (2) Mixing & Blending Equipment; (3) Kettles & Steamers; and (4) Ranges, Ovens, Broilers, Fryers, & Grills. Ask the kitchen personnel which items are used most often and least often. Which items serve multiple purposes?

SCIENCE

Cooking Technology
Research a type of equipment used for cooking. Focus on comparing equivalent models of the same type of equipment available today (example: compare existing open-burner ranges).

Holding & Service Equipment

READING PREVIEW

Key Concepts

- Understanding equipment for holding food
- Understanding equipment for serving food

Vocabulary

- chafing dish
- heat lamp
- holding cabinets
- hot plate
- hotel pans
- plate cover
- service cart
- sneeze guards
- steam table
- tray stands

> **"S**ervice equipment plays a big role in creating the perfect dining experience, the same way the right sauce adds the perfect finish to a dish. **"**
>
> – Mary Frankini

Holding Equipment

The look, taste, temperature, and texture of food when it is presented can delight customers or disappoint them. Restaurants and other food-service businesses use special equipment to hold food at the appropriate temperatures for customers. These businesses also use special equipment to make it easier for the staff to deliver and present food to customers.

In a fast-food restaurant, food is prepared and packaged. It is typically held under special lamps to keep it warm or in refrigerated cases to keep it cold. No special equipment is required to serve the food. The counter person assembles the food on a tray or in a bag. The customer is satisfied when food is up to standards and served in a quick and friendly way.

In a cafeteria, buffet restaurant, or banquet hall, the equipment for holding food also provides a way to display the food for diners to make their selections. A customer is satisfied by the look, variety, and quality of the food and by the convenience of choosing it directly.

Mary Frankini
The Culinary Institute of America

FIGURE 3-13 ▶
Salad Bar in a School Cafeteria
A refrigerated unit keeps salad bar items cold.
Interpreting Illustrations *Why would a cafeteria with a sneeze guard need service staff to move food forward more often than in a setting without a sneeze guard?*

With buffet or cafeteria service, **sneeze guards** protect foods. These are see-through barriers that allow customers to see food but eliminate the possibility of cross-contamination caused by a sneeze. Customers select food by reaching under the guard.

Food-service establishments use holding equipment to hold food at safe temperatures. As you know from Chapter 1, the temperature danger zone is between 41°F and 135°F, so hot foods must be held above 135°F and cold foods must be held below 41°F. Chafing dishes, steam tables, and hold lamps are used to keep food hot.

- **Chafing Dish.** Used to hold just one or two food items, a **chafing** (CHAYF-ing) **dish** is typically a stand, a water pan, an insert pan, and a lid. Most chafing dishes use sterno (or other fuel) to heat water in the water pan. When the water is heated, it keeps the food in the insert pan at an even temperature. Because they are often used by customers to serve themselves, chafing dishes are usually very decorative.

▲ *Chafing Dish*

CULINARY **SCIENCE**

AHHHH – CHOO!

What happens when you are standing in front of a salad bar and the inside of your nose gets a tickle? Something—maybe a strong odor, pepper, or that nasty cold of yours—is irritating your nose. A message is sent to a special part of your brain called the sneeze center, which then sends a message to all your muscles involved in the amazingly complicated process called sternutation (stern-u-TA-shon), or sneezing.

Sneezing is actually an attempt by the body to expel irritating particles from the nose. And the body does a very good job, indeed! Sneezing can send tiny particles, including germs, speeding out of your nose at up to 100 miles an hour!

So in the 1950s, when restaurants began developing salad bars and other types of quick-serve dining, companies developed sneeze guards. Originally, sneeze guards were just straight glass panels held by a wooden structure at head height. But soon sneeze guards were being made of decorative stained glass, leaving less and less room for

▲ *Sternutation*

customers to reach for food. Today, sneeze guards come in many sizes, but all must adhere to strict standards established by the National Sanitation Foundation and enforced by state and county Health Departments.

- **Hot Plate.** Typically used to hold coffee and water, a **hot plate** uses an electrical heating element to keep beverages at the appropriate temperature.

- **Holding Cabinets and Covered Racks.** Available in a variety of sizes, **holding cabinets** and covered racks can hold trays of food or trays containing plates. While both holding cabinets and covered racks move easily on wheels, holding cabinets are usually completely enclosed and insulated to maintain a stable internal temperature. Some holding cabinets are specifically for hot or cold food and plug into an electric outlet to maintain their temperature.

◀

**FIGURE 3-14
Covered Rack**
This covered rack contains trays that can hold plates of food awaiting service.
Inferring What advantage does a covered rack offer when you are serving a large group?

- **Heat Lamp.** Another way to keep food hot is to use a **heat lamp**. These lamps use special bulbs and are placed directly above the area where food is held.
- **Steam Table.** Resembling a large table with a deep, hollow top, a **steam table** is used to keep food hot. Hot water is placed in the top and heated. A grid above the steam accommodates a number of hotel pans of different sizes (hotel pans are discussed later in this section). The steam from the water keeps food hot for service. Large steam tables usually have a thermostat to control the heating elements that maintain the desired temperature.

Refrigerated holding and display units or ice-filled cases are used to keep food cold. In buffets, areas serving cold items might include salad bars, sandwich bars, or dessert bars. The refrigerated unit holding these food items is similar to a steam table except that the unit uses refrigeration rather than steam. Some restaurants use containers or units filled with ice. Bowls can be placed in the ice. In some restaurants, fish or seafood is placed directly on the mounded ice.

Hotel pans are stainless steel or plastic containers typically used for holding and storing food. Hotel pans come in various standard sizes that can be combined easily in steam tables and other serving equipment that is designed to be used with hotel pans.

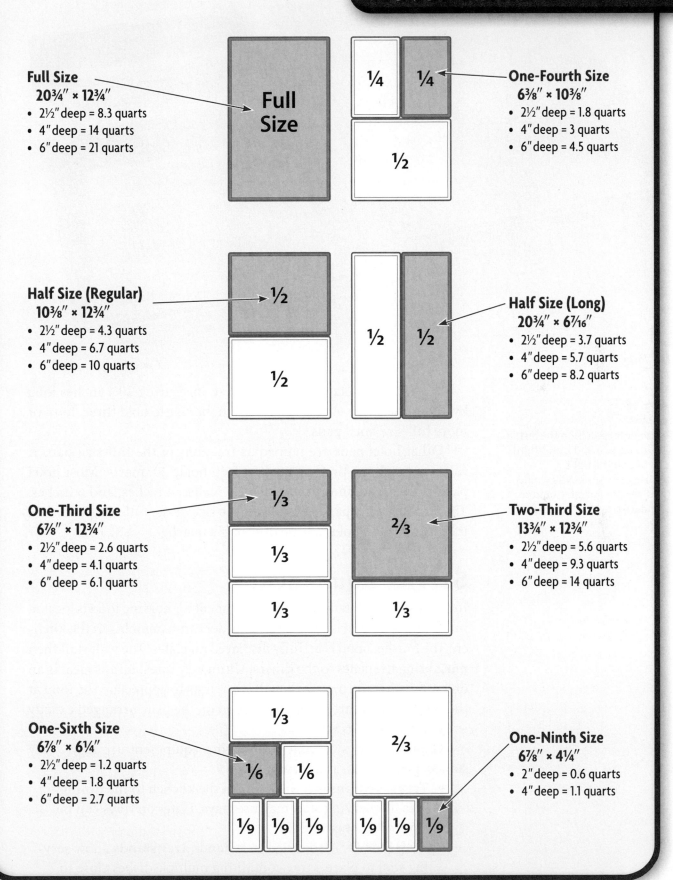

Full Size
20¾″ × 12¾″
- 2½″ deep = 8.3 quarts
- 4″ deep = 14 quarts
- 6″ deep = 21 quarts

One-Fourth Size
6⅜″ × 10⅜″
- 2½″ deep = 1.8 quarts
- 4″ deep = 3 quarts
- 6″ deep = 4.5 quarts

Half Size (Regular)
10⅜″ × 12¾″
- 2½″ deep = 4.3 quarts
- 4″ deep = 6.7 quarts
- 6″ deep = 10 quarts

Half Size (Long)
20¾″ × 6⁷⁄₁₆″
- 2½″ deep = 3.7 quarts
- 4″ deep = 5.7 quarts
- 6″ deep = 8.2 quarts

One-Third Size
6⅞″ × 12¾″
- 2½″ deep = 2.6 quarts
- 4″ deep = 4.1 quarts
- 6″ deep = 6.1 quarts

Two-Third Size
13¾″ × 12¾″
- 2½″ deep = 5.6 quarts
- 4″ deep = 9.3 quarts
- 6″ deep = 14 quarts

One-Sixth Size
6⅞″ × 6¼″
- 2½″ deep = 1.2 quarts
- 4″ deep = 1.8 quarts
- 6″ deep = 2.7 quarts

One-Ninth Size
6⅞″ × 4¼″
- 2″ deep = 0.6 quarts
- 4″ deep = 1.1 quarts

▲
Figure 3-16
Hotel Pans
A full-size hotel pan is on the left; a two-third size pan and a one-third size pan are on the right.
Recognizing Patterns Why would the food-service industry tend to use standard sizes for hotel pans?

The full-size hotel pan is the largest, measuring 20¾ inches long by 12¾ inches wide. A steam table might be able to hold three, four, or more full-size hotel pans.

Other hotel pans are named as fractions of the full-size pan. A full-size hotel pan that is 6 inches deep holds 20 quarts. Most hotel pans are available in three depths: 2½ inches, 4 inches, and 6 inches. The smallest hotel pan is one-ninth the size of the full size pan, is 2½ inches deep, and holds a little over half a quart.

Service Equipment

In a full-service restaurant, most equipment for holding food is located in the kitchen. Food is prepared and orders are assembled in the kitchen. The finished food is artfully displayed on plates. The wait staff then must bring the plates to the diners. Ultimately, a restaurant meal is an orchestrated performance that allows guests to appreciate the food at the right temperature, with all the food on the plate arranged exactly as the kitchen intended.

Common types of tableside serving equipment are trays, tray stands, plate covers, and service carts.

- **Trays.** To transport dishes from the kitchen to the dining area, the serving staff may use trays. Plates on trays can be covered or uncovered.
- **Tray Stands.** Also called jack stands, **tray stands** allow serving staff to place a tray containing multiple dishes close to

table where the dishes will be served. Tray stands are usually made of wood or metal and can be folded when not in use. Some stands have a shelf to hold a tray of dirty dishes.

- **Plate Covers.** When serving staff must travel a significant distance to bring food to the customer, a plate might be covered with a **plate cover** to keep the food warm. When the plate has been set on the table, the plate cover will be removed.

- **Service Carts.** There are various types of service carts. Generally a service cart is used in the dining area to carry food or provide a work surface for carving, plating, or assembling dishes beside a table. A flambé cart (also called a guèridon) is a specialized type of service cart that holds an open burner for finishing a dish with a flaming sauce or cooking an omelet. A pastry cart displays a selection of desserts. A chafer cart holds a chafing dish with food that is kept warm. A salad cart lets wait staff prepare a salad as diners look on.

▲ *Plate cover*

Reading Checkpoint *Name four types of tableside serving equipment.*

3.4 ASSESSMENT

Reviewing Concepts

1. What is a steam table?
2. Name four common types of tableside serving equipment.

Critical Thinking

3. **Solving Problems** List as many combinations of different size hotel pans as possible that occupy the space of one full-size pan (examples: 2 half-size long pans; 1 regular half-size pan and 2 one-fourth size pans).

4. **Drawing Conclusions** Why would a restaurant try to keep the lids of chafing dishes closed as much as possible when serving?

5. **Applying Concepts** A sneeze guard obviously benefits the customer, but does it benefit the food establishment? Explain your answer.

Test Kitchen

Divide into two teams. Have one team role-play serving food from hot and cold holding equipment. Have the other team role-play customers in a rush. Switch roles after ten minutes. Record your observations as both servers and customers.

SCIENCE

Steam Tables

Research steam tables (including prices). Some questions you might consider: Why does a steam table heat evenly? How is the heat maintained at a constant temperature? What happens if the water in the steam table evaporates? What precautions are built in to avoid water evaporation? What sizes are available? When were steam tables invented? Do all steam tables use standard-sized hotel pans?

Review and Assessment

Reviewing Content

Choose the letter that best answers the question or completes the statement.

1. An arrangement of equipment and tools for accomplishing a specific set of culinary tasks is a
   a. work line
   b. workstation
   c. workflow
   d. work section

2. A small broiler, used primarily for browning and melting foods is called a
   a. convection oven
   b. griddle
   c. salamander
   d. deck oven

3. Which of the following cooks food with a heat source from above?
   a. deck oven
   b. oven
   c. broiler
   d. flattop range

4. How is a chafing dish used?
   a. to heat many hot food items
   b. to transport dishes from the kitchen
   c. to hold one or two hot food items
   d. to place in a steam table

5. Which of the following is the first step for cleaning electrical food-preparation equipment?
   a. Soak the machine in hot soapy water.
   b. Disassemble the machine according to manual directions.
   c. Carefully wash the blade.
   d. Turn off and unplug the machine.

6. What is the primary difference between a planetary mixer and a spiral mixer?
   a. A planetary mixer is smaller and sits on a countertop.
   b. A planetary mixer is larger and sits on the floor.
   c. The mixing bowl of a planetary mixer does not move; only the mixing tool moves.
   d. The mixing bowl of a planetary mixer moves; the mixing tool does not move.

Understanding Concepts

7. What is involved in mise en place and why is it important for efficient work flow?

8. How do workstations use refrigerated drawers and undercounter reach-ins to increase efficiency?

9. What is the difference between mixing and blending? Provide an example.

Critical Thinking

10. **Applying Concepts** Review the safety guidelines for food temperatures in Chapter 1. Explain how holding equipment helps maintain these guidelines.

11. **Forming a Model** Identify the work-line arrangement of your home's kitchen (or a kitchen with which you are familiar). Provide a sketch of the kitchen with storage, preparation, and cooking equipment labeled.

Culinary Math

12. **Solving Problems** A restaurant's meat grinder can grind 6 pounds of meat in 2 minutes. A single serving of ground meat at the restaurant is 6 ounces. About how long will it take to grind enough meat for one night's service, which is 200 servings?

13. **Forming a Model** A steam table has room for three full-size hotel pans. How many combinations of hotel pans can you put together if the restaurant wants the first space to use two regular size half pans and the third space to be a full-size pan? The restaurant does not have any one-ninth or one-sixth size pans.

On the Job

14. **Predicting** A chef working on the grilling station always arrives at work late and doesn't have time to complete mise en place for his workstation before customers start arriving. What are the consequences of the chef's late arrival for customers? For the restaurant? For the chef?

15. **Applying Concepts** A restaurant received a load of beef that is intended for use for tonight's dinner. Your infrared thermometer indicated that the temperature of the beef when it was received was 43°F. Would you accept this delivery? Explain your answer.

LAB ACTIVITY

Project 3: Cleaning Preparation & Cooking Equipment

Answer these questions when your class works through Project 3.

- Which piece of food-preparation equipment took the longest to clean? The shortest?

- Which piece of cooking equipment took the longest to clean? The shortest?

- What is the most efficient way to clean your school's kitchen, including all the food-preparation and cooking equipment, on a daily basis?

- How long does it take to clean all of your school's preparation & cooking equipment on a daily basis?

- Is longer-term maintenance (weekly, monthly, yearly) required for any food-preparation or cooking equipment? If so, how is it scheduled?

TEST PRACTICE

Choose the letter that best answers the question or completes the statement.

1. What activities are included in the concept of mise en place?
   A gathering raw materials required by your station
   B preparing raw materials so they are ready to be used by your station
   C making sure your station has all the equipment and tools required
   D all of the above

2. "Lowboy" is another name for a (an)
   A oven
   B broiler
   C undercounter reach-in refrigerator
   D tray stand

3. What type of heat does a flattop range provide?
   A indirect, less intense heat that can't be quickly adjusted
   B direct heat that can be quickly adjusted
   C hot air that is circulated around the food
   D steam heat that provides an even heating surface

4. What of the following sizes is not typically available for hotel pans?
   A three-quarter size
   B one-ninth size
   C one-sixth size
   D A and B

5. Which is the least common type of shelving material?
   A stainless steel
   B wood
   C galvanized steel
   D high-impact plastic

6. What is the common width of an aisle in a storage area?
   A 1 to 2½ feet
   B 3 to 4 feet
   C 60 inches
   D 6 feet

7. What is the maximum height and maximum depth for storage shelves?
   A height 5 feet, depth 24 inches
   B height 5 feet, depth 18 inches
   C height 6 feet, depth 18 inches
   D height 6 feet, depth 24 inches

8. What amount of ingredients is typically stored in a refrigerated drawer or undercounter reach-in?
   A enough for one hour
   B enough for a few hours or a night
   C enough for two days
   D enough for no more than one week

Using Knives

READING PREVIEW

Key Concepts

- Identifying parts of a knife
- Selecting the appropriate knife
- Using a knife properly
- Making the cut
- Maintaining knives

Vocabulary

- batonnet
- bolster
- boning knife
- box grater
- brunoise
- chef's knife
- chiffonade
- cleaver
- cube
- diagonal cut
- dice
- fermière
- filleting knife
- forged blade
- gaufrette
- granton edge
- grit
- heel (of blade)
- honing
- julienne
- lozenge
- mandoline
- oblique cut
- paring knife
- paysanne
- rivet
- rondelles
- serrated edge
- scimitar
- slicer
- spine (of blade)
- stamped blade
- steel
- tang
- taper ground edge
- trueing
- tournée
- utility knife
- whetstone

> **"W**ho you are is completely reflected in your knives—if they're sharp, if they're clean, and if they're put away in the proper manner. **"**
>
> – Gray Kunz

Identifying Parts of a Knife

Probably no other kitchen tool is as important to a chef as a knife. To use this important tool well, a chef must know how each knife is constructed. A chef must know about the wide variety of knives, each designed for a specific task. A chef must know how to use a knife properly and how to make the cuts that are required for particular dishes. Finally, a chef has to know how to maintain a knife.

A knife is constructed from several parts—each of which determines how the knife feels in the chef's hand, how it is best used, and how long the knife will last.

The Blade The blade is the cutting surface of the knife. The blade of a high-quality professional knife is made of a single piece of metal that has been forged or stamped into its desired shape.

Gray Kunz, Chef and Owner
Café Gray, New York, NY

A **forged blade** is made from a single piece of heated metal that is dropped into a mold and then pounded and cut into shape. A **stamped blade** is made by cutting blade-shaped pieces from sheets of previously milled steel.

Blades are usually made of stainless steel or high-carbon stainless steel, but modern knives sometimes use ceramic material, or titanium. Stainless-steel blades are very hard and durable. They are made of chromium and carbon steel. They don't rust or discolor but are hard to sharpen. High-carbon stainless-steel blades are a mix of iron, carbon, chromium, and other metals.

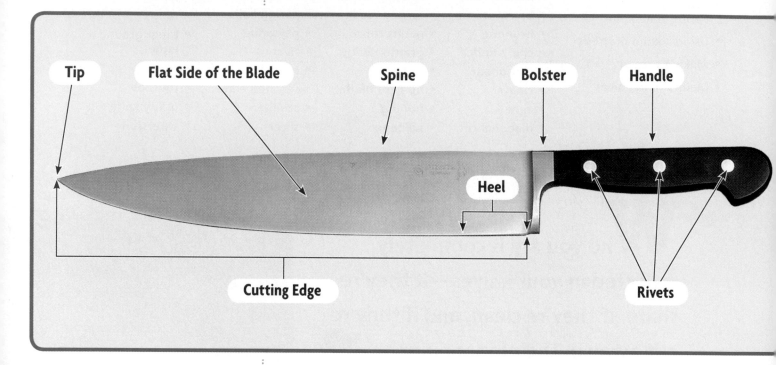

The blade of the chef's knife has several distinct parts:

- **Tip.** Used for fine work, paring, trimming, and peeling. The tip can also be used to core fruits and vegetables or to score items so they will marinate or cook more evenly.

- **Cutting Edge.** Used for slicing, carving, and making precision cuts. The most common type of cutting edge for general use is a **taper ground edge**, in which both sides of the blade taper smoothly to a narrow V-shape.

- **Heel.** Used for cutting tasks that require some force. The **heel** of the blade is the widest and thickest point of the blade.

- **Bolster**. Located at the heel of the blade, at the point where the blade and handle come together. The **bolster** gives the blade greater strength and durability.

- **Spine.** The non-cutting edge of the blade is called the **spine** of the knife.
- **Flat side of blade.** Used to crush garlic.

The Tang The **tang** is the continuation of the blade into the knife's handle. Tangs can be either full or partial. A full tang is as long as the whole knife handle. Knives used for heavy work, such as chef's knives and cleavers, should have a full tang. Knives used for lighter work may have a partial tang that does not run the entire length of the handle.

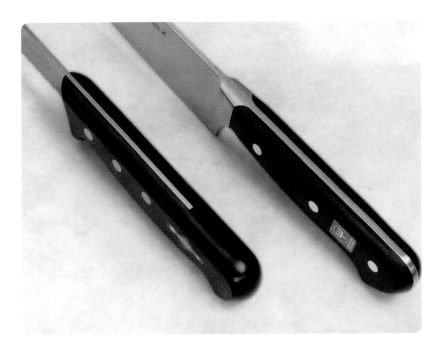

◀

FIGURE 4-1
Different Types of Tangs
The knife on the left has a partial tang; the knife on the right has a full tang.
Drawing Conclusions *Why would a knife with a full tang be used for heavy work?*

The Handle Knife handles are made of various materials, including hard woods with very tight grain, such as walnut and rosewood; textured metal; and composite materials. Some are cushioned to make long hours of work less fatiguing.

Wooden handles are attached to the blades with **rivets**. If rivets are visible on the handle (they aren't always), they should lie flush with the surface of the handle to prevent irritation to the hand and to avoid creating pockets where microorganisms could gather. Composition handles are molded onto the tang.

Because you will be holding your knife for extended periods, be sure the material and the shape of the handle feel comfortable in your hand. Many manufacturers offer a range of handle sizes.

 **Reading Checkpoint** *What are the main parts of a knife?*

Selecting the Appropriate Knife

There are almost as many types of knives as there are types of food. Each aspect of a knife—the length and flexibility of the blade, the type

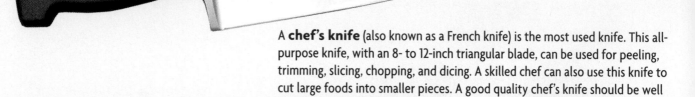

Types of Knives

Chef's Knife

A **chef's knife** (also known as a French knife) is the most used knife. This all-purpose knife, with an 8- to 12-inch triangular blade, can be used for peeling, trimming, slicing, chopping, and dicing. A skilled chef can also use this knife to cut large foods into smaller pieces. A good quality chef's knife should be well balanced, with the weight of the blade equal to the weight of the handle.

Utility Knife

A **utility knife** is a smaller and lighter version of a chef's knife, with a 5- to 7-inch blade. It is used for light cutting, slicing, and peeling.

Paring Knives

A **paring** (PAIR-ing) **knife** is the second most frequently used knife. It has a 2- to 4-inch blade and is used mainly for peeling and trimming fruits and vegetables.

A **tournée** (TOUR-nay) knife is a type of paring knife with a curved blade, making cutting rounded surfaces easier. It is also known as a bird's beak knife.

Boning Knife

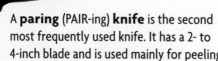

A **boning knife** is used to separate raw meat from the bone. The blade is usually about 6 inches long and is thinner than the blade of a chef's knife. The narrow blade allows you to work around bones, between muscles, and under gristle. Some boning knives have an upward curve; others are straight.

Filleting Knife

A **filleting** (fill-AY-ing) **knife** is specially designed for filleting fish. It has a very flexible blade.

of cutting edge, the strength of construction—is finely designed for a specific task.

 **Reading Checkpoint** *What are the eight basic types of knives?*

Slicers

A **slicer** has a long thin blade with a rounded or pointed tip. It is used to make smooth slices in a single stroke. The blade may be flexible or rigid.

Some slicers have a **serrated** (SER-a-ted) **edge**—a row of teeth that make it easy to slice foods with a crust or firm skin.

Some slicers have a **granton** (GRAN-ton) **edge**, which means a series of ovals have been ground along the edge of the blade. Smoked salmon or moist meats sliced with this knife will not stick to the blade.

Cleaver

Cleavers have rectangular blades and vary in size. They can be used for many of the same applications as a chef's knife.

Scimitar

The long, curved blade of a **scimitar** (SIM-ah-tahr) makes it ideal for cutting through large cuts of raw meat when making them into steaks, cutlets, or medallions.

Using Knives Properly

Remember when you first learned how to write? First you had to concentrate on holding the pencil and shaping each letter. With practice, writing became automatic and you developed your own unique signature. That is just like learning to use a knife properly. First you have to concentrate on holding the knife properly and shaping each item. Before long, using your knife becomes automatic and you develop your own unique style.

Holding the Knife

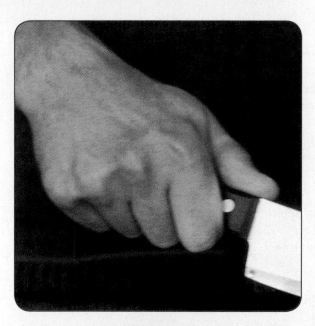

◄ Method 1: Grip the handle with four fingers and hold the thumb firmly against the blade's spine. This method gives you more power.

▲ Method 2: Grip the handle with all four fingers and hold the thumb against the side of the blade. This method gives you more control.

◄ Method 3: Grip the handle with three fingers, resting the index finger flat against the blade on one side and holding the thumb on the opposite side. This method gives you most control.

Your choice of knife grip depends on the particular task, the specific knife, and your personal preferences. There are the three basic grips. While one hand holds the knife and makes the cuts, the other hand controls the food you are cutting.

▲ When cutting an object on the cutting board, tuck the fingers under the knuckles slightly and hold the object, with the thumb held back from the fingertips. The knife blade rests against the knuckles, making it impossible to cut the fingertips.

◀ When cutting fish, meat, and bread, the guiding hand can be placed on top of the food to keep it from slipping. Hold your hand flat on the upper surface of the food and exert a little pressure.

The guiding hand ▶ is also used to hold a carving or kitchen fork when disjointing or carving cooked meats and poultry. The tines of the fork can either be laid across the surface or inserted directly into the food to hold it in place.

▲ Sometimes while peeling or trimming, you may find yourself holding the food in the air, above the cutting surface. The guiding hand will hold and turn the food against the blade. Make sure the food, your hands, and the knife handle are all dry.

 **Reading Checkpoint** *What are four ways the guiding hand is used in cutting with a knife?*

Knife Safety

1. Always hold a knife by its handle.

2. Never try to catch a falling knife.

3. When passing a knife to someone else, lay the knife down on a work surface and allow the other person to pick it up.

4. If you must carry an unsheathed knife in the kitchen, hold it straight down at your side with the sharp edge facing behind you.

5. Never borrow a knife without asking permission, and always return it promptly after using it.

6. Do not allow the blade of a knife to hang over the edge of a table or cutting board.

7. Do not use a knife as a tool to open bottles, loosen drawers, and so on.

8. Do not leave knives loose in areas where they cannot easily be seen or wouldn't be found normally (in a filled sink, under tables, on shelves).

9. Never store or use a knife above waist level.

10. Always cut away from your body.

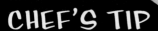

CHEF'S TIP

SAFE SLICING

To slice safely, place the flat side of the food down so it won't slip. For rounded or irregular food, cut off a piece to create a flat surface.

Making the Cut

The purpose of using a knife is to make a food smaller and to shape a food. Small, uniform pieces will cook evenly; large, irregularly shaped pieces won't. A uniform size also makes the finished product visually attractive.

Sometimes preliminary trimming, peeling, or squaring off is necessary to make the actual cuts easier. Foods with a uniform texture once they are peeled and trimmed (such as potatoes, carrots, celery, and turnips) can be cut by using the techniques described here. Foods that grow in layers (such as onions) or have pits, cores, or seeds (such as avocados or apples) all require special variations of these techniques. Meat, fish, and poultry that are still on the bone also call for special cutting and carving techniques. Special cutting techniques for these foods are covered in other chapters.

The basic cutting techniques are:

- Slicing
- Chopping and mincing
- Shredding and grating

Slicing Slicing cleanly through food should be no problem if a knife is properly sharpened. Simply guide the knife through the food, keeping the knife straight and even and letting the knife do the work. Adjust the length of your stroke and the pressure you exert on the food to suit the texture of the food you are slicing.

When you make clean, even slices, you can cut a wide range of foods from fruits and vegetables to meat and fish. Choose your knife carefully. Longer, thinner blades are best for very fine cuts or slices. Smaller blades are easier to manage with smaller foods.

Other food-preparation equipment, such as meat slicers or specialty disks for food processors, can be used for slicing. These are especially helpful when a large number of uniform slices are required. A special slicing tool called a **mandoline** (MAHN-duh-lihn) is sometimes used for very precise slicing. It has extremely sharp blades that can be adjusted to achieve precise cuts and thicknesses.

Chopping and Mincing Chopping usually refers to cutting food into pieces that are roughly but not exactly the same size. Although chopping is sometimes used interchangeably with the word "mincing," minced food is generally smaller than chopped food. To chop or mince, keep the tip of the knife in contact with the board and lower the knife firmly and rapidly, making repeated small cuts until you get the desired fineness.

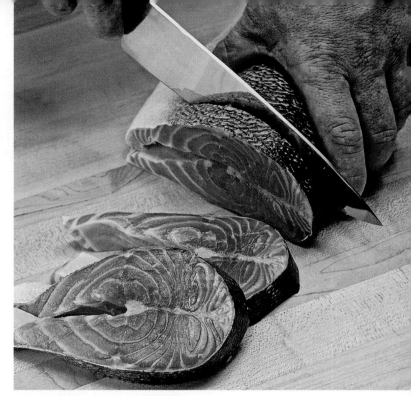

▲
FIGURE 4-2
Slicing
The knife must be properly sharpened to slice correctly.
Predicting *Based on your experience, what happens when you try to cut with a dull blade?*

▲ *Mandoline*

◀
FIGURE 4-3
Chopping versus Mincing
Chopping (left) results in larger pieces than mincing (right).
Predicting *If you added chopped onions to a recipe calling for minced onions, how might the final dish be changed in taste and texture?*

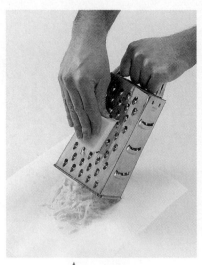

▲ Box grater

Shredding and Grating You can shred or grate items coarsely or finely. Some foods can easily be shredded with a chef's knife. However, other more specialized tools, including slicers, mandolines, and mixers or food processors (with attachments) can also be used, particularly if a large amount of shredded food is required.

Grating is often done with the grater attachments on food processors and mixers. You could also use a **box grater**, a special hand tool for grating. Specialized graters are available for specific tasks, such as grating nutmeg, cheese, or ginger.

Precision Cuts Precision cuts are used when nearly perfect uniformity is required. The ability to produce neat, even cuts shows your skill and craftsmanship. More importantly, it means food cooks evenly and retains the best possible flavor, nutrition, color, and appearance as it cooks. Some precision cuts are:

- **Rondelles.** Pronounced rahn-DELLS, **rondelles** is a French term meaning "rounds." The round shape is the result of cutting through any cylindrically shaped vegetable, such as a carrot or cucumber. To make rondelles, first trim and peel the vegetable. Then slice through the vegetable to make round pieces, or rondelles. Make sure each rondelle is the same thickness.

FIGURE 4-4 ▶
Rondelles
Slice through the vegetable to produce a rondelle.
Applying Concepts *Why should each rondelle be the same width?*

- **Variations of Rondelles**. Rather than cutting straight down to make a rondelle, you can cut down diagonally to make a **diagonal cut.** This exposes a greater surface area of the vegetable and is often used for Asian-style dishes. Some variations on the rondelle cut, such as ripple and **gaufrette** (go-FRET) cuts, require special blades on a mandoline, food processor, or slicer.

CHEF'S TIP

SHREDDING GREENS
When cutting tight heads of greens, such as lettuce or cabbage, cut the head into halves or quarters and remove the core before cutting shreds with a chef's knife.

◀
FIGURE 4-5
Using a Mandoline to Make a Gaufrette Cut
"Gaufrette" is French for "waffle."
Predicting *How do you think the taste and texture of a fried gaufrette potato would differ from a French fry?*

- **Chiffonade.** Used primarily to cut leafy greens and other ingredients into very fine shreds, the **chiffonade** (shiff-en-ODD) cut is done by hand. Chiffonade is different from shredding. The cuts are much finer and more uniform.

BASIC CULINARY SKILLS

Making a Chiffonade Cut

1 Remove stems, if stems are tough.

2 Stack several leaves on top of each other.

3 Roll tightly.

4 Slice the rolled leaves, using very narrow parallel cuts to produce fine shreds. Hold the rolled leaves tightly.

- **Julienne and Batonnet.** Both the **julienne** (JU-lee-ehn) and the **batonnet** (bah-tow-NAY) cuts are long, rectangular cuts that both showcase a chef's cutting skills and allow the vegetables to cook evenly. French fries are a type of julienne cut. Fine julienne cuts are about 1/16 inch thick, julienne cuts are about 1/8 inch thick, and batonnet cuts are about 1/4 inch thick.

BASIC CULINARY SKILLS

Making Julienne & Batonnet Cuts

1. **Trim vegetables** so their sides are straight. This makes it easier to make even cuts.

2. **Slice vegetables lengthwise**, using parallel cuts of the proper thickness (1/8 inch for julienne, 1/4 inch for batonnet).

3. **Stack the slices**, aligning the edges.

4. **Make parallel slices** through the stack (1/8 inch apart for julienne, 1/4 inch for batonnet).

CULINARY HISTORY

The Oldest Tool Known to Man

Stone cutting tools unearthed in Kenya are believed to be nearly 3 million years old. They are considered the oldest man-made tools.

The first knives were made mainly from flint, a particularly hard stone.

Once humans learned mining skills, soft metals such as copper, lead, and gold were extracted from ore. Unfortunately, these soft metals did not make strong knives.

By about 3500 BC, copper was being melted with tin to form bronze. Iron was blended with the other metals to give items more strength and to resist rusting. Eventually, carbon was added and a metal known as carbon steel was developed. It resembled modern wrought iron.

At first, steel was used mainly for weapons. But by about 1500 AD, steel knives, forks, and spoons were used by wealthy people as cutlery. By the end of the 1800s, carbon steel of a consistent quality could be produced on a large scale. In the early 1900s, advancements in steel manufacturing made knives more durable and flexible—able to withstand the rigorous use of professional chefs today.

Research

Research the history of metals, paying particular attention to the development of carbon steel.

◀ *Stone Age knife with serrated edge*

- **Oblique Cut.** The **oblique** (o-BLEEK) cut creates a piece in which the cut sides of a vegetable are neither parallel (side by side) nor perpendicular (at right angles). This effect is achieved by rolling the vegetable after each cut (which is why the cut is sometimes called a roll cut). This cut is used for long, cylindrical vegetables such as carrots. There are no specific dimensions for the oblique cut—the angle at which you choose to make the cuts is up to you, but the angle should be consistent with each piece.

BASIC CULINARY SKILLS

Making an Oblique Cut

1. Make a diagonal cut to remove the stem end of the peeled vegetable.

2. Roll the vegetable 90 degrees (a quarter-turn).

3. Slice the vegetable, using the same diagonal cut as you used in step 1, forming a piece with two angled edges.

4. Roll the vegetable 90 degrees and repeat the diagonal cut. Continue until the entire vegetable has been cut.

- **Dice.** When you cut a **dice**, you produce a cube-shaped piece of food. The smallest dice is called a **brunoise** (brewn-WHAZ), which means "to brown" in French. A brunoise is also known as a fine dice and is about ⅛-inch square. A fine brunoise is even smaller, only about ¹⁄₁₆-inch square.

BASIC CULINARY SKILLS

Dicing

1. Trim and peel the food, if necessary.

2. Cut into slices. Make slices the thickness you want the finished dice to be.

3. Stack slices on top of each other.

4. Make parallel cuts of the same thickness as you used in step 2. This produces sticks.

5. Place sticks side-by-side.

6. Make parallel cuts across the sticks, holding them in place by using your guiding hand.

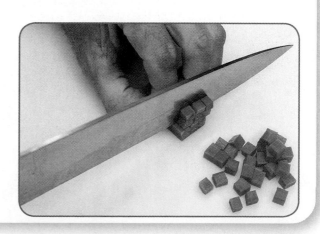

A medium dice is about ½-inch square, and a large dice, also called a **cube**, is at least ¾-inch square but can be larger.

- **Paysanne and Fermière.** These cuts are generally used in older, more traditional dishes, as can be seen in their names. **Paysanne** (pahy-SAHN) means "peasant" in French and

Sample Cuts

Rondelles ▶
Thickness varies

◀ **Brunoise (Fine Dice)**
⅛ x ⅛ x ⅛ inch

Diagonal Cut ▶
Thickness varies

◀ **Small Dice**
¼ x ¼ x ¼ inch

Oblique Cut ▶
Size varies

◀ **Medium Dice**
½ x ½ x ½ inch

Turned ▶
2 inches long

◀ **Large Dice (Cube)**
¾ x ¾ x ¾ inch

Fine Julienne ▶
1/16 x 1/16 x 1 to 2 inches

◀ **Lozenge**
½ x ½ x ¼ inch

Julienne ▶
⅛ x ⅛ x 1 to 2 inches

◀ **Paysanne**
½ x ½ x ⅛ inch

Batonnet ▶
¼ x ¼ x 2 to 2½ inches

◀ **Fermière**
⅛ to ½ inch

fermière (FARM-ee-air) means "farmer." A paysanne cut starts with a batonnet that is ½-inch thick. Cut the batonnet at ⅛-inch intervals so you have a flat ½-inch square that is only ⅛-inch thick. A fermière has a bit more rustic look. To make this cut, start with a batonnet that shows the curved or uneven edges of the vegetable. Cut the batonnet into pieces that are ⅛- to ½-inch thick.

- **Lozenge.** The **lozenge** (LOZ-enj) cut is a diamond-shaped cut that is most often used in garnishes. To make this cut, start with slices that are about ¼-inch thick. Cut the slices into strips about ½-inch wide. Holding your knife at an angle to the strip, make parallel cuts to produce a diamond shape.

- **Turned.** The turned cut is one of the most time-consuming cuts. It requires a series of precise cuts. The turned cut comes from the French verb tourner, meaning "to turn." Vegetables are cut into 2-inch pieces and are turned and cut so the end result is a football-like shape. Classic turned vegetables have seven sides, but the number of sides depends on the vegetables used. Turned vegetables can also have a flat bottom and only three or four curved sides.

 **Reading Checkpoint** *What are the three basic cutting techniques?*

Maintaining Knives

The mark of professional chefs is the attention they give to their tools. They keep knife edges in top condition by honing the knives frequently as they work, sharpening them when needed, taking them to a knifesmith when an edge needs to be rebuilt, and storing them properly. No professional chef would ever drop a knife into a sink of dishwater or put a knife away dirty.

Sharpening Knives with a Stone You give a knife an edge by using a sharpening stone (also called a **whetstone**). Stones are used to sharpen the edge once it has grown dull through ordinary use.

Sharpening stones are available in a variety of sizes, textures, and materials—both natural and manufactured. The relative coarseness or fineness of the stone's material is referred to as its **grit**. Large stones—some with several sides and a well for lubricating oil—can accommodate large and heavy blades. Smaller stones are more difficult to use on longer knives but are easier to transport.

FIGURE 4-6
Sharpening Stones
A three-faced stone is mounted on a rotating frame. Other sharpening stones have different grits on each side.
Applying Concepts *When would a triple-faced stone be preferable to a two-faced stone?*

Some chefs believe a knife blade should be run over a stone from the heel to the tip; others believe it should be run over the stone from the tip to the heel. Similarly, some chefs prefer to use a lubricant such as mineral oil on their stones, while others swear by water. Whichever way you prefer to run the blade over the stone, it is important to be consistent in the direction of the stroke. Water or mineral oil helps reduce friction as you sharpen your knife. Be consistent in the type of lubricant you use.

When using a sharpening stone, use a 20-degree angle for chef's knives and knives with similar blades. You may need to adjust the angle slightly to properly sharpen thinner blades, such as slicers, or thicker blades, such as cleavers.

CULINARY MATH

Measuring Angles

Angles are measured in degrees. Here's an easy way to remember an angle: think of a clock.

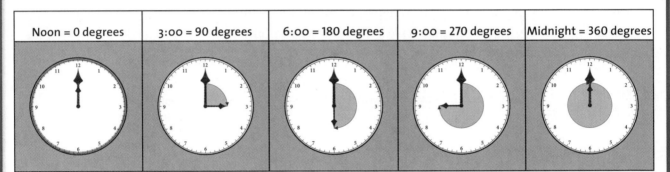

Noon = 0 degrees	3:00 = 90 degrees	6:00 = 180 degrees	9:00 = 270 degrees	Midnight = 360 degrees

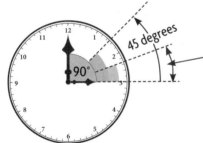

For a 20-degree angle, think of the distance about halfway between 0 and 45 degrees.

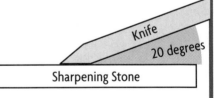

Honing Knives with a Steel Between sharpenings, you maintain a knife's edge with a steel. A **steel** is a textured steel or ceramic rod used to keep the blade straight and to smooth out irregularities. A steel is also known as a butcher's steel or a straightening steel. Steels are not used to sharpen a knife's edge. They are used to straighten the edge, because with use, the knife's edge starts to roll over to one side. The process of straightening the knife's edge is called **honing** or **trueing**. Good chefs are in the habit of using a steel before they start any cutting task, as they work, and again before they store their knives.

Sharpening a Knife

1 Position the stone to keep it from slipping.

2 Lubricate the stone with mineral oil or water. The duller the blade, the coarser the grit of the stone you will need to start.

3 Run the entire edge over the stone gently. Use the coarsest grit you think you will need. Keep the pressure on the knife even and hold the knife at the correct angle (about 20°). Use your guiding hand to maintain constant pressure.

4 Make an equal number of strokes on both sides of the blade. Use about 10 strokes.

5 Switch stones. Use an equal number of strokes on the stone with the next finer grit.

6 Finish sharpening. Use an equal number of strokes on the finest stone.

7 Hone the knife to remove any burrs.

8 Clean and sanitize the knife and clean the stone before use or storage.

There are several honing techniques. The Basic Culinary Skill shown here is a method that is particularly suited to a beginning chef. Whichever method you use, always work in the same direction on each side of the blade. Always use a light touch, stroking evenly and consistently. Lay the blade against the steel; don't slap it. You should hear a light ringing sound. A heavy grinding sound means you are using too much pressure.

Keeping Knives Cleaned and Sanitized To keep your knives safe and in good condition, you must clean and sanitize them. Knives can harbor pathogens, but regular and thorough cleaning and sanitizing removes pathogens before they can affect foods.

Clean knives in hot soapy water and dry them thoroughly between cutting tasks as well as after use and before storage. Sanitize the knives by wiping down the handle and blade with a sanitizing solution so the knife does not become a site for cross-contamination.

Don't clean knives in a dishwasher. Wooden handles can warp or split. Edges can be damaged by jostling or by extreme water temperatures. Never drop a knife into a sink when cleaning pots. The knife could be dented or nicked by a heavy pot.

Storing Knives Proper knife storage prevents damage to the blade and harm to unwary individuals. There are a number of safe, practical ways to store knives: in knife kits or cases and in wall or tabletop-mounted racks.

▲ *Steel*

Honing a Knife

1 Hold the steel in a vertical position with the tip resting on a non-slippery surface.

2 Position the heel of the knife against one side of the steel, near the handle.

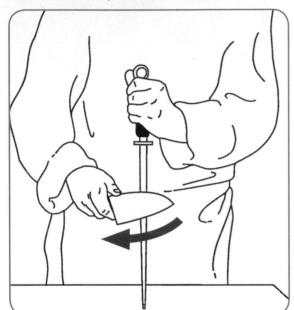

3 Draw the knife down the shaft of the steel and out from the steel so the entire knife blade, including the tip, is honed. Maintain light pressure and use an arm action, not a wrist action, to draw the knife smoothly down the steel.

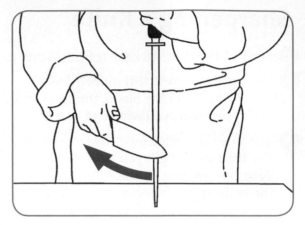

4 Repeat a few times for the first side of the knife.

5 Repeat steps 2, 3, and 4 with the other side of the knife. Use the same number of strokes as you used on the first side.

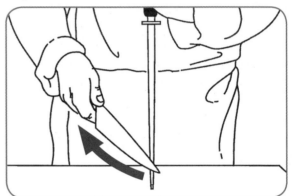

6 Clean and sanitize the knife.

FOCUS ON SAFETY

Cutting Board Safety

To keep the board from slipping or rocking as your work, lay it on a clean, dampened towel or rubber mat. Working on a warped cutting board is dangerous because it cannot be kept stable.

- Knife guards or sheaths add an extra level of protection, especially when knives are stored loose in drawers.
- Choose a knife kit constructed of materials that are easy to clean and sanitize.
- Steel and rubber slotted holders are sanitary and can be washed and sanitized in the dishwasher.
- Mount slotted hangers on the wall, not on the side of a table where an exposed blade might be a safety hazard.
- Clean and sanitize sheaths, knife cases, and slotted knife holders often.

Maintaining the Cutting Surface Cutting boards should always be used when cutting foods. Cutting boards should be flat, with a smooth surface. If they become chipped or gouged, they should be either resurfaced or re-placed. Wipe the board frequently as you work to remove peels, trim, and other debris.

When you switch from one type of food to another (from chicken to lettuce, for exam-ple), you should clean, rinse, and sanitize the board. Today, many kitchens use color-coded boards to help prevent cross-contamination. (These were discused in section 1.2 of this text.)

If the cutting surface is a butcher block top or other large surface, first wipe down the entire surface with a scrub brush or scrubbing pad and a container of clean, soapy water. Using a scraper, lift away any residue. Wipe down the board carefully with a clean, damp cloth to remove any traces of soap. Finally, wipe down the entire surface with a clean cloth that has been wrung out in a sanitizing solution. To prevent sanitizing so-lution from becoming dirty too quickly, wipe down the board with a damp, clean cloth before swabbing with sanitizing solution.

▲
FIGURE 4-7
Knife Kit
A knife kit is a safe and practical way to store and transport your knives.
Drawing Conclusions *Why might a chef be interested in transporting his or her knives?*

 **Reading Checkpoint** *When is a sharpening stone used to maintain a knife?*

4.1 ASSESSMENT

Reviewing Concepts

1. What are the main parts of a knife?
2. What are the eight basic types of knives and how are they used?
3. What are four ways the guiding hand is used in cutting with a knife?
4. What are the three basic cutting techniques? Describe each.
5. When is a sharpening stone used to maintain a knife? When is a steel used?

Critical Thinking

6. **Drawing Conclusions** Why do you think chefs tend to use a chef's knife more than any other kind of knife?
7. **Comparing and Contrasting** What is the difference between a julienne cut and a batonnet cut?
8. **Inferring** Do you think a professional chef would tend to own a triple-faced sharpening stone?

Test Kitchen

Slice, chop, and dice a carrot, using a chef's knife. Now cut the same size pieces by using a paring knife. What are the differences?

LANGUAGE ARTS

Pronouncing French Terms

Many terms in the culinary world are French. Team up with a student who knows French, if possible. Practice your pronunciation of the French terms from this section: chiffonade, rondelles, julienne, batonnet, paysanne, tournée, gaufrette, fermière, and brunoise. When you are satisfied with your pronunciation, define each term.

4.2 Using Smallware

READING PREVIEW

Key Concepts

- Selecting hand tools for specific tasks
- Selecting cookware for specific tasks
- Cleaning and sanitizing smallware

Vocabulary

- bain marie
- balance scale
- bi-metallic-coil thermometer
- braising pan
- casserole
- channel knife
- colander
- conical sieve
- conveyor belt dishwasher
- cookware
- corer
- crêpe pan
- custard cup
- double boiler
- drum sieve
- fish poacher
- food mill
- gratin dish
- gauge
- heat transfer
- kitchen shears
- liquid-filled thermometer
- melon baller
- microplane
- omelet pan
- palette knife
- Parisienne scoop
- pâté mold
- portion scale
- purée
- ramekin
- ricer
- roasting pan
- rubber spatula
- saucepan
- saucepot
- sauté pan
- sauteuse
- sautoir
- sheet pan
- single-rack dishwasher
- skimmer
- smallware
- soufflé dish
- steamer
- stockpot
- terrine mold
- thermistor thermometer
- thermocouple thermometer
- tongs
- turner
- undercounter dishwasher
- warewashing station
- whip
- whisk
- wok
- zest
- zester

"Use the right tool for the job. For a chef, this can make all the difference. The right spoon, the right whip, the right pan—you depend on these tools every day. **"**

– Prem Kumar

Prem Kumar
The Culinary Institute of America

Hand Tools

Hand tools, pots, and pans are often called **smallware**. The type of smallware used by a chef depends on the types of tasks the chef performs in the kitchen.

Culinary hand tools come in a huge variety. Although some hand tools are used in a home kitchen, others are more specialized and are not often seen outside a professional kitchen.

Overall, hand tools can be broadly broken down into five general categories (specialized tools for baking and pastry are discussed in Chapter 17):

- Cutting and slicing tools
- Shredding and grating tools
- Mixing and cooking tools
- Straining, draining, and processing tools
- Measuring tools

Cutting and Slicing Tools There are many specialized hand tools for cutting and slicing food. Often the food served by a food establishment influences the types of specialized hand tools the establishment uses. For example, an Italian restaurant might require an olive pitter. A restaurant that specializes in apple-based products might require a specialized apple peeler, an apple corer, and an apple cutter.

Shredding and Grating Tools Knives can be used to shred and grate food. There are also special shredding and grating attachments for food processors and mixers. As you learned in the previous section of this chapter, general-purpose hand tools such as the box grater and mandoline can also be used for shredding and grating. A **microplane** is another general-purpose tool for grating food.

There are also specialized hand tools for grating specific types of food. A nutmeg grater, for example, is a small grater used specifically to grate nutmeg. Other specialized types of graters include a cheese grater and a ginger grater. Different types of graters and microplanes, whether specialized or general purpose, produce different types of results—from a coarse grate to a fine grate.

Mixing and Cooking Tools Chefs use mixers, blenders, and food processors to mix or blend food. They also use individual hand tools for mixing ingredients. When food is cooking, chefs use hand tools to stir the food to make sure that it is properly cooked. They also use hand tools for removing cooked food from the cookware in which it was cooked. Most of the mixing and cooking tools serve multiple purposes.

FIGURE 4-8
Microplane
A microplane being used to grate a lemon for lemon zest.
Comparing/Contrasting *When would you use a microplane to create lemon zest and when might you use a zester?*

▼

Cutting and Slicing Tools

▲ Peeler

A peeler cuts a thin layer from vegetables and fruits more efficiently than a paring knife. Peelers have a swiveling blade that moves easily over contours of food. If the blade is sharpened on both sides, it peels when moved in both an upward and a downward motion. Peelers are also used to make delicate garnishes, such as carrot or chocolate curls.

▲ Melon Baller

A **melon baller** scoops out smooth balls from melons, cheese, and butter. A melon baller with a scoop at each end, one larger than the other, is called a **Parisienne** (pah-REE-see-ehn) **scoop.**

▲ Pizza Cutter/Pastry Wheel

This handy tool is used to cut pizzas and pastry.

▲ Channel Knife

A **channel knife** is used to cut grooves lengthwise in a vegetable such as a cucumber or carrot. A rondelle cut from the grooved vegetable has decorative edges that resemble a flower.

◄ Olive Pitter

Olive pitters remove the olive pit by plunging a small rod through the olive. An olive pitter can also be used for pitting cherries.

▲ Zester

A **zester** cuts away thin strips of the zest of citrus fruit peels. The **zest** is the colored outer layer of the peel.

▲ Kitchen Shears

Kitchen shears are handy for many kitchen chores, such as cutting string and butcher's twine, trimming artichoke leaves, cutting grapes into clusters, and trimming herbs. Poultry shears, a heavy-duty type of kitchen shears, can cut through the tight joints and ligaments of poultry.

▲ Corer

Used to remove the core of an apple or pear in one long, round piece, **corers** can also be used to remove eyes from potatoes or the stem and core from tomatoes.

▲ Fish Scaler

A fish scaler is used to remove the scales from a fish.

Mixing and Cooking Tools

Mixing Bowls ▶

Mixing bowls are usually made of a nonreactive material such as stainless steel. Glass, ceramic, or earthenware bowls may not be sturdy enough to use in a professional kitchen. (They can be used to serve prepared food.)

◀ Whisk

A **whisk** is a hand tool with thin wires in a sphere or an oval shape. It is used to add air to mixtures. Very round whisks add a large amount of air and are sometimes called balloon whisks. A narrower whisk is often referred to as a **whip**. Whips often have thicker wires and are used to blend sauces or batters without adding too much air.

▲ Palette Knife

A **palette** (PAL-et) **knife** (also called a straight or flat spatula) has a long, flexible blade with a rounded end. It is used for turning cooked or grilled foods and spreading fillings or glazes. (It is also used in baking.)

▲ Turners

A **turner** (also called an offset spatula or a flipper) has a broad blade and a short handle that is bent to keep the user's hands off hot surfaces. The blade can be perforated or unperforated. It is used to turn or lift hot foods.

Rubber Spatula ▲

A **rubber spatula** (SPAT-chew-la) has a broad, flexible tip. It is sometimes called a scraper, and is used to scrape food from the inside of bowls and pans. Some have a tip that can withstand high temperatures.

Skimmers ▶

A **skimmer** has a perforated surface and is used to skim impurities from liquids. It is also use to remove cooked food or pasta from a hot liquid.

◀ Spoons

Spoons are used for mixing, stirring, scooping, and serving foods. They may be wooden or stainless steel; and may be solid, perforated, or slotted.

▲ Tongs

Tongs are very useful for picking up hot items such as meats or large vegetables. They are also used for the sanitary serving of such items as cookies or ice cubes.

▲ Kitchen Fork

A kitchen fork is used to move small pieces of meat from a grill or a broiler and to hold larger pieces of meat when cutting them.

Straining, Draining, and Processing Tools

Drum Sieve ▲

A **drum sieve** (SIV) is a tinned-steel, nylon, plastic, or stainless-steel screen stretched on an aluminum or wood frame. A drum sieve (also called a tamis) is used to sift dry ingredients or purée very soft foods.

Food Mill ▲

A **food mill** strains and purées foods at the same time. (To **purée** (pure-AY) is to process the food until it has a soft, smooth consistency.) A food mill has a flat, curving blade that is rotated over a disk by a hand-operated crank. Professional models have interchangeable disks with holes of varying sizes.

◄ **Conical Sieve**

A **conical** (CON-i-cal) **sieve** (also called a chinois, china cap, or a bouillon strainer) is also used to strain or purée foods. It is a very fine mesh sieve shaped like a cone.

Colander ►

A **colander** (COL-un-der) is a large, perforated stainless steel or aluminum bowl, with or without a base, that is used to strain or drain foods.

◄ **Ricer**

A **ricer** is a device in which cooked food, typically potatoes, is pushed through a pierced container, resulting in rice-like pieces.

Funnel ▲

A funnel is used to pour liquid from a large to a smaller container. Funnels come in various sizes and materials.

Straining, Draining, and Processing Tools There are many specialized hand tools for straining and draining foods. These tools are used with dry or liquid ingredients as well as with food that is in liquid. The delicate mesh of some strainers can be easily damaged. Never drop them into a sink, where they could be crushed or torn.

Chefs use mixers, blenders, and food processors to process foods, but they also use specialized hand tools for food processing. The hand tools often allow a chef to exercise more control over the processing of food, control that would be impossible in a powerful electric tool.

Measuring Tools Measuring is essential in every recipe, not only so a dish is prepared correctly, but also to help control the size and cost of a single portion. Measuring tools measure one of the following:
- Weight
- Volume
- Temperature

Hand Tools

Measuring Weight

◀ **Portion Scale**
A non-digital **portion scale** measures the weight of a small amount of food or an ingredient (typically a portion). Portion scales can typically be reset to zero so you can allow for the weight of a container or weigh more than one ingredient at a time.

Digital Scale ▲
A digital scale (also called an electronic scale) provides a read-out of the weight. Digital scales are usually considered more accurate than other types of scales. A small digital scale is often used as a portion scale.

Balance Scale ▶
A **balance scale** is typically used for weighing baking ingredients. The ingredients are placed on the left side and weights are placed on the right side. When the sides balance, the ingredients weigh the same as the weights.

Hand Tools

Measuring Volume

▲ Measuring Cups and Spoons
Small stainless-steel measuring cups range from one-fourth cup to one cup. Stainless-steel measuring spoons range from one-fourth teaspoon to a tablespoon. Both the measuring cups and the spoons can be used to measure the volume of dry or liquid ingredients.

Volume and Liquid Measures ▲
Volume measures are typically made from metal and marked to show fractions. Volume measures are made in 8-, 16-, 32-, 64-, and 128-ounce sizes and are often marked every 4 or 8 ounces. Liquid measures also measure volume, but usually have a pouring lip to make pouring liquids easier. They are usually transparent glass or plastic and come in 1-cup, 1-pint, 1-quart, 2-quart, and 3-quart sizes.

Ladle ▲
A ladle is used to portion liquids, such as sauces and soups. Ladles will hold 1 to 16 ounces, depending on their size. Look for the measurement on the handle.

Measuring Temperature

◀ Thermistor Thermometer
A **thermistor** (therm-IS-tor) **thermometer** uses a resistor (a type of electronic semiconductor) to measure temperature. Thermistor thermometers give a fast reading (about 10 seconds) and can measure the temperature in thin and thick foods. They are not designed to stay in the food while cooking.

◀ Bi-Metallic-Coil Thermometer

A **bi-metallic-coil thermometer** uses a metal coil in the probe to measure temperature. Bi-metallic-coil thermometers are available in an oven-safe version that can stay in food while cooking. They give slower readings (1 to 2 minutes) and should be used for food that is at least 2 to 2½ inches thick. An instant-read version is not oven-safe and gives a reading in 15 to 20 seconds.

◀ Thermocouple Thermometer
A **thermocouple** (THER-mo-cup-ul) **thermometer** uses two fine wires within the probe to measure temperature. Thermocouple thermometers give the fastest readings (2 to 5 seconds) and can measure the temperature in thin and thick foods. They are not designed to stay in the food while cooking.

◀ Liquid-Filled Thermometer
Liquid-filled thermometers are the oldest type of thermometer. They have either a glass or metal stem filled with a colored liquid. They are designed to stay in the food while cooking. Because they can present a safety hazard, glass stemmed thermometers are less commonly seen in professional kitchens.

Calibrating a Thermometer

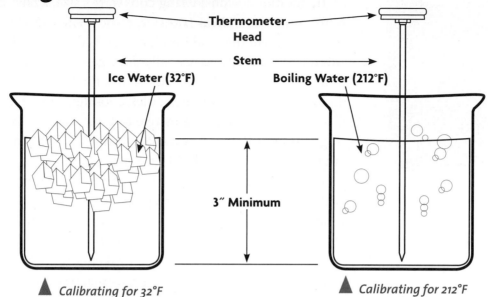

Thermometer Head

Stem

Ice Water (32°F)   Boiling Water (212°F)

3″ Minimum

▲ *Calibrating for 32°F*   ▲ *Calibrating for 212°F*

Most professional bi-metal thermometers are calibrated by using a wrench and the adjusting nut under the dial. Calibration involves making sure the thermometer actually records the temperature accurately. For true accuracy, distilled water should be used. The boiling point is also affected by how far you are above sea level. Calibrate a thermometer before its first use, if it is dropped, or at regular intervals whenever its accuracy is in question. For specific calibration instructions on all thermometers, consult the manufacturer's instructions.

Research

1. Check with the local Cooperative Extension Service or Health Department for the exact temperature of boiling water for your area's atmospheric pressure.

2. Fill a glass with crushed ice. Add distilled water until you have at least 3 inches of water. Stir well. Insert the thermometer and wait until the temperature is finalized (this depends on the type of thermometer you are testing). Without removing the thermometer, adjust it until the dial reads 32°F.

3. Fill a pot with at least 3 inches of distilled water. Heat to boiling. Using tongs and an oven mitt, hold the thermometer in the boiling water. Be careful not to scald your hand. If possible, adjust the thermometer while it is in the boiling water until the dial reads 212°F. It may be necessary to take the thermometer out of the water, adjust, and test again until the thermometer is calibrated.

 **Reading Checkpoint** *What are the five general categories of hand tools used in the kitchen?*

Cookware

Pots and pans are often referred to as **cookware**. Pans usually have flat bottoms, one long handle, and low sides that may be curved or straight. Pots are usually taller than pans and have straight sides. They usually have two handles.

No single type of cookware fits the needs of every chef. For a particular cooking task, a chef must first consider the size of the cookware. Foods should fit the pan comfortably without touching each other.

CHEF'S TIP

AVOIDING WARPS

To keep pots, pans, and oven cookware from warping, never subject them to temperature extremes (leaving them over direct heat for long periods) or rapid temperature changes (plunging a hot pot into water).

▲ *Cast iron skillet*

▲ *Pan with nonstick coating*

Another consideration for chefs is that some cookware is made from materials that react with food.

In addition to considering cookware's size, a chef must also keep in mind the rate of **heat transfer,** or how efficiently heat passes from the cookware to the food inside it. This is determined partially by the cookware's material and partially by its **gauge** (GAGE), or the thickness of the material. The thinner the gauge, the faster the cookware heats, but the faster it cools off. For quick cooking, choose a pan that transmits heat quickly and is sensitive to temperature changes. Moderate gauge works well. For slow cooking, choose a pan that holds heat well and transmits heat evenly. Heavy gauge is best.

Pans used in ovens are produced from the same basic materials used to make stovetop pots and pans. However, because the oven's heat is indirect, it is also possible to use glass and ceramic pans and molds without risk of cracking and shattering them.

For every cooking task, a chef must choose cookware that is an appropriate size, made from appropriate material, and in an appropriate gauge. Commonly used materials for cookware include:

- **Copper.** Transfers heat rapidly and evenly. Because copper can react with high-acid food to create toxic substances, most copper pans are lined with a nonreactive metal. Copper discolors quickly. Proper upkeep requires a lot of time and labor.
- **Cast Iron.** Holds heat well and transmits it very evenly. Cast iron is brittle, however, and must be treated carefully to avoid pitting, scarring, and rusting. Cast iron is sometimes coated with enamel to increase its life and make cleaning easier.
- **Stainless Steel**. Although a poor and uneven heat conductor, stainless steel is often used for cookware because it is easy to clean. Sometimes copper or aluminum is sandwiched in the bottom of the pan or pot to improve heat conductivity. Stainless steel will not react with foods.
- **Steel**. Other types of steel (blue steel, black steel, pressed steel, and rolled steel) transmit heat very rapidly and are preferred when food must be heated quickly. These pans are generally thin and are prone to discoloration.
- **Aluminum.** An excellent heat conductor, aluminum is a soft metal that wears down quickly. It also reacts with foods. When a metal spoon or whip is used to stir a white or light-colored sauce, soup, or stock in an aluminum pot, the food may turn gray. Treated aluminum (often referred to as "anodized aluminum") tends not to react with foods and is very popular.
- **Nonstick Coatings.** A final consideration for chefs is the use of nonstick coatings in cookware. Nonstick coatings can be useful in cookware but require the use of wooden, plastic, or silicon utensils to protect the surface and extend the pan's life.

Stovetop Cooking

▲ Stockpot

A **stockpot** is a large pot that is taller than it is wide and has straight sides. Some stockpots have a spigot at the base so the liquid can be drained off without lifting the heavy pot.

▲ Saucepot

A **saucepot** is similar in shape to a stockpot, although it is not as large. Saucepots have straight sides and two loop-style handles to ease lifting.

▲ Saucepan

A **saucepan** has straight or slightly flared sides and a single long handle.

▲ Sauté Pans

A **sauté pan** is a shallow, general-purpose pan that comes in two types. A **sauteuse** (SAW-toose) is a wide shallow pan with sloping sides and a single long handle. A **sautoir** (SAW-twahr) has straight sides and a long handle and is often referred to as a skillet.

▲ Wok

A **wok** has high, sloped sides, which make it great for quick stir-frying. Once one ingredient cooks, you can push it up the sides, leaving the hot center free for another ingredient.

▲ Omelet Pan or Crêpe Pan

An **omelet pan** or **crêpe** (KRAYP) **pan** is a shallow skillet with very short, sloping sides. A nonstick coating is often used in these pans.

▲ Double Boiler

A **double boiler** is actually a pair of nesting pots. The bottom pot is filled with water and heated, providing steady even heat for the top pot. A double boiler is often referred to as a **bain marie** (BANE ma-REE).

▲ Steamers

A **steamer** is a set of stacked pots or bamboo baskets with a tight-fitting lid. The upper pots or baskets have perforated bottoms so steam can gently cook or warm the contents of the pots or baskets. In a metal steamer, water is placed in the bottom pot and it is placed on the range. Bamboo steamers are generally placed over water in a wok.

▲ Fish Poacher

A **fish poacher** is a long, narrow, metal pan with a perforated rack used to raise or lower the fish so it doesn't break apart.

Oven Cooking*

Roasting Pan ▶
A **roasting pan** is used for roasting and baking. Roasting pans have low sides and are made in various sizes. Roasting racks are placed inside the pan to hold foods as they cook so the bottom, sides, and top of the food all are cooked evenly.

Sheet Pan ▶
A **sheet pan** is an all-purpose baking pan. Sheet pans are shallow, rectangular pans with sides that are generally no higher than one inch. They may be full, half, or quarter size.

Terrine Mold ▶
A **terrine** (teh-REEN) **mold** is traditionally made of pottery but can also be made of metal, enameled cast iron, or ceramic. Terrines are produced in a wide range of sizes and shapes; some have lids.

Braising Pans and Casseroles ▲
A **braising** (BRAY-zing) **pan** and a **casserole** (CASS-a-roll) typically have medium high walls and lids to keep the moisture in. They may be made of various materials.

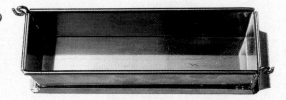

▲ **Pâté Mold**
A **pâté** (pa-TAY) **mold** is a deep, rectangular metal mold. Some pâté molds have hinged sides.

Gratin Dish ▲
A **gratin** (GRAW-ten) **dish** is a shallow ceramic, enameled cast iron, or enameled steel baking dish.

Soufflé Dish, Ramekin, and Custard Cup ▶
A **soufflé** (so-FLAY) **dish**, **ramekin** (RAM-I-kin), or **custard cup** is round and straight-edged. All three come in various sizes. Disposable versions made of aluminum are common.

*Baking pans used in making bread, pastries, and desserts are discussed in Chapter 17.

 *What are some types of cookware used for stovetop cooking? For oven cooking?*

Cleaning and Sanitizing Smallware

Some food-service establishments clean smallware by hand. Other establishments use a dishwasher to clean smallware.

Washing by Hand Even though smallware can be cleaned by hand, it is still important to thoroughly clean and sanitize it to prevent cross-contamination. A three-compartment sink is required for thorough cleaning and sanitizing. Some sinks with counter space provide holding areas for dirty and clean dishes. Dish carts often double as holding areas.

Garbage disposals are mounted in sink drains. They grind up food from rinsed dishes and cookware. Manufacturers recommend against grinding solid bones, fruit pits, and other large, hard objects. Be careful to keep silverware out of disposals.

FIGURE 4-9
Three-Compartment Sink
A three-compartment sink is used for scrubbing pots and pans. **Applying Concepts** *Why is it important to replace the sanitizing solution according to the manufacturer's instructions?*
▼

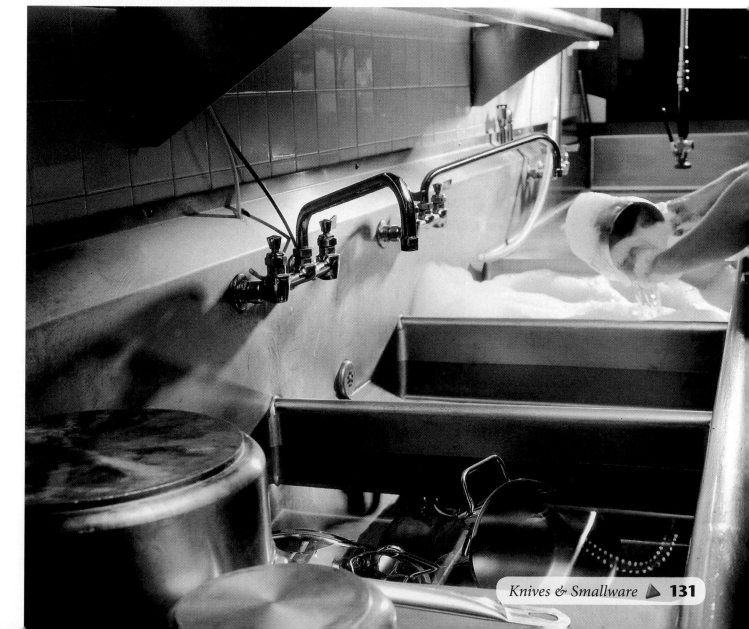

First, scrape food waste into a lined garbage can. Then rinse in a sink. Some sinks have a disposal, which may run in batches or continuous mode.

Using a three-compartment sink, follow these general steps to clean and sanitize most smallware:

1. Clean and sanitize the sink area.

2. Scrape and pre-rinse smallware.

3. Fill the first sink with 110°F water and detergent. Wash the smallware thoroughly with a brush. Drain and refill the water as needed.

4. Fill the second sink with water that is also about 110°F. Rinse the smallware to remove all traces of detergent.

5. Fill the third sink with water at the temperature specified by the manufacturer of your sanitizing agent. Add the recommended amount of sanitizing agent (chlorine or iodine). Submerge the smallware in the third sink for about 30 seconds.

6. Remove and air-dry smallware in a clean area. (Do not towel-dry. This can recontaminate smallware.)

FIGURE 4-10 ▶
Conveyer Belt Dishwasher
These dishes are emerging from a conveyer belt dishwasher.
Applying Concepts *Why is it important for the dishwasher to use water at high temperatures in the process of washing smallware and dishes?*

Dishwashers A food-service business needs to clean a flow of dirty tools, pots and pans, and dishes every day. The business usually establishes a **warewashing station** (also called a scullery) that provides rinsing, washing, and holding areas. The station also includes trashcans, sinks, garbage disposals, and professional dishwashing equipment. The dishwashing staff scrape and rinse plates and load the dishwasher. The equipment uses water at a high temperature to sanitize smallware and dishes. Clean dishes are then held on carts or shelves, ready for the wait staff.

Typically, three types of dishwashing equipment might be used in a professional kitchen:

- **Undercounter Dishwashers.** An **undercounter dishwasher** holds portable dish racks that allow for the easy transfer of clean and dirty dishes. Specialized glass washers are available.
- **Single-Rack Dishwashers.** A **single-rack dishwasher** processes small loads of dishes quickly. Scraped and rinsed dishes are placed in the upper compartment. The washer begins when the door is closed. Clean dishes are ready in minutes.
- **Conveyer Belt Dishwashers.** A **conveyor belt dishwasher** can process a high volume of dishes as a continuous flow.

Reading Checkpoint *What is the general method for cleaning and sanitizing smallware?*

> ## CHEF'S TIP
> **SPECIAL CLEANING AND SANITIZING**
>
> Smallware such as wooden utensils, cast iron pans, and rolled steel pans require special cleaning and sanitizing procedures. Consult the manufacturer's directions before cleaning these items.

4.2 ASSESSMENT

Reviewing Concepts

1. Identify the five general categories of hand tools.
2. List six types of cookware used for stovetop cooking.
3. What is a warewashing station?

Critical Thinking

4. **Applying Concepts** Explain the concept of heat transfer and gauge as it applies to cookware.
5. **Comparing/Contrasting** List the pros and cons of aluminum, stainless-steel, copper, and cast iron cookware
6. **Inferring** Why is a ladle regarded as a measuring tool?

Test Kitchen

Slice two ounces of cheddar cheese, using a chef's knife. Shred the same amount of cheese, using a mandoline. Grate the same amount of cheese, using a box grater (or the disks on a food processor). Compare the results and the amount of effort required to produce those results.

SCIENCE

Heat Transfer

Gather four 12-inch skillets: a cast iron skillet, an aluminum skillet, a stainless-steel skillet, and a copper skillet. Turn the stove burner to high. Place one tablespoon of water in each skillet. Use a stop watch to record the amount of time it takes for the water to begin to sizzle after you place each skillet on the burner. Place only one skillet on the burner at a time and make sure to use an oven mitt when handling hot skillets. Analyze your data to rank the skillets' ability to transfer heat.

Review and Assessment

Reviewing Content

Choose the letter that best answers the question or completes the statement

1. Professional quality knife blades are most often made from
   a. steel
   b. pure iron
   c. stainless steel
   d. high-carbon stainless steel

2. Which one of these is not found on a knife?
   a. stirrup
   b. tang
   c. rivets
   d. bolster

3. Which one of these knives has a long, thin blade?
   a. chef's knife
   b. slicer
   c. scimitar
   d. cleaver

4. Which one of these cuts is most time-consuming to execute?
   a. julienne
   b. batonnet
   c. turned cut
   d. rondelle

5. Which material is the poorest conductor of heat?
   a. aluminum
   b. copper
   c. cast iron
   d. stainless steel

6. Which utensil is used to make melon balls?
   a. zester
   b. Parisienne scoop
   c. palette knife
   d. mandoline

7. Which cookware has straight or slightly flared sides and a single long handle?
   a. stockpot
   b. wok
   c. saucepan
   d. saucepot

Understanding Concepts

8. What are the basic parts of a knife?

9. List at least seven knife safety points.

10. What are the three basic cutting techniques?

11. Name and describe at least five precision cuts.

12. What is the difference between sharpening and honing a knife? When is it appropriate to sharpen knives? Hone them?

13. List the five general categories of hand tools and provide an example of each.

14. List five examples of cookware for stovetop cooking and five examples of cookware for oven cooking.

Critical Thinking

15. **Comparing/Contrasting** If you could choose only two types of knives for your use in the kitchen, what would they be? Why?

16. **Comparing/Contrasting** Of the five general categories of hand tools, which do you think is the most important? Why?

On the Job

17. **Applying Concepts** You are cooking a roast beef in an oven and want to make sure that it is cooked perfectly. What type of thermometer would you use? Describe how you would use the thermometer and what advantages your choice would have compared to other thermometers.

Culinary Math

18. **Solving Problems** A carrot has been squared off. it is now 4 inches long and 1 inch thick. You need to cut it in a medium dice. About how many individual diced squares will the carrot produce?

Project 4: Knife Skills

Answer these questions when your class works through Project 4.

- How sharp were your school's knives when you started?
- Did honing the knives make a difference?
- Which type of knife did you find most comfortable?
- What is the hardest precision cut for you to make?
- What is the easiest precision cut for you to make?
- How fast was your team able to complete the cuts?
- How did the other teams judge your cuts?
- How much food did you waste in making the cuts?

TEST PRACTICE

Choose the letter that best answers the question or completes the statement.

1. Which knife is also known as a bird's beak knife?
   A chef's knife
   B slicer knife
   C tournée knife
   D filleting knife

2. A mandoline is used for:
   A precise slicing
   B sharpening knives
   C honing knives
   D making a turned cut

3. The angle to use for sharpening a chef's knife on a sharpening stone is
   A 10 degrees
   B 20 degrees
   C 45 degrees
   D 90 degrees

4. This cut is used on long, cylindrical vegetables. The vegetable is cut on a diagonal, turned 180 degrees, and cut again on the same diagonal, forming a piece with two angled edges.
   A oblique cut
   B turned cut
   C batonnet cut
   D paysanne cut

5. A chiffonade cut is usually used for:
   A long, cylindrical vegetables
   B leafy greens
   C tomatoes and other juicy vegetables
   D potatoes

6. A ricer is used to
   A hold rice after cooking
   B cook rice
   C drain rice
   D process potatoes into rice-like pieces

7. A sauteuse is
   A similar in shape to a stockpot, although not as large
   B a wide shallow pan with sloping sides and a single long handle
   C a pan with straight sides and a long handle
   D a pan with high, sloped sides that is used for stir frying

8. The third compartment in a three-compartment sink holds
   A sanitizing solution
   B rinse water
   C distilled water
   D a detergent solution

9. A chinois is another name for
   A a sauteuse
   B a ramekin
   C a conical sieve
   D a drum sieve

10. A large dice, or cube, is
    A ¼ inch on all sides
    B ½ inch on all sides
    C ¾ inch on all sides
    D 1 inch on all sides

Culinary Basics

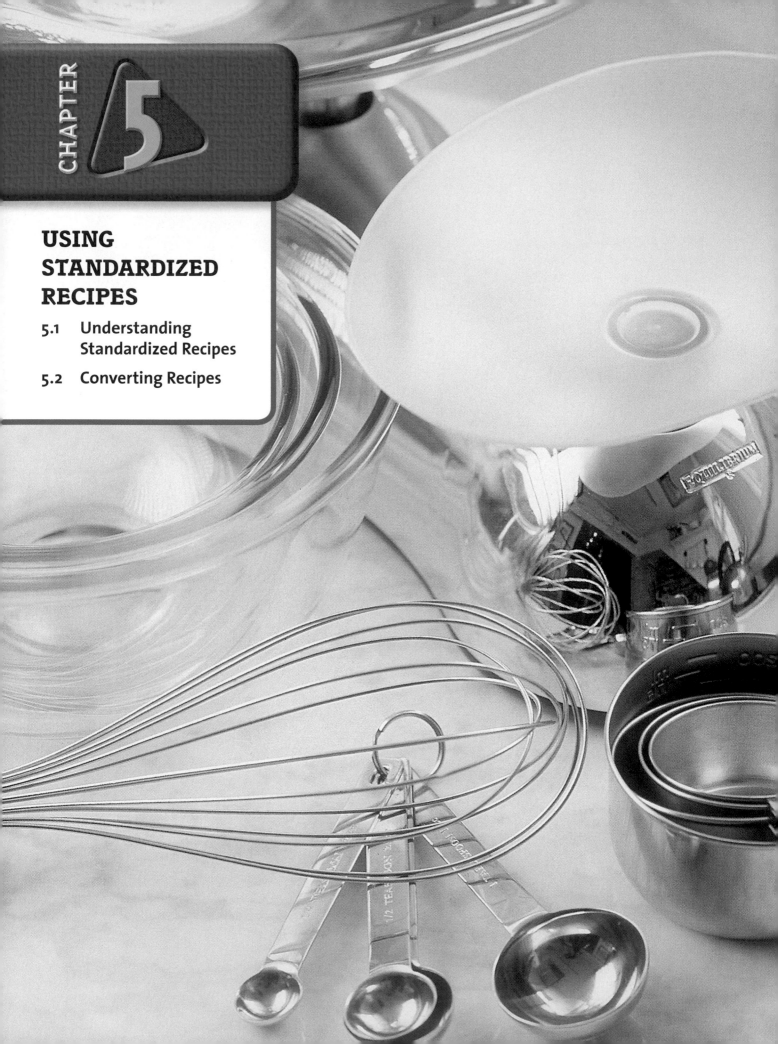

USING STANDARDIZED RECIPES

5.1 Understanding Standardized Recipes

5.1 Understanding Standardized Recipes

READING PREVIEW

Key Concepts

- Learning how kitchens find recipes
- Understanding the sections of a standardized recipe
- Reading recipes
- Understanding measurement conventions and systems
- Understanding measuring techniques

Vocabulary

- metric system
- portion
- recipe
- standardized ingredients
- standardized recipe
- tare weight
- volume
- yield

"Recipes do more than tell you how to make a dish. They help you select ingredients and equipment, organize your work, and track food costs.**"**

– Katherine Polenz
The Culinary Institute of America

Finding Recipes

A **recipe** is a written record of the ingredients and preparation steps needed to make a particular dish.

Recipes can be grouped for easy retrieval in a recipe category. Kitchens, magazines, cookbooks, and chefs create their own categories. Recipe categories could be based on regional dishes, ethnic dishes, dishes based on the main ingredient, and the part of a menu for which the dish is suited.

Chefs collect and adapt recipes from a number of sources (including collecting them from other chefs and restaurants).

Common Recipe Categories

Organizing Idea	Possible Recipe Categories
Regional or Ethnic Recipes	Mediterranean, Texas, Russian
Historic Recipes	Medieval England, Colonial America
Recipes Using a Specific Main Ingredient	Fish, Chicken, Broccoli, Mushrooms
Recipes for Specific Parts of a Menu	Starters, Main Dishes, Side Dishes, Desserts
Recipes for Specific Types of Meals	Breakfasts, Budget Lunches, Quick Dinners
Recipes Using a Specific Cooking Method	Stew, Stir Fry, Barbecue

Five common sources of recipes are:

- **Cookbooks.** Among the best sellers in publishing, cookbooks are available in bookstores and libraries. Most cookbooks specialize in a specific category of dishes.
- **Periodicals.** Newspapers and magazines that target the general public, gourmets, and restaurateurs often feature recipes.
- **Food Producers and Manufacturers.** It makes sense that the producers of food and the manufacturers of food-service equipment would offer recipes to encourage the use of their products.
- **Cooking Contests.** A variety of organizations sponsor cooking contests. They generally publish winning recipes in cookbooks, in periodicals, and on the Internet.
- **The Internet.** The Internet contains many free recipes and recipe databases, often from cooking channel shows.

 *What are recipe categories?*

Standardized Recipes

A **standardized recipe** is a recipe designed to suit the needs of an individual kitchen. Using and writing standardized recipes is a big part of a professional chef's work.

Purpose of Standardized Recipes Standardized recipes help food-service businesses because standardized recipes:

- Support consistent quality and quantity.
- Encourage efficient purchasing and preparation.
- Reduce costs by eliminating waste.

Recipes on the Internet

The Internet is such a big source of cooking information that a person hardly knows where to begin. Of course, typing keywords into a search engine will produce a host of suggestions. (Try entering "tomato soup" in the search box at www.google.com or www.yahoo.com. You'll probably find over 1 million references!)

Visiting well-established Web sites can help you see how information is organized. One such site is www.epicurious.com. Epicurious is affiliated with Condé Nast, the publisher of the food-oriented magazines *Gourmet* and *Bon Appétit*. Epicurious, which bills itself as "the world's best recipe collection," started building its database of menus in 1994. The name "Epicurious" is partially drawn from "Epicurus," the Greek philosopher. The term "Epicure," someone who enjoys the finest

▲ *Epicurious Web site*

things, comes directly from his name, as does the term "Epicurean."

Research

Visit a culinary Web site like www.epicurious.com. Investigate their recipe categories. Print out three recipes, each from a different recipe category. Describe the standardized recipe format used by Epicurious.

- Enable the wait staff to answer guests' questions accurately and honestly. (For example, the type of oil used in a dish may matter very much to a guest with allergies.)

Sections of a Standardized Recipe Standardized recipes may include a number of sections. *The red sections listed below appear in most standardized recipes.*

- **Title.** The title of the recipe identifies the food item or dish.
- **Recipe Categories.** By identifying possible recipe categories, you can group and organize recipes in a way that makes retrieval easier. Sometimes recipes for simple items or items used in other recipes are classified as basic recipes. For example, a restaurant might have a basic recipe for boiled rice, baked potatoes, or a sauce.
- **Yield.** The **yield** of a recipe describes the measured output, expressed as one or more of the following: the total weight, the total volume, or the total number of portions. A **portion** is the serving size for one person expressed in pieces, weight, or volume.
- **Ingredients List.** This is one of the most important elements of a recipe. Ingredients are listed in the order in which they are needed. The ingredients list contains the name and amount of the ingredients you need. It may include advance preparation required (for example, trimming, peeling, dicing, melting, and cooling). It may also indicate a specific variety or brand.

FOCUS ON NUTRITION

Learning from Recipes

Recipes often list nutritional information about each dish. You can see how ingredients translate into calories, fat, carbohydrates, protein, vitamins, and minerals.

Blueberry Muffins

| **YIELD: 1 Dozen Muffins** | **SERVING SIZE: 1 Muffin** |

Ingredients

16 oz (3¾ cups)	All-purpose flour (plus 2 Tbsp to coat berries)
1½ tsp	Double-acting baking powder
½ tsp	Salt
¼ tsp	Nutmeg, ground
4 oz (½ cup)	Butter at room temperature
8 oz (1 cup)	Sugar
1	Egg, large
6 fl oz	Milk
½ tsp	Vanilla extract
1 cup	Blueberries, washed and patted dry
Optional	Cooking spray

Equipment

- **Appliances:** Oven, standing mixer with paddle attachment
- **Cookware:** Muffin tins, paper muffin tin liners, cooling rack
- **Hand Tools:** Scale *(optional),* measuring cups and spoons, sifter, mixing bowls, whisk, rubber spatula, 2-oz scoop

Method

1. Preheat the oven to 400°F.
2. Line muffin tins with paper liners or spray them lightly with cooking spray.
3. Sift together 16 oz flour with the baking powder, salt, and nutmeg.
4. Blend the milk, egg, and vanilla extract in a separate bowl.
5. In a standing mixer with a paddle attachment, cream together the butter and sugar until very light and smooth, about 2 minutes.
6. Add the flour mixture in three additions, alternating with the liquid ingredients, mixing on low speed and scraping down the bowl to blend the batter evenly.
7. Increase the speed to medium and mix until the batter is very smooth, another 2 minutes.
8. Mix 2 Tbsp flour with berries to coat them evenly.
9. Fold the blueberries into the batter, distributing them evenly.
10. Fill each muffin cup ⅔ full with batter using the 2-oz scoop.
11. Bake until the top of the muffin springs back when lightly pressed, 18 to 20 minutes.
12. Cool the muffins in the muffin pan on cooling racks for 5 minutes. Then remove them from the muffin pan and finish cooling them on the rack.

Serve warm or at room temperature. If desired, remove paper liner from muffin before serving. Store in an air-tight container with lid.

Recipe Categories

Muffins, Breakfast Foods, Blueberries

Chef's Notes

1. Coating blueberries with flour keeps them suspended in the batter so they don't all fall to the bottom of the muffin.
2. Shake baking powder before using. Ingredients can separate and need to be mixed for muffins to rise properly.

Potentially Hazardous Foods

- Egg
- Milk

HACCP

- Keep cold ingredients chilled below 41°F.

Nutrition	
Calories	195
Protein	3 g
Fat	9 g
Carbohydrates	26 g
Cholesterol	39 mg

- **Equipment.** A recipe will often list the equipment required for preparing, cooking, storing, holding, and serving an item. This information may be a separate list or may be indicated in other parts of the recipe. Often a recipe will not specify any particular equipment and you will need to use your understanding of basic kitchen procedures to pick appropriate equipment.
- **Method.** This portion of a recipe includes the detailed steps required to make the dish. It may also list appropriate equipment and critical control points for safe food handling.
- **Service.** A recipe may include portioning information (if this information is not already listed in the Yield section of the menu), finishing and plating instructions, appropriate accompaniments (side dishes, sauces, and garnishes), and proper service temperatures.

CULINARY MATH

Weight or Volume?

On the Blueberry Muffin recipe on the previous page did you notice that there are two amounts shown for the flour, butter, and sugar? That's because the first measurement is for weight and the second measurement is for volume. But how do you know when a measurement is a weight and when it is a volume?

In a standardized recipe, dry ingredients that are more than a few tablespoons are usually shown by weight, not by volume. So, for example, the 16 ounces of flour in the blueberry muffin recipe on the next page is one pound of flour (16 ounces = 1 pound, see "Weight Measurements" on page 147). However, the blueberry muffin recipe also shows the equivalent volume measurement of 3¾ cups. The rule is: When a measurement for a dry ingredient is in ounces, it's a weight measurement. If you don't have a scale, you need to convert the weight into volume (and this will differ for every ingredient).

Research

Weigh 16 oz of flour and 16 oz of puffed rice. Measure the volume of these equal weights. Can you see why it is important not to confuse a weight measure with a volume measure?

- **HACCP.** As you learned in the first chapter of this book, HACCP requires identification of critical control points, specific points in the process of food handling where you can prevent, eliminate, or reduce a hazard. A recipe may list these critical control points (CCPs) separately or they may be included in the Method or Service sections. CCPs sometimes occur in the list of ingredients when potentially hazardous foods such as eggs or milk are used. Often when the recipe mentions temperatures and times for preparation, holding, storage, and reheating, a CCP is involved.

FOCUS ON SAFETY

Critical Control Points

Before you begin preparation, check the Method section for critical control points where specific temperatures or careful handling is essential to food safety.

Reading Checkpoint *What elements appear in all standardized recipes?*

Reading Recipes

It is important to read a recipe before you begin preparation. This helps you work efficiently. You can plan your work and prepare the dish correctly. To understand and apply standardized recipes, use the "PRN" method for reading recipes.

> ## PRN Method for Reading Recipes
>
> **P**review   To get the big picture.
>
> **R**ead   To focus carefully on the specifics of the recipe.
>
> **N**ote   Write any adjustments and plans for preparation.

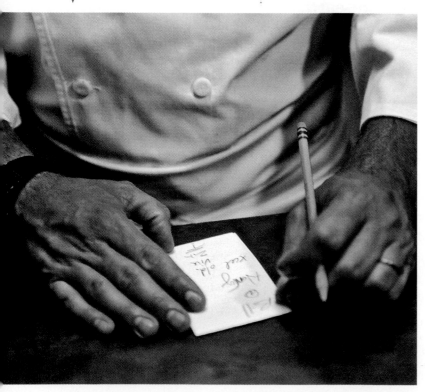

FIGURE 5-1
Writing Notes
A chef writes notes about recipe adjustments or plans for preparation.
Inferring *Why would a chef write down notes about adjustments to a recipe rather than just remembering the changes?*

Some of the questions you may need to ask yourself as you read through a recipe are:

- **Yield.** Does the recipe make enough or too much? (See the next section of this chapter to change the yield of a recipe.)
- **Ingredients.** Are you familiar with all the ingredients? Do you have all the ingredients? If not, can substitutes be used? Are you familiar with the appropriate pre-preparation of all the ingredients? Some recipes may not list all the pre-preparation steps; they rely on your knowledge to make appropriate choices.
- **Method.** Are you familiar with the techniques listed in the Methods section? Do you have all the necessary equipment? If not, is there an alternate method and will further adjustments be required in timing? (Chapter 8 will describe most cooking methods called for in standardized recipes.)
- **Timing.** Do you have to adjust the recipe's timing? Which ingredients have to be prepared in advance? Do you need to pre-heat equipment?

- **Serving and Holding.** What do you do with the finished product? Do you have the appropriate accompaniment or garnish? Check any service and critical control point instructions.

If any of the questions you asked during your preview and read-through make you adjust the recipe in any way, jot down the changes you will make in the recipe.

 **Reading Checkpoint** *Describe the PRN method for understanding a recipe.*

Measurement Conventions and Systems

Measurement Conventions Recipe ingredients are listed in a recipe according to one of three measuring conventions: count, volume, or weight.

- **Count.** When an ingredient is listed in the recipe based on the number of whole items, it is measured by count. Count is good for measuring **standardized ingredients**, those ingredients that have been processed, graded, or packaged according to established standards. Eggs, shrimp, and butter, for instance, are standardized ingredients. For nonstandardized ingredients, count is less accurate. The weight of a peeled and cored apple, for example, depends on the size of the apple and the amount of waste. Similarly, one chef's small garlic clove might be another's chef's medium garlic clove.

- **Volume.** The measurement of the space occupied by a solid, liquid, or gas is its **volume**. Volume measurements are best for measuring liquids and small amounts of dry ingredients such as spices or baking powder. Hand tools such as measuring cups, measuring spoons, ladles, and scoops are used to measure the volume of an ingredient.

- **Weight.** The weight of ingredient is the measurement of its mass, or heaviness. Scales can weigh any ingredient, liquid or dry. Weight measures are typically preferred to volume measures because weight can be measured with greater accuracy.

FIGURE 5-2
Reading a Clear Measuring Cup
Read a glass measuring cup on a flat surface. Read with the mark at eye level.
Drawing Conclusions *Why do you think volume measurements might be less accurate than weight measurements?*

Measurement Systems Weight and volume may be measured by using either the U.S. system or the **metric system**.

In the U.S. system, volume is measured in terms of teaspoon (tsp), tablespoon (Tbsp), fluid ounce (fl oz), cup (c), pint (pt), quart (qt), and gallon (gal). In the metric system, volume is measured in terms of milliliter (ml), and liter (l).

In the U.S. system, weight is measured in terms of ounce (oz) and pound (lb). In the metric system, weight is measured in terms of milligram (mg), gram (g), and kilogram (kg).

Some recipes indicate quantities with very simplistic abbreviations. For example, one teaspoon might appear as 1 tsp or simply 1 t.

FIGURE 5-3 ▶
Using Scales
Scales usually display weight by using the U.S. system or the metric system.
Predicting *When might it be helpful to be able to display both weight systems?*

Volume Measurements

Volume Measure	Metric Equivalent*	U.S. Equivalents*
U.S. SYSTEM		
1 teaspoon (tsp)	5 ml	⅙ fl oz
1 tablespoon (Tbsp)	15 ml	½ fl oz *or* 3 tsp
1 fluid ounce (fl oz)	30 ml	2 Tbsp *or* 6 tsp
1 cup	< ¼ l	8 oz *or* 16 Tbsp
1 pint (pt)	< ½ l	2 cups *or* 16 fl oz
1 quart (qt)	< 1 l	2 pt *or* 32 fl oz
1 gallon (gal)	> 3¾ l	4 qt *or* 128 fl oz
METRIC SYSTEM		
1 milliliter (ml)	1 ml	⅕ tsp *or* 0.0338 fl oz
1/4 liter	250 ml	8.5 fl oz *or* > 1 cup
1 liter (l)	1000 ml	1.1 qt

*U.S./metric conversions are approximate. 1 fl oz = 29.58 ml

Weight Measurements

Weight Measure	Metric Equivalent*	U.S. Equivalents*
U.S. SYSTEM		
1 ounce (oz)	28 g	
¼ pound	112 g	4 oz
½ pound	224 g	8 oz
¾ pound	336 g	12 oz
1 pound (lb)	454 g	16 oz
METRIC SYSTEM		
1 milligram (mg)	0.001 g	
1 gram (g)	1 g	
⅛ kilogram	125 g	4.4 oz > ¼ lb
¼ kilogram	250 g	8.8 oz > ½ lb
½ kilogram	500 g	17.6 oz > 1 lb
1 kilogram (kg)	1000 g	2.2 lb

*U.S./metric conversions are approximate. 1 oz = 28.35 g

One tablespoon might appear as 1 Tbsp or 1 T. One cup might appear as 1 c. One gallon might appear as 1 gal or 1 G.

 **Reading Checkpoint** *About how many grams are in a ¼-pound hamburger patty? About what fraction of a kilogram is a 1-pound loaf of bread?*

Measurement Techniques

Use these techniques to assure accuracy.

- **Dry Volume.** Overfill the measuring container and scrape off any excess. Some recipes call for packing (compressing) ingredients such as brown sugar.
- **Liquid Volume.** Set a clear measuring cup or other clear container on a flat surface. Reading with your eye at the level of the mark, fill to the mark.
- **Weight.** Choose a scale that suits the size of your food. Some scales are best for measuring ounces, others for pounds.

When using a food scale, be sure to account for the **tare weight**, the weight of the container holding the food. Place the container on the scale and reset the scale to zero. If your scale cannot be reset, note the tare and subtract it after weighing the food.

FOCUS ON SANITATION

Measuring Up

To avoid cross-contamination, clean and sanitize measuring tools between uses. Never let food come in direct contact with the scale. Always use a food tray, container, paper barrier, or plastic wrap on the scale.

Measurement Techniques

Measurement	Technique	Tools
Dry Volume	1. Overfill container. 2. Scrape off excess.	Measuring cups, measuring spoons
Liquid Volume	1. Set container on flat surface. 2. Fill to correct mark. 3. Inspect with eye level at mark. 4. Adjust as needed.	Graduated containers, measuring cups, measuring spoons
Weight	1. Set the tare. 2. Place food in container on scale. 3. Read weight and add or remove food.	Scale, food trays or containers to hold food on scale

 **Reading Checkpoint** *How would you measure ½ cup of flour? ½ pound of flour?*

5.1 ASSESSMENT

Reviewing Concepts

1. What is a recipe category? Give three examples of recipe categories.

2. What sections appear in most standardized recipes?

3. What are the steps in the PRN method for reading recipes?

4. How many quarts are in a gallon? Pints in a quart? Cups in a pint? Fluid ounces in a cup?

5. What is tare weight and why is it important in weighing ingredients for a standardized recipe?

Critical Thinking

6. **Classifying** List two foods that fit in more than one recipe category, and list the categories.

7. **Inferring** Explain how standardized recipes encourage efficient purchasing and preparation.

8. **Solving Problems** About how many liters are in a gallon?

TEST KITCHEN

Working in groups, record both the metric and U.S. weights of ¼ cup of each of the following: flour, white sugar, peanuts, popcorn, cooked white rice, dry white rice, water, fruit juice, and honey. Discuss the differences in weight between identical volume measurements. Discuss any differences in recorded weights by different groups.

LANGUAGE ARTS

Writing a Standardized Recipe

Write a standardized recipe for a simple dish you know how to prepare. Include all the sections that typically are used in a standardized recipe and as many other sections as you can.

Converting Recipes

READING PREVIEW

Key Concepts

- Scaling recipes up or down
- Scaling recipes by portion size
- Finding recipe yield based on available ingredients
- Using scaled recipes

Vocabulary

- denominator
- numerator
- recipe conversion factor (RCF)
- scale (a recipe)

> **"S**caling a recipe isn't rocket science. But it isn't straight math either. The more you know about how foods behave when you cook them, the more accurate you can be.**"**
>
> – John Reilly
> The Culinary Institute of America

Scaling Recipes Up or Down

Some days you may need to make more than your recipe calls for. Other days, you may need to make less. What do you do when your recipe's yield doesn't match your needs?

You can scale the recipe. To **scale** a recipe means you change the amount of ingredients to get the yield you need. You can scale up to increase the yield or scale down to decrease it.

Scaling a Recipe Up or Down

To scale a recipe up or down:

1. Find the **recipe conversion factor (RCF).**

$$RCF = \frac{\text{yield you want}}{\text{yield of original recipe}} = \frac{\text{new yield}}{\text{old yield}}$$

2. Multiply each ingredient amount by the RCF.

Try scaling a recipe now. First, you will scale up a basic recipe for boiled white rice. Then you will scale the recipe down.

White Rice, Boiled

YIELD: 20 Servings	SERVING SIZE: ½ Cup

Ingredients

5 cups	White rice
2½ tsp	Salt
10 cups	Water

Method

1. Combine ingredients in a pot.
2. Stir and bring to a boil.
3. Cover, reduce heat, and cook until all water is absorbed.

Recipe Categories
Basic Recipes, Rice, Side Dishes

Scaling Up Your kitchen's basic recipe for boiled white rice yields 20 servings (each serving is ½ cup). However, you need 40 servings. How much of each ingredient do you need?

To scale the recipe up:

1. Find the RCF.

$$RCF = \frac{new\ yield}{old\ yield} = \frac{40}{20} = 2$$

2. Multiply the amount of each ingredient by the RCF (as shown in the following table).

Scaling Up

Ingredient	Old Amount	RCF	New Amount
White Rice	5 cups	× 2	= 10 cups
Salt	2½ tsp	× 2	= 5 tsp
Water	10 cups	× 2	= 20 cups

Converting Fractions

When we scaled a recipe up, the RCF was 40/20. You can change the form of this fraction to make multiplication easier.

You can either convert the fraction to a decimal, or you can simplify the fraction. Both methods give the same results.

Converting a Fraction into a Decimal

Divide the **numerator** (top number) by the **denominator** (bottom number).

$$\text{Numerator} \rightarrow \frac{40}{20} = 2 \leftarrow \text{Denominator}$$

Simplifying a Fraction

Divide both the numerator and denominator by the same factor.

$$\frac{40 \div 10}{20 \div 10} = \frac{4}{2}$$

Continue dividing until the fraction is in a convenient form. You can use a different factor, provided you divide both the numerator and the denominator by the same factor. This time, divide the numerator and denominator by 2.

$$\frac{4 \div 2}{2 \div 2} = \frac{2}{1} = 2$$

To make 40 servings, you will need 10 cups of rice, 5 teaspoons of salt, and 20 cups of water.

Scaling Down You will again use the basic recipe that yields 20 servings of boiled white rice. However, this time you need only 6 servings of boiled white rice. How much of each ingredient do you need?

To scale the recipe down:

1. Find the RCF.

$$RCF = \frac{\text{new yield}}{\text{old yield}} = \frac{6}{20} = \frac{3}{10} = 0.3$$

2. Multiply the amount of each ingredient by the RCF (as shown in the following table).

Scaling Down

Ingredient	Old Amount	RCF	New Amount
White Rice	5 cups	× 0.3	= 1½ cups
Salt	2½ tsp	× 0.3	= ¾ tsp
Water	10 cups	× 0.3	= 3 cups

Multiplying Fractions

When you scaled down the recipe, you had to multiply a fraction (2½) by the RCF, which can be shown as a fraction or as a decimal.

Multiplying Fractions

Convert whole numbers and fractions into one single fraction.

$$2\tfrac{1}{2} \text{ tsp} = \frac{2}{1} + \frac{1}{2} = \frac{4}{2} + \frac{1}{2} = \frac{5}{2} \text{ tsp}$$

Multiply this fraction by the RCF expressed as a fraction. Multiply the numerators and then the denominators.

$$\begin{aligned}\text{Numerator} &\rightarrow 5 \times 3 = 15\\ \text{Denominator} &\rightarrow 2 \times 10 = 20\end{aligned}$$

Then simplify the fraction.

$$\frac{15 \div 5}{20 \div 5} = \frac{3}{4}$$

Multiplying a Fraction by a Decimal

Convert the fraction to a decimal. (Convert whole numbers and fractions into one single fraction. Then divide the numerator by the denominator.)

$$2\tfrac{1}{2} \text{ tsp} = \frac{2}{1} + \frac{1}{2} = \frac{4}{2} + \frac{1}{2} = \frac{5}{2} = 2.5 \text{ tsp}$$

Multiple the amount of the ingredient by the RCF.

$$2.5 \text{ tsp} \times 0.3 = 0.75 \text{ tsp}$$

Convert the decimal to a fraction, using 100 as the denominator.

$$0.75 \text{ tsp} = \frac{75}{100} \text{ tsp}$$

Then simplify the fraction. In this case, you can divide both the numerator and the denominator by 25.

$$\frac{75 \div 25}{100 \div 25} = \frac{3}{4}$$

To scale down the recipe to make only 6 servings, you will need 1½ cups of rice, ¾ teaspoons of salt, and 3 cups of water.

 **Reading Checkpoint** *What is the formula for the recipe conversion factor?*

Scaling Recipes by Changing Portion Size

A food service establishment may decide to change its portion size. Perhaps it is offering a main dish as an appetizer and wants to reduce the portion. Perhaps the kitchen wants to increase the size of a portion because customers have complained that the portion is too small.

When you scale a recipe by changing the portion size, you always work with the recipe's

FIGURE 5-4 ▶
Different Portion Sizes
Different rice-based dishes require different-sized portions of rice.
Classifying *Can you think of dishes that might require large portions of rice? Small portions of rice?*

yield. Remember that a recipe's yield can be expressed as the number of portions multiplied by the size of a portion.

Scaling a Recipe by Changing Portion Size

To scale a recipe based on a new portion size:

1. Find the old yield.

> Old yield = old number of servings × old portion size

2. Find the new yield.

> New yield = new number of servings × new portion size

3. Find the RCF.

$$RCF = \frac{\text{new yield}}{\text{old yield}}$$

4. Multiply each ingredient amount by the RCF.

Your kitchen's basic recipe for boiled white rice yields 20 servings of ½-cup portions. But you need 40 servings of ¾-cup portions. How much of each ingredient do you need?

To scale the recipe based on the new portion size:

1. Find the old yield.

> Old yield = number of portions × size
>
> Old yield = 20 servings × $\frac{1}{2}$ cup = 10 cups

2. Find the new yield.

> New yield = number of portions × size
>
> New yield = 40 servings × $\frac{3}{4}$ cup = 30 cups

3. Find the RCF.

$$RCF = \frac{\text{new yield}}{\text{old yield}}$$

$$RCF = \frac{30}{10} = \frac{3}{1} = 3$$

4. Multiply the amount of each ingredient by the RCF.

Ingredient	Old Amount	RCF	New Amount
White Rice	5 cups	× 3	= 15 cups
Salt	2½ tsp	× 3	= 7½ tsp
Water	10 cups	× 3	= 30 cups

For 40 servings, with each portion measuring ¾ cup, you need 15 cups of rice, 7½ teaspoons of salt, and 30 cups of water.

 **Reading Checkpoint**   *What are the steps for scaling a recipe when the portion size is changed?*

Scaling Recipes Based on an Available Ingredient

Occasionally a restaurant may need to scale a recipe to match the amount of a key ingredient available. This might happen because the restaurant purchased a large amount of an ingredient that is in season, for example, or because the restaurant receives a last-minute reservation and needs to plan the menu.

Scaling a Recipe Based on an Ingredient

To scale a recipe based on an ingredient:

1. Express the ingredient amount in the recipe and the ingredient amount that is available in the same measure.
2. Find the RCF.

$$RCF = \frac{\text{available ingredient amount}}{\text{ingredient amount in recipe}}$$

3. Find the new yield.

$$\text{new yield} = \text{old yield} \times RCF$$

4. Find the new amounts of each ingredient.

$$\text{new amount} = \text{old amount} \times RCF$$

Your restaurant has just rented its banquet room at the last minute. You have 5 pounds of organic, skinless, boneless chicken breasts available. Will that be enough to serve 40 portions of your restaurant's special chicken dish? The recipe calls for 18 ounces of chicken breast and yields 12 cups of the dish. Portions are 1½ cups, so this recipe yields 8 servings.

To scale the recipe based on the available chicken:

1. Express the old and new ingredient amounts in the same measure.

   Old (recipe) amount of chicken = 18 oz

   New (available) amount of chicken = 5 lb

   There are 16 oz per lb, so 5 lb = 80 oz

2. Find the RCF.

   $$RCF = \frac{\text{new amount}}{\text{old amount}} = \frac{80}{18} = \frac{40}{9} \text{ or } 4.44$$

3. Find the new yield.

   new yield = old yield × RCF

   new yield = 8 servings × 4.44 = 35.52 servings

Using only the 5 pounds of chicken you have on hand, you will have only about 35 servings—not enough for the 40 guests. After you made this recipe-scaling calculation, you could decide to purchase enough chicken for five more servings, you could reduce the serving size, or you could alter the recipe to decrease slightly the amount of chicken required.

 **Reading Checkpoint** *How do you scale a recipe based on an available ingredient?*

Using Scaled Recipes

When you make a recipe larger or smaller, preparation factors can change. You may need to cook the dish at a different temperature or for a different time. You may need a pan of a different size. You also may need to adjust the seasonings.

Cooking Temperature and Time Use the original cooking temperature and time as starting points. Watch closely for the results you want. Check for the correct internal temperature of food. When cooking several dishes in an oven together, expect a longer cooking time. (You could also try raising the temperature about 25°F.) When baking

CULINARY **MATH**

Changing Measurement Units

A magazine recipe for a shrimp dish serves 3. You want to scale down the recipe for a single serving, so your RCF is ⅓.

$$\text{RCF} = \frac{\text{new yield}}{\text{old yield}} = \frac{1}{3}$$

Your next step is to multiply each ingredient amount by the RCF.

The new amounts that are highlighted in the table are not very convenient. There is no measuring tool for 1/9 or 1/12 of a cup. And most measuring spoons do not include ⅓ or ⅔ of a tablespoon.

To convert these inconvenient measurements to ones that are easier to use, you will need to find equivalent units. (In the previous section of this book, measurement equivalents are listed in the two tables "Volume Measurements" and "Weight Measurements.")

Scaling Down

Ingredients	Old Amount	RCF	New Amount
Shrimp, large, cleaned	1½ lb	× ⅓	= ½ lb
Butter	⅓ cup	× ⅓	= 1/9 cup
Garlic, minced	4 Tbsp	× ⅓	= 1⅓ Tbsp
Green onions, thinly sliced	6	× ⅓	= 2
Stock, fish	¼ cup	× ⅓	= 1/12 cup
Lemon juice	2 Tbsp	× ⅓	= ⅔ Tbsp
Parsley, fresh, chopped	2 Tbsp	× ⅓	= ⅔ Tbsp

▲ *Shrimp scampi*

To convert 1/9 cup to a convenient equivalent:
Find equivalents for 1 cup.

1 cup = 16 Tbsp

1 Tbsp = 3 tsp

so, 1 cup = 16 × 3 = 48 tsp

You could find the equivalent in tablespoons, but because 1/9 cup is a small amount, you should find the equivalent in teaspoons.

Find the equivalents for 1/9 of a cup in teaspoons.

1 cup = 48 tsp

1/9 cup = 48/9 tsp

1/9 cup = 5 tsp

a half recipe of bread, cakes, or pies, the cooking time may be about ⅔ to ¾ of the original time.

Pan Size Choose a pan that comes closest to keeping the ingredients at the same depth as the original. If you are doubling a recipe, use a pan that has double the volume.

Sometimes your pot will not maintain the original ingredient depth. When this happens, you may need to adjust the time, temperature, and amount of liquid.

Seasonings When adjusting seasonings, especially salt, start with less than you expect to need. Season to taste, a little at a time. Taste after adding more. For example, to double a recipe, start with about 1½ times the original amount of seasonings. Then adjust to taste. If you record the amounts you add, you can revise the recipe for use again.

Limits on Scaling Recipes Some recipes do not scale well. For instance, delicate foods (such as soufflés) or baked items that use yeast (such as breads), do not scale well. In general, do not scale recipes that prepare a single large item, such as cakes, pies, or breads. For these recipes, scale to get a pre-preparation list, but cook several batches to meet your needs.

Recipes cannot be scaled indefinitely. Some chefs recommend never scaling up or down beyond a factor of 4. More cautious chefs stay within a factor of 2. Large-scale changes require adjustments to equipment and method for the recipe.

 **Reading Checkpoint** *How can scaling a recipe change preparation methods?*

5.2 ASSESSMENT

Reviewing Concepts

1. How do you scale a recipe up?
2. How do you scale a recipe by changing the portion size?
3. How do you scale a recipe based on an available ingredient?
4. Can all recipes be scaled up or down?

Critical Thinking

5. **Solving Problems** A recipe yields 10 servings. You want to serve 15. If you keep the serving size the same, what is the RCF?
6. **Relating Concepts** If you increase the number of servings but decrease the serving size, what will happen to the total yield? Explain your answer and include an example.
7. **Inferring** Why might you need to increase oven temperature and cooking time when baking several items at once?

Test Kitchen

Bring in a recipe you like. Scale up the ingredients list as though you were going to make enough for the class. Compare the amount of the main ingredient you need to the amount your school kitchen has on-hand. Would the school kitchen have enough of the ingredient to allow you to make the recipe? If not, scale the recipe based on the amount of the main ingredient that is currently available.

SOCIAL STUDIES

Origin of American Measurements

Research the history of the American system for measuring weights, liquid volume, and dry volume. Compare and contrast the American system and the English system. Describe your findings.

Review and Assessment

Reviewing Content

Choose the letter that best answers the question or completes the statement.

1. What is a standardized recipe?
   a. a recipe that makes one portion
   b. a recipe that is the same in every cookbook
   c. a recipe that makes four portions
   d. a recipe tailored to the needs of an individual kitchen

2. A standardized recipe yields 10 servings and requires ¼ cup of beaten egg. You want to serve 30. How much egg should you use?
   a. ¾ cup
   b. 1⅓ cups
   c. 3 cups
   d. 12 cups

3. Which is an optional part of a standardized recipe?
   a. recipe categories
   b. yield
   c. ingredient list
   d. method

4. A standardized recipe yields 2 quarts. You want to serve 10 servings of 2 cups each. What RCF should you use to scale the recipe?
   a. ¼
   b. ⅖
   c. 2½
   d. 10

5. Which of the following are not equivalent measures?
   a. 1 cup = 8 ounces
   b. 1 cup = 10 tablespoons
   c. 1 quart = 2 pint
   d. 1 tablespoon = 3 teaspoons

6. A standardized recipe uses ½ cup of minced garlic to make 20 servings of ¾ cup each. How much minced garlic should you use to make 15 servings of ½ cup each?
   a. 2 tablespoons
   b. 4 tablespoons
   c. ½ cup
   d. 1 cup

Understanding Concepts

7. Explain the PRN method for reading a recipe.

8. Describe a situation that would require you to scale a recipe by the number of portions. Explain how to do this.

9. What is the purpose of recipe categories? Name two or more categories that could fit a recipe for egg salad.

10. Explain how and why you might adjust a recipe after scaling it.

11. What is an accompaniment? What accompaniments might you serve with a grilled cheese sandwich?

Critical Thinking

12. **Drawing Conclusions** Why is it necessary to read the mark in a clear measuring cup at eye level?

13. **Predicting** A recipe is scaled up by a factor of 1.5. What is the RCF to scale the larger recipe back to its original size? If the larger recipe served 24, how many did the smaller recipe serve? Show your work and explain your answers.

Culinary Math

14. **Solving Problems** The food tray on a kitchen's meat scale weighs 8 ounces. An assistant weighs 2 pounds of beef for stew, but forgets to set the tare. How much beef (measured in ounces) will go into the stew? If the stew must serve 8, how much beef will go into each serving? How much smaller is the beef serving than expected? Explain the consequences to the restaurant for the assistant's mistake.

On the Job

15. **Applying Concepts** Your supervisor scales up a stew recipe for 4 to serve 10. She hands you a copy of the recipe with the new amounts written in pencil. You notice the original recipe called for 1 pound of beef, and the new recipe calls for 3 pounds of beef. Does this seem right? Are you sure? What should you do?

Project 5: Scaling a Recipe
Answer these questions when your class works through Project 5.

- Can you scale up a recipe?

- What factors in a recipe can cause problems when scaling a recipe up?

- As a measuring concept, how precise is a measurement by count—and how do you overcome this imprecision?

- Does a recipe made by weighing ingredients taste the same as a recipe made by using volume measurements?

- Will your team's scaled-up recipe taste as good as another teams' recipes—and what accounts for the difference?

- How good are your notes made by using the PRN method compared to what you learned at the end of the process of scaling up your recipe?

TEST PRACTICE

Choose the letter that best answers the question or completes the statement.

1. Select the false statement about standardized recipes:
   A   They support consistent quality.
   B   They help make preparation more efficient.
   C   They cost a little more to use.
   D   They help inform guests about ingredients.

2. A standardized recipe yields 1 gallon. You want to serve 32 servings of 8 fluid ounces each. What RCF should you use to scale the recipe?
   A   ⅙
   B   ¾
   C   1.333
   D   2

3. Which statement about measurement systems is true.
   A   A kilogram is about the same size as a pound.
   B   One cup equals 16 tablespoons.
   C   The metric system is more accurate than the U.S. system.
   D   Volume measures are used only for liquids.

4. You have 1 liter of chopped celery. A standardized recipe for celery soup calls for 250 milliliters of celery and serves 6. How many servings can you make by using a scaled recipe?
   A   over 40
   B   24
   C   6
   D   1½

5. Which of the following recipe categories are organized by ingredients?
   A   stew, grill, barbecue
   B   fish, cod, vegetables
   C   accompaniments, sauces, condiments
   D   starters, main dishes, desserts

6. A standardized recipe for beet salad uses 8 ounces of cooked sliced beets to make 30 servings of ½ cups each. How much beets should you use to make 12 servings of ¾ cup each?
   A   about 1 ounce
   B   about 2 ounces
   C   about 5 ounces
   D   about 14 ounces

7. A recipe is scaled up by an RCF of 2.5. If the original recipe served 8, how many does the scaled-up recipe serve?
   A   18
   B   20
   C   26
   D   32

Sensory Perception

READING PREVIEW

Key Concepts

- Explaining the role of the five senses in tasting food
- Identifying the ways a food's flavor can change
- Describing the flavor of foods

Vocabulary

- aromatic
- flavor
- opaque
- savory
- taste
- translucent
- umami

"**C**uisine is only about making foods taste the way they are supposed to taste. "
— Charlie Trotter

The Five Senses

Human beings have five senses: taste, sight, smell, touch, and hearing. Each of our senses plays a role in helping us taste our food. Not only do our senses help us identify the food we are eating, but they also help us decide if food is ripe or a dish is properly cooked.

The Sense of Taste Our sense of taste depends on food coming in contact with our tongue as we chew or swallow. The taste buds covering our tongue allow us to distinguish among five tastes:

- Sweet
- Sour
- Salty
- Bitter
- Umami

You may not be familiar with the taste of **umami** (OO-mam-ee). It is also referred to as the taste of **savory** (SAY-va-ree). This flavor, which is best thought of as meaty or brothy, was discovered in the early twentieth century by a Japanese professor. The most common example of umami is the food additive MSG (monosodium glutamate). Umami is often found in protein, some vegetables, and fermented foods, such as soy sauce.

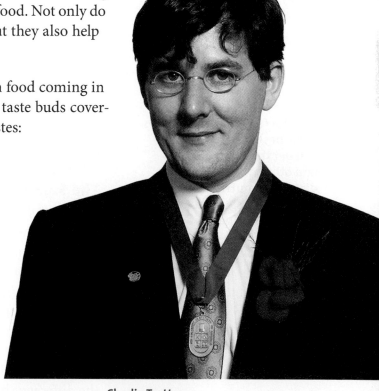

Charlie Trotter
Charlie Trotter's, Chicago, IL

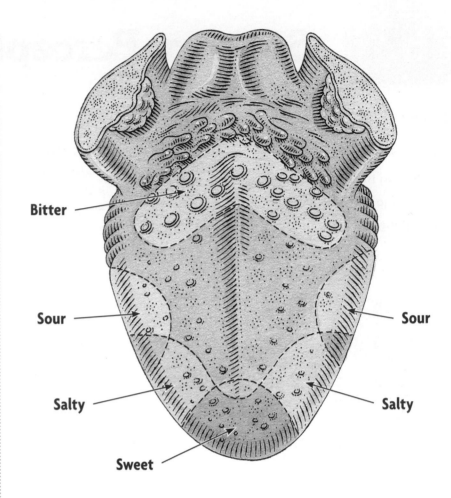

FIGURE 6-1 ▶
Sense of Taste
Specific areas of the tongue are most sensitive to sweet, sour, salty, and bitter tastes. Umami doesn't have a specific location on the tongue.
Applying Concepts *Which part of your tongue might be most affected when you taste a grapefruit?*

Bitter

Sour — Sour

Salty — Salty

Sweet

The Sense of Sight Typically, our first experience of food uses our sense of sight. We tend to prefer foods that look good. Foods that are ripe have the most appealing colors. Foods that are neatly cut and beautifully arranged are more appealing than foods that are not. That is why you hear chefs say "people eat with their eyes" and talk about "feeding the eye." If something doesn't look good, people may not want to try it.

The Sense of Smell When it comes to food, smell is an extremely powerful sense. We check foods for ripeness by smelling them. We monitor how quickly foods are cooking by the smell coming from the stove or the oven.

We can distinguish among thousands of different smells or aromas. Foods with especially strong smells are referred to as **aromatic** (air-o-MAT-ic). Have you noticed that if you have a cold and can't smell things, it is very hard to tell what you are eating? That's because what we think of as the taste of a food is often strongly influenced by our sense of smell. The aroma of a particular food is one of the ways we tell the difference between foods that are similar in appearance and taste. For example, an orange and a tangerine are very similar in appearance but different in smell.

The Sense of Touch Touch is the way we experience a food's texture and its temperature. We use our sense of touch, along with sight and smell, to help identify when foods are fully ripe or properly cooked. Some foods soften as they ripen or cook, while others become more firm.

The texture of food plays an important role in determining how food tastes to us. Very thick or chewy foods stay in our mouths longer than foods that are thin and swallowed quickly. That means we have more time to taste and smell the thicker food. Fatty, oily, or rich foods also coat our mouths. These foods seem to have a fuller flavor than very lean or watery foods.

Our sense of touch is also the way we experience such sensations as the burn of hot peppers, the cooling effect of mint, the drying or puckering effect tea has on the inside of our mouth, the numbing sensation of cloves, and the fizz of carbonated beverages—to name only a few of the ways food feels when we eat it.

▲ **FIGURE 6-2**
Food Texture
Think of the combination of textures in this fried chicken. **Applying Concepts** *What can a crisp, crunchy crust on chicken tell you about its flavor?*

The Sense of Hearing Hearing is also an important aspect of our food experience. For example, crisp foods make a loud crunch as we cut or bite them. When a food sizzles on a platter, we expect it to be very hot.

Chefs use their sense of hearing to help them keep track of how quickly foods are cooking. They can distinguish the sounds of a fast boil or a lazy simmer. They can also tell when the sounds of food cooking in the oven means the oven is too hot or too cool.

 **Reading Checkpoint** *What are the five senses?*

Changing a Food's Flavor

Taste is a word we can use in more than one way. As we just learned, taste refers to the sensation we experience through our taste buds when we put a food in our mouth. Taste is also the word we use when we mean the taste of the food in addition to its smell. **Flavor** refers to the way a food tastes, as well as its texture, appearance, doneness, and temperature. In practical terms, taste and flavor are used almost interchangeably.

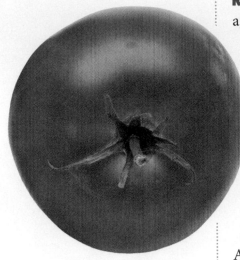

Ripening or Aging The flavor of any food changes as it ripens or ages. Food that is not fully ripe may have a bitter or bland taste because it has not developed completely. When it is ripe, it will have the richest flavor. As food ages, the flavor continues to change until it reaches a point where we consider the food spoiled or rotten. The natural aging and ripening process of any food changes the way it tastes to us. For example, a green tomato has a tart taste, a ripe tomato tastes sweet, and an overripe tomato tastes fermented.

Temperature The temperature of a food also plays a part in how it tastes to us. Very cold food seems less flavorful than warm or hot food. As foods get warmer, it is easier for us to taste and smell. A tomato that you take right out of the refrigerator doesn't have as intense a flavor as one that has been sitting on the counter at room temperature.

Preparation and Cooking When we prepare or cook food, we change it from its original state. The change may be quite simple. For instance, a ripe tomato may simply be sliced. Cutting the tomato changes the way it tastes, even though it is not a big change.

If we take the same tomato and cook it in a pan until it turns a deep brown, we've made a more significant change to the way the tomato tastes. If we chop the tomato and cook it until it is soft but not brown, it has an entirely different taste.

As you learn more about the different ways you can cook food, you will find that each cooking technique produces its own characteristic taste. Cooking is one of the most significant ways we can change the taste of food. We can improve the flavor of food when we cook it, but we can also ruin its flavor.

 **Reading Checkpoint** *What are three ways you can change the flavor of food?*

Describing Flavor

When we describe how a food tastes, we are usually talking in broader terms than just which tastes and aromas a food has. Typically, we are also considering the way the food appeals to all of our senses. When we talk about a food or a dish in this way, we are talking about its flavor.

The Way Flavor Looks When you look at food, you can make some predictions about its flavor. Food that looks fresh and unblemished or has good color usually has the best flavor. We look for a good shape, one that is appropriate for the food. Additionally, the look of food is

usually changed during cooking. Here are some descriptive words we might use to describe the way food looks:

- **Opaque** (o-PAKE), meaning light does not pass through it
- **Translucent** (trans-LU-cent) meaning some light will pass through it
- Transparent or clear
- Colors, such as red, yellow, green, brown, white, ivory, or orange

The Way Flavor Smells There are hundreds, perhaps thousands, of words you might use to describe the way food smells. The way food smells before you eat it is sometimes quite different from the way it smells once you put it in your mouth.

One of the most obvious ways to describe a smell is to describe a similar smell. For example, you might say a food item smells like a lemon, like vanilla, like toast, or like mushrooms. Some other descriptive words relating to the way food smells are:

- Perfumed
- Pungent
- Earthy
- Stale
- Musty
- Fresh
- Strong
- Intense

The Way Flavor Feels Texture is the way food feels when we touch it, cut it, or bite into it.

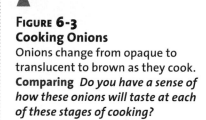

FIGURE 6-3
Cooking Onions
Onions change from opaque to translucent to brown as they cook.
Comparing *Do you have a sense of how these onions will taste at each of these stages of cooking?*

Some descriptive words for a food's texture are:

- Firm, hard
- Soft, yielding, melting
- Crisp, crunchy, crumbly
- Airy, frothy, foamy
- Thick, heavy, dense
- Watery, thin
- Warm, hot
- Cool, cold

The Way Flavor Sounds

The sounds food makes gives you a clue about its flavor, too. Here are some descriptive words for the way a food sounds:

- Snap
- Sizzle
- Pop
- Crackle
- Crunch
- Fizz

 **Reading Checkpoint** *List several words you can use to describe how a food looks, smells, feels, and sounds.*

6.1 ASSESSMENT

Reviewing Concepts

1. What are the five tastes our taste buds allow us to distinguish?
2. What are three ways the flavor of food can be changed?
3. List several words you could use to describe "flavor" as it applies to each of the five senses.

Critical Thinking

4. **Classifying** Think about your favorite food. Which tastes are included in it?
5. **Comparing/Contrasting** Name a food that is more attractive to you hot and less attractive cold. Name one that is more attractive cold than hot.
6. **Classifying** Which of the senses, other than taste and smell, is most important to you in considering flavor. Explain your answer.

Test Kitchen

Cut an apple, an onion, and a radish each into a small dice. Divide into groups of two. While one person is blindfolded and holding his or her nose, the other person should feed the blindfolded person a small amount of each of the foods, asking the blindfolded person to identify the food. Reverse roles. Record the results.

SCIENCE

Umami

Research the discovery of the taste of umami. Who discovered the taste? When was the discovery made? What does the name mean in Japanese? What foods are considered to have a strong umami taste?

Seasoning & Flavoring Foods

READING PREVIEW

Key Concepts

- Understanding why foods are seasoned
- Identifying and using common seasoning ingredients
- Differentiating between seasoning and flavoring food

Vocabulary

- black pepper
- high-sodium food
- iodized salt
- kosher salt
- monosodium glutamate (MSG)
- rock salt
- sea salt
- seasonings
- sodium chloride
- table salt
- white pepper

"Where would we be without salt?"

— James Beard

Seasoning Foods

Seasonings are ingredients you add to a food to improve its flavor. Seasoning ingredients are added in such small quantities that you usually cannot taste the individual seasoning ingredients. If you add just enough seasoning, however, you will notice an improvement in the flavor of the food. Chefs season food to improve its flavor in one of the following ways:

- **Enhancing Natural Taste.** Sometimes, you add a seasoning to make the natural taste of the food more intense or noticeable. In other words, you are enhancing the food's taste. For example, if you cook pasta in plain water without any salt, the pasta won't have much flavor. But if you add just a little salt to the water, the pasta tastes more like pasta.
- **Balancing Tastes.** Sometimes, a seasoning helps to overcome very strong tastes, especially sour, sweet, or bitter tastes. This is sometimes referred to as balancing the tastes in a dish. Vegetables that are very bitter taste less bitter when you add some salt to them. Sour foods such as lemon juice taste less sour if you add a bit of sugar. Sweet foods taste less sweet if you add a bit of salt. Once the strong taste is reduced a little, it is easier to taste other ingredients or flavors in the dish.

James Beard
Food Critic, Cookbook Author

- **Cutting Richness.** Seasonings can also change the way a very rich or fatty food tastes. A little lemon juice or vinegar improves the taste of mayonnaise by making it taste less rich or oily. You may hear this referred to as cutting the richness or oiliness of a dish.

✓ **Reading Checkpoint** *Why do chefs season food?*

Types of Seasoning Ingredients

Seasoning starts with some basic ingredients. There are four basic types of seasoning ingredients:

- Salt
- Pepper
- Sugar and light-flavored sweeteners
- Acids

When you season a food, you add just enough of one or more of these ingredients to change the food's basic taste, but not enough to add a whole new taste.

Salt Salt is an important seasoning. Its chemical name is **sodium chloride** (SO-dee-um CHLOR-ide). It is used in all cuisines and in all countries. You can add it to foods before you cook them, as you cook them, or at the table. When salt is used in very small amounts, it enhances the flavor of a food. In addition to salt, you can also use very salty food, or **high-sodium food,** as a seasoning in a dish. Some high-sodium foods commonly used in the kitchen include soy sauce, Parmesan cheese, bacon, and olives.

Salt can be found underground, where it is mined. Some mines dissolve the salt with water and then pump the salt-saturated water out of the ground. The water is allowed to evaporate and the salt remains. Salt is also found in sea water. The water is allowed to evaporate, leaving behind grains or flakes of salt.

Salt lasts almost indefinitely in dry storage. The only real concern is that the salt may become damp and turn into a hard cake. To keep this from happening, store salt in a cool, dry place in a sealed container.

- **Table Salt**. Salt that is refined to remove other minerals or impurities is referred to as **table salt**. This type of salt is processed to give it a fine, even grain. A small amount of a starch is added to keep the salt from turning into clumps. Iodine may be added to table salt as a nutritional supplement. The salt is then called **iodized** (EYE-oh-dized) **salt**.
- **Sea Salt**. Made by evaporating seawater, **sea salt** is usually not significantly refined, which means it contains additional minerals and other elements found in seawater. This often

▼ *Table salt* ▼ *Sea salt*

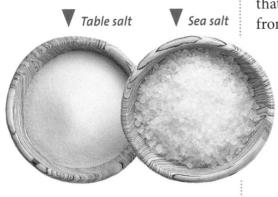

CULINARY SCIENCE

Osmosis

Salt changes food. It draws out water, blood, and other impurities and it kills pathogens. This preserves food by drying it out and makes it less susceptible to spoilage. To keep foods safe to eat when there was no refrigeration, our ancestors used salt to remove as much water as possible.

The process by which salt accomplishes these changes is known as osmosis. Osmosis is the movement of water through a cell wall to equalize the concentration of salt on both sides of the wall. For example, when you salt a piece of meat, the fluid inside the meat travels through the meat's cell wall in an effort to dilute the salt on the other side of the cell wall. So the meat loses fluid.

However, osmosis occurs in both directions. First it draws fluid out of the cell. But when there is more fluid outside the cell than inside it, the fluid flows back into the cell, taking along the dissolved salt. Getting the salt inside the cell, where it can kill harmful pathogens, is the essence of salt-curing foods. That is how foods such as ham, bacon, and dry sausages are preserved. Because of osmosis, salt often meant the difference between life and death for our ancestors.

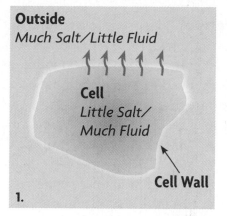

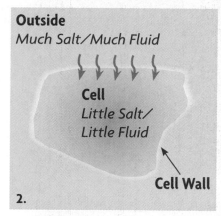

Outside
Much Salt/Little Fluid

Cell
Little Salt/ Much Fluid

Cell Wall

1.

Outside
Much Salt/Much Fluid

Cell
Little Salt/ Little Fluid

Cell Wall

2.

1. Fluid moves through cell wall diluting salt outside cell.
2. Fluid, with dissolved salt, moves back into cell, equalizing fluid on both sides of wall.

Research

Research the process of osmosis as it applies to salting food. In your report, relate osmosis, FAT TOM, water activity (Aw), potentially hazardous foods, and pathogen growth.

---

gives sea salt a slight color. Sea salt is available in grains of varying sizes, from extremely coarse crystals to flakes to a fine grain.

- **Kosher Salt**. A salt made without any additives, **kosher** (KOH-shure) **salt** is sold in coarse or fine grain styles. Kosher salt is typically flakier than table salt. Many chefs like to use kosher salt for general cooking purposes because it is additive-free. To substitute kosher salt for table salt, use twice the volume of kosher salt as called for in the recipe.

- **Rock Salt**. Less refined than table salt, **rock salt** is generally not used for consumption. Its most common use in the kitchen is in ice cream makers or as a bed for certain items, especially oysters or clams that are served on their shells.

- **Monosodium Glutamate (MSG)**. Although not actually a salt, **monosodium glutamate** (mon-oh-SO-dee-um GLUTE-ah-mate), abbreviated as **MSG**, is used in much the same way as salt. MSG provides the umami taste rather than the salty taste and is often associated with Chinese or Japanese food.

▲ *Rock salt*

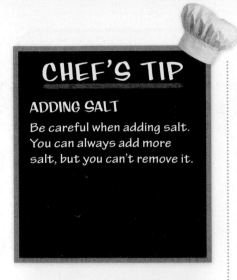

▲ *Black pepper*
Whole, cracked, and ground

▲ *White pepper*
Whole and ground

MSG enhances the meaty or brothy flavor in meat, poultry, fish, and vegetables. The source of MSG is seaweed.

Pepper In most people's mind, salt and pepper go together. They are the most widely used seasonings in the world. Pepper is actually a spice that is often used in small amounts as a seasoning. Typically only black pepper and white pepper are used as seasonings. (Other types of pepper are discussed in the next section, "Herbs, Spices, & Aromatics.") Pepper is slightly hot and brings out the flavor in food.

- **Black Pepper.** From the dried, unripe berries of the pepper vine, **black pepper** is available as whole berries, cracked, or ground. Grinding pepper as it is needed is preferable because the taste is fresher and more aromatic.

- **White Pepper**. When the ripe pepper berries are allowed to dry and their husks are removed, you have **white pepper**. Usually, white pepper is used for light-colored sauces. White pepper is available in the same forms as black pepper, and, just as with black pepper, grinding pepper fresh is always preferred.

Sugar and Light-Flavored Sweeteners Sugar enhances the flavor of dishes—from salad dressings, to tomato sauce, to vegetables and even meat. As a seasoning, you should add only a small amount of sugar to a dish. Sugar with distinctive flavor (such as brown sugar) is used as a flavoring agent, not as a seasoning. Sometimes a light-flavored liquid sweetener, such as light corn syrup, light honey, or light maple syrup, is used rather than sugar.

Acids Lemon or orange juice, vinegar, and wine are all examples of acids you can use to season food. Acids have a sour or tart flavor. In addition to seasoning food, acids can also improve the appearance and texture of food. For example, adding lemon juice when you cook an artichoke keeps it from turning brown. Adding vinegar to the water when you poach an egg gives the egg a better shape.

 **Reading Checkpoint** *Name four types of seasonings.*

Flavoring Foods

When you season a food, you try to improve the food's unique flavor without changing it significantly. When you flavor a food, you change the food's flavor. You add other flavors to the food's original flavor. Some chefs refer to the process of flavoring foods as "layering flavors," adding flavor on top of other flavors to create a new pleasing combination of flavors.

Here's an example that demonstrates the difference between seasoning and flavoring. If you add a small amount of salt to the water you use to cook rice, the cooked rice will simply taste like cooked rice. That means it has been properly seasoned. However, if you add a lot of salt, the cooked rice will take on the distinct and easy-to-identify flavor of salt. Salt has become a flavoring in the dish, not a seasoning. In this case, the difference between an ingredient used as a seasoning and one used as a flavoring is a question of how much you use.

Many ingredients or combinations of ingredients can be used to flavor foods. Each flavoring ingredient is added to a dish at a specific time and in a specific manner to develop a desired flavor in the dish. Some of the basic guidelines for using flavorings are discussed in the next section.

FIGURE 6-4
Salting Water
Adding salt to water prior to cooking pasta
 Applying Concepts *How can adding salt to water change the flavor of pasta?*

 **Reading Checkpoint** **What is the difference between seasoning a food and flavoring a food?**

6.2 ASSESSMENT

Reviewing Concepts

1. What are three reasons chefs season foods?
2. What are the four basic types of seasoning ingredients?
3. What is the difference between seasoning a food and flavoring a food?

Critical Thinking

4. **Comparing/Contrasting** Describe the differences between table salt, kosher salt, and sea salt.
5. **Inferring** Why would only light-flavored sweeteners be used as seasonings?
6. **Classifying** Which type of pepper would you typically use for a light-colored sauce? Why?
7. **Predicting** Will there be times when a chef might want an unbalanced taste or very rich dish? Explain your answer.

Test Kitchen

Divide into four teams. Teams will make a salsa of a medium dice of tomatoes and a fine dice of onions, with three times as much tomato as onion. Then they will divide the salsa into two portions. Teams will focus on one type of seasoning ingredient. Use the seasoning ingredient only to season the first portion, but then use it to flavor the second portion. Evaluate the amounts required for seasoning versus flavoring.

SCIENCE

Iodized Salt

Research the history of iodized salt. When was iodine first added to salt? Why was this done? Are there any problems associated with the use of iodized salt?

6.3 Herbs, Spices, & Aromatics

READING PREVIEW

Key Concepts

- Identifying and using herbs
- Identifying and using spices
- Identifying and using additional aromatic ingredients
- Preparing and using aromatic combinations

Vocabulary

- battuto
- bouquet garni
- Cajun trinity
- cured foods
- herbs
- matignon
- mirepoix
- sachet d'épices
- spice blends
- spices
- standard mirepoix
- white mirepoix

> **"H**erbs are like brilliant jewels that add sparkle to any dish. **"**
>
> – Anita Eisenhauer

Herbs

Herbs are the leaves and stems of certain plants. They are used to flavor a wide variety of foods. Some are considered sweet; others are thought of as savory.

Certain herbs or combinations of herbs are associated with particular cuisines. The taste and smell of basil and oregano, for example, might make you think of Italian foods. Tarragon and chives are often used in French cooking. Cilantro and parsley are important herbs in Chinese cooking. Oregano and mint are key flavors in Greek cooking.

Selecting and Storing Herbs Fresh herbs have intense flavors. When you select a fresh herb, smell it to check for a good aroma. As a fresh herb ages, its flavor gets weaker. Fresh herbs should also have a good color. The leaves should be intact. Bruised or wilted leaves and leaves that have become pale or turned yellow will not have the best flavor. Stems should be firm

Anita Eisenhauer
The Culinary Institute of America

and not split. If the roots are still intact, as they may be on herbs such as cilantro or dill, they should be dry, not soft or wet.

Store fresh herbs in the refrigerator, wrapped loosely in a damp paper towel in a loosely closed plastic bag. Use fresh herbs within a few days for the best flavor.

Many herbs are sold as either dried or ground leaves. Some are sold as a powder. Drying the herbs drives out the moisture in the herb, concentrating the herb's flavor. Be sure to smell dried herbs before you use them. They should have a pleasant smell. If they smell musty or have practically no aroma, they are probably too old to be of any use in cooking.

Buy just enough dried herbs to last six months. Store them in tightly sealed containers, away from heat, moisture, and direct sunlight.

Using Fresh and Dried Herbs Review your recipe to find out when to add fresh herbs. Some recipes call for whole sprigs, some for leaves, and some for only stems. Rinse and dry herbs before chopping them or adding them to a dish. If your recipe requires cut herbs, cut them as close as possible to the time you need them. Once you cut a fresh herb, it starts to lose some of its flavor.

Whole sprigs and stems are usually added to a dish at the start of cooking so the herb can gently flavor the entire dish. For a more intense flavor, chopped or whole fresh leaves are added to a dish at the end of cooking.

Dried herbs often have a more intense flavor than fresh ones because they contain less water. (There are some exceptions. Dried chives, chervil, and parsley have a less intense flavor than the fresh herb.) In general, you can substitute one teaspoon of a dried herb for every tablespoon of fresh herbs called for in a recipe. Most dry herbs need to be added to the dish early on as you cook so the liquid in the dish rehydrates them and the herbs can flavor the dish.

FIGURE 6-5
Adding Basil to Tomato Sauce
Fresh basil or oregano is often added to tomato sauce.
Comparing/Contrasting *Why might adding fresh basil to a finished sauce give a different flavor than adding dried basil when you start to cook the sauce?*

Herbs

Basil ▶

Basil (BAY-zill) has pointed green leaves. Purple varieties and large- or small-leafed varieties are available. Some varieties have the aroma of cinnamon, clove, lemon, or other flavors. Uses include flavoring sauces (including pesto sauce), salad dressings, chicken, fish, and pasta. Basil is also used to flavor oils and vinegars.

◀ Bay Leaf

Bay leaves are smooth and rigid. They may be available fresh but are typically used dry. Bay leaves retain their flavor even after drying. Bay leaves are used to flavor soups, stews, stocks, sauces, and grain dishes. Remove bay leaves from the prepared food at the end of the cooking process.

Chervil ▶

This member of the parsley family has dark green, curly leaves. Dried chervil (CHER-vil) has far less flavor than fresh. Chervil has a flavor similar to parsley with a hint of licorice. It is one of the herbs typically used in the French blend of herbs referred to as "fines herbes" (FEENZ erb).

◀ Chives

Chives belong to the onion family and have a subtle but savory flavor. Chives grow as long, hollow stems. The flowers or buds have a more intense flavor and are sometimes used to flavor or garnish a salad. Dried chives have far less flavor than fresh chives. Chives are typically minced or snipped before they are added to a dish.

Cilantro ▶

Cilantro (see-LAHN-troh) is very similar in shape to flat-leaf parsley. The leaves have scalloped edges. The flavor is fresh, tangy, sharp, and distinctive. It is used in many Asian, South American, and Central American dishes. It is also known as Chinese parsley.

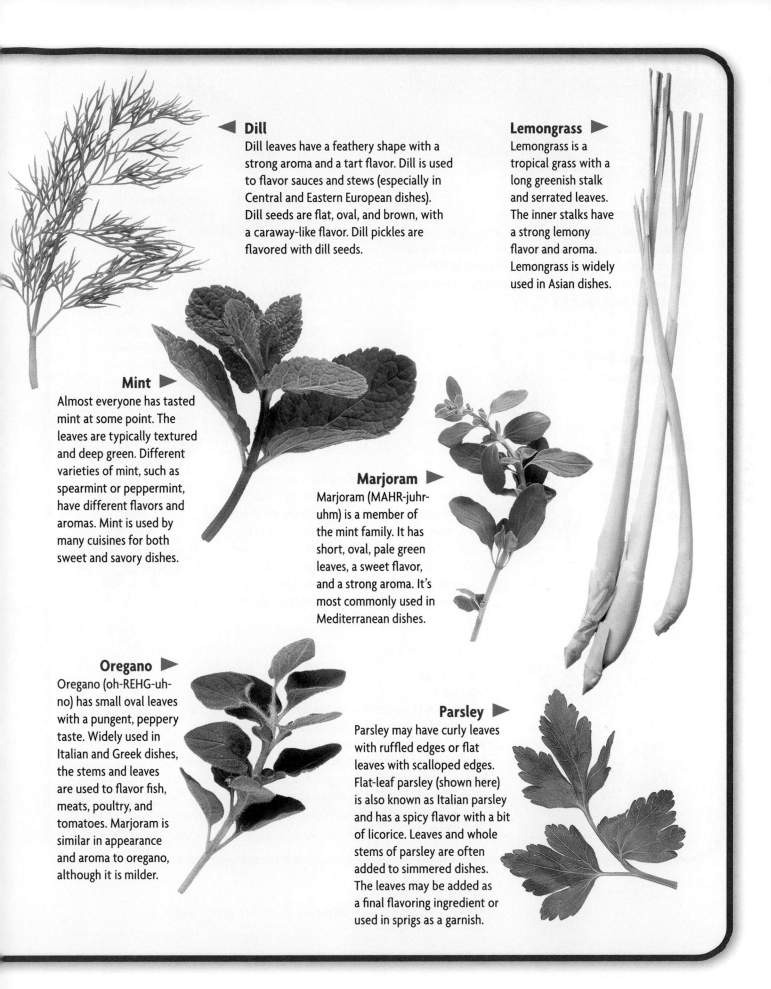

Dill

Dill leaves have a feathery shape with a strong aroma and a tart flavor. Dill is used to flavor sauces and stews (especially in Central and Eastern European dishes). Dill seeds are flat, oval, and brown, with a caraway-like flavor. Dill pickles are flavored with dill seeds.

Lemongrass

Lemongrass is a tropical grass with a long greenish stalk and serrated leaves. The inner stalks have a strong lemony flavor and aroma. Lemongrass is widely used in Asian dishes.

Mint

Almost everyone has tasted mint at some point. The leaves are typically textured and deep green. Different varieties of mint, such as spearmint or peppermint, have different flavors and aromas. Mint is used by many cuisines for both sweet and savory dishes.

Marjoram

Marjoram (MAHR-juhr-uhm) is a member of the mint family. It has short, oval, pale green leaves, a sweet flavor, and a strong aroma. It's most commonly used in Mediterranean dishes.

Oregano

Oregano (oh-REHG-uh-no) has small oval leaves with a pungent, peppery taste. Widely used in Italian and Greek dishes, the stems and leaves are used to flavor fish, meats, poultry, and tomatoes. Marjoram is similar in appearance and aroma to oregano, although it is milder.

Parsley

Parsley may have curly leaves with ruffled edges or flat leaves with scalloped edges. Flat-leaf parsley (shown here) is also known as Italian parsley and has a spicy flavor with a bit of licorice. Leaves and whole stems of parsley are often added to simmered dishes. The leaves may be added as a final flavoring ingredient or used in sprigs as a garnish.

▲ Rosemary
Rosemary has needle-shaped leaves. It has a pungent, resinous flavor, similar to pine needles. Rosemary stems, also known as branches, are sometimes used as skewers for grilled or broiled foods. Dried rosemary is almost as pungent as fresh rosemary.

▲ Sage
Fresh sage leaves are oval and are covered with soft threads, giving the leaf a silvery, furry appearance. It has a pungent, slightly bitter, musty mint flavor and is often added whole to stews and soups. It is also used to flavor roast meats or poultry. Dried sage is often referred to as rubbed sage.

Savory ▶
Savory has small, narrow, gray-green leaves and a bitter, pungent flavor that resembles thyme and rosemary. It is available fresh and dried.

Thyme ▶
Thyme (TIME) has very small gray-green oval leaves. It has a lemony, minty flavor with overtones of rosemary. Some varieties have special flavors such as nutmeg, mint, or lemon. Thyme is used to flavor soups and stews. Whole sprigs or chopped leaves may be used. Dried thyme retains much of the flavor of fresh thyme and is widely available.

◀ Tarragon
Tarragon (TAHR-uh-gon) has narrow, pointed, dark green leaves with a strong licorice flavor. The stems are often added as a flavoring for simmered dishes and sauces. The leaves are typically chopped before they are added as a final flavoring ingredient. Tarragon is often used with chicken, fish, veal, and egg dishes. It is typical in many French-style dishes. Although dried tarragon does not have as strong a flavor as fresh tarragon, it has a potent aroma.

✓ **Reading Checkpoint**   *What are herbs? Give five examples.*

Spices

Spices are aromatic ingredients added in small amounts to foods to give them a specific flavor. They are the seeds, bark, roots, stalks, or fruits of a wide range of plants. Many of the spices we take for granted today, such as cinnamon or pepper, were once so costly that only rich people could afford them.

Although not all spices can be purchased whole, you should try to purchase whole spices whenever you can. Whole spices last longer than spices that are already ground. Ground spices lose their aroma or fragrance more quickly. Whole peppercorns, for instance, can last for several years in dry storage, but ground black pepper starts to lose its flavor after about six months. You can always grind whole spices as you need them.

Spices are sometimes added to a dish whole and then strained out. In other dishes, spices are ground and then cooked in a little oil or other fat to distribute the flavor evenly through the dish. Often, spices are added directly to the dish as it cooks. Recipes usually indicate when and how to add spices to a dish. Spices are also used to flavor oils or vinegars, which are themselves used to flavor dishes.

CHEF'S TIP

CHECK FRESHNESS

Be sure to check spices before you use them. Rub them between your fingertips and then smell them. If the flavor is strong and pleasant, they are still fresh enough to use.

CULINARY HISTORY

Spice Routes

Spices such as cloves, saffron, and cinnamon were highly prized. In the Middle Ages using spices was a show of wealth. But why were spices so valuable just a few hundred years ago? It all has to do with transportation and trade.

First, the Chinese established a trade route, known as the "Silk Road," that linked the East with the Middle East. Merchants would travel in caravans along a number of routes, carrying spices, silks, and gems.

Merchants along the way purchased goods and carried them further west. By the time a spice such as cinnamon had traveled from China or the Spice Islands to Europe, it had changed hands many times. Of course, the price went up each time.

The locations where the spices were grown were jealously guarded secrets. Outlandish stories were often told to Europeans to keep them from getting their hands on the spices. For example, Romans, anxious to find a less expensive source

▲ *Caravan on the Silk Road*

for cinnamon, were told by Chinese merchants that the sweet spice had to be harvested from remote caves that were guarded by fierce bats.

Research

Research which spices were transported on the Silk Road in the Middle Ages. Provide a detailed description of (or the recipe for) a dish from the Middle Ages that would have used one or more of these spices.

Spices

Allspice ▶
Small brown berries that are ground for use as a spice. Allspice lives up to its name. It has a flavor and aroma that is a mixture of cinnamon, clove, nutmeg, ginger, and pepper. Allspice is typically available cracked or ground. Also known as Jamaican pepper, allspice is typically used in spicy, fragrant Jamaican jerked chicken.

Caraway Seeds ▶
A member of the parsley family, the caraway plant is actually an herb. However, the plant is best known as the source for caraway seeds. These small crescent-shaped seeds have a nutty, peppery, licorice taste. They are widely used in baked goods and savory dishes.

Cardamom ▶
These long, light green or brown pods contain a seed that has a pungent, musty, lemony flavor. Cardamom (CARD-uh-mom) is available in whole pods or ground. It is used widely used in Indian dishes.

Cinnamon ▶
Cinnamon is the inner bark of a small evergreen tree that originally came from India and other eastern countries. It has a sweet flavor and aroma. It is sold ground or in rolled-up sticks. It is used in a number of desserts. It is also an important flavoring in many savory dishes.

Cloves ▶
Cloves (CLOVS) are the unopened bud of a tropical evergreen tree. Individual cloves are brown and are shaped like nails (which is why the Romans gave them the name "clavus," the Latin word for nail). Cloves are extremely aromatic, with a sweet, astringent flavor. Like cinnamon, cloves are considered a sweet spice. Cloves are sold whole or ground.

Cumin ▶
Cumin (COO-min) is the crescent-shaped seed of a plant in the parsley family. It has a strong, distinctive earthy flavor and aroma that is often associated with Mexican cooking. Cumin is available whole or ground and is also used in Middle Eastern and Indian dishes.

Fennel ▶

With its feathery foliage, fennel looks like dill. It has a pronounced licorice flavor and is used fresh or dried. The oval seeds are used in Italian and Central European cuisines for baked goods and savory dishes. Fennel seeds are usually sold as whole seeds.

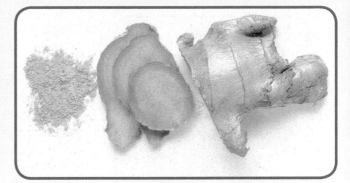

▲ Ginger

Ginger is a tall tropical plant, but only the gnarled root is used as a spice. Ginger root must be peeled to be used. Fresh ginger has a distinctive peppery, sweet flavor with hints of lemon and rosemary and a strong, spicy aroma. Powdered or ground ginger is made by drying fresh ginger root and then pulverizing it. Ginger is used in Asian and Indian cuisines for both sweet and savory dishes.

Mustard ▶

Mustard is a member of the cabbage family, and its leaves are eaten as a vegetable. However, its seeds have an earthy hot flavor and a pungent smell. There are yellow, red, and black

varieties of mustard seeds. Each has a distinctive taste. Mustard is sold as whole seeds or as a powder. The whole seeds are used in Indian cuisine.

Nutmeg and Mace ▶

The seed of the nutmeg tree, nutmeg is oval and has a smooth texture. Mace is the lacy coating that surrounds the seed. Both have a sweet flavor and are highly fragrant.

Nutmeg tastes best when it is freshly ground, using a special grater. Both nutmeg and mace are available ground as well. They are used in both sweet and savory dishes.

◀ Peppercorns

Peppercorns are the berry of the pepper vine, which originally came from India and Indonesia. Small amounts are used as seasoning, along with salt. Larger amounts can be used to flavor a dish. Besides black and white peppercorns, which were discussed in the previous section of this book, there are also green and pink peppercorns. Green peppercorns are unripened peppercorns that are pickled or freeze-dried. They have a soft texture and a sour taste. Pink peppercorns, which are available dried or pickled, are actually not peppercorns. They are the dried berries of a South American rose, and have a bitter, piney flavor.

Spices

◀ **Peppers**

Native to the Americas, peppers are vegetables. They have a wide range of colors and flavors ranging from sweet to extremely hot. Hot peppers are often referred to as chile peppers or chiles. Both sweet and hot peppers are dried and then ground to create a variety of sweet or hot spices. Paprika, for example, is a blend of dried red chiles with a flavor that can range from sweet to hot. Ground peppers are used as a spice in Central Europe, Spain, Italy, and the Americas.

Saffron ▶

Saffron is produced by drying the inner part of the crocus, a small purple flower. Saffron has a distinctive spicy, honeyed, but slightly bitter flavor and a strong, pungent aroma. Saffron not only flavors foods, it also gives them a deep yellow color. Saffron threads are usually crushed before they are added to a dish. Powdered saffron is also available.

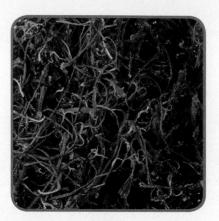

Curry powder, chili powder, and pumpkin pie spice are all examples of **spice blends**, made by combining a variety of spices (and often herbs as well). Dry rubs for seasoning meats or poultry before they

FIGURE 6-6 ▶
Curry Powder
Curry powder is a blend of up to twenty herbs and spices.
Drawing Conclusions *What do you achieve when you combine many herbs and spices (including cinnamon, chiles, fennel seeds, ginger, and cumin) into a spice blend such as curry powder?*

roast are another type of spice blend. Many spice blends are prepared and packaged for sale. Some chefs prefer to make their own spice blends so they can control the amount and type of spices in the blend. Spice blends are typically ground for an even texture, but some include whole spices and seeds.

 **Reading Checkpoint** *What are spices? Give five examples of spices.*

Additional Aromatic Ingredients

Herbs and spices usually have strong and distinctive aromas. However, chefs sometimes use additional aromatic ingredients to add more flavor and aromas to a dish. The three basic types of additional aromatic ingredients used in cooking are:

- Aromatic vegetables and fruits
- Aromatic liquids
- Cured and smoked foods

Aromatic Vegetables and Fruits You can add aromatic vegetables to a dish for some additional flavor and aroma. Plants in the onion family, including garlic, green onions, and leeks, are the most common aromatic vegetables. Other vegetables prized for their aromas include mushrooms and celery. Tomatoes can be used for their aroma. They may be simply chopped and added to the dish or, to intensify their flavor, they can be cooked in the oven or in a pan over direct heat.

Fruits—especially citrus fruits such as lemons, limes, and oranges—are often used to add flavor and aroma to a dish. You can add just the zest (the outer peel) or the juice. You can also use dried fruits such as raisins or apricots to add flavor and aroma to a dish.

Aromatic Liquids Chefs use a variety of liquids in cooking everything from soup to vegetables to grains. Broths and stocks (concentrated broth-like liquids) add aroma to a dish. Other aromatic liquids a chef might use are wines, brandies, and liqueurs. Usually, these are heated to evaporate the alcohol and concentrate the taste.

Flavorful oils, including flavored olive oil, sesame oil, and walnut oil, can also be added to a dish to increase flavor and aroma. These oils are usually not allowed to cook for long in a dish. Getting them too hot for too long cooks away their delicate aroma.

Extracts are made by soaking aromatic ingredients such as vanilla or lemon in alcohol. Extracts can also be added in small amounts to a dish to increase flavor and aroma.

FIGURE 6-7
Pork and Beans
Smoked ham and a bouquet garni
are added to beans.
Predicting *How will the ham
change the flavor of the beans?*

Cured Foods **Cured foods** are foods that are preserved by drying, salting, pickling, or smoking (such as ham, bacon, or salted anchovies). They add a savory flavor and aroma to a dish, and they may also add saltiness. Cured foods are strongly flavored. They are usually added when you begin cooking a dish so they can flavor the dish evenly.

 *What are the three types of additional aromatic ingredients commonly used in cooking?*

Aromatic Combinations

Any time you use more than one flavoring or aromatic ingredient in a dish, you've made an aromatic combination. Some specific combinations are used frequently in the kitchen. The three most common are

- Mirepoix
- Sachet d'épices
- Bouquet garni

Mirepoix Mirepoix (MEER-pwah) is a combination of vegetables used as an aromatic flavoring ingredient in many dishes. You can cut the vegetables in mirepoix into large or small pieces. To determine how big the pieces should be, read over the recipe to find out how long the mirepoix will cook in the dish. Long-cooking dishes call for large pieces of mirepoix. Dishes that cook quickly need mirepoix that is cut into small pieces or thin slices.

By making a few changes to the ingredients in a mirepoix, you can produce a variety of aromatic combinations. The most common types of mirepoix or mirepoix-like aromatic combinations are:

- **Standard Mirepoix.** Used for a variety of stocks and soups, a **standard mirepoix** typically includes the following ingredients (by weight): 2 parts onion, 1 part carrot, and 1 part celery. For brown stock, soup, gravy, or stews, a tomato paste or tomato purée is often included in the mirepoix.
- **White Mirepoix.** A **white mirepoix** is used to flavor white stocks and soups that should have a pale ivory or white color. Parsnips replace the carrots. Leeks may replace some of the onions.
- **Cajun Trinity.** Used in many Creole (KREE-ol) and Cajun (CAGE-uhn) dishes such as gumbo, a **Cajun trinity** is a combination of onion, celery, and green pepper.
- **Matignon.** This mirepoix-like aromatic combination contains onions, carrots, celery, and ham. **Matignon** (mah-tee-YOHN)

Mirepoix

1. **Rinse** onions, carrots, and celery.
2. **Trim** all ingredients.
3. **Cut** ingredients to the correct size.
4. **Add** mirepoix at the correct time. (Consult your recipe.)
5. **Cook** long enough to flavor the dish.

 See Recipe Card 1, "Mirepoix."

Standard mirepoix ingredients: onion, carrot, and celery

is not strained from the dish, so it is important to peel all vegetables and cut all ingredients into a neat dice. Mushrooms, herbs, and spices may also be required by your recipe. Matignon is sometimes known as "edible mirepoix."

- **Battuto.** Used in Italian soups, sauces, stews, and meat dishes, **battuto** (bah-TOOT-oh) includes a cooking fat (olive oil, chopped lard, pancetta, or fatback) with garlic, onions, parsley, carrots, and celery. Green peppers are also commonly added.

Sachet d'Epices and Bouquet Garni Sachet d'épices and bouquet garni are two classic aromatic combinations used in many dishes.

- **Sachet d'Epices.** A **sachet d'épices** (SAH-shay DAY-pees) is a mixture of fresh and dried herbs and dried spices that is tied up in a piece of cheesecloth to make a small bag. Sachet d'épices means "bag of spices" in French. A standard sachet d'épices includes peppercorns, dried thyme leaves, and fresh parsley stems.
- **Bouquet Garni.** Another combination of aromatics, a **bouquet garni** (boo-KAY GAR-nee) uses fresh herbs rather than dried herbs. It also usually includes an aromatic vegetable such as leeks, garlic, or scallions. The ingredients in a bouquet garni may also include sprigs of fresh thyme, fresh parsley stems, rosemary, and citrus peels. Leek leaves or a citrus peel may be used as a wrapper instead of cheesecloth. The ingredients are then tied up.

 **Reading Checkpoint** *What are the three most common types of aromatic combinations?*

▲ *Bouquet garni*

Sachet d'Epices

1 **Measure** peppercorns, thyme, and parsley.

2 **Wrap** the sachet d'épices ingredients in a square of cheesecloth.

3 **Tie** the cheesecloth with string to make a bag.

4 **Add** to the dish.

5 **Simmer** until the dish is aromatic. (Consult your recipe.)

6 **Remove** and discard.

 See Recipe Card 2, "Sachet d'Epices."

6.3 ASSESSMENT

Reviewing Concepts

1. What are herbs? Give five examples.
2. What are spices? Give five examples.
3. Aside from herbs and spices, what are the three additional types of aromatic ingredients commonly used in cooking?
4. What are the three most common types of aromatic combinations?

Critical Thinking

5. **Comparing/Contrasting** Using fennel as an example, describe when you would consider it an herb and when you would consider it a spice.
6. **Communicating** Of the herbs and spices listed in this section, which is your favorite? Describe the flavor of your selection.
7. **Comparing/Contrasting** How does a Cajun trinity differ from a standard mirepoix?

Test Kitchen

Divide into four teams. Each team will finely mince a different herb, either chives, oregano, tarragon, or rosemary. Mix the herb with 2 Tbsp of salted butter at room temperature. Spread on toast. Cut into enough squares for the class to sample. Rank the taste from most favorite to least favorite. Tally the results for the class.

SOCIAL STUDIES

Myths about Herbs and Spices

Research a particular herb or spice. Write a description of any myths or legends related to the herb or spice you chose. Research how the herb or spice acquired its name and whether it has historically been associated with any medical or health benefits.

6.4 Condiments, Nuts, & Seeds

READING PREVIEW

Key Concepts

- Identifying and using condiments
- Identifying and using nuts and seeds

Vocabulary

- condiments
- nuts
- seed
- tahini

> "**S**alsa . . . recently surpassed catsup as America's best-selling condiment. "
>
> – Michael J. Weiss
> "The Salsa Sectors," *Atlantic Monthly*, May 1997

Condiments

Condiments (CON-di-ments) are prepared mixtures we use to season and flavor foods. A condiment is something extra, served on the side and added by the individual diner to suit his or her own preferences. (Condiments can also be used as ingredients in a preparation.) A condiment can change the flavor of a dish by adding spicy, savory, sweet, sour, salty, or umami tastes to food. Condiments may also add color, texture, or even a temperature contrast, to further enhance the way a dish looks and tastes.

Sometimes condiments are selected just to add a new taste to a familiar favorite. For example, a pineapple salsa condiment might be served with a grilled chicken breast.

However, many dishes are served with a traditional condiment (for example, mustard with hot dogs). Mustard, ketchup (also called catsup), hot sauce, Worcestershire (WUSS-ta-shur) sauce, and steak sauce are all examples of traditional condiments you might choose to serve with meats, fish, or poultry dishes. Dressings, dips, and spreads can also be used as traditional condiments. For example, blue cheese dressing is often the traditional condiment served with Buffalo-style chicken wings, and salsa is traditionally served with chips.

▲ *Tabasco sauce*

▲ *Peanut butter on bread*

Think of these traditional condiments. For a taco, you usually choose from a variety of traditional condiments including taco sauce, sour cream, shredded lettuce, sliced green onions, chopped tomatoes, grated cheese, and pickled jalapeno peppers. For sushi, you usually can pick pickled ginger, wasabi, and soy sauce as condiments.

Selecting and Storing Condiments You can purchase fresh or perishable condiments or make them from scratch. When purchasing bottled, jarred, or canned condiments, be sure the container is intact and there are no leaks, bulges, or dents. Be sure perishable condiments are kept in the refrigerator.

Using Condiments Some condiments have extremely pungent or hot flavors. They are typically served in very small amounts. Others have sweet or mellow tastes. The portion size for any condiment can vary greatly from one dish to another and from one restaurant to another. The basic rule of thumb is to offer enough of the condiment so the guest can enjoy it with each bite of the main dish.

Before using a condiment, check it carefully and taste it. This gives you a chance to add more seasonings or flavorings, if necessary. It also allows you to detect any sour or off odors that might mean the condiment is past its prime.

 Reading Checkpoint   *What is a condiment?*

Nuts and Seeds

Nuts are the fruit of various trees. The only exception is the peanut, which grows underground in the root system of a bean-like plant. Nuts are available in the shell or shelled. They are available uncooked, roasted, or blanched (cooked quickly in boiling water and then quickly cooled). Shelled nuts are available whole, halved, sliced, slivered, or chopped. Nuts and seeds are also used to produce butters, such as peanut butter or sesame paste, which is also called **tahini** (ta-HEE-nee).

A **seed** is the part of a plant that can grow into a new plant. Seeds come from a variety of plants, including herbs, flowers, and vegetables. The way a seed is used determines how we classify it. For example, some seeds are used in the same way you use a nut—in larger quantities, for their nutty taste and crunchy texture. Sesame seeds and poppy seeds are two examples. Other seeds are used the same way you use a spice—in smaller quantities, as a flavoring. Mustard seeds, cumin, nutmeg, and fennel seeds are some examples.

India

India is an Asian country with cultural and culinary ties to China and Southeast Asian countries. Some of India's most important culinary influences came from Persia (modern-day Iran and Iraq) and Indonesia (the famous Spice Islands Christopher Columbus set out to find).

Northern India is a noted agricultural area, growing many types of grains. These are featured in an amazing diversity of breads, which are a significant part of any Indian meal. The southern part of India is famous for its fragrant basmati (bahs-MAH-tee) rice, which is a perfect accompaniment to the spicy and often hot southern food. In fact, the further south you travel in India, the hotter the food becomes.

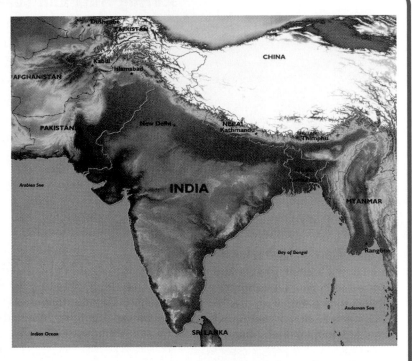

Vegetables are very important in Indian cuisine. There is a strong vegetarian tradition, especially in areas where the primary religion discourages

▲ *Indian spices*

meat-eating. Condiments, including pickled vegetables, chutneys, and other relishes, are indispensable in a typical Indian meal.

Dairy foods are common in Indian cooking, making this cuisine different from that of most other parts of Asia. Ghee (GEE), a form of butter, is widely used to cook foods. Mustard seed oil and coconut oil are also important cooking fats. Yogurt and buttermilk are used on their own and as ingredients in other dishes. Indian cuisine also features a fresh cheese, known as paneer (pah-NEER).

Curries and roasts are important Indian cooking techniques. A curry is a stew that may feature meat, fish, or chicken, or a combination of vegetables. It is flavored with a combination of spices and often finished with yogurt. Roasts are prepared in special ovens known as tandoors (tan-DOERS), which reach extremely high temperatures.

Above all, Indian cooking is noted for its use of herbs and spices. Spice blends, known as masalas (ma-SAH-las), may contain a dozen or more herbs and spices, including mustard seeds, chiles, cinnamon, cloves, ginger, saffron, nutmeg, and bay leaves. Different types of curries are seasoned by different styles of masalas. Throughout India, the selection of spices for a masala is a personal matter. Each family may have its own formula, one that distinguishes their food from the food of their neighbors.

Storing Nuts and Seeds Nuts and seeds are best stored in a cool, dry, dark storage area. If nuts and seeds are received in vacuum packaging, they will last almost indefinitely. Loose nuts and seeds or opened packages, however, can become rancid quickly. You may be able to keep nuts still in the shell for up to six months. Unroasted nuts, sometimes referred to as raw nuts, can last up to three months in dry storage. Roasted nuts start to lose their quality after about a month. Sliced or chopped nuts have the shortest shelf life, usually no more

Nuts and Seeds

▲ Almond

Pale tan with a pitted, woody shell, an almond is teardrop-shaped. Bitter and sweet types are available. Bitter almonds must be cooked. Sweet almonds have a distinctive taste and smell and can be used raw or cooked.

Cashew ▶

A cashew (CASH-yew) is kidney-shaped, sweet, and butter-flavored, with a high fat content. It is always sold shelled, because its skin contains irritating oils similar to those in poison ivy. Cashews are often used for snacking.

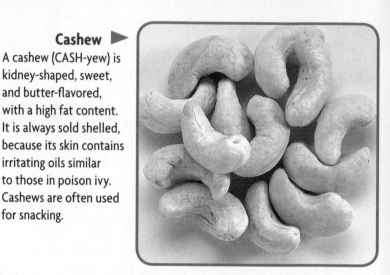

◀ Chestnut

A chestnut is a fairly large nut that is round to teardrop-shaped. Chestnuts must be cooked. They have a high starch content and are used in both sweet and savory dishes.

▲ Hazelnut

This small, nearly round nut has a distinctive rich, somewhat sweet taste. It is widely used in desserts because it complements chocolate and coffee.

than three to four weeks. To keep them for longer periods, store them in sealed containers in the freezer.

Pastes made from nuts and seeds (such as almond paste, nut butter, tahini, and poppy seed paste) will keep in an unopened container for several months. Once the container is open, you can store them in dry storage for up to six weeks. Some butters or pastes can be kept in the refrigerator for up to two months or in a freezer for up to three months. Check them for fresh, pleasant aromas before using.

◀ Macadamia

The macadamia (mac-a-DAME-ee-ah) nut is nearly round. It has a very hard shell and is usually available shelled. It has a rich, buttery flavor and a high fat content.

▲ Peanut

Although the peanut is a seed that grows underground in a pod, it is usually treated as a nut. Peanuts are available in their shell or shelled, raw or roasted. Peanuts are often used for snacking, and peanut butter has made many of us familiar with the nutty taste of a roasted peanut.

Pine Nut ▶

These small, cream-colored, elongated nuts are the seeds from a Mediterranean pine. They have a distinctive, rich, slightly piney flavor and a high fat content. They are used in both sweet and savory dishes.

▲ Pecan

Pecans are often sold whole in their smooth, thin, hard, tan shells. The golden brown kernel has a high fat content and a nutty, sweet taste. It is often used in sweet dishes, such as pecan pie.

Using Nuts and Seeds Nuts and seeds are often roasted or toasted to bring out more flavor. It is easy to overcook or scorch nuts if you aren't paying close attention. When toasting nuts, keep them in motion by stirring them or swirling the pan. As soon as nuts or seeds start to turn color or become fragrant, remove them from the heat. Immediately pour them into a cool container. Otherwise, the heat held by the pan will overcook them. Overcooked nuts and seeds become too bitter to use in cooking.

Nuts and Seeds

▲ Pistachio
The pale green color of the pistachio nut distinguishes it from other nuts. It is typically available whole, shelled and unshelled. The hard tan shell is sometimes dyed red when sold whole. The delicate but distinctive taste of pistachio is used in many desserts. It is also a favorite snacking nut.

Poppy Seeds ▶
Poppy seeds are tiny, round, black seeds of the poppy flower. They have a sweet, nutty flavor and are used primarily in baked goods.

◀ Sesame Seeds
These small, flat, oval seeds may be black or tan. Sesame seeds have a rich, nutty flavor and are widely used in baking.

▲ Walnut
A walnut has a hard, wrinkled shell enclosing a nut with two tender sections. Walnuts are oily, with a mild, sweet flavor. They are used in sweet and savory dishes and are also used in snacking. White walnuts, or butternuts, and black walnuts are North American varieties. Butternuts are richer tasting, and black walnuts are stronger tasting.

Toasting Nuts, Seeds, or Spices

1 **Shell** nuts or seeds.

2 **Add** to a dry, hot sauté pan.

3 **Stir** constantly.

4 **Toast** until aromatic and slightly brown.

5 **Transfer** to a cool bowl.

 **Reading Checkpoint** *How do you toast nuts, seeds, or spices?*

6.4 ASSESSMENT

Reviewing Concepts

1. What is a condiment? Give three examples.
2. How do you toast nuts, seeds, and spices?

Critical Thinking

3. **Communicating** Do you have a favorite condiment? Describe what flavor it adds to the dishes with which you normally use it.
4. **Comparing/Contrasting** Compare and contrast two nuts with which you are familiar in terms of their taste, texture, smell, and appearance.
5. **Recognizing Patterns** Explain why poppy seeds are discussed under the nuts category, fennel seeds are discussed under the spices category, and dill is discussed under the herb category.

Test Kitchen

Divide into four teams. Each team will use a small amount of one of the following untoasted nuts: almonds, pine nuts, sesame seeds, and pecans. Set aside half of the nuts and toast the remaining half. Compare the untoasted nuts with the toasted nuts. Taste the nuts from other teams. Individually evaluate each of the nuts (both toasted and untoasted), ranking them from most favorite to least favorite. Tally the results for the class.

SCIENCE

George Washington Carver

Research some of the culinary uses for peanuts suggested by George Washington Carver. Did he invent peanut butter? Were some of Carver's culinary uses of peanuts later produced commercially? How many of these culinary uses were patented by Carver? Write a report describing your findings?

Review and Assessment

Reviewing Content

Choose the letter that best answers the question or completes the statement.

1. What is umami?
    a. an herb
    b. a flavor
    c. a nut
    d. a spice

2. Which of the following is not included in a standard mirepoix?
    a. onions
    b. carrots
    c. green pepper
    d. celery

3. A condiment is a
    a. flavoring served on the side and added by the individual diner
    b. spice combination used in Italian soups and sauces
    c. spice combination used in Cajun cooking
    d. type of seasoning ingredient

4. When you say a cooked onion is translucent, you are saying that
    a. flavor from the onion has blended with other ingredients in a dish
    b. aroma from the onion has blended with other ingredients in a dish
    c. light passes through the cooked onion
    d. light does not pass through the cooked onion

5. Which of the following is not a reason chefs season foods?
    a. To change the food's flavor
    b. To cut richness
    c. To balance taste
    d. To enhance natural taste

6. In general, you can substitute how much of a dried herb for every tablespoon of fresh herbs called for in a recipe?
    a. 2 tablespoons
    b. 2 teaspoons
    c. 1 teaspoon
    d. ½ teaspoon

Understanding Concepts

7. What are the five tastes our tongue can distinguish?

8. What are the three reasons why chefs season food?

9. What are the four basic types of seasoning ingredients?

10. What is the meaning of opaque? Of translucent?

11. How does a sachet d'épices differ from a bouquet garni?

12. What is a condiment?

Critical Thinking

13. **Comparing/Contrasting** What is the difference between seasoning and flavoring?

14. **Comparing/Contrasting** What is the difference between a standard mirepoix and a white mirepoix?

Culinary Math

15. **Relating Concepts** A recipe that yields 10 servings calls for 3 tablespoons of fresh rosemary. You are scaling the recipe up to serve 40 people and you don't have any fresh rosemary. How much dried rosemary should you use?

16. **Relating Concepts** You are making a standard mirepoix for a large quantity of soup. The mirepoix will be cooked in the soup for a long time. The recipe calls for 40 ounces of onions. What other ingredients are required? How much of those ingredients will be needed? How should you cut the mirepoix ingredients?

On the Job

17. **Forming a Model** You are making a light, white-colored soup. The recipe calls for the addition of a mirepoix. What ingredients would you use in the mirepoix?

18. **Communicating** You cooked a well-seasoned and flavorful dish. It was presented to a diner who immediately requested ketchup to put on it. What should you do?

RECIPE CARDS

Use the following Recipe Cards to test your culinary skill.

1. Mirepoix

2. Sachet d'Epices

3. Bouquet Garni

LAB ACTIVITY

Project 6: Aromatic Combinations
Answer these questions when your class works through Project 6.

- Can you make your own aromatic combination of at least three herbs and spices?

- Do individual herbs and spices in an aromatic combination blend, or do they each retain their own flavor?

- In an aromatic combination, does one herb or spice seem to determine the overall taste?

- Do you associate a specific herb or spice with a specific cuisine?

- Do some herbs and spices taste bad on their own but much better in an aromatic combination?

- Do some herbs and spices taste good on their own but not as good in an aromatic combination?

TEST PRACTICE

Choose the letter that best answers the question or completes the statement.

1. What is the chemical name for salt?
   A sodium
   B sodium iodine
   C sodium chloride
   D potassium chloride

2. Which of the following is not true about monosodium glutamate?
   A It has a salty taste.
   B It is abbreviated as MSG.
   C It is not actually a salt.
   D It enhances a meaty or brothy taste.

3. Which herb has needle-shaped leaves?
   A sage
   B rosemary
   C oregano
   D thyme

4. Which spice is a root?
   A cumin
   B cinnamon
   C saffron
   D ginger

5. Which of the following ingredients would not be included in either a white mirepoix or a Cajun trinity?
   A carrots
   B green pepper
   C parsnips
   D leeks

6. What is another name for sesame paste?
   A umami
   B marjoram
   C chervil
   D tahini

7. What is the difference between a standard mirepoix and a matignon?
   A A matignon includes parsnips.
   B A matignon includes ham.
   C A standard mirepoix includes green peppers.
   D A standard mirepoix includes carrots.

8. Which type of salt is the least refined?
   A sea salt
   B table salt
   C monosodium glutamate
   D kosher salt

GETTING READY TO COOK

READING PREVIEW

Key Concepts

- Understanding mise en place
- Organizing your work
- Sequencing and simplifying work
- Setting up a workstation

Vocabulary

- assignment
- deadline
- mise en place
- setting priorities
- strategies
- tasks
- timeline
- work flow
- work sequencing
- work simplification

> **"Y**ou can tell a lot about the quality of a cook's work before the pan ever hits the fire, just by looking at their mise en place. **"**
>
> – Jonathan Zearfoss

Understanding Mise en Place

Mise en place (MEEZ AHN PLAHS) is a French phrase that means to put in place. Professional cooks and chefs use it to represent the activities they might perform to get themselves, their ingredients, and their equipment ready to start cooking. Mise en place can easily be thought of as a to-do list, but for a true professional, it is much more than that. A complete mise en place helps you determine not just what ingredients you need and what you need to do, but also when you need to do specific tasks, where you need to do the work (for instance, on the stove or at a work table), and how to go about getting everything done for a deadline.

Chefs consider a thorough and complete mise en place vital to their success. You can think of mise en place as a collection of good work habits. Developing good work habits takes concentration, effort, and practice. Once these good habits are established, however, mise en place has several important benefits. You'll be more organized and efficient. You'll be more confident about your work. Your work will have better quality.

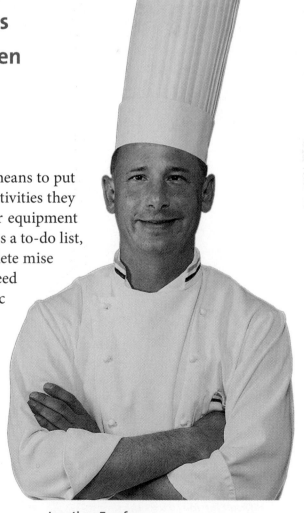

Jonathan Zearfoss
The Culinary Institute of America

Basic mise en place skills also include the cutting techniques necessary to prepare a variety of ingredients; the preparation of certain mixtures to season, flavor, or thicken foods; and some common cooking and mixing methods. More advanced mise en place skills include the ability to prioritize work so you are doing the right things at the right time.

 **Reading Checkpoint** *What is the translation of the French phrase "mise en place"?*

Organizing Your Work

Mise en place is ultimately a way to organize your work. When your work is organized, you make better use of your time. But the only way to be organized is to plan your work.

Planning Your Work Planning your work involves three initial steps:

▲ FIGURE 7-1
Planning Your Work
Taking the time to plan your mise en place is critical.
Applying Concepts *Would it be difficult for you to take the time in a busy kitchen to plan adequately?*

- **Determine Your Assignment.** To make a good plan, you first need to know your **assignment**, the food for which you will be responsible. For example, if you are the grill cook in a restaurant, you know you need to prepare all the grilled foods on the menu. This may include appetizers, main dishes, side dishes, and sometimes even desserts. Your assignment may be to prepare specific menu items. Or, your assignment may be to prepare basic ingredients used in different menu items. After receiving your assignment, read over the recipes for the items on which you will be working. You need to gain a basic idea of the recipes. (Use the PRN ("Preview, Read, Note") method for reading recipes from Chapter 5.) Pay attention to how long food needs to cook or cool and whether you need special equipment, such as a food processor or a slicer.

- **Prepare an Inventory.** After you are familiar with your assignment, your next step is to prepare a written inventory of what you have on hand. Then prepare a written inventory of the things you do not have on hand. The inventory should include ingredients, smallware, and equipment. The sooner you know about a missing ingredient or tool, the sooner you can get it and the less your work will be interrupted.

- **Break Your Assignment into Tasks.** Your next step is to break your assignment into written **tasks**, smaller jobs that lead to completion of your assignment. Tasks can be further broken down into smaller tasks.

Here's an example of the relationship of tasks to an assignment. Imagine you are catering a party. Making the lasagna is your assignment. Your major tasks include cooking the lasagna noodles, making tomato sauce, grating mozzarella cheese, preparing a ricotta cheese filling, and assembling the lasagna. You can break some of these major tasks into smaller tasks so you can organize your work more efficiently. For instance, to make the tomato sauce, you accomplish the minor tasks of chopping onions, garlic, and tomatoes.

Breaking your assignment into tasks also helps you fine-tune the list of equipment you need for each task. For example, to boil lasagna noodles, you'll need a big pot as well as a colander to drain the noodles.

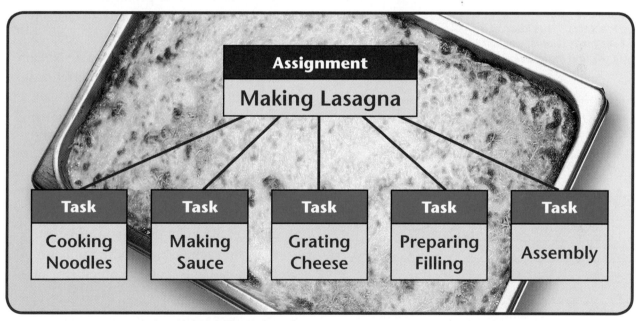

| Assignment |
| Making Lasagna |

| Task | Task | Task | Task | Task |
| Cooking Noodles | Making Sauce | Grating Cheese | Preparing Filling | Assembly |

To make the tomato sauce, you'll need a chef's knife, a cutting board, a saucepan or saucepot, and a mixing spoon. To make the filling, you'll need a bowl, measuring equipment, and a mixing spoon. To cook the lasagna, you'll need a baking dish and some aluminum foil. To serve the lasagna, you'll need a knife, plates, and a spatula.

Reviewing Your Lists One of the important benefits of good mise en place is that it allows you to work on more than one task at the same time. As you look over your major and minor tasks, you may notice that several recipes call for the same ingredient. If you add up what you need for all the recipes, you may find you can take one trip to the storeroom or refrigerator instead of making a separate trip for each task.

FIGURE 7-2
Breaking Down Tasks
A list of tasks for making lasagna.
Applying Concepts *What task would you complete first?*

As you review your list of tasks, you may notice that some tasks can be grouped together but that certain activities need to take place at certain times. Sometimes you need to pay close attention to something as it cooks. Other times, you can leave things to cook on their own. A big pot of water, for example, can take a long time to come to a boil, but you certainly don't need to watch it until it boils. Once you have the water on the heat, you can start another task.

Making a Timeline A **timeline** is a schedule that tells you when certain tasks have to be completed. The beginning of your timeline is the time you start working. The end of your timeline is the time your work has to be completed. The completion time is your **deadline**. You fill in the timeline by working backwards from your deadline to decide when other tasks need to be finished.

A timeline requires you to:

- Create a list of tasks for which you are responsible.
- Know roughly how long it takes you to perform the tasks.
- Know how long it takes to cook the food (the recipe usually provides this).
- Know how long to cool or rest a dish before it can be eaten (again the recipe often will tell you this).
- Know how long you can hold food or a prepared item before it begins to lose quality.

To determine a timeline, follow these steps:

1. **Review your recipes.** Make a list of all the steps involved in preparing a complete mise en place. Jot down your time estimate for each task, including time to collect ingredients, collect equipment, and clean.

2. **Combine tasks.** Look for every recipe that calls for chopped garlic and add together the amounts you need.

3. **Assign a deadline for each task.** If you are a lunch cook, all the items you are responsible for preparing must be finished before the dining room opens its doors at 11:30. You can work backward from your deadline to determine your work schedule. Certain tasks must be finished before you can start certain other tasks.

FIGURE 7-3
Timeline
Your deadline is 7:00.
Solving Problems *If the lasagna has to bake for 1½ hours, when do you need to put it in the oven?*

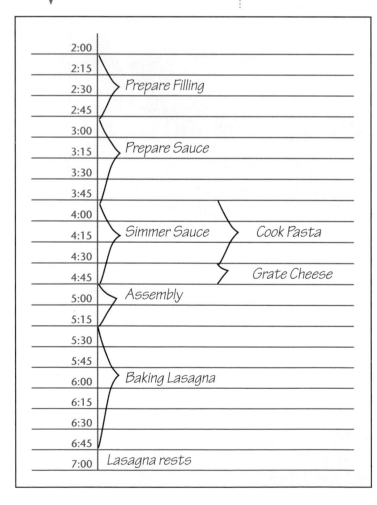

2:00	
2:15	
2:30	Prepare Filling
2:45	
3:00	
3:15	Prepare Sauce
3:30	
3:45	
4:00	
4:15	Simmer Sauce Cook Pasta
4:30	
4:45	Grate Cheese
5:00	Assembly
5:15	
5:30	
5:45	
6:00	Baking Lasagna
6:15	
6:30	
6:45	
7:00	Lasagna rests

4. **Prioritize the work.** Once you know when something must be completed, you can begin to prioritize tasks so you do them in the most efficient sequence.

Let's say it is 2:00 in the afternoon. You are serving lasagna at 7:00 this evening. Your recipe says it takes 1½ hours to bake the lasagna. It also says you should let the lasagna sit for 15 minutes before you serve it. That means on your timeline, the lasagna comes out of the oven at 6:45. It goes into the oven at 5:15. Assume it takes you 30 minutes to fill the pans. That means the noodles, sauce, filling, and cheese must be ready to use by 4:45. So you have 2½ hours to get all those items ready.

CULINARY MATH

Personalizing a Timeline

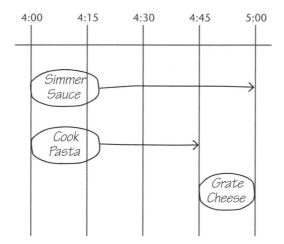

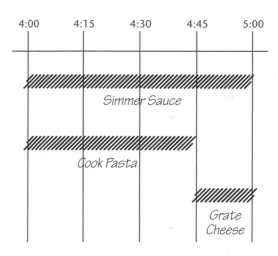

▲ *Portions of two sample timelines*

Not everyone interprets information in the same way. This is true with timelines. Figure 7-3 shows a timeline charted against a table that is broken down in 15-minute time periods. Does this make the most sense to you? Does it adequately show the starting and ending times for the various major and minor tasks involved in the preparation of this dish? Does it show which tasks are going on at the same time?

Experiment

Using the data in Figure 7-3, construct a timeline that shows all the major and minor tasks for the lasagna being prepared. Try to make the timeline as useful for yourself as you possibly can. You don't have to use the table format shown in Figure 7-3. You can use multiple colors, brackets, balloons—anything that makes your timeline helpful and understandable for you. Compare your timeline with classmates' timelines.

Setting Priorities Mise en place means that you work efficiently so everything is done at the right time. To accomplish this goal, you need to decide which tasks are the most important. This is referred to as **setting priorities**. Those tasks that are important are given a higher priority; those that are less important have a lower priority. You need to think about your timeline as you set priorities.

One type of high-priority task is any task you need to get finished before you can start another task. Another type of high-priority task is one that takes a long time to finish. A low-priority task is one that does not have a relationship to another task and that does not involve a great deal of time. You could do this type of task at any point in your timeline and still make your deadline.

Here's how to think about priorities. You need to make the lasagna sauce and filling, grate the cheese, and cook the noodles in 2½ hours. For your first priority, you decide to start the task that takes the longest time—making the sauce. Short tasks, such as grating the cheese, can be done last, or you can fit them in while the sauce simmers or the pasta water comes to a boil.

Problem-Solving Strategies A good mise en place is one that includes **strategies,** the skills and techniques you will use to get the job done. One of the most basic of all strategies is having a written plan. If you write down your plan, you can use it throughout the day as a reminder. A strategy for getting everything ready on time is to make a timeline. A strategy for working on more than one thing at a time is to prioritize tasks.

A strategy for coping with the unexpected is equally important. Just like the other strategies, problem-solving strategies are something you can learn with practice. No matter how good your written plan, however, there is a good chance something unexpected will happen. There might be a power outage. Someone might fail to show up for work. The delivery truck might be delayed. The pan you like to use for your tomato sauce might be in use somewhere else in the kitchen. When you are faced with these kinds of problems, you need to adjust your plan. Coping with the unexpected can be the best way to learn a new skill or might lead to a better way to do something.

 **Reading Checkpoint** *How do you prepare a timeline?*

Sequencing and Simplifying Work

Work Sequencing An important aspect of mise en place is **work sequencing**. Work sequencing means doing the right thing at the right time. When you make a timeline and set priorities for individual tasks, you can use that information to create a work sequence. If your work is properly organized, or sequenced, you don't have to stop and wait for something while you are in the middle of preparing a recipe or serving a dish. As you think about your work sequence, look for the following:

- Dishes that can cook without being watched constantly
- Dishes that need a long time to prepare

- Tasks that can be interrupted or completed in a short time
- Tasks that cannot be interrupted or dishes that require constant attention as they cook

Foods that need a long time to chill, brown, come to a boil, or marinate need to be taken care of early in the day. While they are chilling, cooking, or marinating, you can do something else. You could perform tasks that take a short time or that can be interrupted while you take a few minutes to do something else. Ingredients that stay fresh or flavorful for only a short period, such as minced herbs or sliced tomatoes, should be cut or prepared as close as possible to the time you plan to serve the dish containing that ingredient.

Simplifying Work Work simplification means that you get things done in the fewest steps, the shortest amount of time, and with the least amount of waste. Chopping all the garlic you need at once, rather than chopping garlic for each individual recipe, is an example of work simplification. One of the most important ways you can simplify your work is by learning which tool can do a specific task most easily.

You can find plenty of ways to save time as you work, if you look for them. The less time you have to spend walking from one place to another, the more time you'll have to get your work done. For example, if you need to get a pot to cook some potatoes, remembering to pick up a colander to drain the potatoes at the same time will save you steps. Try to get as many things accomplished on a single trip as you safely can.

 **Reading Checkpoint** *What is work sequencing?*

Setting Up a Workstation

Your workstation is the place in the kitchen where you gather together the tools and ingredients you need to prepare your mise en place, cook, or serve foods. When you set up your workstation properly, you should not have to leave the area while you work. You should use your mise en place lists as reminders so you don't have to make several trips to get what you need or retrieve something you forgot.

FIGURE 7-4
Last-Minute Preparation
Fresh ingredients stay flavorful for only a short period of time.
Drawing Conclusions *Should your timeline reflect the time needed to prepare fresh ingredients at the last minute?*

FIGURE 7-5
Work Flow
Arrange your work in an orderly sequence.
Predicting *How can organizing your work logically help you work faster?*

The way you set up a workstation depends on the type of work you need to do. You need different tools and ingredients while you are preparing your mise en place than you will when you are preparing foods to serve. You need holding containers when you are preparing foods, pots and pans while you cook, and plates when you serve. You may also need a variety of hand tools, such as spoons, whisks, spatulas, peelers, or ladles.

Once you have all the ingredients, tools, and equipment you need, take the time to arrange them so they are easy to reach as you work. You should also try to put them into a logical order. This order is known as the **work flow** for a specific task. For example, if you are peeling and chopping onions, you might put all the unpeeled onions in a bucket on the left side of your workstation. Next to the bucket, you might place a cutting board. You might put a container to hold the peels above your cutting board and a container to hold the peeled onions to the right of the board.

 **Reading Checkpoint** *How do you set up a work flow for a specific task?*

7.1 ASSESSMENT

Reviewing Concepts

1. What is mise en place?
2. What are the three initial steps involved in planning kitchen work?
3. What is work sequencing?
4. How do you set up a work flow for a specific task?

Critical Thinking

5. **Drawing Conclusions** Why would chefs think that a thorough and complete mise en place is vital to their success?
6. **Inferring** One of the benefits of good mise en place is that it allows you to work on more than one task at a time. Why is that important?
7. **Solving Problems** You have a number of small tasks that all have to be done at the same time. How would you indicate them on your timeline?

Test Kitchen

Pick a recipe that uses at least six ingredients and that can be completed in less than eight hours. Prepare an inventory based on the ingredients available in your school's kitchen, break your recipe into major and minor tasks, and then construct a timeline to plan your cooking.

SCIENCE

The Critical Path

In the 1950s, various companies and the Federal Government developed the Critical Path Method, a method for managing projects. It shows which activities are critical to maintaining a schedule. Research the Critical Path Method. Describe who developed it and when, and how it relates to preparing a timeline.

Learning to Work Together

READING PREVIEW

Key Concepts

- Communicating effectively
- Receiving and giving criticism
- Using feedback effectively
- Maintaining courteous and professional communications

Vocabulary

- effective criticism
- feedback
- nonverbal feedback
- verbal feedback

> **"T**hinking like a team and working like a team is the only way to succeed in the restaurant business. **"**
>
> – Gregory Zifchak

Communicating Effectively

No matter how small a restaurant's staff may be, it is crucial for everyone to be able to share information. When information goes both from others to you and from you to others, you are communicating. Effective communication means more than simply talking. It also involves the three elements of effective communication: listening, asking questions, and using the language of the kitchen.

Listening The first rule of effective communication is to listen to what others are saying to you. When you listen to someone, give that person your full attention. Look directly at the person as he or she talks. To be sure you correctly heard what was said, repeat what you heard. Many kitchens have a policy of "echoing" or "parroting." This means that you always acknowledge an order from the chef by saying, "Yes, chef," and repeating the order.

Asking Questions Always ask for more information or an explanation if you aren't completely sure what you've been asked to do. When you ask a question, make it as specific as you can.

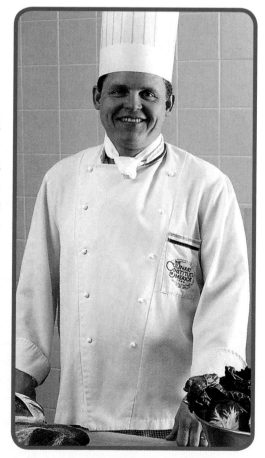

Gregory Zifchak
The Culinary Institute of America

▲
FIGURE 7-6
Listening Skills
Give your full attention when listening.
Inferring *Is the waitstaff in the picture giving the chef their complete attention?*

Pay close attention to the answer and be certain you understand it. If you hear words you don't understand or if you aren't sure about where something is located or when something needs to be done, ask for more information.

A good way to make sure you remember the answers to your questions is to jot down a few notes to remind yourself about them. Keep a small notebook and a pen or pencil with you so you can write notes or look back over old notes you've already written.

The Language of the Kitchen Learning to use the language of the culinary profession is an important start. Throughout this book, you will be introduced to the terms professionals use, including the proper names for techniques, preparations, and equipment. Using these terms properly helps you communicate with others effectively and efficiently.

✓ **Reading Checkpoint** *Name three elements of effective communication in the kitchen.*

Receiving and Giving Criticism

No matter how much experience you have or how long you have been working in a professional kitchen, you can learn a great deal from a specific type of communication known as criticism. Criticism, in this sense, is not used in the standard way we often see it used—as a type of personal attack. **Effective criticism** not only points out what went wrong or where things could be better, but also indicates how you can improve.

Receiving Criticism When you are on the receiving end of criticism, you may feel uncomfortable or even angry, regardless of how carefully the person criticizing you is speaking. Keep in mind that the point of criticism in the workplace is to make your work better.

Remember to listen carefully to criticism. Use basic listening skills when you are receiving criticism. Ask questions if you are not sure what the criticism means or why it is directed at you. Give yourself a chance to think about the criticism before you respond.

Giving Criticism Giving effective criticism to someone else is an important part of working with others. For criticism to be effective, you need to give it carefully.

Try not to criticize someone when you are feeling angry or frustrated. Find a quiet time and place where you won't be disturbed. Stay calm and keep your voice and your temper even. Avoid using negative terms or using words that might sound as though you are making a personal attack on someone.

Keep your criticism focused on specifics. One way to be sure your criticism doesn't turn into a personal attack is to think about the exact changes you want to see and then to clearly state improvements that need to be made.

Effective Criticism

Receiving Criticism	Giving Criticism
Remember criticism's purpose is to make your work better.	Stay calm; don't criticize when angry or frustrated.
Listen carefully.	Avoid negative terms.
Ask questions if you don't understand.	Focus on specifics.
Think before you respond.	Clearly state what improvements are required.

 **Reading Checkpoint** *What is effective criticism?*

Using Feedback Effectively

Feedback is a review of your work. You can get feedback from many different sources and in many different ways. Your co-workers, your boss, and your customers all give you feedback.

Some forms of feedback are spoken; this is referred to as **verbal feedback**. Other forms of feedback are not spoken; this is referred to as **nonverbal feedback**. However, just because feedback isn't said out loud doesn't mean it is not important. Be aware of things around you, such as the facial expressions and body posture of your co-workers, your customers, or your boss and whether plates are empty or full when they come back from the dining room.

Compliments and Complaints One form of feedback comes in the form of compliments or complaints. A compliment tells you that you are doing something correctly. A complaint tells you that you are doing something incorrectly. Both complaints and compliments are personal opinions, of course, but that does not mean you shouldn't pay attention to them.

FIGURE 7-7
Feedback
This communication features both verbal and nonverbal feedback.
Interpreting Illustrations *What kinds of nonverbal feedback do you see in this picture?*

Taking Action When you receive either a compliment or a complaint, you can use it to improve the quality of your work. A compliment is always pleasant, but you can do more with it than simply feel good about yourself. Think about what you did to earn the compliment so you can repeat it. Beyond that, you should also consider the ways you could make your work even better.

A complaint should rarely be ignored. Be honest with yourself about why someone might have made the complaint. Then you can make a change and improve.

 **Reading Checkpoint** *What are the two types of feedback?*

CULINARY HISTORY

The Vatel Society

Chefs, cooks, and other food-service professionals around the world have formed organizations honoring François Vatel (FRAN-swah vah-TEL), the seventeenth century chef to the Prince of Condé (con-DEH) in Chantilly, France.

In April 1671, the Prince of Condé was to have a three-day visit from the Sun King (Louis the 14th). Etiquette demanded that the King and his followers should receive the finest hospitality, which would cost a huge amount of money. But the prince was bankrupt!

Vatel understood how crucial this visit was. He believed that if he managed the visit well, the prince might yet emerge from his financial troubles. So Vatel negotiated with the suppliers for ingredients and planned wonderful banquets and entertainment.

According to letters written at the time, the King was completely charmed. But there were a few problems. A fireworks display failed. There were not enough roasts for every table, so Vatel supplemented the meat with mushrooms. When there were problems with a custard sauce planned for dessert, Vatel substituted whipped cream. The cream was so popular, it became known as "Chantilly cream" and still is served to this day.

▲ *Chantilly cream being applied to a cake.*

Vatel planned a final banquet that featured fish. On the morning of the banquet, he woke at 4:00 to discover only two small deliveries of fish had been made. Vatel believed his honor, and the honor of his prince, had been damaged beyond repair. He was found dead a few hours later when a servant came to tell him the rest of the fish had arrived.

Research

Research the history of François Vatel. Would effective communication have helped Vatel know when the fish deliveries were due?

Courtesy and Professionalism

Courtesy is the way you show respect for others. Professionalism is the way you show respect for your work.

Courteous Behavior in the Kitchen The kitchen can be a busy and dangerous place to work. The respect you show to others is one of the ways to make your work easier and more efficient. Some simple acts of courtesy include making eye contact, cleaning up after yourself, and offering help to others when they need it. Courteous behavior is usually repaid by courteous behavior. If you treat your co-workers with respect, you can expect similar behavior in return.

Professionalism Courtesy is an important part of professionalism. Professionalism also means that you are maintaining standards for your work and for your behavior. Professionals are concerned with a working environment that does not discriminate against others because of the way they look. They show their professionalism by using products and equipment safely and avoiding waste. They are fair with others and direct in their communications.

 **Reading Checkpoint** *What are some of the simple acts of courtesy you should perform in the kitchen?*

7.2 ASSESSMENT

Reviewing Concepts

1. What are the three elements of effective communication in the kitchen?
2. How do you receive criticism effectively? Give criticism effectively?
3. What are the two types of feedback?
4. List three acts of kitchen courtesy.

Critical Thinking

5. **Inferring** Why is it important to listen carefully in the kitchen?
6. **Drawing Conclusions** Why should criticism be focused on specifics?
7. **Inferring** Aside from being courteous, is there another reason you should offer to help someone who needs it, if possible?

Test Kitchen

Have a class volunteer write down an order for eight main courses, with special instructions, and eight sides (an example: a hamburger, medium rare, with ketchup and pickle, no mayonnaise, and cole slaw). In a separate room, or out of hearing from the rest of the class, have a class member listen to the order by using effective listening skills. Continue passing the order from one class member to the next, always out of hearing from the remainder of the class. Compare the order as heard by the last class member to the order as it was originally given. Were there differences?

LANGUAGE ARTS

The Language of the Kitchen

Where would you look for unfamiliar words you encountered in the kitchen? The best approach is to use a dictionary or encyclopedia for culinary arts, cooking, or food. Write a report on the available culinary dictionaries or encyclopedias.

> "**G**ood cooking doesn't stop at the pan. You have to feed your guest through the eye first, so your presentation skills are very much part of your total culinary skill set. "
> – Russell Scott

Russell Scott
The Culinary Institute of America

Presenting Foods

Just as you need a good mise en place to get ready to prepare and cook foods, you also need a good mise en place before you can serve foods to guests. Presenting foods beautifully is a way to entice guests before they even take a single bite.

Basic Guidelines When guests sit down in a restaurant for a meal, they expect that the food will arrive in a reasonable amount of time, that it will be the food they ordered, that it will be at the right temperature, and that it will taste good. The way you put food into a dish or on a plate is referred to as your **plate presentation.** It is one way you can be sure the food gets to the table tasting and looking the way it should. There are three basic rules for plate presentation:

- Hot foods hot, cold foods cold.
- Plates neat, with no drips or smudges.
- Food attractive and appealing.

Basic Mise en Place for Service To prepare your mise en place for service, think about how food will arrive at the table. Then, gather the items you need and arrange them in the area where you will be serving food. Everything should be clean, neatly organized, and within easy reach.

You need plates to serve most entrees and appetizers. You need bowls or cups to serve a soup, stew, or chili. To serve foods on a buffet line, you need hotel pans. For a reception, you may need platters or trays. Some dishes call for a sauce or condiments served in a cup or bowl. All this smallware needs to be on hand and in easy reach.

You usually need hand tools to lift food onto a plate. Ladles or spoons are used for liquid food such as sauces. Salads are often served with tongs or scoops. Sandwiches and other foods that are put together by hand call for food-handling gloves. Gather enough hand tools to last until you are finished serving food. Some foods are ready to serve as they come from the pan. Others may need to be sliced, cut, scooped, or arranged. You may use a variety of hand tools in addition to spoons and tongs. Carving knives (as well as carving forks, cutting boards, and a steel) should be part of your mise en place if you need to cut slices of food. Learning to use any specialized tools for presentation is a fundamental part of your mise en place for food presentation.

Finally, put a container of hot water and paper toweling on your workstation so you can clean the rims of plates, if necessary. Use towels once, and then throw them away.

Reading Checkpoint — *What are the three basic rules for plate presentation?*

Portioning Foods

Portioning foods properly means serving the correct amount of a particular food. A portion of food is the same thing as a serving of food when it comes to putting food on a plate to serve a guest. Portion sizes can vary from one restaurant to another and from one food to another. Portion sizes for the same food should never vary at the same restaurant, however. This is especially true when the same food is being served to more than one guest sitting at the same table.

Importance of Portioning One of the complaints you may hear about a restaurant is that the portion size changes from day to day. This might make guests feel they are being overcharged. Consistent portioning makes your guests feel confident they are paying a fair price.

Serving the right amount of food every time you serve it is important for several reasons. Proper portioning makes it easier to plan your work. You can also reduce the amount of food that is wasted.

The key to portioning food is measuring the portion accurately by using the appropriate tools.

Tools for Portioning As you assemble your mise en place for service, remember to include the appropriate tools for portioning food. Ladles and scoops have already been mentioned as part of your mise en place for presenting food. They are also used to measure out portions. With a portion scale, you can measure out consistent portions of sliced meats or poultry. To select the right tool for a portioning job, you need to know what you are serving and what the proper portion size is for that food.

You can also think of the plates, bowls, cups, or hotel pans you use to serve food as a kind of portioning tool. To select the right serving pieces for a dish, you need to know how the correct portion ought to look when it is served on your plates. For instance, your kitchen may serve eight ounces of soup instead of six because six ounces of soup looks skimpy in your restaurant's soup bowls.

▲
FIGURE 7-8
Portioning Ice Cream
Each scoop of ice cream should be very close to the same size.
Predicting *How would you feel as a customer if your scoops were different sizes?*

 **Reading Checkpoint** *Name several portioning tools you can use during service.*

Temperature

You need to cook and cool food to safe temperatures. You also need to serve food at the temperature that lets your guests most fully enjoy it. Chefs use a number of techniques and tools to get foods to the best temperature for service.

Keeping Foods at the Best Temperature Hot foods should be at least 135°F. If you are serving a food as soon as it comes from the oven, grill, or pan, it will already be hot enough. If you prepare a food ahead of time, you may keep it warm in a steam table. Some foods are kept warm in a low oven. Set the temperature of the oven or steam table to at least 135° and keep an instant-read thermometer on hand to check the food's temperature periodically.

Cold foods should be below 41°F, frozen foods below 32°F. Some foods, such as cheese, are most enjoyable when they are only slightly chilled or are at room temperature. These foods are held in the refrigerator, but before they are served, they should sit at room temperature long enough to lose their chill. Frozen foods, such as ice cream or sherbet, can be transferred to the refrigerator to soften slightly so they have a better consistency and a fuller flavor.

Plates If you put hot soup in a cold soup bowl, the bowl will warm up and the soup will cool down. If you put a cold salad on a hot plate, the plate will cool down and the salad will warm up. To keep foods at the best temperature for service on their way from the kitchen to the table, warm or chill the plates before putting food on them.

Heat plates by arranging them in a place where they will be warm, such as near the stove or under a heat lamp. Have clean side towels on hand to hold the hot plates safely. Chill plates for cold dishes by stacking them in a refrigerator or other cool place.

 **Reading Checkpoint** *How does the temperature of a plate affect the temperature of the food served on it?*

FOCUS ON SAFETY

Check the Temperature
Even though equipment such as steam tables and soup warmers often have dials to control temperature, the dials are not always accurate. Don't rely on the equipment's temperature setting. Use an accurate instant-read thermometer to check food.

Textures, Colors, and Shapes

When you cook food, you change not only its flavor but also its texture, color, and shape. Some cooking techniques make food firm or crunchy. Others make food soft and tender. Some techniques change food from a pale color to a deep brown. Some food takes on a distinct and recognizable shape. You can highlight all these changes when you present a plate to a guest.

Texture Keeping hot food crisp generally means keeping it dry by holding it in uncovered pans. A rack keeps even the bottom of each piece dry and properly crunchy. Keep the food warm, but not so hot it starts to dry out. Usually a temperature of around 160°F is best.

The way you combine food on a plate is another way you can maintain or even improve its texture. A few crackers add a crunchy texture to a bowl of soup. Serving smooth sauces over food makes it more tender. Putting a sauce under crispy food keeps it from becoming soggy.

To keep cold food crisp, hold it in covered containers or well wrapped in the refrigerator. The covering keeps moisture in the food so it doesn't wilt, soften, or dry out. The cold temperature keeps it firm.

Food such as soups, sauces, or stews can develop a skin on the surface. To prevent a skin from forming, keep the food covered or topped with a little butter or oil. Skim off the skin or any fat that rises to the surface before you serve the food.

▲
FIGURE 7-9
Keeping Foods Crisp
Putting a sauce under food keeps crispy food crispy.
Predicting *What would happen had you poured the sauce over this dish?*

Color on the Plate

Including colorful green, white, yellow, orange, and red vegetables adds more than color to a plate. It improves the nutritional value of the dish and adds additional textures and shapes to the plate.

Colors   To get the right color in a food, you need to cook it properly. Recipes instruct you to cook foods until they change color. Each dish has a color that tells you it is properly cooked. Once you've achieved that color, you need to serve the dish before the color starts to change.

When every food on the plate is the same color, the plate can look boring. Adding a few bright colors makes the plate more interesting and attractive. If everything on a plate is brown or white, you could add a vegetable with a bright green color for contrast.

Shapes and Arrangements   The purpose of shaping and arranging foods before you serve them is to make them look more appealing. In some cases, the size and shape of the food you are putting on the plate can even help you determine what size and shape your plate should be. In other cases, the size and shape of your plate might determine the size and shape of the food you are serving. The color of the plate, the size of the border or rim on the plate, and any design or texture on the plate is part of your presentation.

To give shape to semi-soft foods, you can scoop or spoon them. Another option is to use a mold.

When you cut foods into a particular size or shape, your tools must be sharp so you make neat, straight cuts. Foods cook more evenly and have a better texture when you cut them properly, and they also look much more attractive.

Some foods look more attractive on one side than they do on the other. The good-looking side, referred to as the **presentation side**, should always be facing up so guests see it.

Arrange food neatly on the plate. A little open space around food allows guests to see and taste food separately. Putting foods right next

---

BASIC CULINARY SKILLS

Using Molds to Shape Foods

1. Fill the mold.
2. Press food into the mold lightly, using the back of a spoon.
3. Put a plate on top the mold. The plate should be upside down.
4. Turn the mold and plate over. The plate should be right side up and the mold should be upside down on the plate.
5. Tap the mold and lift it from the food.

to each other or on top of each other blends them together (which, of course, for some dishes is desirable).

By arranging foods in different ways, you can also create different effects. For example, to make a piece of meat or fish look larger, you can slice it and spread the slices in a fan shape. When the food covers more of the plate, it looks like a bigger portion. You can also put something under a food to lift it up. Height is another way to change the appearance of a food.

Plates can be arranged so they are either symmetrical or asymmetrical. To make a symmetrical arrangement, imagine a line running through the center of the plate. If you have equal numbers of items placed on both sides of the plate, the arrangement is **symmetrical** (sym-MET-rih-cull). If you have unequal numbers of items on either side of the plate, the arrangement is **asymmetrical** (AY-sym-met-rih-cull).

FIGURE 7-10
Symmetrical Arrangement
Arranging food symmetrically on a plate.
Classifying *Would an asymmetrical arrangement be as pleasing to the eye?*

 **Reading Checkpoint** *What is a symmetrical arrangement? An asymmetrical arrangement?*

7.3 ASSESSMENT

Reviewing Concepts

1. What are the three basic rules for plate presentation?
2. Name two types of portioning tools you can use during service.
3. How does the temperature of a plate affect the temperature of the food served on it?
4. What is a symmetrical plate arrangement?

Critical Thinking

5. **Drawing Conclusions** Why is it important to be concerned with the way food is presented?
6. **Inferring** Why might a kitchen choose to avoid putting sauce over the presentation side, choosing instead to put the sauce under the item?
7. **Relating Concepts** What kinds of plated food might be most suitable for a symmetrical arrangement? What kinds of food might be more suited for an asymmetrical arrangement?

Test Kitchen

Divide into groups of two. Using the same main course, each group will create a plate presentation. Groups can use different sides, sauces, garnishes, or anything available in the kitchen and available to the other groups. When all plates have been presented, discuss the presentations and vote on the most appealing one.

SOCIAL STUDIES

China Dishware

Research the origins of the word "China" as it applies to china dishware. How long has it been made? How is it made? Are there differences in quality in this type of dishware? Is dishware of this sort made today?

Review and Assessment

Reviewing Content

Choose the letter that best answers the question or completes the statement.

1. Which of the following is not one of the initial steps involved in planning kitchen work?

     a. determine your assignment
     b. develop strategies
     c. prepare an inventory
     d. break your assignment into tasks

2. Work sequencing means

     a. doing the right thing at the right time
     b. doing all cooking at one time
     c. arranging tools in a logical order
     d. getting things done in as few steps as possible

3. Which of the following is not true about receiving criticism?

     a. You should remember the purpose of criticism.
     b. You should ask questions.
     c. You should listen carefully.
     d. You should respond immediately.

4. Plate presentation is

     a. the presentation of an empty plate to be filled in the kitchen
     b. the final presentation to the chef before the dish is served to the customer
     c. the way you put food into a dish or on a plate
     d. the presentation of an empty plate to be filled on a buffet line

5. Which of the following is not a tool used for portioning?

     a. ladles
     b. knives
     c. scoops
     d. portion scale

6. Hot foods should be at least what temperature?

     a. 115°F
     b. 125°F
     c. 135°F
     d. 145°F

Understanding Concepts

7. What is an asymmetrical plate arrangement?

8. What is mise en place?

9. What does it mean to portion food?

10. What is the presentation side of a prepared food?

11. What is the beginning and end of a timeline?

Critical Thinking

12. **Applying Concepts** Why is it important to prepare an inventory of both the ingredients you have and the ingredients you do not have?

13. **Drawing Conclusions** Why are timelines, setting priorities, and sequencing work important concepts for everyone working in a kitchen?

Culinary Math

14. **Solving Problems** You are using a 4-oz ladle for portioning chili. You have 1½ gallons of chili. How many portions do you have?

15. **Applying Concepts** One of your dishes requires 2 oz of an ingredient; another of your dishes requires 4 oz of the same ingredient. You expect to prepare about 45 of the first dish but only 25 of the second dish. To simplify your work, you want to make only one trip to cold storage, where the ingredient is kept. How much of the ingredient should you take from cold storage?

On the Job

16. **Applying Concepts** Can you apply the concept of mise en place to everyday living? Explain your answer.

17. **Communicating** A dish wasn't ready when it should have been and caused a problem. It wasn't your fault, but the chef was frustrated and criticized you. What should you do?

LAB ACTIVITY

Project 7: Mise en Place

Answer these questions when your class works through Project 7.

- Can you break the assignment into tasks? The major tasks into minor tasks?

- How many of the ingredients did your school kitchen have on hand? Were any ingredients missing?

- Were all the smallware, hand tools, and equipment for the assignment on hand?

- Did you work out a timeline that made sense? How did your timeline compare with those of other class members?

- What does it feel like to do the mise en place for just one dish? Are you more confident or less confident about preparing the dish?

- What would it be like to do mise en place for four or five dishes all being prepared at the same time?

TEST PRACTICE

Choose the letter that best answers the question or completes the statement.

1. The literal translation of the French term mise en place is
   A   to listen carefully
   B   to place on a dish or plate
   C   to put in place
   D   to work smart

2. A timeline starts when you start working and ends at your
   A   assignment
   B   deadline
   C   task
   D   mise en place

3. Doing the right thing at the right time is
   A   work sequencing
   B   mise en place
   C   work simplification
   D   work flow

4. Which of the following is not a basic rule for plate presentation?
   A   Hot foods hot, cold foods cold.
   B   Plates neat, with no drips or smudges.
   C   Food attractive and appealing.
   D   Foods not touching.

5. Which of the following is not true?
   A   Portion sizes should not vary from food to food at a restaurant.
   B   Portion sizes often vary from one restaurant to another.
   C   Portion sizes for the same food should never vary at the same restaurant.
   D   Consistent portioning makes your guests feel confident about the price.

6. Below what temperature should cold foods be served?
   A   49°F
   B   41°F
   C   35°F
   D   32°F

7. Keeping hot foods crisp generally means keeping them
   A   dry
   B   hot
   C   moist
   D   covered

8. If you have an unequal number of items on either side of the plate, the arrangement is
   A   unprofessional
   B   bad presentation
   C   asymmetrical
   D   symmetrical

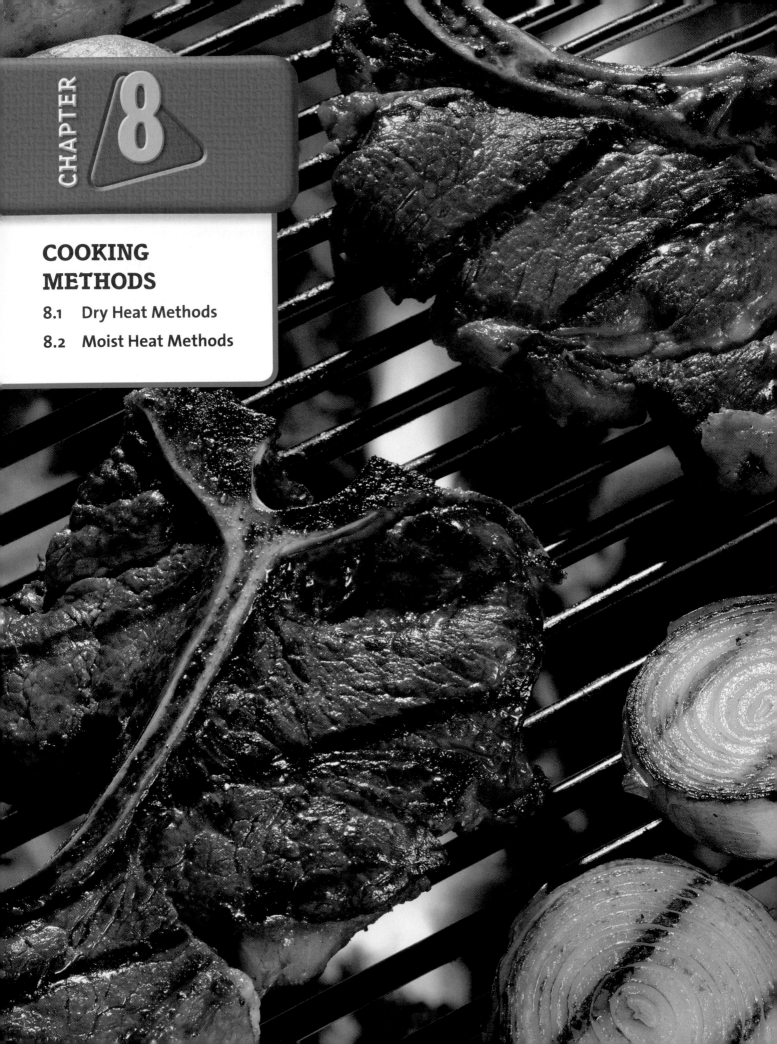

COOKING METHODS

8.1 Dry Heat Methods

8.2 Moist Heat Methods

8.1 Dry Heat Methods

READING PREVIEW

Key Concepts

- Understanding how dry heat affects food
- Identifying and using a variety of dry heat methods
- Determining doneness in foods prepared by dry heat methods

Vocabulary

- baking
- batter
- broiling
- caramelize
- carryover cooking
- conditioning the pan
- deep frying
- dry sautéing
- grilling
- Maillard reaction
- nutritive value
- pan broiling
- pan frying
- radiant heat
- recovery time
- roasting
- sautéing
- searing
- smothering
- standard breading
- stir frying
- sweating
- water bath

> **"I**s there any greater challenge than producing the perfect grill or barbecue? It must have a crust that gleams and crackles, an interior that is perfectly tender and moist, and a flavor that demands attention. **"**
>
> – Chris Schlesinger
> Owner, East Coast Grill & Raw Bar, Cambridge, MA
> Author, *License to Grill* and *Let the Flames Begin*

How Dry Heat Affects Foods

Any cooking method changes the way food looks and tastes. It also changes the nutrition food provides when we eat it.

Methods of Heat Transfer In the dry heat methods, heat is transferred, or conducted, to the food in one of the following ways:

- By rays that come from a glowing, or red hot, heat source such as burning coals, flames, or a hot electric element; this type of heat transfer is called **radiant** (RAY-dee-uhnt) **heat**
- By metal that conducts heat from a burner to the food
- By oil that is heated when a pan transfers heat from the burner to the oil

Changes to Food When you cook food by using a dry heat cooking method, you can see, feel, and taste the changes in food. Another important change is not so easy to detect. These are changes to the food's nutritional value. These four changes—to the food's color, texture, flavor, and nutritional value—may be minimal or dramatic, depending on the food you are preparing and the technique you choose.

The heat source in these methods causes the outside of the food to dry out as it cooks. When the surface is dry, it changes color. Often foods prepared by using dry heat methods have a golden or deep brown color. As foods brown, the flavor on the outside becomes more intense. The color on the inside of the food also changes as you cook, although not as dramatically as the outside.

Food that contains sugar changes colors when sugars on the surface start to turn brown, or **caramelize** (CAR-muh-lyze), when they get hot enough. Protein-rich foods, such as meats, also become brown as they cook. When proteins turn brown as they cook, it is referred to as the **Maillard** (MY-yard) **reaction**.

When the heat comes in contact with the surface of food, the outer layer of the food stiffens. Sometimes you can see and feel a distinct crust. The crispy skin on a roasted chicken, the crunchy breading on a piece of deep-fried fish, and the crisp outer layer of a French fry are all examples of how dry heat methods change the texture of a food. Eggs, meats, fish, and poultry all become firm as they cook. Other food may become softer. Onions, for instance, change from a crisp texture to a very soft, almost melting texture.

Maintaining Moisture in Food When you prepare food for dry cooking, you can take steps to combat the drying effect of the heat. For example, you could dust food with flour to help it stay dry as it cooks. Food such as meat or vegetables that you plan to grill or broil could be soaked in oil, flavorful liquids, aromatics, herbs, and spices before cooking to add moisture. You could also coat food in a batter or breading before frying it. One of the best ways to maintain moisture in food is to avoid overcooking it.

▲
FIGURE 8-1
Caramelizing Food
Cooking onions until their sugar caramelizes, turning a golden brown.
Predicting *If the onions are caramelized on the outside, does that mean their insides are cooked?*

Nutritional Value The carbohydrates, proteins, and fats in food supply us with energy. However, food also provides other things, such as vitamins and minerals, that we need to stay healthy. When you consider all the benefits food might have for our bodies, you are talking about food's nutritional value, which is also referred to as its **nutritive** (NEW-tri-tiv) **value**.

Applying heat to any food can make it lose some of its nutritional value. The longer food cooks, the more nutritive value it loses. Food cooked very quickly with one of the dry heat methods loses relatively few vitamins and minerals. Although cooking can take away some of a food's nutritional value, it can also add something to food that was not there before cooking. One of the most significant ways that some dry heat cooking methods change the nutritional value of food is requiring fat to be added to the food as part of the cooking process.

 **Reading Checkpoint** *How does caramelizing differ from the Maillard reaction?*

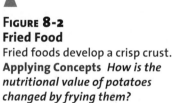
Figure 8-2
Fried Food
Fried foods develop a crisp crust.
Applying Concepts *How is the nutritional value of potatoes changed by frying them?*

Dry Heat Methods

There are eight basic dry heat methods of cooking. As an aid to memory, these methods are often grouped into the following related pairs:

- Grilling and broiling
- Roasting and baking
- Sautéing and stir frying
- Pan frying and deep frying

Grilling and Broiling **Grilling** is a dry heat method in which food is placed on a rack for cooking. Grilled foods have a robust, smoky taste. The heat source is located below the rack holding the food. The heat source could be charcoal, gas, wood (in the form of chunks or logs), or an electric or infrared heating element. The radiant heat from the heat source heats up the metal in the rack enough to cook the food (creating the dark grill marks that are the sign that food was cooked on a grill rack). The radiant heat also cooks the parts of the food that are not in direct contact with the rack.

Figure 8-3
Perfect Grill Marks
To create perfect crosshatch grill marks: (1) Place meat diagonally, presentation side down. (2) Pick up meat halfway through cooking the presentation side and reposition it in the opposite direction. (3) Turn over. It may not be necessary to crosshatch the other side.
Applying Concepts *What does a crosshatch design on a grilled steak contribute to the customer's enjoyment?*

A griddle is sometimes used to prepare grilled food. However, rather than having an open rack over the heat source, a griddle uses a solid, flat metal plate above the heat source. Food that is cooked on a griddle may be referred to on a menu as grilled or griddled.

Broiling is similar to grilling, except the heat source is located above the food. When you put food into a broiler, it cooks from the heat of the broiler rack as well as from the radiant heat given off by the heat source above the rack. The heat in a broiler is typically a gas flame or an electric or infrared heating element.

Roasting and Baking Roasting and **baking** are dry heat techniques in which food is cooked by hot air trapped inside an oven. As the hot air comes in contact with the food, the surface of the food

BASIC CULINARY SKILLS

Grilling and Broiling

1 **Oil the grill** or rack by using an oil-soaked cloth.

3 **Place food on the grill** or rack, with the presentation side facing down. Brush with sauces or glazes if your recipe calls for them.

2 **Heat the grill** or broiler.

Continued on next page

Grilling and Broiling Continued

4 **Turn** the food.

5 **Cook on second side** until properly cooked.

6 **Serve** very hot directly from the grill on heated plates.

 See Recipe Card 4, "Broiled Sirloin Steak."

begins to heat up and dry out. Eventually the surface starts to take on a deeper color. The food's texture changes as it goes from raw to cooked. Meats, fish, and poultry tend to become firmer as they cook, while vegetables and fruits become softer.

In terms of the basic method of heat transfer, there is no significant difference between baking and roasting. We eat "baked" potatoes, although it would be just as accurate to call them "roasted" potatoes.

The difference between roasting and baking has more to do with the size of the food we are preparing. Generally, roasting indicates you are preparing a whole item or large piece of food. Baking typically means you are preparing smaller pieces of a larger food. A chicken you cook whole in the oven is referred to as a "roasted chicken." But the same chicken cut into pieces and cooked in the oven is referred to as "baked chicken."

Baking also includes dishes that are mixtures and cooked in the oven. Examples of this type of baking include scalloped potatoes and pasta dishes such as lasagna. Baking also includes items produced in the bakeshop, such as cakes, cookies, pies, and breads. These foods cook in part by being exposed directly to the heated air trapped in the oven. They also cook in part from contact with the pan that holds them. The material in the pan transfers the heat from the air to the food inside the pan.

Roasting and Baking

1 **Heat** the oven.

2 **Sear** the food in a hot pan on the stovetop or in a very hot oven, if your recipe calls for it. ("Searing" is a variation of sautéing and is discussed later in this section.)

3 **Roast or bake** the food, uncovered, until it is properly cooked.

4 **Baste** the food as it roasts or bakes.

5 **Rest** the food before slicing or carving.

 See Recipe Card 5, "Roast Chicken with Pan Gravy."

When meats are roasted or baked, they are sometimes seared before being placed in the oven. Searing is a type of sautéing and is discussed later in this chapter.

The heat in an oven is not as intense as the heat generated by a grill, a broiler, or even a burner on the stovetop. At times, however, it still may be too intense for delicate food. Chefs control oven heat by putting food in a pan or baking dish and then setting that pan in a larger pan. Then they add enough water to the larger pan to come up around the sides of the smaller pan. This is known as baking foods in a **water bath**. Because the water can only come up to 212°F, it insulates and protects the food. A water bath is often used when a chef wants the finished item to have a creamy, smooth consistency.

Sautéing and Stir Frying Sautéing (SAW-tay-ing) is a cooking technique that cooks food quickly, often uncovered, in a very small amount of fat in a pan over high heat. Food that is suitable for sautéing is typically quite tender and thin enough to cook in a short time. Food is often coated with seasoned flour before sautéing. Sautéed foods are cooked primarily by contact with the pan. The fat you use helps to keep the food from sticking to the pan. It can also add some flavor to the food if you choose a flavorful fat such as butter or olive oil.

Roasting over an Open Fire

▲ *Antonin Carême 1784–1833*

People in prehistoric times often roasted food on sticks over an open fire. This method of cooking remained popular even when people, and cooking, moved into buildings. Large cuts of meat, even whole animals, were placed on a stick or pole, known as a spit, over the fire. Eventually, the spit was made out of metal rather than wood. It was set up so heat radiating from the fire would cook the food. Cooks turned the spit so food would cook evenly—and that took lots of work.

Cooking near the flames of an open fire was also dangerous. Antonin Carême, a famous French chef who lived from 1784 to 1833, describes what it was like in the kitchens of his time:

Imagine yourself in a large kitchen before a great dinner. There one sees twenty chefs at their urgent occupations, coming and going, moving with speed in the cauldron of heat. Look at the great mass of burning charcoal. … Add to that a heap of burning wood in front of which four spits are turning, one of which bears a sirloin weighing forty-five to sixty pounds, another a piece of veal weighing thirty-five to forty-five pounds, the other two for fowl and game.

Research

Research the life of Antonin Carême. Describe his childhood, what caused him to become a chef, what kinds of dishes he cooked, and for whom he cooked his dishes.

When you sauté food in a pan on a burner, you should let the pan heat up first, even before adding any oil. Chefs refer to this step as **conditioning the pan**. Once the pan is hot, you can add oil. The oil will heat up very quickly so you can start cooking right away. If you add food to a cold pan with cold oil, it will stick to the pand and your food will absorb more oil, altering its taste.

When you add food to a sauté pan, the pan cools off. The more food you add, the longer the pan takes to get hot again. The time it takes for the pan to heat up again is called the **recovery time**. The success of a sauté has a direct relationship to the recovery time. A short recovery time means foods will develop good color and flavor.

Turn sautéed food halfway through cooking. Resist the temptation to move food around unless it is cooking too quickly or starting to get too dark.

CHEF'S TIP

"JUMP IN THE PAN"

The word "sauté" comes from a French verb that means "to jump." Sautéed food cooks so quickly that you can imagine it simply jumping into the pan and then out of it, on to a plate.

BASIC CULINARY SKILLS

Sautéing

1 **Coat food** with flour, if indicated in your recipe. Otherwise, blot the food dry and season it.

2 **Heat the pan** over direct heat.

3 **Add oil** or cooking fat. Use only a small amount.

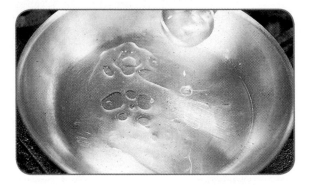

4 **Add food** to the hot pan. Do not crowd food.

5 **Cook the first side.** Do not disturb until the food is halfway cooked.

6 **Turn food** once.

7 **Complete cooking** on the second side until properly cooked.

 See Recipe Card 6, *"Sautéed Chicken Breast with Herb Sauce."*

You can vary the steps in sautéing to produce different effects. There are four important variations of sautéing:

- Stir frying
- Searing
- Pan broiling
- Sweating and smothering

Stir frying is very similar to sautéing, but there are some basic differences. One of the most obvious differences is the pan you use. Stir fries are made in woks, pans with round bottoms and high sides. Foods for a stir fry are usually cut into small strips so they can cook quickly. You turn sautéed food only once, but when stir frying you constantly stir and toss food as it is cooking to make sure it cooks quickly and evenly. Stir frying is an important cooking method for Asian dishes.

Searing (SERE-ing) means you cook food, usually uncovered, in a small amount of hot fat just long enough to color the outside of the food. This can be done to give food, such as a cut of meat, a rich brown color (often before roasting it). Another application for searing occurs when you are preparing a large amount of food, as you might for a banquet. Food is seared to give it good color on the outside, and then it is put in the oven to finish cooking. Food is turned often to avoid burning.

Pan broiling is very much like sautéing except that you use no fat. The food is uncovered and cooked over high heat. This method is used for foods that have a high fat content, such as bacon. Fat that is released by the food is poured off as it forms. This is sometimes referred to as **dry sautéing.**

Sweating calls for lower heat than you would use for sautéing, searing, or pan broiling. Food, typically vegetables, is cooked uncovered over a low heat in a small amount of fat. The food softens, releases moisture, and cooks in its own juices, but is not allowed to brown. Another difference between sweating and sautéing is that you should stir foods more often when you sweat them. **Smothering** is a variation of sweating in which the pan is covered. This increases the amount of juices that are retained in the pan.

Pan Frying and Deep Frying When **pan frying**, food is cooked in hot oil in a pan. The amount of oil you use in pan frying is more than you use for sautéing. The oil should be deep enough to come halfway up the sides of the food you are cooking. So, for example, if the food is one inch thick, you need half an inch of oil in the pan. As with sautéing, you turn foods only once as they pan fry to finish cooking.

▲
FIGURE 8-4
Stir Frying
Stir frying is an important cooking method for Asian dishes.
Applying Concepts *How does stir frying differ from sautéing?*

Barbecue

The southern United States has a rich culinary tradition reflecting influences from around the world. But perhaps the greatest southern culinary tradition is barbecue.

Barbecue is a cooking style that cooks food with smoke over an indirect heat source, which retains the meat's juices and provides a smoky taste. More than just a style of cooking, barbecue is also the name of a social gathering.

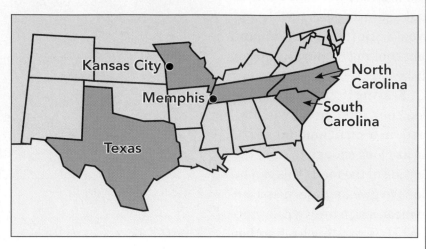

There are intense debates about what barbecue truly is. In the United States, you can find four distinct styles of barbecue:

- **Carolina Barbecue.** Cuts of pork are featured in a Carolina barbecue. In the eastern Carolinas, the sauce is traditionally made from vinegar and seasoned with salt, black pepper, crushed or ground cayenne, and other spices. In the western Carolinas, small amounts of ketchup, molasses, Worcestershire sauce, and spices are added to the basic vinegar sauce. The area around Columbia favors a mustard-based sauce.

▲ *Memphis barbecue*

- **Memphis Barbecue.** Pork ribs are typically featured in a Memphis barbecue. Sauces here are typically tomato-based and somewhat sweet. The sweetness comes from the addition of molasses. Some Memphis barbecue sauces also include mustard.

- **Kansas City Barbecue.** Although pork is featured in Kansas City barbecue, there is also a strong tradition of barbecuing other meats, including beef (no doubt a result of Kansas City's role as a meat-packing center). The thick, tomato-based style of Kansas City barbecue sauce has become the prototype for commercial sauces sold nationwide.

- **Texas Barbecue.** Beef is featured in a Texas barbecue. Beef brisket is considered the most traditional. Sauces in Texas are generally not as sweet as Kansas-style barbecue sauces. Some sauces are thin and made primarily from vinegar and spices like Carolina sauces, though they are usually given a Texas flair by adding chilies and peppers. Other sauces are thicker (though not as thick as Kansas City sauces). Some barbecue fans in Texas serve the sauce as a condiment rather than brushing it on the meat as it cooks.

Research

1. Find two different types of barbecue recipes in cookbooks or on the Internet.

2. Review the ingredients used in the recipes and determine the style of the barbecue (Carolina, Memphis, Kansas City, or Texas).

3. Prepare each of the recipes (including the sauce). Evaluate the results.

You can partially cook thick or dense foods by pan frying them on both sides until golden and crisp. They can finish cooking, uncovered, in the oven. If you cook them entirely in the pan on the top of the stove, the outside might overcook before the food cooks all the way through.

In pan frying, you must heat the oil to the temperature specified in the recipe. Use a thermometer to check the temperature. Most foods are pan fried at about 350°F. If you add food to oil that is not hot enough, the cooked food will be pale and absorb the oil, making it greasy. If the oil is properly heated, food will turn out crisp and golden on the outside and seal the moisture and juice on the inside.

Foods that are most often pan fried are naturally tender and moist. Vegetables, fish, chicken, veal, and pork are common choices.

Pan-fried foods are usually coated before you add them to the oil. There are three basic coating options:

- **Seasoned Flour.** The simplest coating is simply flour that has been seasoned with salt and pepper. To coat the food, you add the food to the flour, turn it until the flour covers the entire surface, and shake gently so any extra flour falls off.
- **Standard Breading.** When a recipe calls for a **standard breading**, it means you dust the food with seasoned flour, dip it in beaten eggs, and then cover it in breadcrumbs (or another crumb mixture). You can add a standard breading to food several hours before you pan fry it if you keep the food in the refrigerator until you are ready to cook it.
- **Batters.** There are many different types of batters, but a **batter** is typically made by blending a type of flour and a liquid. To coat a food with batter, first you coat the food with flour (or cornstarch) and shake off any excess. Then dip the food into the batter until the food is entirely covered. Batter-dipped foods need to go into the pan immediately, so be sure the oil is hot and you are ready to cook before you start dipping food into the batter. Different recipes for batters can produce different textures, from a beer batter to a tempura batter.

Foods are also cooked in hot oil when you are **deep frying**, but with deep frying, the oil completely covers the food. Typically the oil is about 350°F to 375°F. Deep-fried foods are typically coated with standard breading or a batter. Foods that are coated with breading are usually lowered into hot oil with a basket. Foods coated in a batter are generally lowered into the oil carefully with a pair of tongs.

FIGURE 8-5
Standard Breading
The breading should cover the entire surface of the food.
Predicting *What might happen if the breading is not applied evenly?*

Pan Frying

1 **Coat the food,** if required by your recipe.

2 **Heat oil** or cooking fat in a pan. It should be half the thickness of the food.

3 **Add food to the hot oil** carefully. Do not allow pieces to touch.

4 **Pan fry the first side** until a golden crust forms.

5 **Turn and finish cooking.** Thick foods can finish cooking, uncovered on a rack, in a 350°F oven.

6 **Drain** excess oil. Blot with a paper towel before serving.

 See Recipe Card 7, "Pan-Fried Veal Cutlets."

When you add food to the hot oil, the temperature of the oil drops. The time it takes to come back to the correct temperature, the recovery time, has an effect on the flavor, color, and texture of food. That is why you should add foods in small batches when pan frying or deep frying.

Deep Frying

1 **Heat oil** in a deep fat fryer or a pot with tall sides.

2 **Blot food** dry.

3 **Coat food,** if your recipe calls for it.

4 **Add food to the hot oil** by using a frying basket or tongs.

5 **Deep fry** until food is an even golden brown and is fully cooked.

6 **Remove food.**

7 **Drain excess oil.** Blot food on a paper towel before serving.

 See Recipe Card 9, "Deep-Fried Breaded Shrimp."

 **Reading Checkpoint** *What are the eight basic dry heat cooking methods?*

Determining Doneness

Knowing when a food is done can be one of the biggest challenges in any of the dry heat methods. Some foods can be prepared to more than one degree of doneness. Steaks, for instance, can be prepared to any doneness the customer requests, from rare to well done. Two important considerations in determining doneness are carryover cooking and resting food after it is cooked.

Carryover Cooking All foods continue to cook after you take them out of the pan, off the grill, or out of the oven. That is because the food holds heat. The remaining heat is enough to continue to cook the food. This process is known as **carryover cooking.**

FIGURE 8-6
Carryover Cooking
Remove food from the heat before it reaches the temperature the customer requested.
Drawing Conclusions *Which will have the greatest amount of carryover cooking, a roast or a steak?*

The amount of carryover cooking depends on the size of the food. Big cuts of meat can hold more heat, so they continue to cook for a longer period. If you measure the temperature of the food at the center as it rests, you would see that it rises from two or three degrees to as many as ten or fifteen degrees.

You can't stop carryover cooking, so you need to plan for it as part of the total cooking process. This means taking food from the pan, oven, or broiler before it is completely cooked. Then the carryover cooking finishes the cooking. If you wait until the food is completely cooked, carryover cooking will overcook the food by the time you serve it to your guests.

Resting Food Chefs allow food to rest after it is cooked, for three important reasons:

- Food cooks properly without overcooking. A resting period gives carryover cooking enough time for the food to reach its proper doneness.
- Food is moister. When food is being cooked, the heat outside the food drives the food's natural juices toward the center. Letting food rest allows the juices to redistribute, moving back to the outer parts of the food.
- It allows time for proper plating and presentation. Letting the food rest gives you a chance to finish any sauce or side dishes you plan to serve with it.

✓ **Reading Checkpoint** *What is carryover cooking?*

8.1 ASSESSMENT

Reviewing Concepts

1. How does caramelizing differ from the Maillard reaction?
2. What are the eight basic dry heat cooking methods?
3. What is carryover cooking?

Critical Thinking

4. **Comparing/Contrasting** What is the difference between grilling and broiling?
5. **Comparing/Contrasting** What is the difference between sweating and smothering?
6. **Applying Concepts** What is the relationship between recovery time and a food's flavor, color, and texture when deep-frying?

Test Kitchen

Divide into two groups. Both groups will deep fry three batches of French fries. The first group will allow a normal recovery time between batches. The second group will ignore recovery time and cook one batch immediately after the other. Evaluate the results.

Woks

Research woks. Describe the materials from which they are constructed, the sizes available, how they are used for cooking, how they should be maintained, and what types of dishes are typically cooked in a wok.

Moist Heat Methods

READING PREVIEW

Key Concepts

- Understanding how moist heat affects foods
- Identifying and using a variety of moist heat and combination cooking methods
- Determining doneness in foods prepared by moist heat and combination cooking methods

Vocabulary

- blanching
- boiling
- braising
- fork tender
- fully cooked
- parboiled
- parcooked
- poaching
- rolling boil
- simmering
- steaming
- stewing

> **"S**teamed foods get a bad rap, but a perfectly steamed dish of fish or vegetables bursts with wonderful flavor, as long as you care enough to do it right. **"**
>
> – Mai Pham

How Moist Heat Affects Foods

Moist heat techniques have a built-in temperature control. Foods are cooked in a liquid. Most liquids will not rise much above 212°F, the boiling point of water. This means that food cooked by using a moist heat method will have a different appearance, flavor, and texture than food prepared by a dry heat method.

Heat Transfer When you cook food with one of the moist heat methods, the food is cooked either through direct contact with a hot liquid or with steam that rises from the hot liquid. The heat is conducted from a heat source (usually a burner) through a pan and then from the pan to the liquid. When the food is added to the liquid, the heat is transferred from the liquid to the food. If the cooking method relies on steam heat, the food is cooked when the heat from the steam is transferred to the food.

Changes to Food Because moist heat is lower than the temperatures you can produce in a hot pan, in hot oil, or on a hot grill, the changes to a food's color on the surface are not as dramatic.

Mai Pham
Chef, Lemongrass Restaurant, Sacramento, CA
Author, *Pleasures of the Vietnamese Table*

The color on the outside of the food is often the same as the color on the inside. This plays a role in the way the food tastes. Instead of developing a roasted or caramelized flavor, foods are often said to have a clean taste.

Foods such as meat, fish, poultry, or eggs become firmer as you cook them. Vegetables, fruits, and grains become softer. A chef uses these changes in texture as a way of determining when food has finished cooking.

Nutritional Value When food comes in direct contact with a hot liquid or steam, the water draws some of the nutritive elements out of the food. You can keep this to a minimum by cutting food as close as possible to the time you need to cook it and cooking it for as short a time as possible.

 **Reading Checkpoint** *How is heat transferred to food in a moist heat method?*

Moist Heat and Combination Cooking Methods

The moist heat cooking methods have many similarities. The major distinctions between them have to do with the foods you choose and the temperatures of the liquid in which the food is steamed or cooked. There are four basic moist heat cooking methods:

- Steaming
- Poaching
- Simmering
- Boiling

Additionally, there are two important combination methods that require the use of both a dry heat method and a moist heat method. These combination cooking methods are:

- Braising
- Stewing

Steaming When **steaming**, you cook food in a closed pot or a large steamer. The steam trapped in the pot or steamer circulates around the food. The heat in the steam is transferred to the food. The food does not come in direct contact with the steaming liquid. Steaming is a gentle, moist heat technique.

Steaming is a good way to retain as many of the food's nutrients as possible. It is a popular technique for preparing many vegetables, but it is also used to prepare more tender, delicate meats and fish, including chicken breasts, whole fish, and shellfish such as clams or lobsters.

To add more flavor to foods as they steam, you can add seasonings, flavorings, and aromatics to the steaming liquid. As the liquid heats up, those flavors are released into the liquid and the steam it produces. The flavor is then transferred to the food.

Poaching, Simmering, and Boiling Food prepared by poaching, simmering, or boiling is completely covered by hot liquid. **Poaching** is used for tender foods (eggs, fish, poultry breasts, and fruits, for instance) and requires a cooking temperature of 160°F to 170°F. **Simmering** is used for tougher cuts of meat, such as corned beef. The temperature of the liquid should be between 170°F and 185°F. **Boiling** is suitable for pasta and certain vegetables. The temperature of the liquid is boiling, 212°F.

Some foods that are actually simmered are referred to as boiled. Don't be misled by the name of a dish. Check the recipe to see what the correct temperature of the cooking liquid is supposed to be for a particular food.

Of course, the most accurate way to check the temperature of the liquid is with a thermometer. Chefs, however, can often tell how hot the liquid is by looking at the size of the bubbles and the rate at which they rise to the surface. When a liquid is boiling rapidly, it is referred to as a **rolling boil**.

▲
FIGURE 8-7
Steaming Food
Food does not come in direct contact with the steaming liquid when steaming.
Drawing Conclusions *Why would contact with the steaming liquid tend to reduce nutrients in the steamed food?*

BASIC CULINARY SKILLS

Steaming

1. Heat water in a steamer or pot until it is steaming.

2. Place food in the steamer pan or rack, leaving enough room for the steam to circulate around all sides of the food.

3. Place the steamer pan in the steamer over the steaming water and cover.

4. Steam until food is properly cooked. Open the steamer as few times as possible.

 See Recipe Card 10, "Tagine of Cod."

How Hot Is the Liquid?

Stage	Description
Poaching	Many bubbles cling to the sides and bottom of the pan. Some motion is visible on top of the liquid, but it seems to be barely moving. 160°F–170°F
Simmering	Size of the bubbles increases and they rise to the surface more rapidly and more frequently. The surface shows more obvious signs of motion. 170°F–185°F
Boiling	Bubbles are very large and rise very quickly to the surface. There is very much motion on the surface. 212°F

BASIC CULINARY SKILLS

Poaching, Simmering, and Boiling

1 Bring liquid to the correct temperature.

- Poaching 160°F–170°F
- Simmering 170°F–185°F
- Boiling 212°F

2 **Add food.** Add additional liquid, if necessary, to keep the food completely covered.

3 Add seasonings and aromatics, if your recipe calls for them.

4 Cook food at a consistent, even temperature to the proper doneness.

5 Lift or strain the food from the cooking liquid.

See Recipe Card 12, "Corned Beef with Cabbage and Winter Vegetables."

Braising and Stewing Braising and stewing are combination cooking methods because they combine a dry cooking method with a moist cooking method. Food is first seared in hot oil (the dry cooking method). This is done to help food keep its shape as it cooks. It also provides the dish with the rich flavor that develops when food is seared in hot oil.

After searing, the food is gently cooked in a flavorful liquid or sauce. **Braising** usually indicates that the food is left whole or in large pieces, with enough liquid to partially cover it. **Stewing** indicates that food is cut into smaller pieces and then cooked in enough liquid to completely cover the ingredients. Perfectly braised or stewed foods have a rich, complex flavor and a tender texture.

BASIC CULINARY SKILLS

Braising and Stewing

1 Heat a small amount of fat or oil in a pan.

2 Add food to the pan.

3 Sear until evenly colored.

4 Remove seared food from the pan.

5 Add mirepoix or other aromatic ingredients and cook in the hot fat or oil.

See Recipe Card 14, "Braised Lamb Shanks."

6 Add cooking liquid to the pan, stir well, and bring to a simmer.

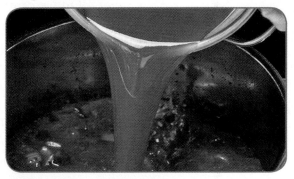

7 Return food to the cooking liquid and cover the pan.

8 Cook at a low simmer until very tender. Turn braised food as it cooks. Add more liquid, if necessary, to keep food appropriately covered.

9 Skim grease and other impurities from the cooking liquid.

Braises and stews are usually made from tougher cuts of meat, whole poultry, and firm-fleshed fish or seafood. You can also braise vegetables and beans. Food that is braised must be able to stand up to the long, gentle cooking process without completely falling apart.

A good braise or stew has a soft texture. The sauce for a braise or a stew is actually nothing more than its cooking liquid. By the time the food is properly braised or stewed, it has released a significant amount of flavor and body into liquid, along with nutrients that may have been drawn out of the food and into the liquid. The result is an intensely flavored, complex sauce.

 **Reading Checkpoint** *What are the four basic moist heat cooking methods?*

Determining Doneness

When using one of the moist heat methods, how do you determine when a food is properly cooked? The answer depends on how that food will be used. For example, if you are cooking the food and serving it right away, you will almost always cook the food all the way through. One exception is eggs, which can be cooked to a range of doneness if the customer makes a specific request. However, if you are using a moist heat method to prepare an ingredient for use in another dish or for a specific type of presentation, you won't cook it all the way through. You need to be able to judge when foods are partially cooked.

Proper Doneness The names for doneness in moist heat and combination cooking methods include:

- Blanched
- Parcooked (or parboiled)
- Fully cooked

Blanching foods involves cooking in a liquid or with steam just long enough to cook the outer portion of the food. When you blanch food, you may see a color change; for instance, blanched broccoli or peas become a bright green. When you use these blanched vegetables, they keep their brilliant colors. Blanching also draws out strong flavors or aromas that might overpower the finished dish. For instance, you might blanch a piece of country-cured ham to make it less salty. Blanching loosens the skin of foods such as tomatoes, chestnuts, peaches, and almonds so they are easier to peel.

To blanch food, bring water or other liquid to a full boil in a pot or a steamer. Add food directly to the liquid or the steamer. Let the food cook just long enough for the change you want. When that

FIGURE 8-8
Blanching Tomatoes
Blanching loosens the outer layer of tomatoes so they are easier to peel after being dropped into ice water.
Writing *Describe how blanching vegetables such as green beans or carrots might help make your work more efficient.*

happens, lift the food out of the liquid or the steamer. Immediately put the food in a container of ice water. This stops the carryover cooking. Drain the food before you store it or use it in another dish.

Parcooked stands for "partially cooked." Parcooked food is typically prepared in the same way as blanched food, using either liquid or steam. The food just cooks a bit longer. Parcooking helps you be more efficient, especially during service, because you only need to cook the parcooked food the remainder of the time required for fully cooked food. For example, if it takes 15 minutes to fully cook a food, and you parcooked it for 10 minutes, you would only need to cook it another 5 minutes for it to be fully cooked. Parcooking is actually a general word for partially cooking a food by any cooking method. Another technique, **parboiled** refers exclusively to partially boiling a food.

Fully cooked food is cooked all the way through, or to the doneness your customer has requested. Be sure to observe the correct temperatures for doneness and remember to allow for carryover cooking.

Test for Doneness Appearance is one of the doneness tests you can use, but it is almost always used in combination with another test. When you are only partially cooking food, the tool you use to test doneness is one of the following: a paring knife, a table fork, or a kitchen fork. A parcooked food may be easy to pierce on the outside, but as you continue to push to the center of the food, there is more resistance. When foods are fully cooked, the knife or fork should slide all the way into the food easily. These foods are said to be **fork tender**.

Reading Checkpoint   *How do you blanch food?*

FIGURE 8-9
Testing for Doneness
Use a paring knife to test for doneness
Predicting *What would happen if you tested for doneness very often?*
▼

8.2 ASSESSMENT

Reviewing Concepts
1. How is heat transferred to food in a moist heat method?
2. What are the four basic moist heat cooking methods?
3. How do you blanch food?

Critical Thinking
4. **Comparing/Contrasting** What are the differences among poaching, simmering, and boiling?
5. **Comparing/Contrasting** What is the difference between braising and stewing?
6. **Inferring** How would parcooking food increase the efficiency of a restaurant kitchen?
7. **Applying Concepts** Which type of cooking would take longer, poaching or simmering? Why?

Test Kitchen
Time how long it takes to cook a batch of green beans completely. Stop carryover cooking. Parcook the same amount of green beans half that time. Stop carryover cooking. Cook the parcooked green beans half the time it took to cook the beans completely. Are these beans cooked completely?

SCIENCE

Healthy Steaming
Research the health benefits of steaming food. Why is it often called the healthiest method of cooking? How does steaming compare with other methods of cooking in terms of maintaining nutritive value?

Review and Assessment

Reviewing Content

Choose the letter that best answers the question or completes the statement.

1. The Maillard reaction occurs when
   a. food that is green turns bright green as it boils
   b. food containing sugar turns brown as it cooks
   c. food containing protein turns brown as it cooks
   d. food that is hard turns soft as it cooks

2. Which of the following is not a method of heat transfer for a dry heat method?
   a. steam
   b. radiant heat
   c. metal of the pan
   d. oil in the pan

3. Which cooking method cooks food quickly, often uncovered, in a very small amount of oil over high heat?
   a. pan frying
   b. simmering
   c. stewing
   d. sautéing

4. Which of the following is not a dry cooking method?
   a. pan frying
   b. simmering
   c. pan broiling
   d. sautéing

5. Which of the following is not a moist cooking method?
   a. sweating
   b. simmering
   c. poaching
   d. steaming

6. What is the first step in stewing?
   a. pan frying
   b. searing
   c. simmering
   d. boiling

Understanding Concepts

7. What is the difference between grilling and broiling?

8. What is the difference between roasting and baking?

9. How do searing, pan broiling, and sweating differ from sautéing?

10. What is the difference between braising and stewing?

Critical Thinking

11. **Recognizing Patterns** How are roasting and braising similar? How are baking and stewing similar?

12. **Applying Concepts** For which type of cooking would you need to be more concerned about carryover cooking, roasting or baking?

Culinary Math

13. **Solving Problems** A recipe for a stew requires 3 cups of carrots with a turned cut. The recipe serves 8 people. You need to serve 50 people. How many cups of carrots should you cut?

14. **Predicting** The internal temperature of a 20-pound roasted turkey increases by about 15°F in the first 10 minutes after it leaves the oven. The internal temperature of a 12-pound turkey increases by about 7°F in the first 10 minutes after it leaves the oven. You are cooking a 16-pound turkey. You want to reach a fully cooked internal temperature of 165°F. Allowing for carryover cooking, at what internal temperature should you take the turkey out of the oven?

On the Job

15. **Applying a Concept** You are in a hurry and need to sauté a large number of ingredients with different textures for one dish. Would you sauté them all at once to save time or add them one at a time to the sauté pan? Explain your answer.

RECIPE CARDS

Use the following Recipe Cards to test your culinary skill.

4. Grilled Sirloin Steak
5. Roast Chicken with Pan Gravy
6. Sautéed Chicken with Herb Sauce
7. Pan-Fried Veal Cutlets
8. Stir-Fried Scallops
9. Deep-Fried Breaded Shrimp
10. Tagine of Cod
11. Poule au Pot
12. Corned Beef with Winter Vegetables
13. New England Shore Dinner
14. Braised Lamb Shanks
15. Yankee Pot Roast

LAB ACTIVITY

Project 8: Moist Cooking Methods

Answer these questions when your class works through Project 8.

- Can you identify poaching, simmering, and boiling by sight?
- What are the differences in a vegetable when it is poached, simmered, or boiled for the same amount of time?
- Can you identify the point when blanching has occurred?
- Do you need to be concerned about carryover cooking when blanching a vegetable?
- Does parcooking save as much time as you expect it would?

TEST PRACTICE

Choose the letter that best answers the question or completes the statement.

1. In terms only of the basic method of heat transfer, what is the difference between baking and roasting?
   A Baking uses a baking pan, which transfers heat.
   B Roasting uses an aromatic liquid to transfer heat.
   C Roasting uses oil to transfer heat.
   D There is no difference.

2. Recovery time is
   A the time it takes for food to become hot when cooking
   B the time it takes for a pan to heat up again after food has been added
   C the time it takes for food to begin releasing moisture
   D the time it takes to remove food from a deep fat fryer

3. The expression "conditioning the pan" refers to
   A cleaning a sauté pan as you are using it
   B adding oil to a pan
   C letting the pan heat up first, even before adding oil
   D adding hot water to a cold pan to increase the speed at which the pan heats

4. Pan broiling is
   A a type of sautéing in which no fat is used
   B a type of sautéing in which water replaces oil
   C a dry heat method using enough oil to come halfway up the food
   D a moist heat method using simmering water

5. For deep frying, the temperature of the oil is typically
   A 212°F
   B 300°F–325°F
   C 325°F–350°F
   D 350°F–375°F

6. Poaching requires a cooking temperature of
   A 160°F–170°F
   B 212°F
   C 250°F–260°F
   D 300°F–310°F

7. When the temperature of the oven may be too intense for a baked food, chefs sometimes
   A blanch the food first
   B turn the oven 50 percent lower
   C bake the food in a water bath
   D sear the food first

UNIT 3

Culinary Applications

READING PREVIEW

Key Concepts

- Selecting and storing eggs
- Preparing and serving egg dishes
- Identifying and storing dairy products

Vocabulary

- albumen
- clarified butter
- coddled eggs
- crème fraîche
- cultured
- custard
- flat omelet
- frittata
- homogenized
- lecithin
- milkfat or butterfat
- omelet
- over egg
- pasteurized
- quiche
- rolled omelet
- scrambled eggs
- shirred eggs
- soufflé
- sunny-side-up egg

"It's hard to imagine a more versatile ingredient than the egg. There are hundreds of recipes for eggs—they show up in everything from sauces to desserts. **"**

— Katherine Polenz
The Culinary Institute of America

Selecting and Storing Eggs

Eggs have been part of our diets long before humans domesticated animals. Centuries ago, we ate eggs from a wide variety of birds, including ducks, geese, quail, swans, and ostriches. Once we domesticated chickens, though, their eggs became the standard by which we cooked, and a staple of our diet. This section is devoted specifically to chicken eggs—how to select the appropriate egg for the dish you are preparing, and how to store your eggs to maintain their quality for the greatest length of time possible.

Egg Anatomy Eggs have three main parts:

- **Shell**. The shell is the hard outer casing that protects the egg inside. Eggshells are porous enough to allow air in and moisture out. The color of the shell doesn't have anything to do with the egg's quality, nutritional value, or flavor. Brown eggs and white eggs simply come from different types of chickens.

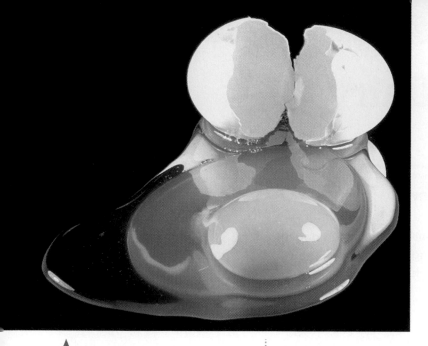

• **White**. The egg white, also called the **albumen** (al-BYOO-men), is made up of protein and water. The white appears clear and has a liquid-like quality in its raw state, but as it cooks, it turns white and hard. Looking closely at the white, you can actually see two separate parts: a runny, nearly flat outer ring and a more round, contained inner ring.

• **Yolk**. The yolk is the yellow center of an egg. It contains protein, fat, and a substance called **lecithin** (LES-i-thin), which serves as a natural emulsifier. The color of a yolk can vary from a pale yellow to a deep golden, depending on the diet of the animal.

FIGURE 9-1
Parts of an Egg
Eggs are a popular breakfast food and an inexpensive source of protein.
Interpreting Illustrations *Can you distinguish the two parts of the white?*

Egg Inspecting and Grading Egg grading is done on a voluntary basis. When a farm calls for an inspection, a grader from the USDA (United States Department of Agriculture) comes and gives a portion of the eggs a good once-over. The shell is the very first thing the graders check. It should be clean and free from cracks or holes. Some of the eggs are broken out of their shells on to plates so the grader can see how firm and high the white is and how much it spreads out on the plate. The grader also notes whether the yolk sits in the center of the white, slides to one side, or flattens out. As an egg ages, the white gets runny and the yolks flatten.

A grader can assign three grades to eggs: AA, A, or B. Once graded, the egg cartons can be marked with the official USDA grading shield.

• **Grade AA**. These are the freshest eggs, with compact whites and yolks that sit high in the center of the whites. Grade AA eggs (also known as "special") have the best appearance in fried or poached egg dishes. The yolks are less likely to break when you separate the eggs into whites and yolks or while you are cooking or turning them.

• **Grade A**. These eggs have a slightly runny white. The yolk is not as high as AA and it is not as centered. Grade A eggs (also known as "extra") are good for dishes where the eggs are blended or whisked and for preparing in the shell. The yolks break more easily than the yolks of Grade AA eggs.

• **Grade B**. Eggs that are Grade B (also known as "standard") have a runny white and a flat, off-centered yolk. They can be used in baking and batters and are used commercially to make liquid, frozen, and dried egg products.

Egg Sizes Egg sizing is also part of the USDA inspection process. There are standard names for egg sizes, and those names indicate the particular weight of the egg. No matter what size egg you are using, the white accounts for two-thirds of the egg's weight and the yolk accounts for the other third. The shell accounts for a little more than 10% of the total weight of the egg. The weights below include the weight of the shell. Remember to subtract that out when factoring what you need for a recipe or conversion.

Egg Sizes and Weights

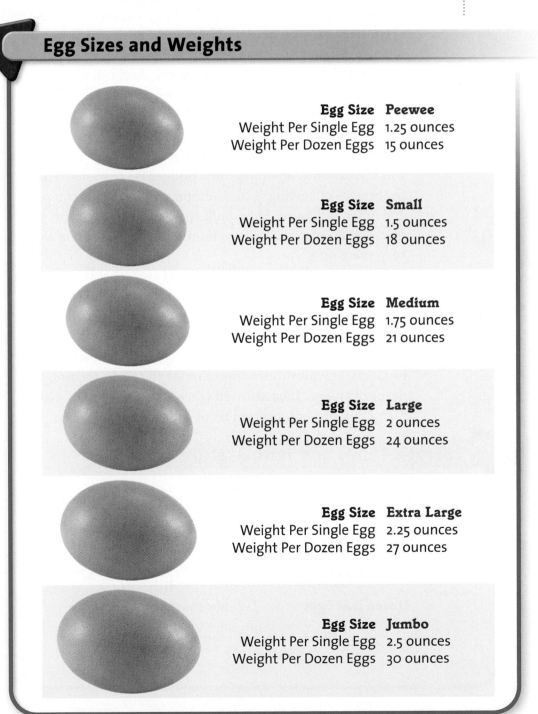

Egg Size Peewee
Weight Per Single Egg 1.25 ounces
Weight Per Dozen Eggs 15 ounces

Egg Size Small
Weight Per Single Egg 1.5 ounces
Weight Per Dozen Eggs 18 ounces

Egg Size Medium
Weight Per Single Egg 1.75 ounces
Weight Per Dozen Eggs 21 ounces

Egg Size Large
Weight Per Single Egg 2 ounces
Weight Per Dozen Eggs 24 ounces

Egg Size Extra Large
Weight Per Single Egg 2.25 ounces
Weight Per Dozen Eggs 27 ounces

Egg Size Jumbo
Weight Per Single Egg 2.5 ounces
Weight Per Dozen Eggs 30 ounces

CHEF'S TIP

CHECK THE DATE

Eggs spoil easily. Egg cartons must display the date the eggs were packed. Do not use eggs that exceed 30 days after the packing date.

▲ *Flat of Shell Eggs*

Buying and Storing Eggs Eggs are sold in a variety of forms. The type of eggs your kitchen stocks depends on several factors: how many people you are cooking for, cost concerns, the way you intend to prepare or use the eggs, and the specific needs of your guests. Eggs are purchased in one of four basic forms:

- **Shell Eggs.** These are fresh eggs, sold in the shell and packed in cartons that contain 6, 12, or 18 eggs. They are also sold in cases; each case contains 12 flats, with 30 eggs on each flat, or 360 eggs per case. If you are checking a delivery of eggs, open the cartons or cases and look at the shells. Remove and discard any eggs that are cracked or broken. Keep shell eggs refrigerated in their original containers. Avoid storing eggs with foods that have strong odors—eggs absorb odors easily.

- **Bulk Eggs.** These eggs are out of their shells and sold in cartons or tubs. You can purchase bulk eggs in different forms: whole eggs (blended yolks and whites), whole eggs with added yolks, yolks only, or whites only. Bulk eggs are **pasteurized**, the process of heating at high temperature to kill bacteria and other pathogens. Store bulk eggs in the refrigerator; store frozen bulk eggs at 0°F. Thaw them under refrigeration to keep them safe.

- **Dried Eggs.** Also known as powdered eggs, these eggs are stored on shelves in the dry storage area of your kitchen. Refrigerate dried eggs after opening the container. To use dried eggs, follow the instructions on the label.

- **Egg Substitutes.** Made either from egg whites or soy-based products, egg substitutes approximate the color, texture, and flavor of an egg. They are used when a customer has a dietary restriction preventing them from consuming egg yolks.

Storage Times and Temperatures for Eggs

Type of Egg Product	Storage Time	Temperature
Shell Eggs	5–7 days	33°–38° F
Bulk Eggs	2–3 days	29°–32° F
Frozen Bulk Eggs	1–2 months	-10°–0° F
Dried	1–2 months	40° F

 **Reading Checkpoint** *What are the four forms in which eggs can be purchased?*

Cooking Eggs

Eggs are probably the most versatile food in the kitchen. Beyond the methods in the following list, eggs are used heavily in baking and pastry work and in the preparation of sauces and soups, also covered later in the book. This section covers the eight basic methods of cooking eggs:

- Eggs cooked in their shells
- Poached eggs
- Fried eggs
- Scrambled eggs
- Omelets
- Shirred eggs
- Quiches
- Soufflés

Eggs Cooked in Their Shells Eggs can be cooked in their shells, producing a variety of results:

- **Coddled**. An ingredient in a modern Caesar salad, **coddled eggs** have warm, thickened whites that are semi-opaque, and the yolk is warm but still very runny.
- **Soft-Cooked**. Also called soft-boiled, these eggs have whites that are barely set and very moist. The yolk is hot but still liquid. They are typically served in the shell in an egg cup. Special spoons may be provided to scoop the egg from the shell.
- **Medium-Cooked**. These eggs have fully set whites. The yolks are thickened and hot. They are served the same way soft-cooked eggs are.
- **Hard-Cooked**. Also known as hard-boiled, these eggs have whites that are completely set and firm. The yolks are also fully cooked and break apart easily when you push on them. Hard-cooked eggs are served as a hot dish at breakfast. They are also served in the form of deviled eggs and egg salad. Cut them into wedges or chop them to use as a garnish for a salad or a vegetable dish.

Eggs are cooked in their shells in simmering water. The shell protects the egg as it cooks. Eggs that are cooked until they are firm keep the shape of the shell even after they are peeled. Hard- and soft-boiled eggs should always be cooked at a steady, gentle simmer. A rapid boil shakes up the egg and can crack the shell. Once that happens, the whites overcook more easily and get tough. The yolk can turn grainy instead of creamy.

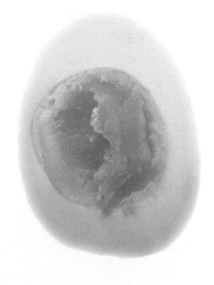

To cook eggs in their shells, lower the eggs into a pot holding enough simmering water to cover them by at least an inch. Cooking times in the following table are counted from the time the water returns to a simmer after you add the eggs.

Cooking Eggs in Their Shells

Doneness	Time (Large Eggs)
Coddled	30 seconds
Soft	3–4 min
Medium	5–7 min
Hard	14–15 min

FIGURE 9-2
Soft-Cooked Egg
A soft-cooked egg is often served for breakfast directly in the shell.
Drawing Conclusions *Why do you think an egg cup is used to serve a soft-cooked egg?*

CHEF'S TIP

GREEN RINGS

The green ring surrounding the yolk in some hard-cooked eggs is a chemical reaction caused by sulfur in the egg yolks. To avoid it, don't overcook the eggs and be sure to peel them as quickly as possible.

Poached Eggs A poached egg is removed from the shell and then cooked in hot water until the white is set but still tender and the yolk is slightly thickened. Poaching, as you remember from Chapter 8, occurs when the liquid is kept at a steady temperature of about 165°F. Temperatures higher than that could produce rubbery whites. Add a small amount of vinegar to the water to keep the egg whites neat and compact.

Use very fresh Grade AA eggs. If you crack the eggs directly into the poaching water, you might break the yolk and spoil the dish. Instead, crack the eggs into cups (one per cup). If the yolks break in the cup, you can still save them for use in another dish.

Slide the eggs out of the cups into the water. The eggs will drop to the bottom of the pan. As they drop, the whites will wrap around the yolks and form an attractive shape.

You can poach eggs to any doneness your customer requests. To prepare poached eggs ahead of time, partially cook them until the white just sets, and then hold them in cold water until needed. When you need the eggs, add them into the cooking water for a minute or two to bring them up to heat and finish the cooking process. They should be served immediately on heated plates.

Fried Eggs A perfectly fried egg is made with a very fresh egg that is cooked quickly in hot oil or butter. The white should be tender and fully cooked. The yolk, no matter how well done, should not break until the guest bursts it with a fork.

You can use just a thin film of oil if you are frying eggs in a non-stick skillet. Keep the heat at about medium high, just hot enough to cook the eggs quickly without scorching them.

There are two types of fried eggs. A **sunny-side-up egg** is cooked in the pan and not flipped. An **over egg** is flipped part way through the cooking process. Over eggs can be cooked over easy, over medium, and over hard (see the description of these levels of doneness on page 251).

CHEF'S TIP

SOUR EGGS

Vinegar added to the egg-poaching water encourages the whites to set, but too much vinegar will flavor the eggs. Use no more than 2 tablespoons per gallon of water.

BASIC CULINARY SKILLS

Poaching Eggs

1 **Bring a pot of water** to 165°F and add some vinegar.

2 **Slide the eggs** into the water.

3 **Poach the eggs** until the white is set, approximately 3–4 minutes.

4 **Lift the eggs** from the water with a slotted spoon or spatula.

5 **Blot the eggs** on a paper towel.

6 **Serve** at once.

See Recipe Card 17, "Poached Eggs."

Frying Eggs

① **Heat the pan** and the cooking fat over moderate heat.

② **Break eggs** into a cup, slide them into the hot fat, and season them.

③ **Baste the eggs**, if desired.

④ **Turn the eggs**, if desired.

⑤ **Cook the eggs** to the desired doneness.

⑥ **Serve** at once.

 See Recipe Card 18, "Fried Eggs."

FIGURE 9-3 ▶
Two Types of Fried Eggs
One sunny-side-up egg served on ham and toast, and two eggs over easy served with bacon, potatoes, and toast.
Communication *Which type of fried egg do you prefer? Why?*

Why Do Egg Whites Cook before the Yolks?

Eggs are made up of long strings of protein molecules. Weak magnetic bonds cause these strings to become tangled into knots. However, a little heat causes these magnetic bonds to break and the knots to become untangled. This allows the protein molecules to form their own new, stronger bonds. Eventually, they form a solid mass. This process is called coagulation.

The white portion of an egg is made up of only proteins and water, so it coagulates at a low temperature, around 145–160°F. Yolks contain more fat and other compounds that have stronger bonds and require more heat to break down. That's why the egg yolk remains raw after the egg whites are cooked.

Experiment

Fry three eggs, producing a different degree of doneness for each. Cook one until the whites are hard but the yolk is completely runny. Cook the next until the yolk is half done, cooked on the outside and runny on the inside. Cook the final egg so the white and the yolk are both completely solid. If you fry the eggs over low heat, you can actually watch as the white coagulates.

The pan is then covered, resulting in a sunny-side-up egg that is fried and steamed. Fried eggs are cooked to three levels of doneness:

- **Easy.** The yolk is warm, runny, and totally unset.
- **Medium.** The yolk is partially set but its center is still slightly runny.
- **Hard.** The yolk is totally set, cooked all the way through.

Scrambled Eggs **Scrambled eggs** are a popular breakfast dish made by mixing the whites and yolks and then stirring them as they cook in a sauté pan or double boiler over low to medium heat. If you stir some water or milk into the eggs before they go into the pan, your scrambled eggs will be fluffier and moister after they cook.

Some garnishes need to be cooked before being added to the egg mixture. Others may be added directly. If you add a garnish, do it while cooking the eggs, not before. The eggs may be broken and scrambled beforehand and then reserved, covered, in the refrigerator until needed. They should not be held more than a day. When serving scrambled eggs, they should be fluffy and moist, but not runny. They should be plated on a warm plate and served immediately.

▼ *Scrambled eggs, ham, asparagus, and toast*

Scrambling Eggs

1 Break eggs into a bowl. Add water or milk, if desired.

2 Season to taste with salt and pepper.

3 Beat the eggs with a fork until evenly blended.

4 Heat the pan and the cooking fat over moderate heat.

5 Add the eggs and stir frequently. Cook over low heat until they are soft and creamy.

6 Serve at once.

 See Recipe Card 19, "Scrambled Eggs."

Omelets An **omelet** is a popular egg dish served at breakfast or brunch. It can be filled or topped with a number of ingredients. Omelets are made by first blending eggs as you do for scrambled eggs. There are two types of omelets: a **rolled omelet**, which you make by stirring the eggs as they cook to keep them tender enough to roll or fold, and a **flat omelet**, which you do not stir but cook slowly for a firmer texture.

The two basic rolled omelet styles are:

- **French Omelet**. Swirl the egg mixture by moving the pan while also stirring the mixture with a fork until small soft moist curds form. Spread the curds in an even layer. The pan's heat sets the eggs on the bottom to make a smooth skin with no large cracks. The omelet is rolled out of the pan on to the plate. Fillings and garnishes are folded into the eggs, stuffed in the middle, or placed on top.
- **American Omelet**. This style of omelet is practical for kitchens that use griddles to prepare most of their egg dishes, but they can also be prepared in an omelet pan. Instead of stirring constantly, the eggs are pushed away from the bottom and sides from time to time. This stirring technique results in larger curds, deep wrinkles, and a bit of browning on the outer layer. American omelets are folded in half instead of rolled. It wouldn't be practical to try to roll something off the griddle.

◀

FIGURE 9-4
Two Types of Rolled Omelets
French omelet is on the left;
American omelet on the right.
Comparing/Contrasting *Describe
the differences in these two
omelets.*

BASIC CULINARY SKILLS

French Omelet

1 **Blend eggs** and add seasonings and garnishes.

2 **Heat a pan** with enough fat to keep the eggs from sticking.

3 **Pour the eggs** into the pan.

4 **Stir the eggs** as they cook until small soft curds form.

 *See Recipe Card 20,
"Plain Rolled Omelet."*

5 **Spread the eggs** into an even layer and add any filling, if desired.

6 **Remove the pan** from the heat and let the eggs rest in the pan.

7 **Shake the pan** to loosen the omelet.

8 **Roll the omelet** out of the pan on to a hot plate.

9 **Serve** at once.

Egg Safety

The risk of getting a foodborne illness from eggs is very low. However, the bacterium Salmonella enteritidis (Se) has been found in a small number of eggs—in 1 out of every 20,000 on average across the United States. The majority of reported salmonellosis outbreaks involving eggs were the result of inadequate refrigeration, improper handling, and insufficient cooking. To ensure that your eggs maintain their high quality and safety:

1. Wash your hands before and after handling eggs and foods that contain eggs.

2. Wash, rinse, and sanitize equipment and work surfaces after handling eggs and foods that contain eggs.

3. Do not use eggs that are broken or cracked, have a slimy feel (may indicate bacterial growth), or have powdery spots that come off on your hand (may indicate mold).

4. Avoid dropping eggshell pieces into a raw egg.

5. Don't keep eggs out of the refrigerator more than 2 hours.

6. Defrost frozen eggs, egg products, and cooked egg dishes safely: in the refrigerator overnight or under running cold water. Use promptly.

7. Cook casseroles and other egg dishes to 160° F. Promptly serve after cooking.

8. Use hard-cooked eggs within 1 week. Use leftover yolks and whites within 3 days. Use cooked egg dishes within 3 or 4 days.

9. Some authorities warn against eating any egg preparation that is not fully cooked.

▼ *Frittata*

The basic flat omelet style is:

- **Frittata** (free-TAH-ta). Also known as a farmer-style omelet (or a tortilla in Spain), a **frittata** is a round, open-face omelet made by pouring beaten eggs into a pan you've preheated over the burner. Once the eggs have cooked and set along the bottom and sides of the pan, you finish cooking the omelet in a hot oven and then cut it in wedges.

Shirred Eggs **Shirred** (SHURD) **eggs** are baked eggs, made by cracking a whole egg into a cup and then cooking it in the oven. They are typically covered with a little cream and topped with breadcrumbs before they are baked. Shirred eggs have firm whites and soft yolks.

Ceramic dishes are the traditional choice for baked eggs because they help cook the eggs evenly and gently. As a further insurance that your eggs will have the best texture, set the filled dishes in a large baking pan and add enough hot water to come up the sides of the dish at least halfway to make a hot water bath.

Quiches A **quiche** (KEESH) is another type of baked egg dish. Eggs are blended with cream or milk, a mixture known as **custard**. The custard is poured into a crust and baked in an oven until the custard is fully cooked. Most quiche recipes include a filling such as cheese, sautéed potatoes or onions, vegetables, or ham.

To check when a quiche is properly baked, insert the tip of a paring knife into the center. If it comes away clean, the eggs are fully cooked and the quiche is ready. Serve hot or at room temperature, as desired.

FIGURE 9-5
Baked Egg Dishes
Spinach quiche and shirred eggs
Comparing/Contrasting *Describe the differences in these two baked egg dishes.*

  Soufflés

Soufflés A **soufflé** (soo-FLAY) is a light, puffed egg dish baked in a ceramic dish. The straight sides of the dish help the soufflé rise up as it bakes. To make a soufflé, you begin by preparing the molds. Rub or brush them liberally with butter to keep the eggs from sticking when the soufflé is served. Next, scatter breadcrumbs or grated cheese over the butter to give the soufflé mixture something to help it rise properly.

The next step is separating the eggs. The yolks are stirred into a base, usually a thick sauce made with milk. The whites are beaten into a thick foam. You combine the base mixture with the beaten whites gently, using a stirring technique know as folding. Folding helps keep air in the egg whites.

As soon as the soufflé is folded together, spoon or ladle it into the prepared dishes and bake in a hot oven.

✓ **Reading Checkpoint** — *What are the basic types of egg cookery?*

Identifying and Storing Dairy Products

Dairy products come in a variety of forms, with a variety of flavors and textures. Each form of dairy product is made up of water, solid particles, and fat, referred to as **milkfat** or **butterfat**. Dairy products are labeled according to the percent of milkfat they contain. Milk and cream are pasteurized and then **homogenized**—a process that evenly distributes and emulsifies the fat particles.

Milk Milk is served as a beverage and also used as an ingredient. There are several forms of milk, from skim milk to whole milk. A number of products are made from milk, including creams, butter, and yogurt. An important type of dairy product, cheese, is discussed in greater detail in Chapter 10.

Milk from cows is the basis of most dairy products, although you may also find goat- and sheep-milk dairy products. Milk is mostly water, with some protein, some sugar, and some fat.

Types of Milk

Form	Description	Type of Container
Whole	Contains no less than 3% milkfat.	Bulk, gallon, half-gallon, quart, pint, ½ pint
Low-Fat	Usually contains 1 or 2% milkfat and is generally labeled accordingly.	Same as whole milk
Skim (Nonfat)	Contains less than 0.1% milkfat.	Same as whole milk
Dry (Powdered)	Milk from which water is completely removed. Made from either whole or skim milk.	50 lbs bulk, 24 oz bulk
Evaporated	Milk that has been heated in a vacuum to remove 60% of its water. May be made from whole, low-fat, or skim milk, with milkfat content as high as 8% to as low as 0.5%.	14.5-oz, 10-oz, or 6-oz cans
Condensed	Evaporated milk that has been sweetened.	Same as evaporated milk

The production of milk is closely regulated. Milk is inspected regularly to be sure it is kept sanitary. Milk and dairy products made from milk are pasteurized to kill harmful bacteria, and then rapidly chilled. Homogenized dairy products are forced through fine screens to break up the butterfat so it won't separate and rise to the top.

Cream and Cultured Dairy Products Cream is thicker, richer tasting, and has a higher milkfat content than milk. It is homogenized and pasteurized, and available in different varieties.

Cultured dairy products such as buttermilk, sour cream, and yogurt are made by adding a specific type of beneficial bacteria to milk or cream. As the bacteria grow, they thicken the milk or cream and give it a tart taste. **Crème fraîche** (krehm fraysh), French for "fresh cream," is similar in flavor and texture to sour cream, but because it contains so much butterfat, it will not curdle in hot soups and sauces the way sour cream and yogurt can.

Butter Butter is made by churning cream until the fat clumps together, squeezing out the water. The best quality butter, grades AA or A, has a delicate, creamy flavor. Salt is often added as a preservative, but it should not be a strong flavor. Lower grades of butter are made from lesser quality cream and may smell a little like cheese.

CHEF'S TIP

NON-DAIRY PRODUCTS

People who are lactose-intolerant and can't digest milk can find milk, cream, yogurt, butter, and cheese made from soy, almonds, or rice. Read the information on the package if you want to substitute them in cooked or baked goods.

Types of Cream and Cultured Dairy Products

Form	Description	Type of Container
Cream, Heavy or Whipping	Contains at least 36% milkfat. Light whipping cream is occasionally available, containing 30 to 35% fat.	Quart, pint, ½ pint
Cream, Light	Contains between 18 and 30% milkfat.	Same as heavy cream
Half-and-Half	Equal parts milk and cream. Contains between 10.5 and 18% milkfat. Used as a lightener for coffee.	Same as heavy cream and in portion sizes
Buttermilk	Thickened, cultured, tangy nonfat or low-fat milk. Used in baking.	Quart, pint
Sour Cream	Thickened, cultured sweet cream. Contains between 16 and 22% milkfat.	Variety of sizes, starting with ½ pint
Yogurt	Thickened, cultured milk. Can be whole, low-fat, or nonfat; flavored or plain.	Variety of sizes, starting with ½ pint
Crème Fraîche	Thickened, cultured, heavy cream with a nutty flavor. Contains 30% milkfat.	Variety of sizes, starting with ½ pint

Clarified Butter

1 Place butter into a cold pot or pan.

2 Heat the pan over a moderate flame.

3 Melt the butter and bring it to a sizzling boil.

4 Boil off most of the water without burning the milk solids.

5 Skim off the foam.

6 Ladle or pour out the clarified butter to remove it, leaving the milk solids at the bottom of the pan.

FOCUS ON NUTRITION

Margarine vs. Butter

Trans fatty acids have been linked to coronary heart disease. Butter contains cholesterol, which is also linked to heart disease. The controversy about using margarine versus butter rages on. Some sources advise limiting your intake of both.

Butter is served as a spread for rolls, breads, and toast and as a topping for pancakes and waffles. You can introduce more flavor and color by blending butter with fruits, herbs, or other ingredients.

Whole butter is made up of mostly butterfat with milk solids and some water. When whole butter gets hot, the milk solids can burn and the butter will start to smoke. To use butter as a cooking fat at high temperatures, you need to remove the milk solids and water, leaving you with what is called **clarified butter**.

Margarine is a butter substitute made from vegetable oils. It comes in many forms, such as regular stick, soft, and whipped. To make margarine, the oils must undergo a chemical transformation which creates what are called trans fatty acids. For culinary purposes, butter is more flavorful than margarine.

Storing Dairy Products Like eggs, dairy products are highly perishable. Most dairy containers are dated to indicate how long the contents will remain fresh. Store dairy products away from foods with strong odors.

 **Reading Checkpoint** *What is the difference between milk and cream?*

Storage Times and Temperatures for Dairy Products

Product	Storage Time*	Temperature
Pasteurized Milk: whole, low-fat, skim	1 week	35°–40° F
Powdered Milk	Unopened: 3 months Reconstituted: 1 week	60°–70° F 35°–40° F
Evaporated Milk	Unopened: 6 months Opened: 3-5 days	60°–70° F 35°–40° F
Condensed Milk	Unopened: 2-3 months Opened: 3-5 days	60°–70° F 35°–40° F
Buttermilk	2-3 weeks	35°–40° F
Yogurt	3-6 weeks	35°–40° F
Heavy or Whipping Cream	1 week	35°–40° F
Light Cream or Half-and-Half	Opened: 1 week Unopened: 4 weeks	35°–40° F
Butter	3-5 months	35°–40° F
Clarified Butter	3 weeks	35°–40° F

*Check expiration dates on products

9.1 ASSESSMENT

Reviewing Concepts

1. What are the four forms in which eggs can be purchased?
2. What are the basic methods for cooking eggs?
3. Describe the difference between milk and cream.

Critical Thinking

4. **Analyzing Information** You're making poached eggs. They keep coming out tasting acidic, and the yolk is totally set. What's going wrong?
5. **Predicting** When butter is not properly clarified, it has solid particles in it. What will happen to this butter when it is used to fry eggs, and how will it affect the flavor of the eggs?
6. **Classifying** You slide an egg on to a pan to fry it. The egg white spreads far out; the yolk is flat and off center. What grade of egg is it?

Test Kitchen

Divide into teams and make omelets. Half of the teams should use a griddle and make an American-style omelet, and the other half should use a pan and make a French-style omelet. What differences do you observe between the American and French omelets? Considering the equipment, length of time needed, and the final product, which method would you use in a restaurant kitchen?

SOCIAL STUDIES

Dairy in Asia

Traditionally, dairy products are not part of the diet in East and South Asia. Research dairy consumption in that part of the world, and try to come up with a theory as to why dairy is unpopular there.

Breakfast Foods & Drinks

READING PREVIEW

Key Concepts

- Preparing pancakes, waffles, and French toast
- Identifying breakfast breads and cereals
- Identifying breakfast meats and potatoes
- Identifying hot and cold breakfast beverages

Vocabulary

- batter
- caffeine
- Canadian bacon
- chicken-fried steak
- continental breakfast
- crêpe
- croissants
- French toast
- hash
- hash browns
- home fries
- muesli
- scone
- smoothie

> **"S**imple things, done well, make all the difference. At breakfast, a perfect cup of coffee might change a single visit to your establishment into a loyal customer. **"**
>
> – Stephen Johnson
> The Culinary Institute
> of America

Pancakes, Waffles, and French Toast

Pancakes, waffles, and French toast are popular, specially cooked breakfast foods. Pancakes and waffles are made from batters. A **batter** is a very wet form of dough made from flour, oil or melted butter, eggs, milk or other liquids, salt, and usually baking powder. Varying the proportions of these ingredients will yield different results, and this is why waffles are fluffy and pancakes are cakey. Pancakes and waffles are served with a variety of toppings, including butter, syrup, fruit toppings, and whipped cream.

Cooking Pancakes and Waffles

1 Sift the dry ingredients together.

2 Combine all the liquid ingredients in a bowl.

3 Add the combined liquid ingredients to the combined dry ingredients. Do not overmix.

4 Coat a griddle or waffle iron with fat and preheat.

5 Ladle the batter on to the cooking surface.

6 Cook the batter until it takes on a golden color and is totally cooked. For pancakes, turn once when bubbles appear on top of the pancake and the edges begin to dry. The second side takes half the time as the first to cook.

7 Serve immediately.

See Recipe Cards 25, "Buttermilk Pancakes," and 26, "Waffles."

French toast is a piece of bread that is dipped in a mixture of milk and eggs and then fried until golden brown on both sides. The mixture often contains sugar, cinnamon, and nutmeg. French toast can be made with different types of bread and is typically served with syrup, fruit toppings, or powdered sugar.

A **crêpe** (KRAYP) is a French pancake. It is created from an extremely thin batter that contains no baking powder, and it is cooked in a special pan over moderate heat. The result is a paper-thin, wrapper-like pancake. Breakfast crêpes are often spread with jam or a fruit mixture and then folded or rolled.

▼ *Crêpes*

Cooking Crêpes

1 **Combine** the eggs, cream, milk, and oil and beat until just blended.

2 **Sift together** the flour, sugar, and salt and place in a mixing bowl.

3 **Add wet ingredients** and mix until smooth, scraping down the bowl as you go.

4 **Add flavoring ingredients** and stir until blended and the batter is smooth.

5 **Rest batter** under refrigeration for up to 12 hours; strain if necessary.

6 **Preheat and butter** a crêpe pan over moderate to high heat.

7 **Add batter** to the pan, swirling the pan to coat it evenly with the crêpe batter.

8 **Cook over moderate heat.** When set, turn over and finish the other side.

9 **Cool crêpes,** if desired. Place on parchment paper and hold cold.

Reading Checkpoint *What are the basic ingredients of a pancake or waffle batter?*

Breakfast Breads and Cereals

A variety of breads are served at breakfast. They can be served as an accompaniment to eggs for a hearty breakfast or with coffee, tea, and juice as a **continental breakfast**. Baking bread is discussed in Chapters 17 and 18. Food-service establishments often use ready-made breakfast breads, including:

- Toasted bread, such as rye, white, or whole wheat bread
- English muffins
- Bagels, made plain or with sesame seeds, raisins, or other ingredients
- **Croissants** (kwah-SAHNTs), which are buttery-rich, crescent-shaped yeast rolls
- Pastries, which are often filled with almond paste, fruit, or cream
- Donuts, which are deep-fried and often ring-shaped
- Muffins, such as corn, blueberry, or bran muffins
- Loaf-style breads, such as banana bread and cran-berry nut bread
- Biscuits, which are light and flakey. A **scone** is a rich biscuit that sometimes contains raisins and is served with butter, jam, or thick cream.

▲ *Continental breakfast with croissant*

CULINARY HISTORY

French Toast

No one knows who first made French toast. A recipe for white bread, soaked in milk and beaten eggs, fried in oil, and covered with honey, dates back to Ancient Rome. Another recipe, from Medieval Italy, calls for sugar and rose-water instead of honey.

Many European countries have simi-lar recipes but different names for the dish we know as French toast. In Spain it is called torriga; in England, it is "Poor Knights of Windsor." In this country, it has been called German toast and nun's toast. One theory for how it was named French toast starts with tavern owner Joseph French in Albany, New York, in 1724. He put the dish on his menu as French toast instead of the grammatically correct "French's toast," leading people, generations later, to be-lieve it was a French dish.

One thing is certain. If you go to France, you won't find French toast on the menu. The French call it pain perdu, meaning "lost bread," based on the tradition of reviving day-old bread with milk and eggs and then cooking it on a hot griddle.

Research

Use the Internet to research some of the historic French toast recipes. How do the recipes compare with today's version of the dish?

Cereal is a breakfast staple for both children and adults. It is also a breakfast choice in restaurants. Preparation of hot cereals, such as those made from oats or wheat, is discussed in Chapter 13. Cold cereals require no preparation. They are generally eaten with milk and topped with fresh fruit such as bananas or berries. Granola is often eaten with yogurt instead of milk. The Swiss version of granola is **muesli** (MYOOS-lee), a mixture of cereal (such as oats and wheat), dried fruit, nuts, bran, and sugar. It is eaten with milk or yogurt.

 **Reading Checkpoint** *What are ready-made breakfast breads and cereals?*

Breakfast Meats and Potatoes

Meat plays a huge part in the American diet, and breakfast is no exception to that rule. A wide variety of meats are served at breakfast, often with both eggs and potatoes. The most common breakfast meats are bacon, sausage, and ham.

- **Bacon**. Salted and smoked meat from the belly of a pig, bacon is available in many forms, such as sliced, thin or thick, or sold in one chunk as slab bacon. Bacon is usually highly fatty and shrinks during cooking. **Canadian bacon** is made from a much leaner portion of the pig. More similar to ham than to regular bacon, it comes in chunks or slices. Bacon is usually cooked in an oven to produce large volumes, but may also be cooked in a pan on low heat.
- **Sausages**. A combination of ground meat, fat, water, and salt, with a variety of flavorings added, sausages are available as both patties and links. Links are wrapped in a casing, which is usually the intestinal membrane of an animal. The standard breakfast link sausage comes to you uncooked. Before cooking it for service, you may want to poach it so it stays together if you plan to slice or dice it. To poach the sausage, prick it with a needle anywhere you see an air bubble. Then submerge it in 165°F water until totally cooked (check this with an instant-read thermometer). After poaching, you can sauté the sausage in a pan or on a griddle.
- **Ham**. Common all over the country and available in many forms, ham used for breakfast is typically smoked, precooked, pre-sliced. Heat it in a broiler or on a griddle before serving.
- **Chicken-Fried Steak.** Popular in the South and Midwest, **chicken-fried steak** is a thin steak dipped into a mixture of egg, milk, and seasonings and then fried like chicken until crisp. It's topped with country gravy and served with eggs and biscuits.

FOCUS ON NUTRITION

Nitrates and Nitrites

Certain preservatives are usually added to sausages and bacon during the curing process. These are called nitrates and nitrites. Although not directly harmful, they break down into nitrosamines at high heat. Nitrosamines are one of the many carcinogens found in cigarettes. The point? Cook your breakfast meats at lower temperatures, and don't eat too much. Or look for products without these preservatives.

- **Hash.** A tasty breakfast combination of chopped meat (typically corned beef), potatoes, and seasonings, **hash** is pan-fried and often served with a poached or fried egg on top.
- **Hash Browns.** A popular side dish, **hash browns** are finely chopped or grated potatoes, pressed down in a pan or on a griddle to brown on one side and then flipped to brown on the other side. **Home fries** are sliced potatoes that are pan-fried, often with chopped peppers and onions.

CHEF'S TIP

DON'T BURN
YOUR BACON

If you are cooking bacon, especially in the oven, and you actually smell the bacon cooking, you have overcooked it. Bacon can be served crisp or tender, but never burned.

FIGURE 9-6
Hearty Breakfast
Bacon, eggs, hash browns, toast, and coffee
Classifying *What are some other breakfast food combinations that can be served together on one plate?*

Reading Checkpoint *How are meats and potatoes used in breakfast dishes?*

Breakfast Beverages

For many people, breakfast is not complete without their beverage of choice. Breakfast beverages either provide additional nutrients or they offer **caffeine**, a chemical found in coffee, tea, chocolate, and sodas that stimulates your body and mind.

- **Coffee**. Coffee is a dark brown liquid produced from running water through roasted, ground coffee beans. Coffee starts as a small, green bean, grown in tropical climates. The beans are harvested by hand and then subjected to a long roasting process. Different flavors are related to the environment where the bean originates, as well as to the roasting process it undergoes. The more a bean is roasted, the "darker" the flavor and the less acidity and caffeine it has. To produce the best possible coffee, you want to start with a whole bean, grind it yourself, and immediately brew coffee from the grind. Also, you should keep coffee for only 20 minutes and then brew a new batch.

FIGURE 9-7 ▶
Coffee
Coffee goes through many stages before it makes it into your cup.
Drawing Conclusions *What gives coffee its familiar dark color?*

▲ *Papaya, berry, and coconut smoothies*

As the coffee sits, the acidity level builds and the flavor of the coffee becomes unpleasant.

- **Tea**. Compared to coffee, tea is lighter in color, contains less caffeine and less acidity, and is actually made quite differently. Tea is made by allowing leaves to steep in hot water, where they release their essential oils slowly, flavoring the liquid. Many ingredients can be used to make tea. In Asian cultures, tea can be composed of fruit zest, spices, flowers, or even bark. Teas made from herbs such as peppermint leaves or chamomile flowers contain no caffeine.

- **Juice**. Available in a variety of market forms, juices are a popular breakfast accompaniment. Fresh fruit or vegetable juice is ideal and nutritious, but not always an option. The cardboard tubes you find in the grocer's freezer are standard frozen concentrate and are combined with water and stirred to produce something near the fresh form.

- **Smoothie**. A **smoothie** is a cold drink made by mixing fresh fruit (such as bananas and strawberries), juice, and ice in a blender until thick and smooth. Smoothies can also contain milk or yogurt. The nutritional value of a smoothie can make it a breakfast substitute—a meal in a glass.

✓ **Reading Checkpoint** *Which breakfast beverages contain caffeine?*

Vietnam

The country of Vietnam is located in Southeastern Asia and has a tropical climate. It is entirely exposed to water on its Eastern border. As such, Vietnamese cuisine uses a lot of fresh seafood. Rice plays an integral role in the diets, as it does in almost all Asian countries. Because France occupied the country for many years, the cuisine has also developed a more Western style than that of other Asian countries. There is prolific use of fresh herbs, citrus, galangal root (a sour, pungent form of ginger), lemongrass, and fish sauce.

A typical Sunday breakfast in Vietnam is quite different from what we are accustomed to. Made with thin vermicelli rice noodles, a savory, complex beef soup called pho (pronounced fuh) is found everywhere, from large restaurants to street vendors. It has certain variations depending on locale, but the most popular form is dark, rich, has hints of roasted anise and clove, and is garnished with

▲ *Breakfast: pho*

fresh cilantro, lime, bean sprouts, pieces of thinly sliced rare beef, and sometimes chili sauce. Slurping loudly, with one's head held just above the bowl, is considered the proper way to consume the dish.

Research

Research the different varieties of pho. Describe how they are made. List the different kinds of ingredients used.

9.2 ASSESSMENT

Reviewing Concepts

1. List the ingredients common to most breakfast batters.
2. Give examples of ready-made breakfasts, describing the components included.
3. Describe the different breakfast meats.
4. List breakfast drinks that do not contain caffeine.

Critical Thinking

5. **Classifying** What types of cooked eggs have a completely cooked white and yolk?
6. **Comparing/Contrasting** Describe the similarities and differences between pancake batter and the liquid mixture used to make French toast.
7. **Comparing/Contrasting** Describe the similarities and differences between bacon and Canadian bacon.

Test Kitchen

Split up into groups. One third of the groups should make pancakes, one third waffles, and one third French toast. Start at the same time, and produce three servings. Compare cooking times. As a chef in a restaurant kitchen, which would you prefer having on the menu?

CULINARY **MATH**

Making Pancakes

You need to make pancakes for 20 people. Each person will eat 2 pancakes; each pancake is made from 4 oz of batter. A single recipe yields 1 qt of batter. How much batter do you need? How many times do you have to scale up the recipe (what is your RCF)?

Review and Assessment

Reviewing Content

Choose the letter that best answers the question or completes the statement.

1. Grade A eggs are
   a. the freshest grade of egg, with a high, centered yolk and tight whites
   b. good for blended egg dishes
   c. used in commercial egg preparations
   d. best for fried egg dishes

2. A French omelet can be described as
   a. flat
   b. round
   c. rolled
   d. baked

3. The biggest difference between cream and milk is
   a. milk has a higher milkfat content than cream
   b. cream is lighter than milk
   c. milk has a slightly more yellow color than cream
   d. cream has a higher milkfat content than milk

4. To make crêpes, you
   a. pour batter into the center of a pan and then cook over medium heat
   b. ladle batter on to a griddle and then cook over low heat
   c. pour batter into the center of a pan and then cook over high heat
   d. swirl batter to coat the bottom of a pan and then cook over medium heat

5. Hash can best be described as a combination of
   a. potatoes and corned beef
   b. ground meats
   c. meat and peppers
   d. potatoes and onions

6. You do not use batter to make
   a. pancakes
   b. waffles
   c. French toast
   d. any of the above

Understanding Concepts

7. Describe the structure of an egg.

8. Compare and contrast poaching eggs and cooking eggs in the shell.

9. Explain how clarified butter is made.

10. What is a continental breakfast?

Critical Thinking

11. **Comparing/Contrasting** What would you do differently if you were preparing an egg over hard versus a sunny-side-up egg?

12. **Classifying** List breakfast options that use ready-made products and fresh ingredients and that require no cooking.

13. **Applying Concepts** What is the best hand tool for pouring batter on to a griddle?

Culinary Math

14. **Relating Concepts** You're preparing scrambled eggs for 10 people. Each person will eat 6 oz of eggs. How many large eggs are needed to feed everyone?

15. **Relating Concepts** A pancake calls for 2 oz of syrup for each pancake. The batter recipe yields 2 gallons, and there are 4 oz of batter to a pancake. Based on the total number of pancakes made from the recipe, how much syrup is needed?

On the Job

16. **Applying Concepts** You only have a griddle for cooking eggs. What type of egg dishes can you prepare?

17. **Problem Solving** You're trying to poach eggs but the yolks keep breaking when they hit the water. How might this be avoided?

RECIPE CARDS

Use the following Recipe Cards to test your culinary skill.

16. Hard-Cooked Eggs
17. Poached Eggs
18. Fried Eggs
19. Scrambled Eggs
20. Plain Rolled Omelet
21. Spinach Soufflé
22. Shirred Eggs
23. Quiche Lorraine
24. French Toast
25. Buttermilk Pancakes
26. Waffles
27. Hash

LAB ACTIVITY

Project 9: Preparing Breakfasts

Answer these questions when your class works through Project 9.

- How did you organize your team?
- Who did the mise en place?
- Did you break down individual cooking tasks?
- How long did each team take to prepare the breakfast?
- Did the division of labor within teams make it more efficient?
- How could you have improved the team's performance?
- How did the various teams' breakfasts taste?
- Was there any link between a team's efficiency and the quality of its breakfast?

TEST PRACTICE

Choose the letter that best answers the question or completes the statement.

1. Which of the following are commonly stored frozen?
   A   shell eggs
   B   bulk eggs
   C   dried eggs
   D   egg substitutes

2. Which of the following egg dishes is made in a skillet?
   A   shirred eggs
   B   soufflé
   C   quiche
   D   frittata

3. Milk that has a fat content at or above 3% is considered
   A   whole milk
   B   light cream
   C   low-fat milk
   D   none of the above

4. A continental breakfast typically contains:
   A   eggs
   B   breakfast meat
   C   breakfast bread
   D   smoothies

5. Which type of egg is cooked in its shell for 30 seconds?
   A   soft-cooked
   B   medium-cooked
   C   hard-cooked
   D   coddled

6. Coffee is ___; tea is ___.
   A   brewed; steeped
   B   caffeinated; decaffeinated
   C   for breakfast; for brunch
   D   made with boiling water; made with simmering water

7. Which part of an egg contains the albumen?
   A   yolk
   B   white
   C   shell
   D   fat

8. Which type of breakfast meat is wrapped in a casing?
   A   bacon
   B   ham
   C   sausage patty
   D   link sausage

10

GARDE MANGER

10.1 Dressings & Dips

10.2 Salads

10.3 Cheese

10.4 Cold Food Presentation

READING PREVIEW

Key Concepts

- Understanding the garde manger station
- Identifying and preparing dressings and dips

Vocabulary

- baba ghanoush
- balsamic vinegar
- basic vinaigrette
- dip
- emulsified vinaigrette
- emulsifier
- emulsion
- extra-virgin olive oil
- garde manger
- guacamole
- herbes de Provence
- mayonnaise
- salad dressing
- salsa
- tapenade
- vinaigrette

> "**S**alad dressings may not require hours of simmering on the stove, but they demand the same level of skill and care on the part of the chef."
>
> – Joseba Encabo

Garde Manger

The **garde manger** (GAHRD mohn-ZHAY), also known as the pantry chef, is the person (or persons) responsible for cold food preparations. In professional kitchens, the term garde manger is typically extended to include all the types of food for which the garde manger is responsible. Today, with diners becoming increasingly familiar with ethnic and imported foods, the garde manger is usually responsible for the foods discussed in this chapter:

- Salad dressings and dips
- Salads
- Cheeses
- Cold food presentations and garnishes

However, kitchens may have different requirements for their particular garde manger station. For example, if a salad requires a grilled chicken breast that is presented sliced and cold on the salad, the grill station would first grill the chicken and then deliver it to the garde manger to cool and use in the salad.

Joseba Encabo (left)
The Culinary Institute of America

Within a particular kitchen, the work flow determines which responsibilities are assigned to the garde manger. Cold sandwiches, cold hors d'oeuvres and appetizers, and preserved meats (all of which are discussed in the next chapter) are often assigned to the garde manger as well.

 **Reading Checkpoint** *What is the garde manger?*

Salad Dressings and Dips

A **salad dressing** is used primarily to flavor salads and, sometimes, to hold a salad together. Many salad dressings are also used as dips. A **dip** is a sauce or condiment served with raw vegetables, crackers, bread, potato chips, or other snack foods. Typically these foods are eaten as appetizers, often while the diner is standing.

Salad dressings and dips fall into five main categories:
- Vinaigrettes (both basic and emulsified vinaigrettes)
- Mayonnaise
- Dairy-based dressings and dips
- Cooked dressings and dips
- Vegetable- or fruit-based dressings and dips

Vinaigrettes A **vinaigrette** (vin-eh-GRETT) is a salad dressing made by combining oil and vinegar into an emulsion. An **emulsion** (e-MULL-shon) is a mixture of uniform consistency made with two ingredients that would otherwise not combine together.

There are two types of vinaigrettes:
- Basic vinaigrette
- Emulsified vinaigrette

A **basic vinaigrette** is a temporary emulsion, typically of some type of oil and some type of vinegar. The process of stirring or vigorously mixing the vinaigrette permits the vinegar and oil to mix together. However, over time, the individual ingredients will separate.

To make an emulsion permanent, an **emulsifier** (e-mull-si-FY-er) is added, resulting in an **emulsified vinaigrette**. Examples of emulsifiers used for salad dressings are egg yolks, mustard, cornstarch, potato starch, or arrowroot. These substances attract both the oil and vinegar in the vinaigrette, thus binding the two ingredients together.

The standard proportion of oil to vinegar in a vinaigrette is three parts oil mixed with one part vinegar. Using an electric blender or mixer forms a basic vinaigrette more quickly and stays emulsified longer than if blended by hand. To keep a basic vinaigrette well blended, mix it before each use.

The principle behind making a good vinaigrette is to achieve a balance between the mouth-coating texture and rich flavor of the oil and the sharp acidity of the vinegar. Because it can be a simple combination of just a few ingredients, a vinaigrette is only as good as its ingredients.

FOCUS ON SANITATION

Storing Salad Dressings
Salad dressings should be stored in tightly covered containers to prevent outside contamination. Make sure they have air circulation and are cooled below 41°F.

FIGURE 10-1
Mise en Place for Vinaigrette
It's important to achieve a balance of textures and flavors in a vinaigrette.
Drawing Conclusions *Why should you try to use the best ingredients possible for a vinaigrette?*

Vinaigrette

1 Combine seasonings, such as mustard and salt.

2 Add vinegar and whisk to blend.

3 Whisk in the oil gradually, in a fine steady stream.

4 Continue blending ingredients until the mixture has a uniform consistency.

5 Adjust seasonings, if necessary.

 See Recipe Card 28, "Red-Wine Vinaigrette."

FOCUS ON NUTRITION

Reduced-Fat Vinaigrette

For a lower-fat, lower-calorie vinaigrette, substitute up to half of the oil called for by the recipe with a lightly thickened vegetable juice, such as tomato.

Although a vinaigrette can be nothing more than oil and vinegar that enhance the flavor of perfect salad greens, a vinaigrette can also be a complex mixture of unusual oils, fruit juices, herbs, and other components that provide a unique flavor experience on their own. Some of the ingredients you can use in creating vinaigrettes are:

- **Olive Oil.** The classic oil used in a vinaigrette is a flavorful olive oil. Olive oil is produced in many grades. Some chefs use a grade designated **extra-virgin olive oil**. This is the finest grade of olive oil, produced by pressing olives once without using any heat. It has a fruity, grassy, or peppery taste with a pale yellow to bright green color and a very low acid content. Other chefs feel that extra-virgin olive oil, because of its expense, is wasted in a vinaigrette where its delicate taste is masked by other ingredients.

The shelf life of extra-virgin olive oil is one year if stored in a cool, dark place, but the fresher it is, the better. For the best flavor, keep olive oil in a dark bottle, capped or corked, and away from direct heat. If pouring from a large can or bottle, pour off as much as you need for the day or the week into a smaller bottle. Keep the larger can or bottle capped, in a cool pantry or cellar.

- **Other Oils.** Although olive oil is a traditional choice for vinaigrettes, many other types of oils can be used. Some that are often used are walnut oil, hazelnut oil, and sunflower oil. Oils that are flavored with herbs and aromatics are also available. Oils should be of high quality for the best flavor and nutritional value. Olive oil and another type of oil are also sometimes mixed together.

- **Vinegar.** A wide variety of vinegars can be used in vinaigrettes. Some of the most common types of vinegars used are red-wine vinegar, white-wine vinegar, cider vinegar, or commercial balsamic vinegar. Commercial **balsamic** (bahl-SAH-mek) **vinegar** has a sweet-sour taste. Vinegars flavored with herbs and aromatics are also available. Most vinegars used in a vinaigrette have a mellow taste.

  A vinaigrette is typically named for the acid used in making it. So, for example, if red-wine vinegar is used, the vinaigrette would be referred to as a red-wine vinaigrette.

- **Other Acids.** Citrus juice, such as lemon, lime, or orange juice, is sometimes substituted for vinegar in a salad dressing. While each type of citrus juice adds acidity, it also adds fruit flavor to the vinaigrette.

- **Mustard.** Of all types of mustards, Dijon (DEE-jhan) mustard is the most commonly used mustard in vinaigrettes. Mustards are the most common type of emulsifier used in creating emulsified vinaigrettes. Prepared mustard can be added to a vinaigrette, but a dry, powdered mustard works just as effectively as an emulsifier. While it makes the emulsion more permanent, mustard, both prepared or dry, also adds a savory, spicy flavor component to the vinaigrette.

- **Herbs.** Fresh herbs can provide another dimension to a vinaigrette. However, herbs discolor and change flavor when added too far in advance. For this reason, add herbs at the last minute.

CHEF'S TIP

TOO CREATIVE?
Although creativity is the mark of a distinguished garde manger, too many seasonings and conflicting ingredients can mask the taste of fine olive oil and good vinegar.

Herbs suitable for use in a vinaigrettes include tarragon, thyme, dill, chives, chervil, mint, basil, or **herbes de Provence** (AIRBS duh proh-VAWNS), a dried herb mixture traditionally associated with France's Provence region that can include such herbs as basil, thyme, marjoram, rosemary, sage, fennel seeds, and lavender.

- **Salt and Pepper.** Salt is important in maintaining the balance of flavor in a vinaigrette. Without adequate salt, a vinaigrette often tastes too harsh. Because it has no additives, kosher salt is often used in vinaigrettes. White or black pepper is also added to a vinaigrette. Even though salt and pepper were added in making the vinaigrette, it is still necessary to taste the salad with the vinaigrette to see if additional salt and pepper are needed.

BASIC CULINARY SKILLS

Mayonnaise

1 Blend egg yolks with a little water.

2 Whisk in one-fourth of the oil a little at time until a creamy and consistent texture forms.

3 Mix in additional flavoring ingredients (such as vinegar, lemon juice, mustard), if using.

4 Add remaining oil gradually, beating continually until soft peaks form.

5 Store in the refrigerator.

 See Recipe Card 33, "Mayonnaise."

- **Sugar.** Vinaigrettes sometimes contain a small pinch of honey or sugar (or other sweetener) to temper the acidity of the vinegar. Honey is also a common component in an emulsified vinaigrette where the honey and mustard combination produce a combination of savory, spicy, sweet, and sour flavors.

Although vinaigrettes are usually thought of as salad dressings, they have many other uses. Depending on the composition of the vinaigrette, it can be used for such things as:

- Adding flavor and moisture when grilling meat or fish
- Dressing cooked vegetables
- Dipping raw or cooked vegetables
- Dressing bean, grain, or rice salads
- Enhancing the flavor of sandwiches

Mayonnaise Mayonnaise (MAY-oh-nayz) is a cold, thick, creamy emulsion of oil and egg yolks. Mayonnaise has many uses in the pantry, either on its own or in combination with other ingredients. For example, combined with vinaigrette, it makes a creamy dressing for salads and other cold foods. Combined with canned tuna, it is used to make tuna salad. Combined with hard boiled eggs, it is used to make egg salad.

Commercial mayonnaise is convenient and has a long shelf life. It suits many purposes but does not compare in flavor or consistency to properly made, fresh mayonnaise. Freshly made mayonnaise is often more richly flavored and looser in consistency than the commercial variety.

Although the recipe for mayonnaise involves only a few ingredients, care is necessary when combining the oil with the egg yolk. Initially, you need to whisk in the oil a drop at a time. The oil must be worked vigorously into the egg to create very small droplets that begin to form the foundation of the emulsion. If the oil is added too quickly and the droplets are too large, an emulsion will not form and the mayonnaise will separate. When about one-fourth of the oil has been incorporated properly, you can add the remaining oil in a steady stream while whisking continually. Whether working by hand with a whisk or using an electric mixer or food processor, you should add the oil very gradually in the beginning and more steadily at the end.

Liquids such as lemon juice, vinegar, or water may be added to adjust for taste and consistency.

Figure 10-2
Mise en Place for Mayonnaise
Making mayonnaise results in a looser, more richly flavored product than most commercial mayonnaise.
Applying Concepts *When might it make sense for a kitchen to use commercially prepared mayonnaise?*

Be sure to add these liquids before the oil is added, to ensure the stability of the emulsion. The mayonnaise is finished when soft peaks form. It may be thinned further by beating in additional water if a dressing consistency is desired. Any additional flavorings, such as chopped herbs, pickles, or capers, can be added to the finished mayonnaise.

Because the egg yolk is raw, mayonnaise must be made and stored with care to prevent contamination. Commercial kitchens typically use pasteurized eggs to prevent the possibility of rapid deterioration and the possibility of salmonella poisoning.

If the mayonnaise begins to separate (chefs refer to this as breaking), the problem can be corrected by gradually incorporating beaten pasteurized egg yolk into the mixture. Introduce the egg yolk slowly, whisking continually until the mixture becomes thick and homogeneous.

Dairy-Based Dressings and Dips Dairy products are sometimes used as the basis for salad dressings and dips. For a dip, you could start with a soft cheese such as cream cheese. (You will learn more

FOCUS ON SAFETY

Pasteurized Eggs
Eggs used for making mayonnaise in an institutional setting should be processed and pasteurized in USDA-inspected plants to ensure against the possibility of salmonella.

Common Mayonnaise Dressings and Dips

Dressing or Dip	Description	Use
Aïoli (aye-YOH-lee)	Garlic mayonnaise, possibly with flavoring such as herbs or sun-dried tomatoes	Cold poached fish, snails, fish soup, boiled meats or cooked vegetables, hard-cooked eggs, salads, or cold meats
Green Goddess	Mayonnaise mixed with tarragon vinegar and anchovies; flavored with parsley, chives, tarragon, scallions, and garlic	Salads, fish, shellfish
Russian Dressing	Mayonnaise mixed with ketchup and possibly relish or pickles	Salads, sandwiches, hard-cooked eggs, cooked meats and vegetables
Tartar (TAR-ter) Sauce	Mayonnaise mixed with dill pickles, capers, onions, lemon juice, or vinegar	Fried fish

about cheeses in section 10.3.) To obtain a thinner consistency, you could use cultured milks such as sour cream, crème fraîche, buttermilk, or yogurt.

FIGURE 10-3
Yogurt and Mint Dip
This refreshing dip is served with raw vegetables.
Applying Concepts *Should you consider whether your guests are sitting or standing when you think about the consistency of a dip?*

CHEF'S TIP

DIPS THAT DRIP

For finger foods served to standing guests, thick dairy dips that don't drip are best.

Dairy-based salad dressings or dips can be flavored with lemons, pepper, poppy seeds, herbs, shallots or other members of the onion family, capers, olives, truffles, nuts, pimiento, pickles, or artichokes. Fruit or vegetable purées are sometimes added to change the color of the dressing or dip, while also adding flavor.

Cooked Dressings and Dips Some cold dishes call for hot dressings. A category of cooked dressings is the type that evolved in America to moisten cole slaw and potato salad. This type of cooked dressing has become popular because it contains little or no oil. Instead, it relies on milk, flour or cornstarch, vinegar, and eggs or mayonnaise. Cooked dressings may include mustard, bacon, or other flavoring ingredients, but they usually have a more acidic flavor than a mayonnaise-based dressing.

A separate category of dips is the light-bodied, warmed Asian dipping sauce served with dumplings. This type of sauce is often based on soy sauce, seaweed, or vegetable stock, and may contain vinegar or some type of wine.

Wilted salads also use cooked dressings. Wilted salads are typically made by pouring a hot vinaigrette on a cold salad so the salad greens become wilted. They often feature other heated components, such as bacon or roasted vegetables. Cooked broccoli, which may be served at room temperature, can be topped with a sizzling dressing made of hot olive oil and garlic. A radicchio (rah-DEEK-kee-oh) salad is traditionally topped with a hot dressing made with olive oil, vinegar, and bacon.

FIGURE 10-4
Wilted Spinach Salad
In a wilted spinach salad, do not allow the greens to lose their texture.
Comparing/Contrasting *How would this salad differ in texture without the bacon? Would it be as appealing?*

FIGURE 10-5
Three Dips
(Clockwise from top) Aïoli, tapenade, and guacamole.
Predicting *Why would you serve three different types of dip at once?*

Vegetable- or Fruit-Based Dressings and Dips

Vegetable- or fruit-based dressings or dips may be cooked or uncooked. They may be puréed, or chunky. In many cases, these dressings and dips can also be used as sauces as well.

- **Salsa.** Usually uncooked, a **salsa** is based on tomatoes or other fruits or vegetables with some tartness or acidity that is heightened by the addition of an acid (vinegar, citrus, or wine). Salsas are flavor-packed and typically also include hot peppers, spices, and herbs.
- **Guacamole.** A Mexican dip, **guacamole** (gwa-kah-MOH-lee) is made from mashed avocado typically seasoned with a combination of lemon or lime juice, tomatoes, cilantro, onions, and chiles.
- **Tapenade.** A dip made from black olives, capers, anchovies, garlic, herbs, lemon juice, and olive oil, **tapenade** (top-en-ODD) is originally from France's Provence region.
- **Baba Ghanoush.** Made from roasted eggplant that has been pureed and seasoned with olive oil, tahini, lemon juice, and garlic, **baba ghanoush** (BAH-bah gha-NOOSH) originated in the Middle East, where it is served as a dip or a spread.

 **Reading Checkpoint** *What are five kinds of dressings or dips?*

10.1 ASSESSMENT

Reviewing Concepts

1. What is the garde manger?
2. What are the five kinds of dressings and dips?

Critical Thinking

3. **Forming a Model** What are the steps in making a vinaigrette?
4. **Communicating** What is an emulsion?
5. **Comparing/Contrasting** What is the difference between a basic and an emulsified vinaigrette?
6. **Forming a Model** What are the basic steps in making mayonnaise?
7. **Comparing/Contrasting** How does a dip differ from a salad dressing?

TEST KITCHEN

Prepare a vinaigrette, using extra-virgin olive oil and red-wine vinegar. Compare it with the flavor of purchased red-wine vinaigrette. Evaluate the differences. Prepare mayonnaise. Compare it with the flavor and texture of purchased mayonnaise. Evaluate the differences.

LANGUAGE ARTS

Descriptive Writing

Research the process used for pasteurizing eggs. Describe what is done to ensure harmful bacteria cannot grow.

READING PREVIEW

Key Concepts

- Understanding the purpose of salads
- Preparing green salads
- Using other ingredients in salads
- Preparing composed salads

Vocabulary

- appetizer salad
- composed salad
- dessert salad
- main-course salad
- mesclun
- salad
- separate-course salad
- side salad
- tossed salad

> **"S**alads used to be just a side dish. Now, they are the center of attention. Even fast food restaurants are making room for salads on their menus. **"**
>
> – Cynthia Ranalli
> The Culinary Institute
> of America

Purpose of Salads

A **salad** is a combination of raw or cooked ingredients, served cold or warm and coated with a salad dressing. Although salads are usually savory, they may also be sweet (as in the case of a fruit salad), or they can contain both savory and sweet elements. In the course of a meal, depending on its ingredients and size, a salad can have one of the following five purposes:

- **Appetizer Salad.** An **appetizer salad** is designed to whet the appetite before the main course. It could be nothing more than a variety of attractive greens with an extra-virgin olive oil and red-wine vinaigrette. But it also could be a more elaborate salad featuring other foods from the garde manger such as cold meat, fish, seafood, or cheese. In America, green salads are often served as appetizer salads.

- **Side Salad.** In informal meals, a **side salad** is served to accompany the main dish. If the main dish is heavy, a light crispy green salad might be an ideal side salad. If the main dish is light, a heavier side salad such as a pasta salad or grain salad would be a good choice. In a banquet situation, the side salad should not use ingredients included in the main dish nor should it use ingredients from an earlier appetizer salad.

FIGURE 10-6 ▶
Side Salad
A salad can contain many ingredients.
Applying Concepts *Is it possible to add too many ingredients?*

- **Main-Course Salad.** In some cases, the main course is a salad. When constructing a **main-course salad**, it is important to provide a balanced meal with a protein source (meat, poultry, fish, beans, or eggs) and a variety of vegetables. In America, substantial main-course salads, often with chicken, fish, or meat, have become very popular. The concept of a salad as a main course is not as common in Italy or France.
- **Separate-Course Salad.** In Italy, a green salad often follows the meat or fish course, especially if another type of salad, such as a seafood salad or a salad of preserved meats and pickled vegetables, was used as an appetizer salad. In France, a green salad usually appears as a separate course, after the main course. These **separate-course salads** are usually light, green salads with a simple vinaigrette or a single vegetable such as asparagus, to refresh the appetite and provide a break before dessert. In a banquet situation, a separate-course salad should not use the same ingredients as were used in an appetizer salad or a side salad.
- **Dessert Salad.** Often featuring fruits, nuts, or gelatin, a **dessert salad** is usually served with a sweetened dressing, a citrus-based dressing, or whipped cream.

Green Salads

A green salad can be used as an appetizer salad, a side salad, a main-course salad, or a separate-course salad. Depending on its purpose, a green salad can consist of just one type of green or many different types of greens. Usually a green salad is a **tossed salad**, which means all the ingredients are combined with dressing.

Types of Salad Greens In terms of flavor, salad greens can be divided into three basic types:

- Mild greens
- Spicy greens
- Bitter greens

Basic Types of Salad Greens

Mild Greens	Spicy Greens	Bitter Greens
Iceberg Lettuce, Boston Lettuce, Bibb Lettuce, Mâche, Romaine Lettuce, Baby Spinach	Arugula (also called Rocket), Mustard Leaves, Watercress, Mizuna	Radicchio, Belgian Endive, Dandelion, Escarole, Chicory, Frisée

The type of greens you use depends on the purpose of the salad in the meal. For example, a side salad might best be kept simple so it refreshes the palate and aids in digestion by providing fiber. On the other hand, a green salad that is an appetizer salad is meant to stimulate the appetite. It might include a variety of greens chosen for flavor, color, and texture attributes.

When constructing an appetizer salad, you should aim for a balance of flavors and texture. For example, if using radicchio, which is crispy and bitter, you could mix in mild but crispy greens such as bibb lettuce or Boston lettuce. Then you could add softer, mild greens such as mâche and complete the salad with a little watercress to add a soft, spicy component.

Some kitchens use prepared mixes of salad greens. Sometimes these mixes have a theme but each has a slightly different taste and texture. For example, **mesclun** (MEHS-kluhn) is a French-style mix that often includes baby red romaine, endive, mâche, radicchio, and arugula. An Asian mixture might include tatsoi, bok choy, baby spinach, mustard, mizuna, and other salad greens.

FOCUS ON NUTRITION

Healthy Greens
Some salad greens have greater nutritive value than others. Iceberg lettuce contains a great deal of water and few vitamins and minerals. Spinach and other salad greens that are a deep green usually have more nutritive value.

Salad Greens

▲ Iceberg Lettuce

▲ Boston Lettuce

Arugula (ah-ROO-guh-lah), also called Rocket ▼

Radicchio (rah-DEE-kee-oh) ▼

▼ Frisée (free-ZAY)

Bibb Lettuce ▲

Romaine (roh-MAIN) Lettuce ▲

▲ Mâche (MAHSH), also called Lamb's Lettuce or Corn Salad

▲ Mizuna (mih-ZOO-nah)

▲ Mustard Leaves (with Flowers)

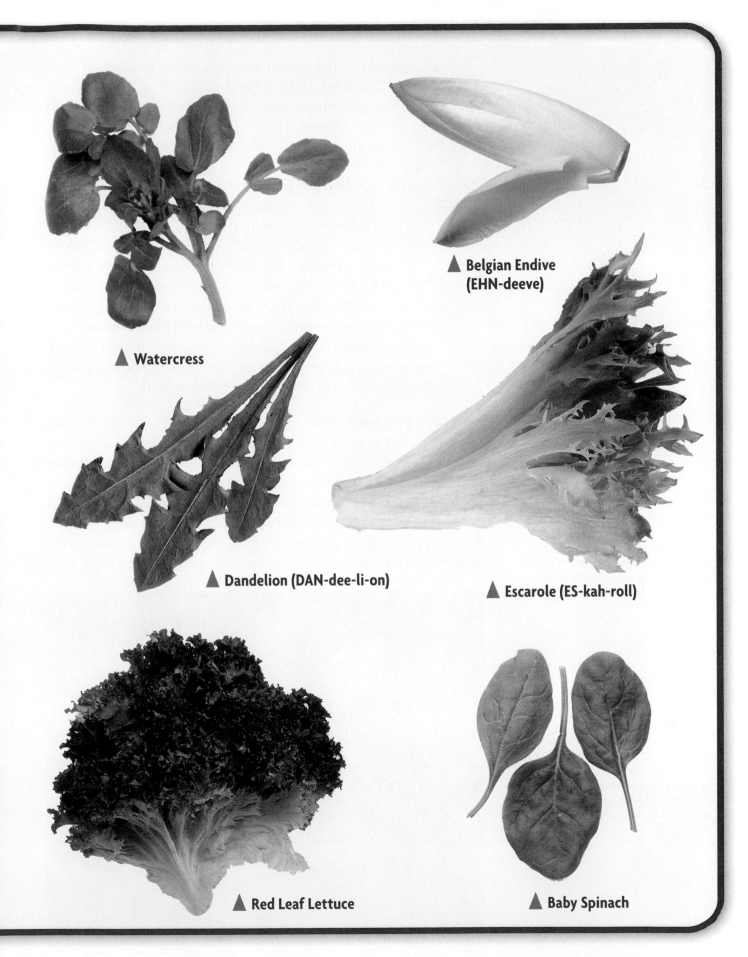

▲ Watercress

▲ Belgian Endive (EHN-deeve)

▲ Dandelion (DAN-dee-li-on)

▲ Escarole (ES-kah-roll)

▲ Red Leaf Lettuce

▲ Baby Spinach

Fresh herbs such as parsley, basil, chives, sorrel, dill, tarragon, cilantro, mint, and chervil are often added to salads as additional flavorings. Certain herbs can serve as the main body of a salad. For example, a Middle Eastern salad uses only parsley as its salad green. Diced tomatoes and green onions are added, and the salad is dressed with olive oil and lemon juice.

Edible flowers are sometimes strewn on top of a salad to provide an interesting visual feature. Edible garden flowers include nasturtiums (nash-TUR-shums), pansies, calendula (cal-EN-dyu-lah), bachelor's buttons, carnations, fuschia (FEW-scha), geraniums, Johnny jump-ups, primroses, roses, sunflowers, and violets.

Edible flowers from herbs are used in the same way as the edible garden flowers. Edible herb flowers include arugula, borage (BORE-age), chives, lavender, mustard, oregano, rosemary, sage, and thyme. Sprouts from beans, grasses, and salad greens are often used in salads as well.

FIGURE 10-7
Salad with Edible Flowers
Edible flowers add visual appeal to a salad.
Inferring *Should you ever put inedible flowers on a salad just for effect, planning to take them off before the salad is actually served?*

Preparing Greens Because greens have a short storage life, they should be used as soon as possible after they are procured, usually within two or three days. They will keep best if washed shortly before use and dried. Once greens are cut or torn, their cut edges oxidize and discolor quickly. Some salad greens, such as spinach or arugula, may need to be washed several times to eliminate the sandy earth in which these ground-hugging greens are grown. You can store dried greens loosely in a clean container covered with a light, damp towel.

FIGURE 10-8
Covering Salad Greens
Cover the cleaned, dried salad greens by placing a damp towel over them before placing them in the refrigerator.
Drawing Conclusions *Why would a restaurant need to have frequent deliveries of salad greens?*

Mixed Green Salad

1 **Rinse greens** thoroughly in cold running water.

2 **Dry** completely in a salad spinner.

3 **Tear or cut** greens into bite-sized pieces.

4 **Dress** and toss well.

5 **Garnish** with ingredients of choice.

 See Recipe Card 36, "Mixed Green Salad."

Greens should be fresh and perky when served. Keep them cool as long as possible before use. Salads should never include wilted leaves or tired sprouts. Dressing should be added at the last minute to ensure that the salad remains crisp.

Matching dressings to green salads is a matter of judgment. Of course, the dressing and the green salad should be compatible, but green salads generally go well with most types of dressings.

Gloved hands are the best utensils for mixing salad components well, but you can also use tongs or large spoons. The dressing should coat the salad ingredients with a light film. A thick or creamy dressing will require more tossing than a vinaigrette. If dressing collects on the bottom of the bowl, there is too much.

Good garnishes make green salads more appealing. Favorite additions to green salads are tomatoes, sprouts, fresh herbs, olives, thinly sliced onions, shredded carrots, cucumbers, mushrooms, and radishes.

CHEF'S TIP

DRY SALAD LEAVES

After rinsing, salad greens should be spun or shaken dry. Excess water in the leaves dilutes the dressing and makes the salad soggy.

They should be fresh and cut into pieces that can be eaten in one bite. Other options are nuts and seeds, shavings of Parmesan cheese, crumbled feta cheese, or sliced hard-cooked eggs. Crisp garnishes such as crumbled bacon or croutons give a boost to green salads. You can make tasty croutons by frying bread cubes in olive oil or by baking seasoned bread cubes in a cool oven.

BASIC CULINARY SKILLS

Croutons

1. Preheat oven to 300°F.
2. Remove crusts from stale sliced bread.
3. Cut into large dice.
4. Toss lightly with olive oil or melted butter.
5. Sprinkle salt and dried herbs (if desired) lightly on the bread.
6. Place on baking sheet.
7. Bake until lightly browned, about 12 minutes.
8. Remove from oven and cool.

9. Store in an airtight container at room temperature.

 **Reading Checkpoint**   *What are the three types of salad greens?*

Other Salad Ingredients

Many ingredients other than greens can be used in a salad. The choice of other ingredients depends on the purpose of the salad and the other dishes in the meal or on the menu.

For example, it is important to consider the connection of a side salad to the main dish. If the main dish is a protein (meat, poultry, or seafood, for example), you might want to use a side salad that focuses on vegetables or starches. If the main dish is a starch, a side salad might focus on vegetables or proteins.

When thinking through a menu, it is also important to have appetizer salads, side salads, and main salads that appeal to a variety of tastes. A diner who orders a substantial main course, such as pot roast, that focuses on protein may be looking for a light appetizer salad. On the other hand, for someone who wants to eat light but desires some protein, a main-course salad with some protein would be ideal.

FOCUS ON **NUTRITION**

Low Calorie?

Salad is not necessarily a diet food. A large amount of a rich dressing or high-calorie additions to a salad can turn even a low-calorie green appetizer salad into a very high-calorie meal.

You can consider four other types of ingredients when constructing salads:

- Vegetables
- Starches
- Proteins
- Fruits and nuts

Vegetables The predominant ingredient in a salads can be raw or cooked vegetables, such as fennel or beets. Raw or cooked vegetables can also be added to green salads. Popular raw vegetable salads include tomato salad, cole slaw, carrot salad, cucumber salad, artichoke heart salad, fennel salad, and mushroom salad. Popular cooked vegetable salads include boiled or roasted beets, roasted peppers, steamed sugar snap peas, blanched green beans, boiled cauliflower, steamed zucchini, boiled turnips, or boiled potatoes.

Depending on the type of the vegetable and the final desired texture, cooked vegetables for salads are typically roasted, grilled, boiled, blanched, or steamed. Some vegetables, such as cabbage, peas, or sugar snap peas are simply blanched for a cooked vegetable salad. Other vegetables may be cooked through. In some cooked vegetable salads, such as German potato salad, the vegetables should still be warm when dressed so flavors combine. Other vegetables, such as zucchini and eggplant, should be dressed at the last minute to avoid sogginess. A chef needs to be aware of the flavor and final texture required by the recipe.

Some cooked salads combine more than one vegetable. Russian salad, called insalata russa (een-sahl-AHT-tah roos-ah) in Italian and or salade russe (sah-LAHDD rooss) in French, is a combination of boiled potatoes, beets, eggs, capers, and often turnips, carrots, peas, and other vegetables. A Russian salad is dressed with mayonnaise.

Starches Salads can feature starchy components, including bread, grains, pasta, and beans.

> ## CHEF'S TIP
>
> ### WATERY SALADS
> Boiled, steamed, or blanched vegetables should be drained thoroughly and dried. Otherwise, cooking water will dilute the salad dressing.

▲
FIGURE 10-9
Cooked Vegetables in a Salad
Grilled eggplant makes a good addition to a tossed green salad. **Predicting** *What other grilled vegetables could be substituted for the eggplant?*

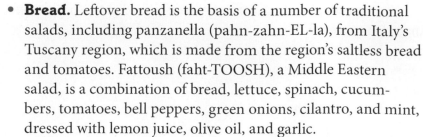

CHEF'S TIP

SALAD TOMATOES

Some tomato varieties with thick skins and few seeds (plum tomato types) are best in sauces. Large slicing tomatoes or thin-skinned tomatoes, such as cherry or grape tomatoes, are best used raw in salads.

- **Bread.** Leftover bread is the basis of a number of traditional salads, including panzanella (pahn-zahn-EL-la), from Italy's Tuscany region, which is made from the region's saltless bread and tomatoes. Fattoush (faht-TOOSH), a Middle Eastern salad, is a combination of bread, lettuce, spinach, cucumbers, tomatoes, bell peppers, green onions, cilantro, and mint, dressed with lemon juice, olive oil, and garlic.

- **Grains.** Many kinds of grains, including cracked wheat, rice, and barley, can be used for salads. Grain salads are best made shortly before they are used, because they absorb the salad dressing easily and can become soggy. They also absorb other flavorings quickly. Tabouli (tah-BOO-leh) is an example of a Middle Eastern grain-based salad. It features cracked wheat.

- **Pasta.** Pasta salads are quite popular. A pasta salad could be the traditional macaroni salad, a couscous salad with lemon, mint, onions, and peppers; or even a Japanese salad made with buckwheat pasta and a peanut-based sauce. A pasta salad often becomes bland in storage. Before serving a pasta salad that has been stored, check its seasoning carefully.

- **Beans.** Beans and lentils make delicious and nutritious salads. They are cooked and served cold or at room temperature. Because beans don't become soggy, they are ideal when advanced preparation is necessary. Virtually any kind of bean can be used individually in salads or combined with other beans (as, for example, a traditional three-bean salad). Beans must be cooked until very tender. They should be dressed close to service time because the acid in a dressing can toughen the beans.

FIGURE 10-10
Starch in a Salad
This Mediterranean salad features chunks of bread with roasted peppers, scallions, and red onion. **Drawing Conclusions** *What do you think the bread contributes to the texture of this salad?*

Protein Protein sources, such as meat, poultry, seafood, and cheese, make excellent additions to warm or cold salads. In some cases, they are the primary focus of the salad. Meat could be roasted, chicken could be grilled, or shrimp could be boiled. No matter how the protein source is cooked, it should be freshly made.

Because seafood is highly perishable and delicate, it should be freshly cooked for use in a salad. If the protein source is cooked in advanced and chilled, the dressing should be added no more than three or four hours before serving. This prevents excessive absorption of the dressing. Ideally, meats, poultry, or seafood used for salads should be moist and tender to the fork. Dressings add flavor; they should not be relied on to return moisture to overcooked food.

Meat, poultry, and seafood salads are served as an appetizer salad or, in a larger portion, as a main-course salad. Because such salads are substantial, they are not typically used as side salads or separate-course salads.

Traditional American-style chicken and seafood salads use a mayonnaise-based dressing. However, other types of protein-based salads, such as grilled chicken salad with Caesar dressing, are becoming more common. There are endless variations on meat, poultry, and seafood salads. Here are some examples:

- Taco Salad
- Steak and Barley Salad
- Cajun-Style Shrimp Salad
- Thai-Style Beef Salad
- Curried Chicken Salad
- Lobster Salad
- Grilled Salmon Salad
- Greek Lamb Salad with Mint
- Seared Scallop Salad

▲
FIGURE 10-11
Protein in a Salad
This mayonnaise-based salad includes shrimp, potatoes, peas, carrots, red pepper, and egg.
Drawing Conclusions *When would you serve this type of salad?*

Fruits and Nuts With the selection of fruits and nuts available today from all over the world, chefs can be highly creative with salads. Once thought of only for dessert salads, fruits are now often featured in appetizer salads and even in main-course salads. An example of an appetizer salad using fruit might be one consisting of pears, blue cheese, a spicy green such as arugula, walnuts, and a rich olive oil without any vinegar. Main-course salads often feature apples or pears. Fruit salads are also sometimes offered on breakfast or brunch menus.

Once cut, fruit deteriorates rapidly. Fruit should be cut close to the salad's serving time. Fruits that turn brown, such as apples and pears, can be placed in a bath of water and lemon juice to prevent discoloration for up to several hours. Lemon juice may create a distraction from the flavors desired in the final salad, however.

▲
FIGURE 10-12
Fruit in a Salad
The slices of orange are an unexpected complement to the endive, watercress, red onion, and fennel.
Analyzing Information *Describe the flavors in this salad and how they balance each other.*

Garde Manger ▲ **291**

Reading Checkpoint *What are the four other types of ingredients to consider when constructing a salad?*

Composed Salads

A **composed salad** is a salad with any combination of ingredients (greens, vegetables, proteins, starches, fruits, or garnishes) that are arranged carefully and artfully on a plate or in a bowl. The entire composed salad can be dressed with one style of dressing, or individual components can be separately dressed with different dressings. The dressing for some or all of the components of a composed salad can be served "on the side"—that is, in a separate container to be applied by the customer.

A composed salad with greens is typically presented as an appetizer salad, a main-course salad, or a separate-course salad. A composed fruit salad can be a dessert course or a main course for breakfast or brunch.

Composed salads present a terrific opportunity for creativity in the garde manger station. Ingredients and garnishes are typically arranged beautifully on a plate or in a bowl, rather than being tossed.

FIGURE 10-13
Composed Salads
French niçoise salad (left) includes tuna, olives, egg, and green beans; Italian Capri salad (right) includes tomato, mozzarella, and basil.
Comparing/Contrasting *Describe the differences between these two composed salad presentations.*

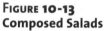

Preparation of a Composed Salad A composed salad often has four component parts:

- **Main Ingredients.** A composed salad often has one or more main ingredients as its centerpiece. The main ingredient could be roasted vegetables, a grilled chicken breast, sliced grilled steak, sautéed shrimp, or a grilled salmon fish filet.

- **Supporting Ingredients.** The main ingredients are often placed on a bed of greens or shredded vegetables. These supporting ingredients can form a base for the main ingredients. For example, the lettuce in a chef's salad carries the main ingredients of hard-cooked eggs, ham, turkey, and cheese strips. Some composed salads include many supporting ingredients artfully arranged on a plate around the main ingredients.

- **Garnish.** The visual appeal of a composed salad is important. The salad should be attractively garnished with ingredients that are appetizing as well as decorative. Consider what ingredients can help to balance or enhance the other ingredients. Choose garnishes with an eye for texture as well as for flavor and color.

- **Dressing.** The dressing should balance the various flavors in the composed salad and be compatible with all the ingredients. It may be served on the side or placed attractively in an individual container as part of the composition. Alternatively, salads may be dressed immediately before service.

When preparing composed salads, focus on balance and contrasts. Ingredients in a composed salad should be arranged with an eye to design. Think of the balance of forms and shapes as you compose and garnish the salad. Of course, nothing can substitute for the freshness and good flavor of the food on the plate, but making the plate interesting and appetizing adds to the pleasure of the dish. Keep these guidelines in mind:

- **Flavors.** Put together various flavors, but make sure they are compatible. Flavors that fight each other are not usually put together on the same plate.

- **Textures.** Combinations of textures make salads appetizing. Crisply cooked crumbled bacon; soft, creamy goat cheese; mild, crisp bibb lettuce; and a tangy vinaigrette, for example, have texture appeal as well as flavor appeal.

- **Colors.** Use color, such as vibrant yellow bell peppers, the purple of radicchio, or the white of endive, to add interest and appeal.

- **Height.** You can create interest by using height as a design element. Sliced vegetables, for example, can be stacked or layered for visual appeal.

CHEF'S TIP

GARNISHES

The quality of the salad in a restaurant usually provides a little preview of what can be expected from the meal to follow. Garnishes should not be an afterthought.

Examples of Composed Salads Some composed salads are so well established that they are among the most popular ordered at restaurants. Other composed salads may depend on seasonal ingredients or special components for which the kitchen is especially known.

Four Popular Composed Salads

Salad Name	Dressing	Ingredients
Chef's Salad	Vinaigrette	Tossed greens; julienned ham, chicken or turkey; cheese; sliced vegetables; and hard-cooked eggs.
Cobb Salad	French dressing	Lettuce (base) with sliced turkey or chicken breast, avocado slices, cheese strips, hard-cooked eggs, tomato, and bacon. Often garnished with blue cheese.
Caesar Salad, with Grilled Chicken	Caesar dressing (olive oil, wine vinegar, egg yolk, garlic, mustard, sometimes anchovies)	Romaine lettuce (base), sliced grilled chicken (main ingredient), and grated Parmesan cheese. Often garnished with croutons.
Niçoise (nee-SWAHZ) Salad	Red-wine vinaigrette	Tuna (main ingredient), with boiled sliced potatoes, tomato slices, hard-cooked eggs, black olives, anchovies, cooked green beans, and sliced bell peppers.

 **Reading Checkpoint** *What is a composed salad?*

10.2 ASSESSMENT

Reviewing Concepts

1. In the course of a meal, what are five purposes of a salad?
2. What are three basic types of salad greens?
3. What ingredients, other than greens, should you consider when constructing salads?
4. What is a composed salad?

Critical Thinking

5. **Comparing/Contrasting** What is the difference between a tossed salad and a composed salad?
6. **Inferring** Why would a dressing for a composed salad often be served separately?
7. **Predicting** In your opinion, does height add interest and appeal to a salad?

TEST KITCHEN

Assemble a collection of as many types of salad greens as you can. Prepare a red-wine vinaigrette. Sample each of the salad greens individually and together, with and without the vinaigrette. Write down your notes about the taste of the various salad greens. Compare your results with classmates.

LANGUAGE ARTS

Descriptive Writing

Research salads from three different countries. Write a standard recipe for your favorite one. Make your recipe and then write a review of your dish.

READING PREVIEW

Key Concepts

- Understanding types of cheese
- Buying, handling, and storing cheese
- Serving cheese
- Cooking with cheese

Vocabulary

- blue-vein cheeses
- cheese board
- cheese cart
- flight of cheeses
- fresh cheeses
- grating cheeses
- hard cheeses
- processed cheese
- rind
- semi-soft cheeses
- soft, rind-ripened cheeses

> **"A** great cheese course is one of the ways that you can set your restaurant apart from the crowd. **"**
>
> – John Fischer
> The Culinary Institute of America

Types of Cheese

Cheese is an important part of the garde manger tradition. With thousands of types of cheeses, a garde manger has a broad spectrum of cheeses from which to choose.

Although cheese can be made from milk from cows, sheep, goats, or water buffalo, there are seven basic types of cheese, based on texture, taste, appearance, and aging:

- Fresh cheeses
- Soft, rind-ripened cheeses
- Semi-soft cheeses
- Hard cheeses
- Blue-vein cheeses
- Grating cheeses
- Processed cheeses

Fresh Cheeses **Fresh cheeses** are moist, soft cheeses that typically have not ripened or significantly aged. These cheeses are used as spreads, eaten with fruits, or used in cooking and baking.

Examples of fresh, unripened cheeses include cottage cheese, cream cheese, farmer cheese, fresh goat cheese (called chevre, SHEHV-ruh), mascarpone (mas-cahr-POHN-ay), fresh mozzarella (moh-tza-REL-lah), feta (FEH-tah), and fresh ricotta (rih-COH-tah).

Because they are fresh, soft cheeses are highly perishable. They should be used as soon as possible after they are purchased.

Soft, Rind-Ripened Cheeses Soft, **rind-ripened cheeses** are soft cheeses that have been ripened by being exposed to a spray or dusting of "friendly" mold. These cheeses are aged until the **rind** (RYND), the surface, develops a soft, downy consistency. The rind, which is edible, provides a delightful contrast in texture and flavor to the interior of the cheese. When fully ripe, a soft cheese should be nearly runny.

Examples of soft, rind-ripened cheeses are Brie (BREE), Camembert (cam-en-BEHR), and Pont l'Évêque (PONT leh-VECK). Many soft ripened cheeses are named after the city or region making the cheese. However, because the names Camembert and Brie are not protected by French law, they are widely used for cheeses produced elsewhere. As a result, the flavor and quality varies of "brie" or "camembert" varies widely.

Semi-Soft Cheeses **Semi-soft cheeses** are more solid than soft cheeses and retain their shape. They may be mild or strongly flavored as a result of the particular process used to make them. There are three types of semi-soft cheeses:

- **Rind-Ripened.** These are semi-soft cheeses whose rinds are washed with a liquid such as grape juice, beer, brandy, wine, cider, or olive oil. The washing produces beneficial bacteria that penetrates and flavors the cheese from the rind to the inside. Examples of rind-ripened, semi-soft cheeses are Muenster (MUHN-stuhr) and Port-Salut (port sahl-OOT).
- **Dry-Rind.** These are cheeses in which the rind is permitted to harden naturally through exposure to air. The rind becomes firm, but the interior of the cheese remains tender. Examples of dry-rind semi-soft cheeses are bel paese (bel pahAYZ-eh), Monterey Jack (MONT-ter-ay JACK), Morbier (MOR-bee-ay), and Havarti (hah-VAHR-tee).
- **Waxed-Rind.** In these cheeses, wax is applied to form a solid shell around the cheese as it

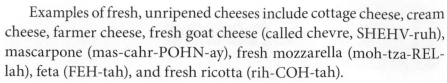

Nutritional Value
Most cheeses contain an average of 60 percent water. They contain fat but are also high in protein and calcium.

FIGURE 10-14
Soft, Rind-Ripened Cheese
When fully ripe, a soft, rind-ripened cheese should be nearly runny.
Predicting *How would you eat a soft cheese that has become runny?*

ripens. The interior of the cheese remains consistently soft. Examples of waxed-rind semi-soft cheeses are the Dutch cheese Edam (EE-duhm) and the Italian cheese Fontina (fon-TEEN-nah).

Blue-Vein Cheeses To make **blue-vein cheeses**, needles are injected into the cheese to form holes in which mold spores multiply. The cheese is salted and ripened in a cave. Roquefort (ROWK-fort) is often called the king of cheeses. It has been made since the Roman times and was the favorite of Charlemagne. Other blue-vein cheeses include Gorgonzola (gore-gon-ZO-la), an Italian cheese, Stilton of England, and Maytag Blue of America. Young blue-vein cheeses are mild in comparison to the aged versions.

◀

FIGURE 10-15
Blue-Vein Cheese
The blue veins in a blue cheese are actually types of a beneficial mold.
Analyzing Information *Does the idea of eating a moldy cheese cause you concern?*

Hard Cheeses **Hard cheeses** have a drier texture than semi-soft cheeses and a firmer consistency. They slice and grate easily. The best-known hard cheeses are probably cheddar cheese and Swiss-style cheeses such as Emmenthaler (EM-en-tah-ler) and Gruyère (gree-YAIR), which have many uses in cooking. Other popular hard cheeses include Colby, Jarlsberg (YAHRLZ-behrg), Provolone (pro-vah-LONE), and Manchego (man-CHE-go).

Grating Cheeses **Grating cheeses** are solid, dry cheeses that have a grainy consistency, making them ideal for grating. They are often grated or shaved onto food rather than cut into slices because of their crumbly texture. However, chunks are also broken off the larger cheese to create bite-size chunks for cheese platters. Grating cheeses are often produced in 75- to 80-pound wheels. Some examples of grating cheeses are Parmigiano-Reggiano (parm-muh-ZHAH-noh reh-zhee-AH-noh), Pecorino-Romano (peh-kuh-REE-noh ro-MON-oh), and the greenish Sapsago (sap-SAY-go) from Switzerland.

Cheeses

Fresh Cheeses

▲ Fresh Chevre
(Goat Cheese)

▲ Mozzarella

▲ Mascarpone

▲ Ricotta

▲ Feta

Soft, Rind-Ripened Cheeses

▲ Brie

▲ Camembert

▲ Pont l'Évêque

Semi-Soft Cheeses

▲ Muenster

▲ Edam

▲ Port Salut

▲ Fontina

▲ Monterey Jack

Cheeses

Hard Cheeses

▲ Cheddar

▲ Gruyere

▲ Jarlsberg

▲ Manchego

▲ Provolone

Blue Cheeses

▲ Roquefort

▲ Stilton

▲ Gorgonzola

Grating Cheeses

▲ Sapsago   ▲ Parmigiano-Reggiano   ▲ Pecorino-Romano

Processed Cheeses **Processed cheese** is made from one or more cheeses that have been finely ground, mixed together with other non-dairy ingredients, heated, and poured into a mold. Processed cheese food is like processed cheese except that it also includes other dairy products. At least 51% of the material in processed cheese food must be cheese. Additional moisture can be added to processed cheese food to make it spreadable.

 **Reading Checkpoint**   *What are the seven basic types of cheese?*

Buying, Handling, and Storing Cheeses

Buying Cheeses A good way to learn about cheeses is from the experts: knowledgeable vendors and the cheese producers themselves. Buy only as much as you need. Once they are cut, cheeses begin to lose quality and should be eaten quickly. This ensures freshness when the cheese is used.

CHEF'S TIP

GRATING CHEESES

Use salty Pecorino with rustic-style dishes; use complex Parmigiano for more refined dishes and sauces.

FIGURE 10-16
Buying Cheeses
The best way to learn about cheese is to ask your supplier.
Inferring *Why would your supplier be interested in educating you about their products?*

FOCUS ON SANITATION

Cheese Work Habits
Knives and other utensils that come into contact with cheese should be washed with hot soapy water between uses throughout the day.

When buying cheeses you should:
- **Examine the Label.** Labels provide information about the type of cheese and its origin, authenticity, ingredients, and date of production.
- **Examine the Rind.** The color of the rind should be natural. Often, the more artificial the color and the more perfect the appearance, the less authentic the cheese may be.
- **Examine the Interior.** The interior should not show any holes or coloring that is not meant to be there. For grating cheeses, be certain they are a healthy straw color and not dried out or powdery.
- **Taste.** You should taste the cheese before buying it, if possible. Make sure it is what you expected.

Handling Cheeses Cut off only as much cheese as you need at a time if you have a large chunk. Store the remainder properly in the refrigerator.

The mold on cheese, unlike mold on most foods, does not contaminate the entire cheese. You can remove any unwanted mold that forms on cheese by trimming it away from the contaminated area. To prevent mold spores from spreading to other parts of the cheese during handling, take care not to bring the moldy area into contact with the rest of the cheese.

Grate cheese only when you need it. Pre-grating cheese causes it to dry out and to lose a great deal of its distinct flavor. You can use box graters or a food processor fitted with a metal blade to grate cheeses.

You can cut fresh and soft cheeses with a cleaned and sanitized wire. Semi-soft, blue, and hard cheeses can be cut with a chef's knife. Traditionally, grating cheeses are not sliced with a knife. Once you cut into a grating cheese, you can use a special cheese chipper with a wooden handle and triangular blade to chip or flake the cheese.

Cheeses must be handled hygienically to prevent potential hazards. Follow these sanitation guidelines when handling cheese:
- Use clean food-service gloves or clean utensils to avoid transferring bacteria from your hands.
- Clean and sanitize work surfaces and other food-contact areas at the end of the day.
- Clean and sanitize equipment used to slice, cut, or otherwise work with cheeses at the end of the day.

CULINARY SCIENCE

Steps in Making Cheese

Cheese making relies on science. Making pasteurized cheese involves the following basic steps:

- **Heating Milk.** Milk is heated to destroy all bacteria (both pathogens and "friendly" bacteria).

- **Adding Starter (Acidification).** A starter is added to the mill, causing it to sour. The starter contains either an acid (such as lemon juice or vinegar) or rennet, an acid-producing substance produced from animal or vegetable sources.

- **Forming Curds.** As the milk sours, the solid matter in the milk forms into solid clumps, or curds. This is called coagulation (co-AG-yew-la-shun).

- **Separating the Curds and Whey.** When the milk has coagulated, it has separated into curds and whey, the remaining liquid from the milk. The whey is drained off, leaving only the curds.

- **Draining and Shaping Curds.** Curds may be placed in bags, baskets, or molds before being placed on racks or hung to drain and dry. Soft cheese is drained and shaped at the same time. Hard cheeses, such as cheddar, are

▲ *Separating curds and whey.*

shaped, drained, and then dried and shaped by pressing.

- **Aging.** Fresh cheeses are not aged. For other cheeses, aging can run from a few days up to several years. Cheeses undergo changes in flavor, texture, and color during ripening. Cheeses may be aged in wax rind, ashes, or leaves. They may be rubbed, washed, or soaked. They may be injected with friendly molds.

Research

Research how a particular type of raw milk cheese is made. Focus on the sanitation issues involved in using nonpasteurized milk.

Storing Cheeses Proper storage ensures freshness for the life of the cheese. Whole cheeses continue to age as long as they are uncut and stored properly. Cut cheeses begin to deteriorate as soon as the inside is exposed to air. Fresh cheeses spoil rapidly, while hard cheeses keep longer because of their low moisture content.

Plastic wrap does not allow cheese to breathe. It is best to wrap cheese in waxed paper or butcher paper and store it in a cool place. Be sure there are no tears or openings in the wrap. Alternatively, the cheese can be placed in a container with a tight-fitting lid. Don't reuse storage wrappings; they have been handled and exposed to the air and counter surfaces. Discard and use fresh wrap.

Reading Checkpoint   *What is the best way to store cheeses?*

CHEF'S TIP

REFRIGERATING CHEESES

Soft cheeses last about two weeks in the refrigerator. Semi-soft cheeses last several weeks. Hard cheeses last about a month. Granular cheeses can last for several months.

Grana Padano

Local cheese makers in northeastern Italy will tell you that their ancestors were making Grana Padano (GRA-nah pa-DAHN-oh), a grating cheese similar to Parmigiano-Reggiano, since before Roman times. These early versions of Grana Padano, called "Grana" for short, were probably made from a mixture of goat's, sheep's, and cow's milk. Cow's milk, which has a high butterfat content and makes a richer cheese, eventually became used almost exclusively to make Grana.

The Romans had a gift for recognizing a good thing when they saw it. They did nothing to stop the tradition of making Grana. But after the Roman civilization fell to successive waves of barbarians, the cheese makers went to the mountains while the barbarians laid waste to the countryside. Eventually, the green valleys grew wild and marshy, and malaria and famine was rampant.

The monks of the Po Valley, specifically Bernardo di Chiaravalle, are given credit for reviving Grana Padano in 1135 A.D. Under Bernardo's direction, the monks redirected water flow, using oxen to both recultivate the land and provide milk for cheese. They perfected and standardized their cheese-making method. Surplus milk was transformed into Grana Padano, a delicious and nutritious food that could be stored for relatively long periods of time without spoiling. The monks called it "caseus vetus," old cheese.

▲ *Sampling a wheel of Grana Padano cheese*

Today, Grana Padano is made in the same areas of Italy, using the same recipe the monks used. Some of the dairy barns have given way to factories where Grana Padano is produced in huge rooms by workers wearing white lab coats and where technicians examine the finished cheeses for unwanted holes by using x-ray machines. But still, Grana Padana looks, and probably tastes, the same as it did way back when the monks were making it in the twelfth century.

Research

Research the history of a particular type of traditional cheese, such as cheddar, Gruyère, or Parmigiano-Reggiano. Describe where it originated, what milk is used, how it is made, how production has changed over time, and how it tastes.

Serving Cheese

Fresh cheeses such as mozzarella should be eaten as soon after they are made as possible because they lose their flavor and creaminess as their moisture evaporates. It is best to purchase them on the same day they are to be used.

Cheeses typically should be served at room temperature. If cheeses have been stored in the refrigerator, they should be left for an hour at room temperature before serving. Set out only as much as you will use. If left out longer than several hours, hard cheeses become oily. Soft cheeses may dry out. Once cheeses are brought to the proper temperature for eating, they should be served immediately and not left out to sit. Individual cheeses are typically served as a separate course in either of two locations within a formal meal:

- **Appetizer Course.** Offering fine cheeses for the appetizer course, or as part of a composed appetizer salad before the meal, provides an opportunity to make a good first impression on a guest.
- **Following a Meal.** In the European tradition, cheeses often follow a meal and are served alongside fruit before a dessert course.

There are three basic ways to serve cheese as a separate course:

- **Individual Cheese.** The advantage of serving a single cheese is that the guest can focus on the appearance, flavor, and texture of a single cheese without being distracted by other offerings on the plate.
- **Multiple Cheeses.** Often, a number of different cheeses are offered at the same time (this is sometimes referred to as a **flight of cheeses**). Sometimes a flight of cheeses includes cheeses of the same variety, thus offering guests the opportunity to sample a range of cheeses from the same base ingredient (for example, goat cheeses). However, an assortment of different types of cheeses is more typical for a flight of cheeses.
- **Cheese Cart.** Some restaurants offer an assortment of cheeses on a **cheese cart**, a cart that is wheeled to the guests' table to give them an opportunity to choose cheeses of different kinds. They can then see them as they make their choice. Typically, a guest orders cheeses and the server arranges them on a plate from the tableside. Bread, crackers, and fruit often accompany the cheeses.

Cheeses are often served on flat marble, china, or wooden platters, sometimes covered with nontoxic leaves (such as grape leaves). No matter which material is used in its construction, the flat platter is typically called a **cheese board**. When serving several cheeses at once, you can place each on separate cheese boards or you can serve them on a single cheese board, leaving plenty of room around each cheese to prevent soft cheeses from running into other cheeses. Provide a separate knife for each different kind of cheese.

FIGURE 10-17
Cheese Board
This cheese board features eight types of cheese, with red and green grapes.
Comparing/Contrasting *What are the advantages and disadvantages of serving so many cheeses at one time?*

CHEF'S TIP

STRINGY CHEESE
Test Parmigiano-Reggiano before using it in cooking. If it becomes stringy when heated, it is too young for cooking.

Bread or crackers and fruit are often served with cheeses. Other foods that pair well with cheeses include cured meats (such as salami or prosciutto), roasted peppers, and cut-up raw vegetables.

Reading Checkpoint *At what temperature should cheeses typically be served?*

Cooking with Cheeses

Although cheese is often used in cooking, heat alters its unique flavor. High heat causes cheeses to become tough and rubbery. As a general rule, use low heat when cooking cheeses. Here are three ways cheeses can be used in cooking:

- **In a Dish.** Semi-soft cheeses are ideal for integrating in a dish because they don't leach excess water the way fresh cheeses can. They should be shredded rather than sliced for easier and

FIGURE 10-18 ▶
Fondue
Vegetables and bread are dipped in cheese fondue.
Predicating *Why would the texture of melted cheese be an important consideration for this dish?*

more even melting. Some cheeses that are particularly suitable for melting include cheddar, Gruyère, and Fontina. Fondue (fon-DUE) is one of the best-known cheese dishes. Made with Emmenthaler or Gruyère cheese, it has a thick, creamy texture and is typically used for dipping cooked or raw vegetables and bread.

- **In a Sauce.** Cheeses can add both body and flavor to sauces. In sauces that call for using aged, complex cheeses such as Parmigiano-Reggiano, use as little heat as possible. Cheese should be stirred into sauces at the last minute.

- **As a Topping or Garnish.** Cheese makes an excellent topping or garnish that complements or offsets the flavors and textures of other ingredients. You can use soft or hard cheeses, or a combination, for topping baked dishes. The properties of soft cheeses such as mozzarella make them excellent for melting. Grating cheeses, such as Parmigiano-Regginao, provide a flavor boost. They can also be shaved for topping or garnish on salads and meat or vegetable appetizers.

 **Reading Checkpoint** *What are three ways cheese is used in cooking?*

CHEF'S TIP

SAVE RINDS

Save rinds from Parmigiano-Reggiano and Pecorino-Romano. Add small portions to soups and cooked tomato sauces for added flavor and texture.

10.3 ASSESSMENT

Reviewing Concepts

1. What are the seven basic types of cheese?
2. What is the best way to store cheese?
3. At what temperature should cheese typically be served?
4. What are the three ways cheese is used in cooking?

Critical Thinking

5. **Classifying** Of the seven types of cheeses, which type are you most familiar with?
6. **Comparing/Contrasting** What is the difference between a fresh cheese and a soft, rind-ripened cheese?
7. **Applying Concepts** Describe three ways of serving cheese during the course of a meal.

TEST KITCHEN

Assemble a collection of as many cheeses as you can, making sure you have a representative of each of the seven types of cheeses. Sample each type of cheese (accompanied by bread, if you wish). Write down your notes about the taste of the various cheeses. Did you have a favorite? Compare your results with classmates.

SOCIAL STUDIES

History of Cheese

Research the history of cheese. What role has it played in history? Who is credited with inventing cheese?

10.4 Cold Food Presentation

READING PREVIEW

Key Concepts

- Identifying types of cold food presentations
- Identifying elements in cold food presentation
- Preparing centerpieces and garnishes

Vocabulary

- antipasto platter
- blinis
- caviar
- cocktail sauce
- cold food presentation
- depurated
- grosse pièce
- on the half shell
- raw bar
- sequencing
- sturgeon

> **"M**aking a beautiful cold platter is a lot like putting together a jigsaw puzzle. Everything needs to fit together to make a delicious and beautiful presentation. **"**
>
> - Pierre LeBlanc

Types of Cold Food Presentations

A **cold food presentation** is a collection of cold foods that are presented in an artful manner, often in a buffet setting. Guests choose for themselves from among the foods, or they indicate their choices to wait staff, who assemble individual plates of food.

Cold food preparations present the garde manger with an opportunity for creative work and artistry. Because cold food presentations must be prepared ahead, the chef has greater control and flexibility than is possible with typical cooking. Cold food presentations may be simple or complex, focusing on one type of food or providing a wide variety of foods. Some examples of cold food presentations are:

- Platters
- Trays
- Raw bars
- Caviar presentations
- Smoked fish presentations

Pierre LeBlanc
The Culinary Institute of America

Platters The garde manger often uses a single large platter of cold food as an opportunity to provide a sampling of cold meats, cheeses, vegetables, fruits, and, perhaps, breads and crackers. A popular choice is the Italian **antipasto** (an-tee-PAHS-toh) **platter,** an assortment of cured meats (such as prosciutto and salami), cheeses, and pickled vegetables. (You'll learn more about cured meats in Chapter 11.)

Fruits are often presented on a platter. Because fruits oxidize and discolor when cut, platters often include whole fruit that can be eaten whole, such as grapes and strawberries. Cheese platters should offer a variety of types, flavors, and textures of cheeses. Cheeses should be offered on cheese boards for easy cutting. Fruits, crackers, and breads often accompany a cheese platter. An assortment of different kinds of salads presents another possibility for creativity.

Trays The garde manger may assemble a cold food presentation on a tray, which is then passed by wait staff or by diners, at the table. A tray is smaller than a platter and usually holds less variety. When assembling a cold food presentation on a tray, take into consideration that the tray will be moving, so the food must be stable and not fall off the tray.

Raw Bars A **raw bar** is a bar or counter at which raw shellfish is served. It is an elegant and luxurious type of cold food presentation. These usually include oysters, and sometimes clams, along with cooked mussels, scallops, shrimp, and lobster. The oysters and clams can be served **on the half shell** (meaning they are opened and served on one of their shells). Other raw seafood that can be served includes shrimp and crab. Fresh lemon, **cocktail sauce** (a dipping sauce of ketchup, horseradish, and possibly Tabasco sauce), or other accompanying sauces are included on the raw bar, as well.

Throughout the world, shellfish is commonly eaten raw. However, raw bars or any service of raw shellfish and other seafood comes with a risk. The restaurant must be aware of possible associated health hazards. By law, all raw shellfish must come from suppliers with a tag detailing the place of origin, the date of harvest, and the wholesale grower and seller. These regulations make it possible to trace any shellfish sold to restaurants in the event of an outbreak of disease.

▲
FIGURE 10-19
Antipasto Platter
An antipasto platter consists of cured meats, cheeses, and pickled vegetables.
Predicating *Do you think you would like the combination of flavors and textures in an antipasto platter?*

High-Risk Eating

Individuals with certain health conditions—such as liver disease, diabetes, cancer, stomach disorders, blood disorders, or immune disorders—who consume raw shellfish or other seafood are at a higher risk than others.

FIGURE 10-20 ▶
Oysters on the Half Shell
A raw bar usually includes oysters on the half shell placed on ice to keep them at the appropriate temperature.
Predicating *Have you ever had raw oysters? If not, do you think you'd like them?*

When purchasing shellfish, follow these guidelines:
- Buy only cultivated shellfish that is raised in clean, controlled environments.
- Buy only depurated oysters, clams, and mussels. **Depurated** (DEP-yew-rate-ed) shellfish have been placed in tanks of fresh water to purge them of their impurities and sand.
- Get to know your suppliers and make sure they sell impeccably fresh shellfish.

▼ *Beluga caviar*

Caviar Presentations **Caviar** is a type of salted fish eggs. In France and the United States, only the eggs from a large fish called a **sturgeon** (STURH-jen) is classified as caviar. Fresh sturgeon caviar should be plump and moist, with a nutty and mildly briny flavor. There are three types of European sturgeon: beluga, osetra, and sevruga. Each provides caviar and each type of caviar has a different flavor and texture.
- **Beluga Caviar.** The beluga sturgeon is the largest type of sturgeon, reaching its maturity at about 20 years, when it may weigh as much as a ton. This long growth period makes the beluga eggs very expensive. Beluga caviar has the largest eggs, which vary in color from light steel gray to dark gray. Beluga caviar is always sold in blue tins or jars.

- **Osetra Caviar.** Brownish with golden highlights, osetra caviar has a nutty flavor that distinguishes it from other caviars. The osetra sturgeon reaches a weight of 500 pounds and matures at between 12 and 15 years. Osetra caviar is always sold in yellow tins or jars.
- **Sevruga Caviar.** The smallest of the three true caviars, sevruga caviar is dark brown, with an assertive flavor. Mature sevruga sturgeon weigh about 150 pounds and mature in 8 to 10 years. It is less expensive than the other two true caviars and is always sold in red tins or jars.

▲ *Osetra caviar*

In America, the black sturgeon provides caviar that is commonly referred to as American caviar. Eggs from fish such as the hackleback, gray paddlefish, white fish, salmon, and lumpfish are also eaten like caviar.

Pressed caviar is made from mature, broken, or overripe eggs. The salted eggs are collected in a linen sack and pressed to release liquid. The result is a spread, which is often used on slices of black bread. It is also included as an ingredient in dishes and in sauces rather than using the more expensive caviar. Pressed caviar is very strongly flavored, with a different texture than other caviar.

Because of the high cost of and luxury associated with caviar, it is typically served for very special occasions. There are time-honored rituals and etiquette associated with serving and eating it. If caviar is served by a restaurant, the garde manger needs to be well informed about buying, handling, and serving it, because of its cost and rarity. Here are some guidelines to handling and serving caviar:

▲ *Sevruga caviar*

- Don't use metal utensils when handling caviar. Metal reacts with caviar, producing an off flavor.
- Chill caviar to 32°F. Because most refrigerators are not this cold, it is usually necessary to keep caviar on ice in the coldest part of the refrigerator. Replenish the ice when it begins to melt.
- Do not open caviar jars until you're ready to use it. Once the jar is opened, the caviar should be served within two to three days.
- Serve caviar in its original container or in a nonmetallic serving bowl. Because it is highly perishable, the container or bowl should be placed on a bed of ice. The best serving platters or plates for caviar are nonmetallic and nonabsorbent, preferably of china.
- Handle caviar carefully to prevent the eggs from breaking.

FIGURE 10-21
Caviar Service
Caviar must be kept cold.
Predicating *Have you ever had caviar? If not, do you think you'd like it?*

- Use special mother-of-pearl, bone, or tortoise shell spoons that are made for handling caviar.
- Serve caviar on lightly buttered white-bread toast or on **blinis** (BLEE-nees), very thin Russian crêpes, accompanied by sour cream.

Lesser quality, non-sturgeon fish eggs are not typically served by themselves. If they are served by themselves, they are served on ice and offered with buttered toast and accompaniments of chopped hard-cooked egg whites, chopped egg yolks (separately from the whites), lemons, and sour cream. It is much more typical for non-sturgeon fish eggs to be used as ingredients or garnishes for other dishes.

Smoked Fish Presentations Smoked salmon and other smoked fishes are often used for cold food presentations. Their natural oils keep their flesh tender and moist. Thinly sliced salmon can be served on toast, black or whole grain breads, or other bread products. Classic combinations include:

- Smoked salmon, minced onion, and capers
- Smoked salmon, chopped hard-cooked eggs, capers, and parsley
- Smoked salmon with caviar-, mustard-, or horseradish-flavored sour cream
- Smoked trout with horseradish sauce
- Smoked sturgeon with caviar

FIGURE 10-22
Smoked Salmon Platter
Salmon is often served with black bread, minced onions, and capers.
Predicating *Have you ever had smoked salmon? If not, do you think you'd like it?*

CULINARY DIVERSITY

Sweden

One of Sweden's most famous dishes, cured salmon, or gravlax (GRAHV-lox), has become a favorite salmon dish for the garde manger. It has a clear, delicate flavor and is easy to prepare.

Like most cured and smoked fish products, gravlax was born of necessity. Fishermen in Sweden and surrounding Scandinavian countries long ago devised this recipe as a way of preserving fish. After filleting the salmon, they covered it with salt and sugar and buried it along a cool, shaded stream while they continued their salmon fishing upstream. Prepared this way, the fish took on a delicate flavor and remained moist and fresh for up to a week. When the fish was cured, the fishermen returned to collect it.

▲ Gravlax

The popularity of gravlax spread to bordering Norway, Finland, and Denmark. Today, it is found on the menus of fine restaurants and hotels all over the world.

Gravlax is still prepared by using sugar and salt, flavored with dill and white pepper, and topped with a weight that acts as a press. After preparation, it is eaten uncooked, accompanied by a sweet-and-sour mustard-dill sauce. Gravlax is an ideal dish for the garde manger station because it is prepared well in advance of serving.

Research

Research the method used for making gravlax. List the ingredients and describe the procedure. Research the traditional sauces that are served alongside it in three Scandinavian countries. Describe each sauce, list the ingredients, and explain the method of presentation.

Reading Checkpoint *What are five common types of cold food presentations?*

Elements in Cold Food Presentation

The garde manger can use cold food presentation as a way to showcase the talents of staff, but design and decoration aren't everything.

The food must be tasty and, ideally, healthful—as well as visually appealing. Serving tools should be both useful and attractive. In addition, thought should be put into creating an attractive and functional table arrangement.

Design Elements for Food Arrangements Although any of the following design elements can be used as a focal point in any sort of plating or food arranging, these design elements should be combined to create energy and interest. Too much repetition, regardless of the element used, is monotonous.

- **Balance.** Balance creates a sense of calm. Use symmetry and evenness in the composition when it comes to shape, color, and texture. Balance the colors, shapes, heights, and textures.
- **Color.** Nothing communicates excitement and vitality like color. Use natural colors, never artificial elements, to stimulate interest. When natural colors are used, you have no need for concern about colors clashing. Use colorful garnishes if the food is dull in color (as meats often are). However, using too much of the same color in an arrangement can be monotonous.
- **Texture.** Glossy surfaces add sparkle. Rough surfaces, such as homemade breads, for example, can reflect a rustic quality. Velvety textures, such as that of fresh mozzarella cheese or the creamy textures of soft cheeses, are seductive. Combining textures is very important when you are designing cold food presentations.
- **Cooking Technique.** Unlike hot foods, cold foods lack the advantage of any significant aroma to entice guests. Certain cooking techniques create enhanced visual appeal suggestive of an aroma. For example, charring or searing meats used for cold salads, or roasting vegetables to give them a warm cast, suggests an aroma, a taste, to your guests. Remember, the chef's saying, "people eat with their eyes"? This is a case of fooling people's noses so they smell with their eyes.
- **Shape and Height.** To communicate abundance and excitement, you can adjust the shape and height of your cold food presentations. You can roll flat foods such as sliced meats and thin breads. You can stack food in interesting arrangements, such as raw or blanched vegetables cut into long, thin strips and formed into haystacks, teepee shapes, or other artistic designs. Grated granular cheeses can be melted in a circular shape on a pan surface and then pinched into little basket shapes for nesting greens or other foods. Pencil-thin breadsticks can jut out of an arrangement of silky prosciutto slices draped over each other on a platter.

- **Focal Point.** You need to provide a center of interest for your presentation. It can be a single item or a combination of items.
- **Strong, Clean Lines.** Whether you use straight rows, angles, or curves, strong uninterrupted lines can be effective design elements. For example, you can create rows of vegetables rather than just placing them randomly or in a jumble. You can arrange sliced foods to form long overlapping lines.

FIGURE 10-23
Presentation Design
Multiple platters were used in this buffet.
Interpreting Illustrations *Do you see any design elements that have not been addressed in this buffet presentation?*

Buffet Table Design The arrangement of items on a buffet table is just as important as the arrangement of food on your platters. Here are some tips for buffet table design:
- Guests should be able to reach food easily.
- Serving utensils and table utensils should be plentiful and within easy reach.

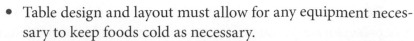

Cross-Contamination
Use gloves, tongs, and other tools when you're setting up or serving a buffet to prevent contaminating food as you work.

FIGURE 10-24
Grosse Pièce
A large portion of this ham has not been cut.
Predicting *Do you see any design elements that have not been addressed in this presentation?*
▼

- Table design and layout must allow for any equipment necessary to keep foods cold as necessary.
- Larger or higher items should be placed behind smaller or lower items on the table surface.

Serving Main Items There are typically two ways to serve the main item in a cold food presentation or a buffet:

- **Slicing and Sequencing.** Slice foods with irregular or tapered shapes to create definite lines when the slices are arranged in a sequence. Arranging slices to overlap one another in the order they were cut is referred to as **sequencing**. When a tapered turkey breast is sliced and sequenced, for example, a regular design with clean lines results.
- **Grosse Pièce.** Serving the main item **grosse pièce** (GROHSS pee-YES) means that a large part of the main item is left unsliced. Grosse pièce means "large piece" in French. A main item can be presented grosse pièce, but the slices cut from the main item can be sequenced.

Serving Tools Serving tools are important for cold food presentations. Although these are functional items, they are set on the table and therefore become part of the presentation. For this reason, you should use dining room tools for a cold food presentation rather than kitchen tools, which may be too large for serving and are certainly not designed for food presentation. Dining room serving tools include ladles, tongs, serving spoons, serving forks, serving spatulas, and serving scoops.

 Reading Checkpoint

What are the two ways that main items are typically served in a cold food presentation or a buffet?

Centerpieces and Garnishes

Two other considerations remain for cold food presentations and for buffets. These are centerpieces and garnishes. They help bring the presentation or buffet together.

Centerpieces A beautiful centerpiece can be a great attraction, communicating excitement and reflecting the artistry in the food presented on the table. They reinforce or magnify the buffet's theme or concept. They help the guests understand the function or meaning of any presentation.

Tall or very large centerpieces must be carefully located. They should never block a guest's view or access to the food. Stabilize top-heavy centerpieces so they don't wobble or fall over. Be certain that all elements of the display are safe when used with food. For example, toxic flowers (such as lilies of the valley) should not be used in a centerpiece where they could drop onto food and someone could accidentally eat them.

One of the most spectacular, but expensive, centerpieces is an ice sculpture. Ice carvings can be purely decorative or they can function as receptacles for food such as cooked shrimp or seafood salads. Individual ice sculptures in the form of decorative cups can hold frozen dishes, fruits, or vegetables.

Ice carving is a highly specialized skill, with the additional challenge that ice melts. However, some ice sculptures can be made easily from molds and assembled into larger pieces. When assembling ice sculptures, plan to use a sturdy base. Set the sculpture in a pan connected to a drain or valve that can capture water from the melting ice and transfer it to a tub. The base can be camouflaged with cloth, edible flowers, plants, or other safe decoration.

▲ *Ice sculpture centerpiece*

Garnishes The purpose of a garnish is to add flavor, color, and texture to individual items, individual dishes, composed platters and trays, and to buffets, in general. A garnish is meant to draw attention to the food, not to overwhelm the food or detract from it in any way.

It used to be that all kinds of things with little eating appeal were used for garnishes simply for color effect. However, because well-trained culinary professionals know the importance of quality in food preparation and presentation, the garde manger thinks of garnishes as food, not simply decoration.

Garnishes cannot be an afterthought. The garde manger needs to put thought into the selection and preparation of garnishes because they must be an integrated part of the dish or presentation. Garnishes should not be boring or overused, like the ho-hum scrap of tired parsley tossed on top of every dish.

Here are additional guidelines for garnishing.

- **Function.** Garnishes should be used to create a visual impression and also to add a taste experience.
- **Flavor.** Garnishes should taste fresh and complement the taste of the item they garnish.

- **Color/Visual Appeal.** Garnishes should be visually attractive as well as good to eat. Typically, they add a different color to the main theme of the dish or presentation. The color of a garnish adds a new effect to the overall dish or presentation (see the chart "Color Effects of Garnishes").
- **Textural Appeal.** Typically, garnishes add a different texture than the dish or presentation with which they are used.
- **Appropriate Size.** Keep scale in mind in designing garnishes. If they are too small in proportion to the food presented, they will look lost on the plate. If they are too large, they compete with the food that should be the focus of the dish or presentation.
- **Special Effects.** Use fanning cuts (on pickles or strawberries, for example), sequencing, julienne or matchstick shapes, spiral cutting (using a spiral cutter), crinkle cuts, rosettes (such as radish "roses"), curls, paper-thin cuts, and molds for soft foods such as aspic or butter, food sculpting, or ice sculpting.

Color Effects of Garnishes

	Color	Effect	Food Garnish
	Green	Freshness and vitality	Chives, parsley, fresh herbs, green sprouts, scallions, greens, limes, green peppers
	Browns and Golds	Warmth, comfort, richness	Lemons, breadsticks, bread products, hard-cooked egg wedges, butter curls, yellow peppers, miniature yellow tomatoes
	Oranges and Reds	Intensity, desire, hunger	Tomatoes, radishes, radicchio, carrots, red or orange peppers, edible nasturtium flowers

Making a Fan Cut

1. Place item on its side on a work surface.

2. Cut in paper-thin slices from tip to stem, leaving the flesh at the base of the stem still attached.

3. Spread the slices out, using your fingers. It should be spread like a fan.

4. Lift the fan carefully onto the plate or platter you are garnishing. Use a knife, spatula, or palette knife. Fruits such as strawberries can also be fanned.

 **Reading Checkpoint** *What are the purposes of centerpieces and garnishes?*

10.4 ASSESSMENT

Reviewing Concepts

1. What are five common types of cold food presentations?
2. What are the two ways main items are typically served in a cold food presentation or a buffet?
3. What is the purpose of a garnish?

Critical Thinking

4. **Drawing Conclusions** Why are only pressed caviar and other types of fish eggs used in cooking?
5. **Compare and Contrast** What design element for food arrangements do you think is most important? Why?
6. **Predicting** How is the appeal of a meat dish improved by the use of a garnish?
7. **Drawing Conclusions** Any service of raw shellfish or other seafood comes with a risk. Why would a restaurant take on that risk?

TEST KITCHEN

Divide into four teams. Each team will create a small platter as a cold food presentation, complete with garnishes. Evaluate other teams' efforts based on the design elements for food arrangements. Tally the results.

SCIENCE

Smoked Fish

Research how fish, such as salmon and trout, are smoked. Focus on such questions as: How long does the process take? At what temperature are they smoked? Is any special type of wood used to produce the smoke? Are herbs or spices used in the smoking process to add flavor? Are there regional or national differences in how fish are smoked?

Review and Assessment

Reviewing Content

Choose the letter that best answers the question or completes the statement.

1. Mayonnaise is
   a. a vinaigrette
   b. an emulsion
   c. a coulis
   d. all of the above

2. The three types of salad greens are
   a. sweet, sour, bitter
   b. mild, spicy, bitter
   c. mild, strong, sweet
   d. sweet, spicy, sour

3. Parmigiano-Reggiano is a
   a. soft, rind-ripened cheese
   b. hard cheese
   c. grating cheese
   d. blue-vein cheese

4. Caviar is
   a. salted eggs from a sturgeon
   b. a type of smoked fish
   c. raw fish
   d. a shellfish, usually eaten raw on the half shell

5. Rémoulade is
   a. a bitter salad green
   b. a type of blue cheese
   c. a mayonnaise-based dressing
   d. a type of sturgeon that produces caviar

6. Mesclun is
   a. a French-style mix of salad greens
   b. a type of soft, rind-ripened cheese
   c. a style of vinaigrette
   d. a type of smoked fish

7. Which of the following is not a fresh cheese?
   a. mascarpone
   b. brie
   c. ricotta
   d. feta

Understanding Concepts

8. What is a vinaigrette?

9. What is a side salad?

10. What is the difference between fresh cheese and a soft, rind-ripened cheese?

11. What is caviar?

12. What is the garde manger?

13. What is the difference between a tossed salad and a composed salad?

14. What are the two methods of serving a main course in a cold food presentation or a buffet?

Critical Thinking

15. **Recognizing Patterns** What is the difference between a hard cheese and a grating cheese?

16. **Predicting** How would you describe the taste of a salad containing radicchio, escarole, endive, and arugula? Based on the taste of the salad, what type of ingredients might you include in a dressing?

Culinary Math

17. **Solving Problems** A recipe for shrimp salad uses 32 ounces of mayonnaise, 8 ounces of lemon juice, and 2 heads of celery for 12 pounds of shrimp. You have only 6 pounds of shrimp. How much of each of the other ingredients is required to make this salad?

18. **Applying Concepts** If the ratio of ketchup to prepared horseradish for cocktail sauce is 7 to 1, how many quarts of ketchup are necessary to make 1 gallon of cocktail sauce? How many quarts of horseradish are necessary?

On the Job

19. **Communicating** A customer indicates she is a vegetarian. She orders a Niçoise salad. Is there a problem? If so, what should you do?

RECIPE CARDS

Use the following Recipe Cards to test your culinary skill.

28. Red-Wine Vinaigrette
29. Russian Dressing
30. Basil Oil
31. Blue Cheese Dressing
32. Pesto
33. Mayonnaise
34. Tarter Sauce
35. Salsa Fresca
36. Mixed Green Salad
37. Chef Salad
38. Caesar Salad
39. Tropical Fruit Salad
40. Potato Salad
41. Pasta Salad with Pesto Vinaigrette
42. Mixed Grain and Bean Salad

LAB ACTIVITY

Project 10: Tasting Cheese

Answer these questions when your class works through Project 10.

- Which cheese do you like the most? The least?

- Which fruit do you like best with the cheeses you tasted, or does it differ based on the type of cheese?

- What are the differences between a soft, rind-ripened cheese straight from the refrigerator and one that has been allowed to reach room temperature? Which do you prefer?

- Can you taste the difference between a mass-produced grating cheese and a grating cheese produced by a small cheese producer? Which do you prefer?

TEST PRACTICE

Choose the letter that best answers the question or completes the statement.

1. The main ingredient in baba ghanoush is
   A   mashed avocado
   B   black olives
   C   eggplant
   D   fresh cheese

2. Which of the following is not a mild salad green?
   A   arugula
   B   mâche
   C   baby spinach
   D   romaine lettuce

3. Which of the following is not a semi-soft cheese?
   A   Muenster
   B   Monterey Jack
   C   Gruyère
   D   Edam

4. Grosse pièce indicates
   A   only large pieces of cheese are used on a cheese plate
   B   seafood will be presented on the half shell in a raw bar
   C   a type of soft, rind-ripened cheese
   D   a large part of the main item is left unsliced

5. Which ingredient is not included in aïoli?
   A   dill pickles
   B   mayonnaise
   C   garlic
   D   herbs or sun-dried tomatoes

6. The smallest of the true caviars is
   A   sevruga
   B   beluga
   C   osetra
   D   American caviar

7. Brie is a
   A   fresh cheese
   B   soft, rind-ripened cheese
   C   semi-soft cheese
   D   blue-vein cheese

8. Depurated oysters are
   A   live oysters
   B   purged of their impurities
   C   flash-frozen
   D   certified, with a tag providing harvest information

CHAPTER 11

SANDWICHES, APPETIZERS, & HORS D'OEUVRES

11.1 Sandwiches

11.2 Appetizers & Hors d'Oeuvres

READING PREVIEW

Key Concepts

- Understanding basic sandwich elements
- Understanding the mise en place for sandwich making
- Understanding the types of cold sandwiches
- Understanding the types of hot sandwiches

Vocabulary

- closed sandwich
- club sandwich
- cubano
- finger sandwich
- foccacia
- grilled sandwich
- hero sandwich
- Kaiser roll
- open-faced sandwich
- panini
- pita bread
- pressed sandwich
- pullman loaf
- tea sandwich
- tortilla
- wrap

"**P**recision counts in sandwich making. Breads, fillings, spreads, and garnishes all need to be kept in balance. "

– Greg Fatigati

Basic Sandwich Elements

Sandwiches have become so popular you can find them on breakfast, lunch, and even dinner menus. You can find them everywhere from diners to fast food restaurants to fancy restaurants. Basically, the incredibly popular sandwich is a combination of four simple elements:

- Bread
- Spread
- Filling
- Garnish

These elements are the building blocks chefs use to create both classic sandwiches and new sandwich variations. The choice of ingredients determines if the sandwich is a nutritious meal or just another high-calorie indulgence.

Bread It is critically important that your bread be fresh and tasty. Using stale or tasteless bread ruins a sandwich. Different types of sandwiches require different types of breads.

Greg Fatigati
The Culinary Institute of America

However, you should never choose bread that is so crusty or hard that it makes the sandwich difficult to eat. Often the type of bread used depends on the type of filling used. The bread must hold the filling without falling apart. For example, a firm, thick slice of bread or a roll is best for a juicy steak sandwich. A softer, thinner slice of white bread is best for delicate tea and finger sandwiches.

Obviously, standard loaves of bread—wheat, white, rye, sourdough, to name only a few—often serve as the base for sandwiches. Some bread used for sandwiches is flavored with herbs, nuts, cheese, or fruit. However, any strong flavoring in the bread should complement the sandwich filling, without dominating or distracting from it.

Other types of types of breads often used in sandwiches are:

▲ White, pumpernickel, and whole wheat bread

FIGURE 11-1
Pita Bread
Pita bread has been cut to form a pocket and the pocket has been filled to capacity.
Predicting *Which types of fillings would work best with the pita bread pockets?*

▼

- **Pullman Loaf.** Baked in a rectangular pan with a lid, a **pullman loaf** is a long loaf. A slice from a pullman loaf is square on all sides. The compact, fine-grain of a pullman loaf makes it easier to slice off the crust or cut the bread into shapes. White and whole wheat pullman loaves are often used for cold sandwiches.
- **Kaiser Roll.** A large, round, crusty roll, the **kaiser** (KIGH-zer) **roll** is also known as a hard roll or a Vienna roll.
- **Focaccia.** A large, flat Italian bread, **focaccia** (foh-KAH-chee-ah) is traditionally flavored with olive oil and herbs.
- **Pita Bread.** A flat round or oval Middle Eastern bread, **pita** (PEE-tah) **bread** is also known as pocket bread. When it is cut in half, each half forms a pocket that can be filled as a sandwich.

- **Tortilla.** Mexico's unleavened bread, the **tortilla** (tohr-TEE-yuh) is a round, flat, bread made of corn or flour. A tortilla looks like a very thin pancake. The filling is often folded or wrapped inside the tortilla.
- **Bagels.** Bagels have become increasingly popular for sandwiches, particularly breakfast sandwiches.
- **Croissants.** The flakey, buttery taste of a croissant helps create a rich-tasting sandwich.
- **Hot Dog and Hamburger Rolls.** These specially created rolls are familiar to anyone who has ever had a backyard cookout.

Spread Spreads add additional flavor and typically act as a moisture barrier for the bread, preventing the moisture from seeping into the bread. However, with some types of sandwiches, it is desirable for the filling to soak the bread, so a spread would not be used. Spreads also keep a sandwich together while adding moisture to it and keeping loose fillings from falling off the bread.

One of the most common spreads is butter. Butter has a rich, smooth flavor and can be perked up by adding spices, peppers, garlic, or other flavorings. Butter is best used as a spread if it is softened so it doesn't tear the bread when it is spread.

Another common spread is mayonnaise. It adds a rich, tangy flavor to sandwiches, and it, too, can be perked up with spices, peppers, garlic, or other flavorings.

Vegetable-based purées made from avocados, olives, roasted peppers, or roasted eggplant can also be used as spreads. Although they reduce fat, purées do not usually provide a moisture barrier to the bread.

Filling The centerpiece of a sandwich is the filling. It can be hot or cold, meal-sized or just enough for a single bite. Attention to detail is what will make your sandwich a success. Salad and other greens should be carefully rinsed and dried, meat and poultry should be properly cooked, cheese should be fresh and not overpowering to other fillings. All slices should be evenly cut.

The filling will determine if you use a spread. The filling will also help you determine what kind of bread you should use. For example, tuna salad or any other mayonnaise-based filling will not require a spread and will require thin, dense bread that is sturdy enough to hold the filling. Sliced meat, particularly if it is dry, will require a generous amount of spread.

Some of the most common fillings are:
- **Meat and Poultry.** When used as the primary filling in a sandwich, meat and poultry can be roasted, fried, broiled, or simmered. They can be served alone or combined with other types of food, such as bacon with lettuce and tomato or Italian sausage with peppers and onions. Meat and poultry can also be made into a mayonnaise-based sandwich salad, such as ham salad or chicken salad.

- **Seafood and Fish.** Tuna and shrimp are commonly made into mayonnaise-based sandwich salads. Many varieties of seafood and fish are broiled or deep-fried for sandwiches and served with tartar sauce.

- **Vegetables.** The emphasis on healthy eating has increased the demand for vegetables in sandwiches. Lettuce, tomatoes, onions, and pickles have always been common on sandwiches. Today you might also use sprouts, peppers, radishes, and cucumbers. In fact, vegetables such as portobello mushrooms are often the primary filling in a sandwich. As a primary filling, vegetables can be grilled, roasted, or served raw. Often a vinaigrette adds flavor to vegetables when they are used as a primary filling.

- **Cheese.** Cheese can be a stand-alone filling, as in the classic grilled cheese sandwich. It is also a favorite combination filling in many other sandwiches. The vast flavor choices range from mild and creamy to pungent and hard. Choose a flavor and texture that complements the other flavors and textures in the sandwich. Low-fat cheeses do not typically melt as well as regular cheese on a hot sandwich and often do not have the same level of flavor.

- **Eggs.** Fried or scrambled eggs are often featured in breakfast sandwiches, along with bacon and cheese, but they can also be used in other types of sandwiches. For example, a French sandwich called croque madame (CROKE ma-DAHM) includes ham, cheese, and a fried egg. Hard-cooked eggs can be made into mayonnaise-based salad sandwiches.

Garnish Garnishes are typically decorative, edible accompaniments on a plate with a sandwich. A garnish should complement the flavor of a sandwich, because the customer often incorporates the garnish into the sandwich itself. For example, lettuce, sprouts, fruit, pickles, relishes, tomatoes, onions, and olives are all side garnishes that could work well as part of the sandwich. Larger garnishes, such as whole vegetables, carrot or celery sticks, pickle spears, or slices of orange or melon, should provide complementary flavors for the sandwich, but are eaten separately.

 **Reading Checkpoint** *What are the four elements of a sandwich?*

Sandwich Mise en Place

Whether you are making many different individual sandwiches or a large amount of the same sort of sandwiches, you need to be organized and perform your mise en place. You will need to wear gloves when constructing sandwiches. There are three steps to performing a mise en place for sandwiches:

- Gathering tools
- Selecting and preparing ingredients
- Organizing the job and the workspace

Gathering Tools Have the following tools on hand:

- Cutting board
- Tongs and spatulas
- Sharp knives, including a chef's knife, a bread knife, and a serrated knife. (Use a very sharp knife to cut sandwiches easily.)
- Serving spoons or scoops for portion control
- Palette knife or butter knife for spreads and mayonnaise-based sandwich salads
- Toaster (if bread will be toasted)

Selecting and Preparing Ingredients In some situations, you will make just one sandwich, when it is ordered. Other times you could be making four, six, or even a hundred sandwiches at a time. No matter how many sandwiches you are making, you still must select the ingredients prior to service. Here are some tips for preparing sandwich ingredients:

- Slice bread and rolls to order. If toasting is required, it's best to wait until assembly to toast.
- Have spreads ready and at a consistency that won't tear the bread. Use a spatula to apply spreads, covering the entire surface.
- Prepare and portion the fillings in advance. Some sandwiches that will be grilled can be assembled in advance and grilled as they are needed.
- Wash and dry salad greens.
- Prepare garnishes in advance.

Organizing the Job and the Work Space As with any mise en place, you must break down the steps involved in making the sandwiches and make sure you rank the tasks in terms of their priority. For example, if you need to cook chicken breasts for a sandwich you will be serving cold, you will need to allow sufficient time not only to cook the chicken but also to bring the chicken down to the correct temperature. Here are some additional guidelines for organizing the job and your workspace:

- Make a list of the steps involved in your recipe, in the order they need to be done. (Remember to use the PRN—Preview, Read, Note—method for reading recipes discussed in Chapter 5.)

▲ *Palette Knife*

- Keep everything you need within reach to save time walking to it.
- Have everything move in one direction, starting with the bread on one side and the finished sandwiches on the other side. (Typically, right-handed people move from left to right, so the bread would be on your left and the finished sandwiches on your right.)
- If possible, prepare multiple sandwiches at one time. Complete them before beginning on the next batch.

FIGURE 11-2
Efficient Assembly Line
Plates move in one direction. When finished they are stored on racks.
Solving a Problem *How does the rack help increase efficiency?*

Reading Checkpoint

What are three steps to performing mise en place for sandwiches?

Cold Sandwiches

A wide diversity of cold sandwiches has developed to suit every taste and appetite. Cold sandwiches are often filled with sliced meats and cheese or mayonnaise-based sandwich salads such as egg salad, chicken salad, and tuna salad. Restaurants typically offer cold sandwiches as a main course, often in combination with a soup or salad. The portability of cold sandwiches makes them a perfect take-out choice as well.

There are six main types of cold sandwiches:

- **Closed Sandwich.** This is what everyone thinks of when they think of a sandwich. A **closed sandwich** is simply two pieces of bread, a bun, or a roll with a filling between them.
- **Open-Faced Sandwich.** When a sandwich is made with one slice of bread and topped with ingredients, it is called an **open-faced sandwich**.
- **Finger Sandwich.** A simple, small sandwich, a **finger sandwich** (also called a **tea sandwich**) is usually made with firm, thinly sliced pullman loaves. Finger sandwiches can be made both as closed sandwiches and as open-faced sandwiches. Because the bread is dense, sandwiches can be cut into small squares, diamonds, rectangles, rounds, and triangles. Pullman loaves are typically sliced lengthwise, filled, and then cut into shapes.
- **Hero Sandwich.** A large closed sandwich, the **hero sandwich** (or simply hero) uses a long thin loaf of bread (often called a hero loaf). Heroes are known by different names in different parts of the country. They can be called submarines, grinders, po' boys, or

▲ *Hero Sandwich*

hoagies. Whatever name you call it, this is a substantial sandwich often filled with thinly sliced meats, cheese, tomatoes, and lettuce, with a variety of garnishes.

- **Club Sandwich.** A double-decker closed sandwich, the **club sandwich** is made with three slices of bread (or toast). It is traditionally filled with chicken (or turkey, ham, or beef), bacon, lettuce, and tomato. These sandwiches are traditionally cut into four triangles, making them easier to eat, and held together with sandwich picks.

CHEF'S TIP

TEA SANDWICHES

Fill open-faced tea sandwiches just before serving to prevent discoloration of the filling. Avoid covering open-faced sandwiches with plastic wrap as the wrap may stick to the filling.

BASIC CULINARY SKILLS

Making a Club Sandwich

1 Toast bread. You will need 3 slices per sandwich.

2 Spread mayonnaise on only 1 side of each slice of toast.

3 Add bottom filling. Layer lettuce, tomato, and bacon.

4 Add second piece of toast, mayonnaise side down.

5 Spread mayonnaise on top of second piece of toast.

6 Add top filling. Layer lettuce and turkey.

7 Add third piece of toast, mayonnaise side down.

8 Secure with sandwich picks.

9 Cut sandwich into quarters. Serve.

 See Recipe Card 43, "Club Sandwich."

CHEF'S TIP

GRILLED MEAT SANDWICHES

Be sure any meat in a grilled pressed sandwich is pre-cooked because a grilled sandwich will only get heated, not cooked.

- **Wraps and Pita Pockets.** A sandwich that is rolled up or otherwise enclosed in an edible wrapper is called a **wrap**. Tortillas or flat round bread are commonly used as the bread. Pita bread is used to make pita pockets. The advantage of a wrap or pita pocket is that they can hold many ingredients and the opening is only at the top. Be careful not to overstuff a wrap or use pieces that are too chunky as this can cause the wrap to come apart.

Reading Checkpoint *What are the six main types of cold sandwiches?*

Hot Sandwiches

There are four main types of hot sandwiches:

- **Sandwich with Hot Filling.** A closed sandwich, a hero sandwich, a club sandwich, and a wrap can all be served with a hot filling. Hamburgers and hotdogs are often served with room-temperature buns, for example. When vegetables such as lettuce or tomato are served with a hot filling, they are often

BASIC CULINARY SKILLS

Making a Wrap

1 Warm a tortilla in a hot skillet for about 15 seconds on each side.

2 Spread puréed black beans on one-half tortilla.

3 Add lettuce, tomatoes, and onions on top of puréed black beans.

4 Add grilled chicken on top of other filling.

5 Roll tortilla closed tightly, starting on the side with the filling.

6 Secure with a sandwich pick. Serve immediately.

The Story behind Peanut Butter and Jelly

Almost always, there's a story behind even the simplest food item. For example, consider the ordinary peanut butter and jelly sandwich.

Although variations of the sandwich have been around since biblical times, legend has it that an Englishman, John Montagu, the fourth Earl of Sandwich, invented the sandwich in 1765. Supposedly he came up with the idea of using bread slices to hold his meat so he could eat while he played cards.

Almost a century later, a St. Louis doctor came up with the idea for peanut butter. He was concerned about his patients who could not chew meat because of dental problems. He ground peanuts into a paste, providing them with a high-protein alternative to meat. The idea caught on and peanut butter was patented.

The next step in our peanut butter and jelly sandwich occurred in 1928. That was the date of the invention of sliced bread. As a result, the popularity of sandwiches soared in America.

The final step in creating the peanut butter and jelly sandwich was World War II. Soldiers were given rations of peanut butter and jelly, and they invented this sweet and savory classic.

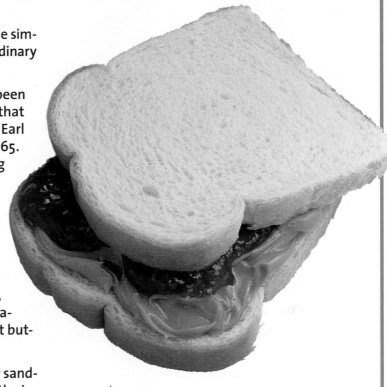

▲ *Peanut butter and jelly sandwich*

As a testament to the popularity of the peanut butter and jelly sandwich, the Peanut Advisory Board estimates that today half of the peanuts grown in the United States are used to make peanut butter.

served on the side until the customer assembles the sandwich. This prevents the hot filling from wilting the vegetable.

- **Grilled Sandwich.** To make a **grilled sandwich**, the sandwich is first assembled and then the outside surface of the bread is spread with butter. The sandwich, also known as a griddled sandwich, is then cooked directly on the heat source, usually a griddle. Grilled cheese and Reuben are examples of grilled sandwiches.

- **Pressed Sandwich.** A sandwich press is used to make a **pressed sandwich**. Sandwiches are toasted on a heavy, two-sided cooking press that compresses and grills them until they are hot and heated through on the inside. The Italian version of a pressed sandwich is called a **panini**. The Cuban version is called a **cubano**.

Open-faced turkey sandwich

• **Hot Open-Faced Sandwich.** Hot open-faced sandwiches are often served on toasted bread, topped with gravy or sauce. In some parts of the country, mashed potatoes are added and the open-faced sandwich is called a hot shot. Eggs Benedict, a breakfast/brunch dish consisting of an English muffin, ham, a poached egg, and sauce is actually a hot open-faced sandwich.

 **Reading Checkpoint** *What are the four basic types of hot sandwiches?*

11.1 ASSESSMENT

Reviewing Concepts

1. What are the four elements of a sandwich?
2. What are three steps to performing mise en place for sandwiches?
3. What are the six main types of cold sandwiches?
4. What are the four main types of hot sandwiches?

Critical Thinking

5. **Predicting** What would happen if you served a hot turkey sandwich with gravy as a closed sandwich on thin slices from a Pullman loaf?
6. **Comparing/Contrasting** Is mayonnaise a better choice than a vegetable purée on a bacon, lettuce tomato sandwich on toast?
7. **Drawing Conclusions** Your tea sandwiches are dried up and hard. What went wrong and how could you have avoided it?

Test Kitchen

Divide into four teams. Each team will prepare a roast beef sandwich, using a different style of bread or wrap. Try to make them as different as possible. Use identical fillings, spreads, condiments, and garnishes. Evaluate the results.

LANGUAGE ARTS

Mouth-Watering Adjectives

Create three flavored spreads for a roast beef sandwich. Write a mouth-watering menu description for each spread that will persuade customers to try it. Use at least three different adjectives in the description for each spread.

Appetizers & Hors d'Oeuvres

READING PREVIEW

Key Concepts

- Identifying types of appetizers and hors d'oeuvres
- Presenting appetizers and hors d'oeuvres

Vocabulary

- appetizer
- brochettes
- bruschettas
- canapés
- carpaccio
- chef's tasting
- crostini
- crudités
- finger food
- hors d'oeuvre
- hors d'oeuvres varies
- pâté
- seviche
- shrimp cocktail
- skewers
- terrine

Olivier Andrieni
The Culinary Institute of America

"**A**ppetizers are meant to stimulate the appetite, not kill it off. 🙷

– Olivier Andrieni

Types of Appetizers and Hors d'Oeuvres

A small, savory, flavorful dish, usually consumed in one or two bites, is called an **hors d'oeuvre** (or-DERV), a French term that means "outside the meal." The same dish, if it were served as the first course in a meal, would be called an **appetizer**. As you can see, the main difference between an appetizer and an hors d'oeuvre is when they are served. There are hot and cold varieties of both hors d'oeuvres and appetizers. Although the same items may be served as either hors d'oeuvres or appetizers, the appetizer portions would tend to be slightly larger than the hors d'oeuvre portion.

The purpose of both an hors d'oeuvre and an appetizer is to stimulate the appetite and set a mood for the meal that will follow. With this in mind, you should offer a variety of flavors and textures that are complementary to the entrée that follows. For example, if you have lasagna for the main course, you might want to avoid serving ravioli as an appetizer.

Hors d'oeuvres are often served with a napkin and eaten with the fingers. When served this way, they are also called **finger food**. Hors d'oeuvres rarely require a fork. Appetizers are usually served on a plate and are often eaten with a fork (although sometimes appetizers are also finger food).

Hot Appetizers and Hors d'Oeuvres

There is an incredible diversity of hot appetizers and hors d'oeuvres. In fact, virtually any type of savory food served in a small portion can be regarded as an appetizer. Any type of food that you can eat with your fingers or in bite-sized pieces could become an hors d'oeuvre. Some common hot appetizers and hors d'oeuvres are:

- **Baked, Sautéed, or Grilled Seafood.** Seafood, particularly scallops and shrimps, are quickly sautéed with herbs and served as an appetizer or hors d'oeuvre.
- **Brochettes.** Meat, fish, poultry, or vegetables can be cooked on **skewers** (SKEW-ers), long, thin, pointed rods made of wood or metal. Small versions of these grilled or broiled skewers of food are called **brochettes** (BRO-shets). The food is usually marinated before cooking. Brochettes are often served with a dipping sauce.
- **Fried Food.** This includes batter-dipped fish, chicken, or vegetables, often served with some type of dipping sauce.

▲

FIGURE 11-3
Hors d'Oeuvre or Appetizer?
Meatballs served on a wooden stick become an hors d'oeuvre. **Recognizing Patterns** *Why would large meatballs be served as an appetizer?*

BASIC CULINARY SKILLS

Vegetable Tempura

1. Heat oil to 375°F.
2. Blot vegetables dry and season.
3. Coat vegetables with batter.

4. Place vegetables in hot oil.
5. Deep fry until batter is golden brown and puffy. Turn, if necessary, to brown and cook evenly.

6. Remove vegetables from fryer with tongs or skimmer.

7. Blot briefly on absorbent toweling.
8. Season, if necessary, and serve at once. Serve with a dipping sauce.

 See Recipe Card 49, "Vegetable Tempura."

- **Pastry and Tart Shells.** Small shells, like tiny pie crusts, can be stuffed with assorted savory fillings and baked. Fillings include custards, meat, poultry, vegetables, cheese, and seafood. Mini pizzas or mini quiches are often created by using pastry or tart shells.
- **Meatballs.** Small meatballs or other highly seasoned ground-meat items are served with toothpicks as hors d'oeuvres. Meatballs are often served in a sweet-sour sauce. Appetizer-sized meatballs are eaten with a fork. Hors d'oeuvre-sized meatballs are often eaten on a skewer or sandwich pick.
- **Pasta.** Small portions of pasta can be served as an appetizer.
- **Grilled, Steamed, Baked, or Roasted Vegetables.** Vegetables such as asparagus, artichokes, peppers, onions, garlic, zucchini, and carrots are cooked and often served with a dipping sauce or dressed with a vinaigrette. Mushroom caps are sometimes stuffed and baked.
- **Dumplings, Egg Rolls, and Spring Rolls.** These are the traditional hors d'oeuvres and appetizers for Asian dinners.
- **Chicken Wings.** Buffalo-style chicken wings are deep-fried after being dipped in a spicy coating. A thin, vinegar-based hot sauce is then poured on them. They are usually served with blue cheese dressing, with celery sticks on the side. Chicken wings can be baked or roasted and flavored in a variety of ways.
- **Crab Cakes.** Crab meat is mixed with mayonnaise, herbs, and spices, formed into patties, and sautéed. Crab cakes are often served with a sauce.

Cold Appetizers and Hors d'Oeuvres It is possible to whet your guests' appetites with something as simple as a slice of smoked salmon on French bread. However, it is just as possible to whet their appetites with a much more elaborate offering, such as a bite-sized crab salad tart with mango chutney. The variety of possible cold appetizers and hors d'oeuvres is endless. The only requirements are that the portion size is appropriate and the appetizer or hors d'oeuvre is complementary to the main course. A significant advantage of cold appetizers and hors d'oeuvres is that you can prepare many of them well in advance. This can be extremely important in a fast-paced professional kitchen. Some common cold appetizers and hors d'oeuvres are:

- **Open-Faced Sandwiches.** Small, bite-sized, open-faced sandwiches are often used as hors d'oeuvres. Crackers or hard breads are often used rather than soft breads. **Canapés** (KAN-up-pays) are bite-sized pieces of bread or crackers with a savory topping. They are used as hors d'oeuvres. Toppings can range from a simple piece of cheese to

▲ *Pizza tarts*

▲ *Spring roll*

▲ *Crab cakes*

▲ *Salmon canapés*

Sandwiches, Appetizers, & Hors d'Oeuvres ▲ **335**

▲ *Bruschetta*

▲ *Crudités*

▲ *Pâté*

an elaborate spread. Larger pieces of bread are used for appetizers. **Bruschettas** (brew-SKEH-tahs) and **crostini** (kroh-STEE-nee) are a type of open-faced sandwich served as an appetizer. They consist of toasted bread drizzled with olive oil and topped with tomatoes, olives, cheese, or other ingredients.

- **Raw Seafood.** This includes just-shucked clams and oysters, served with a variety of sauces.
- **Cold Cooked Seafood. Shrimp cocktail,** cold, steamed shrimp served with a spicy cocktail sauce, is a traditional cold appetizer. **Seviche** (seh-VEE-chee), also spelled ceviche, the Latin American dish of fish and seafood that is cooked in citrus juice and flavored with onions, chiles, and cilantro, is another traditional cold appetizer or hors d'oeuvre.
- **Smoked Fish, Meat, or Poultry.** Often served with bread, condiments, and a sauce, smoked fish, meat, or poultry make an elegant appetizer or hors d'oeuvre.
- **Raw or Cured Meats.** This includes prosciutto and **carpaccio** (car-PAH-chee-oh). Carpaccio is raw beef sliced very thinly and dressed with a sauce. Cured meats are sometimes served with complementary fruits, such as melons.
- **Pickled Vegetables.** Usually included as part of an antipasto plate, marinated or pickled vegetables complement other hors d'oeuvres and appetizers.
- **Cold Grilled or Roasted Vegetables.** Vegetables that have been grilled or roasted are often served cold (or at room temperature).
- **Salads.** Small-portioned salads, including mayonnaise-based salads, are outstanding served as appetizers.
- **Cheese.** Cubes of cheese with sandwich picks make ideal hors d'oeuvres.
- **Raw Vegetables.** Vegetables that have been cut into bite-sized pieces are called **crudités** (kroo-deh-TAYS). They are often served with dips.
- **Pâtés and Terrines.** A **pâté** (pah-TAY) is a well-seasoned, baked mixture of ground meat, fish, poultry, or vegetables. Although pâtés can be served hot, they are usually served cold. They have a texture that ranges from a creamy spread to a crumbly meatloaf. You can cook pâtés in a crust or in a mold, which is called a **terrine** (teh-REEN). When pâté is served in its mold, the pâté is called a terrine.

 **Reading Checkpoint**

What is the difference between an appetizer and an hors d'oeuvre?

Presenting Appetizers and Hors d'Oeuvres

Presenting Appetizers Appetizers are presented to customers when they are seated, so it is acceptable to require the use of a fork, spoon, or even a knife.

Here are some general guidelines for presenting appetizers:

- **Use Small Portions.** Appetizer portions should be small. They are supposed to stimulate the appetite, not satisfy it.
- **Use the Correct Balance of Seasonings.** The correct balance of seasoning at the beginning of the meal affects the palate for the rest of the meal. If the flavor of the appetizer is overpowering, it takes away from the enjoyment of the courses that follow.
- **Make a Good First Impression.** Appetizers provide the customer's first impression of the food. Garnish should be minimal, yet add a touch of flavor and texture as well as color. The appetizer should be plated in an artistic and neat manner.
- **Consider a Chef's Tasting.** Appetizers are sometimes presented in a **chef's tasting**. This is a sampler plate with an assortment of different appetizers. The portions are often only one bite, just enough to sample the various appetizers.

 **Reading Checkpoint** *What are four guidelines to remember when presenting appetizers?*

Presenting Hors d'Oeuvres Hors d'oeuvres can be served buffet style, on platters, or on individual plates. Platters are usually used for events where guests are standing and the platters are circulated by the wait staff. (This type of service is referred to as butler service.) Because people often have glasses in their hands, only one hand is free. The best hors d'oeuvres for these occasions are ones that do not require a plate or utensils. In addition to being served before a meal, hors d'oeuvres are often the only food offered at parties and receptions. The same guidelines apply for both.

Here are some general guidelines for presenting hors d'oeuvres:

- **Use Fresh Ingredients.** Ingredients must be at the peak of freshness. Although trimmings or leftover ingredients can be used in hors d'oeuvres, they should be perfectly fresh.
- **Make Hors d'Oeuvres Bite-Sized.** One or two bites are the ideal size.

FIGURE 11-4
Stuffed Mushrooms
Mushrooms stuffed with breadcrumbs, garlic, and parsley. **Recognizing Patterns** *Why is this an appetizer and not an hors d'oeuvre?*

FOCUS ON SAFETY

Double-Dipping
When serving hors d'oeuvres, always provide a spoon to discourage guests from double-dipping (dipping a chewed portion of food in a communal dipping sauce). Double-dipping increases the hazards of pathogens passed from the guests' hands and mouths to the food.

CULINARY DIVERSITY

Spain

One of Spain's most famous dishes, tapas (ta-PAHS), are small dishes of food served as snacks. Tapa means "to cover," and the first tapa is rumored to have been a slice of ham served on top of a glass of sherry, supposedly to keep the flies out. Eventually, restaurant owners discovered that the saltiness of the ham spurred beverage sales and tapas became a Spanish tradition. Today, most regions in Spain have their own specialty tapas.

Spaniards enjoy tapas before lunch, which is often 2:00 or later, and again before dinner, sometime after 8:00. They walk from one restaurant to another, stopping to enjoy tapas and a beverage. Tapas are typically eaten while standing, making them hors d'oeuvres. There are hot and cold tapas, and it isn't unusual for a small local restaurant to have six to eight different kinds of tapas in warming trays and more cold or room-temperature tapas available. Typically, tapas are very strongly flavored. Common tapas include anchovies, sardines, or mackerels in olive oil; meatballs in tomato sauce; eggs in mayonnaise;

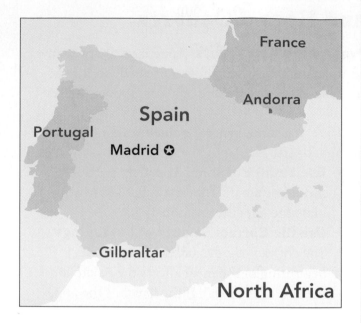

pork in tomato sauce; omelets; shrimp in hot garlic oil; squid in tomato sauce; slices of garlic or smoked-ham sausages; and slices of cheese. It is rare to see a tapas selection that does not include one or more types of olives. And bread is usually available, if only to sop up some of the delectable sauces served with the tapas.

▲ *Refrigerated display case containing tapas in Madrid, Spain*

Research

1. Tapas are increasingly being offered in the United States. Research a restaurant in the United States that is offering tapas on a regular basis. Describe how tapas are used on the menu and what types of tapas are offered.

2. Home cooks are also beginning to cook tapas as hors d'oeuvres or appetizers. Research a cookbook or website that offers tapas recipes. Make three of the recipes, with at least one of the recipes being for a hot tapa, and evaluate the results.

- **Complement Other Foods.** Hors d'oeuvres should complement the other foods served, yet be different enough to avoid being repetitive.
- **Don't Mix Hot and Cold Items.** Hot and cold items should never be presented on the same plate or platter. Use multiple plates or platters if you are offering both hot and cold appetizers.
- **Consider an Hors d'Oeuvres Varies.** Hors d'oeuvres are sometimes presented as an **hors d'oeuvres varies** (or-DERV vair-REEZ). This is a variety plate for one person with a combination of hors d'oeuvres on it, usually fewer than 10 small offerings.

FIGURE 11-5
Hors d' Oeuvres Platter
This attractive platter contains a variety of cold hors d'oeuvres.
Applying Concepts *What rules of cold food presentation are shown in this hors d'oeuvres platter?*

 **Reading Checkpoint** *What are two tips for presenting appetizers? What are two tips for presenting hors d'oeuvres?*

11.2 ASSESSMENT

Reviewing Concepts

1. What is the difference between an appetizer and an hors d'oeuvre?
2. What are at two tips for presenting appetizers? What are two tips for presenting hors d'oeuvres?

Critical Thinking

3. **Comparing/Contrasting** You are serving hors d'oeuvres at a party where people will be standing. You are considering seafood brochettes, chicken wings, or canapés. Which would you choose? Explain why.
4. **Analyzing Information** After a meal, a guest complained to the chef that the appetizer had too much garlic and basil. The main course was a gently poached chicken with a delicate sauce. Was the customer correct? Explain your answer.

Test Kitchen

Make a mayonnaise-based seafood salad for a cocktail party and divide it in half. Serve half as canapés and half as an appetizer salad. Taste the canapés while standing using one hand. Taste the appetizer salad while seated and using a fork. Which presentation method is preferable?

CULINARY MATH

Serving Hors d'Oeuvres

You are planning hors d'oeuvres for a corporate party. Seventy-five people will be attending, and the client estimates that each person will eat ten hors d'oeuvres. If there are five waiters, how many hors d'oeuvres will each waiter eventually serve?

Review and Assessment

Reviewing Content

Choose the letter that best answers the question or completes the statement.

1. What is a pullman loaf?
   a. a type of meatloaf
   b. a vegetable terrine
   c. a rectangular loaf of bread
   d. a sequenced arrangement of bread and meat

2. What is focaccia?
   a. a flat Italian bread traditionally flavored with olive oil and herbs
   b. seafood that is "cooked" in citrus juice
   c. a flat Middle Eastern bread that forms a pocket
   d. a large, round, crusty roll

3. What is finger food?
   a. food served with a napkin and eaten with the fingers
   b. long, thin sandwiches shaped like fingers
   c. large sandwiches with mayonnaise-based sandwich salads
   d. food that is prepared entirely by hand

4. Hors d'oeuvres varies are hors d'oeuvres that
   a. vary according to the day of the week
   b. vary according to the daily specials
   c. are a mixed variety on one plate
   d. vary according to the season

5. Canapés are
   a. bite-sized vegetables often served with dip
   b. meat, fish, or vegetables cooked on a skewer
   c. open-faced sandwiches consisting of toast, olive oil, and tomatoes
   d. bite-sized pieces of bread or crackers with savory toppings

6. Bruschettas are
   a. bite-sized vegetables often served with dip
   b. meat, fish, or vegetables cooked on a skewer
   c. open-faced sandwiches consisting of toast, olive oil, and tomatoes
   d. bite-sized pieces of bread or crackers with savory toppings

Understanding Concepts

7. What are the four elements of a sandwich?

8. What is the purpose of a spread in a sandwich?

9. What is a finger sandwich?

10. What is a pressed sandwich?

11. What is the difference between an appetizer and an hors d'oeuvre?

12. What is a canapé?

13. What are crudités?

14. Why is correct portion size important for appetizers?

Critical Thinking

15. **Applying Concepts** One dish has two small crackers with pâté on them and the other dish has a slice of pâté cut from a terrine. Which is more likely to be an appetizer? Why?

Culinary Math

16. **Analyzing Information** You need 10 pounds of jumbo shrimp to make 100 canapés. It is estimated that each guest will eat two of the canapés. How many guests will 20 pounds of shrimp feed?

On the Job

17. **Writing** Your boss wants to advertise free "finger food" that would be available for a two-hour period in the bar. Write a simple but appetizing description of three types of finger food that could be featured. Because these will be free, they must be inexpensive items.

18. **Drawing Conclusions** The spa menu at a health club features a low-fat wrap. You decide to omit all fat and fill the wrap with slices of tomato, cucumbers, peppers, and a portabella mushroom marinated in balsamic vinegar. Customers complain that the sandwich is too messy. What could be wrong?

 LAB ACTIVITY

Use the following Recipe Cards to test your culinary skill.

43. Club Sandwich
44. Muffaletta Sandwich
45. Chicken Salad Sandwich
46. Reuben Sandwich
47. Tuna Melt
48. Open-Faced Turkey Sandwich
49. Vegetable Tempura
50. Shrimp Tempura
51. Seviche of Scallops
52. Crab Cakes

Project 11: Sandwich Basics

Answer these questions when your class works through Project 11.

- Which type of filling did the teams decide on?
- Which team's bread choice was your favorite? Your least favorite?
- Which team's spread was your favorite? Your least favorite?
- Which team's garnishes (or accompaniments) was your favorite? Your least favorite?
- How did teams vary the filling?
- Which sandwich was the most successful overall?

TEST PRACTICE

Choose the letter that best answers the question or completes the statement.

1. What is a Kaiser roll?
   A   a German-style wrap, with sausages
   B   a type of wrap, featuring ham
   C   a round, crusty roll
   D   an egg roll, with pork inside

2. When organizing your sandwich-making workspace, you should
   A   put bread on one side and move everything in one direction
   B   put bread and all other ingredients in front of you
   C   put bread and all other ingredients on a rack above you
   D   put bread on tray and walk tray from station to station until sandwiches are constructed

3. A "chef's tasting" is
   A   the sample a chef tastes to adjust seasonings
   B   one plate with several hors d'oeuvres to sample
   C   one plate with several small portions of appetizers to sample
   D   the test meal a chef prepares and serves to staff prior to cooking it for paying customers

4. A croque madame is a
   A   delicate French tea sandwich featuring butter and cucumbers
   B   a French canapé with caviar
   C   crusty French bread flavored with herbs
   D   a French sandwich that includes ham, cheese, and a fried egg

5. What is not another name for a hero sandwich?
   A   long john
   B   submarine
   C   grinder
   D   hoagie

6. Crudités are
   A   vegetables cut into bite-sized pieces
   B   raw slices of beef, sliced thinly and dressed with sauce
   C   a type of open-faced sandwich with a savory topping
   D   bite-sized pieces of bread with a savory topping

7. Buffalo wings are usually served with
   A   a vinaigrette
   B   blue cheese dressing and celery
   C   onion dip and French fries a type of open-faced sandwich with a savory topping
   D   barbecue sauce and cole slaw

FRUIT & VEGETABLES

READING PREVIEW

Key Concepts

- Identifying types of fruit
- Selecting and storing fruit
- Preparing fruit
- Cooking fruit
- Serving fruit

Vocabulary

- clingstone
- compote
- essential oils
- ethylene
- freestone
- fritters
- individually quick frozen (IQF)
- maturation
- pith
- ripening
- stone

"**P**astry chefs know that working with seasonal fruit is a big advantage. The flavors are richer and the colors more vibrant. "

— Stephane Weber
The Culinary Institute of America

Types of Fruit

The fruit of a plant ensures the survival of the plant, because every fruit contains a seed (in some cases, hundreds of seeds) that can grow into a new plant. In the culinary sense, fruit is typically eaten as is or used to make sweets and desserts. But there are numerous exceptions to the rule. Fruit is also used in savory dishes, for instance.

Fruit grows on trees, bushes, or vines. Every fruit has a stem end, which is the place where the fruit was attached to the tree, bush, or vine it grew on. The blossom end is opposite the stem.

The seed is surrounded by the fruit's flesh. Melons and similar fruit have a lot of seeds located in a center pocket. Apples and pears have relatively few seeds, and those seeds are found in the center part of the fruit known as its core. Plums, peaches, and apricots have a single seed that is protected by a hard pit, sometimes known as a **stone**. Strawberries have seeds on the outside of the fruit.

▲
Figure 12-1
Fruit Anatomy
Here you can see all the parts of an apple.
Interpreting Illustrations Can you identify all the parts of the apple?

The fruit's skin protects the flesh while the fruit grows and ripens. In some cases, the skin acts as a signal that the fruit is ripe and ready to eat. Ripe fruit has the most vivid colors; until a fruit ripens, it appears green.

You can eat the skin of some fruit, such as apples, pears, plums, and grapes. Other fruit has skin that is either too tough or too bitter to eat (bananas, oranges, and melons, for instance). The heavy outer skin of fruit such as watermelon and pineapple is sometimes referred to as the rind.

Apples Apples are one of the most widely available fruit. Some varieties, such as Red Delicious, Gala, and Pink Lady, are best for eating fresh. Other varieties, such as McIntosh, are best for cooking; they become very soft when cooked and are used for applesauce or apple butter. Baking apples, such as Rome Beauty, hold their shape, making them a good choice for pie and pastry fillings. Varieties such as Golden Delicious, Braeburn, and Granny Smith are good for eating, cooking, and baking. These are referred to as general-purpose apples.

Apples should be firm, with good color. There should be no bruises or soft spots, and the fruit should feel heavy for its size.

Berries Blueberries, strawberries, blackberries, and raspberries are probably what you think of first when you think about berries. They grow on bushes and have a short season. Look for good color, with no bruising or mold. If the packaging is stained with juice, the fruit has probably been damaged in delivery. If a few berries turn moldy, the rest of the container may go bad quickly. Keep berries as dry as possible until you are ready to serve or cook them.

Cranberries are firm and very tart berries that hold and freeze well. They are almost always cooked before they are served. In addition to these familiar berries, this category also includes gooseberries, boysenberries, and currants.

Citrus Fruit Citrus fruit includes oranges, grapefruits, lemons, and limes. There are four basic types of oranges:

- Loose-skinned oranges with easy-to-peel skins, such as tangerines, Minneolas, and clementines
- Sweet oranges, which are large and easy-to-eat, with relatively few, if any, seeds, such as navel oranges
- Juicing oranges, which are also sweet but have thin skin, lots of juice, and many seeds
- Bitter oranges, with heavy rinds and a bitter taste, used to make marmalade

Apples

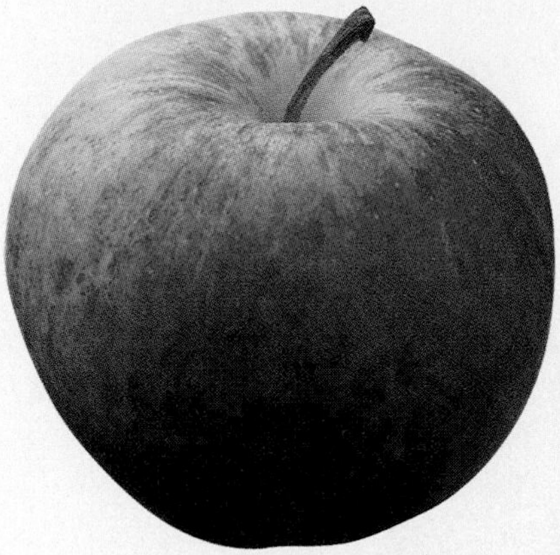

▲ Braeburn

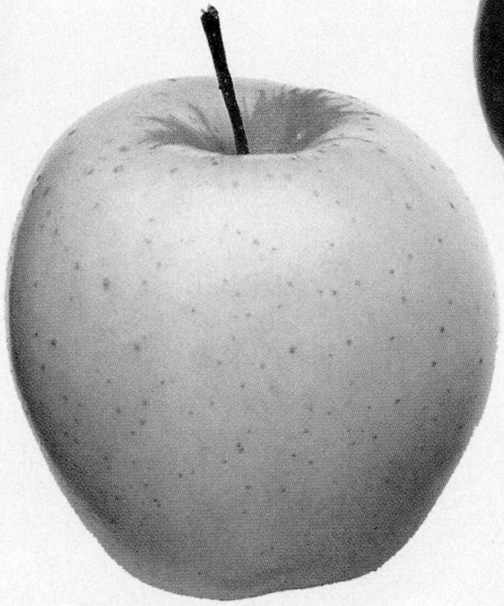

▲ Golden Delicious

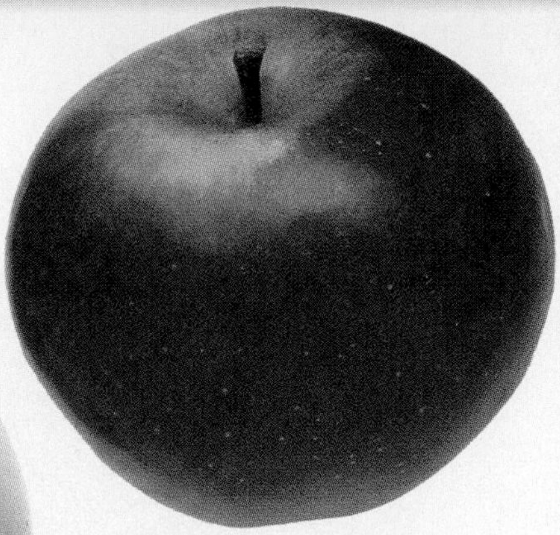

▲ McIntosh

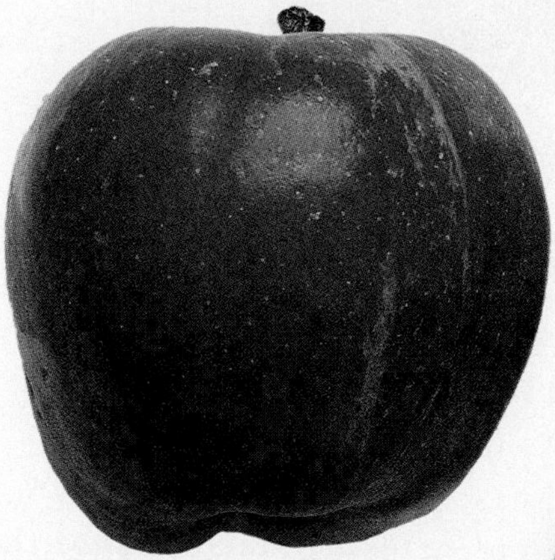

▲ Red Delicious

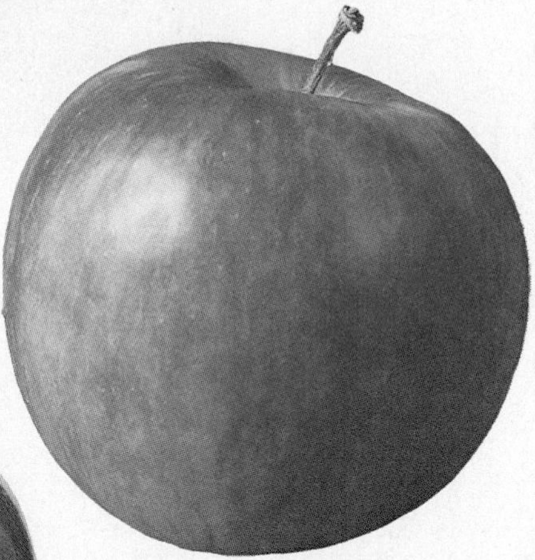

▲ Pink Lady

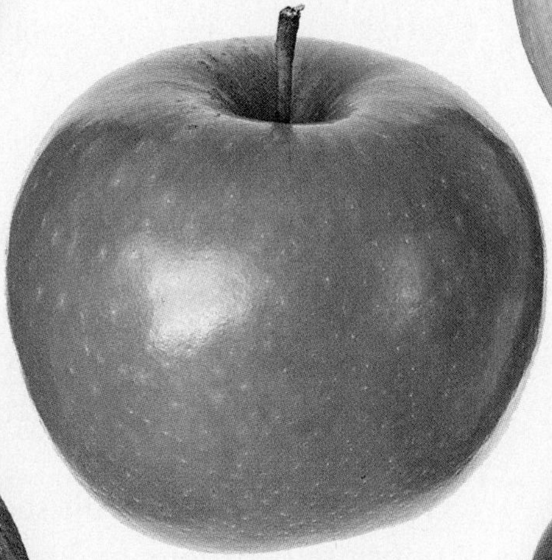

▲ Granny Smith

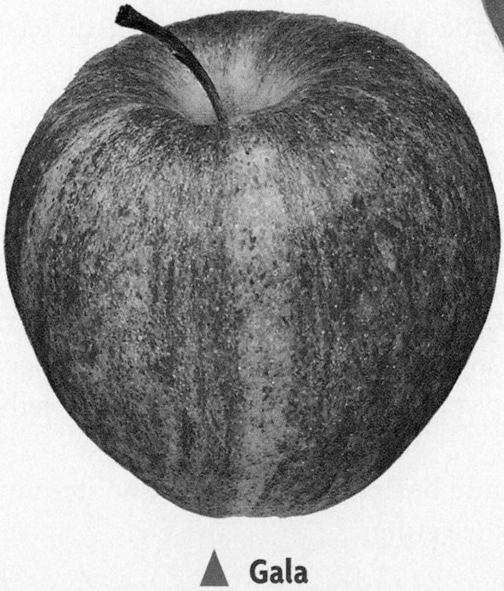

▲ Gala

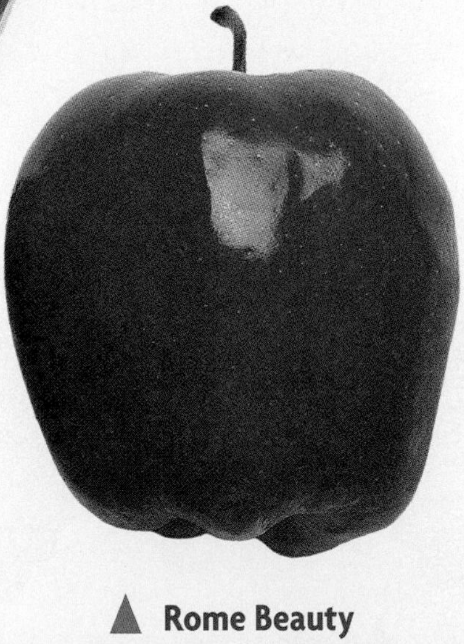

▲ Rome Beauty

Berries

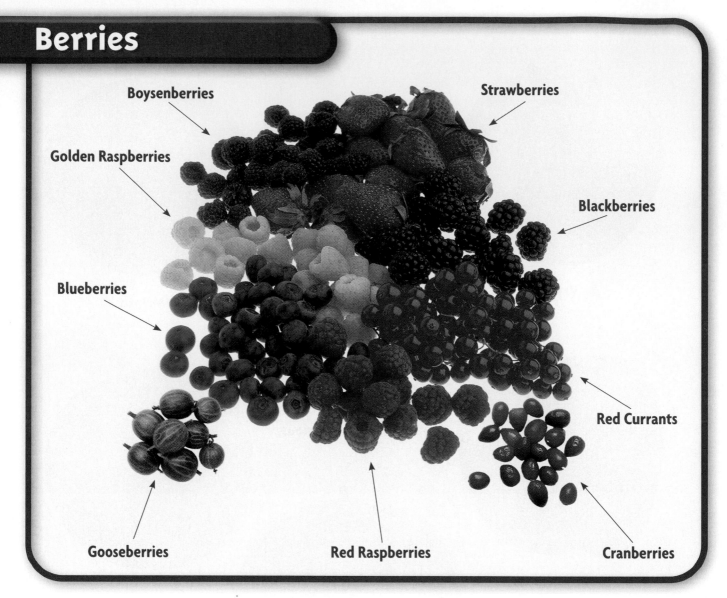

Boysenberries

Strawberries

Golden Raspberries

Blackberries

Blueberries

Red Currants

Gooseberries

Red Raspberries

Cranberries

Citrus fruit has a bright skin that contains its **essential oils**. These oils, which evaporate quickly, give the fruit its distinct aroma and flavor. Just below the outer skin is the white, bitter, and indigestible layer called the **pith**.

Good quality citrus fruit should have good color and aroma, no soft or bruised portions, and no signs of mold.

▲ *Green and red grapes*

Grapes Grapes are juicy berries that grow in clusters on vines or shrubs. They are grown to produce table fruit, wine, and other products. Table fruit may be red, purple (or black), or green, with or without seeds. Concord grapes are used to produce juices, jellies, and preserves.

Grapes should be firmly attached to the stem with no shrinking or shriveling.

Citrus Fruit

Orange

Grapefruit

Lemon

Lime

Tangerine

Clementine

Minneola

Ugli Fruit

Kumquat

Pears Pears are similar to apples in many respects. They grow on trees and have sweet, cream-colored flesh and a core of multiple seeds. Their skin color can range from mottled brown to pale green to deep red.

Like apples, pears are a popular winter fruit because they can be stored successfully in cold storage for several months without overripening or losing their quality.

Stone Fruit Cherries, apricots, plums, peaches, and nectarines are stone fruit. They all contain a hard pit that covers a central seed or

Pears

▲ Anjou

▲ Red Bartlett

▲ Seckel

▲ Bosc

▲ Comice

▲ Asian

kernel. Peaches and apricots have a fuzzy skin that is typically removed before cooking the fruit. Plums are sold in many varieties. Purple or red plums are typically eaten as fresh fruit. Italian plums and Damson plums are best for cooking and baking.

Clingstone fruit is a type of fruit with flesh that clings tightly to the pit, making it difficult to cut the flesh away cleanly. **Freestone** fruit has flesh that separates easily from the pit. Peaches and nectarines come in both clingstone and freestone varieties.

Stone Fruit

Apricot ▲

Cherry ▲

▲ Nectarine

▲ Peach

Santa Rosa Plum ▲

▲ Damson Plum

Melons There are several varieties of melons, each differing in size, taste, color, and skin texture. Melons grow on small shrubs and sit directly on the ground, giving one part of the rind a white, faded patch where it doesn't get any sun. Some melons soften slightly at the stem end when they are ripe. Others have a smooth stem, showing that the melon ripened on the vine long enough to slip off the vine.

Good quality melons should be firm and heavy for their size. Check for a sweet aroma.

Melons

▲ **Casaba**

▲ **Cantaloupe**

▲ **Crenshaw**

Rhubarb Although technically not a fruit, rhubarb is often treated as one. Its red celery-like stalks are extremely tart and used primarily in jams and pies with a considerable amount of sweetener.

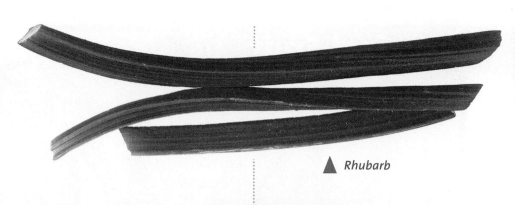

▲ *Rhubarb*

Watermelon ▶

▲ **Honeydew**

▲ Cavendish Bananas

▲ Plantains

Bananas

Bananas are the most popular tropical fruit, grown on trees in bunches. We are most familiar with the yellow Cavendish variety, but there are many others. Red bananas are short and very sweet. Plantains are mild, starchy, and typically cooked like a potato—fried, boiled, or mashed.

▲ Red Bananas

▲ **Fig**

Figs are a small green or dark blue teardrop-shaped tree fruit with extremely sweet flesh filled with many tiny seeds. They are eaten fresh or dried.

▲ **Date**

Dates have papery skin, very sweet flesh, and a long, narrow seed. They are eaten fresh or dried.

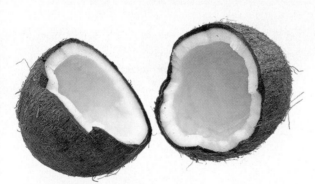

▲ **Coconut**

This brown, hard-shelled fruit grows on a palm tree. It has flesh that is brilliant white, sweet, and somewhat grainy.

Kiwi ▲

The thin, brown, fuzzy skin of the kiwi covers sweet green flesh and a white core surrounded by miniscule black seeds.

◄ **Guava**

The thick skin of the guava (GWAH-vah) ranges in color from yellow to deep purple, and the sweet, fragrant flesh can be pale yellow to bright red.

▲ Mango
With deep yellow, sweet-tasting flesh and skin ranging from red to green, mangos have a large flat seed in the middle of the fruit.

▲ Papaya
The papaya (puh-PI-yuh) is pear-shaped with a yellowish skin, juicy sweet-tart orange flesh, and a core of black seeds.

▲ Passion Fruit
Very fragrant, with tart, golden flesh and tiny edible black seeds, passion fruit is covered in a dark purple skin.

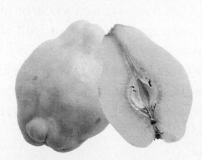

Star Fruit ▲
With a unique star shape when cut across its ridges, star fruit has waxy golden skin, yellow flesh, and a sweet-tart flavor.

▲ Persimmon
The persimmon (puhr-SIM-muhn) has red-orange skin and flesh, creamy texture, and tangy flavor.

Pineapple ▲
With diamond-patterned skin and sword-like leaves that sprout from the top, pineapple has sweet-tart, extremely juicy flesh. It grows on a large palm tree and is picked when ripe. It should smell fragrant, be slightly soft to the touch, and have no browning at the tips of the leaves. Overripe pineapples have soft or dark areas on the skin.

Quince ▲
A quince (KWIHNS) is like a cross between an apple and a pear in flavor and appearance. It has yellow skin and tart flesh that is often used for making jams and jellies.

Pomegranate ▲
The pomegranate (POM-uh-gran-uht) has deep red skin. Inside, the fruit has a good deal of white pith and pockets of hundreds of seeds. Each seed is covered in red pulp that has a sweet-tart flavor.

Tropical and Exotic Fruit Depending on availability, you can often find tropical and exotic fruit at the grocery and at specialty stores.

> ✓ **Reading Checkpoint** *What are the common attributes among all fruit?*

Selecting and Storing Fruit

Fresh fruit can be purchased ripe or unripe, depending on how and when it will be used. It might be grown locally or be shipped from other parts of the world. Fruit is also available in a variety of forms.

Market Forms of Fruit Fruit is sold in a variety of forms. You can buy whole fresh fruit as individual pieces (a single lemon) or bunches (grapes or bananas). Fruit is also sold in containers of varying sizes and shapes: pint or quart baskets, pecks, bushels, cartons, boxes, and crates.

The quality of most fruit is directly related to its growing season. A peach purchased in the dead of winter can't match the flavor, color, texture, aroma, and nutritional value of a peach you buy in the summer, at the peak of its growing season. Most fruit has a relatively short growing season, and some fruit is perishable, lasting only a few days even under ideal storage conditions.

Fresh fruit may also be processed before it is sold. Some examples are stemmed strawberries, sliced or cubed melon, or citrus segments.

Dried fruit has an extremely long shelf life and still contains the majority of the flavor and sweetness of the fresh form. Raisins (dried grapes), prunes (dried plums), dates, and figs are just some of the fruit sold in a dried form. Dried fruit may be sweetened to produce candied or crystallized fruit.

Frozen fruit may be **individually quick frozen (IQF)**, which means that the fruit is frozen whole or in slices or chunks, without any added sugar or syrup. Frozen fruit is also sold as a purée (sweetened or unsweetened) or as a paste. Some frozen fruit is packed in syrup.

Canned fruit options include fruit cocktails (a combination of fruit that has been peeled, sliced or cut, cooked in a syrup, and canned), whole or sliced fruit packed in syrup or juice, and fruit fillings, purées, and pastes.

The Ripening Process Chefs need to understand how fruit grows and ripens. This information helps them select and store fruit so that it is as delicious and nutritious as possible, and also to assure that as little fruit as possible is lost to spoilage.

Fruit that is left to grow on the vine, tree, or bush until it has reached its full size has reached **maturation**. A fully mature fruit has not necessarily finished ripening, however. **Ripening** means that the fruit has developed the brightest color and deepest flavor, sweetness, and aroma. That's why people sniff fresh melons and peaches. Some fruit also softens and gets juicier as it ripens. That's why people squeeze plums or apricots.

Depending on the type of fruit and the way it is to be processed, some fruit must ripen before being picked, such as apples and peaches. Other fruit is picked after maturing but before ripening. Bananas are a good example of a fruit that is picked mature but while it is still green. Kept at room temperature, bananas ripen to a golden yellow.

Fruit ripens because of a gas it gives off, known as **ethylene** (EH-thih-leen). Once the ethylene has ripened the fruit, it continues to affect the fruit. Ripe fruit continues to change and eventually becomes too soft and overripe. If left to ripen for too long, it will eventually turn rotten.

CHEF'S TIP

RIPENING IN A BROWN PAPER BAG

Place the unripe fruit in a paper bag, along with an apple or a banana. Twist the bag shut and keep at room temperature just until the fruit begins to soften.

Grading Fruit After produce is harvested, it is graded by the USDA's Agricultural Marketing Service (AMS). Fresh fruit is judged on its size, shape, weight, color, and the presence or absence of defects such as splits in the skin. Fresh fruit is given the following grades:

- **U.S. Fancy.** Premium quality produce.
- **U.S. No. 1.** Good quality produce that is not quite as perfect as Fancy grade.
- **U.S. No. 2.** Medium quality produce.
- **U.S. No. 3.** Standard quality produce.

The grade of the fruit does not necessarily tell you anything about the fruit's flavor. U.S. No. 2 or 3 fruit does not look as nice as U.S. Fancy, but if you are planning to cut up the fruit to make a pie or a sauce, its appearance doesn't matter as much as its flavor. However, a dessert that features a whole pear or peach may demand the higher grades of either Fancy or No. 1.

▲

FIGURE 12-2
Ripening Process
Bananas are green when picked and yellow when they ripen, and they begin to turn black as they overripen.
Classifying Overripe bananas are most typically used for banana bread. Can you guess why?

Frozen fruit may receive slightly different grades:
- **U.S. Grade A.** Equivalent to U.S. Fancy for fresh produce.
- **U.S. Grade B.** Above-average quality (also known as Choice).
- **U.S. Grade C.** Medium quality (also known as Standard).

For more information on individual produce, go to AMS's standards website: www.ams.usda.gov/standards.

Storing Fruit You need to take the proper steps to preserve the ideal quality of your fruit for as long as possible.

Most fruit is stored under refrigeration. This slows down the ripening process slightly. Be sure that any produce is kept dry. Some fruit, especially apples and pears, gives off generous amounts of ethylene. Store apples and pears away from other fruit, because the ethylene can cause the other fruit to rot.

Some fruit can pick up odors from other foods. Other fruit produces strong odors that can affect foods stored nearby, especially dairy products. Try to keep fruit separated from other perishable goods, when possible.

Store frozen fruit in the freezer until you are ready to use it. Keep canned and dried fruit in the dry storage area of the kitchen. Once you open the packaging for dried fruit, close it tightly or transfer the fruit to a container with a tight-fitting lid to keep it from becoming overdry and also to keep bugs away.

 **Reading Checkpoint** *What happens to fruit when it ripens?*

Preparing Fruit

Whenever you are working with fresh fruit that is not going to be cooked before you serve it to your guests, remember to wear gloves. Cleaning is always the first step in preparing fruit. Once you have cleaned the fruit, you can perform other steps as needed and in the order that makes the most sense. For instance, you may peel a pineapple before you core it, but it might be easier to remove the pit from a mango before you cut away the skin.

Cleaning Even though fruit is not a potentially hazardous food, the skin can carry a number of pathogens. In addition, fruit is exposed to chemicals, dirt, animals, and pests while growing and while being prepared for sale. That makes cleaning fruit properly very important.

Use cold water and a gentle touch to avoid bruising fruit while handling it. Fruit with heavy rind may need more vigorous cleaning; use a brush to scrub away any residue on the skin. Very delicate fruit, such as raspberries, should be delicately rinsed at the last possible moment to be sure that the fruit doesn't become waterlogged.

Peeling, Seeding, and Trimming Some fruit has inedible skin or rind. Pull off the peel if it separates easily from the fruit, such as bananas or oranges. Preparing fruit often involves removing skins, cores, seeds, stones, and stems.

- **Removing Skins.** Use a peeler or paring knife to cut away the skins of apples or pears that have been treated with wax, or skins that are too fuzzy or hairy to eat fresh (peaches or kiwi), or for fruit that you intend to cook. To remove heavy rinds from melons or pineapples, use a chef's knife. Cut between the rind and the flesh, making sure to leave as little flesh on the rind as you can. Pineapples have small "eyes" that should be cut completely away before cutting the fruit into pieces.
- **Removing Cores.** To remove apple or pear cores, cut the fruit in half from the stem to the blossom end and use a melon baller to scoop out the core.
- **Removing Seeds and Stones.** To remove seeds from melons, cut the fruit in half and scoop out the seeds and membranes with a serving spoon. Use the tip of a paring knife to remove seeds from citrus fruit. To remove the hard stone from cherries, use a cherry pitter. To pit plums, peaches, and nectarines, use a paring knife to cut around the fruit, through the skin and flesh, and up to the pit. Hold the piece of fruit with both hands and twist the halves in opposite directions.
- **Removing Stems.** To remove the stems of strawberries, use the tip of your paring knife. Cut around the stem, angling your knife toward the center of the berry, to remove just the top and the white part around it.
- **Zesting.** The peel on citrus fruit can be grated or cut into thin strips to produce citrus zest. The zest is cut from just the bright colorful part of the peel, however. The white part of the skin (the pith) is very bitter and should not be used. Zest is highly aromatic and can be used as a seasoning or as a garnish.

FIGURE 12-3
Peeling Apples
Use a paring knife or peeler to remove skin.
Drawing Conclusions What other parts of an apple can you trim by using a paring knife?

FOCUS ON SAFETY

Using Frozen Fruit

In some recipes, you can use frozen fruit without thawing. When you do need to thaw frozen fruit before using it, remember to follow safe food-handling procedures for thawing, as described in Unit 1.

Cutting Fruit for Service Some fruit is cut into wedges, slices, chunks, or cubes for service. Be sure to use a very sharp knife so that your cuts are clean. This not only helps the fruit's appearance, it also maintains the fruit's quality because you lose fewer juices.

One special way of cutting fruit is to make it into small rounds or balls. Use a Parisienne scoop or melon baller. Twist the scoop into the flesh to cut away a ball of the fruit. Make cuts evenly over the surface of the fruit. Cut away the layer of fruit that is left behind to make a clean layer and a second surface to cut into.

Juicing and Puréeing Fresh fruit can be juiced and puréed. Handheld juicers, including a special tool known as a reamer, can be used to juice citrus fruit. To make juice from fruit such as apples or pears, you need to use a juice extractor. A fruit purée is made by putting prepared fruit (peeled, trimmed, or seeded as necessary) into a blender or food processor. If the fruit is soft and juicy, you can make the purée without adding more liquid. If the fruit is hard or low in moisture, you may need to precook it or add more liquid as you purée.

Preparing Dried Fruit Dried fruit can be served as is, without any advance preparation. However, you may need to soften it before you add it to a dish or a baked item. The procedure for softening dried fruit is to put it in a bowl, cover it with a warm or hot liquid, and let it sit until it swells and softens slightly. Drain the fruit before serving. This process of restoring moisture to dried fruit is called rehydration.

 **Reading Checkpoint** *What are the basic tasks involved in preparing fruit for service?*

Cooking Fruit

Fruit can be prepared by a variety of dry and moist heat methods. Dry heat methods include grilling or broiling, sautéing, frying, and baking. Moist heat options include poaching and stewing. Before you start, review your recipe to determine how you should prepare the fruit. Some methods are best for fruit that is fully ripe, and others are better with fruit that is not completely ripe.

- **Grilling and Broiling.** Grilled fruit can be cut into slices, left whole, or threaded on skewers. To protect tender or delicate fruit, you can brush it lightly with a little melted butter. To give fruit a rich glaze, sprinkle it with sugar or brush it with a little honey or maple syrup. Place the fruit directly on the grill. To broil fruit, arrange it on a sheet tray that you've either buttered lightly or lined with parchment. Broil or grill the fruit just until it has a rich aroma and caramel color.

- **Sautéing.** Sautéed fruit is typically peeled and cut into pieces, and then cooked over medium to high heat in butter. Adding sugar produces a rich glaze on sautéed fruit. Bananas, pineapples, peaches, and plums are all good options. Sautéed fruit may be served on its own or as a filling for crepes, a topping for pancakes, or a kind of sauce for ice cream.
- **Frying.** Pieces of fruit can be coated in batter and then fried to make **fritters**. Instead of batter, you may apply a coating of cake crumbs, chopped nuts, or shredded coconut.
- **Baking.** Fruit can be baked in a number of different ways. A baked apple for instance, may be simply cored and then baked until tender. To add more flavor, you can fill fruit before baking; chopped nuts or dried fruit are common options. Another way to make baked fruit more interesting is to top with a sauce or with whipped cream.
- **Poaching.** Poached fruit is cooked in a liquid, usually with some sugar and other flavorings until it is tender. The fruit should still hold its shape. You can serve poached fruit hot or cold, accompanied by the poaching liquid or not. Poaching can be the first step in preparing fruit to use as filling for pies or tarts.

CULINARY HISTORY

The Influence of Alice Waters and Chez Panisse

In 1971, in Berkeley, California, just north of San Francisco, Alice Waters opened her restaurant Chez Panisse. Mirroring the long-standing European practice, Chez Panisse focused on local ingredients—the best and freshest available in the Bay area. The restaurant challenged its chefs and delighted its customers with menus that changed almost daily and featured organic ingredients.

▲ *Typical farmer's market*

of using foods grown locally had been lost because food from all across the world is available in everyone's supermarket, all year long. Now more people are exploring their local farmer's markets, resulting in an explosion in the number of farmer's markets around the country. And more restaurants now feature, if not focus on, the use of fresh, local ingredients.

Alice Waters' vision and the continued success of her restaurant have influenced how America thinks about food. She has made chefs turn their attention to seasonal, locally grown foods. The concept

Research

Research local farms and farmer's markets in your area. Find out if any of them grow unusual varieties of produce or organic produce.

Poaching Fruit

1 **Prepare** the fruit by trimming, peeling, and cutting as necessary.

2 **Simmer** the liquid, along with any flavoring ingredients called for in your recipe.

3 **Place** the fruit into the liquid. Add more liquid, if necessary, to barely cover the fruit.

4 **Simmer** over low to moderate heat. Allow the liquid to come up to a simmer temperature of 170°F.

5 **Poach** the fruit until tender and flavorful.

6 **Cool** the fruit in the cooking liquid, drain, and serve or store.

See Recipe Card 54, "Poached Peaches"

Puréeing Fruit

1 **Prepare** the fruit as necessary.

2 **Poach** the fruit, if your recipe says to, with sweeteners and flavorings.

3 **Purée** to the desired consistency and adjust the flavoring.

4 **Serve** or store the purée.

See Recipe Card 55, "Applesauce"

- **Stewing**. Though similar to poaching, stewed fruit is often served with its cooking liquid. An example of a stewed fruit dish is a **compote**, which is made from slow-cooking fresh or dried fruit.
- **Puréeing Cooked Fruit.** Fruit purées can be made from poached or stewed fruit. Use a food processor or blender to make a smooth and light purée. Use a food mill for a more textured consistency. For the smoothest, most delicate texture, strain the purée through a fine-mesh sieve. Fruit purées are used as a sauce or as an ingredient in other dishes. Fruit soups are often nothing more complicated than purées that have been thinned with fruit juice or cream.

 **Reading Checkpoint** *What are the moist and dry heat methods for cooking fruit?*

Serving Fruit

Fruit plates and salads are a popular way to serve fruit. Other dishes include fruit cocktails, a mixture of fruit served in syrup. Serve these dishes in chilled cups or bowls. Fresh fruit can be served as a garnish with entrées and desserts. Examples include fresh berries on a chocolate cake or a slice of melon with an omelet at breakfast or even sliced peaches on a bowl of cold cereal.

FOCUS ON NUTRITION

Fruit for Your Health

Fruit is a valuable source for a number of important nutrients, including vitamins, minerals, and fiber. Most people should aim for several servings of fruit throughout the day.

CULINARY MATH

Trim Loss

In the food industry, people are very concerned about how much usable product you get after you cut up your ingredients. The amount of scraps you produce when cutting something is called trim, and the percentage of trim to your whole product is called trim loss.

To calculate trim loss, follow these steps:

1. Weigh the initial product.
2. Process your product per recipe instructions.
3. Weigh the trim.
4. Divide the trim weight by the total weight of the product.
5. Convert the number into a percentage.

Example

Product = 16 oz

Trim = 2 oz

2 ÷ 16 = 0.125 = 12.5%

▲ *Chocolate fondue*

Fruit has the fullest flavor when served at room temperature, so if possible allow it time to lose the chill from the refrigerator by sitting at room temperature for a few minutes.

Fruit is sometimes paired with meats, fish, or poultry. Grapes, raisins, plums, prunes, apricots, and other fruit can be added as a filling or stuffing or added to a sauce. Fruit purées are also featured with savory dishes; cranberry sauce is served with turkey, applesauce with potato pancakes.

One popular fruit offering is a dessert fondue. Bite-size pieces of fresh fruit are dipped into a warm sauce, such as chocolate, caramel, or butterscotch sauce. Fresh fruit coated in a hard chocolate shell is served as a confection.

✓ **Reading Checkpoint** *How might fruit appear on a dinner menu?*

12.1 ASSESSMENT

Reviewing Concepts

1. List the basic parts of a peach.
2. Describe the changes that occur when fruit ripens.
3. What should be the first step of every preparation involving fruit?
4. List the dry heat methods you can use to cook fruit.
5. How can fruit be presented as an appetizer for dinner?

Critical Thinking

6. **Communication** Oranges are often gassed to produce a vivid orange color. Why do you think this is done?
7. **Drawing Conclusions** Why is fruit generally peeled before poaching?
8. **Classifying** Which fruit might be good for sautéing?

Test Kitchen

Divide into four teams. Each team will poach a different fruit. Prepare a single piece of fruit, of roughly the same size and weight (trim down the fruit if needed). Measure out equal amounts of poaching liquid (such as apple cider). Using the same size pans, place the fruit in the pan, and pour the liquid on top. Set the pan over moderate heat and poach the fruit. Carefully monitor the temperature so it stays at roughly 165–170F. Predict which will take the longest. Were you right or wrong? Suggest some reasons for the outcome.

LANGUAGE ARTS

Essay Writing

Review this section. Using one additional resource, write a one-page essay, about 350 words, discussing the definition of a fruit, the standard anatomy, and how a fruit develops from a flower to maturity.

READING PREVIEW

Key Concepts

- Identifying types of vegetables
- Selecting and storing vegetables
- Preparing vegetables
- Cooking vegetables
- Serving vegetables

Vocabulary

- capsaicin
- heirloom plant
- tomato concassé
- tuber

> **"C**hefs today have the opportunity to work with farmers in their own communities to provide their guests with vegetables that are fresh, locally grown, and in season. **"**
>
> – Eve Felder
> The Culinary Institute of America

Types of Vegetables

Vegetables are plants, and we eat different parts of the plant, from the bottom to the top, including the roots, stems, leaves, flowers, and seeds. A number of vegetables are technically fruit, such as tomatoes. Their culinary use is the reason they are included in this section. Some vegetables are eaten raw; some must be cooked. Some vegetables are served as an accompaniment to other foods or used as an ingredient in a dish.

Like fruit, vegetables are versatile, colorful, and available in many varieties. The need to prepare and serve good-tasting vegetables is increasing as more people focus on healthy eating.

Avocados Actually a fruit, avocados are one of the few produce items that contain substantial amounts of fat. The inedible skin can vary in color from brown, in the case of the ripe Hass avocado, to green, like most other varieties. The flesh is creamy and buttery. Once cut, the flesh begins to turn brown almost instantly. To counteract this, avocados are usually not cut until the last possible moment.

FIGURE 12-4 ▶
Avocados
A ripe avocado is firm but yields slightly to gentle pressure.
Communicating How have you seen avocados prepared and served?

Cabbages The cabbage family provides a wide range of vegetables. Included are cabbages, Brussels sprouts, broccoli, and cauliflower.

Cabbage varieties include red and green cabbage, which should be heavy for their size, with tightly packed leaves. Savoy cabbage and Chinese cabbage (such as napa cabbage and bok choy) have leaves that are more loosely packed than red or green cabbages.

When choosing vegetables from this family, look for good uniform color, stems that are not split, and leaves that are not dried out.

Gourds The gourd family includes cucumbers, eggplant, and the many varieties of summer squash and winter squash.

- **Summer Squash.** Varieties include zucchini, yellow squash, and pattypan squash. Like cucumbers and eggplants, summer squash are picked when immature to take advantage of their tender flesh, seeds, and skins. Typically, all parts of these vegetables may be eaten, but you may opt to remove the seeds and skin if they are slightly tougher than desired. The larger and older these vegetables grow, the thicker and tougher their skins, the dryer their flesh, and the larger their seeds.

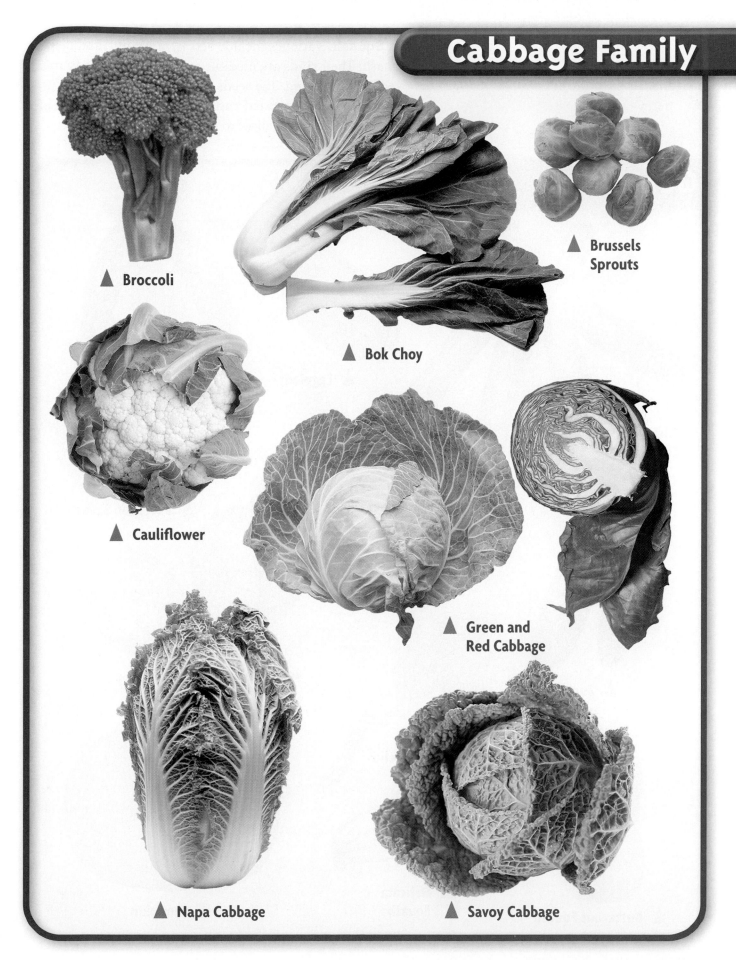

Cabbage Family

▲ Broccoli

▲ Bok Choy

▲ Brussels Sprouts

▲ Cauliflower

▲ Green and Red Cabbage

▲ Napa Cabbage

▲ Savoy Cabbage

- **Winter Squash.** Varieties include acorn, butternut, and delicata squash. Their rinds are inedible and their large seeds are removed before serving. The seeds of some winter squash, such as pumpkins, are toasted and eaten like nuts. The flesh of winter squash is usually yellow to orange in color.

Gourds

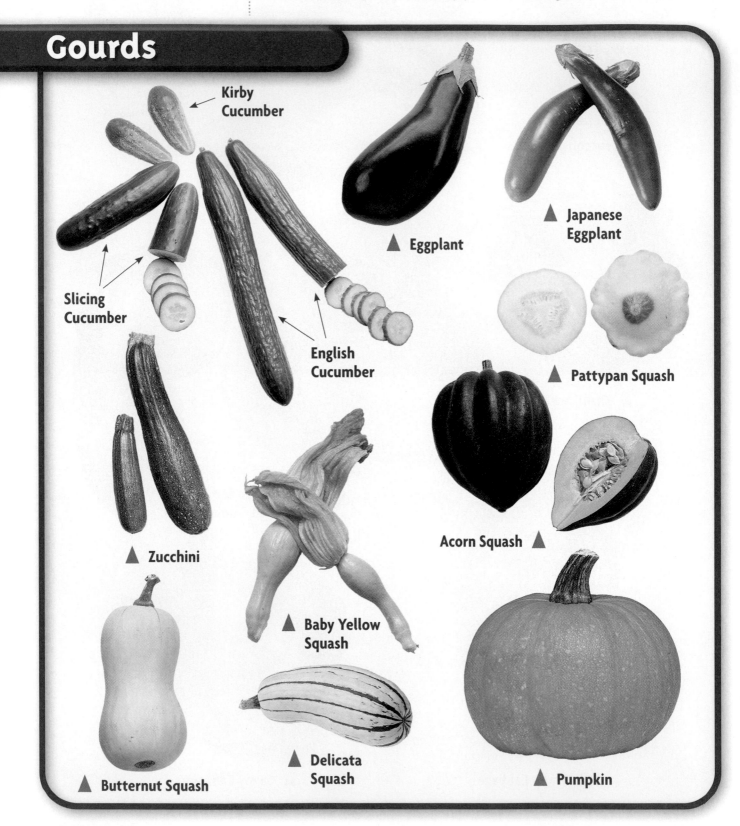

Kirby Cucumber

Slicing Cucumber

English Cucumber

▲ Eggplant

▲ Japanese Eggplant

▲ Pattypan Squash

▲ Zucchini

Acorn Squash ▲

▲ Baby Yellow Squash

▲ Butternut Squash

▲ Delicata Squash

▲ Pumpkin

Leafy Greens Leafy greens include salad greens, discussed in Chapter 10, and green vegetables used for cooking. These include spinach, Swiss chard, turnip greens, and two leafy members of the cabbage family, collards and kale. Cooking greens are often sautéed, steamed, or braised. Selection criteria and handling practices for cooking greens are similar to those for lettuce.

Leafy Greens

▲ Spinach

▲ Swiss Chard

▲ Turnip Greens

▲ Collard Greens

▲ Kale

Mushrooms Mushrooms can vary significantly in size, shape, color, and flavor. For a long time, the only widely available mushrooms were white mushrooms (also sold as button mushrooms or Parisian mushrooms). Today, more varieties are being successfully farmed, which means many so-called "wild" varieties are actually farm-raised.

Cultivated mushroom varieties include white mushrooms, portobello, cremini (kray-MEE-nee), shiitake (shee-TAH-kay), and oyster mushrooms. Wild mushroom varieties include porcini (pohr-CHEE-nee), chanterelles (shan-tuh-REHLS), morels (muh-REHLS), truffles, and many other varieties.

Select mushrooms that are firm, without soft spots, blemishes, or breaks in the cap or stem. Keep mushrooms under refrigeration. Cover with lightly dampened paper towels, not plastic wrap, to keep them fresher long. Keep mushrooms as dry as possible until ready to cook.

Mushrooms

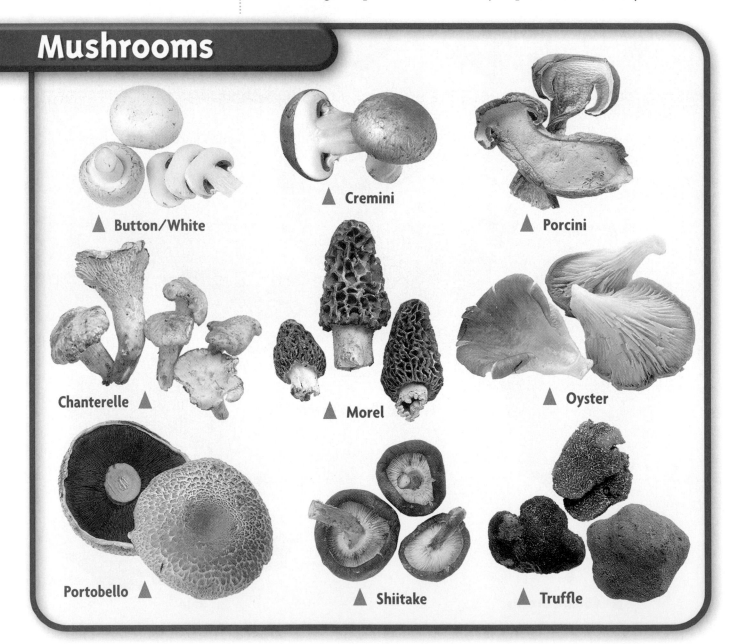

▲ Button/White

▲ Cremini

▲ Porcini

Chanterelle ▲

▲ Morel

▲ Oyster

Portobello ▲

▲ Shiitake

▲ Truffle

Onions The onion family includes garlic, shallots, and two main categories of onions: green (fresh) and dry (cured).

- **Green Onions.** Scallions and leeks are green onions. They have a tender white bulb. In some varieties, the green portion of the onion is edible (scallions, for instance), while in others it is discarded (leeks). Chives are also a type of green onion, although their main culinary application is as a fresh herb. The outer layers of green onions should be firm and not overly dry or torn. The roots should be firm and flexible. Rinse well and dry thoroughly immediately prior to cooking.

- **Dry Onions.** These range in size from tiny pearl onions to large red or yellow onions. They have juicy flesh covered with layers of dry, papery skin that may be white, yellow, or red. Select dry onions, garlic, and shallots that are heavy for their size and have tight-fitting skins.

Onion Family

Garlic

Red Globe Garlic

Yellow Onion

Red Onion

Scallions

Leek

White Onion

Shallots

Pearl Onions

Peppers There are two basic types of peppers: sweet peppers and chiles.

- **Sweet Peppers.** Sometimes called bell peppers because of their shape, all sweet peppers start out green, but some varieties ripen into other colors -- green, red, and yellow being the most common. Sweet peppers of various colors have similar flavors, though red and yellow varieties tend to be sweeter.

Sweet Peppers

Orange Bell Pepper

Yellow Bell Pepper

Red Bell Pepper

Green Bell Pepper

- **Chiles.** These are grown in various sizes, colors, and levels of spice or heat. **Capsaicin** (cap-SAY-ih-sin) is the compound that gives a chile its heat, and it is most potent on the white ribs inside the pepper. Generally, smaller chiles are hotter. In addition, you may work with canned, dried (whole, flaked, and ground), or smoked chiles. Some popular chile varieties, from mild to hot, are Anaheim, poblano, jalapeno, cayenne, Scotch bonnet and habanero.

Look for firm peppers and chiles that feel slightly heavy for their size. The skin should be tight and glossy, with no puckering or wrinkling. The flesh should be relatively thick and crisp.

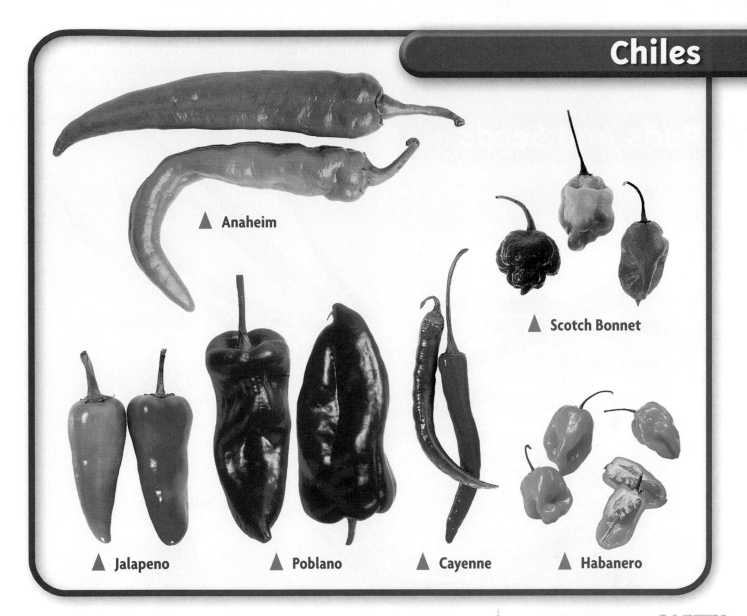

▲ Anaheim

▲ Scotch Bonnet

▲ Jalapeno   ▲ Poblano   ▲ Cayenne   ▲ Habanero

Pods and Seeds Pod and seed vegetables include peas, beans, and bean sprouts, as well as corn and okra. All varieties are best eaten young, when they are at their sweetest and most tender. Once picked, the natural sugars in the vegetable start to convert into starch. Many varieties of peas, beans, and corn are sold in their dried form as well, as discussed in Chapter 13.

Some beans and peas have edible pods; some do not.

- **Edible Pods.** Sugar snap peas, snow peas, green beans, and wax beans all have edible pods. The same is true for the French green bean, haricot vert (ar-ree-koh VEHR), and the Chinese long bean. They are all picked when the pod is still fleshy and tender enough to eat.
- **Inedible Pods.** Green peas, fava (FAH-vah) beans, and lima beans are removed from their inedible pods before eating.

FOCUS ON SAFETY

Handling Chiles

Take appropriate precautions when handling chiles. Wear gloves while cutting chiles. Wash cutting surfaces and knives (including handles) immediately after you finish cutting chiles. Wash your hands well with soap and water. Avoid touching your eyes, lips, or other sensitive areas.

Select fresh beans and pea pods with firm and crisp texture, bright color, and no wilting or puckering. Corn husks should be green and adhere tightly to the ear; the silk should be brown to black, but quite dry.

Pods and Seeds

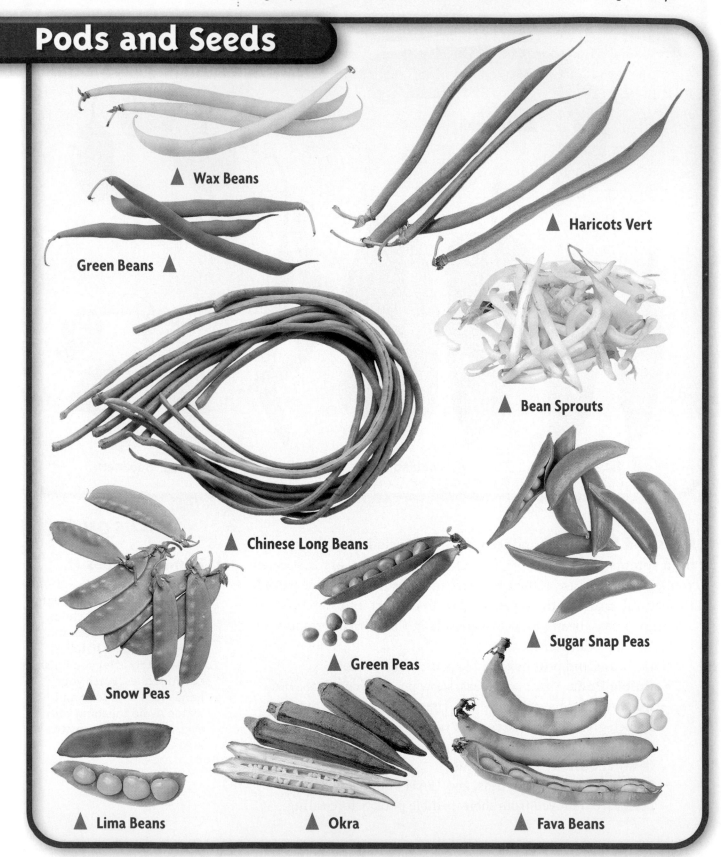

▲ Wax Beans

▲ Haricots Vert

Green Beans ▲

▲ Bean Sprouts

▲ Chinese Long Beans

▲ Sugar Snap Peas

▲ Green Peas

▲ Snow Peas

▲ Lima Beans

▲ Okra

▲ Fava Beans

Root Vegetables Root vegetables grow underground. They serve as nutrient and moisture reservoirs for the tops of the plant. They are rich in sugars, starches, vitamins, and minerals. Popular root vegetables include beets, carrots, parsnips, radishes, and turnips. Roots you might not be familiar with include celeriac (seh-LER-ee-AK), which tastes like celery, and the large Asian daikon (DI-kon) radish.

If root vegetables arrive in the kitchen with their green leafy tops still attached, check for a good color and texture in the leaves. The root end of the vegetable should be firm and dry.

Roots

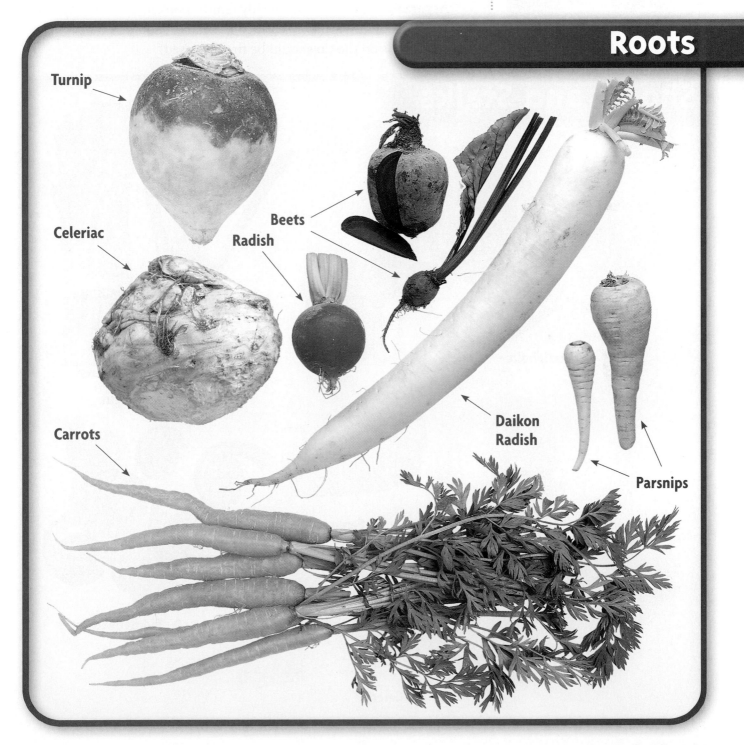

Turnip

Celeriac

Radish

Beets

Carrots

Daikon Radish

Parsnips

Shoots and Stalks Artichokes, asparagus, celery, fennel, and fiddleheads are examples of shoot and stalk vegetables. Fiddleheads are part of an edible fern.

Artichokes are green bulbs comprised of many layers of leaves surrounding a mass of hair-like tendrils, called the choke. The heart of the artichoke is the part attached to the stem. Only the lower part of the leaves and the heart are eaten. Artichokes are actually undeveloped flowers. If left on the stalk, they bloom into beautiful, giant, purple flowers.

Asparagus is a member of the lily family. Look for firm, fleshy, full stalks, with no browning or wilting. The stalks should bend slightly; the small buds on the tip should be firmly closed.

Shoots and Stalks

▲ Artichoke

▲ Fennel

▲ Asparagus

▲ Fiddlehead Ferns

▲ Celery

CULINARY HISTORY

Travels of the Tomato

Probably no other plant has traveled as rocky a road to acceptance and universal appeal as the tomato. An ancestor of our current tomato grew wild in the Andes in South America, possibly as early as 700 A.D. Many years later, in the 1500s, Spanish explorers brought tomato seeds back to Spain. The seeds were eventually brought to Italy and France.

Yet the tomato was not highly regarded in its early years and some even considered it poison. In 1544, naturalist Petrus Matthiolus referred to the tomato as the mala insana, the "unhealthy apple." In his description, he says it is eaten like an eggplant, "fried in oil with salt and pepper." In 1585, Castore Durante offers a similar recipe in his botanical text, Herbario Nuovo, published in Rome. "They are eaten the same way as eggplants, with pepper, salt, and oil, but give little and bad nourishment." Pietro Antonio Michiel of Venice wrote, "If I should eat this fruit, cut in slices in a pan with butter and oil, it would be injurious and harmful to me." Early recipe books recommended cooking tomatoes for three hours to make them safe to eat.

The French appreciated the appearance of the early tomato, which looked like a small golden berry. They had no interest in it as food, but enjoyed growing it. The Italians continued to experiment with it both in the garden and in the kitchen. As a result, by 1700, the marble-sized "golden apple"

▲ Tomato plant

had evolved into a red fruit closer in size and appearance to the plum tomato of today.

Despite the chill with which it was first received, the tomato is now a symbol of Italian cuisine and a basic cooking ingredient used around the world. And tomato lovers everywhere now take great pleasure in what was once considered unthinkable: eating tomatoes raw!

Research

Research the use of tomatoes in early America. Focus on Thomas Jefferson's interest in tomatoes.

Tomatoes Tomatoes are actually fruit and are grown in hundreds of varieties, varying in size, color, shape, flavor, and texture. All have juicy flesh, edible seeds, and smooth, shiny skin. Tomatoes grown commercially are picked unripe and allowed to ripen in transit, but most chefs prefer to find locally grown vine-ripened varieties because of their rich flavor and juiciness. Beefsteak tomatoes are slicing tomatoes best used fresh in salads and sandwiches. Cherry tomatoes and pear tomatoes are also served fresh in salads and cold platters. The egg-shaped plum tomato, and the tomatillo (tohm-ah-TEE-oh), are typically used in sauces and other cooked dishes. Tomatillos, which are green even when ripe, have a papery skin that is removed before use.

FIGURE 12-5 ▶
Heirloom Tomatoes
Heirloom tomatoes come in all shapes, sizes, and colors.
Predicting What might the benefits be of serving heirloom tomatoes?

Gaining popularity in the market these days are heirloom tomatoes. An **heirloom plant** (it can be a fruit or vegetable) is a variety that existed many years ago, before produce was grown for mass-market consumption. Grown from heirloom seeds that have been saved by farmers who want to grow some of these original varieties, heirloom tomatoes are tender, sweet, and juicy.

Tomatoes

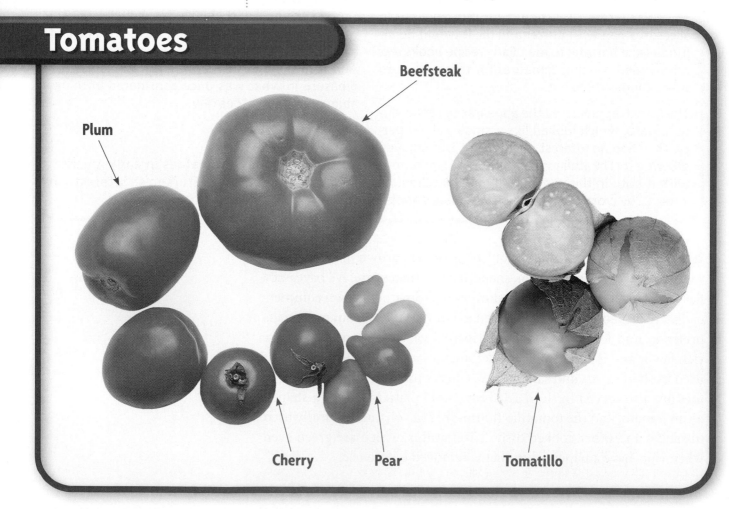

Beefsteak

Plum

Cherry

Pear

Tomatillo

Tubers A **tuber** is a fleshy portion of certain plants that usually grows underground. Potatoes are the most common type of tuber. Most tubers fall into one of the following three categories:

- **High-starch/low-moisture potatoes.** This category includes russet potatoes (also called Idaho), which are used for baking. They are granular and dry after cooking, and they are preferred for baking, puréeing, and mashing. They are also excellent for frying because the low moisture content makes them less likely to splatter or absorb grease. Their natural tendency to absorb moisture makes them a good choice for scalloped or other casserole-style potato dishes.

- **Low-starch/high-moisture potatoes.** This category includes red-skinned potatoes, yellow potatoes (such as Yellow Finn and Yukon Gold), all-purpose potatoes, boiling potatoes, and heirloom varieties such as purple potatoes and fingerlings. They are referred to as waxy, because they hold their shape even after they are cooked until tender. They are a good choice for boiling, steaming, sautéing, oven roasting, and braising or stewing, as well as in salads and soups. New potatoes (any potato that is harvested when less than 1½ inches in diameter) are also high in moisture. Their naturally sweet, fresh flavor is best showcased by simple techniques such as boiling, steaming, or oven roasting.

- **Yams and Sweet Potatoes.** Both varieties of tuber are similar and often confused with one another, but they are actually different plant species. Sweet potatoes have tapered ends, deep orange flesh, dense texture, sweet flavor, and thin, smooth skins. Use the same cooking techniques suggested for low-starch/high-moisture potatoes. True yams are starchier, dryer, and less sweet than sweet potatoes. They have rough, scaly skin and are somewhat blocky in shape, with pale to deep yellow flesh. Use the same cooking techniques suggested for high-starch/low-moisture potatoes.

Select tubers that are firm and the appropriate size and shape for their type.

Reading Checkpoint *How are roots and tubers different from all other vegetables?*

Selecting and Storing Vegetables

Fresh vegetables are ready to eat or cook when purchased, with the exception of avocados or tomatoes, which may need to ripen at room temperature. Vegetables must be selected and stored with care to assure the best flavor and freshness. They are available in a variety of forms.

CHEF'S TIP

POTATO TEST
Check the starch content of potatoes by preparing a brine (11 parts water to 1 part salt, by weight) and then placing the potatoes in the brine. Those that float contain less starch. Those that sink contain more starch.

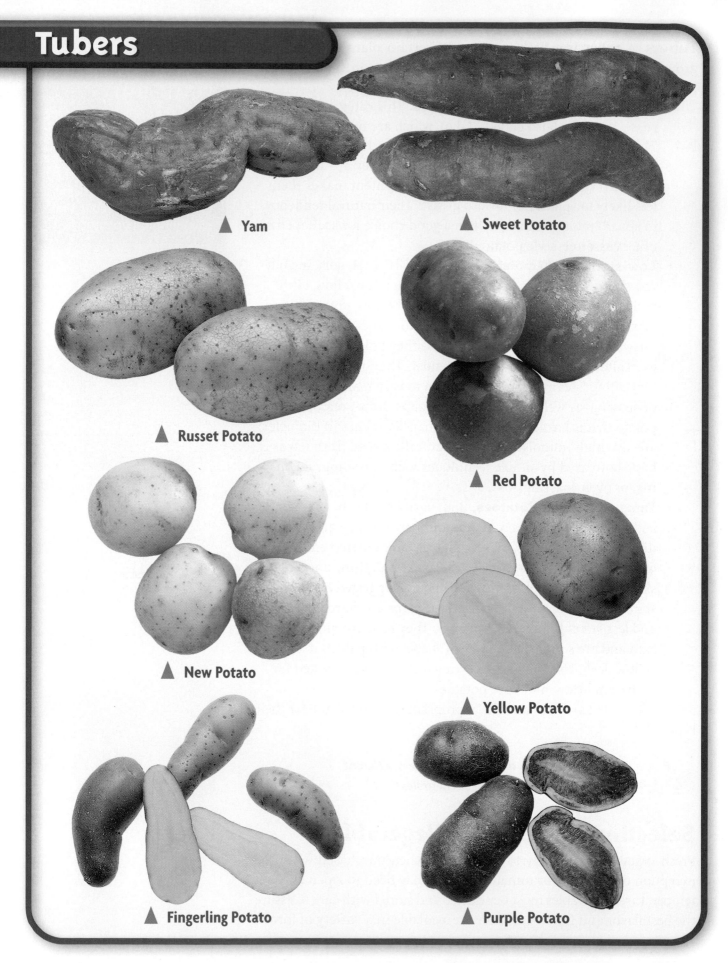

▲ Yam

▲ Sweet Potato

▲ Russet Potato

▲ Red Potato

▲ New Potato

▲ Yellow Potato

▲ Fingerling Potato

▲ Purple Potato

Market Forms Fresh vegetables are sold by weight and count, as well as in boxes, crates, and bags. Some fresh vegetables are peeled, trimmed, and cut before they are packaged and sold. In addition to fresh vegetables, you may also work with canned vegetables, such as canned tomatoes or corn, that are packed in salted water. Dried vegetables commonly used in the kitchen include tomatoes, mushrooms, and chiles.

Like fruit, vegetables are graded for quality by the USDA's Agricultural Marketing Service (AMS). The grade is awarded based on the appearance of the vegetable and its color, shape, and size. Grade designations are most often seen on packages of potatoes and onions. For example, U.S. No. 1 is the grade you will most often see. Potatoes are also assigned a letter (A, B, or C) to indicate their size: "A" indicates potatoes with a diameter ranging from 1⅞ to 2½ inches, "B" indicates 1½ to 2¼ inches, and "C" indicates less than 1¼ inches.

Always try to select vegetables that feel firm and have good color and unblemished skin. And, also as with fruit, chefs should select vegetables according to the manner in which they are going to be used, as well as the price and quality of the produce. When fresh vegetables are out of season, chefs often rely on frozen vegetables instead of depending on more expensive, less flavorful imports.

Storing Vegetables Store vegetables properly to extend their life and maintain their quality.

All fresh vegetables, with the exception of potatoes, tomatoes, avocados, dry onions (including garlic and shallots), and winter squash, are considered perishable and should be kept under refrigeration. Wrap them loosely to keep them from getting too wet.

When fresh root vegetables such as carrots and beets have their leafy tops still attached, remove the tops to keep the vegetables from turning soft or shriveling too quickly. Trim any small roots before storage. To prevent moisture loss, keep roots dry and do not peel them. Store under refrigeration.

Keep unripened avocados at room temperature until they soften enough to use. Store tomatoes at room temperature, if they are still whole, to maintain their flavor.

▲
FIGURE 12-6
Receiving Fresh Vegetables
Vegetables and other produce are packed in boxes and crates for transportation.
Interpreting Illustrations What might the chef be checking for?

Store all tubers in dry storage with good ventilation and away from direct light, heat, and moisture. If potatoes are stored in conditions that are not appropriate, they may soften, wither, develop green spots, or even sprout. Green spots and sprouts in potatoes can be poisonous—discard such potatoes.

Onions, garlic, and shallots should be stored in the same way as potatoes, but keep them separate to avoid flavor transfer. Store them in baskets, bags, or boxes that permit air to circulate.

Winter squash should also be stored in a cool, dark place and will last for several weeks without deteriorating in quality.

Any vegetable that has been trimmed, peeled, or cut should be treated as a perishable food. Keep them refrigerated until you are ready to serve or cook them, and be sure to use them before they have a chance to go bad.

Reading Checkpoint *Which vegetables should be stored under refrigeration?*

Preparing Vegetables

Cleaning is always the first step in preparing vegetables. Once the vegetables are cleaned, you can cut and trim them as needed. Just as when

BASIC CULINARY SKILLS

Trimming and Dicing Onions

1 Cut away a thin slice from the stem and root ends of the bulb with a paring knife, making a flat surface on both ends.

2 Pull away the peel by catching it between your thumb and the flat side of your blade. Trim away any brown spots from the underlying layers.

3 Cut the onion in half from the root end to the stem end. Lay half the onion, cut side down, on the cutting board.

4 Make evenly spaced cuts (¼-inch for a small dice, ½-inch for a medium dice, ¾-inch for a large dice), running lengthwise, with the tip of a chef's knife. Leave the root end intact.

Continued on next page

Trimming and Dicing Onions *continued*

5 Make two or three horizontal cuts parallel to the work surface, from the stem end to the root end, but do not cut all the way through.

6 Make even, crosswise cuts working from stem end up to the root, cutting through all layers of the onion.

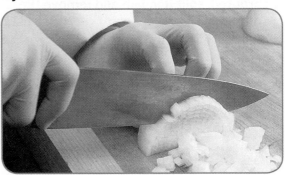

working with fruit, always wear gloves when you prepare fresh vegetables that are not going to be cooked before you serve them.

Cleaning All fresh vegetables, even if they will be peeled before cutting, must be cleaned thoroughly. Washing removes surface dirt as well as bacteria and other contaminants. Leafy vegetables can contain sand and dirt, and even bugs. Celery and leeks are always dirty at the root.

BASIC CULINARY SKILLS

Trimming and Mincing Garlic

1 Separate garlic cloves by wrapping an entire head of garlic in a towel and pressing down on the top.

2 Loosen the skin from each clove by placing a clove on the cutting board, placing the flat side of the blade on top, and hitting the blade with a fist or the heel of your hand.

Continued on next page

Trimming and Mincing Garlic *continued*

3 Peel off the skin and remove the root end and any brown spots. If the clove has sprouted, split it in half and remove the sprout.

as for loosening the skin, but this time apply more force.

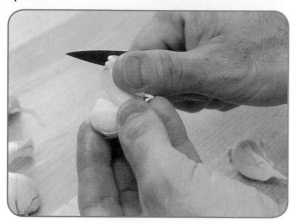

4 Crush the cloves by laying them on the cutting board and using the same technique

5 Mince the cloves by using a rocking motion. To mash the garlic, hold the knife nearly flat against the cutting board and press down.

They also trap dirt between the leaves and stalks. To clean vegetables, run them under cold water. As with fruit, special solutions are available for cleaning vegetables. Wash vegetables as close as possible to preparation time.

Trimming Remove the peels from vegetables if necessary with a swivel-bladed peeler, a paring knife, or a chef's knife. Remove woody stems from such vegetables as mushrooms, asparagus, artichokes, and broccoli.

Onions and garlic are key ingredients in many types of food preparations. It's important to master the techniques for preparing, trimming, and cutting them. They taste best when they are cut as close as possible to the time they are used.

Tomatoes are one of the most commonly used vegetables in the kitchen. They are often peeled, seeded, and then diced. This preparation is what chefs call **tomato concassé** (kon-kah-SAY).

CHEF'S TIP

GARLIC ODOR

To remove garlic odor from your hands, wash them thoroughly and then rub them on a stainless steel surface, preferably under running water. Stainless steel contains the mineral nickel which neutralizes the garlic odor.

 **Reading Checkpoint** *What is the first step in preparing fresh vegetables before cutting and trimming?*

Tomato Concassé

1 Cut a small "X" in the bottom of the tomato with the tip of a paring knife. Do not cut too deeply into the flesh.

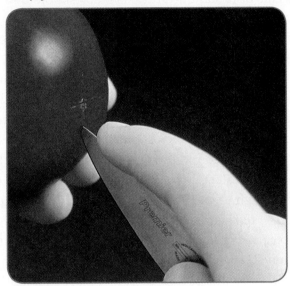

4 Cut the tomato in half at its widest point.

5 Squeeze or scoop out the seeds gently.

6 Dice by making lengthwise cuts, horizontal cuts, and then crosswise cuts.

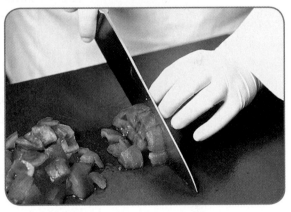

2 Blanch in boiling water for about 15 seconds (or slightly longer if the tomato is unripe). Place tomatoes into a bowl of ice water to stop the cooking.

3 Pull away the skin with a paring knife.

Cooking Vegetables

There are distinct differences in how tender a vegetable should be when it is properly cooked. The proper doneness is determined by how you intend to serve or use the vegetable, the vegetable's characteristics, regional or ethnic preferences, and cooking technique.

There are four levels of doneness for vegetables:

- **Blanched.** Vegetables are blanched for 30 seconds to 1 minute. Blanching is appropriate for vegetables served cold or for those that will complete cooking in a separate process (braising, for instance).
- **Parcooked/parboiled.** Vegetables are cooked to partial doneness to prepare them to be finished by grilling, sautéing, or stewing.
- **Tender-crisp.** Vegetables are cooked until they can be bitten into easily but still offer a slight resistance and sense of texture.

- **Fully cooked.** Vegetables are quite tender, although they should retain their shape and color. If boiling vegetables to make a purée, boil them until they mash easily.

Boiling and Steaming Vegetables Properly steamed and boiled vegetables have vivid colors and identifiable, fresh flavors. Most vegetables are best when simmered, not cooked at a full boil. Add enough salt to develop a good flavor (a standard ratio is 1 tablespoon of salt for every gallon of water).

To preserve the best flavor, texture, and nutritional value of vegetables, serve them as soon as possible after you cook them. Drain well so that any finishing or flavoring ingredients will cling to the vegetable.

Sometimes you will need to at least partially prepare vegetables ahead of time. To preserve the quality of vegetables, chefs use a technique known as refreshing or shocking. As soon as the vegetables are cooked, drain them in a colander and then immediately transfer them to a container filled with ice water. This stops the cooking process. Leave them there just long enough to chill; then drain once again. Store refreshed vegetables in the refrigerator until you are ready to use them.

To steam vegetables, use a large pot with a tight-fitting lid and a steamer insert, a tiered steamer, or a convection or pressure steamer for large quantities. The amount of liquid required depends on both the type of equipment you are using and how long the vegetable takes to cook: the shorter the cooking time, the less liquid needed.

Puréeing Vegetables Chefs use vegetable purées for a variety of purposes: flavoring and coloring another dish, thickening a sauce, or as the basis for a sauce or soup. Vegetable purées can be made from any vegetable tender enough to chop fine enough for a soft, loose texture. Cook the vegetable by the desired technique until tender. (Very tender green vegetables should be briefly blanched to set their colors.) Drain them well before you start to purée them. Equipment options for purées include a food processor, blender, food mill, or sieve.

Taste and evaluate the purée. Some may require additional liquid for a good texture; others may benefit from simmering until they reduce slightly. A variety of ingredients may be added for additional flavor, richness, texture, or color: eggs, cream, butter, spices, herbs, flavorful oils.

Glazing Vegetables Really a finishing technique, glazing vegetables generally incorporates aspects of boiling, steaming, and sautéing and potentially even roasting and baking. The classical method of glazing vegetables is to parcook your vegetables in water, then make the glaze in a separate pan, and finally toss your vegetables in the glaze and serve. You can, however, start the vegetables in the cooking liquid (stock works best), and once they are close to tender, add the butter (and sugar if desired) to form the glaze. Alternatively, you can place all the ingredients in a moderate-temperature oven and cook them until the vegetables are tender and the glaze has formed. The last method is a little tricky because your measurement and timing have to be exact to get it right.

Braising and Stewing Vegetables Vegetable stews and braises may include just one vegetable or a combination. Stewed or braised vegetables literally cook in their own juices. Stews and braises should be fork tender or, in some cases, meltingly soft. These dishes tend to hold well; some even improve after resting. The vegetables in a stew are customarily cut into small pieces. Vegetables for a braise may be parcooked or blanched to set their colors and improve the flavor or texture of the finished braise. (Review the basic braising and stewing techniques in Chapter 8).

BASIC CULINARY SKILLS

Glazing Vegetables

1 **Bring the liquid to a simmer** and season or flavor as the recipe instructs.

2 **Sweat** or smother the vegetables and any aromatics in a cooking fat or in the cooking liquid, if desired.

3 **Pour** or ladle enough cooking liquid into the pan to properly cook the vegetables.

See Recipe Card 58, "Glazed Carrots"

4 **Cover** the pan and cook until the vegetables are done.

5 **Remove** the cover and let the cooking liquid continue to reduce to make the glaze.

Roasting and Baking Vegetables Roasted vegetables have a deep flavor, the result of cooking in the dry environment of the oven. Even relatively dry or starchy vegetables cook properly with no added moisture. Roasting is often used to prepare squashes, yams, eggplant, or beets.

Preheat the oven to the right temperature. Some vegetables roast best at a low temperature for a long period of time; others are best for short periods at high temperatures.

Scrub and pierce vegetables you are baking whole. Piercing them allows steam to escape; otherwise, they can burst.

Add seasoning to cut or peeled vegetables before roasting. Marinades, butter, and oil are often used both to add flavor and to help brown the vegetables for a rich flavor. Stuffing mixtures (rice, bread, mushroom, forcemeat, or sausage, for example) can fill scooped-out vegetables (zucchini, mushrooms, eggplant, or tomatoes).

BASIC CULINARY SKILLS

Making Vegetable Braises or Stews

1 **Cook the aromatic vegetables** in a cooking fat, beginning with members of the onion family.

2 **Add the remaining ingredients** in order, stirring as necessary.

3 **Adjust seasoning and consistency** of the dish as needed.

4 **Stew or braise** the vegetables until flavorful, fully cooked, and fork tender.

5 **Serve** immediately or hold for later use.

 See Recipe Card 59, "Ratatouille"

Grilling and Broiling Vegetables The intense heat of grills and broilers gives vegetables a rich, bold flavor. The basic procedures for grilling and broiling, including proper grill maintenance and applying sauces or glazes, apply to grilled and broiled vegetables. Grilled vegetables have a distinctive charred flavor and deeply browned exteriors.

High-moisture or tender vegetables (mushrooms, zucchini, or tomatoes) can be grilled from a raw state, but dense or starchy vegetables (squash, potatoes, or fennel) may require preliminary cooking to reach the proper doneness on the grill. Soft and pre-cooked hard vegetables may be marinated briefly before cooking. If a marinade has been used, it can be served as an accompanying sauce.

Frying and Sautéing Vegetables Sautéing and stir frying are used both as the primary cooking technique for high-moisture vegetables (leafy greens, mushrooms, soft-skinned squash, for instance) and as a finishing and reheating technique for vegetables parcooked by boiling, steaming, or baking. These techniques lend themselves to a layering of flavors and ingredients.

Match the cooking temperature to the vegetables you are cooking. To gently finish vegetables in cream or butter, use relatively low heat. To get some browning or to retain crispness, use high heat.

BASIC CULINARY SKILLS

Deep Frying Vegetables

1. Heat the oil in a deep fryer or kettle.
2. Add the vegetables to the hot oil, using a basket or tongs.

4. Remove and drain; season if necessary.

3. Fry the vegetables until fully cooked.

See Recipe Card 67, "French Fried Potatoes"

Choose a cooking fat that complements the flavor of the vegetable. Oils such as olive, peanut, canola, corn, or safflower can be used, as well as whole or clarified butter. Use seasonings and aromatics to heighten the vegetable's flavor. Use garnishes to add color or texture.

If you are sautéing or stir frying a combination of vegetables, add those that require the longest cooking time first and end with those that require the least.

Pan fried vegetables may be breaded or coated with flour or batter. Properly done pan-fried vegetables have a golden or brown, crisp exterior, with the interior tender to the bite and very hot. The coating, if any, is crisp and light. Sauces or other accompaniments add complementary or contrasting flavor and texture.

Perfectly fried vegetables include crisp chips, hearty croquettes, and tender vegetables with a light crunchy batter or breading.

Potato Purées The technique of preparing light and flavorful potato purées rests on three basic concepts: choosing the right potato (high-starch/low-moisture varieties are best), getting the potatoes dry before

BASIC CULINARY SKILLS

Puréeing Potatoes

1 Cook the potatoes by steaming or boiling.

2 Dry the potatoes in a pot over low heat or in the oven on a sheet tray until no more steam rises.

3 Purée the hot potatoes until they are smooth.

4 Stir in finishing ingredients, such as seasonings, warmed milk or cream, or whole butter.

See Recipe Card 68, "Whipped Potatoes"

5 Serve as desired or reserve for later use.

you purée them, and having all the ingredients hot when you combine them into the finished purée.

One note about equipment. Use a potato masher, wooden spoon, sieve, potato ricer, or food mill to purée potatoes. A blender or food processor will overwork the potatoes, making them too loose and thin.

 **Reading Checkpoint** *What are the techniques for cooking vegetables?*

Serving Vegetables

The technique you use to prepare and serve vegetables can produce dramatic differences in flavor, texture, color, and nutritive value. For example, although acorn squash is often roasted or puréed, it can also be gently stewed in cream, or grilled and served with a salsa. Cucumbers, most commonly considered a vegetable to be eaten raw, may be steamed, sautéed, or even braised. You can prepare vegetables by all the basic cooking techniques outlined in Chapter 8, making them among the most versatile and interesting options on the menu.

Vegetables are more than just side dishes. They can be featured on their own as an appetizer or main course or served as an accompaniment to meat or fish. They are the foundation of many soups and sauces and an important ingredient in many other preparations. As more customers look for meatless or vegetarian options, your skills in vegetable cookery will assure that vegetables need never be an afterthought.

 **Reading Checkpoint** *How can vegetables be used as more than a side dish?*

12.2 ASSESSMENT

Reviewing Concepts

1. What is a tuber and how does it grow?
2. Which vegetables are stored at room temperature?
3. What is tomato concassé?
4. What level of doneness are puréed vegetables?
5. In addition to being a side dish, how else can vegetables be used?

Critical Thinking

6. **Predicting** Suggest a reason why onions should not be stored in a small refrigerator.
7. **Solving Problems** What's a good tool for pulling away the peel from onions and garlic?
8. **Classifying** Which types of peppers would be good for salads?

Test Kitchen

Split into three teams. Each team will boil the same amount of green beans in the same amount of water. Team 1 adds nothing to the water. Team 2 adds ¼ cup of salt per gal of water. Team 3 adds 2 tsp of baking soda per gal of water. Blanch for 2 minutes, and shock in ice water. Which has the brightest color? The best flavor? The best texture?

CULINARY MATH

Measuring Volume Yields of Cuts

Small-dice a carrot, medium-dice another, and large-dice a third. Weigh a 4 oz portion of each. Measure the volume of each portion. Evaluate the result.

Review and Assessment

Reviewing Content

Choose the letter that best answers the question or completes the statement.

1. Every fruit contains:
   - a. a seed
   - b. flesh
   - c. skin
   - d. all of the above

2. Which of the following vegetables should be stored at room temperature in a dark place?
   - a. tomatoes
   - b. yams
   - c. asparagus
   - d. green leaf cabbage

3. Which of the following two items are essential ingredients to form a glaze?
   - a. cooking liquid
   - b. seasoning
   - c. thickener
   - d. cooking fat

4. Which of the following ingredients is not used in poaching fruit?
   - a. cooking liquid
   - b. sweetener
   - c. flavoring
   - d. cooking fat

5. Which fruit should be stored at room temperature?
   - a. apples
   - b. oranges
   - c. bananas
   - d. berries

6. What is a good flavor tip for boiling vegetables?
   - a. add salt to the water
   - b. add sugar to the water
   - c. cook at a full boil
   - d. all of the above

7. Which of the following should not be stored under refrigeration?
   - a. tomatoes
   - b. potatoes
   - c. avocados
   - d. all of the above

Understanding Concepts

8. Describe the difference between a mature piece of fruit and a ripe piece of fruit.

9. List the anatomy of a plant, using a different vegetable as an example of each anatomical feature.

10. Should apples be stored separately from other fruit? Why or why not?

11. How can fruit be used in savory dishes?

12. Explain the difference between a clingstone and a freestone fruit and give an example of each.

Critical Thinking

13. **Predicting** What might happen to a banana left over the weekend in a lunchbox with an apple?

14. **Classifying** Why is some fruit, such as a tomato, referred to as a vegetable?

15. **Drawing Conclusions** Which potato would be best for oven roasting, a russet or a red-skin potato, and why?

Culinary Math

16. **Solving Problems** An 8 oz apple is peeled, cored, and sliced for a pie. The scraps weigh 1 oz. The recipe calls for 32 oz of sliced apples. How many whole apples are needed to make the pie?

17. **Applying Concepts** Small-diced carrots take up half the space of large-diced carrots. If a 10 oz carrot, large-diced, yields a cup, how much would a 12½ oz carrot yield if small-diced?

On the Job

18. **Solving Problems** You are working the dessert station and have run out of pears for your poached dessert. You have oranges, apples, and pineapple in the walk-in cooler. Which is the best substitute?

19. **Drawing Conclusions** A stewed dish you are preparing contains the following ingredients: onion, eggplant, zucchini, and corn. Which item would you add to the hot oil first?

Use the following Recipe Cards to test your culinary skill.

53. Fruit Coulis
54. Poached Pears
55. Applesauce
56. Broiled Pineapple
57. Steamed Broccoli
58. Glazed Carrots
59. Ratatouille
60. Corn Fritters
61. Grilled Vegetables Provençal-Style
62. Baked Acorn Squash with Cranberry-Orange Compote
63. Braised Romaine
64. Boiled Parslied Potatoes
65. Baked Potatoes
66. Potatoes au Gratin
67. French Fried Potatoes
68. Whipped Potatoes

Project 12: Cooking Potatoes

Answer these questions when your class works through Project 12.

- Does a potato have a consistent texture when cooked by using different methods?

- Does a potato have a consistent taste when cooked by using different methods?

- Do some cooking methods require more time and effort than others, even when you're using the same ingredient?

- How much difference do seasonings, flavorings, and condiments make to the basic taste of the potato?

- Which method of cooking potatoes could have the most problem with overcooking? Which method could have the most problem with undercooking?

TEST PRACTICE

Choose the letter that best answers the question or completes the statement.

1. Which of the following vegetables is actually a fruit?
   A   acorn squash
   B   avocado
   C   beet
   D   yam

2. Which of the following is not a member of the stone fruit family?
   A   apricot
   B   peach
   C   cranberry
   D   cherry

3. Of which family is cauliflower a member?
   A   gourds
   B   roots
   C   tubers
   D   cabbages

4. To which vegetable is a scallion most similar?
   A   cucumber
   B   carrot
   C   leek
   D   asparagus

5. Which cooking method is used for tomato concassé?
   A   blanching
   B   roasting
   C   baking
   D   steaming

6. A plantain is a type of:
   A   squash
   B   banana
   C   potato
   D   melon

7. Which of the following is not stored at room temperature?
   A   avocado
   B   banana
   C   tomato
   D   orange

8. Which of the following fruit can be zested?
   A   apple
   B   kiwi
   C   lime
   D   all of the above

GRAINS, LEGUMES, & PASTA

13.1 Rice & Other Grains

READING PREVIEW

Key Concepts

- Understanding grains and grain processing
- Selecting and storing grains
- Preparing grains
- Presenting grains

Vocabulary

- barley
- bran
- brown rice
- bulgur
- converted rice
- cornmeal
- cracked grain
- endosperm
- farinaceous
- germ
- grains

- grits
- hominy
- hominy grits
- hull
- husk
- instant oats
- kernel
- masa harina
- meal
- milling
- oat groats

- oatmeal
- parcooked grain
- pearl grain
- pearl barley
- pilaf
- polenta
- posole
- processed grain
- quick-cooking oats

- quinoa
- refined grains
- risotto
- rolled oats
- rye berries
- rye flakes
- Scotch barley
- wheat berry
- whole grain
- wild rice

"The history of any cuisine always rests upon a grain: rice throughout Asia, wheat throughout the Mediterranean, and corn throughout the Americas. **"**

– David Kamen

Grains

Grains are the seeds of grasses that human beings have learned to cultivate for food. These particular grasses, known as cereal grasses, are prized for their ability to produce grain. In fact, grains are basic foods in almost any cuisine. Grains provide the majority of calories and nutrients in most diets. American food guidelines, and guidelines throughout the world, concentrate on grains as the foundation of a healthy diet.

Parts of a Grain Grains have several layers when they are first removed from the grasses on which they grow. To make grains easier to cook, digest, and store, some or all of these protective layers are removed. Removing these layers is the first step in processing grain into food. Although each type of grain is different, grains are basically composed of four parts.

David Kamen
The Culinary Institute of America

Grains, Legumes, & Pasta ▶ **393**

CULINARY SCIENCE

Parts of a Grain

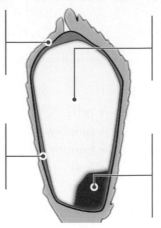

Husk or Hull
Tough protective outer seed coat. The edible seed, without its husk or hull, is typically referred to as the **kernel.**

Bran
Second layer. Contains dietary fiber, an important part of a balanced diet.

Endosperm
Largest part of the grain. Made up almost entirely of carbohydrates, or starch.

Germ
Contains most of the grain's oils, vitamins, and minerals. This is the part of the grain that sprouts to form a new plant.

Grains are not the only foods that are high in starch, of course. Beans and some vegetables, such as potatoes, are also starchy. Nutritionists and cooks sometimes refer to grains, along with these other starchy foods, as a food group called **farinaceous** (fare-eh-NAY-shus) foods.

Processed Grains We don't eat grain just as it comes from the grass. A grain undergoes a number of steps to make it into food.

- **Processed Grains.** Grains that have been prepared to use as food are called **processed grains.** Often grains are cut, crushed, rolled, or ground as part of the processing. This is referred to as **milling.** Some steps in processing are important to make the food digestible or able to store well. Some steps are performed to change the flavor, texture, color, or shelf life of the grain.

- **Whole Grains.** When just the husk or hull is removed from a grain, the grain is referred to as **whole grain** or minimally

FIGURE 13-1 ▶
Farinaceous Foods
Grains, breads, pastas, and legumes are all farinaceous foods.
Drawing Conclusions *How are all these foods alike?*

processed grain. Whole grains typically take longer to cook than most processed grains. To make whole grains easier and quicker to cook, they can be partly or fully precooked by boiling or steaming the grain. Grains treated this way are called **parcooked grains.** ("Parcooked" means partially cooked.) They can be dried or toasted after parcooking.

- **Refined Grains.** Highly processed grains are known as **refined grains**. The more the grain is processed, the more its layers are stripped away. Refined grains have less nutritional value than whole grains because they have fewer vitamins, minerals, and fiber.

- **Pearl Grains and Other Refined Grains.** One of the parts of the grain that is often removed in the refining process is the bran. Removing the bran makes the grain lighter in color and quicker to cook. A grain that has been scrubbed of its bran is referred to as a **pearl grain.** Another part of the grain that is often removed is the germ. Removing a grain's germ removes oils, vitamins, and minerals, but helps improve the grain's shelf life because the germ's oils tend to turn rancid quickly.

**FIGURE 13-2
Processed Wheat**
Each type of processing creates a different texture and taste.
Interpreting Illustrations *Which forms of wheat are familiar to you?*
▼

- **Cracked Grain.** Grain can be further processed by cutting or crushing the kernel into smaller pieces. Whole kernels that are cut into very large pieces are known as **cracked grain** and have a very coarse texture. Cracked wheat is an example of a cracked grain made from a minimally processed grain. Bulgur wheat is an example of a cracked grain made from a parcooked grain.

- **Meal.** Processed grain can also be ground into fine particles by rolling the grain between steel drums or between stone wheels. Grains that are milled into fine particles this way are known as **meal.** An example of this is cornmeal. If grain has been partially cooked, it may be rolled to produce flakes instead of being ground.

Reading Checkpoint *What are the four parts of a grain?*

Grains, Legumes, & Pasta ▶ **395**

Selecting and Storing Grains

Each type of grain has its own tastes and textures. However, the way a specific grain is processed also changes a grain's taste and texture. The three major types of grain are:

- Rice
- Wheat
- Corn

Rice Rice is one of the most important grains in the world. When rice is harvested, the hull is removed by passing the rice through rollers. Once the hull is removed, the rice still retains the bran. Rice that retains some or all of its bran is called **brown rice**. Brown rice has a slightly nutty taste and takes longer to cook than white rice. If the

Types of Rice

▼ Long-Grain Rice

Long-grain rice is four to five times longer than it is wide. Typically fluffy and dry when cooked, it separates easily and does not stick together. Examples: Basmati (bahs-MAH-tee) and Thai Jasmine.

▼ Medium-Grain Rice

Medium-grain rice is shorter than long-grain rice. It is moister than long-grain rice after it is cooked and tends to stick together. Example: Calrose. This example of medium-grain rice is a brown rice (the bran remains on the rice).

▼ Short-Grain Rice

Short-grain rice is nearly round. This type of rice has a relatively high starch content and is quite sticky after it is cooked. Example: Arborio (ar-BOH-ree-oh) and sweet or glutinous rice.

▼ Wild Rice

Wild rice is the seed of a marsh grass. Although it is not related to other rice, it is cooked like them. When wild rice is harvested, it is left to soak for a period of time; this is known as the curing process. After the grain is cured, it is toasted to dry it out. Toasting prepares the grain for storage. It also gives wild rice its toasty flavor. The last step of processing wild rice is removing the hull.

milling process continues long enough to remove all of the bran, the result is white rice.

Rice can also be partially cooked before the hull is removed. After the grain is softened in hot water, it is dried and then milled to produce either brown or white rice. Rice that is parcooked in this way before milling is known as converted rice and has a slightly different taste and texture.

Different varieties of rice produce grains with different lengths and shapes. Each type of rice can be processed as white rice (without its bran) or as brown rice (with its bran).

Wheat Wheat is an ancient grain that grows abundantly in parts of Europe, Asia, and North America. It was first cultivated thousands of years ago and has evolved into a number of different types.

Forms of Wheat

▼ **Wheat Berries**

The whole kernel of wheat. A **wheat berry** is not hulled, polished, or steamed. Wheat berries are usually soaked overnight before being cooked to shorten their cooking time.

▼ **Cracked Wheat**

Made by crushing wheat berries into pieces.

▼ **Bulgur**

Bulgur (BUHL-guhr) is made from steamed whole wheat berries that are then crushed into small pieces. Bulgur is often used to make a traditional Middle Eastern salad known as tabouli (tuh-BOO-luh).

▼ **Wheat Bran**

Made from the bran surrounding the wheat kernel.

Corn Corn is the only grain that is eaten both fresh and dried. Dried corn is prepared in many ways. Some types of dried corn products are made from kernels that are soaked in a solution of lye. The lye makes it easier for us to digest some of the important nutrients in the corn. Some varieties of corn produce white kernels and others produce yellow kernels.

The forms of corn in the following list may be made from either color of corn.

- **Hominy** (HOM-uh-nee) is a whole dried corn kernel that has the hull and germ removed.
- **Posole** (poh-SOH-leh) is the whole kernel with the germ and bran still intact and soaked in an alkaline solution to make the hull softer and easier to digest. Pozole is another common spelling for this type of corn.
- **Cornmeal** is finely ground corn. When whole corn is ground into meal, it is called **grits** in America. Grits can be ground into coarse, medium, or fine particles. **Hominy grits** are grits made from hominy, so they do not contain the hull or germ. Cornmeal made from posole is known as **masa harina** (MAH-sah ah-REE-nah). **Polenta** (poh-LEHN-tah) is an Italian term for cornmeal.

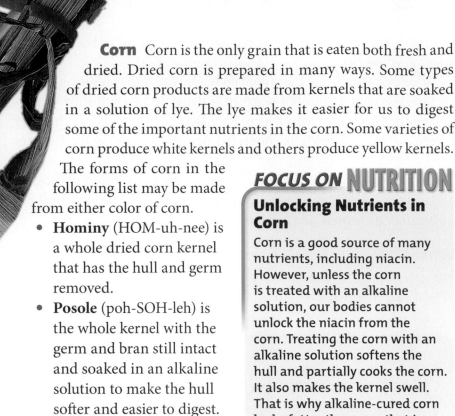

◄ **FIGURE 13-3**
Varieties of Corn
An ear of corn with its husk still attached, shown with corn kernels, grits, and cornmeal.
Analyzing Information *Can you identify the hominy?*

FOCUS ON NUTRITION

Unlocking Nutrients in Corn

Corn is a good source of many nutrients, including niacin. However, unless the corn is treated with an alkaline solution, our bodies cannot unlock the niacin from the corn. Treating the corn with an alkaline solution softens the hull and partially cooks the corn. It also makes the kernel swell. That is why alkaline-cured corn looks fatter than corn that is dried without this treatment.

Additional Grains Oats grow well in areas that are too cold for growing wheat, rice, or corn, or where the soil is poor. Oats are sold in many forms.

- **Oat groats** are the whole grain of the oat, with the hull removed.
- **Oatmeal** is coarsely ground oats that are cooked as a hot cereal or used in baking.
- **Rolled oats** are made by steaming groats and then rolling them into flat flakes. Rolled oats are also called old-fashioned oats. **Quick-cooking oatmeal** is rolled oats cut into smaller pieces to reduce cooking time.
- **Instant oats** are rolled oats that have been partially cooked and then dried before being rolled again.

Barley is a grain that looks like a doubled grain of rice. It is most commonly sold as **pearl barley**, which means it has been milled several

The Goddess of Grain

The word "cereal" doesn't just mean corn flakes, puffed rice, or oatmeal. It is a general term used to refer to all grains. Grains, and the ground meal made from grains, were very important to early civilizations—so important, in fact, that grain was sometimes used in place of money.

In early civilizations, many festivals and feasts were dedicated to grains. Most early cultures believed a powerful god or goddess controlled the harvest of grains. That meant any grain-related festival was also usually dedicated to a god or goddess. Offerings were made to the god or goddess asking for good weather and growing conditions. Storytellers would tell how the god or goddess gave grain to humans in the long distant past. In fact, the word "cereal" is based on the name of the Roman goddess of agriculture, Ceres.

Today we still observe some of the old customs associated with Ceres. Throwing grains of rice at a new bride dates back to ancient Roman times when people sprinkled grains of barley around the temples dedicated to Ceres.

CERES

Research

Research the relationship between a culture, nation, or people (past or present) and the grain associated with that culture, nation, or people. List and describe at least two dishes from that culture, nation, or people that prominently feature that specific grain. Make one of the dishes you have described.

times to completely remove the outer husk and the bran. **Scotch barley**, which is also called pot barley, is also milled, although the bran is not completely removed.

Rye is sold as a whole grain known as **rye berries**. If the berries are put through a roller, the result is **rye flakes**.

Quinoa (KEEN-wah) is a high-protein grain that was originally grown in South America. It has a round kernel and becomes fluffy and light when you cook it. Before cooking quinoa, put it in a bowl of cold water and rub it between your palms for a few minutes. Repeat until the water is clear.

Storing Grains Grains are dry goods. They should be kept dry during storage. Hold them in containers with tight lids if they are removed from their packaging. Keep them above floor level in an area that is cool and dry.

Oats

Oats are commonly available as: groats, oatmeal, rolled or old-fashioned oats, quick-cooking oatmeal, instant oats, oat flour, and oat bran.

Barley

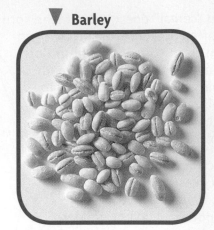

Barley is commonly available as pearl barley, Scotch or pot barley, and barley flour.

Rye

Rye is commonly available as: rye berries, rye flakes, and rye flour.

Quinoa

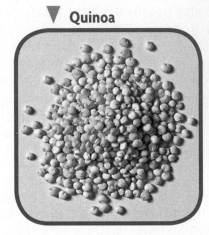

Quinoa is commonly available as whole kernels.

Some whole grains, especially those that still contain some or all of the bran or germ, can lose their quality quickly. They should be stored in the refrigerator or freezer if they must be kept for more than a few weeks.

Reading Checkpoint *Name the three major types of grain.*

Preparing Grains

There are several ways to prepare grains. Each involves a different method of adding liquid. When grains are fully cooked by either steaming or boiling, they should be tender to the bite. Some types of grain separate from each other easily. Other grains may be sticky and clump together. Fluffy grains are perfect for soaking up juices. Sticky grains are easy to eat with chopsticks.

Boiling or Steaming Grains Boiled grains are made by simply stirring a measured amount of grain into a large pot of boiling salted water. The grains are simmered until tender.

Steamed grains are made by stirring a measured amount of grain into a measured amount of liquid. The amount of liquid is just enough for the grain to absorb. The pot is covered as the grain cooks. When steamed grains finish cooking, there should not be any liquid to drain away.

Preparing Cereals and Meals Cooked grain meal (such as cornmeal and oatmeal) is made by stirring the grain into a simmering liquid. Cereals and meals are stirred throughout their cooking time in order to develop a creamy, smooth texture. It is important to add the meal to the simmering liquid properly so the dish does not become lumpy.

Some cooked meals are stiff enough to pull away from the sides of the pot and are relatively heavy in texture. Others remain liquid enough to pour easily.

BASIC CULINARY SKILLS

Boiled or Steamed Grains

1 Bring liquid to a boil.

2 Add salt and other seasonings as directed by your recipe.

3 Add grain all at once. Stir to separate grain.

4 Reduce heat. Simmer until grain is fully cooked and tender. Cover the pot if you are steaming the grain.

5 Drain grain through a colander if you are boiling the grain.

6 Fluff grain with a fork to test for doneness.

7 Serve grain while very hot.

 See Recipe Card 69, "Boiled Rice."

"Mush" and "porridge" are general-purpose names for cooked grain meal. They may be made from almost any type of grain. Cooked meal is known by different names in different parts of the world. Grits, for example, is the name for the cornmeal porridge served in the United States, while polenta is the name of the cornmeal porridge enjoyed in Italy.

BASIC CULINARY SKILLS

Mush (Porridge)

1 Bring liquid to a boil.

2 Add salt and other seasonings as directed by your recipe.

3 Add cereal or meal in a thin stream, stirring constantly.

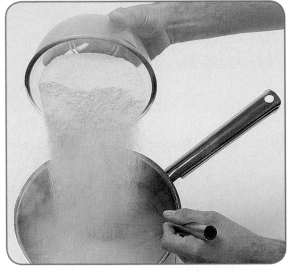

4 Reduce heat to a simmer and cook, stirring as necessary, until done.

5 Adjust seasonings. Add any additional ingredients suggested by your recipe.

6 Serve cereal while very hot. (Or cool properly to serve later.)

 See Recipe Card 70, "Polenta."

Preparing Pilaf Originally from the Middle East, **pilaf** (PEE-lahf) is a grain dish in which the grain—usually rice—is first sautéed in a pan, usually with oil or butter, before adding a hot liquid. It is then covered and cooked over direct heat or in the oven.

In pilaf the grains remain separate and take on a nutty flavor from the initial sautéing of the grain. The grain has a slightly firmer texture than if it had been prepared by boiling.

Cooking Grain

Type of Grain (1 cup)	Liquid	Simmer Time	Yield
Rice			
Long-grain white rice	1½–1¾ cups	18–20 minutes	3 cups
Long-grain brown rice	3 cups	40 minutes	4 cups
Short-grain white rice	1–1½ cups	20–30 minutes	3 cups
Short-grain brown rice	2½ cups	35–40 minutes	4 cups
Wild rice	3 cups	30–45 minutes	4 cups
Converted rice	2–2½ cups	20–25 minutes	3 cups
Wheat			
Wheat berries (Soak overnight)	3 cups	1 hour	2 cups
Bulgur wheat (as pilaf)	2½ cups	15–20 minutes	2 cups
Cracked wheat	2 cups	20 minutes	3 cups
Grits			
Whole hominy (Soak overnight)	2½ cups	2½–3 hours	3 cups
Hominy grits	4 cups	25 minutes	3 cups
Cornmeal, polenta, grits	3–3½ cups	35–45 minutes	3 cups
Oats			
Oat groats	2 cups	45–60 minutes	2 cups
Rolled oats, old fashioned oats	1½ cups	15–20 minutes	1½ cups
Quick-cooking oats	1½ cups	5 minutes	1½ cups
Barley			
Pearl barley	2 cups	35–45 minutes	4 cups
Scotch barley	2½ cups	50–60 minutes	4 cups
Other			
Quinoa	1–1½ cups	10–12 minutes	3½–4 cups

Pilaf

1. Heat oil or butter in a pan.

2. Add onions and sauté, stirring frequently, until softened.

3. Add grain all at once and sauté, stirring frequently, until well coated with oil or butter.

4. Add liquid to the grain and bring to a simmer. Stir the grain to keep it from clumping together or sticking to the pan.

5. Add any remaining flavorings, such as bay leaf or thyme, according to your recipe.

6. Cover the pot and finish cooking the pilaf either on the stovetop over low to moderate heat or in the oven. Do not stir the pilaf as it cooks.

7. Test a few grains for doneness. They should be tender, but not soft and mushy. If there's a hard white speck in the middle, it's undercooked. Grains should separate easily.

8. Remove from heat. Let the pilaf rest, covered, for 5 minutes.

9. Uncover the pot. Use a fork to fluff the grain and release the steam.

10. Adjust seasonings and serve the pilaf while it is very hot.

 See Recipe Card 71, "Rice Pilaf."

Preparing Risotto Risotto (rih-ZOT-toh) is an Italian rice dish typically made with arborio rice, a special type of short-grain rice with a round shape that becomes creamy when cooked. Just as with a pilaf, the rice is sautéed. Then a small amount of liquid is added to the rice and stirred until it is absorbed. More liquid is added gradually and the rice is stirred constantly. This makes a creamy dish. A properly cooked risotto has a soft, almost pourable consistency.

Risotto

1. Heat oil or butter in a pot.

2. Add onions and sauté, stirring frequently, until softened.

3. Add rice all at once and sauté, stirring frequently, until well coated with oil or butter.

4. Add one-fourth of the liquid to the grain and bring to a simmer. Stir constantly until the rice has absorbed all the liquid.

5. Add remaining liquid in three more additions, stirring and simmering until the grain absorbs one addition of liquid before you add the next one.

6. Remove the pot from the heat and stir in butter and any other ingredients called for in your recipe.

7. Serve the risotto at once.

See Recipe Card 72, "Risotto."

 **Reading Checkpoint**   *What are the steps in preparing a pilaf?*

Presenting Grains

Grains are versatile. They can be served hot or cold, at any meal, as a side dish, an entrée, or an appetizer.

Hot Grain Dishes Many grain dishes are best when they are served as soon as possible after they are cooked. Serve hot grain dishes on heated plates so they will hold their heat. Grains can be seasoned, flavored, and garnished to make them more interesting and flavorful. Hot grain dishes can be served as an entrée, a side dish, or an appetizer.

Cold Grain Salads Many grains are served cold as a salad. Rice, barley, and cracked wheat are some examples. Grains to use in a salad must be fully cooked and tender.

CHEF'S TIP

PILAF AND RISOTTO

Pilafs and risottos call for large amounts of liquid. If you heat the liquid in a separate pot before you add it to the grain, the cooking time is reduced because the liquid is already at a simmer.

The cooked grains are then combined with a dressing or other sauce along with additional ingredients such as vegetables, fruits, or meats. Serve grain salads on chilled plates. Cold grain salads are typically served as a side dish or as an appetizer.

 **Reading Checkpoint** *What is the correct way to serve a hot grain dish?*

FIGURE 13-4 ▶
Tabouli
A cold Middle Eastern salad that consists of bulgur, chopped tomatoes, parsley, mint, and scallions.
Classifying *Is this a warm-weather presentation or a cold-weather presentation?*

13.1 ASSESSMENT

Reviewing Concepts

1. What are the four common parts of a single seed of grain?
2. What are the three major types of grain?
3. What are the basic steps involved in boiling or steaming grains?
4. Why are grains regarded as being versatile?

Critical Thinking

5. **Comparing/Contrasting** What is the difference between masa harina, polenta, and hominy grits?
6. **Applying Concepts** Why do wheat berries take longer to cook than bulgur?
7. **Comparing/Contrasting** What is the difference between rolled oats and instant oats?

Test Kitchen

Prepare steel-cut oats, rolled oats, and instant oats. Time the preparation of each. Taste each finished cereal for taste and texture. Evaluate the results in terms of preparation time, taste, and texture.

SCIENCE

Parts of Grains

Research the individual seeds of rice, wheat, corn, oats, barley, rye, and quinoa. Draw and label the parts of each seed. For each grain, describe which component parts of the grain are removed by various types of processing.

READING PREVIEW

Key Concepts

- Identifying legumes
- Selecting and storing legumes
- Preparing legumes
- Presenting legumes

Vocabulary

- aflatoxin
- beans
- hummus
- legume
- lentils
- peas

> ❝**W**hether served as a simply flavored dish or made into complex stews or casseroles, beans have a place of importance, though not always of honor, in nearly every great cuisine.❞
>
> – Bill Phillips

Bill Phillips
The Culinary Institute of America

Legumes

A **legume** (LEG-yoom) is a plant with a double-seamed pod containing a single row of seeds. Depending on the variety of legume, people eat the seeds or the seeds together with the pods. As you know from Chapter 12, legumes such as green beans, where the seeds are eaten with the pods, are treated as vegetables. This chapter deals with legume seeds that are removed from the pod and dried. After they are dried, the seeds can be stored for long periods and then cooked by boiling them in water until tender enough to chew and digest easily.

There are three types of legumes. Dried legumes that are longer than they are round are called **beans**. Examples are navy beans, kidney beans, and fava beans. Legumes that are round are called **peas**. Examples of peas are black-eyed peas, green peas, and chickpeas, which are also known as garbanzo (gar-BAHN-zoh) beans or ceci (cheh-chee).

The third type of legume is called **lentils**. They are shaped like round disks. Peanuts, although we think of them as a type of nut, are really a type of bean.

Reading Checkpoint   *What are legumes?*

Selecting and Storing Legumes

Good-quality legumes have a uniform size and smooth skins. Most legumes are sorted and cleaned when they are packaged. A package should have a minimum of shriveled or crushed legumes.

Selecting Legumes Dried legumes are sold in bags, boxes, or packages. The packaging should be intact, with no rips or tears. You can buy legumes in packages of varying sizes.

Canned legumes have usually been cooked and should be soft and ready to eat. They should arrive in cans that are free of dents. The cans should not bulge, and there should be no signs that the contents of the can have started to leak. Beans come in various size cans.

Storing Legumes Buy legumes in quantities that will last for no more than one month. Legumes continue to age as they are held in storage. Very old legumes may have a musty flavor. Old legumes also take more time to soak, require more water to cook properly, and may take longer to cook.

Store legumes in airtight and moisture-proof containers. Keep the containers in a cool, dry storage area, at least 6 inches off the floor.

If dry legumes become damp during handling or storage, they can develop a dull or furry coating of mold. There is no way to get rid of the mold once it has formed. Legumes that are infected with this mold may develop a dangerous toxic substance known as an **aflatoxin** (aff-la-TOX-in).

Reading Checkpoint   *Why is it important to store legumes properly?*

Preparing Legumes

All dried legumes need to be sorted and rinsed before cooking. Most also need soaking time for softening.

Sorting and Rinsing Dry Legumes Sort and rinse legumes before cooking them. This step removes anything you don't want in the dish you are making, such as small stones. You can also get rid of any legumes that have shriveled or cracked. Never use a legume that is moldy.

Legumes

▲ Great Northern
White beans used to make soups and stews as well as baked beans.

▲ Kidney Beans
Dark red beans, available in various sizes.

▲ Chickpeas
Round legume with a tan color, popular in Middle Eastern dishes.

▲ Fava Beans
Large, flat beans that are green when fresh and brown when dried. Also known as broad bean.

▲ Black-Eyed Peas
Round, beige legume with a pronounced black dot, which is referred to as the "eye."

▲ Lentils
Lentils can be brown or red. They are popular in Indian cooking.

▲ Black Beans
Shiny, small beans, sometimes known as turtle beans, used in Caribbean and South American dishes.

▲ Split Peas
Split peas can be green or yellow. Also known as a field pea. Popular in soups.

▲ Pinto Beans
Pinto beans have a streaked red-and-white skin. They are used in many Mexican dishes.

SORTING BEANS

An efficient way to sort beans is to spread them in an even layer in a shallow pan. Work from one end to the other in rows, pushing each row toward one end of the pan to keep them from mixing with the unsorted beans.

Once you have sorted the legumes, put them in a large container. Add enough cold water to cover them completely. Stir them in the water to loosen any dirt. Legumes that are light enough to float to the top of the water either are very dry or may have been attacked by insects that eat out the inside of the bean. It's usually best to eliminate these.

Pour the legumes into a colander so water can drain away. Then rinse with fresh, cool water.

CULINARY SCIENCE

Dehydrating and Rehydrating Foods

When you let a food dry out, whether by accident or on purpose, the food shrinks and gets lighter. This happens because the food is losing moisture. And although this is good if you want to keep the food from spoiling, it is not so good if you want to eat the food. To make the food moist enough

▲ *Three types of dried beans*

to chew and enjoy, you need to put moisture back into the food.

Dehydration (taking moisture out of foods) is a traditional method of preserving foods. It works especially well with grains and legumes, although it is also common for mushrooms, fruits, sausages, meats, and fish.

Sometimes your job as a cook is to turn dried foods into flavorful, moist, and tender dishes. Steaming, boiling, and simmering techniques all add water to

foods, so these are the most appropriate cooking techniques. You may need to give these techniques a boost by soaking dried foods in cold water. No matter how you put dried foods and water together, what you are doing is rehydrating them.

You know that dried foods are properly cooked when they are tender enough to bite into easily. More than just getting softer, some dried food also gets bigger and plumps up. It weighs more than it did before you added water to it. Dried food changes in three ways when you rehydrate it:

- Size (or volume)
- Weight
- Texture (dry versus moist and tender versus hard)

The difference in texture is obvious. When you bite into food, you are testing its texture. To measure the change in volume and weight, you can use both a measuring cup and a scale.

Experiment

Measure the volume of a 1-pound batch of navy beans by using a measuring cup. Completely prepare the beans, using the long-soak method. After cooking the beans, measure the volume increase and the weight increase. Convert the increases to a percentage. By what percent did the beans increase in volume? In weight?

Soaking Dry Legumes Beans and other legumes have a protective skin. Soaking legumes before cooking softens the skin so they will cook more quickly. Most legumes need to be soaked before cooking. Some, such as lentils and split peas, are ready to boil without soaking. If a recipe requires that you soak the legumes, use one of these techniques:

- **Quick-Soak Method.** Combine the sorted and rinsed beans in a large pot with enough cold water to cover them by about 2 inches. Bring to a boil; then remove the pot from the heat, cover tightly, and let the beans soak for about 1 hour. Drain the beans and rinse once more before cooking them.

- **Long-Soak Method.** Combine sorted and rinsed beans in a large container with enough cold water to cover them by about 3 inches. Refrigerate the beans as they soak. See the following table for soaking times. Drain the beans and rinse once more before cooking them.

Dried legumes can be stored at room temperature for quite a long time. However, once you cook them, legumes need to be handled like other potentially hazardous food. Cool cooked legumes quickly if you must store them. Keep them at a safe temperature during service so pathogens do not make the foods unsafe to eat.

Using Canned Legumes Canned legumes are already cooked. During the canning process, the legumes are combined with a liquid to keep them moist. Before using canned legumes in a recipe, pour them out of the can into a colander and rinse them well. Rinsing away the canning liquid reduces the legumes' sodium content.

▲
FIGURE 13-5
Rinsing Beans
Put sorted beans in a large container with enough water to cover them.
Applying Concepts *Why do you put sorted beans in a large container before rinsing them?*

 **Reading Checkpoint** *How do the quick-soak method and the long-soak method for preparing legumes differ?*

Presenting Legumes

Bean dishes are an interesting part of many cuisines. They may be served as a side dish, as a soup, as a main dish, or as an appetizer. Some bean dishes are served hot and others are served cold.

Legume Dishes You can serve legumes directly after they are simmered. They are also often cooked together with other ingredients to make a stew, soup, or chili.

Soaking and Cooking Times for Legumes

Legume	Soaking Time (Long-Soak Method)	Cooking Time
Black beans	4 hours	1½ hours
Black-eyed peas	No soaking necessary	1 hour
Chickpeas	4 hours	2–2½ hours
Fava beans	12 hours	3 hours
Great Northern beans	4 hours	1 hour
Kidney beans (red or white)	4 hours	1 hour
Lentils	No soaking necessary	30–40 minutes
Peas, split	No soaking necessary	30 minutes
Peas, whole	4 hours	40 minutes
Pinto beans	4 hours	1–1½ hours

▲ **FIGURE 13-6**
Rice and Beans
Red kidney beans and black-eyed peas with rice and vegetables.
Inferring *Why are dishes such as red beans and rice often described as a healthy alternative to meats?*

Cooked legumes can be mashed or pureed after they are cooked. **Hummus** (HOOM-uhs), for example, is a popular Middle-Eastern spread made from mashed or pureed chickpeas that are seasoned and served with pita bread, chips, or raw vegetables. Refried beans are made by mashing beans and cooking them with a fat such as lard or oil. Beans can be added to soups as an ingredient or the soup can be made primarily from beans. Examples of bean soups include Senate bean soup, a Caribbean-style black bean soup, and split-pea soups.

Adding Cooked Legumes to Other Dishes Throughout the world, dishes that combine grains and legumes provide an important way of maintaining a healthy diet. Grain and legume combinations can be served as a main dish or as a side dish. Examples include red beans and rice and "Hoppin' John," a dish made with rice and black-eyed peas.

Cooking Dry Legumes

1 Sort and rinse legumes before preparing them.

2 Soak legumes, if necessary, using either the long-soak or quick-soak method.

3 Place in a pot and add cold water to cover legumes by about 2 inches.

4 Bring to a boil. Stir occasionally to keep from sticking to the pan.

5 Continue boiling until legumes are nearly tender.

6 Skim the foam to improve the flavor of the finished dish.

7 Add salt, as well as any acidic ingredients (tomatoes, vinegar, citrus juices, for instance) called for by your recipe, during the final third of cooking time.

8 Cook until tender enough to mash easily. However, the skins should still be intact.

9 Drain fully cooked legumes or cool and hold them in their cooking liquid for later use.

See Recipe Card 73, "Stewed White Beans."

Combining legumes and grains is a good, inexpensive way to increase protein, fiber, and vitamins in your diet. A meal of rice and beans, for example, contains more fiber, vitamins, and minerals than meat. It contains less fat, especially saturated fat, than meat. And, far from adding cholesterol to your diet as meats do, rice and beans actually help your body clear out cholesterol.

Legume Salads After legumes are fully cooked and tender, they can be cooled and prepared as a salad. Legume salads are often served as a side dish or as part of an appetizer. To make a legume salad, combine the cooked and drained legumes with the desired dressing or sauce. Add additional ingredients such as herbs, chopped tomatoes, onions, and other vegetables. Serve legume salads on chilled plates.

Most dressings added to legumes in a salad contain either vinegar or lemon juice. This toughens the skin of the legumes. To keep the texture of legumes in salads creamy and soft, make the salad as close as possible to the serving time.

 **Reading Checkpoint** *Name several ways you might present cooked legumes.*

Figure 13-7
Lentil Salad
A cold Greek salad made with green lentils, black olives, and lemon juice.
Solving Problems *Can you think of an additional ingredient that you might consider adding to this salad?*

13.2 ASSESSMENT

Reviewing Concepts

1. What are legumes?
2. Identify three types of legumes. Briefly describe each.
3. How do you typically prepare legumes for cooking?
4. How can you use legumes in creating various dishes?

Critical Thinking

5. **Comparing/Contrasting** What are the major differences between the quick-soak method for preparing legumes and the long-soak method?
6. **Applying Concepts** If some stored beans have mold growing on them, would you feel safe in using other beans from the same storage container?
7. **Predicting** Restaurants sometimes hold a bean salad for days. Assuming that the salad is held at a safe temperature, is this a good idea? Explain your answer.

Test Kitchen

Prepare dried beans using the quick-soak method and the long-soak method. Compare them in terms of flavor and texture with a can of prepared beans that have been rinsed. Evaluate the results.

SOCIAL STUDIES

Winter-Time Legume Dishes
Because legumes are inexpensive, easily stored, and highly nutritious, they are often used as an important part of the winter diet. Research hearty legume dishes suitable for a winter dinner. Describe the dish. Make sure to indicate the country or region in which the dish originated. If possible, make the dish.

13.3 Pasta

READING PREVIEW

Key Concepts

- Identifying types of pasta
- Preparing pasta
- Presenting pasta

Vocabulary

- al dente
- dumplings
- extruded
- fettuccini
- gnocchi
- lasagna
- lo mein
- macaroni
- pasta
- pierogi
- ravioli
- semolina flour
- spaetzle
- tagliatelle
- tortellini
- udon
- wontons
- wrappers

> **"M**y mother introduced me to pasta. True to the Italian saying that food is first eaten with the eyes, then the mouth, she transformed flour and eggs into ribbons, curls, butterflies, half-moons, and angel hair. **"**
>
> – Julia della Croce

Types of Pasta

Pasta is Italian for dough. The term is also used to describe the category of starchy foods made from shaped dough that includes flour and liquid. Pasta is typically cooked in boiling or simmering water. Almost every cuisine has some dish that is similar to pasta. The names of the dishes vary, but the concept—starchy foods made from shaped dough that includes flour and water—remains the same. The variety of names is just an imaginative way to dress up one of the world's simple staple foods.

The term pasta is most often associated with Italian cuisine. **Macaroni** is another common name used to refer to pasta in general. It, too, is associated with Italian cuisine. Wheat flour is commonly used in Italian pasta.

Asian-style pastas are more often known as noodles, as are the pastas made in some parts of France and Germany. Asian-style noodles often use flours made from beans or rice.

Julia della Croce
Ultimate Pasta, 1999

Figure 13-8
Flavored Fresh Pasta
Adding vegetables, herbs, and spices to pasta changes its flavor and color.
Solving Problems *What additional ingredients might you choose to get the colors in the pastas shown here?*

▼

Dumplings are made from dough that is soft enough to drop into a pot of boiling water. **Spaetzle** (SHPET-zuhl) is a popular Austrian and German dumpling. **Gnocchi** (NYOH-kee) is an Italian dumpling. **Pierogi** (peer-OH-gee) are Polish half-moon shaped dumplings. They can have a sweet or a savory filling and can be fried or boiled.

Pasta is made in a wide variety of shapes and is available in two forms:

- Fresh pasta
- Dried pasta

Fresh Pasta Fresh pasta consists of dough made by blending flour with a liquid such as water or eggs. The dough is soft enough to knead by hand, but stiff enough to hold a shape. Fresh pasta should feel smooth and supple. It should not appear dry or crumbly. It can be rolled into thin sheets and cut into shapes. After cooking, fresh pasta has a delicate texture.

Fresh pasta may be plain or it may be flavored with vegetables, fruits, spices, or herbs. These additional ingredients add both flavor and color to the pasta.

If your kitchen does not make its own dough, fresh pasta can usually be purchased. Fresh pasta is typically available commercially in sheets and in ribbon shapes such as **fettuccini** (feht-too-CHEE-nee) or **tagliatelli** (tag-lee-ah-TEHL-ee). Many Asian-style pastas, such as **udon** (oo-DOHN) or **lo mein** (low mane) noodles, can also be purchased fresh. **Wrappers** are another type of pasta used frequently in Asian cooking. Wrappers are sold in squares, rounds, and rectangles. They can be made from wheat or rice flour.

Fresh pasta or noodles are often dusted with cornstarch to keep the sheets or strands from sticking together. Keep fresh pasta in its packaging in the refrigerator or the freezer.

Dried Pasta Dry pasta is also made by blending flour with a liquid such as water or eggs to create dough. However, the dough is usually too stiff to shape by hand, so most dry pastas are made by machines. These pasta-making machines can create the same flat ribbon shapes found in fresh pastas. The dough can also be **extruded** (pushed through an opening in a pasta-making machine) to make special shapes, such

Soba Noodles (Dry)
Soba noodles are made from buckwheat flour and have a brown color. They are popular in Japanese cooking.

Flat Pasta (Dry)
Flat pasta is usually made from semolina flour and water. Flat pasta shapes include linguini (pictured here) and fettuccini. They may be sold as straight strands or in "nests."

Wrappers (Fresh)
Wrappers can be made from wheat or rice flour. They are used to make a variety of Asian-style dishes.

Egg Noodles (Fresh)
Egg noodles are made from wheat and eggs. They have a flat shape after they are cooked. They may have curly edges and are available in many sizes, from fine egg noodles to broad noodles.

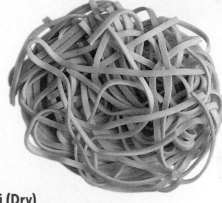

Rice Vermicelli (Dry)
This Asian pasta is made from rice instead of wheat. The noodles are very white after cooking.

as elbow macaroni, spaghetti, or penne. The shaped pasta is then dried until it is hard and brittle. Dry pasta should have an even color and break cleanly without bending.

Italian-style pasta is usually made with **semolina flour** (seh-muh-LEE-nuh), pale yellow flour made from durum (DUR-um) wheat. Durum is very hard wheat that has a high protein content and makes an elastic dough. Semolina flour give pasta a pleasing, chewy texture after it is cooked.

Flours from other grains—including rice, chickpeas, buckwheat, quinoa, and millet—can be used to make dry pastas. These pastas have unique flavors and textures. They may be important to have on hand if you need to cook for people on a wheat- or gluten-free diet.

As with fresh pasta, dry pasta can also be flavored with a number of different ingredients to give them a special color or flavor.

Pasta is sold commercially in packages of various sizes, from 1-pound boxes to bulk packaging. Store dry pasta either in its original packaging or in airtight and moisture-proof containers in a cool, dry

Dried Pasta Shapes

Shells ▼

Elbow Macaroni ▲

Penne (PEN-nay) ◀

Manicotti (man-uh-KOT-tee) ▶

Rigatoni (ree-gah-TOE-nee) ◀

area. Keep pasta off the floor so pests cannot get into the packages. Do not let the packaging or the pasta become damp.

 **Reading Checkpoint** *In what forms is pasta available?*

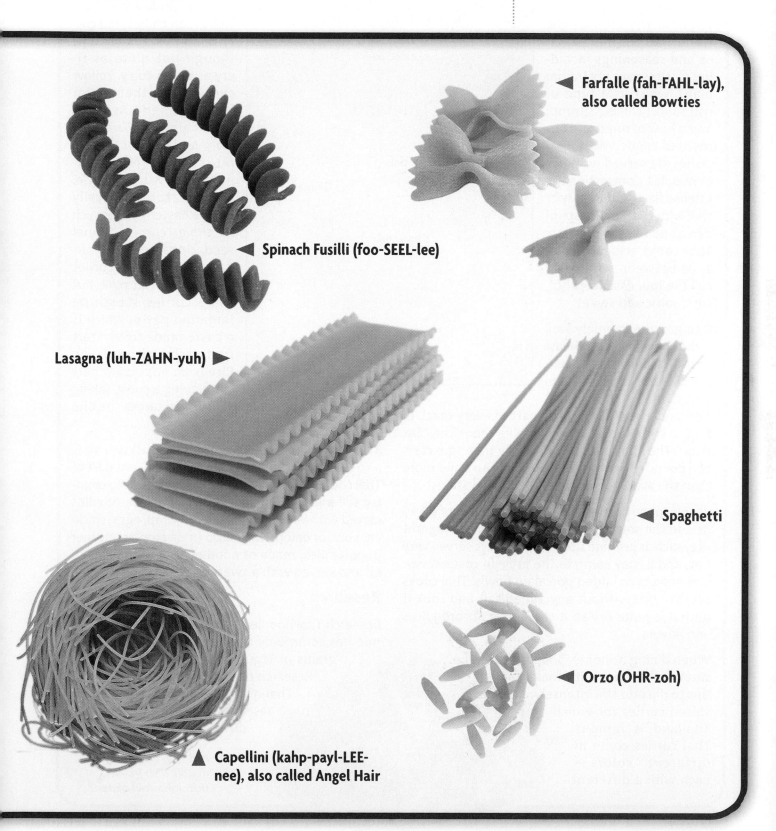

◀ **Farfalle (fah-FAHL-lay), also called Bowties**

◀ **Spinach Fusilli (foo-SEEL-lee)**

Lasagna (luh-ZAHN-yuh) ▶

◀ **Spaghetti**

◀ **Orzo (OHR-zoh)**

▲ **Capellini (kahp-payl-LEE-nee), also called Angel Hair**

Thailand

The cuisine of Thailand has recently been growing in popularity all over the world. Traditional Thai dishes and seasonings including curries; **nam pla (**nahm plah), which is a type of fish sauce; chilies; shrimp; and a host of dried and fermented foods. Most Thai dishes are served with rice or noodles. Contrasting the intense flavors of a curry or chili with the bland taste of rice or noodles is one way Thai cooks achieve a balance between what they call the four essences: hot, sour, salty, and sweet.

Rice grows extremely well throughout all of Southeast Asia. Thailand is at the center of the Southeast Asian peninsula. Throughout Thailand, rice is the central part of every meal. In fact, a common greeting is "Kin khao!" or "Eat rice!" The Thai people eat nearly three quarters of a pound of rice every day—nearly 40 times more than the average person in the United States.

People in the northern part of Thailand favor sticky rice. In the south, they prefer long-grain fragrant rice, such as jasmine rice. Rice is always served very hot, and it may come to the table in covered woven baskets or lidded porcelain bowls. Thai cooks prepare rice without any added salt and cook it until it is quite dry so it can better absorb juices and flavors.

When dining at home, people may make small balls of rice with their fingertips to dip into the intensely spiced curries for which Thailand is famous. Thai curries come in different colors— each with a different

level of spiciness. Green curry includes the hottest green chilies; red curry is also extremely hot, though not quite as fiery as green curry. Yellow curries get their color from turmeric, a spice that came to Thailand from Malaysia or Burma. **Mussaman** (MUSS-ah-mahn), or Muslim-style, curry features typically Middle Eastern spices such as clove, cumin, fennel seed, cinnamon, and cardamom. Most Thai curries include coconut milk, but some curries substitute tamarind paste, which is a paste made from a tart fruit with a citrus flavor. Rice is an important part of enjoying a curry. Taking a bite of rice cools your mouth and tames the bite of the chilies in the curry.

Rice, along with wheat, beans, and buckwheat, is also made into noodles, another significant part of Thai cooking. Street vendors throughout the country sell **pad thai** (pahd tie), a dish of rice noodles served with bean sprouts, dried shrimp, eggs, chicken, pork, or onions. **Mee krop** (mee crop) is another popular dish, made of noodles that are puffed in oil and served with a sweet dressing.

Research

Research Thai noodles. What are the names of the noodles commonly used in Thai cooking? What grains or legumes are they made from? Research recipes for different styles of Thai noodle dishes. Based on your research, prepare a Thai noodle dish.

◀ *Pad Thai is a traditional noodle dish found throughout Thailand.*

Preparing Pasta

Preparing pasta involves first making the pasta dough and preparing the actual pasta. After that, the pasta is boiled before it is presented. Using commercially prepared pasta saves you the time and effort of making fresh pasta dough and then rolling out the dough to make pasta.

Fresh Pasta Dough Fresh pasta dough is simple to prepare. After making the dough, you need to let it rest before rolling it out with a pasta machine or a rolling pin.

Boiling Pasta Boiling pasta softens it so it is easy to eat. Fresh pasta is already moist when it goes into the pot, so it cooks very quickly. You can usually cook fresh pasta as you need it.

Dried pasta, on the other hand, typically takes longer to cook, so you may need to prepare the pasta ahead of time and then reheat it in simmering water immediately before you serve it. To hold pasta for later service, rinse or submerge it in cold water until it is well chilled. After it is chilled, drain it thoroughly and mix it with a little oil.

BASIC CULINARY SKILLS

Fresh Egg Pasta

1 Combine flour and salt in a bowl. Make a well in the center.

2 Add liquid (usually eggs and water) in the well. If your recipe calls for oil, add it with the liquid ingredients.

3 Pull flour into the liquid, stirring by hand until a loose mass forms. Work as rapidly as possible. Adjust consistency with additional flour or water as needed.

4 Turn dough out onto a floured work surface.

5 Knead until the texture becomes smooth and elastic.

Continued on next page

Grains, Legumes, & Pasta ▶ **421**

Fresh Egg Pasta *Continued*

6 Gather and smooth the kneaded dough into a ball. If the ball is too large for your pasta machine, you can cut it.

7 Cover dough. Let it rest at room temperature for at least 1 hour.

8 Roll dough into thin sheets. Cut into desired shapes by hand or by using a pasta machine.

9 Cook pasta. Or store in a refrigerator for up to 2 days.

 *See Recipe Card 75, "Fresh Egg Pasta."*

Transfer the pasta to a storage container, cover it, and keep it refrigerated until you are ready to reheat it for service.

Dried semolina pasta is traditionally cooked **al dente** (al DEN-tay). This Italian expression means "to the tooth," and it is used to describe pasta that is cooked only until it gives a slight resistance when you bite it. The pasta should be neither too soft nor too hard.

 Reading Checkpoint *What are the steps in boiling pasta?*

Presenting Pasta

Pasta is an extremely popular food. It can be served hot, as an appetizer, as the main course, or as a side dish. It can also be served cold in salads. Pasta is also added to other dishes, such as soups.

Adding Sauce to Pasta Combining pasta with a sauce is perhaps the most common way to present pasta. Different pasta shapes are traditionally paired with different types of sauces. Long, thin shapes, such as spaghetti or linguini, are traditionally paired with a smooth, thin

Boiling Pasta

1 Bring a large pot of water to a boil and add salt. Use at least 1 gallon of water for every pound of pasta. Add 1 ounce of salt (2 tablespoons) to every gallon of water.

2 Add pasta and stir until it is softened, submerged, and separated.

- Fresh and filled pasta is best when prepared in simmering, not boiling, water.
- Dried pasta is cooked at a boil throughout the entire cooking time.

3 Cook until done, stirring occasionally. Pasta that is served immediately is cooked until fully tender. Pasta that will be baked, reheated, or held in a sauce should be slightly undercooked.

4 Drain pasta in a colander as soon as it is cooked.

5 Serve pasta immediately with a sauce or toss the pasta with oil, chill, and store for later service.

sauce that can cling to the pasta, such as a tomato sauce or a cream sauce. Sometimes the sauce is as simple as good olive oil. Extruded tube-shaped pasta shapes such as rigatoni or penne are most often paired with chunkier sauces. Pasta shapes with wrinkles or ridges, such as fusilli, are also used with a chunky sauce.

CHEF'S TIP

USING A PASTRY BAG

Use a pastry bag to add a soft filling to pasta. The bag should not have a tip. Spoon the filling into the bag. Then twist the large end of the bag to force the filling into the pasta. Stop twisting to stop pressing out the filling.

FIGURE 13-9
Making ravioli or tortellini
Adding filling to fresh pasta rounds.
Applying Concepts *How can this method be used to make either ravioli or tortellini?*

▼

To add a sauce to pasta, first drain the pasta well after cooking to remove any water that is still clinging to it or that is trapped inside tube-shaped pasta. Extra water dilutes the flavor of the sauce and might make it too thin to cling to the pasta properly.

There are two methods for combining cooked and drained pasta with a sauce:

- You can add the pasta directly to the sauce and then toss them together. This is typically done in a sauté pan over medium-high heat. This method of combining sauce and pasta guarantees that the pasta dish is very hot when you serve it.
- You can ladle the sauce over the drained pasta on a heated plate. You need to make sure that the pasta, the sauce, and the bowl or platter are very hot. Otherwise, the pasta will cool off too quickly.

Baked Pasta Dishes To assemble a simple baked pasta dish such as macaroni and cheese, you combine the pasta with the sauce and any other fillings. With any baked pasta dish, make sure to slightly under-cook the pasta. The pasta will finish cooking as it bakes.

Lasagna (luh-ZAHN-yuh) is a layered pasta dish. To put it together, you put layers of sauce, pasta, and filling into an oiled dish. You may add a topping, such as grated cheese or breadcrumbs. The dish is baked until the pasta is fully cooked and tender. All the ingredients, including the sauce and fillings, should be very hot. If there is a topping, it should be golden brown.

Filled Pasta Dishes Pasta shells can be filled with various foods, including cheese, meats, seafood, and vegetables. Dried pasta is filled after the pasta is cooked. Fresh pasta is typically filled before it is cooked.

To add a filling to dried pasta, you first need to cook the pasta. Leave it slightly undercooked if you are planning to cook the pasta again after it is filled. Drain the pasta and cool it so you can handle it without burning yourself. Then spoon or pipe the filling into the pasta.

Ravioli and tortellini are two familiar Italian-style filled pastas made with fresh pasta. **Ravioli** (rav-ee-OH-lee) is Italian for "little wraps." Ravioli is made by layering a filling between two sheets of pasta and then cutting out filled squares, rounds, or rectangles. **Tortellini** (tohr-te-LEEN-ee) is Italian for "little twists." Tortellini is made by cutting out circles or squares of fresh pasta, adding a filling, and then folding and twisting the dough to get a specific shape.

Other cuisines also have a strong tradition of filled pastas. **Wontons** (WAHN-tahns) are a type of Chinese tortellini made with a fresh pasta wrapper. They are often served as appetizers or in soups.

To make filled pasta using fresh pasta, you can make your own dough or you can buy commercially prepared fresh pasta sheets or wrappers. After fresh pasta is filled, simmer it until the pasta is tender and the filling is very hot.

Serve filled pasta as is, with a sauce, or use it as a garnish for a soup. Filled pasta can be served immediately with a sauce or it can be baked with a sauce and then served.

**FIGURE 13-10
Saucing Pasta**
Pasta shells with meat sauce.
Applying Concepts *Why is this sauce a good choice to pair with this pasta shape?*

 **Reading Checkpoint** *What are the two ways to combine cooked pasta with sauce?*

13.3 ASSESSMENT

Reviewing Concepts

1. What is the difference between fresh and dried pasta?
2. How does cooking fresh pasta differ from cooking dried pasta?
3. What are the two methods for combining cooked and drained pasta with a sauce?

Critical Thinking

4. **Comparing/Contrasting** What are the advantages and disadvantages of using fresh versus dried pasta in a restaurant?
5. **Recognizing Patterns** What type of sauce would be best suited for farfalle pasta?
6. **Drawing Conclusions** Can you think of any disadvantages of adding pasta directly to the sauce before serving (as opposed to ladling the sauce over the cooked and drained pasta)?

Test Kitchen

Prepare a batch of fresh fettuccini and a batch of dried fettuccini. Compare the cooking time. Taste the finished pasta and evaluate the differences between the two pastas.

SOCIAL STUDIES

Origin of Pasta

Research the history and origins of pasta. Describe your findings. Indicate which pasta dishes today resemble the most ancient pasta dishes.

Review and Assessment

Reviewing Content

Choose the letter that best answers the question or completes the statement.

1. The edible seed of grain without its husk or hull is called the:
   a. germ
   b. kernel
   c. bran
   d. endosperm

2. Which of the following is not a legume?
   a. lentil
   b. chickpea
   c. oat
   d. pinto bean

3. Italian style pasta is usually made with what kind of flour?
   a. buckwheat flour
   b. rice flour
   c. semolina flour
   d. corn flour

4. A pearl grain is grain that:
   a. is round
   b. has been scrubbed of its bran
   c. has been boiled
   d. has been soaked in a solution of lime

5. The quick-soak method for cooking black beans involves letting the beans soak for:
   a. 12 hours
   b. 4 hours
   c. 1 hour
   d. ½ hour

6. Hominy is the whole dried kernel of what grain?
   a. wheat
   b. rice
   c. oats
   d. corn

7. Bulgur is:
   a. made from corn that has been soaked in a solution of lime
   b. made from parcooked rice
   c. made from steamed whole wheat berries that are crushed
   d. made from steamed groats that are rolled into flat flakes

Understanding Concepts

8. What does the term farinaceous mean?

9. What is the difference between a legume and a grain?

10. What is fresh pasta?

11. What is a whole grain?

12. Is a lentil classed as a legume or a grain?

13. Which type of grain is more processed: a whole grain or a refined grain?

14. Why are legumes sorted before being rinsed?

Critical Thinking

15. **Comparing/Contrasting** What is the difference between preparing grains by boiling them versus preparing them by steaming them?

16. **Predicting** You are planning to make filled pasta using large, dried shell pasta. After filling, the pasta will be baked. To what degree of doneness will you cook the pasta before it is filled? Explain your answer.

Culinary Math

17. **Solving Problems** A 10-serving recipe for lasagna calls for 14 ounces of ricotta cheese. How much cheese is required to make 65 servings?

18. **Applying Concepts** If a 10-serving recipe calls for 2½ pounds of spaghetti, how much pasta is a single serving?

On the Job

19. **Applying Concepts** If you ran an Italian restaurant, which method of adding sauce to pasta would you prefer? Explain your answer.

20. **Communicating** A customer asks you the difference between rice pilaf and risotto. How would you answer? (Remember that the customer wants to know not only how they differ in preparation but also how they differ in flavor and texture.)

RECIPE CARDS

Use the following Recipe Cards to test your culinary skill.

69. Boiled Rice
70. Polenta
71. Rice Pilaf
72. Risotto
73. Stewed White Beans
74. Refried Beans
75. Fresh Egg Pasta
76. Couscous with Lamb and Chicken Stew
77. Pasta alla Carbonara
78. Tortellini
79. Lasagne
80. Macaroni and Cheese
81. Soba Noodles with Sesame

LAB ACTIVITY

Project 13: Preparing Rice

Answer these questions when your class works through Project 13.

• Do you think different types of rice absorb varying amounts of water as they cook?

• Do different types of rice have different cooking times?

• Do some types expand more than other types?

• What are the differences in taste and texture between long-grain rice and short-grain rice? Between brown rice and white rice?

TEST PRACTICE

Choose the letter that best answers the question or completes the statement.

1. Basmati rice is what type of rice?
   A   wild rice
   B   long-grain rice
   C   medium-grain rice
   D   short-grain rice

2. What is the cooking time for fava beans?
   A   12 hours
   B   4 hours
   C   3 hours
   D   1 hour

3. What is spaetzle?
   A   a type of grain
   B   a type of legume
   C   a type of pasta
   D   a dangerous toxic substance that can develop on legumes

4. Masa harina is made from:
   A   posole cornmeal
   B   semolina flour
   C   rice flour
   D   hominy grits

5. Using the long-soak method, how long should lentils be soaked?
   A   12 hours
   B   4 hours
   C   1 hour
   D   No soaking is necessary

6. Semolina flour is made from:
   A   bulgur
   B   cracked wheat
   C   durum wheat
   D   wheat berries

7. What portion of the grain contains most of the grain's carbohydrates?
   A   germ
   B   endosperm
   C   bran
   D   hull

8. What is orzo?
   A   a type of pasta
   B   a type of rice
   C   a type of legume
   D   a type of barley

9. What ingredient in corn cannot be used by our bodies unless the corn is first treated with lye?
   A   bran
   B   posole
   C   niacin
   D   fiber

10. How much salt should be added to every gallon of water used to boil pasta?
    A   ½ teaspoon
    B   1 teaspoon
    C   1 tablespoon
    D   1 ounce

STOCKS, SAUCES, & SOUPS

READING PREVIEW

Key Concepts

- Identifying basic ingredients for stocks
- Identifying types of stocks
- Preparing and storing stocks
- Using stocks

Vocabulary

- brown stock
- double-strength stock
- fish fumet
- fonds de cuisine
- glaze
- gravy
- neutral stock
- shellfish stock
- stock
- stock base
- vegetable stock
- white stock

> **"S**tock is liquid gold. **"**
> – Robert Danhi

Basic Ingredients for Stocks

A **stock** is a flavorful liquid used primarily to prepare soups, sauces, stews, and braises. The quality of a stock plays a major role in the quality of the soups and sauces you make with that stock. In fact, stocks are such an important part of classic French cooking that they are known as **fonds de cuisine** (FAHN duh kwee-ZEEN), which translates as "foundations of cooking."

Stocks are produced by simmering together the following basic types of ingredients:

- Bones, shells, or vegetables
- Mirepoix (and, often, additional aromatic ingredients)
- Spices and herbs
- A liquid (typically water)

Bones, Shells, or Vegetables The major ingredient in any stock determines its flavor, color, and body. A stock will use one of these major ingredients:

- **Beef and Veal Bones.** Use bones with some meat still clinging to them to give the stock a richer flavor.
- **Poultry Bones.** Use necks, wing tips, backs, or a cut-up chicken.
- **Fish Bones.** Use bones from flounder, sole, or any other lean white fish.
- **Shellfish Shells.** Use lobster, shrimp, or crayfish shells.

Robert Danhi, Executive Chef
Two Chefs on a Roll, Carson, CA

- **Vegetables.** Use a combination of vegetables for a rich, balanced flavor. Avoid starchy vegetables (potatoes or hard squash) to keep the stock from becoming cloudy. Also avoid vegetables that "bleed" such as beets.

Mirepoix Most stocks include a mirepoix. Remember from Chapter 6 that a combination of onions, carrots, and celery is a "standard mirepoix." A mirepoix in which parsnips replace the carrots (and often leeks replace some of the onions) is called a "white mirepoix." Some stock recipes call for additional aromatic ingredients such as dry white wine, mushrooms, leeks, garlic, tomato paste, or even ham. Different types of stocks will call for different mirepoix and different combinations of aromatic ingredients.

Spices and Herbs Dried spices such as whole peppercorns give stocks a pungent aroma. Fresh or dried herbs such as bay leaf, thyme, or parsley stems also provide aroma to stocks. Individual recipes will list the specific spices and herbs a stock requires. Remember to tie dried herbs and spices up into a sachet d'épices. Fresh herbs are tied into a bouquet garni. (Sachet d'épices and bouquet garni are discussed in Chapter 6.)

Liquid Most stocks begin with cold water, never hot water. This prevents cloudiness. It also allows the flavor and nutrients to be gently and evenly extracted as the liquid moves from cold to the beginning of simmering.

FIGURE 14-1
Basic Ingredients for Stock
Ingredients for a chicken stock
Applying Concepts *Is this a white stock or a brown stock?*

▼

Reading Checkpoint *What are the four types of basic ingredients used in stocks?*

Types of Stock

A stock is named for its major ingredient (and in the case of brown and white stocks, how that major ingredient is prepared). There are five basic types of stock:

- A **brown stock** is made from bones that are roasted until they have a deep reddish-brown color. Using roasted bones causes the stock to have a dark brown color and a fuller "roasted meat" flavor. Brown veal stock, made from roasted veal bones, is the most common type of brown stock.

- A **white stock** is made from unroasted bones. Some chefs blanch the bones by simmering them in water before starting to make the stock. White beef stock is sometimes called **neutral stock** because it has a very mild, unassertive flavor.

- A **fish fumet** (fyoo-MAY) is made by cooking fish bones in a little oil until they turn opaque (known as sweating) before adding water, mirepoix, spices, and herbs.
- A **shellfish stock** is made from shellfish shells that are sautéed in a little oil until they turn a deep vivid red before adding water, mirepoix, spices, and herbs.
- A **vegetable stock** contains a variety of vegetables that are cut or sliced before simmering.

 **Reading Checkpoint**   *What are the five basic types of stock?*

Five Basic Types of Stocks

Stock	Description	Ingredients for 1 Gallon of Stock
Brown stock	Roasted meat flavor, deep reddish-brown	8 pounds of roasted bones (meat or poultry) 1 pound of mirepoix 4 to 6 ounces tomato paste 1 sachet d'épices 6 quarts cold water
White stock	Mild flavor, almost colorless when hot	8 pounds of unroasted bones (meat, poultry, or fish) 1 pound of mirepoix 1 sachet d'épices 6 quarts cold water
Fish fumet	Fish flavor, very light color, translucent but not perfectly clear	11 pounds of fish bones (sweated) 1 pound white mirepoix 1 bouquet garni 4 quarts cold water
Shellfish stock	Seafood flavor, red to orange-red color, translucent but not perfectly clear	11 pounds of shells (lobster, shrimp, or crayfish) 1 pound mirepoix 1 sachet d'épices 6 quarts cold water
Vegetable stock	Varies according to vegetables selected	4 pounds of combined vegetables 1 pound mirepoix 1 sachet d'épices 4 quarts cold water

Preparing and Storing Stocks

As with most culinary efforts, much of the work of making a good stock is preparing the ingredients properly and choosing the right equipment to use. There are, however, three keys to success when simmering a stock:

- Keep the stock at a gentle simmer.
- Skim any foam or froth.
- Simmer long enough for a full flavor.

Preparing Bones Purchase beef or veal bones cut into short lengths. Pieces about 3 inches long are best. This releases more flavor into the stock.

White and brown stocks can use other types of bones. For lamb, venison, or pork bones, use the same simmering time as veal bones. For turkey, pheasant, or duck bones, use the same time as chicken bones.

The following additional preparation steps also play an important part in developing the best color and flavor.

- **Browning Bones.** Place the bones in a hot roasting pan and roast at 375° F or higher until the meat clinging to the bones turns a deep brown. Remove the bones and pour off the extra fat. Dissolve any drippings that accumulate in the roasting pan in a little water and then add them back to the stock.
- **Blanching Bones.** The purpose of blanching bones is to keep the color of a stock very pale or white. Place the bones in a large pot with enough cold water to cover them by about 3 inches. Bring the water to a simmer. Immediately drain and rinse the bones.

FIGURE 14-2
Sweating Fish Bones
Cook bones and mirepoix until they soften and begin to release moisture.
Drawing Conclusions *If you sweat the bones first, what type of stock are you making?*

- **Sweating Bones.** The flavor of a fish fumet is intensified by sweating the bones in a small amount of fat. Sweating, as you remember from Chapter 8, involves moderate heat. The goal is to gently cook the fish bones along with the mirepoix until they soften and begin to release their moisture. The flesh clinging to the bones becomes opaque. You may also hear this step referred to as "smothering," because the lid is left on the pot. Leave the bones in the pot and add the liquid and other ingredients.

Preparing Mirepoix Choose the ingredients for your mirepoix according to the type of stock you are making. A standard mirepoix (onions, carrots, and celery) is used for brown stocks. A white mirepoix (onions, leeks, celery, and parsnips) omits the carrots to keep white stock pale in color.

Cut the mirepoix into a size and shape that best suits your stock's cooking time. For stocks that cook for more than one hour, cut the mirepoix into a medium or large dice. For stocks that simmer less than one hour, cut the mirepoix into a small dice or thin slices.

Preparing a Sachet d'Epices or a Bouquet Garni

Wrap the ingredients for a sachet d'épices in a small piece of cheesecloth and tie the cheesecloth securely into a bundle with string. Gather together the ingredients for a bouquet garni into a bundle, wrap the bundle once or twice with string, and then tie the string securely.

Choosing Equipment

The main piece of equipment for preparing a stock is a stockpot. Stockpots are taller than they are wide. This helps them concentrate flavors in the stock. The stockpot should hold all of the ingredients and the liquid with at least 3 inches of space at the top. Check the bottom of the pot and choose one with a flat surface. For very large quantities of stock, restaurants often use a steam-jacketed kettle. As stock simmers, you will need a skimmer or flat spoon to skim foam from the surface. Removing foam from the surface keeps the stock clear.

Restaurants often use a stockpot with a spigot for draining the stock out of the pan without stirring up the other ingredients. If your pot does not have a spigot, you will need a large ladle to scoop the stock from the pot. To help keep the stock clear, try to disturb the bones as little as possible while you drain the stockpot or ladle out the stock.

When the stock is finished, you will need to strain it. To strain a stock, ladle or drain the stock carefully through a sieve or a cheesecloth-lined colander into containers suitable for cooling.

Preparing Fish Fumet

Fish fumet has a more noticeable flavor than a white stock made with fish bones. This increase in flavor is because the bones and the mirepoix are allowed to sweat before the water is added. Adding other aromatic ingredients such as dry white wine or mushrooms can also add more flavor. Fish bones are very delicate and release their flavor more quickly than animal or poultry bones. This means that the simmering time is shorter—45 minutes to 1 hour is enough for a good stock. When the cooking time is this short, you can add the sachet d'épices along with the cold water.

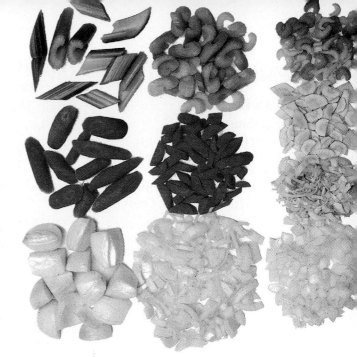

▲
FIGURE 14-3
Cutting Mirepoix
Cut the mirepoix into a shape that best suits the stock's total simmering time.
Recognizing Patterns *Why is mirepoix cut very fine for a fish fumet?*

▲
FIGURE 14-4
Stockpot
A steam-jacketed kettle with a spigot
Predicting *How can a spigot help improve a stock's appearance?*

More for Less

If you skim stock as it simmers, you remove most of the fat. Any remaining fat is easy to lift away once the stocks have chilled, making them virtually fat-free. Chefs trying to cut fat in dishes such as mashed potatoes, stuffings, or even vinaigrettes can substitute this fat-free stock for cream, butter, or oil. The result may be more flavorful than the original dish, with less fat.

FIGURE 14-5 ▶
Peeling Shrimp
Remove shrimp shells and reserve the meat for later use.
Applying Concepts *Why would a shellfish stock use a regular mirepoix, not a white mirepoix?*

Preparing Shellfish Stock Lobster, shrimp, and crayfish shells turn a deep red when they are sautéed in oil. This deepens the stock's flavor. The mirepoix (often with the addition of tomatoes) is also sautéed long enough to produce a deep color. Like fish bones, shellfish shells require only 45 minutes to 1 hour of simmering time to flavor a stock. Therefore, you should add the sachet d'épices when you add the cold water.

Preparing Vegetable Stock Vegetable stocks cook in 30 to 60 minutes if the vegetables are cut into small dice or thin slices. This is long enough to extract the flavor from the vegetables, but short enough to avoid developing a strong or bitter flavor. There are two optional steps you can use to vary the flavor and color of a vegetable stock. The vegetables can be allowed to sweat over low heat, in the same way that you sweat fish bones for a fumet. Or, you can roast the vegetables until brown, as you would for a brown stock.

BASIC CULINARY SKILLS

Brown Stock

1 Prepare the bones, mirepoix, and tomatoes.

2 Roast the bones, mirepoix, and tomatoes until they have a rich brown color.

3 Combine the roasted ingredients with cold water in a stockpot. Add water to dissolve drippings in the pan and add to the stockpot.

4 Simmer over medium heat for the recommended time.

5 Skim the surface to remove any foam.

6 Add sachet d'épices during the last 30 to 45 minutes of simmering time.

7 Strain the stock.

8 Cool the stock to below 41°F. Store in the refrigerator.

 See Recipe Card 82, "Brown Veal Stock."

White Stock

1 **Prepare** the unroasted bones and mirepoix. If you are blanching the bones, blanch them now.

2 **Combine** the ingredients with cold water in a stockpot.

3 **Simmer** over medium heat for the recommended time.

4 **Skim** the surface to remove any foam.

5 **Add** sachet d'épices during the last 30 to 45 minutes of simmering time.

6 **Strain** the stock.

7 **Cool** the stock to below 41°F. Store in the refrigerator.

 See Recipe Card 83, "Chicken Stock."

Using Prepared Stock Bases A **stock base** can be purchased in a highly concentrated form or as a powder or cube. These bases are made according the manufacturer's instructions and brought to a simmer. You can use them instead of stocks or you can add them to a stock you made yourself to give a weak stock more flavor.

Good quality stock bases from a manufacturer are made from the same basic ingredients as you would use to prepare your own stocks.

Nutrition Facts

Serving Size 1 cup (240ml)
Serv. Per Container about 4

Amount Per Serving

Calories 20	from Fat 0
	% Daily Value*

Fat 0 g	
Sodium 330mg	14%
Total Carb. 5 g	2%
Sugars 1 g	
Protein 0 g	

Nutrition Facts

Serving Size 1 Cup (9g) [1 Tbsp dry]
Servings Per Package 8

Amount Per Serving

Calories 30 Calories from fat 10	
	%Daily Value*
Total Fat 1g	2%
Saturated Fat 0g	0%
Cholesterol 0mg	0%
Sodium 780mg	33%
Total Carbohydrates 3g	1%
Dietary Fiber <1g	
Sugars 1g	3%
Protein 2g	

▲

FIGURE 14-6
Stock Bases
Labels from two brands of prepared stock base
Analyzing Information *Which of these stock bases relies more on sodium for flavor?*

However, some lower-quality stock bases list high-sodium ingredients on the label, ahead of meats, poultry, or vegetables. Use the highest quality stock base for the best results. For better results from a prepared stock base, simmer the base with meat and vegetable trimmings.

Storing Stocks Stocks that are not used immediately should be cooled and stored as quickly as possible after they are made. Cool stocks in an ice bath or with a chill wand. Once the stock is cool, transfer it to storage containers. Be sure to add a label with the stock's name and the date it was made. All stocks should be stored in the refrigerator or freezer.

✓ Reading Checkpoint   *What are the three keys to success when making stocks?*

CULINARY SCIENCE

Convection

Convection is one of the ways that heat travels through gases or liquids. A pot of stock simmering on the stove is a good example of using convection. As the stock pot sits on the burner, the pot gets warmer. Once the stock pot becomes hot, the liquid closest to the bottom heats up and begins to rise. Eventually, the warmed liquid rises to the top. Then, it starts to cool. As it cools, it falls. This constant rising and falling motion is known as *convection*.

You see convection beginning to take place when tiny bubbles form on the sides and bottom of a pot. After a while, the bubbles rise to the top of the pan. The hotter the liquid, the larger the bubbles, and the more action in the pot.

❝This constant rising and falling motion is known as convection.❞

You can influence convection when you stir foods. This is known as *mechanical convection* and helps keep the heat more even for a more consistent temperature.

As liquid moves from the bottom of the pot to the top, it can trap impurities and grease, eventually taking them to the top of the pot. That is why you skim away the impurities to make a clear, clean stock.

Experiment

Bring a large amount of water to a boil using a glass pot or pan. Add a few drops of food coloring. Analyze the color pattern for convection as the food coloring travels through the pot of water.

Using Stocks

Choosing the Right Stock Recipes often indicate the type of stock that should be used. A specific type of stock is selected to add the desired flavor, color, or texture to a dish.

- Use white or poultry stocks for dishes that should be a white or ivory color.
- Use a stock made from the same type of meat or fish featured in the recipe. For instance, use chicken stock for poached chicken breasts or fish fumet for poached fish.
- Use a brown stock for dishes that should be a dark color.
- Use a neutral stock to add body without adding a noticeable flavor. For instance, use white beef stock to make a vegetable soup or to cook beans.

Reducing Stocks To concentrate a stock's flavor and give it more body, a stock can be reduced. To reduce a stock, you simmer the stock in order to cook away some of its liquid. If the stock is simmered until only half of the original water remains, it is a **double-strength stock**. If it is simmered until it has an intense flavor and a very syrupy consistency, it is called a **glaze**.

 **Reading Checkpoint** *What is a double-strength stock?*

BASIC CULINARY SKILLS

Reducing Stock

1. Test the stock (see Chef's Tip).
2. Rapidly simmer the stock. Transfer the stock to a smaller pot, if necessary, after it has reduced.
3. Continue simmering until half the original amount of stock remains. The stock has been reduced. It is now a double-strength stock.
4. Strain the double-strength stock.
5. Cool the double-strength stock to below 41°F. Store in the refrigerator.

Making a Glaze

1. **Rapidly simmer** the double-strength stock.

2. **Continue simmering** until the stock is reduced by half.

3. **Check the consistency** of the stock.

   A glaze is thick enough to cling to the front and back of a spoon and very syrupy. If the stock is not yet syrupy, continue to reduce it until it has the correct consistency.

4. **Cool** the glaze to below 41°F. Store in the refrigerator.

14.1 ASSESSMENT

Reviewing Concepts

1. What are the four types of basic ingredients used to make stocks?
2. Identify the five basic types of stocks. Briefly describe each.
3. What are the basic steps involved in preparing a brown stock?
4. What is a glaze and how is it prepared?

Critical Thinking

5. **Drawing Conclusions** Why is it necessary to cool stocks and glazes below 41°F?
6. **Comparing/Contrasting** What is the difference between the preparation of a brown veal stock and a white beef stock?
7. **Predicting** How will the flavor, color, and aroma of a vegetable stock change if you use roasted vegetables in the stock?

Test Kitchen

Prepare chicken stock from unroasted bones, mirepoix, and sachet d'épices. Make chicken stock from a purchased base. Taste the finished stocks and evaluate the results.

LANGUAGE ARTS

Descriptive Writing

Research five techniques of notable chefs for making stocks. Describe how each chef's technique is similar and how each is different. Assume that your audience is your fellow students and is familiar with the technique for making stock presented in this textbook. Focus on communicating specific details as clearly as possible so your audience can use the results of your research in their own cooking.

14.2 Sauces

READING PREVIEW

Key Concepts

- Identifying basic ingredients for sauces
- Preparing thickeners for sauces
- Identifying types of sauce
- Preparing and storing sauces
- Presenting sauces

Vocabulary

- béchamel sauce
- brown sauce
- chutney
- compound butter
- coulis
- demi-glace
- derivative sauces
- espagnol sauce
- grand sauces
- hollandaise sauce
- jus de veau lié
- liaison
- nappé
- purée
- refined starch
- relish
- roux
- salsa
- starch slurry
- tempering
- velouté

"**A** sauce should never be considered a disguise or a mask. Its role is to point up, prolong, and complement the taste of the food it accompanies, to contrast with it, or to give variety to its presentation. "

— Julia Child

Basic Ingredients for Sauces

A sauce is a liquid served with foods to add more flavor, color, texture, and eye appeal to the food. Sauces are made from three basic types of ingredients:

- Liquids
- Aromatics and seasonings
- Thickeners

Liquids The main ingredient in a sauce is typically a flavorful liquid such as a stock. In fact, stocks are the main liquid ingredient in many sauces. The flavor of the stock should match the flavor of the food you plan to serve with the finished sauce. For example, chicken stock is the best choice for a sauce to be used with a chicken dish. Shellfish stock is used in a sauce with seafood dishes.

Julia Child
Mastering the Art of French Cooking, 1961

▲
FIGURE 14-7
Serving Sauces
Sauces can be served over food, under food, or on the side.
Communicating *How do you prefer sauces? Why?*

Sauces made with a stock get both their flavor and some of their color from the stock.

Other ingredients can be used in place of some or all the stock in a sauce. Milk or cream, for example, can be the main liquid ingredient in some sauces. They give sauces a creamy flavor and a white color. Sometimes egg yolks and butter are used in place of some of the stock. Some vegetables, such as tomatoes, mushrooms, and bell peppers, contain enough moisture to be used as the main liquid ingredient of a sauce without using any stock.

Aromatics and Seasonings Sauces need to be very flavorful. In addition to the flavor from the liquid ingredient, other ingredients need to be added to the sauce as it cooks. Aromatic vegetables, including shallots, onions, leeks, and mushrooms, are often added to a sauce as it cooks. Small amounts of aromatic liquids, such as wine or brandy, are sometimes added.

There are many seasoning options for sauces—the most basic are salt and pepper, but your sauce recipe may indicate others. Herbs, spices, and mustard are some of the most common types of seasonings found in sauces.

Thickeners Sauces must be thick enough to coat foods. Recipes often call for ingredients that will help thicken a sauce.

Roux (roo) is a cooked paste made from wheat flour and a fat. The starch in the flour thickens the sauce. However, in addition to starch, flour also contains proteins and other elements that do not help thicken the sauce and will need to be skimmed from the sauce as it simmers. The fat in the roux adds some flavor to the sauce, so it is common to use a flavorful fat, such as butter, when preparing a roux.

A **starch slurry** is a mixture of a refined starch and cold water. A **refined starch** is made from a starchy ingredient such as corn, rice, or potatoes that is processed to remove all elements except the starch. A refined starch is also known as pure starch. A starch slurry is a good choice as a thickener when you want to make a sauce that is very clear.

A **liaison** (lee-AY-zohn) is a mixture of cream and egg yolks that are added to a sauce at the end of cooking time. Liaisons add a creamy flavor, golden color, and a light thickness to a sauce.

A **purée** (pyur-AY) is a very fine paste made by cooking a flavorful ingredient until it is very soft and then straining it or using a food processor or blender to chop it very fine. A purée is soft and smooth, with a liquid consistency. Sauces made from vegetable purées are sometimes described as self-thickening, because they do not need an added thickener.

 **Reading Checkpoint** *What are the three basic types of ingredients used to make a sauce?*

CHEF'S TIP

CHECKING ROUX

To check if roux is cooked out, take a small taste of the sauce (use proper tasting procedures). Hold it against the roof of your mouth with the tip of your tongue. It should feel very smooth, with no cereal taste.

Preparing Thickeners

Sauces are noted not only for their flavor and color, but also for their consistency. A good sauce is thick enough to coat foods. A sauce that has been thickened properly is described as **nappé** (nah-PAY), a French word that means "coating" or "covering." For your sauce to achieve the correct consistency, your sauce recipe may call for a roux, a starch slurry, or a liaison.

Roux Roux is made by cooking equal parts of fat and flour together. All-purpose flour is the most common choice for the flour in a roux. Clarified butter is the most common choice for the fat.

A roux is identified by its color. The longer a roux cooks, the darker its color will be. White roux is made with oil instead of butter and is cooked for a short time to give it a very white color. Pale or blond roux is made with clarified butter and is cooked longer than white roux for a golden color. Brown roux is made with clarified butter and oil. It is cooked long enough to give it a deep brown color. The lighter the roux, the more it thickens; the darker the roux, the less it thickens. There are two ways to add roux to a sauce:

- Add a cooler liquid to the hot roux. Make the roux and, while it is still hot, gradually add a cooler liquid to it. Whisk the mixture as you add the liquid to smooth out any lumps that may form.
- Add a cooler roux to a hot liquid. Have the liquid at a simmer. Break cold roux into small pieces and put them in a bowl. Add enough hot liquid to dissolve the roux. Whisk well to completely dissolve the roux. Pour the dissolved roux into the simmering liquid.

▲ **Figure 14-8**
Roux
Roux can be cooked to a variety of colors.
Analyzing Information *Which color of roux would you choose for a light- or ivory-colored sauce?*

Roux

1 **Measure** the ingredients.

2 **Heat the fat** in a heavy gauge skillet.

3 **Add the flour** all at once and stir to combine. There should be no lumps and the roux should not look greasy or be too stiff.

4 **Cook the roux**, stirring constantly, until it has the correct color.

5 **Use immediately** or store in a refrigerator.

See Recipe Card 87, "Roux."

How Much Roux?

Consistency Desired	Description	Amount of Roux
Light	Lightly coats a spoon. Pours easily. Used as the base for some soups.	10 to 12 ounces per gallon (depending on type of roux)
Medium	Clings to food and coats it evenly. Pours easily, but is not runny. Used for most sauces.	12 to 14 ounces per gallon (depending on type of roux)
Heavy	Stiff enough to mound when dropped from a spoon. Does not pour easily. Used to hold ingredients together (for example, a heavy sauce could bind a baked macaroni and cheese dish).	14 to 16 ounces per gallon (depending on type of roux)

Sauces thickened with roux need to simmer at least 45 minutes to remove the starchy or pasty taste and gritty feel of the flour. You may hear this referred to as "cooking out the roux."

Use the right amount of roux to get the right consistency for the sauce. The less roux you add, the lighter the consistency. The more roux you add, the heavier the consistency.

Starch Slurries Starch slurries thicken liquids more quickly than roux. To make a starch slurry, stir the refined starch (typically cornstarch or arrowroot) together with a cold liquid until the starch is dissolved and the mixture has the consistency of heavy cream.

Add a starch slurry gradually to a simmering liquid. Continue to simmer after the starch slurry has been added, whisking or stirring until the liquid is thickened. Starch slurries typically thicken simmering liquids in two or three minutes.

Liaison To make a **liaison**, you blend cream and egg yolks in a bowl until they are very smooth. The liaison will be added to a hot liquid, but before you can do that you need to use a special technique called **tempering** to warm the liaison. If you don't temper the liaison, the egg yolks could overcook or scramble when they first enter the hot liquid. To temper a liaison, gradually stir or whisk a few ladles of the hot liquid into the liaison. Add enough to bring the liaison close to the temperature of the simmering liquid. When the liaison is warmed enough, you can add it to the rest of the hot liquid. Continue to simmer very gently just long enough for the egg yolks to lightly thicken and form a sauce. Do not let the sauce come to a full boil.

 **Reading Checkpoint** *What are three thickeners used to prepare sauces?*

Types of Sauces

The Grand Sauces There are hundreds of different types of sauces. However, classic cookbooks written for chefs describe five **grand sauces** (these are also called mother sauces or leading sauces):

- Brown sauce
- Béchamel sauce
- Velouté sauce
- Tomato sauce
- Hollandaise sauce

A **brown sauce** has a rich brown color and is typically served with meats. The three basic types of brown sauce are espagnol sauce, demi-glace, and jus de veau lié. **Espagnol sauce** (ess-spah-NYOL) is a brown sauce made by thickening a brown veal stock with a roux.

Demi-glace (DEH-me-glahs) is made by simmering espagnol sauce with an equal amount of brown veal stock until the sauce is intensely flavored and thick enough to coat foods. **Jus de veau lié** (JHOO duh voh lee-AY) is made by simmering a brown stock with flavorings and aromatics and, in some cases, additional bones or meat trimmings to intensify the stock's flavor. Jus de veau lié is thickened with a starch slurry.

Béchamel sauce (BAY-shah-mell) is a white sauce made by thickening milk with a white roux. Béchamel is sometimes flavored with onions, cloves, and bay leaves.

Velouté (veh-loo-TAY) sauce is a white sauce made by thickening a poultry, fish, or shellfish stock with a blond roux. The type of stock you use determines the type of velouté you make: chicken stock for chicken velouté, fish stock for fish velouté, and so forth.

Tomato sauce is made by simmering tomatoes and flavoring ingredients such as basil or garlic until the tomatoes are soft enough to purée. A French-style tomato sauce includes some stock and may be thickened with roux. Italian-style tomato sauces do not include stock or roux.

BASIC CULINARY SKILLS

Roux-Thickened Sauce

1. **Warm** the liquid. Add aromatics or seasonings if your recipe calls for it.

2. **Combine** the liquid and the roux.

3. **Whisk** until there are no lumps.

4. **Simmer** for about 45 minutes.

5. **Strain** the sauce.

6. **Return** to a simmer.

7. **Add** finishing ingredients, if required by your recipe. Adjust seasonings.

 See Recipe Card 89, "Velouté Sauce."

Hollandaise sauce (HOLL-uhn-daze) is made by blending melted or clarified butter into slightly cooked egg yolks. Lemon juice and vinegar add flavor to the sauce. Hollandaise is a type of sauce that is sometimes referred to as a warm emulsion sauce. As you remember from Chapter 10, an emulsion is made when two ingredients that don't normally mix together are blended so that one of the ingredients is suspended evenly throughout the mixture.

Hollandaise sauce can be tricky to make. If it gets too hot, the eggs will begin to scramble. The first sign that eggs are beginning to scramble is that they will look like very small clumps or threads in the sauce. If there aren't too many clumps, you can rescue the sauce by immediately taking it off the heat and adding a bit of cold water. Whisk the sauce until it looks smooth again, then continue to add the butter over gentle heat. If the sauce has a lot of clumps, you will need to strain it and then begin again with fresh egg yolks. This time, use the strained hollandaise to replace the warm clarified butter.

CHEF'S TIP

OILY HOLLANDAISE

If hollandaise sauce looks oily, you are adding butter too quickly. Stop adding butter. Whisk over barely simmering heat until the existing butter is absorbed into the yolks.

BASIC CULINARY SKILLS

Purée Sauce

1 **Prepare** aromatic and main vegetables.

2 **Sauté** the aromatic vegetables.

3 **Add** the main vegetables. Add liquid, if necessary.

See Recipe Card 90, "Tomato Sauce."

4 **Simmer** until the vegetables are very tender.

5 **Add** additional seasonings or aromatics.

6 **Remove** bouquet garni, sachet, or bay leaf.

7 **Purée** to the appropriate smoothness.

8 **Return** to a simmer.

9 **Add** finishing ingredients, if required by your recipe. Adjust seasonings.

Warm Emulsion Sauce

1 Combine egg yolks with liquid.

2 Cook over barely simmering water in a stainless steel bowl, whisking constantly, until the yolks are thickened and warm.

3 Add warm clarified butter very gradually, still working over the barely simmering water. Whisk constantly as you add the butter.

4 Add a small amount of warm water when the sauce becomes stiff.

5 Add lemon juice, salt, and pepper after all the butter is blended into the yolks.

6 Strain the sauce. Keep warm for service.

 See Recipe Card 91, "Hollandaise Sauce."

Brown Sauce Derivatives

Name	Preparation	Serve With
Red Wine Sauce	Simmer brown sauce with red wine, minced shallots, cracked peppercorns, thyme, and bay leaf. Strain and season before serving.	Grilled red meats (also with fish in contemporary cooking)
Mushroom Sauce	Sauté sliced mushrooms in butter until tender, add brown sauce, and simmer until flavorful.	Beef, veal, poultry
Robert Sauce	Sauté minced onions in butter until tender, and add white wine. Simmer until wine cooks away. Add brown sauce and simmer until flavorful. Finish with pinch of sugar and mustard.	Grilled pork

Derivative Sauces Grand sauces can be used as the main ingredient in another sauce. The grand sauce is combined with other seasonings or garnishes for a specific flavor, color, or texture. Sauces made this way are known as **derivative sauces** because they are derived from or based on a grand sauce. Other terms commonly used for derivative sauces include small sauces or compound sauces. The following tables show some of the classic derivative sauces.

Velouté Sauce Derivatives

Name	Preparation	Serve With
◀ Suprême Sauce	Sauté sliced mushrooms in butter until tender. Add velouté and cream, simmer, and strain.	Poultry, fish
Aurore Sauce	Simmer velouté with tomato purée.	Eggs, white meats, poultry
Shrimp Sauce	Simmer velouté with cream. Add cooked shrimp and whisk in whole butter just before serving.	Fish, certain egg dishes

Béchamel Sauce Derivatives

Name	Preparation	Serve With
Onion Sauce	Sauté minced onions in butter until tender. Add béchamel sauce and heavy cream. Simmer until thickened and flavorful.	Veal, pork, poultry
Lobster Sauce	Simmer béchamel sauce with cream until thickened and flavorful. Add diced lobster meat, and season with cayenne pepper.	Lobster, fish
◀ Mornay Sauce	Add grated Gruyère and Parmesan cheeses to béchamel. Cook over low heat until cheeses melt. Whisk in butter just before serving.	Veal, poultry, vegetables

Hollandaise-Style Sauces

Name	Preparation	Serve With
Béarnaise Sauce	Simmer tarragon vinegar, chopped tarragon, shallots, and peppercorns until liquid cooks away. Add water; then strain into the egg yolks and prepare as for a hollandaise. Finish with minced tarragon leaves.	Grilled meats
Mousseline Sauce	Fold whipped heavy cream into hollandaise sauce.	Boiled fish, asparagus
Royal Glaçage Sauce	Fold together equal parts of velouté, hollandaise, and whipped heavy cream. Use as a coating, and then lightly broil the dish to brown before serving.	Poached white meats, fish

Miscellaneous Sauces Today, chefs are making a great number of sauces that are not based on the grand sauces. These are often referred to as miscellaneous sauces. Some miscellaneous sauces are served hot; others are served cold.

- A **compound butter** is made by softening butter and blending it with ingredients such as minced herbs, shallots, ginger, citrus zest, or spices. To use a compound butter as a sauce, put slices of it on top of broiled or grilled meats. Compound butters can also be added to hot cooked pastas or vegetables. The food's heat melts the butter so it coats the food.
- A **coulis** (koo-LEE) is a thick puréed sauce, usually made from vegetables or fruits. Italian-style tomato sauces for pasta dishes are an example of a coulis-style sauce. For additional richness, coulis and purées may include a bit of cream just before they are served.
- A **gravy** is similar to the grand sauces but usually includes pan drippings produced by meats as they roast. These drippings are simmered with a stock or broth, and a thickener, such as roux or a starch slurry, is added to thicken the gravy. Gravies are often made in smaller batches than grand sauces.
- A **salsa** is a cold sauce made from a combination of vegetables, typically tomatoes, onions, peppers, and chilies. They are typically seasoned with salt, pepper, and lime juice. Salsas are often served as a dip with chips or vegetables but are also used as a topping or an ingredient in other dishes. They can be served with a wide range of foods, including meats, eggs, vegetables, grains, and legumes.

- A **relish** or a **chutney** is a sauce with a noticeably chunky texture that is typically served with meats, poultry, or fish. These sauces can be served hot or cold and are typically made from fruits, vegetables, or a combination of fruits and vegetables. Relishes and chutneys are often seasoned with a combination of sweet and sour ingredients, such as vinegar and sugar. They may be made from raw or cooked ingredients. Some versions are sweet, others are savory, and some are very spicy.
- A wide range of sauces, including barbecue sauce, applesauce, cocktail sauce, and tartar sauce, fall under the category "specialty sauces." These sauces can be used as an ingredient in another dish or served as a topping or dip.

 **Reading Checkpoint** *What are the five grand sauces?*

Preparing and Storing Basic Sauces

Preparing sauces requires patience and attention to detail. With all the work involved in making sauces, it makes sense to store an excess amount correctly for later use.

Equipment Used in Preparing Sauces Using the correct equipment when making a sauce is important. Choose saucepans that hold the sauce comfortably with enough room to stir the sauce and skim it if necessary. Check the bottom of the pan to make sure it is very flat. Warped pans will develop hot spots that can burn or scorch the sauce. Avoid aluminum saucepans for white sauces because the sauce may become discolored. Additionally, aluminum pans react with sauces that contain acidic ingredients (such as tomatoes or lemons), creating a potential health hazard.

Sauces that need to be strained should be poured through a sieve. The smoother you want the finished sauce to be, the finer the sieve should be. Using cheesecloth in a sieve gives you the smoothest sauce.

The equipment you use to purée a sauce depends on the amount of sauce you are preparing and the texture you want in the finished sauce. A food mill will produce an even but slightly coarse texture. Food processors and blenders make a finer purée.

FIGURE 14-9
Using Cheesecloth in a Sieve
Using cheesecloth in the sieve gives a velvety texture to a finished sauce.
Drawing Conclusions *Why do you think fine restaurants emphasize the quality of their sauces?*

CULINARY DIVERSITY

France

Perhaps no country is more associated with food and cooking than France. In fact, there are two distinct types of French cooking: the high-level restaurant cooking known as haute cuisine (OHT kwee-ZEEN), which means "high cooking," and everyday cooking, which is often influenced by local ingredients and traditions.

Haute cuisine has its origins in restaurants of the 1850s when elaborate meals of many courses were served to the aristocracy and upper classes. This type of cooking was very rigid. Dishes were prepared in specific ways and given specific names. That way, when customers ordered a dish in a restaurant they could know what they were ordering.

Sauces play a major role in haute cuisine. In fact, the concept of the grand sauces and their derivatives is from haute cuisine. Auguste Escoffier, in his important guide to haute cuisine, Le Guide Culinaire, first published in 1902, lists 221 types of sauces! In this groundbreaking guide, Escoffier rarely lists a preparation of meat without also listing a sauce, a garnish, and perhaps an accompanying dish or two.

French everyday cooking—or, as it's known in French, cuisine bourgeoisie (kwee-ZEEN bour-shwa-ZEE)—is often influenced by the ingredients available within a specific region. For example, bouillabaisse (BOOL-yuh-BAYZ), a type of fish soup, comes from Provence in southern France, bordering on the Mediterranean. Alsace, famous for its cabbage and pigs, is also famous for chacroute garnie (shoo-KROOT GAR-nee),

a dish made from sauerkraut, pork sausages, and ham.

These two styles have been blended in many restaurants, creating a cuisine that is simpler than haute cuisine but more complex than everyday cooking.

Research

Research four classic sauces that are not listed in this chapter. List the name of the sauce and indicate what grand sauce is used in making the sauce. Describe the flavoring ingredients used in making each of the sauces. Then name the foods each sauce is typically served with and the cooking method most often used to prepare these foods.

◄ Bouillabaisse

Storing Sauces You can serve a sauce as soon as you have finished preparing it. To keep a sauce hot during a meal, transfer it to a holding container and keep it very warm. Sauces that contain eggs should be kept warm but not too hot. If they overheat, the eggs will continue to cook and can give the sauce a lumpy or curdled appearance.

Some sauces can be stored for a few days, although sauces containing eggs cannot be stored. To cool and store a sauce, put it in a metal container and set it in an ice bath. Make sure the container is stable so you can stir the sauce. Remember that stirring a food as it cools helps it cool faster and keeps it safe. You can read more about the correct way to cool foods in Chapter 1, "Sanitation."

 **Reading Checkpoint** *When should aluminum sauce pans be avoided?*

Presenting Sauces

Sauces add flavor, moisture, color, and sheen to other foods. When you pair the right sauce with a food, it enhances the dish by either making the flavor of the food more intense or adding a contrasting flavor. Here are some guidelines for presenting sauces:

- Serve sauces at the right temperature. Hot sauces should be at a simmer (around 180°F) when they are presented. Sauces thicken as they cool and their flavors are not as pronounced as when they are hot. A cool sauce could also cool off the main item.
- Reheat stored grand sauces properly. Put the sauce in a heavy-bottomed saucepan and place the pan over low heat. Stir the sauce until it softens.

CHEF'S TIP

HOLDING SAUCE
A sauce thickened with a starch slurry typically does not hold on a steam table as well as a roux-thickened sauce.

FIGURE 14-10
Presenting Sauces
Serve enough sauce to flavor and moisten the dish.
Inferring *Can there be too much sauce on a dish?*

Tasting Sauces

It's important to taste sauces both when they are made and when you reheat them. A food worker should never use a utensil more than once to taste food that is being sold or served.

Then increase the heat to high and bring the sauce to a full boil for 3 minutes.

- Hold sauces properly. Sauces that have been thickened with either a roux or a starch slurry can develop a skin on the surface when you hold them in a steam table. To prevent a skin from forming, put a thin layer of clarified butter on the surface, or cover the container tightly. Remove and discard any skin that does form. Warm emulsion sauces and sauces finished with a liaison should be warm but not hot enough to overcook or curdle. Keep them in a warm water bath.

- Season sauces properly. Be sure to taste sauces after you reheat them to check their flavor. Salt and pepper are the most common choices to season foods, but read your recipe to see if you need to adjust other ingredients as well, such as citrus juices, wine, or fresh herbs.

Reading Checkpoint *At what temperature should a hot sauce be served?*

14.2 ASSESSMENT

Reviewing Concepts

1. What are the four types of thickeners used in making sauces? Briefly describe each.

2. Describe the steps in making a roux.

3. What are the five grand sauces?

4. What types of sauces cannot be stored?

5. In what two ways can a sauce enhance a food?

Critical Thinking

6. **Predicting** What will happen to a béarnaise sauce if it gets too hot?

7. **Analyzing Information** What is the grand sauce used as the base for the light-colored sauce that uses Gruyére and Parmesan cheeses?

8. **Comparing/Contrasting** What is the difference between an espagnol sauce and a jus de veau lié?

Test Kitchen

Make three different batches of béchamel sauce. Use 10 ounces of blond roux for the first batch. Use 12 ounces of blond roux for the second batch. Use 16 ounces of blond roux for the third batch. Evaluate each of the batches for thickness. Which do you think has the best consistency for a soup? Which would you choose for a sauce?

 **CULINARY MATH**

9. A recipe for a chicken velouté sauce calls for 12 ounces of roux for a 1-gallon batch. How much roux do you need for 4 gallons of sauce?

10. Your recipe for béchamel has a medium consistency and uses 12 ounces of roux for a 1-gallon batch. How much roux would you need to make a béchamel with a heavy consistency?

> "**S**oups fill your mouth completely and instantly, giving you a simultaneous experience of aroma, texture, taste, and temperature. "
>
> – Wayne Almquist

Basic Types of Soup

Soups are liquid foods served in a bowl and eaten with a spoon. Serving a soup at the beginning of a meal provides an opportunity to make a good first impression on a guest. Preparing and serving soups will help you learn more about basic culinary techniques, seasoning, garnishing, and serving foods.

Soups are an effective way to use material that has been trimmed from other foods and can help reduce the overall food cost in the kitchen. Soups also allow you to feature seasonal foods. Most menus feature at least one selection of each of these two basic types of soup:

- Clear soups
- Hearty soups

Clear Soups Clear soups are richly flavored, aromatic liquids. The goal for any clear soup is to produce a very clear liquid. The flavoring ingredients you add to the soup as it simmers are strained out and are not served. Typically, starchy ingredients are not used in clear soups because they make the soup cloudy. There are two basic types of clear soups: broths and consommés.

Wayne Almquist
The Culinary Institute of America

CHEF'S TIP

SOUP DU JOUR

Soup du jour (de ZHOOR) means "soup of the day." Many restaurants change their soups daily to adapt to changing weather, seasons, or special events—or simply to add variety.

Figure 14-11
Seasonal Soup
Soups allow you to feature seasonal foods.
Drawing Conclusions *Why would a restaurant want to feature seasonal foods?*

▼

A **broth** is a clear, thin soup made by simmering a combination of meats, vegetables, aromatics, and water until you have a liquid with a good color and flavor. The flavoring ingredients are strained from the liquid and the result is a broth. The greater the care you take with a broth as it simmers, the clearer it will be. Almost all the fat is removed from a broth, although a few droplets of flavorful fat are common on a good broth. **Bouillon** (BOOL-yohn) is the French term for a broth. You may be familiar with dehydrated bouillon cubes. These are a form of instant broth.

A **consommé** (KAHN-soh-may) is a very clear soup that is completely fat-free. Consommés are a more refined broth, made by blending a good broth or a stock with a combination of ingredients, referred to as the **clarification**. The clarification adds flavor and color to enhance the broth, but the most important purpose of a clarification, and the reason for its name, is to clear the soup by trapping any fine particles in the broth or stock.

Broths and consommés can be served on their own as a soup. You can add a simple garnish, such as herbs, diced cooked meats, or cooked noodles. Changing the aromatic ingredients and including a specific garnish can change these soups from a simple broth or consommé into a specialty soup. Specialty soups are soups that are associated with a specific country, region, or ethnic group. Some examples of clear specialty soups include wonton soup, hot and sour soup, or matzo ball soup.

Hearty Soups Hearty soups have a thickened broth. In hearty soups, the liquid called for in the recipe is an important part of the soup, but it is not the only important element. The main flavoring ingredients remain in the soup, sometimes left whole and sometimes puréed.

Hearty vegetable soups are soups with broth and a significant amount of vegetables (and often meats, pasta, and other ingredients). If you were preparing a broth, you would strain these ingredients out first. For a hearty vegetable soup, you leave them in the soup. The addition of starchy ingredients (rice, barley, potatoes, or pasta, for instance) thickens the soup slightly. The broth is typically not clear. A number of specialty soups fit the description of hearty vegetable soups. Minestrone (mee-ness-TROH-nay) is an example of a specialty soup that is a hearty vegetable soup from Italy. Borscht (BOHR-sht) from Russia or Poland and Manhattan clam chowder from the United States are other specialty soups that are hearty vegetable soups.

A **cream soup** is a noticeably thick soup with a velvety smooth texture. Cream soups are made by combining a broth or stock with the main flavoring ingredient (or a combination of flavoring ingredients). You may need to add a thickener such as roux, arrowroot, or cornstarch for a very smooth soup with an even texture. Some soups are made from ingredients that thicken the soup adequately by themselves; potatoes and some fruits are examples. Cream soups typically have the consistency of heavy cream and are opaque. Cold cream soup options include the classic vichyssoise (vee-shee-swahz) (a cold cream soup made from potatoes and leek) and fruit soups (such as apple soup or strawberry soup). New England clam chowder is a specialty soup that is a cream soup.

A **purée soup** is made by simmering a starchy ingredient (beans, dried peas, potatoes, or starchy vegetables) along with additional vegetables, meats, or aromatics in a broth or other liquid until they are tender enough to mash easily. The entire soup is puréed to the appropriate texture. Some purée soups are deliberately left chunky (for instance, black bean soup). Others are puréed until they are as smooth as a cream soup (for example, split pea soup).

A **bisque** (bisk) gets its color and flavor from lobster, shrimp, or crayfish shells. (A crayfish is a small fresh-water, lobster-like shellfish.) The shells are cooked until they are brightly colored. After you add broth or stock, a thickener, vegetables, and aromatics, you simmer the soup until it is thick and very flavorful. The soup is puréed, including the shells; then strained and finished with cream.

 **Reading Checkpoint**   *What are the two basic types of soup?*

> **CHEF'S TIP**
>
> **ADDING CREAM TO SOUPS**
>
> When making a large batch of cream soup, prepare the soup up to the point where you add cream. Cool the soup. Then reheat only as much soup as you need and add cream only to that amount.

FIGURE 14-12
Clear or Hearty?
A garnished clear soup and a hearty vegetable soup.
Comparing/Contrasting
Compare how the vegetables in these two soups are cooked.

Preparing Soups

You could spend months or years making nothing but soups and never repeat a recipe. Soups can feature a huge variety of ingredients, alone and in combination. However, making soup requires only a few basic skills. They are the same skills used in preparing stocks and sauces: selecting ingredients, careful simmering and skimming, puréeing, and thickening with a starch or a liaison.

Choosing Equipment for Soups A soup pot with a flat, heavy-gauge bottom is the basic piece of equipment for making most soups. In addition to a soup pot, you may need other equipment. Use wooden or metal spoons to stir soups and prevent scorching. Use sieves or colanders with cheesecloth to strain soups. If your soup needs to be puréed, use a food mill, a blender (either counter top or immersion style), or a food processor.

Making a Broth The goal for any clear soup, whether it is a broth or a consommé, is to produce a very clear liquid. A selection of flavorful ingredients is the starting point for a good broth. Keeping a broth at a slow, even simmer helps to extract the most flavor from the ingredients. Careful skimming removes the impurities that make a broth cloudy.

BASIC CULINARY SKILLS

Broth

1 Prepare ingredients.

2 Add cold liquid to cover the main ingredient.

3 Add remaining ingredients.

4 Bring to a simmer.

5 Maintain a slow, gentle simmer. Skim to remove any foam that rises to the surface.

Continued on next page

Broth *Continued*

6 Taste the broth from time to time. Adjust the seasonings.

7 Add aromatics such as a bouquet garni or sachet d'épices during the final 30 to 45 minutes.

8 Strain the broth.

 See Recipe Card 93, "Chicken Broth."

Making a Consommé Consommés differ from broths because they use a clarification to clear the broth. The ingredients for the clarification are selected according to the flavor and color you want in your finished consommé. Ground meat, poultry, or fish is blended with egg whites, finely chopped or ground vegetables, herbs, and an acid.

BASIC CULINARY SKILLS

Consommé

1 Prepare the clarification ingredients.

2 Blend the clarification ingredients together. They must be very cold.

3 Add cold stock or broth to the cold clarification in a soup pot.

Continued on next page

Consommé *Continued*

4 Bring to a simmer slowly, stirring the consommé occasionally to keep the clarification from sticking and scorching.

5 Stop stirring the consommé when the clarification ingredients start to form a large soft mass (the raft).

6 Break a small opening in the raft, after it forms (if it hasn't broken open on its own).

9 Simmer the consommé for the recommended time.

10 Ladle the consommé out of the pot. You can make a slightly larger opening in the raft, but don't break the raft apart.

7 Lower the heat. Very small bubbles will rise to the surface through the hole in the raft.

8 Baste the raft while the consommé simmers by gently ladling some of the consommé over the top of the raft.

11 Strain the consommé through a very fine sieve, cheesecloth, or filter.

12 Skim or blot any fat on the surface of the consommé.

 See Recipe Card 94, "Consommé."

Typical acids are tomatoes, lemon juice, or wine. This mixture is referred to as a clarification before it is cooked with a broth or stock. Once the consommé reaches a simmer, the clarification is referred to as a **raft**, because it floats on the top of the consommé like a raft on water.

Making a Hearty Soup Although a clear soup usually calls for all the ingredients to be added to the pot at the same time, hearty soups are made by adding ingredients in a particular order. Begin with the aromatic ingredients, such as onions, garlic, or leeks. Add the rest of the ingredients in order, starting with those that take the longest to cook and ending with those that take the least amount of time to cook.

Hearty Soup

1 Prepare ingredients.

2 Sauté aromatic ingredients (mirepoix, mushrooms, onions, bacon, garlic, and similar ingredients).

3 Add a flavorful liquid.

4 Add roux, if your recipe calls for it.

5 Add the remaining ingredients (including sachet d'épices or bouquet garni) in a sequence that ensures they will be cooked to the correct point of doneness.

6 Simmer gently, stirring frequently so the soup doesn't stick to the pot.

7 Skim the surface to remove foam or fat.

8 Taste the soup as it cooks, adjusting seasonings and consistency as necessary.

9 Continue simmering until all the ingredients are fully cooked, very tender, and very flavorful.

10 Remove the sachet d'épices or bouquet garni and discard.

11 Purée the soup, if your recipe calls for it.

12 Add finishing ingredients or garnishes, if your recipe calls for it.

 See Recipe Card 95, "Cream of Broccoli Soup."

 **Reading Checkpoint** *What is the difference between making a broth and making a consommé?*

Reheating and Serving Soups

When soups are served at the right temperature, they have the best possible flavor, texture, and color. If you've made enough soup to last for more than one day, you will need to reheat the soup. Then you will need to hold it at the right temperature until it is served to a customer.

Figure 14-13
Reheating Soup
A thin layer of water or broth
helps avoid scorching thick soups
as they reheat.
Solving Problems *Why are soups
reheated over direct heat, not in
a steam table?*

▼

Reheating Soups Reheat all soups over direct heat, not in the steam table. Use a heavy-gauge pot and place the pot on a burner. Clear soups can simply be brought to a boil over high heat.

To warm thinner hearty soups, put them into a pot over medium heat and stir frequently. Be careful. Most hearty soups have starchy ingredients; the starch can stick to the bottom of the pot and easily burn.

Thick hearty soups such as cream soups, purées, or bisques need extra care. For them, pour a thin layer of water or broth into the pot before you add the cold soup. Warm the soup over low heat until it is softened and warmed through. Once the soup is warm, you can increase the heat and bring it to a simmer, stirring frequently.

Serving Soups To serve a soup properly, you will need to hold it at the optimum temperature that keeps it safe but also maintains the right flavor, color, and texture.

- Keep hot soups very hot. For safety, all soups must be held at 165°F. Place them in containers in a steam table or a bain

Figure 14-14 ▶
Holding Soups for Service
A soup should be brought to the
table as soon as it is ready.
Solving Problems *What should
you do if a soup is not hot
enough to serve?*

marie of hot water. Check the temperature of hot soups in the steam table periodically to be sure they are not getting cool.

- Keep cold soups very cold. Place cold soups in containers and hold them in a cold bain marie filled with ice.
- Keep soups covered. Covering the container prevents cross-contamination. A covered container of soup is also less likely to develop a skin. Covering the container helps keep hot soups hot and cold soups cold.

Garnishing Soups

A garnish adds an extra dimension to a soup. A fresh garnish such as herbs or grated citrus zest can add flavor or freshness. A garnish such as diced meats, grated cheese, or noodles can add substance to the soup. A garnish such as a dollop of cold sour cream on a hot soup or a crunchy crouton on a purée soup can add contrast. Even the crackers often served with soups are a type of garnish.

An item that is cooked in the soup is not considered a garnish but is a component of the soup. To be considered a garnish, a cooked item is added to the soup after it is cooked.

- Prepare garnishes properly and hold them at the appropriate temperature. All garnishes should be small enough to fit in a spoon so they are easy to eat.
- Garnishes such as fresh herbs, sour cream, grated cheeses, and croutons do not need to be heated before adding them to the soup. Other garnishes may need to be hot when you add them to the soup so the garnish does not cool down the soup.
- Garnish soups right before they are served. Add garnishes and finishing ingredients to batches or individual portions as close to the time of service as possible.
- Serve crisp accompaniments on the side. Crackers, breadsticks, and similar crisp breads are often served with soups to offer a texture contrast.

▲
FIGURE 14-15
Cold Tomato Soup with Garnishes
Crisp garnishes provide contrasting textures to the soup.
Applying Concepts *What other ways could you garnish this soup?*

Garnishes for Clear Soups Broths and consommés have a wide range of garnishes. If the garnish for a clear soup needs to be cooked, prepare it separately from the broth or consommé. Otherwise, the garnish will cloud the broth, particularly if the garnish contains a starch.

Garnishes

Clear Soups

▲ **Chicken Broth**
Garnish: Chicken, pasta, carrot, celery

▲ **Fish Broth**
Garnish: Sea bass, carrot, watercress, ginger

▲ **Beef Consommé**
Garnish: Thin rings of onion

▲ **Wonton Soup**
Garnish: Wontons (dumplings), noodles, cilantro

▲ **Vegetable Broth**
Garnish: Lettuce, cucumber, carrot, parsley

Garnishes for Hearty Soups A popular garnish for a hearty soup is a **crouton** (CREW-tahn), a small cube of bread that is toasted or fried until crisp and golden brown. There are many other options for garnishing hearty soups. Bisques often include diced cooked seafood.

Hearty Soups

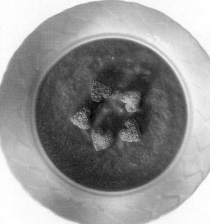

▲ **Carrot-Ginger Soup**
Garnish: Heart-shaped croutons

▲ **Black Bean Soup**
Garnish: Tortilla chips, bacon, cheese, sour cream, cilantro

▲ **Soupe au Pistou (French Vegetable Soup)**
Garnish: Pistou (basil sauce)

▲ **Lobster Bisque**
Garnish: Lobster, tarragon

▲ **Mulligatawny Soup (Spicy Indian Curried Soup)**
Garnish: Wild rice, coconut milk, cilantro

Cream soups are often garnished with small pieces of the main ingredient (for example, cooked broccoli for a cream of broccoli soup).

 **Reading Checkpoint** *How are soups held for service?*

CULINARY HISTORY

Soups and Sops

The word "soup" comes from "sop." A sop is a moistened piece of bread. Soups originally included slices of dry or stale bread because bread was too valuable to waste. Once it was too stale or dry to eat, the bread was used in other dishes. The bread might have been simmered in the soup as a thickener, or it might simply have been placed in the bottom of the bowl before broth was ladled over it.

The soups we enjoy today still bear the imprint of earlier soup-making techniques. One classic soup that follows this tradition is onion soup gratinée (grah-teen-nay). A toasted piece of bread, often topped with grated cheese, is floated on a rich broth chock-full of golden brown onions. The soup is baked until the bread and cheese forms a crust, known in French cooking as a gratinée.

Another soup that betrays its culinary history through its name is a bisque. Bisques can be thickened with cooked rice, potatoes, potato starch, or a roux. However, the first bisques were thickened by crumbling a type of stale biscuit into the soup to make it thicker and more substantial.

Today, many soups are thickened with ingredients other than bread, but the combination of soup and bread is still an important part of soup preparation and service. We often garnish soups with croutons, which are just cubes of toasted bread. We serve crackers or breadsticks with soups to offer texture and contrast.

▲ *Onion soup gratinée*

Research

Use a classic cookbook or the Internet to research the history of bisques. Describe how recipes for bisque have changed over time.

International Soups

Here are some international soups with which you might not be familiar:

Waterzooi (VAH-tuhr-zoh-ee) ▶
A Belgian soup of chicken, vegetables, and seasonings that are blended into a rich sauce of cream, butter, and egg yolks, garnished with lemon slices and parsley, and served with crusty bread. Fish is occasionally used instead of chicken.

Mulligatawny (muhl-ih-guh-TAW-nee)
Shown on page 463.
An Indian soup adapted by the British, made of curried chicken or vegetable stock with coconut milk, pieces of chicken, onion, carrots, celery, and garnished with cilantro.

Soupe au Pistou (soup oh pees-TOO)
Shown on page 463.
From the Provençal region of France, a white bean and vegetable soup garnished with pistou (pesto in Italian cuisine), which is made of basil, parmesan cheese, garlic, and olive oil.

Borscht (BOHR-sht)
A Russian soup made from fresh beets. It can be prepared sweet and served cold with a sour cream garnish; or it can be savory with meat, cabbage, potatoes, and other vegetables and served hot.

14.3 ASSESSMENT

Reviewing Concepts

1. Identify the two basic types of soup. Briefly describe each.
2. Explain the process of using a clarification in making a consommé.
3. Describe the differences when reheating clear soups and hearty soups.
4. Identify three things that a garnish can add to a soup.

Critical Thinking

5. **Predicting** What would happen to a clear broth if you simmered potatoes in it?
6. **Comparing/Contrasting** What is the difference between a purée soup and a cream soup?
7. **Applying Concepts** Describe five ways you could garnish your favorite soup.

Test Kitchen

Make three batches of cream of potato soup. For two batches, prepare the soup up to the point of adding the cream and then chill the soup. For the third batch, prepare the soup completely, adding the cream, and then chill it. The next day, reheat the soup that already includes the cream. Reheat one of the remaining batches and, when it is hot, add the cream. For the last batch, add the cream before you begin heating it. When all the soups are hot, taste and evaluate them.

LANGUAGE ARTS

Descriptive Writing

Research three different types of chowder. Write a description of each type of chowder, pointing out their similarities and differences.

Review and Assessment

Reviewing Content

Choose the letter that best answers the question or completes the statement.

1. White stock is made from
   a. white onions
   b. unroasted bones
   c. white rice
   d. all of the above

2. Béchamel sauce is a
   a. brown sauce
   b. derivative sauce
   c. grand sauce
   d. puréed sauce

3. For safety, all hot soups must be held at
   a. 212°F
   b. 100°F
   c. 350°F
   d. 165°F

4. A sauce that has been thickened properly is described as
   a. nappé
   b. slurry
   c. roux
   d. coulis

5. In a roux, the balance of fat to flour is
   a. two parts fat to one part flour
   b. four parts fat to one part flour
   c. one part fat to one part flour
   d. three parts fat to one part flour

6. A bisque gets its color and flavor from
   a. lobster, crawfish, or shrimp shells
   b. beets
   c. black beans
   d. split peas

7. A liaison is a mixture of
   a. onions, parsnips, and celery
   b. fat and flour
   c. cream and egg yolks
   d. refined starch and cold water

Understanding Concepts

8. Describe the difference between a brown beef stock and a white beef stock.

9. Compare and contrast béchamel and velouté.

10. What is the difference between a broth and a consommé?

11. Describe the general process for making a roux-thickened sauce.

12. Describe the technique of tempering a liaison before you add it to a hot liquid.

Critical Thinking

13. **Recognizing Patterns** Which stock would be darker: a vegetable stock made from fresh vegetables or a vegetable stock made from roasted vegetables? Explain your answer.

14. **Predicting** You have reheated a cream soup. Is it likely that you will need to adjust the seasonings? Explain your answer.

Culinary Math

15. **Solving Problems** A recipe for 1 gallon of brown beef stock uses 8 pounds of roasted bones, 1 pound of mirepoix, 4 to 6 ounces of tomatoes, and 6 quarts of water. How much of each of these ingredients is required to make 2½ gallons of brown beef stock?

16. **Applying Concepts** How much roux is required to make a half-gallon of a sauce with a medium consistency?

On the Job

17. **Applying Concepts** A customer who is allergic to dairy products orders a dish featuring Mornay sauce. Does the sauce present a problem for the customer? Explain your answer.

18. **Inferring** What is the disadvantage for a restaurant in having a dish that features béarnaise sauce on its menu every day?

RECIPE CARDS

Use the following Recipe Cards to test your culinary skill.

82. Brown Veal Stock
83. Chicken Stock
84. Fish Fumet
85. Court Bouillon
86. Vegetable Stock
87. Roux
88. Jus de Veau Lié
89. Velouté
90. Tomato Sauce
91. Hollandaise Sauce
92. Béchamel Sauce
93. Chicken Broth
94. Consommé
95. Cream of Broccoli Soup
96. Shrimp Bisque
97. Black Bean Soup, Caribbean-Style
98. Minestrone

LAB ACTIVITY

Project 14: Preparing Tomato Sauce
Answer these questions when your class works through Project 14.

- Do you think the ingredients you use in a sauce make a difference in the taste of the sauce? For example, would you taste the difference between fresh tomatoes and canned tomatoes?

- Do you think the sauce's method of preparation makes a difference in the overall quality of a sauce?

- Does the texture make a difference?

- Which variation in ingredients and preparation pay off when you consider its time and difficulty?

TEST PRACTICE

Choose the letter that best answers the question or completes the statement.

1. What is another name for neutral stock?
   A consommé
   B chicken stock
   C white beef stock
   D vegetable stock

2. Which of the these sauces are a velouté derivative?
   A mushroom sauce
   B supreme sauce
   C mousseline sauce
   D Robert sauce

3. Which of the following should be completely fat-free?
   A consommé
   B bouillon
   C broth
   D bisque

4. How many pounds of fish bones are required for 1 gallon of fish fumet?
   A 3 pounds
   B 5 pounds
   C 8 pounds
   D 11 pounds

5. A stock should be cooled to below what temperature before storing?
   A 41°F
   B 35°F
   C 31°F
   D 0°F

6. A liaison is a mixture of
   A onions, carrots, and celery
   B onions, parsnips, and celery
   C cream and egg yolks
   D refined starch and cold water

7. To keep the color of a white beef stock very pale, some chefs
   A sweat the bones
   B blanch the bones
   C simmer longer
   D use a white roux

8. A starch slurry is a good choice for a thickener when
   A you need to thicken a cold sauce
   B you want to make a sauce that is very clear
   C you are making a white sauce
   D you are making a tomato-based sauce

15

FISH & SHELLFISH

15.1 Fish

15.2 Shellfish

READING PREVIEW

Key Concepts

- Identifying basic types of fish
- Selecting and storing fish
- Preparing fish
- Matching cooking methods to fish

Vocabulary

- anadromous fish
- belly bones
- cross cuts
- deep poaching
- drawn fish
- en papillote
- farm-raised fish
- fillet
- flat fish
- freshwater fish
- glazed fish
- goujonette
- headed and gutted fish
- lox
- pan-dressed fish
- paupiette
- pin bones
- PUFI mark
- quarter fillets
- round fish
- saltwater fish
- shallow poaching
- steaks
- tranche
- whole fish
- wild fish

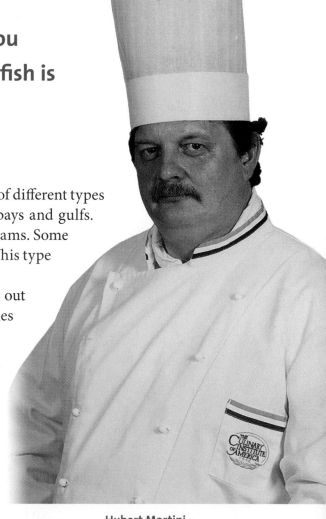

> **"T**here is nowhere to hide when you are cooking fish. The quality of your fish is everything. **"**
>
> – Hubert Martini

Types of Fish

When you say fish, you could be referring to any of thousands of different types of fish. **Saltwater fish** live in oceans, seas, and the water of bays and gulfs. **Freshwater fish** live in freshwater ponds, lakes, rivers, and streams. Some fish live part of their lives in saltwater and part in freshwater. This type of fish is known as **anadromous** (ann-AH-drom-us) **fish.**

Farm-raised fish are raised in ponds or in penned waters out in the ocean. Fish that are captured in nets or on fishing lines in open water are referred to as **wild fish**. While wild fish are seasonal food that can vary greatly in quality from season to season, farm-raised fish have a consistent quality year-round because their diets and living conditions are more precisely controlled.

One of the biggest challenges in identifying fish is that a single fish can have many different names, depending on the part of the country you are in. However, what matters most to a chef is how the fish will taste when it is cooked. The most important factors in deciding how to cook a fish are its fat content and its body type.

Hubert Martini
The Culinary Institute of America

Fat Content Fish don't have much fat, and the fat they do have is different from the fat found in animals that live on the land. The fat in fish gives each type of fish its distinctive flavor. The higher the fat content, the stronger the fish's flavor. Fish that swim constantly have more fat and darker-colored flesh than fish that stay in one place. In terms of fat content, there are three types of fish:

- **Lean Fish.** With light-colored flesh, a mild flavor, and a delicate texture, lean fish easily separates into flakes once it is cooked. Lean fish tend to stay relatively still, living and feeding at the bottom of the ocean.
- **Moderately Fatty Fish**. With a richer, more deeply flavored flesh than lean fish, moderately fatty fish have a texture that is somewhat firmer than lean fish. They also separate into flakes when they are cooked.
- **Fatty Fish.** Many fatty fish are saltwater fish, who swim over great distances. Their flesh is the most deeply flavored and colored.

Body Type From a chef's perspective, fish have three basic body types:

- **Round Fish.** With eyes on both sides of their heads, **round fish** swim in an upright position, belly down and back up. The skin on the belly is usually paler and the skin on the back and sides is darker.
- **Flat Fish.** With both eyes on the same side of their heads, **flat fish** swim close to the bottom. They are wider than they are thick.
- **Non-Boney and Other Fish.** Some of these fish have cartilage (CART-ti-ledj), a flexible material, rather than bones. Others are unusual fish that don't fit in other categories.

 **Reading Checkpoint** *Based on fat content, what are the three types of fish?*

Selecting and Storing Fish

Fish are extremely perishable. They need to be kept chilled and iced from the moment they are caught. Fish must be checked for quality when they arrive at the kitchen. Professional kitchens are required to keep any certificates and invoices for the fish they receive.

Inspection and Grading Fish (and shellfish) are inspected by the National Marine Fisheries Service (NMFS), a part of the National Oceanic and Atmospheric Administration (NOAA). The NMFS is charged with inspecting all fish that is processed for sale, including fish caught in the wild and fish that is farm-raised. The NMFS even inspects fishmeal that is intended for use as animal feed.

Lean Flat Fish

Dover Sole ▲
Flesh is fattier and firmer than other members of the flat fish family. Baked, broiled, poached, sautéed, or steamed.

Lemon Sole ▲
Also called English sole, blackback flounder, and winter flounder. Light, slightly sweet, delicate flesh. Baked, poached, or sautéed.

Halibut ▲
Dense, snow-white flesh, with a fine texture and mild taste. Halibut has the highest fat content of all low-fat fish. Baked, broiled, fried, grilled, poached, sautéed, or steamed.

Others

Fluke (Summer Flounder)
White, flaky flesh, with a delicate flavor and texture. Baked, poached, or sautéed.

Gray Sole (Witch Flounder)
Light, slightly sweet, delicate flesh. Baked or poached.

Rex Sole
Delicate, creamy white flesh, with a distinct flavor. Poached or sautéed.

Rock Sole
Firm and creamy white flesh. Baked, poached, or sautéed.

▲ **Turbot (TUR-bow)**
Delicate flavor with a firm texture. Baked, broiled, fried, grilled, poached, steamed, or sautéed.

Lean Round Fish

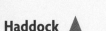

Haddock ▲
Firm texture, low fat, with a mild flavor. (The skin is left on fillets to distinguish them from Atlantic cod.) Poached, baked, sautéed, or pan-fried. Also salted or smoked.

Alaskan Pollack ▲
Also called Pacific pollack and snow cod. Light gray, flaky flesh with a mild flavor. Also smoked or processed to make Surimi (soo-REE-mee), a Japanese product shaped, flavored, and colored to resemble various types of shellfish, such as crab and shrimp.

Atlantic Cod ▲
Thick, white flesh with a mild flavor. Roe, cheeks, and chins are delicacies. Shallow poached, baked, pan-fried, or deep-fried. Also smoked, cured, salted, or dried.

Moderately Fatty Round Fish

Weakfish ▲
Also called sea trout. Sweet, delicate flesh. Poached, baked, sautéed, grilled, broiled, or steamed.

Black Sea Bass ▲
Also called rock sea bass. White, firm flesh, with a delicate texture. Poached, baked, deep-fried, or sautéed. Also pickled. Commonly served whole, using tableside presentation.

Striped Bass ▲
Coarse texture, large flakes, with flavorful flesh. Broiled, grilled, poached, baked, deep-fried, or sautéed. Also pickled. Extremely versatile.

Red Snapper ▲
Also called American snapper. Firm texture. Poached, baked, sautéed, grilled, broiled, or steamed

Atlantic Grouper ▲
Varieties: yellowfin grouper, yellowmouth grouper, black grouper, and red grouper. Sweet, white flesh. Poached, baked, broiled, steamed, or deep-fried. Also used in chowders.

Others

Walleyed Pike (Pike Perch)
Mild flavor, low fat content, with a firm texture. Broiled, sautéed, poached, steamed, baked, or stewed. Also used in soups.

Vermillion Snapper (Beeliner)
Often substituted for red snapper, though smaller; less flavorful. Poached, baked, sautéed, grilled, broiled, or steamed.

Tilefish
Firm yet tender flesh. Poached, baked, broiled, deep-fried, or pan-fried. Available whole and drawn or as fillets.

Fatty Round Fish

Rainbow Trout ▲
Firm, off-white flesh with a mild flavor. Poached, baked, broiled, fried, grilled, or steamed. Often stuffed. Generally sold head-on.

Atlantic Salmon ▲
Deep, pink flesh; high fat content. Poached, baked, broiled, steamed, or grilled. Also smoked. Raw in sushi. Used in dips and soups.

Coho Salmon ▲
Also called silver salmon. Similar in taste and texture to Atlantic salmon. Poached, baked, broiled, steamed, or grilled. Also smoked. Used in dips and soups.

Bluefin Tuna ▲
Dark red to reddish brown flesh, with a very distinct flavor when cooked. Baked, broiled, grilled, or sautéed. The most sought-after fish for sushi and sashimi (with consistently high prices).

Pompano (PAHM-pah-noh) ▲
Also called cobblerfish and palmenta. Delicate, beige flesh that turns white when cooked, with a complex flavor and medium fat content. Poached, baked, broiled, grilled, fried, or steamed. Expensive.

◀ **King Mackerel**
Also called kingfish. High fat content, finely textured and flavorful flesh. Baked, broiled, grilled, or sautéed. Also smoked.

Spanish Mackerel ▲
Delicate flesh. Baked, broiled, grilled, or sautéed. Also smoked.

Others

Albacore Tuna (AHL-ba-cor)
Light red to pink flesh that is off-white when cooked, with a mild flavor. Baked, broiled, grilled, or sautéed. Often canned and sold as "white tuna."

American Shad
White, sweet flesh, with a high fat content. Poached, baked, broiled, grilled, or sautéed. Also smoked. Eggs (roe) are considered a delicacy.

Artic Char
Dark red to rose or white flesh. Poached, baked, broiled, fried, grilled, or steamed. Often stuffed.

Bluefish (Blue Runner)
Dark, oily, strongly flavored flesh, with a fine texture. Baked or broiled.

Brook Trout (Speckled Trout)
Delicate and buttery flesh. Poached, baked, broiled, fried, grilled, or steamed. Often stuffed.

Chinook Salmon (King Salmon)
Medium to dark red flesh. Smoked, poached, baked, broiled, steamed, or grilled. Used in dips and soups.

Dolphinfish (Mahi Mahi, Dorado)
Pink to tan flesh turns off-white when cooked; firm texture with a large flake; sweet, delicate flavor. Baked, broiled, grilled, pan-fried, or sautéed.

Sockeye Salmon (Red Salmon)
Dark red flesh. Poached, baked, sautéed, grilled, broiled, or steamed.

Non-Boney and Other Fish

Monkfish ▲

Also called anglerfish, devilfish, frogfish, and goosefish. Very firm, mild white flesh. Baked, broiled, grilled, fried, sautéed, or pan-fried. Commonly sold as tails and fillets. Low yield when sold head-on. Livers are popular in Japan.

Eel ▲

High-fat, firm flesh, with a rich, sweet flavor. Broiled, fried, or stewed. Also smoked.

American Catfish ▲

Firm flesh, with a mild, sweet flavor. Poached, baked, broiled, grilled, steamed, stewed, deep-fried, or pan-fried. Also smoked. Commonly sold headless and skinless.

Anchovy ▲

Silver skin; soft, flavorful flesh. Deep-fried or pan-fried whole. Also smoked or marinated. Sold canned (packed in oil or salt) and dried. Used as a flavoring additive and garnish. When whole, best less than 4 inches in length.

John Dory ▲

Also called Saint Peter's fish. Firm, bright white flesh, with a delicate flavor and fine flake. Poached, grilled, or sautéed.

Sardine ▲

Silvery skin; delicate fatty flesh. Broiled, grilled, or deep-fried whole. Also marinated, salted, smoked, or canned. Available whole or dressed. When whole, best less than 7 inches in length.

Skate ▲

Also called a ray. White firm flesh, with a sweet flavor. Poached, baked, fried, sautéed. Fins (called wings) produce two fillets. The upper fillet is generally thicker than the lower one.

▲ Tilapia (til-AHP-ee-ah)

Also called mudfish. Off-white to pink flesh; flavor is very mild. Poached, baked, broiled, grilled, or steamed.

Others

Swordfish

Very firm, dense flesh, with a distinct flavor. Baked, broiled, grilled, or sautéed. Available skinless and headless, or as fillets or steaks.

Sturgeon

Firm, high-fat flesh, with a rich, delicate flavor. Baked, braised, broiled, grilled, or sautéed. Also smoked. Eggs used for caviar.

Mako Shark

Firm, pink to white flesh, with a sweet flavor. Poached, baked, broiled, grilled, fried, or sautéed.

CULINARY **SCIENCE**

Left- or Right-Eyed Fish?

When flat fish first hatch, they are shaped like round fish and are nearly transparent. They float on the water currents. Being transparent is most likely a way the fish have evolved to escape predator fish that might eat them.

The fish stay transparent as long as they are surviving on the food supplies in their yolk sacs. Once they begin to eat actual food, they start to change. Gradually, one eye starts to move across the fish's skull until eventually both eyes are on the same side of the head. The backbone and the skeleton also start to migrate, staying in line with the eyes.

Some fish have both eyes on the right side (right-eyed flat fish) and some have both eyes on the left (left-eyed flat fish). The skin on the side of the fish that has the eyes begins to darken and take on more color, usually a color that is very similar to the bottom surface. The skin on the side of the

▲ *Fluke*

fish opposite the eyes (the blind side) stays light; that is, the side of the fish that faces down toward the bottom.

Research

Research the life cycle of a flat fish. Make sure to discover if it is a left-eyed or right-eyed fish.

The NMFS has established three types of evaluation for fish:

- Type 1 is an evaluation for quality and wholesomeness.
- Type 2 is an evaluation of the accuracy of the labeling and weight.
- Type 3 is an evaluation of the sanitation of the processing facility itself.

If a facility passes a Type 1 inspection, it receives a mark from the United Sates Department of Commerce known as a **PUFI mark**, which stands for Processed under Federal Inspection. (Processors of fish and shellfish often pay for inspections that ensure adherence with HACCP guidelines, cleanliness, and safety.)

Grades are assigned as part of a voluntary program. Only fish and shellfish that receive a PUFI mark are eligible for the highest grade, which is US Grade A. These fish and shellfish are of the highest quality, with good shape, flavor, and aroma. Grade B is considered good quality, and fish graded C is considered fairly good quality. Grades B and C are used primarily for processed or canned products.

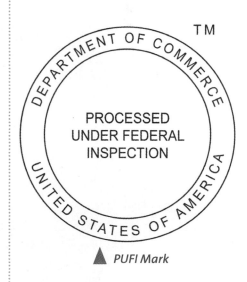

▲ *PUFI Mark*

Market Forms In fish markets, fish is sold in a variety of forms:

- **Whole Fish.** The fish as it was caught, completely intact and still including the stomach, is referred to as a **whole fish**. Whole fish that has the stomach removed is referred to as a **drawn fish** (or a drawn whole fish). If the head is also cut off, the fish is referred to as **headed and gutted fish**. A **pan-dressed fish** has the fins removed, and sometimes the head and tail are also cut off. Pan-dressed fish are usually small enough to fit easily in a pan and make a single serving.
- **Cross Cuts or Steaks.** A large drawn fish can be cut into sections. Large sections are known as **cross cuts**. Small cross cuts, pieces portioned for a single serving, are known as **steaks**. Because they are a cross cut, steaks contain at least a portion of the spine and may contain other bones.
- **Fillets.** A boneless piece of fish is called a **fillet** (FILL-eh). The skin may be left on or it may be removed, depending on the type of fish.
- **Frozen Fish.** **Glazed fish** is a whole fish that has been dipped in water and then frozen several times to build up a layer of ice. Fish fillets and steaks are also sold already trimmed, cut into portions, and then packaged and frozen.
- **Canned Fish.** Canned fish is completely cooked and packed in cans. Tuna and salmon are two common types of canned fish.
- **Salted, Cured, and Smoked Fish.** Salt cod is made by filleting cod, soaking it in a salty brine, and letting it dry. Cured fish is also brined or coated with salt. The fish takes on a salty and savory flavor. **Lox** is cured salmon.

Selecting Fish Whole fish should pass the following tests for freshness:

- **Smell the Fish.** The fish should have a clean, sweet, sea-like smell. If the fish doesn't smell good, it has failed the most important of all the tests.
- **Check the Temperature.** Fish should be received at a temperature of 41°F or less.
- **Look at the Fish.** Check for a good overall appearance: a clear slime, no cuts or bruising, and pliable fins. The scales (if there are any) should tightly adhere to the fish. If the fish still has its head, look at the eyes. They should look full, not shrunken or dried out.

FIGURE 15-1
Cross Cuts
Cutting directly across the fish results in a cross cut. Often cross cuts include bones.
Predicting *As a customer would you prefer a cross cut or a fillet?*

- **Press on the Fish.** The flesh should rise quickly after being pressed. It should not hold onto the mark.
- **Open the Gills and the Belly.** The gills, located near the fish's head, are the way it breathes. Once the fish is caught, the gills start to turn brown and may become slimy. If the guts have been removed, check inside the fish. The fish should be clinging to the bones, especially along the backbone.

Fish begin to lose moisture once it is cut. A small amount of liquid in the bottom of a container is hard to avoid, but there should not be a deep layer. Fish fillets and steaks should be packed in clean containers when you receive them.

If you are checking fillets or steaks for quality, look at the individual pieces. They should be neatly cut and of an even size. The fish should look moist and have very few if any cracks. If the skin is still attached to the fish, it should look moist and have no tears or punctures.

Storing Fish Before you received any fish, its quality and wholesomeness was someone else's responsibility. From the moment you accept a fish, its quality and wholesomeness become your responsibility.

Fresh fish lasts only a few days, even under the best storage conditions. Fish needs to be keep very cold and moist, but not wet. Whole fish, including drawn or pan-dressed fish, need to be stored in a bed of shaved ice.

To store whole fish:

1. Put a layer of shaved ice in a perforated hotel pan or container, preferably made of stainless steel.

2. Pack some ice into the belly cavity of the fish, and then put the fish belly facing down on the bed of shaved ice in the perforated container.

3. Mold the ice tightly around the fish.

FIGURE 15-2
Selecting Fish
Steps in checking for freshness. Press on the fish (left). Check the gills (middle). Check the belly (right).
Applying Concepts *What would you do if you doubted the freshness of a fish you were about to serve?*

CHEF'S TIP

WHY SHAVED ICE?

Shaved or flaked ice fits more tightly around the fish, reducing its contact with the air and keeping it cold. Make sure to permit melting ice to drain away from the fish.

Aquaculture

You may have read stories in the news about farm-raised fish, and you've probably seen farm-raised fish for sale in grocery stores. Aquaculture, the raising of fish and shellfish in a controlled environment, is actually an ancient practice. Ancient Chinese manuscripts describe the practice of raising fish. Ancient Egyptians may also have practiced aquaculture and passed their skills on to the Romans. The Romans raised oysters in beds, and as the Roman Empire expanded throughout Europe, they carried this knowledge along with them.

Until the 18th century, fish or shellfish for aquaculture were captured when they were immature. They were transferred to ponds and allowed to grow to maturity. Modern aquaculture is different. Rather than capturing fish, the male and female fish are collected when they are ready to spawn. The fish eggs and sperm are pressed out of the fish and then mixed together so the eggs become fertilized. Once the eggs are fertilized, they are raised in carefully controlled conditions.

Initially, only luxury items such as shrimp and oysters were raised this way. Today, more and more species are being farm-raised. Concerns have been raised about fish that have been genetically altered for quick growth. There are worries that the farmed fish might escape from their pens and drive out the

▲ *Raising fish on a fish farm*

wild species. There are also concerns about potentially toxic materials that are eaten by farmed fish and, in turn, eaten by us. Some chefs also feel that the taste and texture of wild seafood is better than that of farmed seafood. Despite all these concerns, it is difficult to imagine how the demand for fish could be met without aquaculture.

Research

Read three articles about farm-raised salmon. Write a paper describing the pros and cons of farm-raising salmon.

---

4. Set the perforated container in a second container to allow water from melting ice to drain away.

5. Re-ice the fish daily.

To store fish fillets:

1. Place the fish in a storage container (stainless steel is preferable, although food-grade plastic is acceptable).

2. Set the container in an ice-filled hotel pan.

◄
FIGURE 15-3
Storing Fish
Perforated hotel pan (left) and
fish stored on a bed of shaved
ice (right).
Drawing Conclusions *Why might
fish be stored with the belly facing
down?*

3. Keep fish fillets away from direct contact with the ice to keep as much flavor and texture in the fish as possible.

To store frozen fish:

1. Do not accept frozen fish with white frost on its edges. This indicates freezer burn, the result of improper packaging or thawing and refreezing of the product.

2. Store frozen fish at -20°F to 0°F until it is ready to be thawed and cooked.

Reading Checkpoint   *What are the five steps for testing for freshness in a whole fish?*

Preparing Fish

Chefs use a variety of techniques to prepare fish before they cook it. They select the technique based on the kind of fish they are preparing.

Filleting Fish Round fish are filleted by using a different technique than flat fish. Of course, many fish are sold already cut into fillets or even filleted and portioned. However, a kitchen may find it can control costs better, and improve the quality of the fish it serves, if it buys whole fish and asks chefs to fillet the fish themselves.

Round fish produce two fillets, one on each side of the backbone. Flat fish can be cut into two fillets or four fillets (which are sometimes known as **quarter fillets**).

Trimming a Fillet You can trim a fish fillet by removing any belly or pin bones. **Belly bones** are found along the thinner edge of the fillet. You can simply slice them away from the fillet. **Pin bones** are found in the middle of the fillet. To locate them, run your finger over the fillet from the head to the tail. Use needle-nose pliers or tweezers to pull out the bones. Pull them in the direction of the head to avoid ripping the flesh.

Filleting Round Fish

1 Place fish on cutting board with the backbone parallel to the side of the cutting board and the head on the same side as your dominant hand (that is, on your right, if you are right-handed).

2 Cut behind head and gill plates, using a fish filleting knife. Angle the knife down and away from the body. Cut to the backbone only. Do not cut off the head.

3 Turn knife, without removing it, so the cutting edge points toward the tail.

4 Run blade down the length of the fish, cutting against the backbone. Avoid sawing the knife back and forth.

5 Remove fillet and lay it skin-side down on the cutting board.

6 Repeat on the second side.

FIGURE 15-4 ▶
Removing Pin Bones
Use needle-nose pliers to pull out pin bones.
Prediction *As a customer, would you be upset if you discovered pin bones in your fillet?*

Filleting Flat Fish (Quarter Fillets)

1 Place fish on cutting board with the head away from you and the tail toward you.

2 Make a cut on one side of the backbone from the head to the tail.

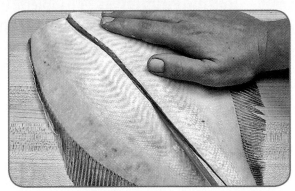

3 Cut along the bones, working from the center to the edge. Keep the blade angled slightly so the cut is very close to the bones.

4 Remove the first quarter fillet and lay it skin-side down on the cutting board. Trim away any internal organs attached to the fillet.

5 Turn the fish around so the tail is toward you.

6 Cut along the bones, working from the center to the edge, to remove the second fillet.

7 Turn the fish over.

8 Remove the bottom fillets, using the same technique as for the first and second fillets.

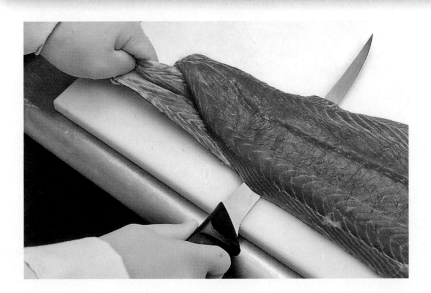

◀

FIGURE 15-5
Removing Skin
The cutting edge of the knife should be against the skin.
Drawing Conclusions *Why might a restaurant want to keep the skin on a fish?*

To remove the skin, lay the fillet parallel to the edge of the cutting surface. Hold the knife so the cutting edge is cutting against the skin and pull it taut with your guiding hand. Push the knife from one end to the other with a slight back-and-forth motion.

Rolling Paupiettes A **paupiette** (poh-PYET) is a thin fillet that is rolled up before it is cooked. This gives the fish a neat appearance and also helps it cook evenly. Paupiettes are generally made from lean fish, such as flounder or sole, although they may be made from some moderately fatty fish, such as trout or salmon. A paupiette is often filled with a stuffing.

FIGURE 15-6
Rolling Paupiettes
Roll the fillet from the head to the tail.
Predicting *As a customer, would you rather be presented with a stuffed paupiette or a thin fillet?*

Cutting Fillets Fillets can be cut into slices, using either an angled cut or a straight cut. By angling the blade as you cut, the cut slice, called a **tranche** (TRAHNSH), will have more surface area. A straight cut, called a **goujonette** (goo-zhohn-NET) or sometimes a fish finger, is usually about the width of a thumb.

FIGURE 15-7
Cutting a Fillet
A slice from a fillet can be angled to create a tranche (left) or cut straight to create a goujonette (right).
Predicting *What cooking methods would be best used with a tranche cut?*

 **Reading Checkpoint** *How do you fillet a flat fish? A round fish?*

Matching Cooking Methods to Fish Types

The basic guideline for cooking fish is: the leaner the fish, the more delicate the cooking method you should choose.

Sautéing Fish

1 Heat pan and cooking fat over moderate heat.

2 Dust fish with flour.

3 Add fish to the pan carefully to avoid splashing.

4 Sauté on the first side until golden.

5 Turn fish once and finish cooking on the second side.

6 Remove fish from the pan and keep fish warm.

7 Pour off fat from the pan, but do not wipe it out.

8 Return pan to heat.

9 Add whole butter and cook until the butter has a nutty smell.

10 Add lemon juice and parsley. Serve the fish very hot with the lemon-butter-parsley mixture.

 See Recipe Card 100, "Sautéed Trout Meunière."

Determining Doneness in Fish No matter what type of fish you are preparing, fish is fully cooked when it reaches an internal temperature of 145°F. At that temperature, the fish will be more firm than when it was raw. The flesh, which is somewhat translucent when raw, will be opaque. Some types of fish may flake when they are done. The flakes should slide apart and appear very moist.

Some people may prefer fish cooked slightly less (especially salmon and tuna), but you should cook fish this way only if the customer specifically requests it or if the menu clearly states that you cook fish to a medium or medium-rare doneness.

Sautéing Sautéing works well for lean fish, including flounder, sole, halibut, and cod. Some moderately oily fish, such as trout, bass, and salmon, are also suitable for sautéing. Denser fish, such as tuna, shark, and swordfish, can also be successfully sautéed.

When sautéing, the more delicate the fish, the lower you should make the temperature. A fragile Dover sole fillet needs less intense heat than a piece of tuna. The small amount of fat used during sautéing keeps the fish moist and flavorful and helps prevent it from sticking to the pan and tearing.

CHEF'S TIP

SIZZLER PLATTER
Some restaurants refer to the broiling pan as a sizzler platter.

Most fish sautés call for the fish to be dusted with flour to create a slight crust, as well as to keep the moisture in the fish from spattering too much when the fish is put into the hot oil. A classic presentation for fish is to dip it in flour, sauté it quickly, and then serve it with a sauce made of butter, lemon, and parsley. The name for this dish is à la meunière (ah la muhn-AIR).

Pan Frying and Deep Frying Frying is a good technique for most lean and some moderately fatty fish. Frying indicates that the fish will be given a coating of some kind, such as a batter or a coating of breadcrumbs or cornmeal. Pan frying calls for more fat in the pan than sautéing does, usually enough to cover about one-third of the fish.

Deep-fried fish are cooked in enough hot oil to completely submerge them. Fish sticks, fish and chips (coated in cornmeal batter and fried), and a fisherman's platter that includes a variety of fish and shellfish are some common fried fish dishes.

Grilling and Broiling Grilling is suitable for virtually all fish, but the fish must be prepared properly for the grill. Moderately oily and oily fish such as mackerel, bluefish, and snapper usually require nothing more than seasonings. A marinade is also a common way to season and prepare moderately oily and oily fish for the grill. Their naturally firm and meaty texture holds up well to the intense heat of the grill. You do need to brush both the grill and the fish lightly with oil to keep the fish from sticking and tearing. Leaner fish can be grilled but you need to use a hand rack. A hand rack is a cooking rack that opens, allowing fish to be inserted, and then closes. It is turned by hand. With a hand rack, you can lift and turn fish so they don't fall apart.

Grilled salmon ▲

Broiled fish can be prepared in the same way as grilled fish. When broiling, the heat is located above the fish instead of below it, so fish usually does not need to be turned. Because it is not turned, fish can be coated with a sauce and then broiled. Fish prepared in this manner is known as au gratin (oh GRAH-ten). If the fish is brushed with butter and topped with breadcrumbs before it is broiled, the dish is known as à l'anglaise (ah lahn-GLEZ).

Baking and Roasting Whole fish, fillets, and steaks can all be cooked in the oven. Whole fish are referred to as being roasted, while pieces are typically referred to as being baked. There is no significant difference between baking and roasting fish.

Baked salmon ▲

To keep the fish moist, it often has some sort of topping or crust. Other possibilities for roasted or baked fish include adding aromatics to the fish as it cooks or even stuffing the whole fish or fillets with a stuffing mixture.

Steaming It is important to cook steamed fish just until it is done. Fish begins to dry out and lose flavor if it is overcooked. Asian cuisines have many classic preparations of whole steamed fish, but you can also steam smaller portions, such as fillets or steaks.

One special adaptation of the steaming technique calls for the fish to be wrapped, usually in parchment paper and often with aromatics and vegetables. Then the package is baked in the oven, causing the water in the vegetables and fish to steam the food. This is referred to as cooking the fish **en papillote** (ahn pap-ee-YOTE).

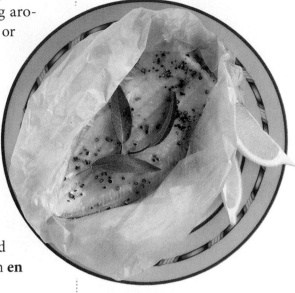

▲ *Sole en papillote*

BASIC CULINARY SKILLS

Broiling Fish

1 Butter or oil a broiling pan lightly.

2 Add a bed of aromatic ingredients, if desired.

3 Season prepared fish and brush with butter.

4 Add a breadcrumb topping or sauce to the fish.

5 Broil a few inches from the heat source, raising or lowering the broiler rack, until

the top is browned and the fish is cooked through.

6 Serve at once on heated plates.

 See Recipe Card 102, "Broiled Lemon Sole on a Bed of Leeks."

Poached trout ▲

Poaching Fish is often poached. If you cook fish in enough liquid to completely cover it, you are **deep poaching** the fish. If you use just enough liquid to create some steam in the pan, you are **shallow poaching** the fish.

Deep poaching is typically used for fish steaks, whole fillets of larger fish such as salmon, or whole fish. Deep-poach fish until they are just cooked through. Keep the temperature of the liquid low so there are only a few small lazy bubbles breaking the surface. The poaching liquid can be reserved to use as a broth or as the base for a soup.

Shallow poaching cooks fish quickly. It is most often used for portion-sized fillets or fillets that have been rolled around a filling. The poaching liquid is almost always used to make a sauce that is served with the cooked fish.

✓ **Reading Checkpoint**   *What is the safe internal temperature for fully cooked fish?*

15.1 ASSESSMENT

Reviewing Concepts

1. Based on fat content, what are the three types of fish?
2. What are the five steps for testing freshness in a whole fish?
3. How do you fillet a flat fish into quarter fillets?
4. What is the safe internal temperature for fully cooked fish?

Critical Thinking

5. **Classifying** Based on body type, what are the three types of fish?
6. **Drawing Conclusions** Explain why a PUFI mark is important in evaluating your supplier of fish.
7. **Recognizing Patterns** Can you see why the leaner the fish, the more delicate the cooking method you should choose for it? Explain.

Test Kitchen

Divide into six teams. Each team will cook the same cut and type of fish in a different way. The cooking options are: sautéing, pan frying and deep frying, grilling and broiling, baking and roasting, steaming, and poaching. Each team must select its own recipe. Evaluate each team's results.

SCIENCE

NMFS

Research the National Marine Fisheries Service (NMFS). Write a report identifying two recent NMFS issues that could affect the quality of our seafood.

15.2 Shellfish

> ## "From shrimp to caviar, we associate seafood dishes with luxury. "
>
> – Ken Arnone

Types of Shellfish

Shellfish are aquatic animals protected by some type of a shell. There are two types of shellfish:

- **Mollusks.** Shellfish that have soft bodies and no skeletons are **mollusks**. Many mollusks are protected by shells, and some have only a small amount of cartilage on the inside of their bodies. Abalones (a-buh-LOH-nee), clams, oysters, mussels, scallops, octopus, and squid are all mollusks. Squid is often called **calamari** (cahl-ah-MAHR-ee).
- **Crustaceans.** The second type of shellfish is **crustaceans** (crus-TAY-shuns), which have jointed exterior shells. Examples of crustaceans are lobsters, crabs, shrimp, and crayfish (also called crawdads).

Fresh and frozen shellfish are available in various forms.

- **Fresh Shellfish.** Fresh shellfish is available from suppliers in the following forms: live, shucked, tails, cocktail claws, and legs and claws.
- **Frozen Shellfish.** Frozen shellfish is available from suppliers in the following forms: shucked, tails, cocktail claws, and legs and claws.

Shucked shellfish means the seafood has been removed from its shell. When you purchase shucked shellfish, you receive the meat along with the shellfish's natural juices, known as its **liquor**.

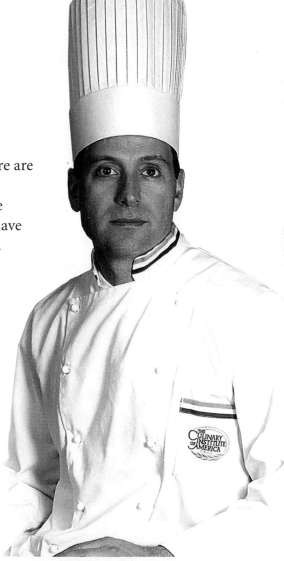

Ken Arnone
The Culinary Institute of America

Mollusks such as oysters, clams, and mussels may be available shucked. Scallops are nearly always sold shucked.

 **Reading Checkpoint** *What are the two types of shellfish?*

Receiving and Storing Shellfish

For any restaurant specializing in shellfish, receiving and storing them is critically important. Few other foods spoil more quickly. It is important to purchase shellfish from reputable suppliers. As discussed in Chapter 10, you should buy only depurated mollusks. (Depurated mollusks have been placed in tanks of fresh water to purge them of their impurities.) Every food-service establishment must keep full records of the fish and shellfish they purchase.

To avoid spoilage, you must store live mollusks, such as oysters or mussels, at a temperature between 35° and 40°F. Do not hold them in fresh water or directly in ice; it will kill them. Mollusks need to be alive when served raw. If they are to be cooked, they must be alive at the beginning of the cooking process.

Live lobsters, crabs, shrimp, and crayfish should be packed in seaweed or damp paper upon delivery. Look for signs of movement, indicating they are still alive. If a lobster tank is not available, lobsters can be stored directly in their shipping containers or in perforated pans under refrigeration until they are to be prepared.

Shrimp is the most popular of all shellfish. It is most commonly available previously frozen or frozen with the heads removed, although you occasionally will find fresh shrimp with their heads on. Shrimp is sold by the number of shrimp per pound. This is known as the **count**.

Clams, mussels, and oysters should have a sweet, sea-like aroma. Look for tightly closed shells. When purchased live in the shell, clams, mussels, or oysters should be delivered in a bag or sack. Store them directly in the bag in a perforated pan and keep the bag tightly closed and weighted to

Crab ▲

Shrimp ▲

Shrimp Counts and Sizes

Count (Shrimp per Pound)	Common Name
10 or fewer	Colossal
11 to 15	Jumbo
16 to 20	Extra-Large
21 to 30	Large
31 to 35	Medium
36 to 45	Small
About 100	Miniature

prevent it from opening. Any open shells should close immediately when they are tapped. Shells that do not close indicate the mollusk is dead and should be discarded, along with any that have broken shells. Store shellfish in their containers under refrigeration as you would fish fillets.

 **Reading Checkpoint** *At what temperature should live mollusks be stored?*

Preparing Shellfish

Thaw frozen shellfish safely by either placing it in the refrigerator until it thaws or putting the shellfish, still in its packaging, in a container and letting cool water run over it in a sink.

Lobster Lobster is best when purchased alive. The first step in preparing a lobster to boil or steam is to kill it. Lobsters can be split before they are broiled or baked.

BASIC CULINARY SKILLS

Preparing Live Lobsters

1 Leave the bands on the lobster's claws.

2 Place lobster, stomach-side down, on a cutting board.

3 Insert the tip of a chef's knife into the base of the head.

4 Pull the knife down, through the shell, splitting the head in half.

5 Reverse the direction of the lobster.

6 Split the tail by starting at your initial cut and cutting through the shell of the tail section.

Removing Meat from a Cooked Lobster

1. **Hold tail section securely** in one hand while holding the body with the other.
2. **Twist your hands** in opposite directions, pulling tail away from the body.

3. **Pull the tail meat out** of the shell. It should come away in one piece.

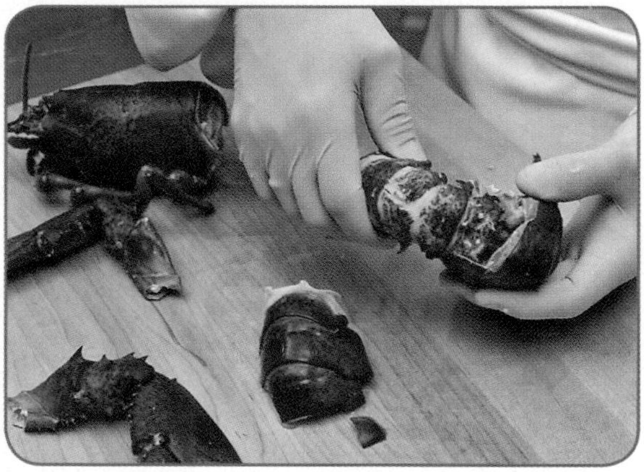

4. **Crack the claws,** using the heel of a chef's knife.

5. **Pry the shell away from the claw meat,** using your fingers. The meat should also come out in a single piece, retaining the shape of the claw.

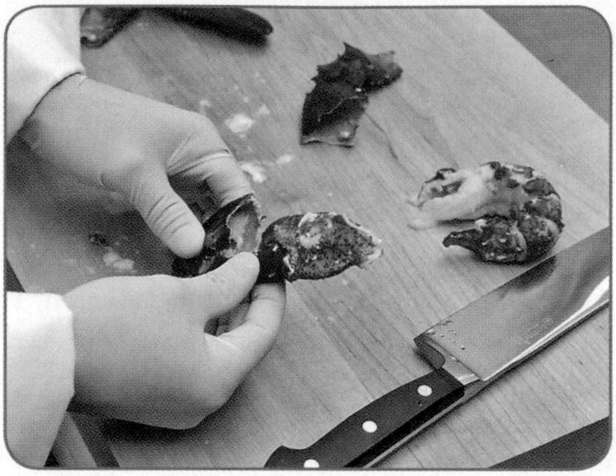

6. **Cut through the knuckles.**

7. **Pull out the knuckle meat.**

New England

Traditional New England cooking is often regarded as hearty comfort food. It draws heavily on the culinary influences of its original settlers, the English. You'll find large cuts of meat cooked either by roasting or by braising (known in New England as a pot roast). As you might imagine, in a part of the United States where winters are long and cold, there are lots of filling, long-cooked dishes that were originally prepared in pots suspended over an open fire or in communal ovens. For example, a traditional Saturday night supper throughout New England is baked beans.

Early New England cooks drew heavily on the resources of the area. They adapted dishes they had been familiar with in their European homes. Homegrown ingredients, such as maple syrup, fiddlehead ferns, and berries, came to play an important role in New England's culinary landscape. The cooks also drew their inspiration from the sea, from the abundant fish and shellfish found along the New England coast. But, perhaps most importantly, New England has been associated with lobsters.

New England clam chowder, a rich and rib-sticking soup made with plenty of fresh clams (often a specific type of clam known as a chowder clam—a larger, tougher clam that is chopped or ground before it is added to the soup). The broth is milk and the thickener is potatoes.

Native Americans showed the early settlers how to use pits to prepare seafood. A shore dinner, as this pit-style of cooking is often known, remains a regional favorite. A shore dinner is prepared by digging a pit in the sand, filling the pit with rocks, and then adding enough driftwood to produce a hot fire. Once the fire burns out and the rocks are hot, a layer of seaweed is added. Then fish and shellfish (including lobsters, of course) are added, often along with aromatic vegetables, potatoes, and corn. Finally, a tarp or cloth is used to cover the pit and trap the steam that comes from the seaweed.

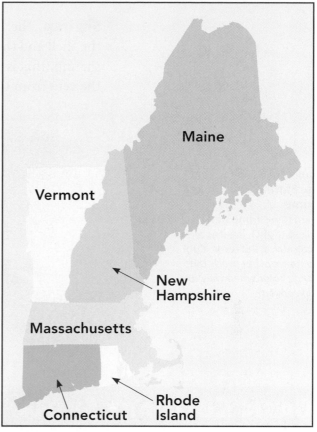

Research

1. Compare recipes for clam chowder from Rhode Island, Maine, and New Hampshire.

2. What are the characteristics of American lobster and how does it compare to lobster from the Mediterranean and Caribbean?

◄ *Maine is famous for its lobsters.*

Once a lobster is cooked and cool enough to handle, you can remove the edible meat to produce a large tail portion and intact claw sections as well as smaller pieces from the knuckles and legs.

Shrimp There are two steps to cleaning shrimp. First, you remove the shell and then you remove the vein that runs along the back of the shrimp (this is actually the intestinal tract of the shrimp). Removing the vein from the shrimp is referred to as **deveining** (dee-VANE-ing).

FIGURE 15-8 ▶
Raw Shrimp and Cooked Shrimp
When raw shrimp (left) is cooked (right), it turns pink. **Recognizing Patterns** *Can you name other foods that change color when they are fully cooked?*

BASIC CULINARY SKILLS

Peeling and Deveining Shrimp

1 Pull the shell away from the shrimp, starting on the underside of the shrimp where the feathery legs are located.

2 Place shelled shrimp on a cutting board, with the curved outer edge of the shrimp on the same side as your cutting hand.

3 Make a shallow cut on the curved outer edge by using a paring or utility knife.

4 Scrape out the vein, using the tip of the knife.

A special tool is available for deveining shrimp, but a paring knife works well too. For shrimp dishes that are grilled or sautéed, you need to clean the shrimp before cooking. When boiling or steaming shrimp, you can clean them either before or after cooking. Shrimp that has been boiled or steamed in the shell are moister and plumper than shrimp that were peeled and deveined before cooking. After cleaning, the shells can be reserved for other uses, such as making shrimp stock, bisque, or shellfish butters.

Clams, Oysters, Mussels, and Scallops Mollusks such as clams, oysters, scallops, and mussels are sold already shucked. However, many restaurants purchase clams, oysters, and mussels live in their shells. These restaurants may use the oysters in a raw bar or they may have dishes that require clams, oysters, or mussels in their shells. It is important, in this sort of restaurant, to be able to open the clams and oysters with ease. Freshly shucked clams and oysters are often used for cooked dishes (shucked mussels are less commonly used). When opening oysters and clams, be sure to reserve any juices. They add great flavor to soups, stews, and stocks.

Mollusks

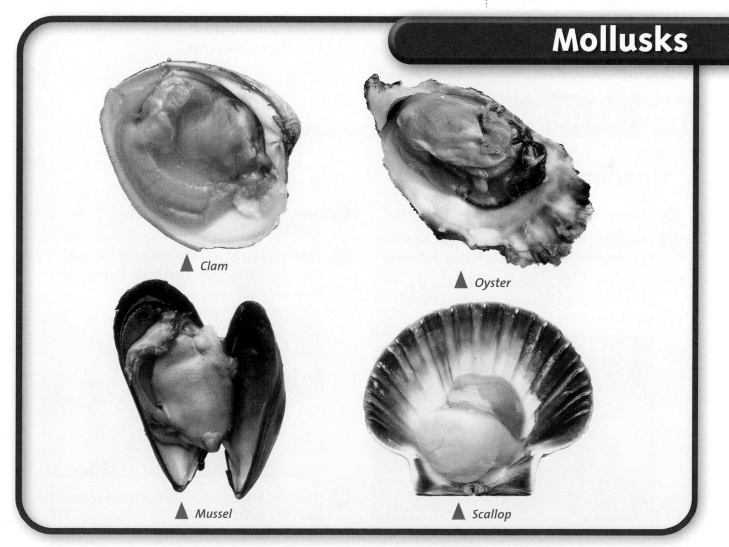

▲ *Clam*

▲ *Oyster*

▲ *Mussel*

▲ *Scallop*

Opening Clams

1. **Wear a wire mesh glove** to hold the clam.

2. **Place the clam in your hand** so the hinged side is facing outward.

3. **Work the side of a clam knife** into the seam between the upper and lower shells. You can use the fingers of your gloved hand to help guide the knife and give it extra force.

4. **Twist the blade slightly,** like a key in a lock, to pry open the shell.

5. **Slide the blade over the inside of the top shell** once it is open, to release the clam from the shell.

6. **Slide the blade under the clam** to release it from the bottom shell.

Opening Oysters

1. **Wear a wire mesh glove** to hold the oyster.

2. **Place the oyster in your hand** or on a cutting board so the hinged side is facing outward.

3. **Work the tip of an oyster knife** into the hinge, holding the upper and lower shells together.

4. **Twist the blade,** like a key in a lock, to break open the hinge.

5. **Slide the blade over the inside of the top shell,** once it is open, to release the oyster from the shell.

6. **Slide the blade under the oyster** to release it from the bottom shell.

◄ **Figure 15-9**
Removing the Beard
Pull the beard away from the shell.
Drawing Conclusions *When preparing a dish with mussels, what are the implications for your mise en place?*

Before using any mollusks, you need to clean them. Clams and oysters are easy to clean. Scrub them well with a brush under cold running water. Discard any that remain open when tapped (this indicates that the clam or oyster has died and can't be eaten safely). If any closed shell feels unusually heavy or light, check it. Occasionally, you will find empty shells or shells filled with clay or sand.

Mussels are rarely served raw. The method for cleaning them before steaming or poaching is similar to the cleaning method used for clams and oysters. However, unlike clams and oysters, mussels have a dark, shaggy beard, which is removed just before cooking. Once the beard is pulled away, the mussel dies. To clean a mussel, hold it under cold running water. Use a brush with stiff bristles to thoroughly scrub the mussel and remove all the sand, grit, and mud from the outer shell. Then, pull the beard away from the shell. Because removing the beard kills the mussel, do not clean the mussel and pull off the beard until you are ready to begin cooking the mussel.

Reading Checkpoint *How do you prepare live lobsters?*

▲ *Steamed mussels*

▲ *Fried clam basket*

▲ *Grilled lobster tails with drawn butter*

Matching Cooking Methods to Shellfish

As discussed in Chapter 10, oysters and clams are often served raw in a raw bar. The clams and oysters are served freshly shucked on the half shell. Aside from being served raw, you can use almost any of the basic cooking techniques when cooking shellfish.

Shellfish has a pronounced flavor, sometimes briny and slightly salty (shrimp and oysters) and sometimes slightly sweet (scallops, crabs, or lobsters). This flavor allows shellfish to pair well with strong flavors, including tomatoes, olives, capers, and ham. You can choose accompaniments for shellfish that contrast with these flavors. Or, you can use a rich cream sauce or even melted butter. Butter that is used as a sauce for shellfish is known as **drawn butter**. It is actually clarified butter. To make it, you melt butter and separate the melted butterfat (the clarified butter) from the milk solids and water.

Lemon wedges are a common garnish for seafood dishes, either added directly to the dish or served alongside the shellfish for the guest to add to taste.

Steaming and Boiling Shrimp, lobsters, crab, and crayfish are typically steamed or boiled. (For crabs, sometimes only the legs are steamed.) After being steamed or boiled, they may be eaten hot or cold. Adding aromatics, including herbs, spices, and vegetables, is a common practice that adds more flavor to the shellfish.

Mussels, clams, and oysters are often steamed. They can be steamed in a steamer, suspended over a simmering liquid. Another way to steam mussels, clams, and oysters is in the marinara style. In this style of steaming, the cleaned shellfish is placed in a pot along with a small amount of flavorful liquid such as a broth. Additional ingredients, including garlic, onions, tomatoes, olives, or even diced ham, are often added. The pot is covered and the liquid is brought to a simmer. The lid traps the steam and the shellfish is cooked in the steam until the shells open. The mussels, clams, and oysters become plump and their edges start to curl.

Frying Clams, oysters, shrimp, and squid can be coated with a batter or breadcrumbs and fried until crisp on the outside. This technique provides a good contrast of flavors and textures for shellfish. Scallops are another type of shellfish that is often fried because the coating protects the sweet, moist flesh of the shellfish while developing a golden, crunchy coating. Be sure to season shellfish before you dip them in batter or add a coating, so they are as flavorful as possible.

Grilling and Broiling Scallops, shrimp, and lobsters are often prepared by grilling or broiling. Use skewers to hold small shellfish such as shrimp or scallops on the grill. Lobsters are typically halved before grilling or broiling.

Sautéing or Stir Frying Sautéed or stir-fried shrimp or scallops are very popular. It is important to cook shrimp and scallops quickly at a fairly high temperature. Shrimp and scallops will often be soaked briefly in a marinade that has a blend of sweet and savory flavorings. The marinade often helps caramelize the cooked shrimp or scallops.

Baking and Roasting Lobster is sometimes baked. Squid and octopus are sometime stuffed and baked. Clams are often topped with a savory breadcrumb mixture and baked. Shellfish are often added to stuffing for fish or poultry. For example, many Thanksgiving turkeys are filled with oyster stuffing. Discard the marinade after soaking the shellfish.

▲ *Stir-fried shrimp*

▲ *Vietnamese stuffed squid*

 **Reading Checkpoint**) *Describe five ways that shellfish is cooked.*

15.2 ASSESSMENT

Reviewing Concepts

1. What are the two types of shellfish?
2. At what temperatures should live mollusks be stored?
3. How do you prepare live lobsters?
4. Describe some of the ways that shellfish can be cooked.

Critical Thinking

5. **Classifying** What type of shellfish are crayfish?
6. **Drawing Conclusions** Why is it important for a food-service establishment to keep full records of the fish and shellfish they purchase?
7. **Recognizing Patterns** What relationship does the count have to the size of shrimp?

Test Kitchen

Divide into six teams. Each team will cook the same size shrimp in a different way. The cooking options are: steaming and boiling, frying, grilling and broiling, sautéing and stir frying, baking and roasting. Each team must select its own recipe. Evaluate each team's results.

SCIENCE

Oysters

Research the life cycle of oysters in the wild. Compare this to the life cycle of farmed oysters. Based on your findings, write a report on oyster farming.

Review and Assessment

Reviewing Content

Choose the letter that best answers the question or completes the statement.

1. Shellfish are
   a. fish with shells
   b. aquatic animals protected by some type of shell
   c. lobsters, but not clams, oysters, or mussels
   d. clams, oysters, and mussels, but not lobsters

2. An example of a mollusk is a (an)
   a. lobster, but not a clam, oyster, or mussel
   b. clam, oyster, or mussel, but not a lobster
   c. shrimp, but not a lobster
   d. oyster, but not a scallop

3. An anadromous fish is a
   a. freshwater fish
   b. saltwater fish
   c. farm-raised fish
   d. fish that spends part of its life in saltwater and part in freshwater

4. An example of a lean flat fish is
   a. Atlantic salmon
   b. lemon sole
   c. Atlantic cod
   d. striped bass

5. An example of a fatty round fish is
   a. Atlantic salmon
   b. lemon sole
   c. Atlantic cod
   d. striped bass

6. A drawn fish is a
   a. whole fish
   b. whole fish with its head removed
   c. whole fish with its head and stomach removed
   d. whole fish with its stomach removed

7. Live mollusks should be stored at a temperature between
   a. 0°F–20°
   b. 20°F–30°
   c. 30°F–35°
   d. 35°F–40°

Understanding Concepts

8. What do you do when you shuck shellfish?

9. What is the relationship between the count of shrimp and their size?

10. Which type of NMFS inspection is the most important for a food-service establishment?

11. At what temperature is a fish fully cooked?

12. What is the difference between shallow poaching and deep poaching?

13. How can you tell if a stored clam, mussel, or oyster is alive?

Critical Thinking

14. **Applying Concepts** What effect would cooking mussels have on your mise en place?

15. **Predicting** With what type of cooking method would you be most likely to use a tranche cut? A goujonette cut?

16. **Comparing/Contrasting** What is the difference between opening clams and opening oysters?

Culinary Math

17. **Applying Concepts** You are making a recipe for broiled shrimp that requires 3½ pounds of extra-large shrimp and serves 20. You need to expand the recipe to serve 60. How many pounds of shrimp do you require? About how many shrimp will that be? About how many shrimp is a portion?

On the Job

18. **Applying Concepts** To increase efficiency, a cook debearded the mussels that will be used for steamed mussels early in the mise en place. The steamed mussels are prepared as they are ordered. Do you have any concerns?

19. **Communicating** A customer has received a salmon steak and sends the fish back because there are bones in it. What should you do?

LAB **ACTIVITY**

Use the following Recipe Cards to test your culinary skill.

    99. Poached Salmon with Asparagus and Basil Sauce

    100. Sautéed Trout Meunière

    101. Flounder à l'Orly

    102. Broiled Lemon Sole on a Bed of Leeks

    103. Poached Trout Paupiettes with Vin Blanc Sauce

    104. Broiled Stuffed Lobster

    105. Mussels Marinara

Project 15: Farm-Raised versus Wild

Answer these questions when your class works through Project 15.

- What were the differences in price between the farm-raised salmon and the wild salmon?

- Did you notice any differences between the two types of raw salmon?

- Did you notice any differences in the cooking of the two salmons?

- Did you notice any differences in the taste or texture of the two salmons?

TEST PRACTICE

Choose the letter that best answers the question or completes the statement.

1. A pan-dressed fish always has its
- **A** head removed
- **B** tail removed
- **C** fins removed
- **D** fillets removed

2. Glazed fish are
- **A** fish dead for over three days
- **B** whole fish dipped in water and frozen
- **C** salted fish in which the salt forms a glaze
- **D** fish with the skin removed

3. Lox is
- **A** cured salmon
- **B** cured trout
- **C** cured red snapper
- **D** cured sole

4. Where are pin bones found?
- **A** near the tail of a fish
- **B** near the head of a fish
- **C** in the middle of a fillet of a fish
- **D** in the center part of a squid

5. Calamari is another name for
- **A** octopus
- **B** squid
- **C** crayfish
- **D** both octopus and squid

6. You typically devein
- **A** lobsters
- **B** squid
- **C** shrimp
- **D** scallops

7. Which mollusk is rarely served raw?
- **A** crayfish
- **B** oysters
- **C** shrimp
- **D** mussels

8. When do you remove a mussel's beard?
- **A** immediately upon receiving it
- **B** within 24 hours of receiving it
- **C** within 24 hours of serving it
- **D** immediately before preparing it

9. What is the count for medium shrimp?
- **A** 21–30
- **B** 31–35
- **C** 36–45
- **D** Over 45

10. Which are not usually purchased by restaurants live in their shells?
- **A** scallops
- **B** mussels
- **C** oysters
- **D** clams

16

MEAT & POULTRY

16.1 Meat

READING PREVIEW

Key Concepts

- Understanding meat inspection and grading
- Identifying various types and cuts of meat
- Receiving and handling meat
- Preparing meat for cooking

Vocabulary

- aged (beef)
- boxed meat
- butterflied
- crown roast
- dry aging
- dry cured
- fabrication (of meat)
- forequarter
- foresaddle
- frenching
- game
- grain (of meat)
- hare
- haunch
- hindquarter
- hindsaddle
- lamb
- marbling
- mutton
- offal
- primal cuts
- quarters (of meat)
- retail cuts
- saddle
- seams (in meat)
- sides (of meat)
- silverskin
- subprimal cuts
- variety meat
- veal
- venison
- wet aging

> **"C**ooking meats properly is a balancing act. You have to match the right method to the cut.**"**
>
> – Johann Sebald
> The Culinary Institute of America

Inspection and Grading of Meat

Meat is one of the costliest items on the menu—but also one of the most potentially profitable. To get the most value from the meat you buy, it is important to understand how to receive, store, and prepare it properly. However, before you can begin this process, you need to understand the inspection and grading process for meat.

Meat Inspection Government inspection of all meat (including game and poultry) is required. In fact, inspections are required at various times—on the farm or ranch, at the slaughterhouse, and again after butchering. Most meat is inspected by federal inspectors. States that have their own meat inspections must meet or exceed federal standards. Both federal and state inspections are paid for with tax dollars.

Federal and state inspectors ensure that:

- Animals are free from disease.
- Farms are operated according to appropriate standards for safety, cleanliness, and health.
- Meat is wholesome and fit for human consumption.

Quality Grading Quality grading, unlike inspection, is voluntary. The US Department of Agriculture (USDA) has developed specific standards that are used to assign grades to meat based on its quality. The USDA also trains graders, ensuring that quality standards are consistent across the country. Because quality grading is voluntary, the individual meat packer—not the taxpayer—absorbs the cost involved in grading meat. Packers may choose not to hire a USDA grader to assign a quality grade. Instead, packers may assign grades based on their own standards. However, those standards must meet or exceed federal standards.

The grade placed on a particular carcass is applied to all the cuts from that particular carcass. Quality graders consider the following (adjusting the standards according to the type of meat being graded):

- The overall shape of the carcass
- The ratio of fat to lean meat
- The ratio of meat to bone
- The color of the meat
- The amount of fat present in the lean flesh (this is known as **marbling** in beef)

Butchering After slaughtering, inspection, and grading, a large animal carcass is butchered. It is first cut into manageable pieces. The exact standards for individual animal types govern where the cuts are made. There are typically two ways to cut up a carcass:

- **Sides and Quarters.** The first cuts made in this type of butchering divide the carcass into sides and then into quarters. **Sides** are prepared by making a cut down the length of the backbone. **Quarters** are made by cutting sides into two pieces and dividing them at specific points. The front quarter is called the **forequarter**. The rear quarter is called the **hindquarter**. Larger carcasses, such as those of beef and pork, are usually cut up this way.
- **Saddles.** This type of butchering divides the carcass into two portions by cutting across the belly. Each portion includes the left and right side of the carcass. Whenever a portion includes both the left and right side of the carcass, the portion is called a **saddle**. The front portion of the carcass is called the **foresaddle**. The rear portion is called the **hindsaddle**. Smaller carcasses, such as veal, are often cut up this way.

FOCUS ON NUTRITION

B Vitamins

Meat is a rich source of important nutrients such as protein. It is also one of the most reliable sources of the B vitamins. In fact, people who do not eat any meat at all may not get adequate supplies of B vitamins unless they take a supplement.

The next step is to cut the quarters or saddles into **primal cuts** (or, as they are sometimes referred to, primals). These are portions that meet uniform standards for beef, veal, pork, and lamb. Primal cuts are then broken down into **subprimal cuts** (or subprimals).

Subprimals can be trimmed, packed, and then sold to restaurants or butcher shops. A restaurant buying a subprimal would need to do additional butchering to break down the subprimal into portion-sized cuts of meat. This type of butchering is called **fabrication**.

Increasingly, however, subprimals are broken down at the packing plant and sold in smaller pieces, referred to as **retail cuts**.

Most food-service establishments buy boxed meat. **Boxed meat** is meat that is fabricated to a specific point (such as primal, subprimal, or retail cuts) and then packed and boxed. At that point, as boxed meat, it is ready to ship for sale to restaurants, butchers, and retail outlets.

FIGURE 16-1
Butchered Sides of Beef
The grade placed on a carcass is applied to all the cuts from that particular carcass.
Drawing Conclusions *Why would a restaurant use retail cuts rather than fabricating cuts from a carcass?*

Common Retail Cuts

Retail Cut	Description
Steak	Portion-sized cut, with or without the bone, that typically includes well-defined portions of lean meat and fat; dry heat methods for cooking.
Roast	Large, multi-portion cut intended for roasting or braising.
Chop	Portion-sized cut that often includes a portion of the rib; both dry heat and moist heat are used.
Cutlet	Thin, tender, boneless portion-sized cut, often taken from the leg or rib; typically requires dry heat methods.
Medallion	Small, round or oval, portion-sized cut often from the rib or loin; typically requires dry heat methods.
Noisette (nwah-ZEHT)	Small, tender, round portion-sized cut, usually from the rib or loin; typically requires dry heat methods.
Emince (EH-manss)	Small, thin, portion-sized cut; typically requires dry heat methods.
Stew Meat	Small chunks, typically .75 to 1.5 inch, of relatively lean meat cut from a variety of the primal cuts; used for stewing.
Ground Meat	Ground meat, including some percentage of fat, from various primals; also referred to as hamburger and minced beef.

Types and Cuts of Meat

The flavor, color, and texture of any meat are influenced by several factors: the amount of exercise the muscle receives, the animal's age, the type of feed it received, and its breed.

Beef The animals used in the beef industry are typically young males (steers) and females (heifers). The older the animal, the less tender the meat.

Specialty beef is available from other countries, such as Kobe (KOH-bay) beef from Japan and Limousin (lee-MOO-zan) beef from France. Specialty beef from the United States includes Certified Angus, natural beef, and organic beef.

Beef may be **aged**, a process that gives meat a darker color, a more tender texture, and a fuller flavor. Boneless cuts such as steaks may be vacuum-packaged and stored under refrigeration for several weeks, a process referred to as **wet aging**. **Dry aging** calls for the side, forequarter, or hindquarter to be hung in a climate-controlled area. Aged beef is expensive due to additional processing costs as well as the significant moisture and weight loss that reduce the ultimate yield.

There are eight USDA (US Department of Agriculture) grades of beef. From the highest to the lowest quality, they are Prime, Choice, Select, Standard, Commercial, Utility, Cutter, and Canner. The top three grades, Prime, Choice, and Select, come from younger beef. Grades lower than Select are generally used for processed meat, such as frankfurters, and are not used in the restaurant or retail industry. The grades most widely sold retail are Choice and Select.

- **USDA Prime.** Only a small percentage of beef is graded Prime. This grade is usually reserved for hotels, restaurants, and butcher shops. Prime beef is the most tender, juicy, and flavorful. It has abundant marbling, which enhances both flavor and juiciness. Prime roasts and steaks are excellent for dry cooking methods (roasting and broiling).
- **USDA Choice.** The most popular quality and the most widely sold grade in retail stores. Choice beef is very tender, juicy, and flavorful. It has less marbling than Prime.
- **USDA Select.** Very uniform in quality, Select beef is gaining in consumer popularity because it is leaner than the higher grades (it has less marbling). Not as juicy or flavorful as Prime or Choice, Select beef is often marinated before cooking or cooked by using moist heat methods.

A beef forequarter contains four primal cuts: the chuck (shoulder), the rib, the brisket and foreshank, and the short plate. The hindquarter also

▲ *USDA Grade Shields*

contains four primal cuts: the loin, the sirloin, the flank, and the round (leg). These primal cuts may be sold individually, or, as is more often the case, they are broken down into subprimal cuts or retail cuts.

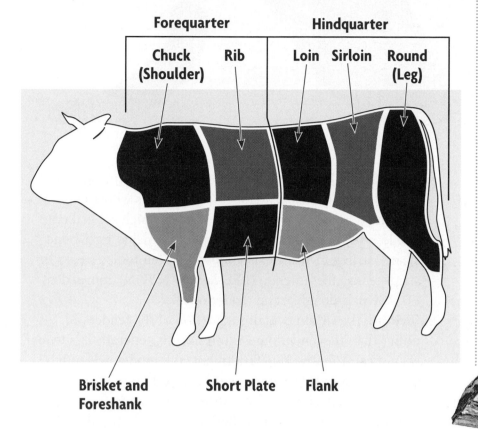

Forequarter

Chuck (Shoulder)   **Rib**

Hindquarter

Loin   **Sirloin**   **Round (Leg)**

Brisket and Foreshank   **Short Plate**   **Flank**

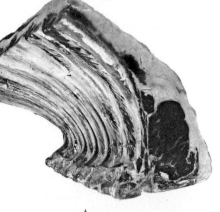

◀ **FIGURE 16-2**
Beef Primal Cuts
Both the forequarter and the hindquarter are broken into four primal cuts each.
Relating Concepts *Have you ever seen one of these cuts in a butcher shop or grocery store?*

▲ *Beef rib*

The following list summarizes the cooking methods and uses for the eight beef primal cuts.

- **Chuck (Shoulder).** Moist heat and combination cooking methods are appropriate for cuts from the chuck primal, which usually need long, slow cooking. The meat is sold as roasts (bone-in or boneless) or cut into steaks. Chuck is often used for stew meat and ground beef.
- **Rib.** Roasting, grilling, broiling, and sautéing are the most common cooking methods for most cuts from the primal rib. The rib is often sold whole. It is also sold in smaller roasts (bone-in and boneless), or cut into steaks such as rib eye steaks.
- **Brisket and Foreshank.** The brisket is typically braised. It is also used to make corned beef. When cured and smoked, it is used to make pastrami. The foreshank is typically braised or used in stews.
- **Short Plate.** This primal cut is under the primal ribs. Short ribs and skirt steak are fabricated from the short plate. Short ribs are often braised, while the skirt steak is cooked with dry heat methods, such as grilling.

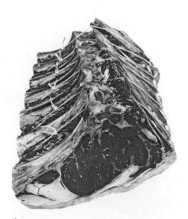

▲ *Rib roast (trimmed and tied)*

▲ Boneless rib eye roast

▲ Beef brisket

▲ Skirt steak

▲ Strip loin (top view)

- **Loin (Short Loin).** The front portion of the loin contains some very tender meat. Most cuts are sold as whole roasts (which are roasted or braised) or steaks (which are grilled). The loin produces a variety of retail cuts, including T-bone steaks, strip loin steaks (also known as Delmonico steaks or strip steaks), filet mignon (FEE-lay me-NYON), tournedos (TOUT-nah-doughs), and tenderloin tips.
- **Sirloin.** The sirloin contains a portion of the tenderloin. Other than the tenderloin, sirloin meat is generally less tender than meat from the loin. Sirloin butt is a moderately tough retail cut. Roasting, grilling, broiling, and sautéing are the most common cooking methods for sirloin cuts.
- **Flank.** Flank steak is below the loin and is almost always sold whole. Flank steak can be grilled, but it is also often braised, sometimes with a stuffing.
- **Round (Leg).** The most common cooking methods for cuts from the round are braising and stewing. Two portions of the round, the knuckle and the eye of the round, can be roasted. Cuts from the round are often made into cubes for stew meat or kebabs. Meat from the bottom round is often ground.

▲ Tenderloin (top view)

▲ Flank steak

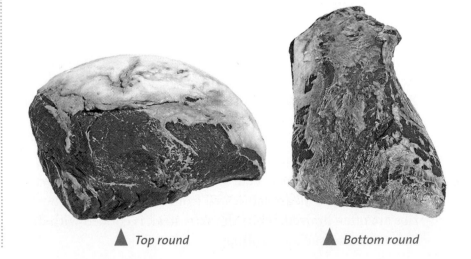

▲ Top round

▲ Bottom round

Kitchens also use cuts other than those from primal cuts. These cuts include organs, such as the liver, as well as some muscles—the tongue, for example. Overall, this type of meat is known as **variety meat**, or as **offal** (AH-full).

Beef Variety Meat

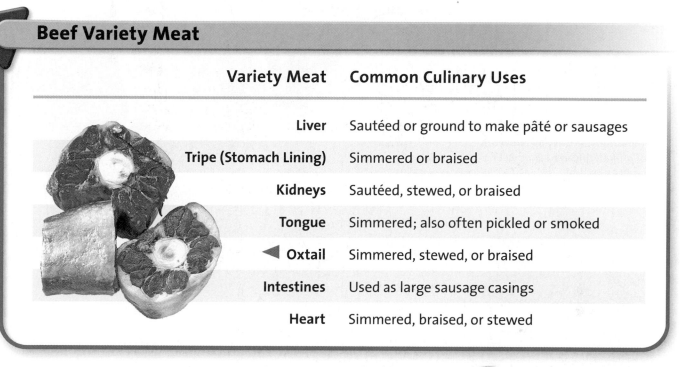

Variety Meat	Common Culinary Uses
Liver	Sautéed or ground to make pâté or sausages
Tripe (Stomach Lining)	Simmered or braised
Kidneys	Sautéed, stewed, or braised
Tongue	Simmered; also often pickled or smoked
◀ Oxtail	Simmered, stewed, or braised
Intestines	Used as large sausage casings
Heart	Simmered, braised, or stewed

Veal Veal comes from a young calf, generally two to three months old. It has delicate, tender flesh that is pale pink in color. Milk-fed veal is no more than 12 weeks old at the time of processing. Veal of this age has received mother's milk or formula only. Formula-fed veal may be up to four months old, but the calf's diet contains no grass or feed.

There are six USDA grades of veal: Prime, Choice, Good, Standard, Utility, and Cull. Only Prime and Choice are used in the restaurant industry or purchased retail. Prime has abundant marbling and is generally very juicy and tender. Choice is somewhat less juicy, less flavorful, and with less marbling.

Veal is usually cut into a foresaddle and a hindsaddle, but it can be split into two sides, similar to beef. The primal cuts for veal are the shoulder (also known as the chuck), shank, rack (or rib), breast, loin, and leg. Variety meat from veal is highly prized, especially the sweetbreads, liver, calf's head, and brains.

The following list summarizes the cooking methods and uses for the six veal primal cuts.

- **Shoulder (Chuck).** Moist heat or combination cooking methods, such as stewing, simmering, and braising, are appropriate for roasts from the shoulder primal. Stew meat and ground meat are commonly made from less desirable cuts.

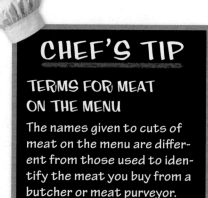

CHEF'S TIP

TERMS FOR MEAT ON THE MENU

The names given to cuts of meat on the menu are different from those used to identify the meat you buy from a butcher or meat purveyor.

▲ *Veal shoulder roast*

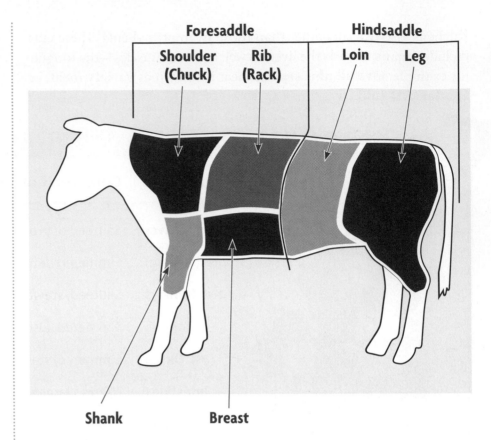

Shoulder (Chuck)   Rib (Rack)   Loin   Leg

Shank   Breast

FIGURE 16-3 ▶
Veal Primal Cuts
The foresaddle is broken into four primal cuts, but the hindsaddle is broken into only two primal cuts.
Comparing/Contrasting *How are veal primals different from beef primals?*

▲ *Veal rib*

▲ *Veal shank*

- **Rib (Rack).** Ribs can be roasted whole (both bone-in and boneless) or they may be broken down into individual chops and cooked by using dry heat cooking methods. A **crown roast** is prepared by tying a rib roast into a crown-shape.
- **Shank.** Meat from the shank is often braised. The meaty shank is used to prepare osso bucco (AW-soh BOO-koh), an Italian method of braising veal shanks with aromatic vegetables.
- **Breast.** The breast (bone-in or boneless) is often stuffed and rolled, before being braised or slowly roasted.
- **Loin.** Prized for its tender meat, the meat of the loin has an even texture. Cuts from the loin are very tender and are suitable for dry heat techniques such as roasting, grilling, broiling, and sautéing. Whole roasts (bone-in), chops, and boneless portion-sized cuts are available. Bones for the roasts or chops

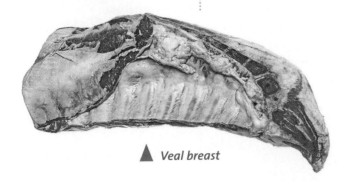

▲ *Veal breast*

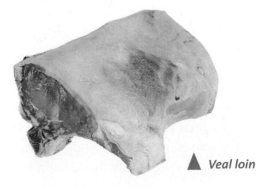

▲ *Veal loin*

are often scraped clean before they are cooked, a technique known as **frenching**.

- **Leg.** Veal legs may be purchased whole and then broken down into their smaller pieces. A subprimal cut from the leg is the top round. Veal from the top round has the best texture and cooks the most evenly.

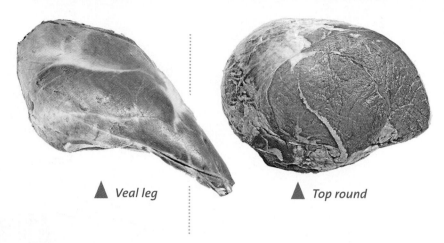

▲ Veal leg　　　　▲ Top round

Veal Variety Meat

Variety Meat	Common Culinary Uses
Sweet Breads (Pancreas or Thymus Gland)	Poached or sautéed
Tongue	Poached, simmered, or braised (and may be pickled or smoked)
Cheeks	Typically braised
Liver	Sautéed or used to make terrines and pâtés
Heart	Simmered or braised
◀ Kidneys	Sautéed, braised, or stewed
Feet	Simmered (feet are often used to give stocks body)

Pork Pork, the meat of domesticated pigs, is some of the most popular meat sold in the United States. Pigs have been specifically bred over many generations to produce the leaner cuts of meat sold today. Pigs are commonly slaughtered when they are most tender, under the age of 12 months.

The USDA grades for pork reflect two quality levels: Acceptable and Utility. Within the Acceptable grade, there are four grades (grades 1 through 4) based on yield. The higher the grade the more meat compared to fat or bone. Generally, a bigger animal has more lean meat. Stores sell only USDA Acceptable, grade 1 or 2 pork. Lower yield or utility grade is mainly used in processed products and is not available in supermarkets. The pork you buy may have quality grades assigned by a meat packer, rather than federal grades. The grading system used by an individual packer must be clearly defined and match or exceed federal standards.

FOCUS ON SAFETY

Certified Pork

Pork can be contaminated with a parasite. Consuming contaminated pork results in trichinosis, a foodborne illness. Pork can also be contaminated with e. coli, salmonella, or toxoplasmosis. Pork labeled "certified pork" has been tested not only for safety, but also for quality and the animals' living conditions.

The pork carcass is split into two halves along the backbone, like beef. However, then it is divided in a slightly different manner from most other meat. Instead of dividing the rib and loin into two portions, the rib and loin are left together in one long primal loin. Other primal cuts include the Boston butt, shoulder, belly, and ham.

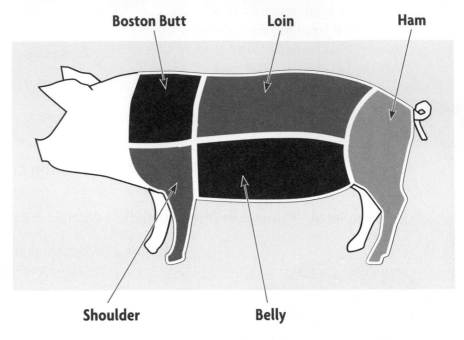

The following list summarizes the cooking methods and uses for the five pork primal cuts.

- **Boston Butt.** This primal cut (bone-in or bone-out) often has regional names, such as daisy ham or cottage butt. Boston butt is used to prepare a specialty ham known as tasso (TA-soh). Common cooking methods for the Boston butt include roasting, sautéing, and stewing. It may also cured or smoked. The smoked version is also known as English bacon.
- **Shoulder.** This primal pork cut is most suitable for stewing and braising (but may, because of the relatively high fat content, be roasted with some success). It is also used for ground pork. Because of the relatively high fat ratio, the shoulder is often used to make sausages. The shoulder is sometimes known as a picnic ham.
- **Loin.** Cuts from the pork loin are tender and suitable for dry heat and quick cooking methods such as roasting, grilling, broiling, sautéing, and pan frying. The meat is sold as whole roasts (bone-in and boneless), chops (bone-in or boneless), and cutlets. The loin may be cured or smoked. It is known in the United States as Canadian-style bacon. Baby back ribs are also part of the loin. They are usually slow cooked by braising or barbecuing.

Figure 16-4
Pork Primal Cuts
The pork loin is left long.
Comparing/Contrasting *How is the pork loin different from loins from other animals?*

▲ *Pork, Boston butt*

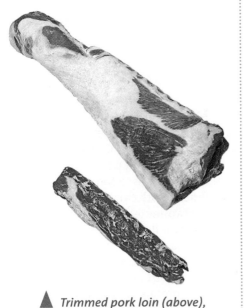

▲ *Trimmed pork loin (above), pork tenderloin (below)*

- **Belly.** Bacon is made by curing or smoking the belly. Dry heat methods, including pan broiling, are appropriate for bacon. Spareribs are also cut from the belly. This very popular cut is sold whole or cut into portions.

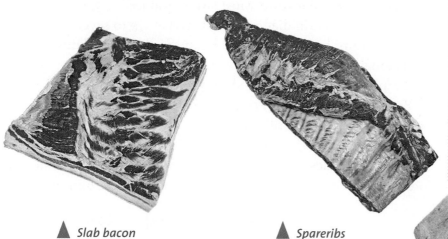

▲ *Slab bacon*　　　▲ *Spareribs*

- **Ham (Leg).** Bone-in or boneless cuts from the ham may be whole roasts, steaks, or portion cuts. Top round is often prepared as thin boneless cuts and sautéed or pan fried. The ham is typically roasted, baked, often with a glaze, or boiled. The shank can be simmered, stewed, or braised. These cuts are often smoked or cured. A ham can be a fresh, cured, or smoked. Prosciutto is **dry cured** (cured by rubbing with salt and often seasonings) and then dried. Smithfield ham is dry cured and then smoked.

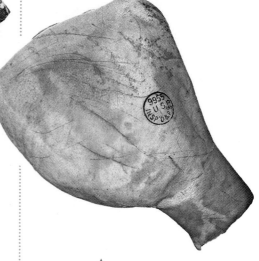

▲ *Ham, top view*

Pork Variety Meat

Variety Meat	Common Culinary Uses
Jowl Bacon	Crumbly form of bacon from the jowl, used for flavoring rather than as slices
Fatback	Clear fat from the back that has no traces of lean meat; used in pâtés and terrines
Neckbones	Smoked; used for flavoring in soups, stews, and broths
Liver	Used for sausages, pâtés, and terrines
Heart	Simmered, braised, or stewed; used for sausages, pâtés, and terrines
Intestines	Used for sausage casings
Kidneys	Simmered, stewed, or braised

Lamb and Mutton **Lamb** is the tender meat produced by young, domesticated sheep. The texture of lamb is a direct result of what the lamb consumes and the age at which it is slaughtered. Milk-fed lamb has the most delicate color and flavor. Grass-fed lamb has a more pronounced flavor and texture. Most lamb produced in the United States is finished on a grain diet and butchered at six to seven months old. The meat from sheep that is over 16 months old is called **mutton**. Mutton is tougher than lamb and has a strong, gamey taste.

Lamb for the restaurant industry and retail consumption is graded Prime or Choice, with Prime the most tender, juicy, and flavorful. Lower grades (Good, Utility, and Cull) are only used commercially.

Like veal, lamb is usually cut into either a foresaddle and a hindsaddle or into sides. There are five primal lamb cuts: the shoulder, the foreshank and breast, the rib (known also as rack), the loin, and the leg.

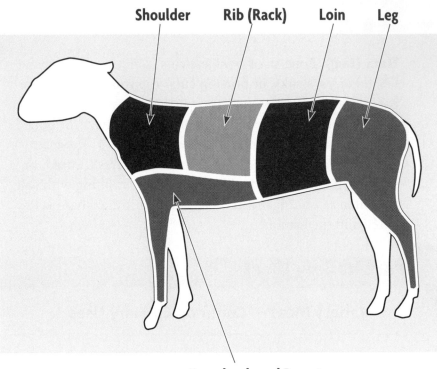

FIGURE 16-5
Lamb Primal Cuts
Lamb is cut into five primal cuts.
Relating Concepts *Which animal does lamb most resemble in terms of its primal cuts?*

▲ *Square-cut shoulder of lamb*

The following list summarizes the cooking methods and uses for the five lamb primal cuts.

- **Shoulder.** Common cooking methods include simmering, braising, and stewing. Cuts are sold as roasts and chops, as well as cubed and ground meat. Some boneless cuts may be roasted or grilled.
- **Foreshank and Breast.** The lamb foreshank is usually braised or simmered. The breast can be braised, simmered, broiled, or grilled.

- **Rib (Rack).** The rib is typically roasted, either as a rack, a crown roast, or a bone-in roast. Chops from the ribs are sautéed, broiled, or grilled. Chops may be single or double-boned. Bones may be frenched before cooking. The breast is usually braised or stewed. It may also be cut into small ribs (often called riblets) and barbecued.

▲ *Full rack of lamb*

▲ *Frenched rack with a single rib chop*

- **Loin.** Meat from the loin is tender and best suited to quick-cooking dry heat methods (sautéing, grilling, or broiling) to achieve the best flavor and texture. Whole cuts (bone-in or boneless) are usually roasted. English chops are bone-in and may be a single- or double-bone cut. Saratoga chops are boneless and may also be single- or double-bone cuts. The boneless cuts may be used for cutlets, emince, medallions, or noisettes.

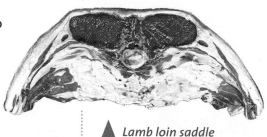

▲ *Lamb loin saddle*

- **Leg.** Some cuts from the leg are tender enough for dry heat methods. Cuts from the leg (sirloin, top round, bottom round, and eye round) can be roasted or braised. The top round is also used to prepare steaks or cutlets. The lamb shank and heel are typically braised, stewed, or simmered. The leg may be **butterflied** (split down the middle and then spread open) and grilled or stuffed and braised.

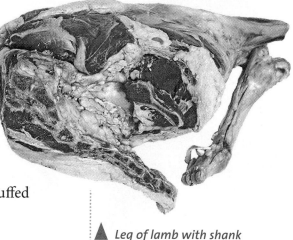

▲ *Leg of lamb with shank*

Lamb Variety Meat

Variety Meat	Common Culinary Uses
Tongue	Simmered, often smoked
Liver	Sautéed; used in pâtés and terrines
Heart	Simmered, braised, or stewed
Kidneys	Simmered, braised, or stewed
Intestines	Used for sausage casings

▲ *Venison shoulder, outside*

▲ *Venison haunch, outside*

▲ *Rabbit, side view*

Game **Game** is a general term for meat of wild mammals and birds. Although the term **venison** can be used as a general term for large game animals, in the United States venison typically refers to the meat from any member of the deer family, including antelope, caribou, elk, moose, reindeer, red-tailed deer, white-tailed deer, and mule deer. Meat from other popular large game, such as buffalo and wild boar, is usually identified as such in a restaurant.

The most popular small game animal is rabbit. It has mildly flavored, lean, tender meat with a fine texture. A **hare** is a type of large rabbit and is usually wild. They can weigh from 6 to 12 pounds. A mature rabbit that has been raised commercially for food typically weighs from 3 to 5 pounds, while a young rabbit weighs around 2½ pounds.

Game that is sold in restaurants is typically raised commercially for food. More game meat, and more varieties of game, is now being farm-raised. Most large game animals produce meat that is dark red and very lean. The flavor, color, and texture of the flesh are a direct result of its age and diet as well as the season.

The same general rules that determine how to cook red meat will typically work for venison and other large game:

- Cuts from less exercised portions such as the loin and the rib may be prepared by any technique. Dry heat methods such as grilling or roasting are frequently used.
- Well-exercised areas of the animal, such as the **haunch** (the hindquarters of a deer, consisting of the leg and the loin), the shank, and the shoulder are best when cooked by moist heat or combination methods. These cuts are also used for preparing pâtés and terrines.

✔ **Reading Checkpoint** *What are the eight beef primal cuts?*

Receiving and Handling Meat

Meat is quite perishable. When you receive it, check its temperature by inserting a thermometer between packages, but do not puncture the packaging.

- Meat should be received below 41°F.
- Meat that has been subjected to previous temperature abuse will be dry or discolored.
- Look for packaging that is clean and intact.
- Check the temperature inside the storage area of the delivery truck.

At the proper temperature and under optimal conditions, meat holds for several days without noticeable loss of quality. Meat can also be

Home on the Range

For most animals that are raised as food, home on the range means living on a factory farm. The high demand for meat, poultry, and dairy products means that these foods need to be mass produced. For the animals, this means living conditions that are far removed from what nature intended. And for the consumer, it can mean food products of poor nutritional value that might also, over time, pose health problems.

▲ *Free-range cattle, a healthier alternative?*

In recent years, many farmers and ranchers are trying something different. They are raising free-range animals. Instead of being confined to cages or pens, these animals are allowed to roam freely outdoors. Instead of eating commercially produced grain feed, they are able to graze on grass and plants in a pasture. Their diet is often organic, meaning it is free of pesticides, antibiotics, and hormones.

Pesticides are toxic chemicals sprayed on crops. They are consumed by animals and then in turn consumed by us. Pesticides can impair the immune system and cause diseases. Antibiotics are given to factory-farmed animals to cut down on disease. Overuse of antibiotics can lead to strains of bacteria that are resistant to drugs. Some factory-farmed animals are also fed hormones to make them grow faster, and cows are sometimes given a hormone to produce more milk. There is growing concern that hormone residues in meat and dairy might be harmful to our health, potentially disrupting our own hormone balance.

Free-range animals fed an organic diet are a quality food source. Research shows that free-range chickens have 21% less fat and 28% fewer calories than factory-raised chickens, and are often juicier and tastier. Their eggs have 34% less cholesterol. The meat from cattle raised on grass instead of grain has 4 to 6 times less fat and more essential nutrients, such as omega-3 fatty acids, vitamin E, and beta-carotene.

Although it takes a lot of grass and a lot of land to raise animals naturally, animals that are truly home on the range offer a healthy alternative food source.

Research

Research grass-fed beef. Compare how it differs in nutritional value, consistency, texture, and flavor to conventional beef.

frozen for longer storage. To keep meat properly chilled and prevent cross-contamination, follow these guidelines:
- Wrap and store meat under refrigeration, below 41°F.
- Hold meat in a separate unit, when possible, or in a separate part of the cooler.

- Place uncooked meat on trays to prevent them from dripping onto other food or onto the floor. Store on the bottom shelf.
- Keep different kinds of meat separated; for example, beef should not come into contact with pork.
- Store vacuum-packed meat directly in its packaging if the packaging has not been punctured or ripped.
- Once meat has been removed from its packaging, rewrap it in air-permeable paper, such as butcher's paper.
- For meat with a short shelf life (variety meat and uncured pork products), cook as soon as possible.

 **Reading Checkpoint**   *At what temperature should meat be stored?*

Preparing Meat

Meat must be prepared before it is served. Some steps are performed before you cook the meat, and some are done after the meat is cooked, before you serve it to a guest.

Trimming Chefs refer to the **grain** of the meat. What they are talking about is the direction that the fibers in the meat are running. Some meat preparation techniques call for meat to be cut across the grain. This means you slice the meat across the fibers. Others techniques call for the meat to be cut with the grain, that is, in the same direction as the fibers.

Some cuts of meat are actually several different muscles. These muscles are connected by a membrane. Chefs refer to these membranes that join the muscles as **seams**. Cutting along a seam helps separate a large cut into smaller pieces.

Many cuts of meat have fat you should cut away before cooking. Visible, or surface, fat is usually trimmed away. Sometimes, however, you may leave a thin layer of fat to provide natural basting, especially during long slow-cooking methods such as roasting or braising. For sautéing and other quick-cooking methods, you should usually remove the fat completely.

Silverskin is a tough membrane that surrounds some cuts of meat. It gets its name from its somewhat silvery color. Silverskin is likely to shrink when exposed to heat. When it shrinks, it can cause meat to buckle and cook unevenly. So before cooking you should remove any silverskin, along with any gristle or tendons (tough connective tissue that holds muscles onto the bones). As you trim meat and poultry, work carefully to be sure you don't cut away edible meat.

Cutting and Pounding Cutlets A cutlet may come from the loin, the tenderloin, or any other sufficiently tender cut of meat, such as the top round. Based on a restaurant's theme or style of menu, different types of restaurants will use different words for a cutlet. Some of the more common terms for a cutlet are scallop; scaloppine (skol-a-PEE-nee), typically used in Italian restaurants; and escalope (eh-SKAL-oph) used in French restaurants.

Cutlets are pounded to make sure they have an even thickness over their entire surface. This allows them to be rapidly sautéed or pan fried. When you make cutlets you need to adjust the weight of the mallet and strength of the blow to match the meat. Veal cutlets require a more delicate touch than pork cutlets, for example.

BASIC CULINARY SKILLS

Making Cutlets

① **Trim meat** completely. Remove all visible fat, tendons, gristle, and silverskin.

② **Cut pieces** of the same thickness and weight (generally ranging from 1 to 4 ounces).

③ **Place meat** between two layers of plastic wrap.

④ **Pound meat.** Use a pounding and pushing motion to pound cutlets to an even

thickness over their entire surface. Do not tear or overstretch the meat.

⑤ **Arrange pounded cutlets** on parchment-lined sheet pan. Keep well chilled until ready to cook.

 See Recipe Card 109, "Pork Cutlet with Sauce Robert."

Preparing Meat for Stewing or Grinding It is usually best to cube meat that you intend to use for stewing or for grinding. This meat is usually tougher and fattier than other meat.

For both stew meat and meat you will be grinding, remove the surface fat and any large pockets of fat. Cut meat along seams. Remove silverskin, tendons, and gristle. Cut meat into cubes of relatively even size and shape. To make meat more tender in a stew, cut against the grain. To prepare meat you will be grinding, make sure your cubes are small enough to slide easily through the feed tube of a grinder.

Grinding Meat Grinding meat calls for scrupulous attention to safe food-handling practices. Observe the following procedures for best results:

- Clean the grinder well and put it together correctly. Make sure the blade is sitting flush against the die. In this position, the blade cuts the food neatly rather than tearing or shredding it.

- Chill all grinder parts that will come in contact with the meat by either chilling them or putting them in an ice bath. Grind the meat into a stainless steel bowl that is placed in a larger bowl of ice.

- Do not force the meat through the feed tube. If the pieces are the correct size, they will be drawn through the tube easily.

- Be sure the blade is sharp. Meat should be cut cleanly, never mangled or mashed, as it passes through the grinder.

- For all but very delicate meat (for example, some types of organ meat), begin with a die that has large openings. The ground meat will appear quite coarse. The lean meat and fat will be visible as separate components in the ground meat.

- Continue to grind through progressively smaller dies until the desired consistency is achieved. The coarse appearance of the meat starts to become finer as the lean meat and fat blend.

FIGURE 16-6
Grinding Meat
Start grinding meat with a die that has large openings.
Relating Concepts *Why would you put the bowl of ground meat in a bowl of ice?*

Tying a Roast

1 **Cut lengths of string** long enough to wrap completely around the meat twice.

2 **Pass one length of string** around the meat and cross one end over the other end.

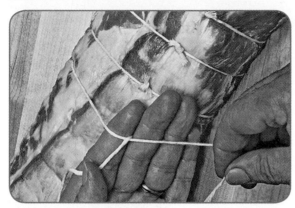

3 **Make a loop** by passing one end around the index finger of one hand.

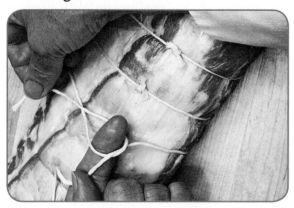

4 **Pass the string underneath itself.**

5 **Push the end of the string through the opening** where your fingertip was.

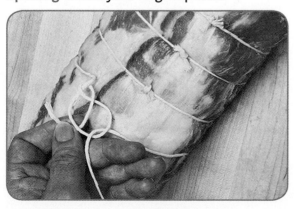

6 **Pull both ends of the string to tighten** until the string is pressing firmly against the meat.

7 **Loop one end of the string** completely around your thumb and forefinger and pull the other end of the string through the loop.

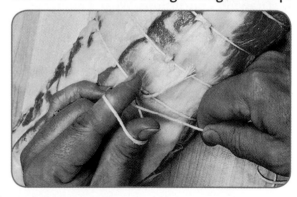

8 **Pull both ends of the string** to tighten securely. Trim any long strings so the knots are neat.

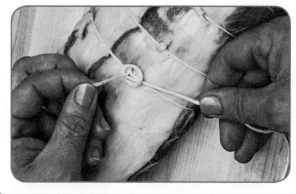

9 **Repeat.** Tie lengths of string at even intervals until the entire piece of meat is securely tied.

Tying a Roast Tying a roast with secure knots that have the right tension is one of the simplest and most frequently required types of meat fabrication. It ensures that the roast will be evenly cooked and that it will retain its shape after roasting.

 **Reading Checkpoint** *How do you make cutlets?*

16.1 ASSESSMENT

Reviewing Concepts

1. What is a primal cut?
2. What are the eight beef primal cuts?
3. At what temperature should meat be stored?
4. How do you make cutlets?

Critical Thinking

5. **Recognizing Patterns** Which animal doesn't have a primal rib cut?
6. **Drawing Conclusions** What advantages does specifying the primal cuts offer to meat packagers, butchers, restaurants, and diners?
7. **Comparing/Contrasting** Compare the appropriate cooking methods for similar primals in two different animals (for example, compare the cooking methods used for beef and veal shoulders, or pork loin and lamb loin).

Test Kitchen

Divide into four teams. Each team will cook patties of a different ground meat, using only salt and pepper as seasonings. Grill or sauté patties to a safe temperature for the meat your are cooking (temperatures will vary). Evaluate the differences between the various types of meat.

SCIENCE

Mad Cow Disease

Research Mad Cow Disease. Write a report on the disease, identifying its causes and the effect it has on humans. Discuss the efforts to keep Mad Cow Disease out of national food chains.

READING PREVIEW

Key Concepts

- Understanding poultry inspection and grading
- Identifying various types and forms of poultry
- Preparing and serving poultry

Vocabulary

- disjointing
- giblet bag
- gizzard
- keel bone
- poultry
- ratites
- suprême
- trussing

> **"C**hicken is like a blank canvas, inviting the chef to explore new flavors and textures from cuisines around the world. **"**
> — Gerard Viverito

Inspection and Grading

Poultry refers to any domesticated bird used for human consumption. Poultry must undergo a mandatory inspection for wholesomeness that is similar to the inspection process for meat. The USDA poultry grades are A, B, and C. Restaurants and retail outlets purchase Grade A poultry.

Raw poultry must be chilled to 26°F during processing. After processing, poultry may be packed as "chilled," "chilled with ice," or "chilled with dry ice." Poultry chilled to less than 26°F is labeled "frozen" or "previously frozen."

 **Reading Checkpoint** *To what temperature must poultry be chilled during processing?*

Types of Poultry

Chicken is the most popular form of poultry, but poultry also includes turkey, ducks, geese, and a number of farm-raised game birds such as pheasant or quail. The following chart summarizes the types of poultry, their weight, their characteristics, and the appropriate cooking techniques used for them.

Gerard Viverito
The Culinary Institute of America

Recently, the family of flightless birds, referred to by their Latin name **ratites** (RAT-ites), have become more popular. This family includes such birds as the ostrich, emu (E-moo), and rhea (RHEE-ah). Their meat is a rich red color, lean, and low in fat. Ratites have been subject to federal inspection since April 2002. The meat is sold as steaks, fillets, medallions, roasts, and ground meat. The tenderest meat is from the thigh. Meat is also produced from the forequarter.

Common Types of Whole Poultry

Type of Poultry	Weight	Characteristics and Cooking Techniques
Chicken, Broiler	1½–2 lb	Very tender; suitable for all cooking techniques
Chicken, Fryer	2½–3½ lb	Very tender; suitable for all cooking techniques
Chicken, Roaster	3½–5 lb	Tender; suitable for all cooking techniques
Chicken, Stewing	3½–5 lb	Not tender; suitable for moist heat and combination methods
Chicken, Capon (Castrated Male)	5–8 lb	Tender; usually roasted
Duckling, Broiler or Fryer	2–4 lb	Very tender; usually roasted but suitable for most techniques
Duckling, Roaster	4–6 lb	Tender; usually roasted
Goose, Young or Gosling	6–10 lb	Tender; usually roasted
Guinea Hen or Fowl	¾–1½ lb	Tender; suitable for most techniques
Pheasant	1½–2 lb	Tender; suitable for most techniques
Rock Cornish Game Hen	¾–2 lb	Very tender; suitable for all cooking techniques
Squab (domestic pigeon that has not begun to fly)	Under 1 lb	Light, tender meat; suitable for sautéing, roasting, grilling (as bird ages, meat darkens and toughens)
Turkey, Young Hen or Tom	8–22 lb	Very tender; suitable for all cooking techniques
Turkey, Yearling	10–30 lb	Fully mature but still tender; usually roasted

Market Forms of Poultry Poultry is sold in a variety of forms. Whole birds have been cleaned and the head and feet removed. You may find a small bag in the cavity of a whole bird, known as the **giblet bag**, which includes the liver, stomach (or **gizzard**), heart, and neck.

Other market forms for poultry are:
- Whole chicken cut into individual pieces (typically breasts, drumsticks, thighs, and a back, but could be half chickens or quarter chickens, as well)

- Breasts (whole breast or half breast, with the skin and bones, boneless, or boneless and skinless)
- Whole legs (typically sold bone-in and with the skin)
- Thighs (sold bone-in or boneless, with or without the skin)
- Drumsticks (sold bone-in, with or without the skin)
- Ground poultry
- Processed poultry (made into such processed items as patties, sausages, or bacon)

Choosing Quality Poultry Poultry should have plump breasts and meaty thighs. The skin should be intact with no tears or punctures. Poultry must be purchased from reputable purveyors and, for optimum quality, kept chilled to below 32°F during storage. Put poultry in drip pans before storing it in the refrigerator so it does not contaminate food stored below it.

 **Reading Checkpoint** *What types of whole chickens are commonly available?*

▲ *Drumstick, thigh, wing, breast*

CULINARY HISTORY

History of Turkeys

Everyone associates the turkey with America's first Thanksgiving. But where did that turkey come from? Most of us probably assume it was a wild turkey one of the colonists shot. However, the turkey on the Pilgrim's table probably came over on the same ship they did. In all likelihood, it was an English turkey.

To understand this, you need to know a little more about turkeys. Turkeys were originally native to North America and Mexico. They were domesticated in Mexico around 200 BC. Returning conquistadors brought turkeys to Spain in 1510. A few years after that, turkeys were brought to English farmers. It was these turkeys, descended from the original Spanish

▲ *Wild turkey*

turkeys, that the Pilgrims brought with them on the Mayflower in 1620. The Pilgrims eventually bred their domesticated turkeys with wild turkeys, developing new, hardier, meatier, and better-tasting turkeys. On Thanksgiving, as you eat your turkey, think of the long journey turkeys traveled to arrive on the first Thanksgiving table.

Research

Research the breeds of turkey today. Compare heirloom, heritage, or legacy breeds with the breeds produced for factory farming. Determine what kinds of turkeys are available in your area.

CHEF'S TIP

KNIFE SELECTION AND CARE

Select the right knife for the task and use a steel before and during work. With a sharp knife, you are less likely to waste poultry. Cuts will be also be neat and straight for better-looking dishes.

Preparing and Serving Poultry

Poultry is one of the most popular of all menu offerings. Basic poultry fabrication techniques can be applied to virtually all types of poultry, not only chicken but also squab, ducks, or turkey. You will, however, need to make some adjustments. Smaller birds require more delicate, precise cuts and a smaller blade. Larger or older birds call for a heavier blade and greater pressure to break through tough joints.

Trussing Poultry One of the most important skills required for cooking poultry is trussing whole birds. The object of trussing, or tying a bird, is to give it a smooth, compact shape so it cooks evenly and retains moisture. There are several methods for trussing poultry. Some involve special trussing needles, some require only string. The method demonstrated in the following Basic Culinary Skills uses only string.

Disjointing Poultry Before or after cooking, poultry can be cut into halves, quarters, or eighths. Overall, this process is referred to as **disjointing**. When you divide a bird in half, you need to cut through the **keel bone**. The two halves of the breast are joined by some cartilage as well as a bone known as the keel bone because it is shaped like the bottom (or keel) of a boat.

Cutting into halves is an especially important technique for use on smaller birds, such as Cornish game hens and broiler chickens, that will be grilled. These birds are small enough to cook through before the skin becomes scorched or charred. One half of the bird is usually enough for a single portion.

Large birds can be further broken down into quarters for portion-sized pieces or into eighths for smaller pieces. If the bones are left in during cooking, they provide some protection against scorching and shrinking. Save the wing tips and backbone for use in the preparation of stock.

Fabricating Skinless, Boneless Breasts The same technique used to make boneless, skinless chicken breast portions can be used for pheasant, partridge, turkey, or duck. If one wing joint, often frenched, is left attached to the breast meat, it may be referred to as a **suprême** (soo-PREM).

Determining Doneness Cooking poultry properly is important. Guests are as aware of foodborne illnesses, and as concerned by them, as chefs are. Fully cooking poultry is an important way to be sure it is safe when you serve it to a guest. When poultry is fully cooked, its juices should be clear, with no trace of pink. When a chicken is properly roasted, you can move the leg easily. You can also test whole poached chickens this way. Of course, the final test is always a thermometer.

Trussing Poultry

1 Remove giblets (if any).

2 Cut off the first wing joints. Also cut away any pockets of fat from the bird's cavity.

3 Stretch skin to cover the breast meat.

4 Pass the middle of a long piece of string underneath the joints at the end of the drumstick. Cross the ends of the string to make an X.

5 Pull the string toward the tail and begin to pull the string back along the body.

6 Pull the string tightly across the joint connecting the drumstick and thigh. Then pull it along the body toward the bird's back, catching the wing underneath the string.

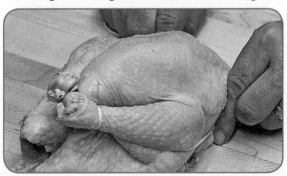

7 Pull one end of the string underneath the backbone at the neck opening.

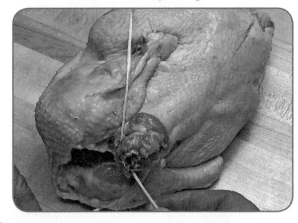

8 Tie the two ends of the string securely.

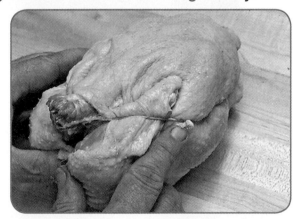

9 The properly trussed bird is ready to cook.

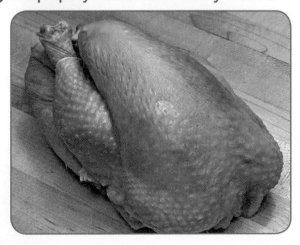

 See Recipe Card 115, "Roast Turkey with Chestnut Stuffing."

Disjointing Poultry

1. **Remove the backbone** by cutting along both sides of it.

2. **Remove the keel bone** by pulling it away from the chicken.

3. **Cut the chicken into halves** by making a cut down the center of the breast to divide the bird in half.

5. **Cut at joints** to separate leg and thigh, wing and breast, if desired. Otherwise, leave in quarters (as shown).

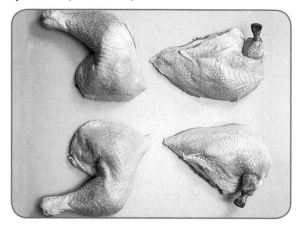

4. **Separate the leg and thigh** from the breast and wing by cutting through the skin just above where the breast and thigh meet.

 See Recipe Card 116, "Southern Fried Chicken with Country-Style Gravy."

FIGURE 16-7 ▶
Testing for Doneness
The chef checks the internal temperature of a roast chicken.
Communicating *What would you serve with this roast chicken?*

The safe internal food temperature for poultry is 165°F. In some restaurants, and for some types of poultry such as duck breast, guests may ask for a specific degree of doneness.

Dry Heat Methods Roast whole chicken, baked chicken parts, grilled or barbecued chicken, and fried chicken are all popular chicken dishes made by dry heat cooking methods.

CULINARY DIVERSITY

Peking (Beijing) Duck

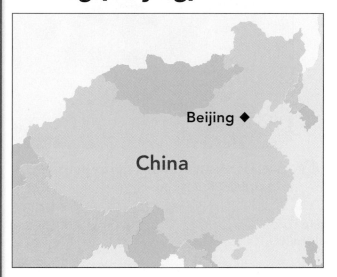

Roast duck can be traced back as far as 1330 in China. When the Ming Dynasty capital was shifted from Nanjing to Beijing in the early 15th century, roast duck was one of the favorites of the imperial court. According to local history, the Bianyfang restaurant in Beijing, which opened in the mid 16th century, was the earliest roast duck restaurant. By the 18th century, Beijing-style roast duck had become a favorite of the upper classes. (Peking duck gained its name from "Peking," the anglicized name of Beijing. Peking duck is now often called Beijing duck.) Eventually a special breed of duck was reared exclusively for the dish.

What makes Peking duck so good? It starts with an air pump! The carcass is inflated, separating the skin from the body. After some seasoning and drying, the duck is roasted in a hot oven. The duck's fat melts away and the skin becomes crispy.

The traditional way of serving Peking duck is as a three-course meal. First the crispy skin is served with small steamed pancakes, raw scallions, hoisin (HOY-sinh) sauce (a thick, brown, sweet-and-spicy sauce made from soybeans, garlic, chiles, and spices), and plum sauce (a spicy, fruity sauce made from plums, chiles, vinegar, and sugar). For the next course, the duck meat is chopped up, stir-fried, and eaten wrapped in fresh lettuce. For the final course, the bones are used for broth.

Research

1. Research recipes for Peking duck. Compare versions for the professional kitchen and the home kitchen.

2. Research restaurants serving Peking duck. Compare how it is served in three different restaurants.

◄ *Peking duck in a pancake*

Boneless Breast Portions

1 Cut along either side of the keel bone, with the breastbone facing up. Use your guiding hand to steady the bird.

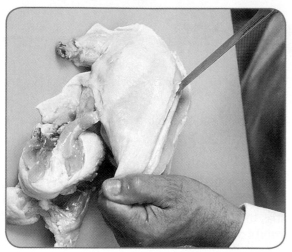

3 Free the meat from the bones, using the tip of the knife. Run the tip of the knife along the bones.

2 Remove breast meat from the rib cage with delicate cuts.

4 Boneless breast portions can be pounded into cutlets, if desired.

 See Recipe Card 114, "Chicken Fajitas."

Figure 16-8 ▶
Variety of Poultry Dishes
Duck with sesame seeds (left), chicken stir-fry with mango (right), turkey tortillas.
Communicating *Which of these poultry dishes looks the most appealing to you?*

All but a few types of poultry are excellent for these methods. Most of the poultry you will find for sale in supermarkets is young, tender, and meaty—perfect for dry heat methods.

When you are roasting whole birds, such as turkey, chickens, ducks, or geese, it can sometimes be difficult to get the dark meat of the legs and thighs fully cooked without overcooking the leaner white meat portions. If you are preparing portions, start the dark meat portions before the white meat portions so both types of meat are finished at the same time.

Moist Heat Methods Any moist heat method or combination heat method is suitable for poultry, including steaming, poaching, simmering, stewing, and braising. Steaming and poaching are often used for lean, tender portions. Shallow-poaching is popular for breast portions because the cooking liquid can serve as the basis for a sauce that can add moisture and flavor to the breast when it is served.

Serving Poultry Poultry is, perhaps, the most popular menu choice in restaurants today. Guests enjoy poultry because of its flavor, but they also choose it because of its perceived health benefits. It is lower in saturated fat and cholesterol than most red meat. Poultry is a versatile food that pairs well with most cooking techniques and is a good vehicle for flavors from around the globe.

 **Reading Checkpoint** *What is the safe internal temperature for cooking poultry?*

16.2 ASSESSMENT

Reviewing Concepts

1. To what temperature must poultry be chilled during processing?
2. What types of whole chickens are commonly available?
3. What is the safe internal temperature for cooking poultry?

Critical Thinking

4. **Comparing/Contrasting** Compare the smallest and largest types of commonly available whole chickens in terms of their size and cooking techniques.
5. **Inferring** Why might it be helpful for a restaurant to purchase whole chickens and disjoint them in the kitchen?
6. **Inferring** Do you think cooking ostrich meat would be more like cooking turkey or more like cooking beef? Why?

Test Kitchen

Divide into four teams. Each team is responsible for locating a simple recipe that uses skinless, boneless breast of chicken. Each team will make its recipe and share the dish with the other teams. Evaluate the differences, focusing on the role that chicken plays in the dish.

SCIENCE

Chicken Breeds

Research the history of three particular breeds of chicken that are used as a food. Write a report on the breeds, including where they originated, how long they have been bred, and any comments on the amount, flavor, color, or texture of their meat.

Review and Assessment

Reviewing Content

Choose the letter that best answers the question or completes the statement.

1. The quality grading of meat is
   a. required by the USDA
   b. required at the state level
   c. required by local governments
   d. voluntary

2. The front portion of a side of beef is typically called the
   a. foresaddle
   b. forequarters
   c. hindsaddle
   d. hindquarters

3. A medallion is a
   a. small round or oval portion-sized cut
   b. large multi-portion cut intended for roasting or braising
   c. small chunk, typically .75 to 1.5 inch, used as stew meat
   d. none of the above

4. Which of the following is not a primal cut for pork?
   a. Boston butt
   b. shoulder
   c. sirloin
   d. belly

5. Meat should be received at a temperature below
   a. 49°F
   b. 41°F
   c. 32°F
   d. 26°F

6. Raw poultry must be chilled to what temperature during processing?
   a. 49°F
   b. 41°F
   c. 32°F
   d. 26°F

7. For optimum quality, poultry should be kept chilled to below
   a. 49°F
   b. 41°F
   c. 32°F
   d. 26°F

8. In poultry, "gizzard" is another name for
   a. the liver
   b. the stomach
   c. the neck
   d. the kidney

Understanding Concepts

9. In terms of poultry, what does disjointing mean?

10. In terms of butchering meat, what is a primal cut?

11. In terms of butchering meat, what is a subprimal cut?

12. What grades of beef are most widely sold in retail outlets?

13. Why are cutlets pounded?

Critical Thinking

14. **Applying Concepts** Why do you chill the parts of a grinder when you are grinding meat?

15. **Predicting** What would happen if you didn't truss poultry before roasting it?

Culinary Math

16. **Applying Concepts** You are making a recipe for a dish that requires 40 oz of lamb stew meat for 10 servings. You are cutting the stew meat yourself from pieces of a lamb shoulder but have experienced a 15% waste due to trimming. About how much shoulder will you need for 50 servings?

On the Job

17. **Applying Concepts** The chef has just asked you to sauté some baby back pork ribs. What should you do?

18. **Communicating** A customer has asked for a rare duck breast. You know that this means the duck breast will not be at a safe internal food temperature. What should you do?

RECIPE CARDS

Use the following Recipe Cards to test your culinary skill.

106. Rib Roast au Jus
107. Roast Leg of Lamb with Mint Sauce
108. Beef Stroganoff
109. Pork Cutlet with Sauce Robert
110. Veal Blanquette
111. Estouffade of Beef
112. Chili
113. Sateh of Chicken with Peanut Sauce
114. Chicken Fajitas
115. Roast Turkey
116. Southern Fried Chicken with Country-Style Gravy
117. Chicken Pot Pie

LAB ACTIVITY

Project 16: Trussed or Not Trussed

Answer these questions when your class works through Project 16.

- How difficult was it to truss the chicken?
- Did the trussing seem to make any difference in the total cooking time?
- How even was the cooking of the trussed chicken? The untrussed chicken?
- Were there differences in the final cooked chickens in terms of flavor? Moisture? Brownness or crispiness of the skins?
- Given the difficulty of trussing a chicken, was it worth it?

TEST PRACTICE

Choose the letter that best answers the question or completes the statement.

1. An emince is a
   A a subprimal meat cut
   B a small, thin, portion-sized cut of meat
   C a pork variety meat
   D another name for a cutlet

2. Subprimals can broken down at the packing plant and sold in smaller pieces called
   A primals
   B boxed meat
   C retail cuts
   D saddles

3. Which of the following is not a lamb primal cut?
   A shoulder
   B flank
   C leg
   D loin

4. Which of the following is not another name for cutlet?
   A scallop
   B scalloppine
   C escalope
   D noisette

5. Another name for offal is
   A variety meat
   B meat from a young cow
   C meat from lamb that has aged over 16 months
   D meat that has passed its safe-serve date

6. When a portion of meat includes both the left and right side of the carcass, it is a
   A side
   B quarter
   C saddle
   D primal

7. A ratite is a
   A bird in the family of flightless birds (example ostrich)
   B castrated male rooster
   C veal variety meat
   D dish made from the veal shank

8. The keel bone joins together the
   A drumstick and thigh
   B wing and body
   C two breasts
   D wing tip and wing

UNIT 4

Breads & Desserts

READING PREVIEW

Key Concepts

- Identifying bakeshop ingredients and their functions
- Identifying and using bakeshop equipment
- Understanding formulas used in the bakeshop

Vocabulary

- all-purpose flour
- baking stones
- bench scraper
- blooming
- bread flour
- cake comb
- cake flour
- chemical leavener
- confectioner's sugar

- corn syrup
- denaturing
- dough divider
- dough sheeter
- egg wash
- formulas
- gelatin
- gluten
- granulated sugar
- knead

- leavener
- loaf pans
- organic leavener
- parchment paper
- pastry bag
- pastry blender
- pastry brush
- pastry wheel
- pectin

- peel
- physical leavener
- proofer
- retarder
- sil pad
- springform pans
- superfine sugar
- tapioca
- tart pans
- tube pans
- turntable

> **"T**he ingredients and techniques used in the bakeshop are incredibly versatile. The challenge to the baker or pastry chef is to use them properly to get the most perfect result. **"**
>
> — Thomas Vaccaro
> Dean of Baking and Pastry Studies
> The Culinary Institute of America

Bakeshop Ingredients

Although they share certain similarities, baking and cooking are fundamentally different. Although a soup, stew, or even a sauté can be changed at virtually any stage of preparation, most breads, cookies, muffins, cakes, or custards need to be put together exactly as the recipe describes before you bake, chill, or freeze them. Once a batter is ladled into the pan, for example, it is usually too late to adjust the amount of salt or change the texture.

Another important distinction between baking and cooking is that most baked goods and desserts require more advance planning. Cakes need to cool and be frosted, custards and puddings need to chill and firm up in the refrigerator, and yeast breads need plenty of time to rise.

Approach baking in a systematic way. Before you begin baking, gather all the equipment and measure out the ingredients called for in your recipe. Read the recipe carefully; you may need to sift dry ingredients together, melt and cool some ingredients, or permit others to warm slightly to room temperature. Plan ahead so your frozen dessert is perfectly chilled when you want to serve it, your pastry dough is ready to roll out when your filling is complete, and a cake is cooled before you start to frost and decorate it.

Ingredients function in specific ways to help determine the final texture, flavor, and color of baked goods. Good bakers know how each ingredient affects the outcome.

Flour Perhaps no ingredient is as important to a baker as flour. The amount of protein and starch in a particular type of flour determines how it will behave in a recipe.

Wheat flour is the most common type of flour used in the bakeshop. It contains the right amounts and types of certain proteins, such as glutenin (GLU-teh-nin) and gliadin (glee-AH-din), which give structure to yeast-raised dough. You should first moisten a wheat flour and then **knead** (NEED) it, working it by hand or in a mixer to distribute the ingredients. Kneading develops **gluten** (GLU-ton), a network of long, stretchy strands that trap the carbon dioxide given off by yeast in the dough. This is what causes yeast-based dough to rise.

Flour also contains starch that thickens when it is heated and absorbs liquids. Different flours contain different types of starch. That is why the results you get when you cook or bake with different types of flour differ greatly. For example, a cornstarch-thickened pudding has a different look and feel than a flour-thickened pudding.

Because of these differences in the proteins and starches in different types of flours, it is important to follow a recipe precisely when selecting flour. Some of the more common types of wheat flour used in baking recipes are:

- **All-Purpose Flour.** A blend of half "soft" (low protein) and half "hard" (high protein) wheat, **all-purpose flour** is probably the most common type of flour used in the bakeshop.

CULINARY SCIENCE

Flour Power

Much of our food supply, including flour, comes from seeds. Scientists often cross seeds to breed new, improved varieties of plants and animals.

Flour that many consider to be the best American flour for baking comes from wheat named Turkey Red. The type of Turkey Red being grown today has been genetically developed from an early strain of seed that was carried to Kansas by Mennonite farmers in 1873. The Mennonites left Germany and then Holland in search of religious freedom. They moved to the Ukraine, and on the way they passed through the Crimea, across the Black Sea from Turkey, where they discovered the prized Turkey Red wheat. Eventually they immigrated to the United States, bringing Turkey Red seeds with them.

The seeds they brought came from several areas of the Ukraine. Turkey Red is a winter wheat, which means it is planted in the fall and grows immediately until the first hard frost comes, when it lies dormant, or "asleep," until it starts to grow again in the spring. This made the seeds all the more valuable because until then only spring wheat, which is planted in the spring and harvested in the late summer, was available in the United States. Until the arrival of Turkey Red, wheat was not planted commercially in the United States.

Turkey Red proved to be a hearty seed that is credited with establishing the wheat industry in Kansas

and turning the region into "the bread basket of America." Turkey Red provided the genetic stock for our modern varieties of wheat.

Research

Research the history of wheat farming in America. Focus on the specific strains of wheat that have contributed to commercial wheat farming.

- **Bread Flour.** Considered "harder" or "stronger" than all-purpose flour because it has more protein in it, **bread flour** is most appropriate for use in most yeast-bread recipes.
- **Cake Flour.** With less protein than either bread or all-purpose flour, **cake flour** is "softer" than the other two flours. It is used in most cake recipes and many cookie and muffin recipes because it provides a less chewy, more tender texture.
- **Whole Grain and Stone-Ground Flour.** Whole grain flour is milled to leave some of the bran intact. Stone-ground flour is milled by using stone mill wheels and is usually produced in small batches. Both whole grain flour and stone-ground flour usually retain more oil and are more flavorful.

To store opened packages of flour, transfer the contents to an airtight container or a large resealable plastic bag to keep out moisture, dirt, and pests.

Unopened packages of white flour keep for up to two years in a cool, dry location. Once opened, they should be used within eight months. Store other types of standard-ground flour (such as potato, rice, rye, oat, or corn flour) in a cool, dry location and use them within two or three months after opening. You could also keep them in the refrigerator for up to six months.

Eggs Eggs contribute proteins, fat, and moisture to baked items. They also provide structure and texture. As eggs are stirred, whipped, or heated, their protein strands unfold and recombine. This creates a network that traps liquids or air, resulting in a texture that can range from a soft foam, such as a meringue, to a sliceable custard, such as a quiche. Other ingredients in the recipe, as well as the way you mix and cook egg-rich dishes, can give a variety of results.

Egg substitutes (powdered or liquid) may be substituted for fresh eggs in some cases. When you use substitutes, you will find some differences in the flavor, color, and texture of the baked goods. Egg substitutes can be refrigerated in unopened containers for up to ten days. Once they are opened, they should be used within three days.

Here are some examples of how eggs are used in the bakeshop:

- When eggs are stirred over direct heat, as when making a custard, the stirring keeps the protein strands short enough to prevent a solid network from forming. This produces a product with a smooth, spoonable consistency.
- When a custard is baked in the oven, the mixture is not stirred as it cooks. This allows longer strands of protein to form, which settle into a firm structure that holds its shape.

FIGURE 17-2 ▶
Brushing with an Egg Wash
Brushing the top of dough with an egg wash before baking gives the product a glossy sheen when baked.
Communicating *What does a glossy sheen add to the final baked product?*

- When eggs are whisked, they trap enough air to make a foam, giving lightness to a soufflé and similar dishes.
- Adding eggs to dough provides the dough with moisture, helping it stick together. Eggs also provide additional protein to the dough for a firmer and drier product after baking. The water in eggs expands when you bake cakes and muffins, helping them to rise.
- Adding egg yolks to dough adds a rich golden color to the final item, from sponge cake to bread to a vanilla sauce.
- Brushing the tops of breads and pastries with an **egg wash**— a mixture of egg and water or milk—before baking gives a glossy sheen. Egg washes that include only the whites become very shiny, and those that include the yolks give a brilliant golden hue.

Eggs are an enormously versatile ingredient, but they are also a potential source of pathogens such as Salmonella. Controlling the temperature of eggs as you cook, cool, and store them is one of the most important ways to keep eggs wholesome. Shell eggs should be refrigerated at a temperature between 33°F and 38°F. Cooking egg dishes to a safe temperature of 165°F also helps prevent illness by killing any pathogens. Cool egg-based dough quickly to keep it from sitting too long in the temperature danger range between 41°F and 135°F.

Leaveners A **leavener** (LEV-en-er) increases the volume of a dough or batter by adding air or other gas. Bakers rely on three basic types of leaveners—organic leaveners, chemical leaveners, and physical leaveners—to raise breads, cakes, and cookies.
- **Organic Leaveners.** Yeast, a tiny single-celled organism, is an **organic leavener.** It must be living to do its work. Like any living organism, yeast needs the right environment in order to live. When the conditions are right, yeast cells grow and reproduce, giving off carbon dioxide and alcohol in the process. Carbon dioxide increases the volume of dough when the yeast is first added to the dough and then again when the dough is exposed to the heat of the oven. This is what gives bread its spongy texture. To grow and reproduce, yeast requires moisture, warmth, and food (in the form of sugar, whether added to the dough or naturally present in the flour). Yeast grows most rapidly between 60°F and 90°F.

CHEF'S TIP

PASTEURIZED EGGS
Pasteurized eggs have been heat-treated and can be used to guarantee food safety in recipes that call for uncooked or semi-cooked eggs (any eggs that are not cooked to the safe temperature of 165°F).

FIGURE 17-3
Yeast Increases the Volume of Dough
Yeast produces carbon dioxide that increases the volume of the dough.
Interpreting Illustrations *Can you see the carbon dioxide bubbles in this rising dough?*

FOCUS ON NUTRITION

Hydrogenation

Most shortenings and margarines contain trans fatty acids, byproducts of hydrogenation, which turns liquid fats into solid fats. Some people are concerned about the health risks of trans fatty acids and search for products without trans fatty acids.

Cooler temperatures slow the yeast down, although they don't kill it. Yeast is destroyed when the temperature of a baked good reaches 137°F.

- **Chemical Leaveners.** Baking powder is a **chemical leavener**. It reacts rapidly to leaven a baked good when it is combined with moisture and heat. When we say that a baked good has been leavened, we mean that the volume of the batter has been increased by the addition of air or gas. Baking soda is similar to baking powder, but it also requires an acidic ingredient. When these leaveners are blended with liquid in a batter, a chemical reaction produces gas that forms bubbles. As the batter settles into a firm structure during baking, these bubbles give the baked item a spongy, springy texture, sometimes known as its "crumb." If baking soda and baking powder are not properly blended into the batter, the bubbles may be too large, resulting in tunnels or big air pockets. Recipes often call for the chemical leaveners to be sifted with the flour and other dry ingredients to break up any clumps and make sure they are mixed well.

- **Physical Leaveners.** Steam and air are **physical leaveners**. When moisture from butter, eggs, or other liquid is heated in a batter, it turns to steam. The steam takes up more space than water. Air also expands when it is heated, thereby leavening a batter. Creaming butter or whipping egg whites incorporates air into a batter, and as items such as cakes or soufflés bake in the oven, the pockets of air are trapped while the batter dries enough to take on a relatively firm structure. The trapped pockets give baked goods height as well as a soft, spongy crumb.

Fat Fat is critical to the success of most baked goods. Fats contribute to a baked good's flavor, texture, and freshness.

- **Flavor.** Some fats, such as butter, lard, and nut oils, contribute their own flavor to baked goods. Other fats, such as vegetable oil, margarine, and shortening, are chosen because they lack flavor. Flavorless fats allow the flavors of other ingredients to come to the front. The fat in a batter or dough also encourages browning on crusts and edges; this provides extra flavor for the baked good.

- **Texture.** Fats determine the texture of baked goods. Depending on the type of fat you use in a baked good and the way it is worked into a batter or dough, the resulting texture may range from meltingly smooth to flaky and brittle. The more fat in the recipe, the softer the batter or dough. Baked goods that are made from soft batters or doughs have a tendency to spread out while they bake. The way batter spreads is important, for example, in making cookies of the right size. Fats also produce a texture contrast, as the outer edges become crisper than the middle of the baked good.

- **Freshness.** Fat extends the life of a baked good by holding in moisture, so the baked good stays fresh longer.

Fats can be divided into two basic types: solid fats, which are firm at room temperature, and liquid fats, which are liquid at room temperature. The texture of solid fats permits them to be worked into the dough or batter. If you melt a solid fat, such as butter or shortening, you can use it in a recipe as a liquid fat. An oil is a pure liquid fat.

CHEF'S TIP

BUTTER & BAKING

When baking, use unsalted grade AA butter. If you substitute a European-style butter, which has a slightly higher butterfat content and less moisture, you may need to add a bit more liquid.

Solid Fats

Fat	Description	Flavor and Use
Butter	Made from cream.	Adds flavor and flakiness to pastry or biscuits.
Lard	Made from refined pork fat.	Has a unique flavor. Makes a very flakey pastry. Substitute it in equal amounts for the shortening or butter in pie dough. Especially good in pastry for savory dishes.
Shortening	Made from vegetable oil that has been processed (hydrogenated) to make it solid at room temperature.	Lacks flavor. Used like butter or lard, but adds extraordinary flakiness.
Margarine	Production process is similar to that of shortening.	Lacks flavor. Used as a substitute for butter.

Liquid Fats

Fat	Description	Flavor
Neutral Oil	Canola, corn, safflower oils.	Lacks flavor.
Vegetable Oil	Blend of neutral oils.	Lacks flavor.
Flavored Oil	Nut oils (walnut, peanut, sesame, almond) and olive oil.	Has a distinctive flavor.

CHEF'S TIP

SUPERFINE SUGAR

In a pinch, you can make superfine sugar by grinding regular sugar in a food processor or blender.

FIGURE 17-4 ▶
Flakey Pie Crust
The flavor and flakiness of a pie crust depends on the type of fat used.
Interpreting Illustrations *Does this pie crust look flakey to you?*

FOCUS ON SAFETY

First Aid for Bakers

Burns are the most common baking hazard. If you are burned, immediately flush the affected area with cool water. Keep a cool compress on the area until it feels more comfortable, and then apply a bandage.

▼ *Brown Sugar*

The mixing method used for a batter or dough often dictates the form a fat must take. Some recipes for cakes and breads require a fat in liquid form—oil, melted butter, or melted shortening. Some recipes call for butter or shortening to be room temperature, and other recipes require the solid fat to be very firm, even chilled, before you add it to other ingredients.

Sweeteners A variety of sweeteners are used in the bakeshop. Different sweeteners behave differently when they are mixed and baked, so it is important to use the type specified in a recipe.

The most commonly used sweeteners are:

- **Granulated Sugar.** Refined from sugar cane or sugar beets, **granulated** (GRAN-u-late-ed) **sugar** is ordinary white sugar.
- **Superfine Sugar.** Granulated sugar that is more finely ground so it dissolves more easily is called **superfine sugar** (also referred to as baker's sugar and castor sugar).
- **Confectioner's Sugar.** Sugar that has been ground into a fine, white, easily dissolvable powder is called **confectioner's** (con-FECK-shun-ers) **sugar** (also referred to as powdered sugar).
- **Brown Sugar.** Thick, dark molasses is combined with white sugar to make flavorful and moist light or dark brown sugar.
- **Molasses.** A byproduct of sugar refining, molasses is a thick, sweet, brownish-black syrup that has a distinctive, slightly bitter flavor.
- **Honey.** Ranging in color from very light to almost as dark as molasses, honey is often identified by the flowers from which the bees gathered nectar.

- **Maple Syrup.** The boiled-down sap of maple trees, maple syrup is graded according to color, body, and flavor. Grade B is richer in flavor than grade A and is suggested for baking.
- **Corn Syrup.** Made from cornstarch, **corn syrup** is a thick, sweet syrup that is available light or dark; the dark has added caramel flavor and color.

Sweeteners provide baked goods with more than sweetness and flavor. They also provide texture. In some cases, they help baked products rise. Sweeteners attract moisture, making baked goods softer and longer lasting than those with little or no sugar. Because of caramelization, sweeteners develop a rich brown color when heated. This adds appealing color, as well as flavor.

Sugar interacts with other ingredients on a chemical level. When combined with liquids, sugar raises the temperature at which the liquid will boil. Adding sugar makes eggs less prone to overcook, even over direct heat.

Adding liquids to hot sugar can cause the sugar to splatter or foam up. To lessen the chances of burning yourself, take the pan away from the heat before you add liquid. Wear oven mitts to protect your hands when you add a liquid, and keep your face partially turned away. Even if the mixture doesn't splatter, the steam can scald you.

Acids Citrus and other fruit juices, wine, vinegar, yogurt, buttermilk, and salt are some of the acids used in baked goods. Acids change the structure of proteins, an effect known as **denaturing** (dee-NAY-tshur-ing). When an acid is added to a protein, the strands that compose the protein either tighten or loosen, depending on the specific proteins the foods contain. By changing the amount and type of acid in a recipe, you can create different textures. For example, adding lemon juice to a cream-cheese tart filling breaks down the texture of the cream cheese so it becomes lighter and spreadable.

Fermenting yeast cells give off alcohol—an acid—to produce a good flavor and texture in breads. The alcohol relaxes the gluten strands so they can stretch while the dough increases in volume and bakes. Acidic ingredients are also added to batters leavened with baking soda to start the leavening action.

Salt Salt is a powerful flavor enhancer and seasoning, even for sweet dishes. In small amounts as a seasoning, salt does not actually add an identifiable flavor to a dish. Instead, it balances other flavors and makes them more vivid. As you add salt in larger quantities, it begins to contribute its own distinctive flavor.

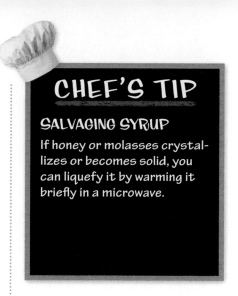

CHEF'S TIP

SALVAGING SYRUP
If honey or molasses crystallizes or becomes solid, you can liquefy it by warming it briefly in a microwave.

CHEF'S TIP

SPECIAL SALTS

In baking, coarse salt and sea salt are used primarily as toppings. The larger crystals add both flavor and texture to breads and rolls.

FIGURE 17-5
Blooming Gelatin
Dissolving gelatin in water is referred to as blooming the gelatin.
Applying Concepts *Would vegetarians eat a product that was thickened with gelatin?*

▼

Salt is important in baking because of the way it reacts with other ingredients. Salt controls the activity of yeast, keeping it from over-fermenting and thereby ensuring a good texture. If the yeast is not controlled, the bread may rise rapidly at first, only to deflate.

Thickeners Bakeshops often use thickeners to give body to liquid mixtures. Some of the most common thickeners are:

- **Cornstarch and Arrowroot.** After being blended with cold liquid, cornstarch and arrowroot are added as thickeners to such dishes as a simmering pudding or pie filling. (You can substitute an equal amount of arrowroot for cornstarch in most recipes.) Both of these thickeners last for up to eight months on the shelf.

- **Gelatin.** A protein processed from the bones, skin, and connective tissue of animals, **gelatin** is used as a gelling agent to thicken and stabilize foams or liquids. Gelatin is widely available in granulated or powdered form, in tins or individual packets (1 package equals 2¼ teaspoons and weighs ¼ ounce). When substituting the less widely available gelatin sheets, use the same weight as you would of powdered gelatin (refer to the package information; different types of gelatin sheets may have different weights). Packages of powdered gelatin desserts contain flavorings and sweeteners in addition to gelatin and cannot be used in place of unflavored powdered gelatin in a recipe. Dissolving gelatin in water is referred to as **blooming** the gelatin.

- **Pectin.** Working like gelatin to thicken a liquid, **pectin** is a substance naturally found in high concentration in certain fruits, especially apples and citrus fruit. Unlike gelatin, pectin does not usually require chilling to reach its full thickening potential, making it well suited for fruit preserves and confections. Also unlike gelatin, pectin requires the presence of both a liquid and the correct amount of acid to thicken properly.

- **Tapioca.** Quick-cooking or instant **tapioca** is made from the cassava root, a starchy tropical tuber. Because tapioca contributes no flavor of its own and imparts transparent gloss to fruit, it is often used to thicken fruit pie fillings and to make pudding.

Bakeshop Equipment

The quality of the equipment you use for baking has a distinct effect on the quality of your baked goods.

Tools for Measuring Scales, thermometers, measuring cups, and measuring spoons are necessary to make accurate measurements in the bakeshop. You can review the various types of measuring tools and the right way to use them in Chapter 4. In addition to these tools, bakers and pastry chefs also use some other measuring tools.

- Wooden dowels of various thicknesses make rolling dough to the proper thickness easier.
- Rulers or tape measures make rolling dough to the proper thickness and dimensions easier. They are also useful when you need to determine the dimensions of a baking pan or mold.
- Timers keep track of time as you bake. The classic dial-type timer works by counting down the time, but some digital timers give you the option of counting time down or up. Some timers allow you to keep track of the baking times for as many as four different items, which is a very helpful feature when you are making multiple batches or a variety of baked goods. Many digital timers have a cord or clip so you can carry them with you if you leave the kitchen.

FIGURE 17-6
Tools for Measuring
Bakeshop measuring tools include a ruler, a timer, and a candy thermometer.
Inferring *How might a bakeshop's specialty influence the types of measuring tools they use?*

CULINARY MATH

A Pint's a Pound?

There's a famous expression, "A pint's a pound the world around," which means that 1 pint by volume (that is 2 cups) of anything weighs 1 pound by weight (that is, 16 ounces). But is this really true?

Research
Weigh 2 cups of flour and 2 cups of sugar. Is a pint a pound? Now try it with water.

Figure 17-7
Marble Work Surface
Fudge cooling on a marble work surface.
Drawing Conclusions *Why is a marble work surface better than a wooden work surface for this use?*

Work Surfaces Two work surfaces are commonly seen in a bakeshop: wood surfaces are required when you want to keep the item you are making warm, and marble surfaces are used when you want to keep the item from getting warm.

Wood surfaces are excellent for kneading bread dough. A wooden surface has a texture that grabs the dough, making it easier to stretch the dough. It is also relatively warm, compared to marble, metal, or even plastic materials.

Marble, on the other hand, is a cool, smooth stone with no texture. It is useful for making items such as chocolates, fudge, or caramels when you don't need to stretch dough and want to keep the item cool as you work it. Marble is very good for rolling out delicate pastry dough and cookies; you can work them more easily with less chance of their warming up and getting too soft.

Tools for Cutting Bakers and pastry chefs use many of the same cutting tools that are used throughout the kitchen, including a basic set of knives. Serrated knives are especially good for slicing breads and cakes without tearing them. Some tools, however, are more common in the bakeshop:

▲ *Bench Scraper and Pastry Blender*

- **Bench Scrapers.** With a rectangular steel blade and capped with a wooden or plastic handle, a **bench scraper** (also called a bench knife) is usually six inches wide. The steel blade has a dull edge but is thin enough to cut through dough. You can use a bench scraper like a knife to cut soft ingredients such as butter or soft cheese or to lift and turn soft or wet dough as you knead it, as well as to transfer ingredients such as chopped nuts from your work surface to the mixing bowl. Bench scrapers also make short work of cleaning off a work surface.
- **Pastry Blenders.** With a crescent-shaped loop of thin wires attached to a handle, a **pastry blender** is used to mix fat into flour when you make a pastry dough. If you don't have one, substitute two table knives to cut the fat into the flour.
- **Biscuit and Cookie Cutters.** Made of thin metal sheets or molded plastic, biscuit cutters and cookie cutters have edges that are sharp enough to cut through pastry or cookie dough cleanly. Biscuit cutters may have straight or scalloped edges; 3-inch cutters are a good basic size. Cookie cutters are sold in a

◄
Figure 17-8
Pastry Blender
A pastry blender is a specialized hand tool for mixing fat into flour. **Drawing Conclusions** *How does a pastry blender help a chef avoid over mixing?*

variety of shapes and sizes; a 3-inch diameter round cutter is very common for rolled and cutout cookies.

Bread-Baking Equipment Bakers use special bread-baking equipment, such as:

- **Baking Stones.** Unglazed ceramic pieces used to line an oven rack are called **baking stones**. These stones or tiles help develop a crisp crust on breads and pizza by holding and transferring the oven's heat evenly. The stones need to preheat along with the oven for best results.
- **Peels.** A large flat wooden or metal paddle used to slide bread onto baking stones and to retrieve them when they are done is called a **peel**. If you don't have a peel, you can use a cookie sheet that has no sides.

Appliances Mixers make baking tasks easier and more efficient. As you may recall from Chapter 3, bakeshops tend to use free-standing mixers, which are capable of mixing and kneading heavy yeast dough. Mixers, food processors, blenders, and other large equipment share space in the bakeshop with other specialized equipment such as:

- **Proofers.** A **proofer** is a special box that holds dough as it rises. Most models have thermostats to control heat and are able to generate steam.
- **Dough Sheeters.** A **dough sheeter** rolls large batches of dough into sheets. Some dough sheeters also roll dough into loaves and cut out doughnuts or croissants.

Yeast Breads, Rolls, & Pastries ▶ **547**

- **Dough Dividers.** A **dough divider** (also called a dough press) cuts a quantity of dough into equal pieces so they can be shaped into rolls.
- **Retarder.** To control fermentation by slowing it down, bakers use a refrigerated cabinet called a **retarder**.

Baking Pans and Molds The surface of a pan has an effect on how items bake. Darker pans produce baked goods with a deep crust color, and those with shiny or light surfaces tend to produce goods with a lighter color. Lining pans properly makes it easier for you to get baked goods out without sticking or tearing.

Bakers use parchment paper to line pans. **Parchment paper** is a grease-resistant, nonstick, heatproof paper. The paper is coated with silicone on one side, allowing baked goods to spread properly and release from the paper easily. It comes in rolls, or precut for use as pan liners.

Bakers also use a special liner made of silicone, sometimes known as a **sil pad**, that can be used over and over again. Silicone can withstand temperatures up to 600°F. Flexible sil pad mats, sold in several sizes, give baking pans a nonstick surface and provide a heat-resistant surface for candy making. Baking pans and molds made of the same material are available in a variety of sizes.

Here are some more common baking pans and molds:
- **Loaf Pans.** Rectangular pans used for simple cakes and quick breads are called **loaf pans**. Mini loaf pans are available for making small loaves. You can buy loaf pans in metal, glass, and ceramic, with or without a nonstick coating.
- **Pie Pans.** Pie pans have sloped sides and are made from aluminum, glass, or earthenware. The sides of the pan may be up to 3 inches tall. The deeper the pan, the more filling you will need. One of the most common sizes is a 9-inch pie pan with sides that are 1½ inches tall. If you prefer to use glass pie pans, lower the oven temperature by about 25 degrees and the baking time by 5 to 10 minutes. Glass conducts heat efficiently, so the edges and bottom of your pie may brown too rapidly if you use the recipe's temperature and baking time.
- **Tart Pans.** Made of tinned steel or ceramic, **tart pans** have short, often scalloped sides and usually have a removable bottom. However, they may be round, square, or rectangular. Some pans have a nonstick coating. Tartlet pans are simply small tart pans, sized to make individual pastries.
- **Cake Pans.** Cake pans are manufactured of tinned steel, aluminum, glass, or silicone. They may have a nonstick coating. Common cake pans range in size from 6-inches to 18-inches.

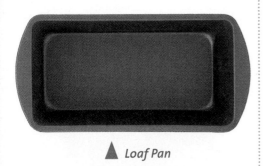

▲ Loaf Pan

▲ Tart Pan

- **Springform Pans.** Consisting of a hinged ring that clamps around a removable base, **springform pans** are used for baking delicate cakes that might otherwise be difficult to unmold, such as a cheese cake..
- **Tube Pans.** With a center tube of metal that conducts heat through the center of the batter, **tube pans** bake heavy batters evenly, without over-browning the outside of the cake. A tube pan (also called an angel food cake pan) works well for batters that need to bake quickly. Tube pans are typically made of thin metal, with or without a nonstick coating. They come in a range of sizes, and the sides may be fluted, molded, or straight.
- **Soufflé Dishes and Custard Cups.** Soufflé dishes, custard cups, and pudding molds are ovenproof ceramic, glass, or earthenware dishes used to bake a variety of dishes. Soufflé dishes have straight, smooth sides that are typically as high as the dish is wide and come in a range of sizes, from 2 ounces to 2 quarts. Custard cups have straight or sloped sides and come in a variety of sizes. Petits pots are custard cups that may have lids. Gratin dishes may be oval or round and have relatively short sides. Pudding molds may have smooth or patterned sides for a special appearance when the pudding is unmolded.

Tools for Pastry Bakers use special tools for working with pastry, such as:

- **Rolling Pins.** Rolling pins stretch dough into thin sheets. Ball-bearing rolling pins have a steel rod extending through the pin and fixed to the handles. Ball bearings on each end of the rod make it easy to roll the pin. Rolling pins may be made of wood, marble, metal, or a synthetic material. Straight (or French) rolling pins are just round rods that are often 16 inches long. They have no handles. Tapered rolling pins are good for rolling dough into circles. Marble rolling pins stay cool, which is helpful to a pie baker or pastry maker. Specialty rolling pins may have grooves or patterns to imprint in the dough as you roll.

▲ **FIGURE 17-9**
Springform Pan
Removing the frame of a springform pan from a cake. **Predicting** *What advantages would a springform pan offer?*

▲ *Tube Pan*

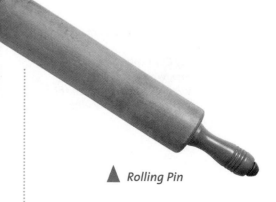

▲ *Rolling Pin*

▲ *Pastry Brush*

▲ *Pastry Wheel*

- **Pastry Brushes.** Used to apply egg wash and to butter pans and muffin tins, **pastry brushes** are made of soft, flexible nylon, silicon, or unbleached hog bristles. Unlike brushes used for paint, pastry brushes have no reservoir in the handle, so they are easy to clean completely after each use. Soak the brush briefly if dried food needs to be loosened, but avoid prolonged soaking. Let the brush air-dry as soon as it is clean. A 1- to 1½-inch wide brush is suitable for most uses. Brushes used for pastry work should be kept separate from those used to apply barbecue sauces, marinades, and other savory ingredients.

- **Pastry Wheels.** A round blade mounted on a handle is called a **pastry wheel**. As you roll the blade over pastry dough, it makes a single, clean cut. The blade may be straight or scalloped to make a decorative edge. You can also use a sharp paring knife or scissors to cut pastry.

- **Pastry Bags and Tips.** A **pastry bag** is a cone-shaped bag with two open ends. On the smaller, pointed end, you apply a decorative tip. Into the larger opening you add dough, fillings, or whipped cream. You squeeze the bag to force the contents through the tip, allowing you to add fillings to pastries, make delicate cookies, and apply decorative finishes to cakes and pastries. Tips that are round or star-shaped are the most versatile, but you can buy specialty tips to make leaves, flowers, and other shapes. Pastry bags are typically made of nylon or plastic. Some bags are designed for only a single use. If your bag is reusable, wash it well in warm soapy water inside and

FIGURE 17-10 ▶
Pastry Bag
Applying whipping cream using a pastry bag.
Relating Concepts *As a customer, would you rather have whipped cream applied this way or spread on the pie with a palette knife?*

out, rinse it thoroughly, and air-dry completely before storing.

- **Metal Spatulas and Palette Knives.** The bakeshop often uses metal spatulas and palette knives with long metal blades and blunt edges. The handle may be offset (angled) to make it easier to lift baked goods from the pan. Palette knives are long and narrow, with a rounded, blunt end. They are good for spreading fillings, icings, and glazes; decorating cakes and pastries; and spreading batter or dough into an even layer before baking. Some palette knives have a serrated edge for slicing cakes into layers.
- **Cake Combs.** Used to create a decorative edge on iced cakes or to give texture to a chocolate coating, a **cake comb** is a triangular or rectangular piece of metal or plastic with serrated edges. The teeth vary in their size and shape, giving you a choice of three or four different effects.
- **Turntables.** Although not essential, a **turntable** makes it easier to decorate cakes. You can easily turn the cake with one hand while the other is free to use the palette knife, pastry bag, or cake comb.

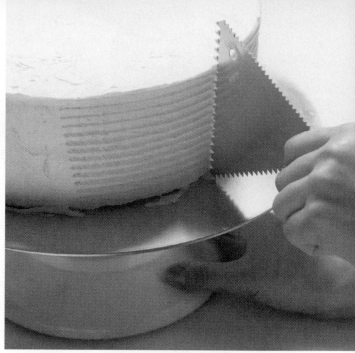

▲
FIGURE 17-11
Cake on a Turntable
Turning the cake with one hand while using a cake comb to create a pattern with the other hand. **Applying Concepts** *Why is it usually more efficient to use a turntable than to move around the cake yourself?*

 **Reading Checkpoint** *What are five of the most common types of baking pans and molds found in the bakeshop?*

Formulas

Bakers and pastry chefs often call their recipes **formulas**. This distinction helps point out the importance of accuracy in all aspects of baking, from measuring ingredients to having them at the right temperature. For success, ingredients must be prepared correctly and combined in the right order, using the right technique.

Bakers' Percentages Baking formulas often include percentages as a type of measurement for ingredients. Any recipe that has been written in percentages shows the baker how each ingredient compares to the total amount of flour. In a formula written in percentages, the flour called for in the formula is considered to be 100%.

If your formula calls for 2 pounds of flour and 1 pound of sugar, the flour is 100% and the sugar is 50%. If the formula calls for 2 pounds of flour and 3 pounds of sugar, the flour is still 100%, but now the sugar is 150%. Knowing how the ingredients relate to each other as a percentage makes it easy for bakers to accurately increase or decrease recipes.

Dry Ingredients Flour, granulated or powdered sugar, baking soda, baking powder, cocoa powder, and similar powdery ingredients are generally referred to as dry ingredients. These ingredients may need to be sifted together, sometimes two or three times, to remove any clumps and to incorporate some air. Sifting also distributes ingredients such as salt and chemical leaveners evenly throughout the baked item.

Wet Ingredients Milk, water, eggs, oil, melted butter, honey, and vanilla extract are all examples of wet ingredients. Be sure you check the formula carefully. Sometimes liquid ingredients are combined and then added to dry ingredients all at once. At other times, they are added in sequence. You may also be asked to add wet ingredients in parts, adding some of the wet ingredients, then some of the dry ingredients, and then some more of the wet ingredients, and so on.

▲
FIGURE 17-12
Sifting Dry Ingredients
Some recipes call for dry ingredients to be sifted.
Drawing Conclusions *Why might it be necessary to sift dry ingredients more than once?*

 **Reading Checkpoint** *What is a baking formula?*

17.1 ASSESSMENT

Reviewing Concepts
1. What are the three types of leaveners?
2. What are five of the most common types of baking pans and molds found in the bakeshop?
3. What is a baking formula?

Critical Thinking
4. **Comparing/Contrasting** What is the difference between a pie pan and a tart pan?
5. **Inferring** In a bakeshop, when would you want to use a fat that lacked flavor?
6. **Classifying** If you were working with chocolates, fudge, or caramel, which type of work surface would you use?

Test Kitchen
Divide into four teams. Each team will locate a baking recipe that is not written as a baking formula. Every team will share a copy of its baking recipe with the other three teams (so each team will have the same four recipes). Each team will then convert the recipes to baking formulas. Compare the results.

SCIENCE

Maple Sugar
Research the history and process of making maple sugar. Discuss how the various grades are made.

READING PREVIEW

Key Concepts

- Identifying basic types of yeast dough
- Understanding the straight dough-mixing method
- Modifying the straight dough-mixing method

Vocabulary

- biga
- brioche
- challah
- chlorine dioxide
- dough starter
- enriched dough
- fermentation
- gluten window test
- hard dough
- hot cross bun
- kuchen
- kugelhopf
- laminated yeast dough
- lean dough
- medium dough
- modified straight dough-mixing method
- pâte fermentée
- pickup
- poolish
- pre-ferment
- rolled-in yeast dough
- scaling
- soft dough
- sourdough
- sponge
- stollen
- straight dough-mixing method
- sweet rich dough
- yeast hydration

> **"F**rom four simple ingredients—yeast, flour, water, and salt—bakers around the world have created an incredible array of breads, rolls, and pastries.**"**
>
> – Richard Coppedge
> The Culinary Institute of America

Basic Types of Yeast Dough

Yeast dough is the blank canvas of baking. You can make it plain or add different ingredients to create everything from bread to cakes. Master the art of basic yeast dough techniques and the sky's the limit.

Lean Dough **Lean dough** (also called **hard dough**) is the most basic type of yeast dough. Only the bare essentials—flour, yeast, salt, and water—are used to make it. Spices, herbs, dried nuts, and fruit may be added, but very little (if any) sugar and fat is included.

Pizza crust, hard rolls, Italian-style bread, and the slender French baguette, with its chewy texture and hard crust, are classic examples of products made with lean dough. Whole wheat, rye, pumpernickel, and sourdough breads are also variations of lean dough. The coarse flour used in these breads makes for a denser texture.

Lean dough can be difficult to handle because little or no fat is used. Commercial bakeries sometimes use chemical dough conditioners such as **chlorine dioxide** (KLOR-ene die-OX-ide) to produce a more stable dough, increase loaf volume, and prevent the loss of leavening.

A pizza crust is made from a lean dough that is stretched or rolled until it is thin. There are several options for shaping the dough once it is properly fermented. You may simply stretch it out by pulling on the edges of the dough. Or you can use a rolling pin to stretch it out. The most entertaining approach calls for the dough to be draped over your fist and repeatedly spun off your fists and into the air. Each time you toss and catch the dough, it stretches a bit more.

▲
FIGURE 17-13
Lean Dough
French baguettes, pumpernickel, and rolls.
Classifying *What percentage of the yeast bread and pastry you eat is made from lean dough?*

Soft Dough The soft slices of Pullman bread, which is typically used for sandwiches, are made with **soft dough** (also called **medium dough**). It is lean dough with sugar and fat added. The amounts of fat and sugar vary from 6% to 9%.

As you know from Chapter 11, Pullman slices get their square shape from the covered loaf pans in which the loaves are baked. You can also use soft dough to make soft rolls that you can shape into knots or cloverleaf balls. Fat and sugar help make soft dough tender when it's baked and give it a soft crust.

Enriched Dough When lean dough is enriched with butter, oil, sugar, eggs, or milk products, it becomes **enriched dough** (also called **sweet rich dough**). Enriched dough has fat and sugar amounts up to 25%, making the dough sweet and rich. The addition of fat and other ingredients changes the texture of the dough, making it softer and a bit more difficult to handle. It also slows down the yeast activity and requires more time for the dough to ferment.

Eggs and butter not only tenderize, but they also create a soft crust and a golden color. The percentage of eggs is important because too many eggs will result in heavy dough. The finished product should have a cake-like texture.

The 240 Factor

The temperature of the air can warm an icy beverage. The friction created by rubbing your knee on a rug can feel like a burn. In the same way, the temperature of the air around dough, as well as friction created by mixing it, affects the dough's temperature.

The temperature of ingredients used to make dough has a direct impact on the temperature of the dough. For example, if you drop a handful of room-temperature raspberries into a chilled glass of lemonade, they will warm the lemonade a bit. Likewise, if you use cold eggs or warm flour, it will affect the desired dough temperature (or DDT, for short). The DDT for yeast dough is typically around 80°F.

The faster you mix dough, the greater the friction created by the beaters and the warmer it makes the dough. Although it is difficult to control the heat generated by beating, the temperature of ingredients such as flour, or the room temperature, you can control the temperature of the water you use.

There is a simple, three-step scientific formula, sometimes called the 240 Factor, for producing the DDT of a yeast dough, based exclusively on controlling the temperature of the water used in the dough:

1. Multiply the desired dough temperature by 3. (Remember, the DDT = 80°F.)

$$80 \times 3 = 240$$

2. Then, add together the current temperature of the flour, the room, and friction (with average friction = 30°F).

Flour = 50°F, Room = 68°F, and Friction = 30°F

Total = 148

3. Subtract the total from 240. The answer is the ideal water temperature.

$$240 - 148 = 92$$

The ideal water should be 92°F.

Calculate

Based on your kitchen's temperature and the temperature of flour in your kitchen, calculate the temperature of the water you should use in making a bread dough.

Enriched dough is used around the world to create some of the best-loved yeast breads, cakes, and rolls, including:

- **Cinnamon Buns.** Sugar and cinnamon are spread on sweet dough that is rolled and then sliced before baking to make cinnamon buns. Raisins are sometimes added to the dough. Drizzled with icing and served warm, these comforting confections have become an American standard.
- **Hot Cross Buns.** A signature cross made of icing tops a **hot cross bun**. These sweet yeast buns originated in England and were traditionally served on Good Friday. They are popular for Easter breakfast, too.
- **Brioche.** A rich French bread, **brioche** (BREE-ohsh) often has a knotted top and is made in individual molds with a fluted base. It can also be made into round loaves or rolls. Brioche dough is used as a crust to wrap cheese, sausage, and other food.

▲ *Brioche*

CHEF'S TIP

SWEET NOTHING

Added fat and sugar make enriched dough moist and soft. Be very sparing with extra flour on the work surface or in shaping the dough because too much flour can toughen the finished product.

- **Challah.** A sweet and airy bread made with lots of eggs, **challah** (HAL-la) is a Jewish bread and it's usually braided. Traditionally served on the Sabbath and holidays, this bread is a treat on any occasion.
- **Stollen.** The traditional Christmas bread of Germany, **stollen** (STOH-len) is a sweet, loaf-shaped yeast bread that is filled with dried fruit and topped with icing and cherries.
- **Kuchen.** Another German original, the popularity of **kuchen** (KOO-ken), a sweet, yeast-raised cake filled with fruit or cheese, has spread throughout Europe and the United States. Kuchen can be served for breakfast, teatime, or dessert.
- **Kugelhopf.** A light yeast cake filled with candied fruit, nuts, and raisins, **kugelhopf** (KOO-guhl-hof) is usually baked in a fluted ring mold. A tradition of Austria, kugelhopf is also associated with Poland, Alsace, and Germany.

FIGURE 17-14 ▶
Variety of Breads
All of these breads were made using enriched dough.
Applying Concepts *How would you use these breads compared to breads made from lean dough?*

 **Reading Checkpoint** *What are the basic types of yeast dough?*

Straight Dough-Mixing Method

The simplest and most common way of mixing yeast dough is called the **straight dough-mixing method.** In this method, you mix all the ingredients for the dough together at the same time. When the ingredients are mixed, either by hand or in a mixer, the yeast starts to develop immediately. Although the process is not difficult, you must pay attention to the following details.

Scaling Ingredients The most accurate way to measure ingredients is to weigh them. When liquids and solids are weighed, it is called scaling. (Some recipes may require you to measure liquids, such as milk and water, with a volume measure.)

Precise measurement is important, because ingredients interact together. Inaccurate measurements in baking alter the balance of ingredients and affect the finished product. For example, the amount of yeast in a recipe is the exact amount needed to raise the dough. Adding too much egg, flour, or other ingredient to the dough interferes with the yeast development. Baker's formulas—in which basic ingredients are listed as percentages, or parts, based on the weight of the flour—are often used for yeast dough.

Yeast Hydration Yeast is an organic leavener, which means it is alive but resting or dormant until it is moistened. The soaking process that activates yeast is called **yeast hydration**. When mixed with a liquid, the cells start to work.

Pickup The first stage of mixing ingredients is called **pickup**. Set the mixer at a low speed to combine the yeast and water. Oil, if it is being used, is added next, followed by the dry ingredients. Shortening, if it is used, goes in last. After everything is combined, increase the mixer speed to medium.

Gluten Development Gluten is one of the proteins in flour. Kneading dough causes a web of gluten strands to stretch and expand. The network of elastic strands that form during gluten development is important because it enables dough to hold in the gas bubbles that are formed by the yeast without breaking through the dough. The gas bubbles allow dough to rise.

Dough that has been properly kneaded is shiny and elastic. To test the strength of the gluten and be sure it is properly developed, you can pinch off a piece of the dough and pull it. It should be stretchy without tearing, and when you hold it up to the light, it should be thin enough for some light to come through. This is called the **gluten window test**.

Bulk Fermentation The organisms in hydrated yeast produce carbon dioxide and alcohol as a byproduct when they have moisture and a food source and are at the right temperature. This is called **fermentation** and it makes the dough rise until double or triple in size. Bread made from under-fermented dough that hasn't risen enough will be flat, while bread made from over-fermented dough will have a yeasty, sour taste.

FIGURE 17-15
Bulk Fermentation
The dough doubles or triples in size during bulk fermentation.
Applying Concepts *Would the dough rise as much if the temperature were lower?*

Straight Dough-Mixing Method

1 **Scaling the ingredients.** Ingredients are precisely weighed.

2 **Hydrating the yeast.** Yeast is activated when combined with water.

3 **Pickup stage.** All other ingredients are added at once with the mixer on a slow speed.

4 **Gluten development and kneading.** Increase the mixer speed to medium until dough begins to catch on the dough hook. Properly kneaded dough is satiny and forms a ball in the mixing bowl. If a small piece is stretched thin, it holds together without breaking (gluten window test).

5 **Bulk fermentation.** Dough will double or triple in size as the yeast ferments.

6 **Folding dough.** Folding and pushing the dough down releases its carbon dioxide.

Pizza Dough

1 Hydrate the yeast in water.

2 Add the flour and salt and mix at a low speed until the dough is evenly moistened. (This is the pickup stage.)

3 Mix and knead the dough by hand on a floured surface or on medium speed in a mixer until the dough is very smooth and springy to the touch.

4 Make a gluten window to test the dough.

5 Transfer the dough to an oiled bowl, oil the surface lightly, and cover.

6 Bulk-ferment the dough until it doubles in size and the dough retains an imprint when pressed with a gloved fingertip.

7 Fold the dough over on itself in several places. The dough is ready to shape into pizza crust at this point.

See Recipe Card 118, "Pizza."

The surface of the dough should be oiled so it won't dry out. The container should also be oiled so the dough won't stick to the sides. Cover the dough with plastic wrap or a clean cloth and leave it to rise in a warm area until the rising is completed.

Folding Dough After the rising is complete, the dough is folded over and turned onto a floured work surface. The dough is continuously folded over on itself to get rid of any more gases. Each piece is gently pushed down a few times to release the carbon dioxide that formed during fermentation. This process helps distribute the yeast evenly. In addition, folding helps create a uniform overall temperature by folding the cooler, outside dough into the warmer center.

The dough is then scaled into pieces for size consistency and baked.

Reading Checkpoint

Describe the straight mixing method for yeast dough.

Modifying the Basic Method

Rather than adding all the ingredients at once, the **modified straight dough-mixing method** adds ingredients in steps. This method provides better distribution for fat and sugar and is particularly useful for enriched dough.

Enriched Yeast Dough Enriched yeast dough may call for modifications to the basic straight dough-mixing method. One very simple change is to use milk in place of the water used in a lean dough.

Once the dough is mixed, it may be softer and stickier than regular lean dough.

Very rich dough may need to be kept cool, even during bulk fermentation, so the extra butter stays in the dough rather than melting and separating out of the dough. This requires that ingredients are mixed in a specific order:

1. Hydrate the yeast and add the flour.

2. Add liquid ingredients (milk, cream, eggs, oils, or melted butter) and sweeteners (honey, sugar, or maple syrup).

3. Mix the dough until all the flour is evenly moistened.

4. Add additional butter (room temperature or softened) gradually (if the formula calls for it) until evenly blended.

5. Continue to mix and knead the dough until it is properly developed.

FIGURE 17-16
Sponge
An overhead view of a developed sponge in the mixing bowl.
Analyzing Information *How can you tell when sponge dough is developed?*

Sponge Mixing Method The sponge method combines one-third to one-half of the formula's total liquid with all the yeast and enough flour to make a very loose dough. This dough is called a **sponge**. A sponge is usually mixed in the same bowl you will use to prepare the entire batch of dough. When the sponge has doubled in size, the remaining ingredients are added to the sponge and mixed to make a dough. Breads made with a sponge have a richer, deeper flavor and an improved texture.

Pre-Ferments A **pre-ferment** (PREE-fer-ment), also called a **dough starter**, is similar to a sponge. Some or all the yeast is mixed with water and some flour to create the pre-ferment. This is allowed to ferment for a specific time and is then added to the dough before its final mixing. The pre-ferment increases the fermentation time, which increases the strength of the gluten in the dough. This adds depth and complexity to the flavor while also extending the shelf life of the bread.

If you want to make a pre-ferment for a dough that does not specify one in the formula, you need to subtract the amount of flour, water, and yeast in the pre-ferment from the total flour, water, and yeast in the formula.

There are several types of pre-ferments. Each has a different flavor and is used for different breads. Some common examples are:

- **Poolish.** Combining equal parts of flour and water (by weight) with some yeast, a **poolish** (poo-LEESH) is then allowed to ferment. The actual amount of yeast varies, depending on how long the poolish will be allowed to ferment. Use less yeast for a long, slow fermentation. A poolish is fermented at room temperature until it doubles in volume and then begins to get smaller (anywhere from 3 to 15 hours). The poolish is added to the rest of the ingredients during mixing.

- **Biga.** An Italian pre-ferment, the process for making **biga** (BEE-gah) is similar to that for making a poolish, but biga is stiffer because it contains less water. A biga usually calls for about one-third to one-half the total amount of yeast called for in the formula. Bigas, like poolish, are allowed to ferment from 3 to 15 hours at room temperature. Before you can add the biga to the rest of the dough, however, you need to loosen it by adding the additional water required by the formula.

- **Sourdough.** With a tangy, slightly sour flavor, **sourdough** pre-ferment is made from wild yeast. The difference between sourdough and most other pre-ferments is that sourdough starter can be kept alive a long time, sometimes hundreds of years.

- **Pâte Fermentée.** A French term that literally means "old dough," **pâte fermentée** (PAHT fer-mahn-TAY), is a piece of dough saved from one batch and added along with the flour, yeast, and liquid. Wrap the pâte fermentée airtight and you can save it in the refrigerator for 48 hours or in the freezer up to 3 months.

▲ *Sourdough bread*

Rolled-In Dough Fat can be used to add flavor to any type of yeast dough. When fat is rolled in or folded into dough (as opposed to being mixed into the dough itself), it adds flakiness. Buttery yeast pastries, such as the classic Danish and croissants, get their feathery flakiness from folding the dough into many thin layers with butter layers in between. The process of rolling in and folding in fat creates layers of dough called **rolled-in yeast dough**. It is also known as **laminated yeast dough** because it is made up of alternating layers of dough and fat (and under a microscope would look like plywood, with all its layers).

The fat layers produce steam in the oven, creating lightness by puffing up the thin dough layers. The dough is rolled into a rectangle, layered with chilled butter, and folded into thirds, like a letter. The process is then repeated. The added handling of rolling and folding means that you should not knead the dough as much as regular yeast dough.

▲ *Danish*

When fruit is added to yeast dough, it releases some sugar into the dough. This could slow the bread's rise. Also, the finer the fruit is chopped, the more likely it is to release sugar, altering the dough's sugar ratio.

Over-handling yeast dough can ruin the finished product, making it tough and chewy.

The final rolled-in dough is then refrigerated to chill the fat again. This dough keeps well in the refrigerator for several days.

Yeast Bread Garnishes Yeast bread garnishes are ingredients that stay separate from the dough's structure while maintaining a distinctive flavor. Some garnishes are mixed into the dough before the dough rises. For example, black olives and cranberries are added to bread dough before it rises. Blueberries and chocolate chips are garnishes added to pastries before the dough rises. Other garnishes are added after the dough has risen, as with filled croissants. The dough is folded or rolled around the garnish.

Garnishes can add crunch and flavor to dough but they can also add extra weight. More yeast may be required, depending on the amount added. It is important to consult your recipe for the precise ratio of a garnish to the flour in the recipe.

Reading Checkpoint *What is a pre-ferment?*

17.2 ASSESSMENT

Reviewing Concepts

1. What are the basic types of yeast dough?
2. What are the basic steps in the straight dough-mixing method?
3. What is a pre-ferment?

Critical Thinking

4. **Comparing/Contrasting** What do both soft dough and enriched dough have that lean dough doesn't?
5. **Predicting** Why is the final product of enriched dough often yellow and lean dough never is?
6. **Comparing/Contrasting** What is the difference between the modified straight dough-mixing method and the basic straight dough-mixing method?

Test Kitchen

Divide into 2 teams. One team will prepare a bread recipe, using active dry yeast. The other team will prepare the same recipe, using instant yeast. All other ingredients should be identical and the amounts should be identical. Compare the results.

 **CULINARY MATH**

Substituting Yeast

To substitute instant yeast for active dry yeast, use .67 times the weight of the active dry yeast for the instant yeast. For example, 1 tsp of active dry yeast = ⅔ tsp of instant yeast. If a recipe calls for 3 tsps of active dry yeast, how much instant yeast would you substitute for it?

Breads, Rolls, & Pastries

Key Concepts

- Dividing and pre-shaping the dough
- Shaping breads, rolls, and pastries
- Baking breads, rolls, and pastries
- Evaluating the quality of yeast breads, rolls, and pastries

Vocabulary

- baguette
- bench boxes
- bench proofing
- boule
- free-form loaf
- injera
- oven spring
- pan loaf
- pan proofing
- scoring

"**F**ashioning dough into rolls and loaves demands a delicate touch. The dough is a living thing right up to the moment you put it in the oven. "

— **Eric Kastel**
The Culinary Institute
of America

Dividing and Pre-Shaping Dough

For large-scale baking, the dough must be divided into equal parts for uniform sizes. Once the dough is divided, it is pre-shaped and allowed to relax.

Cutting and Scaling Dividing dough into pieces that are of uniform size is important for quality control. Scale each piece, using the bench scraper to add pieces of dough or remove excess to get the exact weight. The dough is fermenting while you work, so the sooner you finish, the better. The divided pieces are smaller and will ferment more quickly than the undivided dough.

It's always easier to use the right tool for a job. Bakers use a bench scraper to divide dough for superior results. Pulling or tearing the dough weakens the gluten.

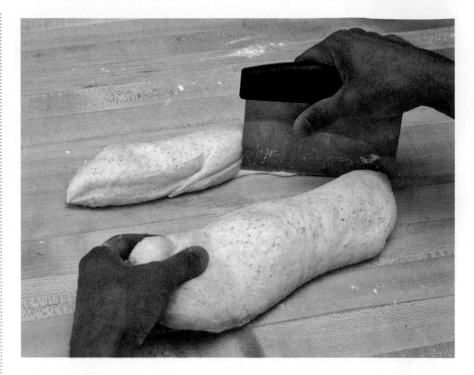

FIGURE 17-17 ▶
Cutting Dough
Use a bench scraper to cut dough.
Predicting *How might the shape of your initial cut be affected by the type of product you are going to make?*

Pre-Shaping After the dough is cut and scaled, you pre-shape the divided dough on a lightly floured surface by covering it with your hands and gently shaping it into tight rounds. The purpose of pre-shaping is to get the dough close to the final shape. You should also use the bench scraper to move and lift the round balls of dough for minimal handling.

Bench Proofing After the dough has been rounded, cover the rounds and let the dough rest until you can stretch it carefully without tearing—usually about 20 minutes. This is called **bench proofing**,

FIGURE 17-18 ▶
Bench Proofing
Dough can be proofed in a linen-lined mold or in a basket.
Inferring *Why is it important that the skin on dough holds in carbon dioxide?*

Pre-Shaping Dough into Rounds

1 Bring edges of the dough together in the middle.

2 Turn over. Tuck any loose dough into the bottom.

3 Cover with your hands and round out the edges.

4 Press edges toward the middle to tighten the ball.

a brief resting period that allows the gluten to relax and makes the dough easier to shape.

Bench proofing can be done on the workbench in bowls covered with cloth or plastic wrap or in covered containers called **bench boxes**. During bench proofing, the dough forms a skin that holds in the carbon dioxide.

 **Reading Checkpoint** *What is the purpose of bench proofing?*

Shaping Breads, Rolls, and Pastries

The shapes of bread, rolls, and pastries are as distinctive as a person's signature. The shape identifies what they are, from the oval of a rye bread to the long and narrow loaf of French bread. Bread can be shaped by the pan it is baked in, such as a loaf pan, or by hand, as with pizza. Some of the shapes look complicated, but once you learn the basic technique, you'll enjoy perfecting it. Another important aspect is that specific shapes complement specific dough qualities.

Begin shaping with little or no flour on the work surface. You want the dough to stay in place, and too much flour will make it slip around. Try to work without interruptions, because the fermentation process is still going on. Also, follow the same order that you used to pre-shape, starting with the first loaf you rounded.

Flat Breads Many cultures throughout the world have a variation of flat bread in their cuisine. The shape of flat bread lends itself to being a carrier for other food, much as we use sliced bread to make sandwiches. For example, in some African countries, such as Ethiopia, a flat bread called **injera** (in-JAH-raw) is traditionally used, instead of utensils, to pick up food and as part of the meal.

FOCUS ON NUTRITION

Green Is Lean
Reduce fat in pizza by using less meat and adding a layer of spinach leaves or other vegetables sautéed in garlic. Use low-fat mozzarella cheese to keep calories under control.

Flat breads can be crisp, soft, puffy, or flat as a cracker. Some examples of flat breads are pita and focaccia. Another example is pizza. Pizza is an Italian word for "pie." When you think about it, a pizza is just a flat bread covered with tomato sauce, mozzarella cheese, or other ingredients. A pizza can be round or rectangular, thick or thin, crispy or chewy. Too much topping on a pizza weighs down the crust, interfering with its ability to bake properly.

Baguettes A **baguette** (bag-EHT) is a long, narrow French bread with a crispy, golden brown crust and a light, chewy crumb dotted with holes. The skinny, cylindrical shape of a baguette provides a maximum amount of crunchy crust.

▲ Flat bread

BASIC CULINARY SKILLS

Baguettes

1. Scale the dough into pieces of the correct size.
2. Reshape the pieces into rounds.
3. Bench proof the dough.
4. Press the dough into a puffy rectangle.

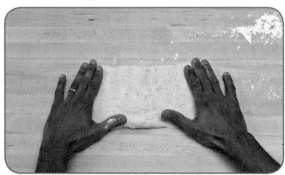

5. Lift the ends of the dough and allow its own weight to stretch it out.

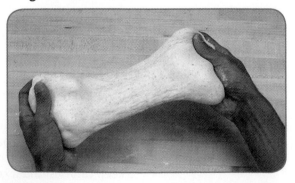

6. Roll the stretched dough into a long cylinder, pressing the seams shut for the best finished loaf.

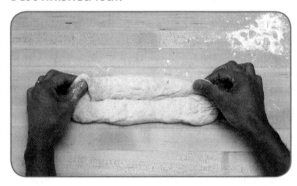

7. Transfer the shaped dough to a baking sheet or a floured cloth.
8. Proof (in a proofer with steam, if possible) until nearly doubled in size.
9. Score the loaf lightly. Brush or mist lightly with water.
10. Bake the dough until a good crust develops and the loaf sounds hollow when you tap the bottom.
11. Cool the loaf on a cooling rack before slicing or serving.

 See Recipe Card 119, "Baguettes."

Free-Form Loaves A **free-form loaf** is not pressed into a mold or a pan. It is shaped by hand into an oval, round ball, and other shape. The French word for ball, **boule** (BOOL), is used to describe a round loaf of bread. You make the shape by pressing dough into a round patty, folding the edges into the center, and pinching them together. You then press the edges of the dough together with your cupped hands, rotating in a circular fashion until a neat ball is formed.

▲ *Boule*

Pan Loaves A **pan loaf** is made by pressing dough into a mold or a pan. The first step to making a loaf shape is pressing dough into a wide rectangle. Then, fold the right side just past the middle and slightly overlap the left side onto the right. Roll down the top edges of the dough and push it away from you with your thumbs. Roll it back and forth into a rectangular loaf shape just a bit longer than the pan. Tuck the ends in before placing the dough in the loaf pan.

Braided Loaves Three tapered ropes of dough are often used to make a braided loaf (although four ropes can also be used). Braided loaves are often made with rich dough. The braids help the bread keep its structure so the bread doesn't flatten. The dough must be firm enough to hold the shape, and the ropes must be of uniform size to make an even braid. Divide the dough into thirds and shape them in the same way as the baguette.

FIGURE 17-19
Braiding Challah Dough
This loaf of challah bread uses three ropes of dough.
Interpreting Illustrations *Can you see how the outside rope becomes the center rope?*

▼

Starting with an outside rope, cross the outside rope over the center rope. Now the center rope is an outside rope and the outside rope is the center rope. Do the same thing with the other outside rope. Repeat until you have used all the bread. Pinch the finished braid ends together and tuck underneath the loaf, toward the center.

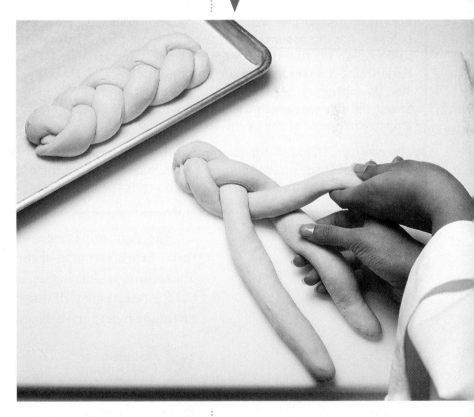

Rolls and Pastries The first step in making rolls and pastries is to cut and scale. Then you round off the dough. Eventually you can use any of the shaping techniques for breads to create free-form shapes or shapes that are a result of a mold or small-sized pan, or even use the braiding technique to create knots and twists. Aside from all the other shaping techniques, some pastries are rolled and sliced.

CULINARY DIVERSITY

Croissants around the World

It's not polite to fight over food, but some people are still arguing over the exact origin of croissants. Hungary, Austria, and France all claim the croissant as their own. The passion for croissants has spread beyond those countries, and interpretations of it exist around the world.

▲ *Croissants in a French bakery*

invention of croissants to the Turk's attempted siege of Budapest.

Marie Antoinette, who later became queen of France, was born in Austria and is reputed to have introduced croissants to the French after she moved there.

It is agreed that the early version of croissants were more bread-like, and the French are credited with introducing the flakey, buttery version the world has come to enjoy today.

There is definitely a French connection, but the Austrians claimed croissants first. Legend has it that the Turk's war with Austria in 1683 led to the creation of croissants. The Turks were digging a tunnel in the night in their attempt to sneak under the protective city walls of Vienna. The Turkish soldiers, having assumed that the city would be asleep, didn't realize that bakers are busiest in the dark hours. A baker alerted officials and the invasion was interrupted. As a reward, the baker who saved the city was given the privilege of creating a pastry in honor of the event.

The crescent shape of the pastry was inspired by the crescent shape on the Turkish flag. A similar story, dating three years later in Hungary, connects the

In England the word "croissant" first appeared in a dictionary in 1899. Italians have a less buttery interpretation that they call a cornetto, or "horn."

Research

Americans have embraced croissants for breakfast, lunch, and dinner. Croissants are everywhere, from fast food restaurants to the frozen food case. Identify five places nationally where croissants are offered, and describe how they are served and sold.

The sight of pastries, with their distinctive shapes, is enough to turn a breakfast buffet, teatime, or coffee break into a special occasion. The techniques for shaping individual pastries are a bit labor-intensive, but the results are well worth it. The distinctive shapes help customers distinguish between different types of pastries.

 **Reading Checkpoint** *Why is the shape of a bread, roll, or pastry important?*

Baking Breads, Rolls, and Pastries

When making yeast dough products, there is a great deal of preparation before you are actually able to bake the product. After you have created and shaped the dough, you have a series of final steps before you are able to bake. Understanding the purpose of these final steps and what happens in the oven during baking gives you better control of the outcome.

Pan Proofing After the dough is shaped, it is allowed to rise one last time. This final rise before baking is called **pan proofing**. During this stage, the dough is allowed to rise about three-quarters of the expected finished product. It will finish rising in the oven.

Washes and Glazes Dough is sometimes covered with an egg wash or glaze before baking to give the crust a shiny appearance. Egg washes give the crust a deeper color. The stickiness of egg washes is used like glue to attach seeds, such as poppy or sesame seeds, to breads.

Some bread is sprayed with water before baking or steamed during baking to create a crispy crust. When bread is given this treatment, an egg wash is not used (because it would just be washed off).

Toppings such as melted butter or warmed, strained fruit preserves can be used as glazes. Sticky buns, for example, have a specific glaze made from the sugary liquid in which the raisins used in the sticky buns are soaked. These glazes are brushed on in the pan just before the product is baked in the oven.

Scoring The top of dough is sometimes cut with slashes to release steam that builds up during baking. This is called **scoring** and it is done to control the tearing that could otherwise occur at the seam on the loaf. The sharp, thin blade of a knife or single-edge razor produces the best results when scoring. Cuts should be between ¼- and ½-inch deep.

CHEF'S TIP

CLEAN CUT
You will get the straightest line if you work fast when you score bread. Slow-motion scoring can drag the dough and create an uneven line.

FIGURE 17-20
Scoring
Loaves of bread with different scoring.
Classifying *Why do customers prefer that specific types of bread are always scored in the same way?*

FIGURE 17-21
Cooling Bread
Loaves of fresh-baked bread cool
on racks in a bakery.
Applying Concepts *Why is fresh-
baked bread cooled on racks and
not on shelves?*

▼

Baking Stages A series of chain reactions begins to take place as soon as dough is placed in an oven. Oven spring and crust formation are the most important of these reactions. The final step in the process is determining doneness.

- **Oven Spring.** The last stage of rising that occurs in the oven is called **oven spring**. This is when the heat expands the carbon dioxide gas in the dough and stretches the gluten into a network of strands that trap steam and the carbon dioxide. This ultimately gives the dough its final shape and allows it to reach full size.

- **Crust Formation.** The crust starts forming as the dough's outer surface dries out. Once the crust is formed, the dough can no longer expand. Steam ovens and a water spray are sometimes used to keep the dough surface moist and delay the formation of crust so full development can occur. This moisture during baking also creates better browning.

- **Determining Doneness.** A golden color and good aroma are both indicators of doneness. Another indicator is a hollow sound when you thump the bread. Generally you should regard the recipe's recommended baking time as a guideline and use actual indicators to evaluate doneness.

Cooling and Slicing Breads Remove breads, rolls, and pastries from their baking pans immediately. Cool bread on a rack before slicing. Hot bread continues to bake until it is cooled, often evaporating excess moisture. Slice bread with a serrated knife after it has cooled. Use a gentle, sawing motion to cut even slices.

 **Reading Checkpoint** *What is pan proofing?*

Evaluating Quality

The final, post-baking stage is when you assess the quality of your product. An evaluation is like detective work where you look for clues to help you understand what happened. Evaluating helps you improve your technique by showing the cause-and-effect relationships of your product's appearance, crumb, and flavor.

- **Appearance.** The golden-brown color of a well-developed crust is the first indication that proper baking has occurred. Special flours, such as rye or oat, will influence color. If the finished product is pale, it has been baked at too low a temperature or it isn't completely done. Dough that has been brushed with an egg wash has a more tender and golden crust than others.

- **Crumb.** Yeast breads should be fairly elastic but easy to bite into. The more eggs, fat, and milk used in the product, the more tender the crumb will be. The more times the dough is allowed to rise, the finer and more even the crumb will be.

- **Flavor.** If there is a strong taste of alcohol, either too much yeast was used or insufficient time was spent proofing before baking. A strong alcohol odor and bland flavor indicate not enough salt was used.

 **Reading Checkpoint** *What is the purpose of evaluating your finished product?*

17.3 ASSESSMENT

Reviewing Concepts

1. What is the purpose of bench proofing?
2. Why is the shape of a bread, roll, or pastry important?
3. What is pan proofing?
4. What makes yeast bread taste like alcohol?

Critical Thinking

5. **Predicting** What would happen if you made a baked product without scaling the dough?
6. **Applying Concepts** Is it a good idea to change the traditional shape of a bread, roll, or pastry? Explain your answer.
7. **Analyzing Information** Your pizza is soggy and didn't rise properly. What might have happened?

Test Kitchen

Divide into three teams. Each team will make a batch of yeast rolls. Team 1 will use an egg wash consisting of egg yolks. Team 2 will use an egg wash of egg whites. Team 3 will not use an egg wash. Bake the rolls and evaluate the results.

SOCIAL STUDIES

Versatile Flat Breads

Flat breads are used in many cultures and in different ways. Research two more examples of flat breads. Indicate the country where the flat bread originated and the food with which it is served.

Review and Assessment

Reviewing Content

Choose the letter that best answers the question or completes the statement.

1. The difference between lean dough and enriched dough is
   a. texture
   b. color
   c. sweetness
   d. all of the above

2. Another word describing rolled-in dough is
   a. layered
   b. rounded
   c. laminated
   d. flattened

3. When ingredients are weighed, it is called
   a. measuring
   b. dividing
   c. the method
   d. scaling

4. In the modified straight dough-mixing method,
   a. ingredients are all mixed at the same time
   b. Half the dry ingredients are mixed with half the wet ingredients, then the other half of the dry ingredients are added, then the other half of the wet ingredients
   c. Liquid ingredients are added to the yeast and flour
   d. dissolved yeast and flour are added last

5. In baking, a sponge is
   a. made with yeast, sugar, and water
   b. a thick, batter-like yeast mixture developed separately
   c. a type of sweet roll
   d. a sweet dessert dough

6. Dough starters start fermentation
   a. before yeast is added
   b. while the oven is preheating
   c. before the final mixing of the dough
   d. before the yeast is packaged

7. Dough garnishes are
   a. decorative designs on the bread
   b. decorations made of dough
   c. part of the dough structure
   d. ingredients that stay separate from the dough structure

Understanding Concepts

8. Why are enriched dough products more tender than lean dough products?

9. What is rolled into laminated dough and how does it contribute to lightness?

10. What does the gluten window test show?

11. What is the difference between bench proofing and pan proofing?

12. What happens when the crust forms during the baking process?

Critical Thinking

13. **Comparing/Contrasting** What is the difference between the straight dough-mixing method and the modified straight dough-mixing method?

14. **Applying Concepts** Your first bread had a very strong smell of alcohol. What went wrong?

Culinary Math

15. **Solving Problems** If it takes you 2 hours to shape 48 baguettes, how many can you do in half an hour? Based on that figure, approximately how long does it take to shape each baguette?

16. **Applying Concepts** You are having 66 guests for breakfast. The serving size per person is 3 mini-Danishes. You are making 6 different fillings. You want to divide the total amount of mini-Danishes by 6 to determine how many of each flavor you will make.

On the Job

17. **Applying Concepts** You are working in a nursing home, and the elderly residents want more whole grains in their diet. You add barley and oats to their favorite bread. What other ingredient may have to be adjusted? Why?

18. **Communicating** Students in your high school cafeteria are concerned about their weight. You have developed a tasty and healthy pizza with low-fat cheese and fresh vegetables for them. Write a brief and playful description of your pizza for the menu board.

RECIPE CARDS

Use the following Recipe Cards to test your culinary skill.

118. Pizza

119. Baguette

120. Focaccia

121. Soft Rolls

LAB ACTIVITY

Project 17: Differences in Flour

Answer these questions when your class works through Project 17.

- Did the doughs rise equally in both the bench proofing and the pan proofing?
- Were there differences in the cooking time or degree of doneness for the rolls made from the various doughs?
- Were there differences in flavor, aroma, and texture among the final baked rolls?
- In your opinion, which dough worked best for this product?

TEST PRACTICE

Choose the letter that best answers the question or completes the statement.

1. Chlorine dioxide is
  A produced by fermentation
  B a dough conditioner
  C a poison resulting from incorrect fermentation
  D a pathogen

2. In the straight dough-mixing method,
  A ingredients are all mixed at the same time
  B wet ingredients are added alternately with dry
  C dry ingredients are mixed first and wet ingredients are added last
  D dissolved yeast and flour are added last

3. Yeast hydration is
  A the excess moisture produced by fermentation
  B the excess moisture produced by a yeast product after baking
  C the soaking process that activates yeast
  D the process of spraying water on a yeast product while baking

4. Pickup is
  A the first stage of mixing ingredients
  B an odor picked up by fermenting dough
  C the process of using a peel
  D the process of rolling out dough

5. Injera is a
  A utensil for rolling out dough
  B type of flat bread
  C utensil for picking up flatbread in an oven
  D type of leavener

6. Poolish is a
  A type of leavener
  B type of flat bread
  C type of dough starter
  D utensil for rolling out dough

7. Pectin is a
  A type of flat bread
  B dough starter
  C leavener
  D thickener

8. A proofer is a
  A special box that holds dough as it rises
  B leavener
  C utensil for spraying water on yeast products in the oven
  D dough starter

9. A boule is a
  A utensil for shaping dough
  B round loaf of bread
  C cylindrical loaf of bread
  D dough starter

Yeast Breads, Rolls, & Pastries ▶ **573**

QUICK BREADS

READING PREVIEW

Key Concepts

- Identifying basic ingredients
- Mixing and baking methods
- Garnishing muffins and quick breads

Vocabulary

- creaming
- crumb topping
- quick bread
- stir-ins
- streusel
- sugar glaze
- well method

"**M**uffins and quick breads are indispensable in any good bakeshop. To make them into signature items, showcase seasonal fruit, special shapes, and even holiday themes."

— Todd Knaster
The Culinary institute of America

Basic Ingredients

A **quick bread** is a type of bread that is quick to make because baking soda or baking powder, rather than yeast, is used for leavening. The result is a batter rather than a dough. The batter can be baked immediately after the ingredients are mixed because there is no need to wait for a fermentation process to occur. Quick breads are usually baked in loaf pans. Muffins can be made from the same batter and baked in individual cup-shaped tins.

Quick breads and muffins may be sweet or savory and can be served throughout the day. They are equally appropriate at simple coffee shops or fancy restaurants. Quick breads freeze well and can be kept in the refrigerator up to a week when tightly wrapped. Muffins are best when served freshly baked and still warm from the oven. They freeze well and should be wrapped in aluminum foil when reheated.

The basic ingredients for muffins and quick breads are:

- **Flour.** All-purpose flour is considered standard for muffins and quick breads. Other types of flour, such as whole wheat, oat, graham, and pastry flour, or cornmeal may be substituted entirely or in part for the all-purpose flour.
- **Sugar.** White sugar, brown sugar, and molasses are typical sweeteners. Granulated sugars add texture.
- **Fat.** Fat provides moisture and tenderness. Either oil or butter may be used.
- **Liquid.** Milk, buttermilk, and water are all used to give moisture to muffins and quick breads.
- **Eggs.** The fresher the eggs, the better the structure they give in baking. Eggs should be at room temperature because this makes them easier to mix into the batter. Be careful not to leave eggs out of the refrigerator for more than two hours.
- **Salt.** Salt is a seasoning providing color and texture. It should not be eliminated.
- **Leavening Agent.** Either baking soda or baking powder can be used in making muffins and quick breads. Both are chemical leavening agents, creating carbon dioxide to make the batter rise. Baking powder starts to lose its ability to leaven within six months and should be tested to make sure it is still active. Mix two teaspoons of baking powder with one cup of warm water. It should fizz.

FOCUS ON NUTRITION

Half the Fat

Applesauce and fruit purée work especially well as fat substitutes when making quick breads and muffins. The fruit fibers hold moisture and the natural sugars promote browning. Substitute purée for up to half the fat.

CULINARY SCIENCE

Baking Powder and Baking Soda

As you know from Chapter 17, baking powder and baking soda are chemical leaveners. When baking soda is combined with a dry acid and a liquid, it creates a chemical reaction that produces carbon dioxide, which makes batter rise.

Baking powder is simply baking soda that is already combined with at least one dry acid, cream of tartar, and some cornstarch. The cornstarch is there to absorb moisture so the chemical reaction doesn't happen before baking begins.

There are usually two acids in baking powder, one that reacts at room temperature to produce carbon

Premium Quality
for your favorite baking recipes

DOUBLE ACTING

BAKING POWDER

NET WT 10 OZ (283g)

▲ *Double acting baking powder*

dioxide, and one that produces carbon dioxide with heat. This is known as "double acting" baking powder.

Baking soda does not contain any acid. It must be mixed with a liquid and an acidic ingredient such as buttermilk, lemon juice, or sour cream to begin releasing carbon dioxide.

Research

Research the history of double action baking powder. When was it first made? How much better is it than the single action baking powder?

Methods of Mixing and Baking

Two basic methods are used for mixing muffins and quick breads, the well method, which is simpler and more frequently used, and the creaming method. A liquid fat such as melted butter or oil is used for the well method. A solid fat such as softened butter or shortening is used for the creaming method.

As you know from Chapter 17, gluten, an elastic protein, develops when flour is combined with liquids. Gluten helps ingredients stick together. However, when too much gluten forms, as it does when batter is overmixed, the batter becomes elastic and cannot rise well. The result will be heavy, misshapen loaves or muffins, dotted with air holes.

Well Method In the **well method**, liquids are blended in one bowl and dry ingredients are sifted in another. Next, a depression (often called a well) is made in the dry ingredients and the liquids are poured into the well. The batter is then mixed minimally. Even if the batter looks lumpy, do only a minimal amount of mixing to avoid overmixing.

Creaming Method In the creaming method, sugar and fat are creamed together, usually with a paddle attachment. **Creaming** is a mixing method in which fat and sugar are combined vigorously to incorporate air. Beating sugar granules into the fat fills the batter with tiny air bubbles that expand in baking and produce lightness in the final texture. This gives muffins and quick breads that use the creaming method a finer texture than products that use the well method.

Eggs are then beaten in, one at a time. It's important that the eggs are at room temperature or they will cause the butter to become firm and reduce creaminess.

As the final step, dry ingredients are sifted together and added to the mixture, alternating with any liquid ingredients.

Preparing and Filling Pans Pans and muffin tins need to be greased, that is, coated with a fat such as butter or a sprayed vegetable oil. This promotes browning and makes muffins and quick breads easier to remove.

▲
**FIGURE 18-1
Picture Perfect**
To make a perfect muffin, you must avoid overmixing.
Predicting *As a consumer, how would you feel if you purchased a misshapen muffin that was filled with air holes?*

FIGURE 18-2 ▶
Before and After
Muffins tins are filled only half way. The finished muffins expand to full size.
Predicting *What would happen if you overfilled the muffin tin?*

Use a portion scooper to ensure a uniform muffin size. Muffin tins should be filled only halfway, because the batter will double in volume and form a dome-shaped top. Overfilling can cause batter to spill over the sides and result in a flat top.

Baking Muffins and quick breads should be baked until the edges begin to shrink from the sides and the top springs back when lightly pressed. A wooden skewer inserted in the middle should come out clean.

Cool loaf breads on a rack before removing the loaves from the pan. Muffins should be removed immediately because steam may become trapped and make them soggy.

 **Reading Checkpoint**   *What is the difference between the well method and the creaming method of making muffins and quick breads?*

Garnishes and Serving Accompaniments

Muffins and quick breads can easily be enhanced with the addition of simple toppings and fillings.

Stir-Ins A wide variety of ingredients can be added to muffins and quick breads to transform a basic recipe into a special treat. Known as **stir-ins**, these ingredients can range from savory to sweet. Shredded vegetables, fresh fruit, nuts, whole grains, meat, cheese, and chocolate are all popular stir-ins.

Creaming Method for Blueberry Muffins

1 Sift flour and baking powder **together.**

2 Cream butter, sugar, and salt **together with a paddle attachment in the bowl of an electric mixer.**

3 Add eggs, one at a time, at low speed. Scrape the sides of the bowl each time.

4 Alternate adding milk with dry ingredients, one-third each time.

5 Remove from mixer.

6 **Fold in blueberries** with a rubber spatula.

7 Portion equal amounts of batter into greased muffin tins.

8 Bake at 400°F for 20 minutes or until lightly browned on top.

9 Remove muffins from tins. Serve warm.

 See Recipe Card 22, "Blueberry Muffins."

Stir-ins should be chopped in proportion to the size of the product being made. If they are too large, they may interfere with the batter's ability to hold together. The quantity of stir-ins should be limited for the same reason. One cup of additions per one cup of flour is the maximum you should use. Stir-ins should be mixed in just enough to distribute them without overmixing.

CULINARY **HISTORY**

Banana Bread Comeback

American social and industrial history is often reflected in the invention and revision of recipes. Banana bread is a good example of this.

A Depression-era housewife is credited with developing banana bread in the 1930s as a way to earn extra income. It's possible that she decided to make the bread to use overripe bananas.

A dramatic shift in attitudes occurred after World War II. Science and technology that was in place for the war effort became available for consumer production. The development of chemical preservatives, artificial coloring, and artificial flavoring caused many new products to be introduced to groceries. This occurred at a time when Americans were eager to embrace all things modern.

As the food processing industry continued to mechanize and reinvent the way food was grown and prepared, the practice of many old-fashioned food traditions, including making home-baked goods, declined. However, the social unrest of the l960s created a culture of rebellion that had a tremendous impact on food. The atmosphere of distrust extended to the food industry, where an increasing number of synthetic products, from hormones for animals to synthetic additives, were entering the food chain. People were encouraged to get back to

▲ *Banana bread*

the basics of healthy and nutritious dining—and banana bread had a comeback.

So when the times "are a-changing" (to paraphrase a Bob Dylan song), so are the tastes.

Research

Research the history of another popular food that has been around for quite some time. Has it, too, had a history that relates to the events in American social and industrial history?

FIGURE 18-3
Cranberry Bread
Cranberries have been added as a stir-in to a sweet quick bread.
Communicating *Do you have a favorite type of quick bread or muffin stir-in?*

▼

Chop or shred any fruit, vegetables, nuts, or other ingredients before you begin mixing your recipe. Muffins and quick bread batters should be baked immediately after they are mixed so the leavening is still active.

Sugar Glazes A **sugar glaze** is a thin liquid made by dissolving sugar in water. It becomes smooth and glossy after setting. Glazes can be flavored with the addition of other ingredients, such as lemon juice or vanilla.

Confectioner's sugar or superfine granulated sugars are commonly used for glazes. In addition to the added sweetness, sugar glazes seal the top and help prevent baked goods from drying out. Glazes are applied with a pastry brush.

Crumb Toppings and Streusels A **crumb topping** is a crumbly mixture of fat, sugar, and flour. A **streusel** (STRU-sel) is a crumb topping that may also include spices and nuts. A careful balance of these ingredients produces a crispy quick bread and muffin topping. Sometimes crumb toppings and streusels are also included as a filling, but the fat is often eliminated as it tends to get pasty when baked.

FIGURE 18-4
Adding a Streusel Topping
A streusel topping adds additional salty, sweet flavor and a special texture to a muffin or quick bread.
Drawing Conclusions *Would you rather have a muffin or quick bread with a streusel topping than one without?*

 **Reading Checkpoint** *What is a stir-in for a muffin or a quick bread?*

Reviewing Concepts

1. Why is a quick bread quicker to make than a yeast bread?
2. How does the well method differ from the creaming method?
3. What is a stir-in for a muffin or a quick bread?

Critical Thinking

4. **Applying Concepts** You are creating a new muffin recipe and you want it to be light and fluffy. Would you use the well method or the creaming method?
5. **Analyzing Information** In an emergency you could substitute baking powder for baking soda, but you could not substitute baking soda for baking powder. Why not?
6. **Drawing Conclusions** A muffin made by using the well method did not rise well and was heavy, misshapen, and filled with air holes. What might have happened?

Test Kitchen

Divide into two teams. Using the same recipe, make muffins. One team will use the well method and the other will use the creaming method. Evaluate the differences, focusing on the differences in texture and flavor.

CULINARY MATH

Converting Loaf Yield into Muffin Yield

Measure the volume capacity of a loaf pan by filling it three-fourths full of water. Then measure the capacity of an individual muffin in a muffin tin that makes 12 muffins by filling it half full of water.

1. Calculate how much muffin batter is required for the muffin tin.
2. How many muffin tins will the batter for a loaf pan fill?

CHEF'S TIP

A STICKY SITUATION
To prevent dates and other sticky stir-ins from adhering to your knife when cutting, first spray the knife with cooking oil.

"The best biscuits and scones need to be both flaky and tender. You have to have your ingredients chilled and work them as little as possible."

— Eric Kastel
The Culinary Institute
of America

Biscuits, Scones, and Soda Bread

Biscuits, scones, and soda bread are all flaky quick breads. They are made from dough that uses flour and a solid fat.

Biscuits Biscuits are small quick breads with little or no sugar. There are three main types of biscuits. However, it seems that every region has its own biscuit variation.

- **Rolled and Cut Biscuits.** Biscuit dough is patted out by hand or rolled out and then cut into circular shapes.
- **Drop Biscuits.** The dough for drop biscuits has more liquid and can be dropped from a spoon onto the baking sheet.

- **Beaten Biscuits.** Beaten biscuits are a Southern tradition that dates back to the 1800s. Unlike regular biscuits, where light mixing creates a flaky dough, beaten biscuits are beaten for a long period and the resulting dough is hard and stiff. According to some old recipes, the dough was put on a tree stump and beaten at length with a rolling pin, mallet, or heavy object.

Scones Scones are sweet, biscuit-like, individual quick breads. The main difference between a biscuit and a scone is that a biscuit is not sweetened and a scone typically is. Scones can also have fruit or nuts added to the dough. Cream scones are richer scones because cream is substituted for the water.

Scone dough is folded into a disk and cut into wedges, diamonds, squares, or rounds. Scones, originally made with oatmeal and cooked on a griddle in a way similar to pancakes, are a Scottish tradition. They are named after the Stone of Destiny (Scone), the place were Scottish kings were once crowned.

Soda Bread **Soda bread** is named for the baking soda that is used to leaven it. An acid ingredient is also added to the mixture, such as buttermilk. The dough is similar to that of biscuits and scones and is shaped into a round loaf. Unlike the American version of soda bread, classic Irish soda bread is not sweetened and does not include eggs, butter, or raisins.

Rubbed-Dough Method Biscuits, scones, and soda bread are made by using the **rubbed-dough method**. Rather than blending butter or some other fat with flour to form a batter, the fat in the rubbed-dough method is cut into chunks, chilled, and then loosely rubbed into the flour. This process promotes flakiness because it prevents the fat from fully combining with the flour.

 Reading Checkpoint *What is the rubbed-dough method?*

Mixing and Baking

Baking techniques can change the attractiveness of a biscuit or scone dramatically. It's important to know how the result is affected by temperature, basic shaping, and egg washes.

FIGURE 18-5
Scones
These scones were made with cream rather than water.
Predicting *How would the use of cream rather than water affect the flavor of the scone?*

Temperature Chilling butter or fat is important in the rubbed-dough method because the coldness keeps the butter or other fat from blending in too much with the flour. Chilled fat contributes to the final product's flakiness because it serves as a temporary barrier between the flour and the liquid in the dough, allowing more space for the leavening gases to expand. Eventually the chilled fat melts during baking, creating spaces for gas bubbles to form and allow a light, flaky structure to take shape.

Additional coldness can be achieved by placing biscuits and scones in the freezer for half an hour or more once they are shaped.

A high temperature in the oven is as important as using chilled fat in the dough. High temperatures help trap steam in the dough layers, giving additional rise and flakiness to biscuits and scones.

Basic Shaping The softness of biscuit dough requires that the work surface, dough, and cutter are all floured generously. However, be careful not to add too much flour or overwork the dough. It will make the biscuits heavy and thick, rather than light and fluffy.

Use long, smooth movements when rolling the dough, lifting the rolling pin before reaching the edges so the dough doesn't get too thin. You will get a greater yield if edges are rolled out straight.

BASIC CULINARY SKILLS

Rubbed-Dough Method

1. **Combine dry ingredients** in a bowl and sift or blend.

2. **Rub cold butter** or other fat into dry ingredients with your fingertips until the mixture looks like coarse oatmeal.

3. **Make a well** in the center of the dry ingredients and pour in the blended liquids.

4. **Gather the dough into a ball** on a floured work surface and gently pat or lightly roll it into the appropriate thickness, about ½ inch for biscuits.

Dough must be cut with a sharp tool, such as a biscuit cutter or a knife. Using a cup or anything else with dull edges squeezes the outside of the dough together, interfering with its ability to rise properly. When cutting out biscuits try to avoid waste. The added handling of re-rolling the scraps will toughen the dough.

◄

FIGURE 18-6
Cutting Biscuits
Use a sharp tool when cutting biscuit dough.
Applying Concepts *How has waste been minimized when cutting out these biscuits?*

BASIC CULINARY SKILLS

Making Laminated Biscuits

① **Roll** the dough out to half the desired thickness.

② **Fold** it into thirds or fourths.

③ **Turn** it so the long side is parallel to the edge of the work surface.

④ **Roll** the dough out again, this time to the desired thickness for baking.

⑤ **Repeat** the process of folding, turning, and rolling the dough one more time.

The Tea Tradition

A hungry duchess is credited with introducing afternoon tea to British society in the 1800s. Anna, the Duchess of Bedford, often got the sinking feeling of an empty stomach in mid-afternoon, hours before dinner was served.

She had a cup of tea and a light snack in her room to satisfy the hunger pangs. One day a visitor arrived and was invited to join her. By the second half of the nineteenth century, afternoon tea had become one of the highlights of Victorian life.

In 1864 a clever manager at the London Bridge branch of the Aerated Bread Company set up a few tables and chairs in the back of the bakery and began serving tea with goods from the bakery. It was a humble beginning for the afternoon teas now being served on fancy linens, fine china, and shiny silver services in elegant hotels and tearooms around the world.

Although the terms "afternoon tea" and "high tea" are often used interchangeably, they are distinctly different meals. Afternoon tea is tea served with a light meal of small savory sandwiches, scones,

▲ *Traditional afternoon tea with tea sandwiches, scones, and cake*

and little cakes. High tea is a heavy meal, often the main cooked meal of the day. It is so substantial it is served on a high table, such as a dinner table, rather than a low tea table that Americans refer to as a coffee table—thus the name "high tea."

Research

Research three restaurants serving tea. Identify the types of food served with the tea.

Sometimes an optional step of folding the dough into thirds, like a letter, or fourths, like a book, is added. This is a type of laminating process (similar to the laminated yeast dough described in Chapter 17) that results in multiple layers. Laminating makes it easier for steam, which is produced during baking, to expand the dough and promote flakiness.

After the dough is shaped, you can brush it with an egg wash. This coating is brushed on baked goods to add gloss and color for a more appealing look.

 **Reading Checkpoint** *How do you make laminated biscuit dough?*

Serving Biscuits and Scones

Biscuits are usually served warm with a meal. Scones are served throughout the day with coffee and tea. Biscuits and scones are both popular for breakfast. In addition, there are occasions with which each is specifically associated.

CHEF'S TIP

COLD CASE

Scone dough can be prepared in advance and refrigerated up to 24 hours before baking. Resting the dough in the refrigerator makes scones tender because it settles the gluten.

Afternoon Tea The custom of taking an afternoon tea break provides an opportunity to slow down and enjoy one of the simple pleasures of life. Afternoon tea served with scones, small sandwiches, and cakes helps boost sagging energy and spirits. In the last decade, the popularity of afternoon tea has led to a booming new business. Teashops are opening across the nation, and scones are quite popular. Scones are served with butter, jam, or thick cream.

Shortcakes Biscuits are the foundation for a dessert called a **shortcake**. Uncooked fruit and some of its juices are spooned between a split biscuit and crowned with a mound of whipped cream to make a shortcake. Soft fruit such as strawberries is ideal for a shortcake.

 **Reading Checkpoint** *What is a shortcake?*

▲
FIGURE 18-7
Shortcake
Mixed berries are used for this shortcake.
Recognizing Patterns *What other type of fruit could have been used for a shortcake?*

18.2 ASSESSMENT

Reviewing Concepts
1. What is the rubbed-dough method for making biscuits and scones?
2. How do you make laminated biscuits?
3. What is a shortcake?

Critical Thinking
4. **Drawing Conclusions** You order "fluffy buttermilk biscuits" from a menu, but hard, flat disks are served instead. What might have gone wrong with the biscuits?
5. **Applying Concepts** Two job candidates are asked to make biscuits. Why does the one who uses the laminating process get hired?
6. **Analyzing Information** The edges of your cut biscuits didn't rise properly. What might have gone wrong?

Test Kitchen
Divide into two teams. Both teams will make biscuits, using the same recipe. One team will roll out the dough once and make non-laminated rolled and cut biscuits. The other team will make laminated rolled and cut biscuits. Evaluate the results.

CULINARY MATH
You are planning an afternoon tea for 24 people. Each guest will be served 2 scones. There's enough dough for 8 disks, from which you are cutting wedge-shaped scones.
1. How many wedges must each disk yield?
2. At the last minute, 8 more guests are added. You can increase the yield by making smaller scones. How many must each disk yield now?

Review and Assessment

Reviewing Content

Choose the letter that best answers the question or completes the statement.

1. Quick breads are
   a. made without yeast
   b. quick to make
   c. made with chemical leaveners
   d. all of the above

2. In the creaming method, which of the following ingredients are creamed together?
   a. eggs and flour
   b. butter and flour
   c. butter and sugar
   d. cream and eggs

3. In the well method
   a. a special mixer blade is used
   b. the edges of the dough are given a special treatment
   c. liquids and dry ingredients are mixed separately and then combined
   d. all ingredients are mixed together at the same time

4. The purpose of the creaming method is to
   a. save time
   b. beat in air bubbles
   c. use less milk
   d. none of the above

5. Scones are usually served with
   a. cold cuts
   b. butter, jam, and thick cream
   c. maple syrup
   d. olive spread

6. Streusel is
   a. a mini-loaf pan
   b. a German word for pastries
   c. a crumb topping
   d. none of the above

7. Biscuits are baked at
   a. low temperature
   b. high temperature
   c. moderate temperature
   d. a combination of high and low

Understanding Concepts

8. How do baking soda and baking powder differ?

9. Why is the well method used more often than the creaming method?

10. How does the rubbed-dough method contribute to flakiness?

11. How do biscuits and scones differ?

12. Why do you use cold butter to make biscuits and scones?

Critical Thinking

13. **Applying Concepts** Why can you substitute baking powder for baking soda in quick breads, but not baking soda for baking powder?

14. **Comparing/Contrasting** What is the difference between the rubbed-dough method of making biscuits and the creaming method of making muffins and quick breads?

15. **Predicting** Which are more likely to be flakier, rolled and cut biscuits or drop biscuits? Explain why.

Culinary Math

16. **Solving Problems** If a quick bread recipe yields 6 cups of batter and a muffin requires ¼ cup of batter, how many muffins will the quick bread recipe yield?

17. **Analyzing Information** You are serving hot biscuits for a 7:30 breakfast meeting. The biscuits require 20 minutes for preparation and 20 minutes for baking. What is the latest you need to be in the kitchen?

On the Job

18. **Analyzing Information** You opened a bakery. Two teashops have opened in nearby towns. They're crowded. Do they give you any ideas to help your bakery?

19. **Communicating** You have created a new muffin for the many health-conscious customers you serve. Write a sign for the window.

RECIPE CARDS

Use the following Recipe Cards to test your culinary skill.

122. Blueberry Muffins
123. Corn Muffins
124. Zucchini Bread
125. Buttermilk Biscuits
126. Cream Scones

LAB ACTIVITY

Project 18: Blueberry Muffins

Answer these questions when your class works through Project 18.

- How does the flavor of the muffins made with buttermilk compare with those made with milk?

- How does the appearance of the muffins made with buttermilk compare with those made with milk?

- Are there any other differences between the two sets of muffins?

TEST PRACTICE

Choose the letter that best answers the question or completes the statement.

1. Quick breads are leavened by
   A   yeast
   B   cinnamon
   C   baking soda and baking powder
   D   the mixer blade

2. When liquid and dry ingredients are mixed separately and then combined, it's called
   A   quick method
   B   well method
   C   creaming method
   D   easy method

3. Streusels are
   A   toppings and fillings
   B   sweet
   C   crumbly
   D   all of the above

4. Scones differ from biscuits because they are
   A   sweet
   B   different shapes
   C   served anytime, often with tea
   D   all of the above

5. Biscuits are made flaky by
   A   beaten method
   B   rubbed-dough method
   C   low baking temperature
   D   long kneading time

6. Biscuits are best when shaped by
   A   paper cups
   B   a glass
   C   sharp tools
   D   a coffee cup

7. What type of flour is considered standard for muffins and quick breads?
   A   cake flour
   B   all-purpose flour
   C   bread flour
   D   whole grain flour

8. Baking powder starts to lose its ability to leaven after
   A   2 months
   B   4 months
   C   6 months
   D   8 months

9. Baking soda contains baking powder and what acid?
   A   lemon juice
   B   alcohol
   C   cream of tartar
   D   buttermilk

10. Muffins should be removed from their muffin tin
   A   immediately
   B   within 10 minutes
   C   within 1 hour
   D   when used or sold

DESSERTS

READING PREVIEW

Key Concepts

- Identifying various types of chocolate
- Working with chocolate
- Making ganache

Vocabulary

- baker's chocolate
- bittersweet chocolate
- chocolate liquor
- coating chocolate
- cocoa butter
- cocoa powder
- compound chocolate
- dark chocolate
- Dutch processed
- ganache
- milk chocolate
- nibs
- semisweet chocolate
- tabling method
- tempering
- unsweetened chocolate
- white chocolate

> "**O**nce you understand how chocolate behaves and you master a few simple skills, it is one of the most rewarding types of specialty work in the pastry shop."
>
> – Peter Greweling
> The Culinary Institute of America

Identifying Different Types of Chocolate

There are three basic types of chocolate: dark chocolate (bittersweet or semisweet chocolate), milk chocolate, and white chocolate. However, there are seven variations of these basic types of chocolate commonly used in baking.

- **Unsweetened Chocolate.** The actual chocolate-making process begins when the cleaned cocoa kernels, known as **nibs**, are milled into a thick paste. (Review the Culinary Science feature on the next page to find out where chocolate comes from.) This paste is called **unsweetened chocolate, chocolate liquor**, or **baker's chocolate**. Unsweetened chocolate is used primarily as a flavoring in recipes. By itself, chocolate is very bitter.

CULINARY SCIENCE

Where Does Chocolate Come From?

Did you ever wonder where chocolate comes from? It is made from the seeds of the cacao tree, which typically grows in tropical rainforests. The process of making chocolate begins with harvesting the ripe cacao pods. These pods, similar in size to a small pineapple, contain about 50 seeds, which are also known as cocoa beans.

Most of the world's cocoa beans (about 80%) come from a variety of cacao tree called the Forastero, grown in Africa. The more expensive and rare beans, prized by chocolate makers, come from the Criollo, a cacao tree grown in Mexico, Central America, South America, and Indonesia. The Criollo bean was first used by the ancient Mayans. It is less bitter and more aromatic than other cocoa beans. Another variety of bean is the Trinitario, developed in Trinidad. It is a hybrid of the Forastero and the Criollo.

After the cocoa beans are harvested, the next step in the chocolate-making process is fermentation. The beans are piled together and allowed to sit for several days to ferment. This is a natural reaction that produces heat and begins to develop the chocolate flavor of the beans.

The fermented beans are then dried. They are spread in the sun for days or weeks to lower their moisture content. This allows them to be stored for long periods of time without spoiling.

The beans are then roasted in an oven to further develop the flavor of the chocolate. This is similar to roasting coffee beans. Roasting is a critical step—too light a roast will not generate a strong flavor and too dark a roast will give the chocolate a burnt, bitter taste. Cocoa beans from different locations have different qualities and flavors, so chocolate makers often blend beans to produce a distinctive mix.

The roasted and cooled beans are cracked to help separate the hard

▲ Cocoa beans shown in the pod and then dried

shell on the outside of the beans. The shell is removed, leaving the cocoa kernels, or nibs. These nibs, like coarsely ground coffee, are the raw material that manufacturers use to grind, blend, and mold into the product we call chocolate.

Research

Cacao trees are grown in tropical rainforests and on sunny farms. Research how cacao trees are grown and how their growing methods affect the local environment.

▲ Beans roasting in large, rotating ovens to release their flavor and aroma

- **Cocoa Powder.** The unsweetened chocolate may be pressed to remove the cocoa butter, leaving dry **cocoa powder**. **Cocoa butter** is the cream-colored fat from the cocoa beans. It is used in the chocolate-making process. Most cocoa powder used in the kitchen is **Dutch processed** (also called alkalized cocoa). This involves reducing the acidity of the cocoa beans before they are ground. The process makes the cocoa powder milder, less acidic, and darker than untreated cocoa. Cocoa powder is commonly used in many baking preparations.

- **Bittersweet and Semisweet Chocolate.** Cocoa butter, sugar, vanilla, and other flavorings are added to chocolate liquor to produce **bittersweet chocolate** and **semisweet chocolate** (both of which are commonly referred to as **dark chocolate**). Because there are no set standards, the amount of sugar in each varies. Bittersweet chocolate, with less sugar than semisweet chocolate, must contain at least 35% chocolate liquor, while semisweet can contain anywhere from 15% to 30% chocolate liquor.

- **Chocolate Chips or Morsels.** The chocolate used to make chocolate chips is a special blend of chocolate. Generally, chocolate chips contain less cocoa butter than other chocolates. This allows them to retain their shape when baked.

- **Milk Chocolate.** In Switzerland, the Nestle Company developed **milk chocolate** by developing a milk powder and then adding it to dark chocolate. Today, milk chocolate must contain at least 12% milk solids and 10% chocolate liquor. Milk chocolate tends to be sweeter than dark chocolate. It is widely used in candies.

- **White Chocolate.** Although not a true chocolate, **white chocolate** is made from cocoa butter, sugar, milk powder, and flavorings. It does not contain any chocolate liquor. It is usually quite sweet.

- **Compound or Coating Chocolate.** Chocolate that is made with vegetable fat instead of cocoa butter is called **compound chocolate** or **coating chocolate**. Replacing the cocoa butter with other, cheaper fats saves the producer money. Compound chocolate is generally easier to use for dipping or glazing and do not require tempering.

FIGURE 19-1
Strongest Flavor?
Bittersweet chocolate, milk chocolate, and white chocolate
Predicting *Of the three types of chocolate, which do you think has the strongest flavor?*

CHEF'S TIP

BOWL OF CHOCOLATE

If chocolate is used regularly in the kitchen, keep a covered bowl of it on top of the oven. The heat from the oven will melt the chocolate and save time when it is used in a recipe.

Working with Chocolate

Dark chocolate, milk chocolate, and white chocolate are available in several forms. The most common is a bar or large block that can be as small as a few ounces to larger than a few pounds. For convenience, many chocolate companies sell their chocolate in small drops, or coins. These cost slightly more than bars but are much easier to weigh and melt.

When chocolate is used to flavor desserts and pastry items, it can be melted and completely incorporated into the item as in a chocolate cake. The chocolate can also be left intact, as in chocolate chip cookies. Or, it can be both incorporated and left intact as in chocolate ice cream with chocolate chips in it.

Melting Chocolate Chocolate melts faster when you use small pieces. This also lessens the chance of burning the chocolate or making it too hot. When melting chocolate, you can use the coins or drops straight from the package; you don't need to cut them into smaller pieces. However, bars or blocks should be chopped into small, even pieces. Use a heavy knife to chop chocolate. Dark chocolate can be extremely hard and difficult to chop.

Place the small pieces of chocolate in a clean, dry bowl. When working with chocolate at any stage, keep the chocolate from contact with water or steam. Water reacts with the starch in cocoa and causes melted chocolate to become very thick. Even one drop of water can make a pound of chocolate unusable.

Place the bowl of chopped chocolate over a pan of simmering water. Stir the chocolate regularly as it is heated to speed the melting and prevent it from getting too hot. The milk solids in milk and white chocolate burn at very low temperatures, so be especially careful not to get them too hot. When melting milk or white chocolate, it is often safest to bring a pan of water to a boil and then turn off the heat. Place the bowl of chocolate in the pan and allow the residual heat to melt the chocolate. Alternately, chocolate may be melted in a microwave. Place the chocolate in a clean, dry, microwave-safe bowl and microwave it for short periods of time at no more than 80%, stirring the chocolate between each heating. This method works well for small batches but is not practical in large-scale production.

Tempering Chocolate **Tempering** is the process of properly crystallizing chocolate. Tempering chocolate is necessary when the chocolate is to be used by itself and not incorporated into a recipe. Tempering gives chocolate a shiny appearance. It prevents the cocoa butter from separating out of the chocolate and causing white swirls or spots. It makes the chocolate stronger, giving it snap. Tempering also makes the chocolate contract as it cools and gives the chocolate a higher melting point. Although the process of tempering requires some skill and practice, the steps are simple and not difficult to master.

Three significant factors are involved in tempering chocolate:

- **Time.** There are no shortcuts in tempering. If the process is rushed, the chocolate will not crystallize properly.
- **Temperature.** Tempering involves both appropriate heating and appropriate cooling to ensure good crystallization.
- **Stirring.** Tempering requires continuous stirring or movement of the chocolate.

Tempering begins by completely melting the chocolate. Bring the chocolate to between 110°F and 120°F. Once the chocolate is completely melted, you need to stir it constantly while it cools. The chocolate should be cooled to around 80°F, allowing the chocolate to begin to crystallize and thicken.

One method professional chefs use to cool chocolate is called the **tabling method**. To use this method, pour approximately half of the warm, melted chocolate onto a marble slab. Then move the chocolate around the marble surface with two metal spatulas to cool it. When the chocolate on the marble begins to thicken, return it to the bowl, combining it with the still warm portion. Then stir the chocolate vigorously to cool the entire bowl, evening the temperature.

▲

FIGURE 19-2
Melting Chocolate
Take care when melting chocolate not to let it get too hot.
Applying Concepts *How does heating chocolate over water keep the chocolate from getting too hot?*

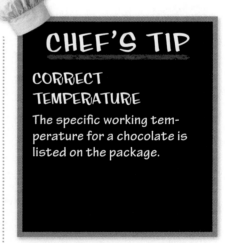

CHEF'S TIP

CORRECT TEMPERATURE

The specific working temperature for a chocolate is listed on the package.

◄

FIGURE 19-3
Cooling Chocolate
With the tabling method, chocolate is spread around a marble surface.
Applying Concepts *Why is a marble surface good for cooling chocolate?*

Heart-Healthy Chocolate?

Recent studies have shown that dark chocolate contains a large amount of antioxidants, which reduce the chance and severity of many types of heart disease. Although these studies show promising results, they are still in the early stages.

The next step is to test the chocolate for temper. The easiest way to test for temper is to dip the tip of a spatula or paring knife in the chocolate. Properly tempered chocolate should become firm, or set, in 3 to 5 minutes. It should set smooth, with no swirls, streaks, or spots on the surface. If the test is successful, the chocolate is ready to be used. It is referred to as being in temper.

If the chocolate is not in temper (meaning that it did not set properly or had swirls, streaks, or spots), table one-third to one-half of the chocolate again. Once it is returned to the bowl, test the chocolate again for temper.

Storing Chocolate Chocolate can be stored for up to a year, if it is stored properly. Four things that should be avoided when storing chocolate are:

- **Heat.** Chocolate should be stored in a cool place. Heat can melt chocolate and cause the cocoa butter to separate out. The ideal temperature for storing chocolate is about 55°F.
- **Moisture.** Moisture will cause the chocolate to become very thick when it is melted. Although chocolate is usually packaged in a paper wrapper, it is a good idea to keep it wrapped in plastic or in an airtight container to prevent moisture in the air from coming in contact with the chocolate.
- **Odors.** The cocoa butter in the chocolate absorbs odors easily. If the chocolate is stored near items that give off strong odors, the chocolate can absorb those odors and have an unpleasant taste.
- **Light.** Avoid storing chocolate in bright light. Light can break down the cocoa butter, causing it to go rancid. The covering of the chocolate should prevent contact with light.

 **Reading Checkpoint**   *What is tempering?*

Making Ganache

Ganache is an emulsion made with chocolate and cream. It is used for fillings in candies and cakes and as a glaze for cakes and pastries. Heavy cream is heated to a boil before it is added to the chocolate. The ratio of chocolate to cream varies, depending on how the ganache will be used. For a firmer ganache, more chocolate is used, and for a lighter, looser ganache, more cream is used. When making a ganache, it is important to remember that it is an emulsion. If the mixture separates or the emulsion breaks, the final product will not have the desired creamy smooth texture.

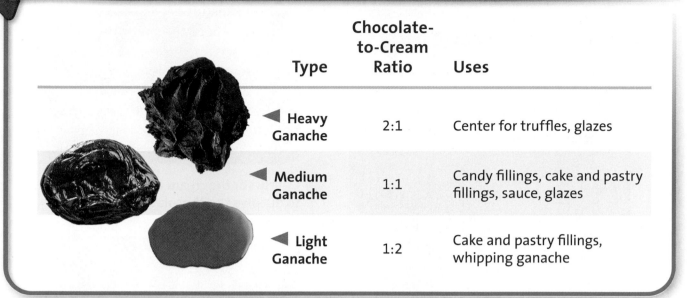

	Type	Chocolate-to-Cream Ratio	Uses
	◄ Heavy Ganache	2:1	Center for truffles, glazes
	◄ Medium Ganache	1:1	Candy fillings, cake and pastry fillings, sauce, glazes
	◄ Light Ganache	1:2	Cake and pastry fillings, whipping ganache

A ganache can be flavored in a variety of ways. The cream used in the ganache can be flavored with vanilla, cinnamon, tea, or herbs. A fruit-flavored ganache is made by substituting a portion of the cream with a fruit puree. Extracts and alcohols can also be added. However, if more than a few drops of liquid are added to the cream, you will need to reduce the cream by that amount so you maintain the appropriate chocolate-to-liquid ratio for your ganache.

When two-thirds of the hot cream and chocolate are initially mixed, an emulsion forms. The mixture should be completely smooth, with no chunks of chocolate. It should have a shiny, elastic appearance. Once the initial mixture has come together, you need to continue adding the cream a little at a time, stirring it in to maintain the emulsion.

You can use the ganache immediately or allow it to cool and thicken before using it. For example, when using a ganache as a glaze, you would use it warm so it remains liquid. For truffles, on the other hand, the ganache should be allowed to thicken in the refrigerator overnight.

If you want to thicken a ganache, allow it to cool at room temperature, stirring the mixture from time to time to ensure that it cools and sets evenly. For light ganache that will be whipped to incorporate air, cool the ganache to room temperature first, stirring occasionally, and then chill the ganache in the refrigerator overnight before whipping.

FIGURE 19-4
Truffles
These chocolate ganache truffles are coated with a tempered chocolate.
Applying Concepts *Why is tempered chocolate used for the coating on these truffles?*

Making a Ganache

1 **Chop chocolate** into small pieces of equal size and put it in a bowl.

2 **Bring cream to a full boil** in a saucepan.

3 **Pour two-thirds of the cream** over the chopped chocolate.

  *See Recipe Card 127, "Chocolate Ganache."*

4 **Gently stir** the cream and chocolate mixture to dissolve the chocolate and create an emulsion.

5 **Add the remaining cream,** a little at a time, to the mixture while stirring until all of the cream has been incorporated.

Reading Checkpoint *What is a ganache?*

19.1 ASSESSMENT

Reviewing Concepts

1. What are the seven variations of chocolate commonly used in baking?
2. What is tempering chocolate?
3. What is a ganache?

Critical Thinking

4. **Predicting** What would happen if you used regular dark chocolate as the chocolate chips in chocolate chip cookies?
5. **Solving Problems** If chocolate that had been stored for a long time was melted and it was too thick, what might have happened to it during storage?

Test Kitchen

Divide into four teams. Each team will make a heavy ganache. Team 1 will use cream. Team 2 will use milk. Team 3 will use water. Team 4 will use orange juice. Compare the texture and flavor of the ganaches.

SOCIAL STUDIES

Chocolate for Everyone

Research how chocolate has moved from being a food reserved for royalty and the elite to become a treat for everyone.

Custards, Mousses, & Frozen Desserts

READING PREVIEW

Key Concepts

- Making custards
- Making mousses and other aerated desserts
- Making frozen desserts

Vocabulary

- aerating
- Bavarian cream
- crème anglaise
- frozen soufflé
- granité
- meringue
- mousse
- parfait
- sabayon
- sherbet
- sorbet
- sugar syrup

"**A** simple mixture of eggs, cream, and sugar can be stirred into a smooth sauce, baked into a silken custard, lightened to make a mousse, or frozen to make ice cream. "

– George Higgins
The Culinary Institute
of America

Custard

A custard is a liquid that is thickened with eggs. As a custard is cooked, proteins in the eggs bond together, giving the liquid more body or thickness. Generally the liquid used is a dairy product—milk, cream, or a combination of the two. Great care must be taken when preparing custard recipes. You need to cook the eggs until they bind the custard, but you also have to avoid overcooking them.

There are three basic types of custards.

- Baked custards
- Stirred custards
- Boiled custards

Baked Custards This is probably the most common type of custard. Cheese cake and pumpkin pie, as well as crème caramel (KREHM KAIR-ah-mehl) and crème brûlée (CREM broo-LAY), are examples of baked custards.

Figure 19-5 ▶
Crème Brûlée
A crème brûlée is a custard topped with a crust of caramelized sugar.
Predicting *Describe the texture of this topping.*

BASIC CULINARY SKILLS

Baked Custard

1 Preheat the oven to 350°F.

2 Heat the milk with half the sugar over medium or high heat.

3 Combine the remaining sugar with the eggs in a bowl.

4 Add one-third of the hot milk to the eggs and whisk together.

5 Add the remaining milk.

6 Strain the mixture through a fine strainer.

7 Pour the custard into ovenproof containers and place the containers into a hotel pan.

8 Place the hotel pan in the oven. Pour warm water into the hotel pan to provide a water bath.

9 Bake until just set. When moved, the custard should jiggle and not look liquid.

10 Remove containers from the water bath, transfer to a sheet pan, and refrigerate.

 See Recipe Card 134, "Bread and Butter Pudding."

Baked custards are made by preparing a mixture of liquid, eggs, and flavoring. The liquid can be dairy or non-dairy, such as pumpkin puree. The eggs are added along with flavorings. The flavorings could be sugar, vanilla, spices, chocolate, herbs, or fruits. Flavorings can be added to the liquid before the eggs or added after the eggs are mixed.

In the recipe, you add hot milk to the eggs. If you added all the hot milk to the eggs at once, the eggs would cook. To avoid cooking the eggs, you add only one-third of the hot milk to the eggs while whisking. This increases their temperature without cooking them. You can then add the remaining milk to the egg mixture without cooking the eggs. This is referred to as tempering the eggs, slowly increasing their temperature to avoid cooking them.

Stirred Custards Stirred custards contain ingredients almost identical to those in baked custards. The difference between the two is how they are cooked. Instead of being baked in the oven, stirred custards are cooked over low heat on the stove. Controlling the cooking and the maximum temperature is extremely important.

BASIC CULINARY SKILLS

Stirred Custard

1 Heat the milk with half the sugar over medium-to-high heat.

2 Combine the remaining sugar with the eggs in a bowl.

3 Add one-third of the hot milk to the eggs and whisk together.

4 Add the remaining milk.

5 Place the pan over low-to-medium heat. Stir the mixture thoroughly with a wooden spoon.

6 Test the consistency of the custard. The custard is finished cooking when it coats the back of a wooden spoon.

7 Remove the pan from the heat immediately and strain through a fine strainer.

8 Place the custard in an ice bath and stir it occasionally to ensure it cools quickly and evenly. Refrigerate after cooling.

 *See Recipe Card 130, "Vanilla Sauce."*

With baked custard, temperature is controlled by keeping the oven temperature low and by cooking the custard in a water bath. With stirred custard, you need to stir the custard continuously as it is heated and to stop the cooking at the right moment. As the mixture cooks, the consistency will change from very liquid or watery to slightly thicker (like heavy cream). When the custard coats the back of a wooden spoon, it is finished cooking. Stop the cooking immediately by placing the cooked custard over an ice bath.

Stirred custard uses a method for making a classic sauce, **crème anglaise** (CREM on-GLAZE), which is often used as a base for ice cream and mousses.

Boiled Custard Boiled custards have the same basic ingredients as baked and stirred custards, but they also include a starch. By incorporating starch, you make the custard thicker than the other types of custards. The starch also allows you to cook the custard to a higher temperature. In fact, the addition of starch requires that you bring the custard to a full boil and cook it for one minute to completely activate the starch and to remove any starchy taste. The boiled custard method is used to make pastry cream and cream pie fillings.

BASIC CULINARY SKILLS

Boiled Custard

1. Heat the milk with half the sugar over medium-to-high heat.

2. Combine the remaining sugar and cornstarch with the eggs in a bowl.

3. Add one-third of the boiling milk to the eggs and whisk together.

4. Add the egg mixture to the pan of milk and stir.

5. Heat the mixture, stirring continuously, until it comes to a boil.

6. Continue boiling the custard for one minute, stirring continuously.

7. Pour the custard into a shallow container.

8. Cover the surface of the custard with plastic wrap and refrigerate.

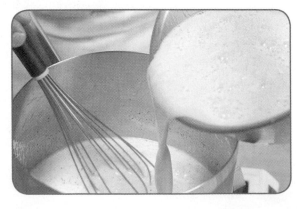

Custard Type	Basic Ingredients	Thickening Agent	Cooking Method	Uses
Stirred	Milk, sugar, eggs	Eggs	Cooked slowly on stove	Sauce, ice cream base, Bavarian cream base, mousse base
Baked	Milk, sugar, eggs	Eggs	Baked in a water bath	Crème brûlée, crème caramel, custard pies
Boiled	Milk, sugar, cornstarch, eggs	Eggs, cornstarch	Cooked on stove	Pastry cream, cream pie fillings

Reading Checkpoint *What are the three types of custards and how are they made?*

Mousses

A **mousse** (MOOSE) is made by adding air to flavored bases, such as chocolate or fruit purees. The term mousse comes from the French word that means fluffy. Adding air to food is referred to as **aerating** (AIR-ate-ing) the food. Aeration (air-AY-shun) makes mousses very light and delicate.

Mousses are used by themselves, as well as for fillings for cakes and other pastries. A mousse is just one type of aerated (AIR-ate-ed) dessert. Other types of aerated dessert include most types of frozen desserts, such as ice cream and sorbet.

Mousses and other aerated desserts are made from four basic components: a flavored base, an egg foam, gelatin, and whipped cream. By varying the type or amount of these components, you can achieve different flavors and consistencies.

- **Bases.** The base is what gives mousses and other aerated desserts their flavor. Fruit mousses are based on fruit purée. Chocolate mousses use melted chocolate or sometimes cocoa powder. A stirred custard can also be used as a base for a mousse. The custard can be flavored with a fruit purée, chocolate, spices, or nuts.
- **Egg Foam.** Mousses use an egg foam to provide their airy texture. The foam can be based on either egg yolks or egg whites. The egg foam is heated to 140°F to ensure it is safe. Use egg yolks to create a sabayon. A **sabayon** (sah-by-YON) is made by whipping egg yolks as they are heated with sugar.

Storing Custards and Mousses

Because custards and mousses contain eggs and dairy products, they should be kept in the refrigerator at all times. In general, custards should be used in 3 days after they're made. You may freeze mousses to prolong their shelf life.

**FIGURE 19-6
Light as Air**
Mousse is prized for being light and airy.
Inferring *Is there such a thing as too airy a mousse?*

Use an egg-white foam to create a **meringue** (mehr-ANG), a mixture of stiffly beaten egg whites and sugar. Because more air can be incorporated into egg whites than into egg yolks, a mousse made with a meringue will be lighter than one made with an egg-yolk foam. Some recipes, such as that for chocolate mousse, use both an egg-yolk foam and one based on egg whites.

- **Gelatin.** Most mousse recipes require gelatin to stabilize the mousse and allow it to hold its shape. The gelatin is soaked in cold water and then melted before adding it to the mousse. The gelatin is usually added to the base, before adding the egg foam.
- **Whipped Cream.** As the last step in making a mousse, whipped cream is folded into the mousse. The cream should be whipped to the soft peak stage and gently incorporated to avoid overworking it, possibly causing the cream to separate.

Three other types of aerated desserts are quite common:

- **Fruit Mousse.** A fruit mousse is prepared by incorporating gelatin and flavoring with fruit purée and then folding in an egg foam and whipped cream.
- **Chocolate Mousse.** Made by folding egg foam and whipped cream into melted chocolate. A chocolate mousse typically does not use gelatin because the cocoa butter in the chocolate acts as a stabilizer.
- **Bavarian Cream.** Similar to a mousse except that it is made without any egg foam, a **Bavarian** (bah-VAR-ee-uhn) **cream** is made from a base of stirred custard (vanilla sauce), fruit puree, or a combination of the two. Gelatin is added to the base and whipped cream is carefully folded in. Bavarian cream is simpler to make, but is denser and less airy than a mousse.

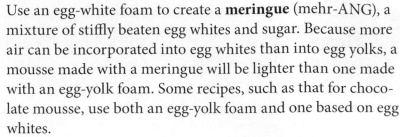

Reading Checkpoint *What are the four basic components of a mousse?*

Frozen Desserts

Frozen desserts include a wide variety of items that, similar to mousses, are aerated to give them a special texture. The texture is also achieved by the ingredients used in the frozen dessert. Five of the most common types of frozen desserts are discussed on the following pages.

Flan

Custard is a wonderful comfort food, enjoyed around the world, and flan (FLAHN) is a delicious example. Flan is a sweetened egg custard, coated in caramel sauce. This rich, creamy dessert originated in Spain and is popular in many countries, including Portugal, Mexico, Cuba, and the Philippines. It is also a favorite in France, where it is called crème caramel, and in Italy, where it is crema caramella. The essential ingredients for this dessert are eggs, milk, and sugar. The typical flavoring is usually vanilla, but its many variations include orange, almond, and pistachio.

▲ *Custard is poured on top of the caramel*

Flan can be baked in a pie dish and served in slices or made in individual-sized ramekins or custard cups. Either way, you first create the caramel sauce by heating sugar and water. The sauce is poured into the bottom of the baking dish and swirled to coat the sides. Then you make the custard and pour it over the caramel base. You place the baking dish in a pan of water and then bake the flan in the oven. When the custard is set, the dish is turned over on a plate and then lifted, covering the cooked custard with the caramel sauce.

The next time you go to a Spanish or Mexican restaurant, order flan for dessert. Or, make it yourself. Just be sure you have enough caramel sauce on the plate for every delicious spoonful of custard.

▲ *Flan served with the bottom up and plenty of caramel sauce*

Research

Find a few recipes for flan. Compare ingredients and flavorings. Make the recipe that interests you most, and evaluate your results.

- **Granité.** Made from a flavored water base, a **granité** (grah-nee-TAY) is made by either stirring the base as it begins to freeze or by scraping the frozen base into a sort of shaved ice. Granités have very large ice crystals. They are often served between courses in a multi-course meal to cleanse the palate. They may also be served as a component to a plated dessert.

FIGURE 19-7
Sorbet
Fruit sorbets garnished with fresh fruit and mint.
Predicting *Why would you garnish a fruit sorbet with the same fruit from which it was made?*

They may be fruit-based or made by flavoring a **sugar syrup** (a concentrated solution of sugar and water). Granité is the French name for this frozen dessert. Granita (grah-NEE-tah) is the Italian name.

- **Sorbet.** Made from flavored bases frozen and aerated in an ice cream maker, a **sorbet** (sor-BEY) is generally fruit-based. As the base begins to freeze, the air is trapped inside the base, creating a smooth, creamy texture.

- **Sherbet.** A variation of a sorbet, a **sherbet** (SHUR-biht) is made similarly, but has a meringue folded into it to further aerate it.

- **Ice Cream.** Ice cream is made by aerating a dairy base in an ice cream maker. Because it uses dairy in the base, ice cream tends to be heavier and richer that granités, sorbets, and sherbets. Ice cream can be made from a vanilla sauce or from sweetened milk or cream.

- **Parfait and Frozen Soufflé.** When a mousse is frozen it is referred to as a **parfait** (par-FAY) or **frozen soufflé**. Both parfaits and frozen soufflés rely on egg foams and whipped cream to aerate them.

The texture of frozen desserts—their hardness, softness, smoothness, or creaminess—is important. The hardness of a frozen dessert is affected by two main factors:

- **Sugar Content.** One important factor—perhaps the most important factor affecting the hardness of a frozen dessert—is its sugar content. Sugar lowers the freezing point of water. The more sugar a recipe has, the softer the frozen dessert will be at 32°F. For example, if you made a sorbet and it came out very hard and brittle, you could melt it, increase the sugar, and reprocess it in the ice cream maker. On the other hand, if the sorbet was very soft, you could melt it, increase the amount of fruit puree (or simply add water) and reprocess. The added water dilutes the sugar in the recipe and allows the sorbet to freeze at a higher temperature.

- **Amount of Aeration.** Another major factor affecting the texture of a frozen dessert is the amount of aeration it receives. The airier the dessert, the lighter and softer it will feel in the mouth. An ice cream maker that spins very rapidly will aerate ice cream or sorbet more than one that is turned very slowly. Granités that are made by stirring by hand will have a much denser and coarser texture than a granité made with the same ingredients but processed in an ice cream machine.

Frozen Soufflé

1 Make a paper collar that circles a ramekin.

2 Whip cream to a soft peak.

3 Combine sugar and water in a sauce pan. Wash sugar crystals off the sides of the pot.

4 Boil the sugar and water solution on a high heat.

5 Place egg whites in a mixing bowl and whip.

6 Pour the whipped egg whites over the sugar solution when the solution reaches 240°F.

7 Whip the mixture until it is room temperature. It forms a meringue.

8 Fold in the fruit purée.

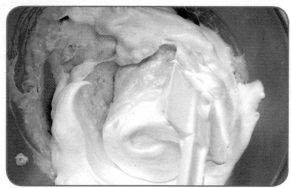

9 Fold in the whipped cream.

10 Fill the prepared ramekin with the mixture.

11 Freeze overnight.

12 Serve. Remove paper collar and dust the top with powdered sugar.

 **Reading Checkpoint** *What are the two major factors affecting the texture of frozen desserts?*

19.2 ASSESSMENT

Reviewing Concepts

1. What are the three types of custard?
2. What are the four basic components of a mousse?
3. What are the two major factors affecting the texture of frozen desserts?

Critical Thinking

4. **Applying Concepts** What is the purpose of tempering the eggs when making a custard?
5. **Comparing/Contrasting** What is the difference between a sabayon and a meringue?
6. **Comparing/Contrasting** What is the difference between a granité and a sorbet?
7. **Comparing/Contrasting** What is the difference between a sorbet and a sherbet?

Test Kitchen

Divide into three teams. Choose a basic baked custard recipe. Team 1 will make the custard using egg yolks only. Team 2 will use egg whites only. Team 3 will use whole eggs. All teams will use the same amount of eggs. Compare the texture and taste of the custards.

SCIENCE

Ice Cream

Research how early hand-turned ice cream makers worked. Report on how they got the liquid cold enough to form ice cream and how they aerated it. Compare that to a modern electric home ice cream maker.

> **L**ayer a basic sponge cake with a filling, add a cookie garnish, and you have an elaborate pastry. It all comes down to a few basic elements.
> — **Alison McLaughlin**
> The Culinary Institute of America

Basic Ingredients of Cookies and Cakes

The characteristics of a cookie or cake are determined to some degree by their ingredients. Each ingredient contributes to the flavor and texture. Four basic ingredients are used for both cookies and cakes:

- **Flour.** The gluten found in flour gives cookies structure. It also adds some flavor and nutritional value. Most cake recipes call for cake flour, which is lower in protein content. This prevents gluten development in the cake, which would make it tougher.
- **Eggs.** Eggs provide structure and moisture.
- **Sugar.** Sugar is predominantly a flavoring agent, but it is also responsible for browning during baking. It helps cookies expand during baking.
- **Fat.** Fat adds moisture and contributes to tenderness and mouth-feel.

The following ingredients are often found in many types of cookies and cakes:

- **Leaveners.** Chemical leaveners for cookie and cake production include baking soda and baking powder.
- **Flavorings.** Flavor agents used in cookies and cakes are almost limitless. Extracts are an easy way to impart flavor without altering a recipe. Citrus zest can be added to give a lemon or orange flavor. You can also use nuts, spices, chocolate chips, and fruit as flavorings.
- **Garnishes.** Garnishes add additional flavor, texture, and eye appeal to cakes and cookies. You can add them to cookie dough or batter before baking or apply them after baking as decorative touches. Garnishes include chocolate chips, nuts, candy pieces, dried fruit, citrus zest, icing, and melted or tempered chocolate.

 **Reading Checkpoint** *What are the four basic ingredients used for both cookies and cakes?*

Types of Cookies

The three main types of cookies are drop cookies, bar cookies, and rolled cookies.

Drop Cookies The most common type of cookie is the drop cookie. **Drop cookies** are made from a firm dough or batter that holds its shape on a sheet pan. Form drop cookies by scooping out a portion of dough and dropping it onto a sheet pan. Most recipes for this type of cookie contain a high percentage of fat. The fat melts during baking to give the cookie its finished shape. A drop cookie can be crispy or chewy, depending on its ingredients and how long it is baked. Two common types of drop cookies are chocolate chip cookies and oatmeal cookies.

There are three special types of drop cookies: icebox cookies, piped cookies, and stenciled cookies.

- **Icebox Cookies.** Often called refrigerator cookies, **icebox cookies** are formed into a cylinder, chilled, and then sliced and baked. This type of cookie is ideal for high-volume production demands. If cylinders have a similar weight and circumference, each cookie is guaranteed to be the same portion and to bake evenly. Cylinders of chilled cookie dough are quick to slice and place on sheet pans. If properly wrapped, the dough can be held in the freezer for two to three months.

▲ *Chocolate Chip Cookie*

▲ *Spritz cookie*

- **Piped Cookies.** Made of soft dough that can be piped through a pastry bag, **piped cookies** can be made into many decorative shapes if you use different pastry tips. The size of the pastry tip is often determined by the consistency of the dough. The thinner the dough, the smaller the tip. Uniform piping is crucial to the success of this cookie's production. Spritz cookies, ladyfingers, and macaroons (mak-uh-ROONS) are among the many types of piped cookies.

- **Stenciled Cookies.** Delicate, wafer-like **stenciled** (STEN-suld) **cookies** are made with batter that can be spread very thin and baked without losing its detailed shape. You form these cookies either by spreading the batter onto sheet pans into stencils to make perfect designs or by spreading the batter free-hand, without any stencil. Ingredients for this type of cookie vary, but recipes often contain a high percentage of sugar and eggs, with very little flour. Stenciled cookies bake quickly and, when you remove them from the oven, they can be rolled, curled, or draped over an object while still warm to form different shapes. A popular stenciled cookie is the tuile (TWEEL). It is frequently used as an edible container or accompaniment to frozen desserts, mousses, and custards.

FIGURE 19-8 ▶
Chocolate Tuiles
Tuiles are rolled into shape while still warm.
Applying Concepts *How might you fill this cookie?*

Bar Cookies **Bar cookies** are made from a soft batter that is spread into a pan before baking. Once baked, bar cookies are cut into individual cookies. Some types, such as lemon bars, are layered with different components. Although bar cookies generally have a shorter shelf life than other cookies (their sliced edges turn stale quickly), they are good for production because they can be portioned into different sizes and shapes.

Twice-baked cookies are a special type of bar cookie. They are made of dough that is formed into a large log-shaped cookie and baked. Once baked, the cookies are cut into slices and baked a second time to attain a very crisp texture. This type of cookie has a long shelf life because of its low fat content. Italian biscotti (bee-SKAWT-tee) are the most common twice-baked cookies. They are very crunchy and are often dipped in chocolate for added flavor.

Rolled Cookies **Rolled cookies** (also called **cut-out cookies**) are made of stiff dough that is rolled flat and then cut into decorative shapes, often using cookie cutters. You can also create them free-hand with the tip of a sharp knife. Cut-out cookies have great eye appeal because of their unique shapes and their garnishing possibilities. However, they are among the most challenging cookies to make because the cookies need to retain their shapes during baking. Cut-out cookies are generally crisp, although some varieties have chewy or soft textures.

Molded cookies are a variation of rolled cookies. They are made with stiff dough that is shaped by hand. The dough can also be stamped, pressed, or piped into carved molds. When making this type of cookie, the dough must be firm enough to hold its shape when baking. Cookie molds come in a variety of shapes and sizes and are commonly made of wood. Many molded cookies are of international origin, such as the German springerle (SPRING-uhr-lee) and English shortbread. Bakeries and pastry shops customarily offer these traditional varieties for special holidays.

 **Reading Checkpoint** *What are the three main types of cookies?*

Making Cookies

Unless otherwise stated in the recipe, cookie ingredients should be at room temperature (70–75°F) before mixing. Cold ingredients (such as butter, eggs, and milk) should be brought to room temperature before adding them to the dough. When added during the mixing process, cold ingredients can cause the dough to separate and lose its uniform consistency.

▲ *Bar cookies*

▲ *Biscotti*

▲ *Cut-out cookie*

Accurately measured ingredients are necessary to ensure dependable baking results. A scale provides the most precise measurements. If in doubt, measure a second time. It is easier to correct a potential baking problem at this point. Once cookies go into the oven, it is too late to correct any problems.

The texture, shape, and structure of a finished cookie rely heavily on the way it is mixed. The two most common mixing methods for cookies are:

- The creaming method
- The foaming method

Preparing Cookie Pans   Many chefs prepare the cookie pans before making the cookie dough. Cookies that are evenly baked and uniform in size require the use of specific pans that are properly prepared. Most bakers prepare their pans before mixing their dough.

- **Selecting a Pan.** Flat, standard-sized sheet pans are suitable for most cookies. Cookies with a high fat content tend to brown easily, so it is good practice to use two stacked sheet pans. This is called **double-panning**. Double-panning creates insulation for cookies, allowing for gentle heating of the bottoms. When preparing bar cookies, use the pan size specified in the recipe. Using a pan with the correct dimensions ensures that bars bake evenly and reach the desired thickness.

- **Preparing the Pan.** Pans are typically lined with either parchment paper or silicone baking mats. Silicone baking mats are ideal for baking cookies. They provide a nonstick surface, can withstand oven temperatures up to 500°F, and are cost-effective because they are reusable. Stenciled cookies, in particular, bake best on silicone mats. For bar cookies, line the

FIGURE 19-9 ▶
Using a Silicone Mat
Cookies are easy to remove from this type of pan liner.
Analyzing Information *How is the chef forming the shape of these cookies?*

pan with parchment paper and leave an overhang on two sides of the pan to act as handles. When properly cooled, the entire bar can be removed from the pan easily and without breakage. If the recipe calls for a greased pan, either spray the surface lightly with a nonstick cooking spray or use clean paper toweling to apply a light coating of fat. (Greasing pans for cookies is not generally recommended; the fat may cause excessive spreading and browning on the bottoms.)

- **Temperature of Pan.** Never portion cookie dough onto hot sheet pans or baking pans. Pans should be at room temperature before they are prepared or filled. If the pans are hot, the cookie dough will start to melt before it goes into the oven. This will result in excessive spreading.

Creaming Method Many cookies are made by using the creaming method. As you know from Chapter 18, to cream means to blend a combination of ingredients together until their consistency is smooth and uniform. Unlike baked products that require a long creaming time to allow for the incorporation of air (such as some sorts of cakes), the mixing time for cookies is short, eliminating the addition of too much air. (Longer creaming times cause increased leavening, which results in light and airy, cake-like cookies.)

BASIC CULINARY SKILLS

Creaming Method for Cookies

1 Place sugar and fat into the bowl of a mixer.

2 Cream the ingredients on medium speed with a paddle attachment until the mixture is smooth.

3 Add eggs in several additions and beat well after each addition.

4 Scrape the bowl with a rubber spatula, when needed, to blend ingredients.

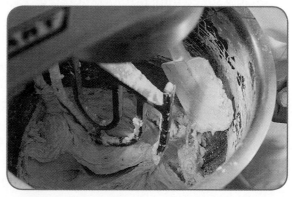

5 Add the dry ingredients all at once and mix on low speed until just incorporated.

6 Add garnishes.

7 Blend until evenly combined. Do not overmix.

A short creaming time prevents cookies from spreading too much during baking. If the dough becomes too warm as it is creamed and shaped, the cookies may spread too much and run into each other on the baking sheet. However, if the dough remains cool until it goes into the oven, cookies will spread at the proper rate. Avoid overmixing. This causes gluten to develop and the cookies will not be as tender, nor will they spread properly. Cookies that are intended to spread during baking will normally contain a significant amount of butter to help encourage their expansion.

Foaming Method The foaming method is used to make several varieties of cookies, including biscotti. The foam in this method is made by whipping eggs and sugar until thick and light in texture. Cookies made with this mixing method tend to use less flour and have a more resilient texture than those made with the creaming method.

BASIC CULINARY SKILLS

Foaming Method for Cookies

1 Place sugar and eggs into the bowl of a mixer.

2 Whip ingredients on high speed, using a whisk attachment, until thick and light.

3 Add dry ingredients and mix on low speed until just incorporated.

4 Add fat, if required by your recipe, and mix on low speed until just incorporated.

5 Scrape the bowl with a rubber spatula, when needed, to blend ingredients.

6 Add garnishes, if required by your recipe.

7 Blend until evenly combined. Do not overmix.

 See Recipe Card 137, "Biscotti."

Shaping Cookies Techniques vary for shaping different types of cookies. With the exception of bar cookies, the manner in which cookies are portioned, shaped, and placed onto the baking sheet will determine how they bake.

- **Drop Cookies.** To portion drop cookies, fill a scoop of the proper size with dough and level it off. Release the dough onto the prepared sheet pan. If stated in the recipe, flatten the mounded dough for a more even spread. Leave 1 to 2 inches of space between the mounds of dough. This gives the cookies enough space to spread during baking. Also, portion the dough into even rows so space is used efficiently.

- **Icebox Cookies.** Chill dough for about 10 minutes. Divide it into manageable portions. Mound each portion onto a separate piece of parchment paper, leaving 2 to 3 inches at each end. Roll the paper around the dough and smooth it into an even cylinder. When the paper is wrapped tightly around the dough, gather the ends of the paper and twist to compact the dough into a log. If the roll becomes flat on one side, round it by gently rolling it again. After the dough is rolled into a cylinder, chill it until it is very firm. Most frozen dough can be sliced directly from the freezer. Use a sharp knife for clean and uniform slices. The thickness of the slices determines the character of the baked cookie. Thin slices will result in a crisp texture, thicker slices will be softer. Place the slices on a prepared sheet pan in even rows, spacing the cookies about 2 to 3 inches apart to allow for spread. Icebox cookie dough can be stored in the refrigerator for up to one week. For longer storage, wrap properly, label the packaging, and freeze until needed.

Figure 19-10
Shaping Icebox Cookies
Roll the cookie dough into an even cylinder.
Predicting *Why should the cylinder of cookie dough be smooth and even?*

- **Piped Cookies.** Place the dough into a pastry bag fitted with the appropriate tip. When the pastry bag is one-half to two-thirds full, twist the top of the bag to seal it. Squeeze the bag to release any air in the tip. Hold the twisted end firmly in one hand. Use the other hand to lightly guide the tip. Apply even pressure to dispense cookies in even rows onto a prepared sheet pan. Maintain consistent pressure while keeping the tip at a constant level to produce uniform cookies. The shape of the cookie determines the angle of the bag. Hold the bag upright for stars and swirls. Hold the bag at an angle for straight lines. To finish each cookie, release the pressure, push down slightly, and then quickly lift the tip away. If the tip is lifted away before the pressure is released, the dough will form a "tail" on the top of the cookie that is likely to become too dark during baking. Use a template to maintain even spacing when you are piping cookies. You can create a template by marking a pattern onto the back of parchment paper. Pipe the cookie dough onto the front of the paper to avoid contamination from ink.

▲ *Piping cookie dough*

- **Stenciled Cookies.** Place the stencil on a silicone-lined sheet pan. Spoon a small amount of chilled batter into the center of the design and use a small offset spatula to spread it evenly to the edges of the stencil. This makes the cookies bake uniformly. Carefully lift the stencil from the sheet pan, scrape off any excess batter, and repeat the process. Spacing depends on the size of the stencil. If you are shaping the cookies free-hand, place the batter on the prepared sheet pan and use an offset spatula to shape. Stenciled cookies are often baked in small batches because they must be wrapped or shaped while hot from the oven.
- **Bar Cookies.** Begin with a properly lined baking pan of the correct size. Use a rubber or offset spatula to spread the batter evenly. Hold the spatula nearly parallel to the surface of the batter while spreading. Spread the dough to an even thickness. The corners and edges will dry out during baking if they aren't as thick as the center.
- **Twice-Baked Cookies.** Place the dough on a prepared sheet pan and form into a log according to the dimensions of the recipe. Gently even out the sides of the log with lightly floured hands. Bake the log until it is a light golden brown and then remove it from the oven and cool for 10 to 15 minutes. The center of the log will be soft when removed from the oven. If indicated in the recipe, lower the oven temperature while the log cools. Using a wide offset spatula, transfer the log to a clean work surface and cut it with a serrated knife crosswise on the diagonal into slices of desired thickness. Return the slices to the sheet pan and position each slice cut side down, one-half inch apart in even rows. Return to the oven and bake to the desired crispness.
- **Cut-Out Cookies.** When rolling cookie dough, always work with chilled dough. Prepare the sheet pans prior to rolling so you can transfer the cookies directly to the pan. Divide the dough into manageable portions. Work with one portion at a time and keep the remaining dough tightly wrapped and refrigerated. When rolling out the dough, if it is soft and delicate, place it between two sheets of parchment paper for easier rolling. If the dough becomes warm while rolling, place it in the refrigerator to chill. When cutting the cookies, press firmly to make clean cuts through the dough; twisting the cutter can cause the cookies to lose their shape. You can place cut-out cookies relatively close together on the sheet pan because cut-outs do not generally spread much. When using cutters of varying sizes and shapes, bake cookies of like sizes together to ensure even baking.

▲ *Biscotti are twice-baked cookies.*

Cut-Out Cookies

1 **Dust** the dough and the work surface lightly with flour. Do not use more flour than needed.

2 **Place the dough** on the board.

3 **Roll out the dough** from the center to the outer edge. Turn the dough often while rolling to keep it an even thickness. Most cookie dough should be rolled ⅛- to ¼-inch thick.

4 **Cut cookie shapes** free-hand or use cookie cutters. Dip the cutting edge of the knife or cutter into flour to keep it from sticking to the dough. To minimize trimmings, place the cutter close to the cut-out holes.

5 **Transfer cookies** to the prepared sheet pan. Maintain even rows for consistency.

- **Molded Cookies.** If the dough is too soft to hold its shape, refrigerate until it is firm enough to work with. To shape by hand, roll dough into smooth balls of a uniform size. Place the balls of dough on a prepared sheet pan in even rows, spacing the cookies about 2 to 3 inches apart. To make stamped cookies, roll the dough according to the cut-out cookie directions, press the prepared stamp into each cookie, and remove quickly. Use a sharp knife to cut the dough into individual portions. Place cookies on a prepared sheet pan in even rows 1 inch apart. To make cookies with a cookie mold, pack the dough into the prepared mold and run a rolling pin over the surface a few times to fill the mold completely. Molds should be very clean so the cookies are clearly imprinted with the design and unmold easily.

Baking Cookies Cookies need to be properly baked to attain their desired shape, size, flavor, and texture. Consider the following factors before placing the cookie dough into the oven:

- **Oven Temperature.** Preheat the oven to the correct temperature before baking cookies. A preheated oven ensures that the cookies bake at the proper rate, spread to the preferred size, and achieve the expected texture, flavor, and color. Preheating an oven normally takes about 15 minutes.
- **Position of Oven Racks.** Generally, when baking only one pan of cookies at a time, center the rack so the cookies are in the middle of the oven for even browning and baking.

▲ *Fully-baked biscotti*

FIGURE 19-11
Cutting Bar Cookies
Bar cookies can be cut into a variety of shapes, including squares, rectangles, triangles, and diamonds.
Communicating *What shape do you prefer? Why?*

▼

When baking multiple sheet pans, leave at least 2 inches around each sheet to allow for even heat circulation.

- **Baking.** Halfway through the recommended baking time, rotate the sheet pans so the part that had been in the back of the oven is now in the front of the oven. This helps achieve even browning and baking. When baking more than one sheet pan at a time, change their positions on the oven racks as well as rotating them. Because most cookies are smaller than other baked goods and often contain a high percentage of sugar, they burn easily. Check for doneness several minutes before the recipe indicates.

- **Determining Doneness.** Because many types of cookies remain on the hot sheet pan for several minutes before transferring to wire cooling racks, they will continue to bake when they are removed from the oven. To account for the carry-over baking, you can remove cookies from the oven when they appear slightly underbaked. The majority of cookies are done when they are light golden brown on the bottom and along the edges. Consult the recipe for specific indications of doneness.

- **Cooling Cookies.** Instructions for cooling vary among recipes. Generally, you should remove cookies from the sheet pan as quickly as possible after baking to prevent further browning. Some cookies, however, are too soft to be removed immediately. When necessary, allow the cookies to cool briefly on the baking pan just until they have set enough to be transferred to a wire cooling rack. Stenciled cookies should be shaped as soon as they are removed from the oven.

Finishing Cookies Finished cookies provide versatility to any food-service establishment. From big, chunky drop cookies to expertly garnished cut-outs, cookies are a part of many catered events, receptions, banquets, buffets, and plated desserts. Many cookies are ready to be served as soon as they cool. However, bar cookies need to be cut and stenciled cookies need to be shaped (if desired). You can also ice or glaze cookies and create sandwich cookies.

- **Cutting Bar Cookies:** Cool bar cookies completely and remove the entire bar from the pan, using the handles of the parchment paper. Place on a clean cutting surface. If glazing or icing, apply the desired amount and chill to firm the glazing or icing before cutting. Use a thin, sharp knife for clean, straight cuts. Wipe the blade of the knife clean between cuts.

- **Glazing or Icing Cookies.** There are several ways to apply glazes and icings to cookies after baking. To eliminate mess and waste, arrange cookies closely together on wire racks placed over sheet pans. Pipe icing or glaze over the surface of the cookies to create a design, or simply drizzle the icing or glaze free-form. Another technique involves spreading icing or ganache on the surface of a cookie with a small offset spatula. You can also dip cookies into melted chocolate or warm ganache. When dipping, allow the excess chocolate or ganache to drain into the bowl. Scrape any extra from the bottom of the cookie and place the coated cookies on wire racks to set until firm.

- **Shaping Stenciled Cookies.** Shape warm stenciled cookies by draping them over various objects to create different shapes. To make a container, for example, you could drape the cookie over an inverted cup. The cookie must be warm and pliable enough to shape without cracking.

- **Sandwiching Cookies.** This process involves joining two cookies together with a thin layer of filling or ice cream. The cookies used for sandwiching should be uniform in shape and thickness. Apply just enough filling to hold the cookies together. Using a small offset spatula, spread the filling so it doesn't quite reach the edge of the cookies; the filling will spread when the cookies are pressed together.

Serving and Storing Cookies Although cookies have always been served with hot beverages and cold milk, they also provide the perfect accompaniment to frozen desserts, mousses, and custards. Their crisp texture is a nice contrast to the creaminess of the dessert. Cookies are an important element of plated desserts. As a combination of various items, such as cool ice cream, warm chocolate sauce, light-as-air whipped cream, and crunchy cookies, plated desserts offer chefs the freedom to create signature desserts. Even with contrasting flavors, textures, and temperatures, the components of a plated dessert are meant to complement one another. Ice cream, chocolate sauce, whipped cream, and a cookie may sound like ingredients found in a common sundae, but when presented in a unique and decorative manner, the dessert becomes a one-of-a-kind creation.

CHEF'S TIP

COOL COOKIES
If stenciled cookies become cool and brittle while shaping, return the pan of baked cookies to the oven to warm briefly.

▲
FIGURE 19-12
Shaping Stenciled Cookies
The baked cookies are draped over cups while they are still pliable.
Predicting *Why is it important to work fairly quickly when shaping a stenciled cookie?*

▲ *Ice cream with biscotti*

The most important step in storing cookies is to cool them completely on wire racks before putting them away. Because cookies contain a significant amount of sugar, and sugar attracts moisture from the air, cookies can turn soggy or stick together if they're not stored in airtight containers at room temperature. To prevent fragile cookies from breaking, store them between layers of parchment paper. Precut bar cookies should be wrapped individually. Most cookies can be frozen for up to 2 to 3 months. They should be wrapped well in plastic, freezer bags, or plastic containers with airtight lids. Remember to date and label the cookies on the outside of the packaging before storing them in the freezer.

 **Reading Checkpoint** *What are the two most common mixing methods for cookies?*

Making Cakes

It is important to have all ingredients for a cake properly scaled out before beginning the mixing process. For any type of cake, it is important to sift all the dry ingredients. Sifting the dry ingredients together helps to mix and combine them. More importantly, it breaks up any lumps in the flour.

The mixing methods used for different cakes greatly affect their texture and density. The method used also affects the specific ingredients called for by the recipe. The three most common mixing methods for cakes are:

- The creaming method
- The warm foaming method
- The cold foaming method

Preparing Pans Most bakers prepare their cake pans before mixing their cake batter. Cakes are baked in a wide variety of pans. Pan types include loaf pans, tube pans, Bundt pans, round pans, and square pans, as well as using new materials such as silicon and special paper molds. For most types of cake, pan preparation is vital. If the pan is not properly prepared, you will not be able to remove the baked cake without damaging it.

Most cake pans are prepared by greasing and flouring them. Take soft butter or shortening and brush it into the pan, being careful to completely cover the pan. After greasing, put a small amount of flour in the pan and move it around to ensure that the flour completely coats the inside. For some cake pans, you can use paper liners.

Creaming Method The creaming method is one of the simplest ways to make a cake batter and is similar to the creaming method for

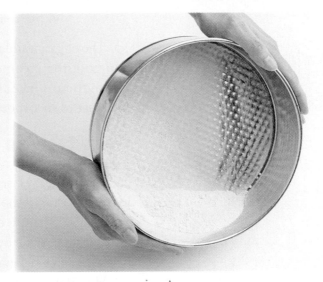

▲
FIGURE 19-13
Preparing Cake Pans
This springform pan is first greased (left) and then coated with flour (right).
Predicting *Why does a springform pan make it even easier to remove a cake without damaging it?*

making cookies. Pound cake is a classic example of a cake made by using the creaming method. Creaming-method cakes tend to be denser and heavier than cakes made by using other mixing methods. The air that is trapped in the fat by creaming creates small pockets of air in the baked cake. The trapped air expands slightly during baking, helping to leaven the cake. In a classic pound cake, for example, the trapped air is the only leavener, so it is important to add as much air as possible during the creaming process.

In the creaming method, you mix the sugar and fat (butter) together until they are very light and fluffy. After the sugar and fat are creamed, add the eggs a little at a time to prevent the mixture from separating and breaking the emulsion.

CHEF'S TIP

WARM BUTTER
Creaming time is decreased if you slightly warm the fat before beginning to cream it with the sugar.

◄
FIGURE 19-14
Emulsifying the Batter
When adding the eggs or other liquids to the fat and sugar in a creaming-method cake, be sure to add them slowly to avoid separating the mixture.
Inferring *How would a cake turn out if the sugar and fat do not emulsify with the eggs?*

The eggs should not be straight from the refrigerator, because they will cool the creamed fat and sugar, increasing the time it takes to cream them. Once all the eggs are incorporated, you add the flour and mix just to incorporate it. Do not overmix the batter.

Warm Foaming Method Sponge cakes are a wide category of cakes that are typically made with a warm egg-foam base. (Angel food cake is made by using the cold foaming method.) The lighter, airier texture is due to the air beaten into the eggs before other ingredients are added. Because eggs are capable of trapping very large quantities of air, cakes made by using the warm foaming method are much less dense than cakes made by using the creaming method.

Heating the egg and sugar mixture dissolves the sugar and loosens the proteins in the eggs, which allows them to accept and hold more air throughout the mixing and baking. When the warm egg and sugar mixture is whipped in a mixer on high speed, it will quadruple in volume, become very pale in color, and have a much firmer texture. This is the egg foam that is so important for this method of mixing.

After the egg foam has reached maximum volume, slow down the mixer to a medium speed and allow to mix for another 15 minutes. This step is called **stabilizing**. After the initial high-speed whipping, the air in the foam is in both large and small bubbles. In the stabilizing step, the continued mixing breaks the large bubbles into smaller ones. This provides a better final texture.

After the egg mixture has stabilized, the dry ingredients are incorporated by hand, folding in several small additions. You must do this very carefully to prevent the tiny air pockets from being broken. A small amount of liquid fat is gently folded in last. The fat will speed up the breaking down of the foam, so it should always be added last.

Cold Foaming Method Angel food cake is made by using the cold foaming method. Angel food cake is a meringue-based cake batter. Its light, airy texture results from the large amount of air that can be beaten into the meringue. Angel food cakes tend to be very sweet because a high sugar content helps stabilize the meringue.

To make an angel food cake, begin whipping the egg whites and slowly add sugar as if you were making a meringue. After whipping the meringue to the soft peak stage, fold in cake flour and more sugar. One important step that sets these cakes apart from other types of cakes is that the pans are not greased. The delicate batter needs to adhere to the sides of the pan as it cools or it will collapse. After filling the pan with the batter, run a knife or spatula around the inside of the pan to get rid of any large air pockets. After baking, the cakes are cooled upside down to prevent collapse.

▲ *Angel Food Cake*

Warm Foaming Method

1. **Prepare** the pans and preheat the oven.
2. **Sift** the dry ingredients.
3. **Combine** eggs and sugar in a bowl.
4. **Place** the egg mixture over a pan of simmering water.
5. **Stir** the egg mixture while it heats.

6. **Remove from the heat** when the mixture reaches 110°F.
7. **Whip** the mixture with an electric mixer on high speed for 5 minutes.

8. **Continue whipping** the mixture on medium speed for 10 to 15 minutes.

9. **Add dry ingredients** in several batches, carefully folding them in.

10. **Combine** a small portion of the batter with the fat and then fold it into the rest of the batter.

11. **Pour** the batter into the prepared pans and put in the oven.
12. **Turn cakes out** of their pans and onto a cooling rack when they are baked.

Baking Cakes No matter which mixing method you use to make a cake, baking is the last step. All types of cakes are delicate mixtures that have trapped air in them. If the cake is not baked immediately after mixing, the air can easily escape before the batter sets. This makes the crumb irregular.

Always preheat the oven to the desired temperature before beginning a cake recipe. Most cakes bake between 350°F and 400°F, although thin sheet cakes are sometimes baked at a slightly higher temperature. After the cake is put in the oven, avoid opening the door to the oven until the cake is about half baked. The change in temperature from hot air escaping can cause the cake to fall.

▲
FIGURE 19-15
Testing Doneness
A sponge cake should spring back when gently touched with a finger. **Inferring** *Why would it be better to test a sponge cake by touching it gently rather than sticking a skewer in it?*

There are several tests to tell when a cake is done. The first and easiest is to look for even browning on the surface. Because most cakes have a large amount of sugar, they get very brown as the sugar caramelizes. As the cake bakes, it will also pull away from the sides of the pan, leaving a small gap. (The exception to this is angel food cakes, which stick to the pan.) If both of these tests are positive, gently touch the top of the cake with the tip of a finger. The small dent should spring back immediately. If the dent remains, the cake needs more time. The last test is to insert a skewer or paring knife into the center of the cake. The tester should come out completely clean, with no moist batter sticking to it.

Once the cake is baked, it should be unmolded. Turn the pan upside down over a cooling rack. If the pan was properly prepared, the cake will drop out of the pan. If the cake is left to cool in the pan, it may become soggy from steam and is likely to stick. If the cake is stuck in the pan, gently run a paring knife around the edge of the pan. After the cake is completely cooled, it can be filled and served. It can also wrapped and frozen for later use.

 **Reading Checkpoint** *What are the three mixing methods used for cakes?*

Building, Icing, and Finishing Cakes

Almost any type of cake can be used to make a filled cake. After the cake is baked and allowed to cool, it is cut into several thin layers. A filling is spread or piped between the layers. The cake is then reassembled. At this point it is ready to be iced. In general, a spreadable icing is used for cakes, but pourable icings such as a liquid glaze, or even rolled icings such as marzipan, may be used.

Building Slice the cake, using a long serrated knife. Try to keep the layers level and even in thickness. After the cake is covered with icing, it is garnished or decorated and is ready to be served. Soak one layer with flavored simple syrup. **Simple syrup** is a mixture of equal amounts of sugar and water that has been brought to a boil to dissolve the sugar crystals. The syrup adds both moisture and flavor to the finished cake. Spread a layer of the filling to be used (jam, buttercream, ganache, mousse, or another filling). Repeat these steps with all the layers of the cake. Do not put filling on the top layer. At this stage, the cake can be finished, wrapped and refrigerated, or frozen for finishing at a later time.

Icing **Buttercream** is an icing that is made by aerating butter, shortening, or a combination of the two with powdered sugar. Buttercream is used to ice and decorate cakes. It is also used as a filling in cakes and pastries. Buttercream is very rich and the amount per serving should be kept small. Most buttercreams have a long shelf life if properly stored. If you use buttercream that was made ahead of time and stored in the refrigerator, it must be warmed and then rewhipped or it will be very stiff and dense.

The most common types of buttercream are American, Italian, French, and German.

- **American Buttercream.** The easiest type of buttercream to make is **American buttercream**. It is just butter that is creamed with powdered sugar. It is denser and richer than the other types of buttercreams.
- **Italian Buttercream.** **Italian buttercream** is made by adding butter to a meringue. After the meringue is made, softened butter is added to it. Italian buttercream is very white, which makes it appropriate for wedding cakes.
- **French Buttercream.** **French buttercream** is made from egg yolks that are whipped. Sugar is added to the whipped yolks and then softened butter is added. Because French buttercream is made with yolks, it has a yellow color.

▲
FIGURE 19-16
Building a Layer Cake
Cream and fruit are used between layers.
Predicting *How would you finish the outside of this cake?*

Pound Cake

Have you ever wondered how pound cake got its name? It comes from the cake's original, easy-to-remember ingredients: a pound of butter, a pound of sugar, a pound of eggs, and a pound of flour. In 1747, Hanna Glasse published this pound cake recipe in *The Art of Cookery Made Plain and Easy*:

Take a pound of butter, beat it in an earthen pan with your hand one way, till it is like a fine thick cream: then have ready twelve eggs, but half the whites; beat them well, and beat them up with the butter, a pound of flour beat in it, a pound of sugar, and a few caraways. Beat it all well together for an hour with your hand, or a great wooden spoon, butter a pan and put it in, and then bake it an hour in a quick oven. For a change you may put in a pound of currants, clean washed and picked.

This might have been considered an easy recipe in the 1700s, but thankfully we no longer have to beat the ingredients with our bare hands for an hour—leaveners and mixers now do the work of aerating and blending the batter for us. And we no longer have to use a pound of each ingredient, though most recipes still call for these proportions to produce the desired result: a rich and satisfying dessert.

Early pound cake recipes sometimes included currants, lemon, nutmeg, brandy, almonds, and other flavoring ingredients. Pound cakes today are

▲ *Marble pound cake*

often vanilla or chocolate flavored. The chocolate is sometimes melted and blended into the batter for a marbleized cake.

Pound cake has a moist texture and slices well. It can be eaten plain, dusted with powdered sugar, or garnished with fruit or ice cream. It is not a fancy cake, but made fresh, with quality ingredients, it is still—centuries after its introduction—a simple favorite.

Research

Research pound cake recipes from the 1700s, 1800s, and early 1900s. Compare recipe instructions and ingredients with a modern-day pound cake recipe.

- **German Buttercream**. **German buttercream** is made from a base of whipped pastry cream. When the pastry cream is cool, butter is added to it. German buttercream is very rich, but a good choice for a cake filling. Because German buttercream is dairy-based, it has a short shelf life and should be made and used in several days.

You can flavor buttercreams in a number of ways. The simplest way is to add an extract or flavor paste when you finish making the buttercream. For example, you can add melted chocolate to make a chocolate buttercream. Because buttercream uses a large amount of sugar, unsweetened chocolate is often the best choice to flavor it. Alcohols, fruit purees, and fruit juices can all be added to a buttercream to flavor it, but take care not to add too much or the mixture is likely to separate.

To ice a cake, begin by applying a thin coat on all surfaces. This is called the crumb coat because it keeps crumbs from appearing in the next coating. Then apply a second, thicker layer of icing to finish the cake. Try to get is as smooth as possible.

Finishing After icing, you can add decorations for visual appeal. Decorations can be very simple, such as combing the sides of the cake with a cake comb. Or, you can get more complicated. For example, you could make intricate piped designs.

Decorations on the top can include a decoration placed on top of each slice. You could also decorate the top with a large design, such as writing "Happy Birthday." In general, it is more appealing to keep decorations small in relation to the size of the cake. If the decorations are large, they tend to overwhelm the cake and make it look top-heavy.

▲
FIGURE 19-17
Piped Designs with Buttercream
Buttercream is a perfect medium to pipe decorations on cakes, but it needs to be the proper consistency to look its best.
Communication *Do you like the basket weave pattern that the pastry chef is applying to this wedding cake?*

 **Reading Checkpoint** *What are the four types of buttercream icing?*

19.3 ASSESSMENT

Reviewing Concepts

1. What are the four basic ingredients used for both cookies and cakes?
2. What are the three main types of cookies?
3. What are the two most common mixing methods for cookies?
4. What are the three most common mixing methods for cakes?
5. What are the four types of buttercream icing?

Critical Thinking

6. **Applying Concepts** Why is it necessary to cream cookie ingredients for only a short period of time?
7. **Drawing Conclusions** Why is simple syrup brushed onto a cake when it is filled?

Test Kitchen

Divide into two teams. Team 1 will make a drop cookie from scratch. Team 2 will make the same variety of drop cookie but use either a cookie mix or a prepared cookie dough. Compare the flavor, texture, and color of the finished cookies.

SOCIAL STUDIES

Wedding Cakes

Wedding cakes are closely tied with different cultures. Research traditional wedding cake styles for France, England, and the United States. Compare and contrast the different traditions.

19.4 Pies, Tarts, & Pastries

READING PREVIEW

Key Concepts

- Making pie and tart dough
- Assembling pies and tarts
- Making pastries by using choux paste
- Plating desserts

Vocabulary

- blind baked
- choux paste
- éclairs
- fluting
- lattices
- rubbed dough method
- streusel
- top crust

"**P**lated desserts challenge the pastry chef to go beyond the standard baked item and find ways to showcase its shapes, colors, and textures."

– Stephane Weber
The Culinary Institute of America

Pie and Tart Dough

The pastry shell is a major component of a pie or tart. It has a large effect on the texture of the final product. Pies and tarts are both made by filling a pastry shell with a fruit, nut, or cream filling. Pies are made in a pan that has tall sides that flare out. Tarts are made in pans that have shorter sides and tend to be vertical. Tart pans may have either straight sides or fluted sides.

Three types of pastry dough are used for both pies and tarts. They are defined by their ingredients and how they are made. They are flaky dough, cookie dough, and crumbly dough.

Flaky Dough Flaky dough is generally used for pies. It is made with flour, water, and butter or shortening. The fat is cut into the dry ingredients and left in small pieces before adding the water. This method is called the **rubbed dough method** because when you make it by hand, you rub the fat into the dry ingredients with your hands. The spaces left by the melted fat when the dough is baked give it a flakey texture. For flavoring, you usually add a small amount of salt and sometimes a small amount of sugar. Flakey dough tends to be pale or white when baked.

Cookie Dough Cookie-textured dough is a sugar cookie type dough made from flour, sugar, fat, and eggs using the creaming method.

▲
FIGURE 19-18
Pie vs. Tart
The apple pie (left) has tall sides that flare out. The pear tart (right) has shorter sides that are typically vertical.
Drawing Conclusions *Which do you think would have a greater ratio of filling to dough, a pie or a tart?*

BASIC CULINARY SKILLS

Rubbed Method Pie Dough

1 **Sift** together the dry ingredients.

2 **Chill** the shortening or butter until very firm.

3 **Cut** the fat into cubes ½-inch square.

4 **Place the fat in the mixing bowl** with the dry ingredients.

5 **Break the fat into smaller pieces** by rubbing the mixture with your fingers in the bowl.

6 **Add the liquid** to the bowl when the pieces of fat are the size of split peas. The liquid should be cold to avoid melting the fat.

7 **Mix** the liquid carefully with the dry ingredients and fat. Mix just until the mixture comes together and forms a ball.

8 **Wrap** the dough in plastic wrap.

9 **Chill** the dough for several hours before using.

 See Recipe Card 145, "Pie Crust."

FIGURE 19-19
Assorted Pies
The texture of a pie is determined mostly by the incorporation of the fat.
Communicating *How important to you is a flaky pie crust?*

▲ *Blueberry filling*

The complete incorporation of the fat is what gives the dough the texture of a cookie. This type of dough is most often used for tarts. The addition of eggs gives this type of dough a golden brown color when baked. This is also known as short dough or tart dough.

Crumbly Dough Crumbly dough is very rich in both fat and sugar. It is typically made from flour, sugar, fat, and eggs. Crumbly dough is very delicate to work with. It can be made by using either the rubbed dough method or the creaming method. When using the rubbed dough method, you work the fat completely into the dry ingredients rather than leaving large pieces of fat before incorporating the liquid.

✓ **Reading Checkpoint** *What are the three types of dough used in pies and tarts?*

Assembling Pies and Tarts

After the dough is made, a pie or tart must be assembled. This involves making a filling, rolling out the dough, filling the pie shell, and, in some cases, topping the pie or tart.

Fillings There are four types of filling for pies: raw fruit filling, cooked fruit filling, cream filling, and custard filling.

- **Raw Fruit Filling.** Raw fruit fillings are made by mixing cut-up fruit with sugar, other flavorings, and either flour or cornstarch. The fruit and other ingredients are tossed together and then placed into an unbaked shell. As the filling bakes, the fruit releases juices that are thickened by the flour or cornstarch. This is one of the simplest methods and is often used for apple pies, peach pies, and berry pies. Raw fruit pies must be prepared and baked as soon as the filling is made or the fruit will begin to break down.
- **Cooked Fruit Filling.** For a cooked fruit filling, the cut fruit is cooked on the stove with sugar and other flavorings. You thicken the liquid released by the fruit by using a cornstarch slurry. Once the filling has cooled, it is placed in an unbaked pie shell. Cooked fruit fillings are used for apple pies, cherry pies, and blueberry pies. Cooked fruit fillings have the advantage of being able to be prepared in advance and stored in the refrigerator for several days before you fill and bake the pie.
- **Cream Fillings.** Cream fillings are made by preparing a boiled custard and filling a pre-baked shell just after it has

finished baking. Classic cream-filled pies include Boston cream pies and lemon meringue pies, as well as chocolate, coconut, and banana cream pies. Because the filling must go into the previously baked shell as soon as it is cooked, pies with cream fillings cannot be made in advance and stored in the refrigerator waiting to be baked.

- **Custard Fillings.** For a custard filling, a liquid is combined with eggs to form a custard, and the raw custard is poured into the shell and baked until set. The shell may either be raw or pre-baked, depending on how long the custard will take to fully set. Pecan pies, pumpkin pies, and quiches are examples of custard fillings. Custard fillings may be made a day or two before baking but should not be stored longer because they contain raw eggs that can quickly spoil.

▲ *Chocolate custard filling*

Rolling Dough No matter which type of dough you use, it should be rested and well chilled before you use it to make a pie or tart. Some tarts are made by pressing the dough evenly into a tart pan. Most pies are made by rolling the dough and placing it into a pie pan.

Roll the pie dough, using plenty of flour to prevent it from sticking to the bench and to the rolling pin. The dough should be rolled to approximately 1/8 inch thick. Roll the dough larger than the pan so there will be enough dough to go up the side of the pan.

Before moving the dough into the pan, brush the excess flour off with a soft brush. Fold the dough in half and then in half again. Gently lift the dough up and place it in the pan. Unfold the dough. Gently work the dough into the pan, being sure to cover all the surface area of the pan. You can then trim off the excess dough with a small knife or by pressing the dough against the edge of the pan to pinch it off.

Pie crusts are usually given a decorative edge, called a **fluting**. This fluting makes the pie more attractive. You can do it by gently squeezing the dough between your fingers or by using a special tool.

CHEF'S TIP

NEED DOUGH?
As a general rule, one ounce of dough is needed for each inch of the pan's diameter.

◀
FIGURE 19-20
Fluting
Fluting can be done by hand or by using special tools.
Drawing Conclusions *Why would a professional bakery or restaurant want its pies to have perfectly fluted crusts?*

▲ Lined shell weighted
with beans

Blind Baking A pie shell is either filled and then baked or it is baked before filling. A pre-baked pie shell is also called a **blind baked** pie shell. Pre-baked, or blind baked, pie shells are used when the filling is either not baked at all or when the pie will be in the oven for a shorter time than it would take to bake the dough.

To blind bake a pie shell, line the shell with parchment paper and fill the paper with weights. The weights may be dried beans, uncooked rice, or special pie weights made from metal or ceramics. Bake the weighted shell in the oven until the dough is baked. The weights keep the pie shell from bubbling.

Assembling After the pan has been lined with dough (and, in some cases, blind baked), it can be filled with the pie filling. Fill the pie higher than to the top of the crust for both raw fruit and cooked fruit fillings. Both of these fillings will tend to shrink when baked. Custard pies should be filled as much as possible. When filling custard pies, it is best to do it as close to the oven as possible because it is difficult to carry the pie filled with the liquid filling. Cream pies are usually topped with meringue or whipped cream to make them look full so they can be filled close to the top of the crust.

Toppings Both pies and tarts can have a variety of toppings, either before baking or after baking. Toppings include a top crust, streusel or crumbs, a lattice, fresh fruit, meringue, or whipped cream.

- **Top Crust.** A large piece of pastry dough that is rolled out and placed on top of the filled shell before baking is called a **top crust**. The rim of the bottom crust needs to be brushed with water before placing the top crust on it. The top crust may be egg washed to give it color and a shiny appearance. Small slits should be cut in several places in the top crust to allow steam from the filling to escape.

- **Lattice.** Made with the same dough as you use to line the shell, **lattices** are rolled-out dough that is cut into strips. The strips are laid across the top of the filling to create a cross-hatch, or lattice, effect. Lattices may be egg-washed for color and shine before baking. A lattice adds an interesting visual effect and allows some of the filling to be visible after the item is baked.

- **Streusel or Crumbs. Streusel** is a mixture of flour, sugar, nuts, oatmeal, or other dry ingredients and butter to create large chunks or crumbs (which is why streusel is often referred to as a crumb topping). These chunks or crumbs are sprinkled over the pie or tart filling to completely cover it before baking. Crumb toppings provide flavor as well as an interesting texture to the pie or tart.

- **Fresh Fruit.** Fresh fruit can make an attractive addition to a pie or tart. After the pie has been baked and cooled, you slice the fruit and arrange it in a decorative fashion on top.
- **Meringue and Whipped Cream.** Cream pies are often covered with either meringue or whipped cream. To cover a cream-filled pie or tart with meringue, prepare the pie or tart. Make a meringue and spread it on completely, covering the filling. Then lightly brown the meringue in a very hot oven, in a broiler, or by using a propane torch. For whipped cream, the sweetened cream is usually piped on the cooled pie in a decorative way.

▲ *Streusel topping*

 **Reading Checkpoint** *What are the four types of pie fillings?*

Pastries Made with Choux Paste

Choux paste (SHOO PASTE) is a very versatile dough or batter. It is used widely by pastry chefs and bakers to create both sweet and savory items. Probably the most widely known pastries made with choux paste are **éclairs** (AY-clahrs) and cream puffs. Éclairs are long, straight pastries that are filled with cream and glazed on top.

Choux paste is made from very basic ingredients—liquid, fat, flour, and eggs. The liquid used is usually water, milk, or a combination of the two. Almost any fat can be used, but you should consider the taste of the fat. For example, if you were making a savory item with the choux paste, lard or bacon drippings might be appropriate as the fat, but they would not be appropriate for a sweet item. Flour is used to give the choux its structure and allows it to trap steam during baking, pushing the choux up and creating the hollow space inside for fillings. Eggs add flavor and moisture.

▲ *Meringue topping*

Choux paste is usually piped out and baked, but it can also be fried and served like a doughnut. In addition to sweet applications, choux paste can be used for savory items, such as hors d'oeuvres or appetizers, because the paste has little or no sugar in it.

After making the choux paste, use it to fill a pastry bag fitted with a large round tip. Pipe out the desired shapes on a parchment-lined sheet pan. You could egg-wash the items to give them more shine and color. Bake the items in a preheated oven until they are completely browned. As they bake, the liquid in the paste turns to steam and pushes the dough apart, creating a hollow in the center. This is where you can put a filling after baking.

Choux Paste

1 Scale the ingredients.

2 Pour the liquid into a saucepan.

3 Cut the fat into small cubes.

4 Add the cubed fat to the liquid.

5 Heat the mixture. Use a medium to high heat.

6 Remove the mixture from the heat when it comes to a full boil.

7 Add the flour all at once and stir it in.

8 Cook the mixture, while stirring, for about 30 seconds.

9 Put the dough in a mixing bowl and stir for a minute to cool it slightly.

10 Add eggs one at a time, allowing them to incorporate after each addition.

11 The paste is done when all the eggs are incorporated. You can then pipe the choux paste into the desired shape.

 See Recipe Card 147, "Profiteroles."

After the choux is baked and cooled, you can fill it. For sweet items you usually use a cream-based filling. The most traditional filling is a flavored pastry cream. You can lighten the pastry cream by folding in whipped cream. You can also use mousses and even ice cream. The cleanest way to fill the choux is to poke a small hole in the bottom and pipe the cream inside, being sure to completely fill it. For some items it may be more appropriate to slice the choux and pipe the filling in.

Choux paste items are usually finished with a glaze or other garnish on top. They may also be finished by dipping the tops in caramel, chocolate, or simply lightly dusting them with powdered sugar.

◀
FIGURE 19-22
Choux + Filling + Glaze = Dessert
Many pastries can be made using different combinations of choux paste shapes, fillings, and glazes.
Applying Concepts *What different choux paste desserts are you familiar with?*

 **Reading Checkpoint** *What are the steps in making choux paste?*

Plating Desserts

Plating desserts is often thought of as the showplace for showing a chef's skill in pastry and dessert making. Plates can range from the very simple, such as a slice of cake or a tart on a plate, to multi-component designs that coordinate a number of flavors, textures, and temperatures. In fact, those three elements—flavor, texture, and temperature—need to be considered when you create a plated dessert.

When thinking about a plated dessert, you also should consider everything added to the plate as adding to the pleasure of eating the dessert. Nothing on the plate should be placed there simply for visual purposes, because it looks good.

A plated dessert starts with the major component of the dessert. This could be a tart, pastry, cake, or some other sweet. The main component should look attractive and interesting.

Try to work with small molds or to cut from a large item in a way that does not look just like a wedge.

After the main component, everything else added to the plate needs to complement and contrast the flavor, texture, and temperature of the main component. You can add a sauce, or several sauces, to the plate to increase flavor. You could use a simple fruit sauce made from a purée and sugar or use a cream sauce, such as crème Anglaise.

Frozen components are often added to provide a major change in temperature. If the main component is warm or room temperature, adding an ice cream or sorbet provides contrast. Using a frozen component can also give the chef an opportunity to add another flavor to the plate. For example, an individual apple tart could be paired with a caramel ice cream. The caramel will work well with the apple flavor and is not a part of the tart itself.

FIGURE 19-23 ▶
More Than Just a Chocolate Tart
The components of this plated dessert offer contrasting flavors, textures, and temperatures.
Drawing Conclusions *Is there anything you would add to or subtract from this arrangement?*

For textural contrast, a small cookie or tuile may be added to the plated dessert. The distinct crunch of a properly made cookie adds to the overall enjoyment of the dessert. This textural change can be especially important if the main component in the dessert has only one texture. This could happen with a mousse or baked custard.

When deciding how to plate a dessert and what other items to put with a main component, you should think about flavor combinations and experiment with several options to come up with the best combination. It is also a good idea to try the plate as your client or customer would and sit at a table to eat it. That way, you can discover which desserts are hard to eat or which flavors and textural combinations just do not work well.

 **Reading Checkpoint** *What are the three elements of a plated dessert?*

19.4 ASSESSMENT

Reviewing Concepts

1. What are the three types of dough used for pies and tarts?

2. What are the four types of pie fillings?

3. What are the steps in making choux paste?

4. What are the three elements of a plated dessert?

Critical Thinking

5. **Compare and Contrast** What is the difference between a pie and a tart?

6. **Compare and Contrast** What is the difference between a cream filling and a custard filling?

7. **Applying Concepts** If your major component is a brownie, what might you do to make a memorable plated dessert?

Test Kitchen

Divide into three teams. Decide on a pie filling. Each team will make a different version of a pie shell and fill it with the same filling. Team 1 will make the pie using a flakey dough. Team 2 will use a cookie dough. Team 3 will use a crumbly dough. Evaluate the pies.

LANGUAGE ARTS

Gather Information

Discuss with four chefs and/or bakers their methods for making flaky pie dough. Compare and contrast their different approaches and tricks for achieving a flaky crust.

Review and Assessment

Reviewing Content

Choose the letter that best answers the question or completes the statement.

1. The chocolate made from cocoa butter, sugar, milk powder, and flavorings is
   a. unsweetened chocolate
   b. semisweet chocolate
   c. white chocolate
   d. coating chocolate

2. Boiled custard is
   a. thickened by eggs
   b. thickened by starch
   c. cooked on the stove
   d. all of the above

3. If a cookie recipe spreads too much when it is baked, it might have
   a. had a long creaming period
   b. too much yeast
   c. been kept too cold
   d. an inadequate amount of butter

4. Sponge cakes are an example of the
   a. creaming method
   b. angel food method
   c. foaming method
   d. rubbed method

5. Choux paste gets its structure from
   a. eggs
   b. butter
   c. flour
   d. cream

6. Granité is a type of
   a. mousse
   b. custard
   c. cake
   d. frozen dessert

7. An oatmeal cookie is a type of
   a. stenciled cookie
   b. piped cookie
   c. drop cookie
   d. bar cookie

Understanding Concepts

8. What is a ganache?

9. What is a sabayon?

10. What type of cookie is made by using the foaming method?

11. What is the base for an angel food cake?

12. In relation to the pie shell, what make a cream pie different from other types of pies?

13. What is the most widely known pastry made from choux paste?

Critical Thinking

14. **Recognizing Patterns** Would a ganache made with white chocolate have a stronger chocolate flavor or weaker than a ganache made with milk chocolate? Explain your answer.

15. **Analyzing Information** What is the difference between a stirred custard and a baked custard?

16. **Comparing/Contrasting** How are bar cookies and twice-baked cookies similar? How are they different?

Culinary Math

17. **Applying Concepts** How much cream is required to make 6 pounds of light ganache?

18. **Solving problems** If a recipe of choux paste makes 42 éclairs and a recipe of pastry cream makes enough to fill 24, how much of each recipe will be needed to fill an order for 84 éclairs?

On the Job

19. **Classifying** A customer has given you a recipe for shoo-fly pie that is made with 1 quart of molasses, 2 cups of sugar, 8 whole eggs, and 4 egg yolks. What type of pie would you consider this filling?

Use the following Recipe Cards to test your culinary skill.

127. Chocolate Ganache

128. Chocolate Fondue

129. Chocolate Truffles

130. Vanilla Sauce

131. Frozen Lemon Soufflé

132. Bavarian Cream

133. Chocolate Mousse

134. Bread and Butter Pudding

135. Vanilla Ice Cream

136. Oatmeal Raisin Cookies

137. Biscotti

138. Marbleized Pound Cake

139. Vanilla Sponge

140. Angel Food Cake

141. Cheesecake

142. Italian Buttercream

143. Layer Cake

144. Common Meringue

145. Pie Crust

146. Apple Pie

147. Profiteroles

148. Fruit Tart

149. Crêpes Suzette

150. Strawberry Shortcake

Project 19: Chocolate, Chocolate, Chocolate

Answer these questions when your class works through Project 19.

- Which type of chocolate did you prefer raw?

- Did the different varieties of chocolate seem to melt differently? Or mix with the cream differently?

- Did the chocolates differ in their coating ability?

- Did the chocolates differ in their flavor and texture?

TEST PRACTICE

Choose the letter that best answers the question or completes the statement.

1. What is another name for unsweetened chocolate?
   A   dark chocolate
   B   compound chocolate
   C   chocolate liquor
   D   cocoa powder

2. Boiled custard is thickened with
   A   potatoes
   B   cornstarch
   C   tapioca
   D   flour

3. Which of the following is an examples of a bar cookie?
   A   biscotti
   B   tuiles
   C   chocolate chip cookies
   D   spritz cookies

4. When using the creaming method, cookies that are intended to spread during baking will normally contain a significant amount of
   A   butter
   B   eggs
   C   salt
   D   liquid

5. Of the following, which requires a blind baked shell?
   A   blueberry pie
   B   coconut cream pie
   C   peach pie
   D   apple pie

6. Which of the following is an important ingredient in an angel food cake?
   A   butter
   B   lard
   C   meringue
   D   shortening

7. Which of the following is not a required ingredient of choux paste?
   A   chocolate
   B   fat
   C   eggs
   D   flour

8. What is not a required ingredient of Bavarian cream?
   A   custard
   B   gelatin
   C   egg foam
   D   whipped cream

Culinary Management

WORKING IN A RESTAURANT

READING PREVIEW

Key Concepts

- Identifying restaurant personnel
- Working the front door
- Greeting and seating diners

Vocabulary

- back of the house
- back waiter
- brigade
- bus person
- captain
- carver
- chef de cuisine
- continuous seating plan
- dining room attendant
- dining room manager
- entremetier
- executive chef
- expediter
- fish station chef
- fixed seating plan
- front of the house
- front waiter
- grillardin
- grill station chef
- line chef
- maître d'
- maître d' hotel
- no-reservation policy
- pastry chef
- pâtissier
- poissonier
- prep chef
- receptionist
- reservation policy
- roast station chef
- rôtisseur
- roundsman
- runner
- saucier
- sauté station chef
- second chef
- server
- sommelier
- soup and vegetables station chef
- soup station chef
- sous-chef
- station chef
- swing chef
- tournant
- trancheur
- vegetable station chef
- wine steward

"**G**ood service, no matter whether the restaurant is upscale, family-friendly, or quick service . . . is simply the ability to make the customer happy."

— Marjorie Livingston
The Culinary Institute of America

Restaurant Personnel

How does everything get done properly in a restaurant? The answer is: Restaurants break down a big task into smaller manageable parts, each carried out by well-trained staff. Typically, the system of staffing a restaurant is referred to as a brigade system. A **brigade** (bri-GADE), is a group of workers assigned a specific set of tasks. The tasks might be related by a cooking method, type of food, or equipment.

Restaurants typically use the brigade system in both the dining room, which is often referred to as the **front of the house**, and in the kitchen, which is referred to as the **back of the house**.

The skills necessary in the front and the back of the house depend on the style of the food establishment. Most restaurants use standard names for personnel within their brigades. These often are based on a classic French brigade system. The specific terms used in a restaurant may vary, based on the size of the restaurant and the type of food and service offered by the restaurant.

Front-of-the-House Brigade A formal restaurant may require some or all of the following professionals in their front-of-the-house brigade. An informal restaurant may require only a few of these professionals. The most common term for the position is listed here first, but common variations (both English and French) are also indicated when appropriate.

- **Maître d'.** The person responsible for running the front of the house is the **maître d'** (MAY-truh DEE), which is short for **maître d'hôtel** (MAY-truh doh-TELL). The maître d' is also called the **dining room manager**. The maître d' is responsible for training service personnel, working with the chef to design the menu, arranging guest seating, taking reservations, and for good public relations with guests.
- **Captain.** At fine dining restaurants, the **captain** is responsible for explaining the menu to guests and taking their orders. The captain is also responsible for the smooth running service in a specific group of tables. The captain may also help serve the food. The captain is always available to the tables in his or her charge and never leaves the dining room.
- **Carver.** In classic service, the person in charge of carving and serving meats or fish and their accompaniments from the meat cart is called the **carver** or the **trancheur** (tran-SHUR). In modern dining rooms, the captain often replaces the carver.
- **Wine Steward.** It is the responsibility of the **wine steward**, who is also called the **sommelier** (suhm-uhl-YAY), to manage the buying and storing of wines, maintain proper wine inventory, counsel guests about wine choices, and serve wine properly at the table.
- **Server.** Second in line of responsibility after the captain, the **server**, sometimes called the **front waiter** often helps the

▲
FIGURE 20-1
Maître d' and Chef
The maître d' works with the chef to design the menu.
Inferring *What kind of personality characteristics do you think a maître d' should possess?*

captain take orders. The server is responsible for making sure the table is set properly for each course, that food is delivered properly to the correct tables, and that the diners' needs are met. The server can take an order to the kitchen, if necessary.

- **Runner.** Depending on the size and formality of the restaurant, the **runner** may deliver food and drinks to the front waiter, clear plates, and refill bread and water. The runner, often called the **back waiter**, provides overall assistance to the server.
- **Receptionist.** In formal restaurants, the **receptionist** assists the maître d' in greeting guests, answering the telephone at the front desk, and taking telephone reservations. In more casual restaurants, the receptionist may replace the maître d' and be referred to as the host or hostess.
- **Bus Person.** In large or formal restaurants where the back waiter assists the front waiter, a separate worker, the **bus person** (sometimes called the **dining room attendant**), is responsible for clearing and cleaning tables.

Back-of-the-House Brigade A formal restaurant may require some or all of the following professionals in their back-of-the-house brigade. Many formal restaurants use French terms to describe their back-of-the-house cooking positions. A chef who has responsibility for a particular type of food is often referred to as a **station chef** or a **line chef**.

- **Executive Chef.** The head chef is called the **executive chef**, or **chef de cuisine** (CHEF duh KWEE-zine). The executive chef commands the kitchen, designs the menu and oversees its execution, as well as overseeing food costs. The executive chef also coordinates the style of service with the maître d' and devises a system for how service staff should communicate orders to the kitchen.
- **Sous-Chef.** The French term **sous-chef** (SU-chef), means under-chef. The sous-chef, also known as the **second chef**, is the executive chef's principal assistant, who is responsible for scheduling personnel and temporarily replacing the executive chef or other chefs as necessary. The sous-chef sometimes acts as the expediter.
- **Expediter.** The **expediter** (ex-PED-eye-ter).accepts orders from the dining room and relays them to the various station chefs. The expediter also reviews the dishes before service to make sure they are correct. The expediter often accepts orders from the dining room, relays them to the various chefs in the kitchen, and reviews the dishes before they are served to the customer.

FIGURE 20-2
Bus Person
The bus person is a vital component in a smoothly running dining establishment.
Communication *What does the performance of the bus person communicate about a restaurant?*

▼

▲ Grill chef

- **Grill Station Chef.** The chef responsible for all the grilled items is the **grill station chef,** also called the **grillardin** (gree-yar-DAHN).
- **Roast Station Chef.** The chef responsible for all the roasted items is the **roast station chef,** also called the **rôtisseur** (roh-tess-UHR).
- **Fish Station Chef.** The chef responsible for preparing and cooking fish and seafood is the **fish station chef,** also called the **poissonier** (pwah-sawng-YAY).
- **Sauté Station Chef.** The chef responsible for sautéed dishes and accompanying sauces is the **sauté station chef,** also called the **saucier** (saw-see-YAY).
- **Garde Manger.** As you know from Chapter 10, the garde manger or pantry chef is the chef responsible for cold food preparations, including salads and salad dressings and cold appetizers.
- **Soups and Vegetables Station Chef.** The chef responsible for hot appetizers, pasta courses, and vegetable dishes is the **soup and vegetables station chef,** also called the **entremetier** (ehn-tray-mee-tee-AY). In larger kitchens, this position is broken into the **soup station chef,** who is responsible for stocks and soups, and the **vegetable station chef,** who is responsible for vegetables and starches.
- **Roundsman.** Working wherever needed, the **roundsman** is a roving chef who may fill in for absent chefs or assists chefs in other stations. This position is also known as a **swing chef.** or **tournant** (toor-NAHN).
- **Pastry Chef.** The chef responsible for making pastry and many other desserts is the **pastry chef,** also called the **pâtissier** (pah-tee-SYAY).
- **Prep Chef.** The chef responsible for preparing ingredients that will be used by other chefs is the **prep chef**. A prep chef washes and peels vegetables and fruits, cuts meat, and does any other work necessary for supporting other chefs.

▲ Pastry chef

Reading Checkpoint

What position is the head of the front-of-the-house brigade? Of the back-of-the-house brigade?

Working the Front Door

The first opportunity a restaurant has to make a good impression is at its front door. The guest's first contact with the restaurant is with the maître d' or the receptionist. Whether that first contact with the customer is made on the telephone or in person at the door, the person making the contact plays an important role. Naturally, a warm telephone conversation or personal reception at the front door makes guests feel welcome and promises a good dining experience before they are even seated at their table.

Telephone Etiquette In the food-service business, you sometimes communicate with people as much by telephone as in person. It can be difficult for a customer to get through to the restaurant or to understand what the restaurant representative is saying. If the person answering the phone is uncooperative or not well informed, the customer is not likely to form a good impression. Callers can become so discouraged that they do not make a dinner reservation. The person assigned to answer the telephone should be trained to keep the following telephone etiquette in mind:

- As much as possible, answer the telephone at the first ring and no later than the third ring.
- Develop an appropriate and brief telephone greeting. For example, "Hello, this is Oliver's Restaurant, Vanessa speaking. May I help you?" Have the greeting written down and placed next to the telephone where it can easily be seen by anyone answering the phone.
- Speak slowly and clearly. Very often people answering the phone speak so fast that callers cannot understand what they say.
- Know the restaurant's hours and location.
- Focus on the person being spoken to until you satisfy their question. Be pleasant and courteous.
- Avoid speaking to anyone else at the same time you are on the phone.
- Avoid putting customers on hold for long. If unable to give your complete attention, ask callers for their telephone number. If they do not give you a number, ask them to call back soon, making sure to give them your name. It is better to call back than not to give your full attention.
- When a caller asks to speak to someone, reply with, "May I ask who is calling?"

▲

FIGURE 20-3
Working the Front Door
The guest's first contact with a restaurant is the maître d'.
Drawing Conclusions *Why is a warm welcome important when greeting customers?*

FIGURE 20-4
Answering the Telephone
Be pleasant and courteous when answering the phone.
Predicting *How would you feel if you were treated discourteously in your first contact with a restaurant?*

▼

CHEF'S TIP

HOLIDAY
RESERVATIONS
Because holidays such
as Mother's Day, Easter,
Thanksgiving, and New Year's
Day are especially hectic for
restaurants, take special
care when taking reserva-
tions for these days.

Reservations Restaurant kitchens need to anticipate how much food to buy and prepare. Dining room managers need to know how many guests to set up for and how many servers will be necessary. Reservations provide information about how many customers to expect and when they will arrive, making it easier for a restaurant to plan. Advance knowledge of how many guests to expect is particularly necessary for busy mealtimes when there might otherwise be too many people for a dining room to handle and not enough food, or too many servers and too much food.

Upscale restaurants usually take reservations because their dining service is often more elaborate and lengthy, their customers do not dine casually, and the customers often travel from a distance to get to the restaurant. When a restaurant takes reservations, it is said to have a **reservation policy**.

Some restaurants don't take reservations. This is referred to as a **no-reservation policy**. They serve customers on a first-come-first-served basis. Most restaurants that do this expect a steady volume of diners or a quick turnover. However, some popular upscale restaurants that have a steady following don't take reservations, which leads to lines of customers waiting to get into the restaurant. Some restaurants view this as a way of generating an image of desirability.

Analyzing the Decision to Take Reservations

Using a Reservation Policy

Advantages	Disadvantages
• Guests can make definite plans for dining in the restaurant.	• Taking and confirming reservations is more labor-intensive initially.
• Restaurant management can plan ahead.	
• Guest traffic flow and table sittings can be staggered, improving traffic flow in the dining room.	• Customers who don't show up for their reservations can throw off planning for both the kitchen and the dining room.
• Food orders can be staggered, enabling kitchen staff to produce dishes with greater attention to detail and consequently higher quality.	
• Less rush and stress in the dining room and kitchen encourages smooth relations between guests and service staff.	• May discourage diners from spontaneously patronizing a restaurant if the expectation is that reservations are required.
• Service staff has greater opportunity to provide better service to diners.	
• Service staff can more easily handle requests for special diets, menu exceptions, birthdays, and so on.	

Many formal restaurants that use reservations will accept guests without reservations when the restaurant is slow. On the other hand, casual restaurants that don't usually take reservations may require them for groups over eight.

The Reception Desk The front desk (also called the reception desk) provides any information necessary to a guest or the dining room for smooth operation. Here you might find the reservation book or computer station, a seating plan for the dining room, copies of the menu and wine list, a logbook or history of daily dining room records, telephone and telephone directory, an answering machine, an employee directory, a credit card machine, maps, emergency numbers, paper supplies, pens, pencils, and other administrative necessities.

Menus should undergo quality control at the reception desk. Menus that are dog-eared, stained, or otherwise unsightly or outdated should be replaced.

Taking Reservations An efficient system for taking and recording reservations should be in place. One way to organize the procedure is to use a preprinted form that can be filled in at the time the reservation is made.

CHEF'S TIP

MESSY MENUS
Sloppy menus are unappealing and signal sloppy service or careless management.

Analyzing the Decision to Take Reservations

Using a No-Reservation Policy

Advantages	Disadvantages
• Eliminates the cost of staff to take and manage reservations.	• The line for a table can discourage potential customers.
• Encourages turnover of tables.	• Diners may become rushed by service staff feeling pressured by people waiting to be seated.
• Tables are not tied up by customers who don't show up for their reservations.	• Extended waiting can cause disgruntled customers and bad publicity.
• Revenue is increased through bar sales to guests waiting to be seated.	• Creates crowding at the entrance.

FIGURE 20-5
Greeting Guests
All guests feel appreciated if they are greeted warmly.
Drawing Conclusions *Why would restaurants use databases to keep track of their regular customers' preferences?*

Reservations should include the following:
- Date when the reservation was taken
- Name of the person taking the reservation
- Date and time for the reservation
- Name and telephone number of the guest
- Number in the party
- Smoking or nonsmoking preferences
- Any special seating requests
- Any special server requests
- Any handicapped seating requests
- Any other special requests (birthday or other occasion, accommodating children, or others with special needs, and so on)

✓ **Reading Checkpoint** *What are the advantages and disadvantages of a reservation policy?*

Greeting and Seating Guests

As the first link in the chain, so to speak, the maître d' or receptionist sets in motion the entire restaurant experience.

Greeting Guests The maître d' or receptionist should greet guests with a warm smile and a professional demeanor. Regular customers will feel appreciated if the person at the front door knows them and refers to them respectfully by name. After the greeting, guests should be asked if they have a reservation and accommodated as soon as possible. The maître d' or receptionist should offer to check coats and wraps before customers are seated.

Seating The maître d' should lead guests to their tables rather than permit them to make their own way. This gives management control over the traffic flow and establishes a relationship between the maître d' or receptionist and the guest.

There are many advantages to a preplanned dining room seating plan. Placement of tables should take into account the flow of server traffic through the room, exit doors, and paths for leading guests to their seats. It should allow for an even distribution of customers, as well as the safe and attractive placement of tables and seats.

A seating plan should create an impression that the room is filled. This is done by seating guests strategically, first at window seats and then in the central area of the room. The plan should allow for servers to move about to set tables and clear dishes without disturbing guests at nearby tables. Diners should be distributed to the wait staff evenly to prevent overload for any one server and to provide an equal opportunity to everyone on duty.

FOCUS ON SAFETY

Clear the Way
Crowding tables together can block the way for bus persons or wait staff, leading to spilling or dropping food. Spills can cause slipping or falling, resulting in injuries.

There are typically two ways to organize seating:

- **Fixed Seating Plan.** By staggering set meal times (such as at 6 p.m., 8 p.m., and 10 p.m.), a **fixed seating plan** enables the kitchen to work at a steady, reliable pace.
- **Continuous Seating Plan.** As long as there are empty tables that turn over regularly, a **continuous seating plan** allows the wait staff to pace themselves and the restaurant to have a steady volume of business, even if checks are not large.

No-Shows and Late Arrivals Customers who don't show up for their reservations, or who show up very late, cause big problems for restaurant management. These customers cause restaurants to lose money and disappoint customers who have had to wait for tables—only to see empty tables in the dining room.

One way of minimizing the likelihood of no-shows or late arrivals is to call the day before to confirm reservations. A restaurant may decide on a policy of giving away a table if guests arrive a half hour late might be better than not filling a table at all—and losing revenue. Of course, you could always allow for bad weather or for regular customers, who should always receive special consideration.

 **Reading Checkpoint** | *What are the two ways to organize seating in a restaurant?*

20.1 ASSESSMENT

Reviewing Concepts

1. What position is the head of the front-of-the-house brigade? Of the back-of-the-house brigade?
2. What are the basic steps involved in taking reservations?
3. What are the two ways to organize seating?

Critical Thinking

4. **Drawing Conclusions** Most upscale restaurants require reservations. Why would the service staff hold tables for guests even if they don't arrive on time? What do you think are the best measures a restaurant can take to protect itself from no-shows without discouraging their repeat business?
5. **Comparing/Contrasting** Compare a fixed seating plan with a continuous seating plan.
6. **Predicting** How will a no-reservations policy in a fine dining restaurant affect customers? Service staff? Kitchen staff?

Test Kitchen

Divide into groups of 10. Each group will be a kitchen brigade, with each individual assuming the role of a specific type of chef at the appropriate location in the kitchen. Using a menu from a local upscale restaurant, your teacher or classmates will order 10 meals from the menu. An expediter will relay the meal orders to the various chefs, who will describe what they must do to prepare the dish.

LANGUAGE ARTS

Descriptive Writing

Research the reservation policies of five different types of restaurants by calling them during their down time. Describe the advantages and disadvantages of each of the policies of the particular establishments you have researched.

READING PREVIEW

Key Concepts

- Identifying serviceware
- Cleaning service utensils

Vocabulary

- china
- cover
- flatware
- glassware
- hollowware
- serviceware
- tableware

> **"C**offee pots, creamers, and salt shakers are part of the dining room 'mise en place.' They have to be perfectly clean and ready to use before the guests arrive. **"**
>
> – Gerard Fischetti
> The Culinary
> Institute of
> America

Serviceware

The dishware and utensils used in the dining room, both on or off the table, are called **serviceware**. The serviceware that is used by customers is sometimes called **tableware**.

Categories of Serviceware Serviceware includes all the dishes and silverware, as well as such things as carving knives, serving spoons, and ladles. Small serviceware is often broken into the following categories:

- **China.** Everything designed to contain food is regarded as **china**. This includes such things as plates, bowls, dishes, cups, saucers, and creamers.
- **Flatware.** All utensils used at the table or for serving are considered **flatware**. This includes all knives, forks, and spoons used at the table or for serving.

- **Glassware.** All glass containers for containing liquids are regarded as **glassware**. This includes water glasses, wine glasses, champagne goblets, cocktail or liquor glasses, beer mugs, pitchers, and carafes.
- **Hollowware.** Large objects, whether decorative or utilitarian, including such things as silver platters, candlesticks, large tea or coffee pots, sauceboats, fondue sets, and cake stands are called **hollowware**.

Service staff also use many tools and utensils in the course of their shift. The restaurant management often posts a list of them to help personnel remember what they are responsible for. These typically include candles or table lights, chairs, china, coffee-making equipment, condiments, creamers, silverware, glassware, side tables, linens, menus, and side stands.

The wait staff must have the tools of their trade with them at all times when they are on duty. Their essential tools include two working pens, a crumber (a device for cleaning crumbs from the table), order forms (for recording customers' orders), a small calculator, and a small notebook.

The Cover In restaurant terms, a **cover** is a complete place setting for one person. It includes china, glassware, and flatware. Follow these general guidelines when setting covers on tables for the most visual appeal and comfort:
- Place settings should face each other across the table, whenever possible.
- Every place setting should be set identically to achieve a consistent look.
- The width of each place setting should be about 18 inches.

Different types of restaurants require different types of covers or place settings. Typically, the cover is preset, with the napkin centered between the flatware. After diners are seated and place their napkins on their laps, their dishes are placed between the flatware.

In fine dining, the cover must be arranged in a specific way:
- On square or rectangular tables, the bottom of the plate, napkin, and flatware should be placed in a straight line, 1 inch from the edge of the table.

FIGURE 20-6
Hollowware
Hollowware includes silver candlesticks, cake stands, platters, and coffee pots.
Predicting *In what type of restaurant would you see hollowware like this?*

FIGURE 20-7
Cleaning a Table
Wait staff using a crumber to remove crumbs from the table.
Predicting *Why would wait staff clean the table when guests were still at the table?*

Working in a Restaurant ▶ 653

▲ Diner

▲ Casual/Family-Style Restaurant

▲ Bistro

▲ Banquet, Set for Four Courses

▲ Fine Dining

- On round tables, the bottom of the plate, napkin, and flatware should be arranged in a straight line with the outermost edges of the cover 1 inch from the edge on either side.
- Cloth napkins can be placed to the right side of the place setting under the flatware on the right side. If the napkin is folded, it can be placed in the middle of the cover between the flatware (if there is no plate) or in the middle of the plate.
- Forks should be on the left; knife and spoon on the right.
- Put only flatware that will be necessary for the meal at each place setting. (Some fine restaurants place no than four pieces of flatware at each place setting at a time. If more flatware is required for additional courses, the wait staff places it in the proper place just before it is needed.)
- Flatware should be arranged in order of use; the pieces needed first are placed on the outside.
- Knives should be placed with the cutting edge toward the rim of the plate. Spoons are placed on the right side of the knife, facing up.
- The butter plate should be placed on the left side of the main course plate and 1 inch from the edge of the table.
- The cup and saucer should be placed on the right of the plate above the flatware; the handle should face to the right, angled slightly forward, toward the diner, and positioned to easily slip into the diner's finger.
- Glassware should be placed to the right of the plate in line with the dinner knife. If additional glasses are necessary, they should be added to the right, angled further from the diner.
- Fine restaurants place any flatware needed for dessert only after the other dishes and utensils are cleared and the table is brushed of crumbs.
- For banquets, dessert flatware should be placed above the plate.

Reading Checkpoint *What is a cover?*

Cleaning Service Utensils

Proper cleaning of service utensils prevents spreading of germs and bacteria, which can thrive in restaurant settings where food is ever-present and attention to detail can lose its priority in the hectic pace of kitchens and dining rooms. Government regulations concerning hygiene are rigorous for restaurants. All personnel should be well informed about them—and should comply with them.

Eating Spaghetti

During the eighteenth and nineteenth centuries, poor people ate spaghetti and other pasta with their hands. When the four-pronged fork was invented by Gennaro Spadaccini, a court official in Naples, pasta became a food fit for royalty as well—because now the royalty could eat it without a loss of dignity.

Today, according to Italian rules of etiquette, pasta and sauce should be served on flat dinner plates, not in a bowl. The proper utensil with which to eat pasta is a fork. A spoon is typically not offered with pasta, unless the sauce is very thin (such as is the case with some seafood sauces). The goal in eating pasta is to twirl a moderate amount of pasta around the prongs of the fork, using the curve of the plate to help twirl the pasta onto the fork.

Research

Research the history of the fork. Explain how people ate before the fork was invented. List a few different kinds of forks and their purposes. Describe how the invention of the fork changed table manners.

Proper cleaning is also important when considering customers. Nothing turns customers away and spreads bad publicity faster than dirty conditions. Dining room floors, walls, windows, and doors should be kept spotless, as should all furniture and tableware. This includes condiment dishes, sugar bowls, cruets, breadbaskets, ash trays, and candleholders.

Washing Tableware Restaurants must comply with local health department regulations for dishwasher water temperature and other standards designed to assure sanitary cleaning conditions.

The high water temperature of any dishwasher is enough to kill bacteria, but the process doesn't automatically guarantee spotless glassware and dishes unless dirty tableware is handled properly before being loaded. Enough detergent should be used and chemical desanitizers can be added during the rinse cycle. At the end of the day, dishwashing areas, spray devices, and rinse pipes should be dismantled and cleaned thoroughly with hot water. Keep the following guidelines in mind when washing tableware:

- China. China should be scraped and rinsed by hand before it is loaded in the dishwasher. This should be followed by a pre-wash rinsing cycle in the dishwasher. For the best circulation of detergent and water, avoid overloading the dishwasher. China with any chips or cracks should be thrown out and replaced.
- Glassware. Before machine washing, it is important to spot-wash glassware by hand to eliminate lipstick marks or any other resistant traces of use. Glassware should be checked again when it is unloaded for any remaining marks.
- Flatware. Rinse and presoak flatware before spreading it out and washing it on a wire rack in the dishwasher. Bunching flatware together in rack sections may prevent water from entirely surrounding each piece and adequately disinfecting and washing it. After washing, flatware should be air-dried and stored to avoid prolonged contact with any airborne contaminants.

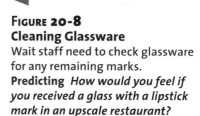

FOCUS ON SANITATION

Customer's Rights
Cleanliness is the right of every customer. Restaurants are obligated to ensure the public's well-being as long as their doors are open.

◄

FIGURE 20-8
Cleaning Glassware
Wait staff need to check glassware for any remaining marks.
Predicting *How would you feel if you received a glass with a lipstick mark in an upscale restaurant?*

Polishing No amount of automatic dishwashing will result in spotless glassware or sparkling flatware. Rinse aids added to the machine along with detergent will help, but only hand polishing removes resistant water spots from glassware and tarnish from silverware.

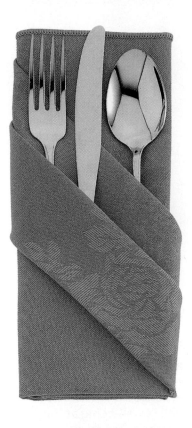

- **Glassware.** If local regulations permit, clean glassware can be exposed to steam and wiped with a clean wiping cloth to polish. The steam can be applied with a steam wand, or racks of clean glassware can be set over chafing dishes filled with steaming water.
- **Flatware.** Stainless-steel utensils should be dipped in hot water and wiped dry with a clean wiping cloth to polish. Place on clean linen napkins and store in closed drawers.
- **Silverware.** Tarnish-removing agents are the best method for polishing silver. However, if these agents are used, the silverware must be thoroughly washed afterwards to remove any trace of chemicals. The silverware should then be wiped with a clean wiping cloth. To store for daily use, place silverware on linen napkins in closed drawers. If silver is not used every day, it should be placed in bags specifically designed for silverware or in airtight containers.

Reading Checkpoint *Why do you need to spot-wash glassware?*

20.2 ASSESSMENT

Reviewing Concepts

1. What is a cover?
2. Why do you need to spot-wash glassware?

Critical Thinking

3. **Predicting** What would happen if flatware were not presoaked before washing?
4. **Comparing/Contrasting** How does a banquet cover differ from the cover of a fine restaurant?
5. **Applying Concepts** On which side of the plate is the fork?
6. **Applying Concepts** On which side of the plate is the butter plate?
7. **Applying Concepts** Where is glassware placed in relation to the plate and the flatware?

Test Kitchen

Working in teams of three, and without viewing other teams, set covers for a family style restaurant, a four-course banquet, and a fine restaurant. Each team member is responsible for setting one of the covers. Compare each team's covers.

Table Settings

Research the history of table settings in a specific nation at a specific time. Focus on the connection between the way the table was set, the types of dinners enjoyed by that particular society, and what this says about the society as a whole.

READING PREVIEW

Key Concepts

- Identifying styles of service
- Serving guests

Vocabulary

- American service
- brunch service
- buffet service
- butler service
- cafeteria service
- counter service
- dupes
- English service
- family service
- French service
- platter service
- room service
- Russian service
- service style
- side-table service
- table service
- take-out service

"**A** dining room professional knows how to work with the kitchen to pace the meal properly according to the needs of the guest. "

— Bill Guillfoyle
The Culinary Institute of America

Service Styles

In the culinary world, when we talk about **service style** or **table service**, we are concerned with how food and drink is delivered to the guest.

Common Service Styles in America There are many styles for table service. Sometimes a combination of styles is used. Some are more formal than others. The four most common types of table service in America are American service, buffet service, counter service, and take-out service.

- **American Service.** The predominant service style in American restaurants, including casual restaurants and banquets, is **American service**. In this style, food is fully prepared and plated on individual serving plates in the kitchen and brought to the dining room. Tables are fully preset. Dishes are served by the right hand at the right side of the guest. This leaves the server's left hand free to carry other plates. American service allows for quick distribution of food by relatively few servers.

▲
FIGURE 20-9
Buffet Service
Buffets offer diners a wide variety of foods to sample.
Drawing Conclusions *How can you control portion size at buffets?*

- **Buffet Service.** Practical for serving a large number of people over a period of time, **buffet service** features servers who stand behind long tables spread with dishes. Servers may serve guests, or guests may serve themselves. This style of service allows for a great variety of dishes. The buffet is a good solution for feeding groups of people meeting in conference rooms or catered dining rooms because it offers a great deal of choice, while permitting guests to mingle. Service requirements are limited, making this method of service economical in terms of labor costs. On the other hand, because guests pay a set price for all they can eat, food cost can be very high. Waste and excess can be controlled if servers, rather than guests, dish out portions. Another possible disadvantage of this system can be the compromised quality of the food if it is left out for a long time. Foods can dry out when exposed to the heat of a chafing dish or steam table. Care must be taken to offer foods that won't spoil or lose their freshness easily when left on the buffet table.

- **Brunch Service.** An efficient way to offer a great deal of choice in a leisurely fashion, **brunch service** is a combination of a buffet-style breakfast and lunch with American service. This system requires an efficient service staff to keep the dining room clean and organized.

- **Cafeteria Service.** Restaurants featuring **cafeteria service** typically offer self-service where diners choose their own foods from behind a counter or barrier. Servers dish out controlled portions from the other side. Guests carry their dishes on trays to their tables, eliminating the need for any servers in the dining room. As with brunch service, the cafeteria method of food service requires service staff to keep the dining area clean, even if customers bring their dishes to a cleanup station or throw out disposables themselves.

- **Counter Service.** The purpose of **counter service** is to provide fast and easy dining away from home. A profitable alternative to table dining, counter service provides fast and easy turnover of guests. As long as condiments are within easy reach of counter stools, diners can easily help themselves. Servers require fewer steps to take and deliver orders, making it easy to serve customers. However, a counter filled with diners can create a hectic situation as servers try to take, place, pick up, and deliver orders in a hurry. Some upscale restaurants have counters where guests can sit casually and have a beverage and appetizers before dinner—or even eat their dinner at the counter.

- **Room Service.** Widely used in hotels, **room service** requires speed and efficiency. The server delivers food to the room quickly to keep it warm and fresh. Every part of the setting and detail of the meal must be delivered at once.

- **Take-Out Service.** Italy, France, and other European countries have had popular, high-quality **take-out service** traditions for years where people buy prepared food as an alternative to cooking at home. Take-out has become wildly popular in America in recent decades. Many people prefer to purchase food to take to their offices or to bring home, rather than eating in a restaurant setting. Where once only the take-out restaurants or casual restaurants offered take-out, now even upscale restaurants sometimes provide take-out menus and options such as food delivery and Internet ordering. Take-out service is sometimes referred to as home-meal replacement service.

Common International Service Styles Some of the more common international service styles are seen in a variety of American restaurants. For example, a casual restaurant might offer a family service style. A fine restaurant might offer a streamlined side-table service. It helps to be aware of all the varieties of service styles.

- **French Service.** Established in the court of Louis XIV in about 1680, **French service** is an elaborate style of service based on serving a meal in three courses: the first, the second, and the dessert. The first course, or the entrée, was timed for the entrance of guests into the dining room. (The French word "entrée" is derived from "enter."). For both of the first two courses, hot dishes were brought into the dining room on silver platters and placed on a side table. Many dishes were prepared or finished off by a specialized server at the table. After each course, the guests left the table while it was cleared, cleaned, and reset for the following course. Servers served courses at the right side of the place setting. The system is based on a clear division of labor, with detailed tasks assigned to carefully trained servers. The first two courses were made up of as many as 40 dishes—including soup, meat, and fish.

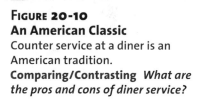

FIGURE 20-10
An American Classic
Counter service at a diner is an American tradition.
Comparing/Contrasting *What are the pros and cons of diner service?*

CULINARY DIVERSITY

Service Traditions

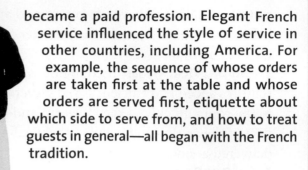

Before the French Revolution, French inns and taverns served simple food often consisting of one dish, usually a stew or plain roasted or boiled meats without sauces. Elaborate dining was the privilege of the wealthy, who retained skilled cooks and servants to cater to them in their homes.

In the 1800s, after the French Revolution, cooks who once worked for noble households brought their skills to restaurants and began to experiment with sauces and to offer more types of food. As the food in restaurants became more refined, so did the service. Where once waiters were low-paid servants for the aristocracy, restaurant service became a paid profession. Elegant French service influenced the style of service in other countries, including America. For example, the sequence of whose orders are taken first at the table and whose orders are served first, etiquette about which side to serve from, and how to treat guests in general—all began with the French tradition.

Research

Research the sequence and manner in which meals are served in various types of restaurants in France today. Describe the relationship between the waiter and the guest in these types of restaurants.

▲ *Platter service*

French service is elegant and leisurely, but it requires costly equipment and a large number of highly trained servers.

- **Side-Table Service.** With **side-table service**, dishes are prepared or finished off at the table. This style of service requires a mobile cart, a burner or heat source for cooking, and a large silver dome for covering food to keep it warm. This special type of French service is theatrical and elegant but labor-intensive and time-consuming. When used today, this service is usually streamlined. Cooking is not done at the table; the food is delivered in covered platters and plated at the side table. In this type of service, dishes are served at the right side of the guest.

- **Russian Service.** Typically used for banquets, **Russian service** is less elaborate than French service, but is elegant and requires skill from the wait staff. The server delivers completely prepared hot food immediately from the kitchen in large platters, quickly but with some ceremony. The idea is to serve guests freshly cooked dishes at the table without the ritual of plating at the side table, saving time without sacrificing quality. Using the right hand, the server places empty plates at the guest's right. After delivering the food to the table in a large platter, the server serves each guest from the left side, using the right hand. This is in contrast to other styles of service where dishes are served at the right side of the guest. Before the food is served from the platter, it is shown to the guest with a serving fork balanced over a serving spoon. This style of service is also called **platter service**.

- **English Service.** Usually offered in restaurants, **English service** is for special groups or private dinners. The table is fully preset and food is delivered on platters to the dining room. The serving dishes are placed on the table or on a table nearby. A server or the host serves soup from a tureen, carves meat, and serves food from the platter to the guests.

- **Family Service.** Probably the most efficient form of table service, **family service** is similar to English service except that food is placed on the table in serving dishes and guests help themselves. Some casual restaurants feature family service to create a homey atmosphere.

- **Butler Service.** Similar to Russian service, **butler service** also has the server bring the platter to the table. However, with butler service, a serving spoon and fork are provided so guests can serve themselves. The server stands at the left of each guest, holding the platter with both hands, moving from guest to guest.

▲
FIGURE 20-11
Butler Service
Guests make their own selections from a platter.
Drawing Conclusions *What type of food might be difficult to serve this way?*

 **Reading Checkpoint** *Describe four common American service styles.*

Serving Guests

In Italy and in France, restaurant service is considered a profession, not just a job. The server should always be professional, no matter what style of restaurant. This means learning the skills of the restaurant service trade and practicing them until confidence is acquired. A server becomes a seamless connection between the dining room and the kitchen. Servers make guests feel welcome and comfortable. They anticipate guests' needs while keeping a respectful distance. Policies for service staff differ from restaurant to restaurant, but these guidelines apply to most restaurants.

Starting the Meal
- Pull out chairs for guests when they are being seated. If they have to leave the table, pull out the chair again for them.
- Greet guests with a smile once they are seated and attend to them as soon as possible.
- Acknowledge children and bring them bread or other designated food at once; a contented child makes a contented parent.

FOCUS ON SAFETY

Tiny Guests
Before offering a booster chair for a small child, check that the chair is clean, that its straps function properly, and that the chair has all its parts.

Writing the Order

- Each restaurant has its own system of numbered guest checks and **dupes** (duplicates orders) for passing orders from the dining room to the back of the house. There may be separate dupes for appetizer and dessert stations. Guest checks need to be very clear, because many people will see them, including the waiter, the person entering the order, the kitchen staff, the guest, the cashier, the manager, and the bookkeeper.
- Certain abbreviations are usually specified by the restaurant for food and beverages.
- Unless some guests volunteer their orders while others are still deciding, start with the ladies, older first, then older gentlemen, followed by other gentlemen, and children last.
- Write down the order for each person in the order in which it will be served. Go over each order with every guest before leaving the table to be sure you have made no mistakes.
- In most restaurants, only one check is written for each table unless guests request otherwise.
- If an order is continued on a second guest check, the first check should be subtotaled and stapled to the second.

▲ *Guest check*

Serving Water and Bread

- Ask guests if they want water immediately after they sit down.
- Fill water glasses as soon as they are half empty.
- If a glass becomes greasy or otherwise soiled from a guest handling it during the course of the meal, replace it with a fresh one.
- Bring bread as soon as possible according to the restaurant's established procedures. Serve from the guest's left onto the butter plate at the left side of the place setting. Lift the bread with a serving fork on the bottom and a spoon on top.

Serving Beverages

- Guests should be asked if they want something to drink as soon as they are seated.
- Take and serve beverage orders in the same sequence as for the food and dessert courses.
- Bring beverages within five minutes after taking the orders.
- Never serve alcoholic beverages to a minor. Breaking the law can cause the restaurant to lose its liquor license and be faced with fines.
- Place beverages on a beverage tray in the order that they should be served. Carry the beverage tray on your left palm.
- Use cocktail napkins only if there is no tablecloth.
- Keep the table clear of unwanted glasses.

▲ *Serving water*

Presenting the Menu

- Mention any specials of the day and inform guests about any dishes on the menu that are not available. This prevents disappointment later.
- Be informed about the menu and any specials of the day so

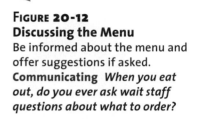

FIGURE 20-12
Discussing the Menu
Be informed about the menu and offer suggestions if asked.
Communicating *When you eat out, do you ever ask wait staff questions about what to order?*

you can answer any questions. Provide details, such as "we make our own soups fresh every day."
- Be prepared to make vegetarian suggestions and to answer any questions about how the kitchen can prepare dishes for people with special diets.
- Be diplomatic but straightforward if asked for suggestions or opinions. Guests appreciate honesty.
- Pass the menus from the right side, with the right hand, after any beverages are brought.

Serving Food

- Anticipate guests' needs.
- Serve orders without delay to make guests feel they are being taken care of and to prevent food from overheating.
- Serve women first and children last.
- Serve guests from their right, with the right hand, unless the restaurant or style of service requires a different approach.
- Check tables after serving courses to see if anything more is needed.
- Keep the table clear of empty plates.
- Pay attention to tables even when you are not serving them directly.

▲ *Pouring coffee from the right*

FOCUS ON SANITATION

Kitchen Cleanliness

For good hygiene, partially empty creamers should be removed, emptied, and sent to the bus tray along with other dirty dishes when a table is cleared.

- Be available as a server, but keep a professional distance when speaking to guests. This means not standing closer than 3 feet and making no personal conversation.
- Be a team player; everything runs more smoothly in a cooperative environment, especially in a hectic dining room.

Course Sequence

- The order in which various courses are served varies based on the type of food, the restaurant, and the country.
- Often the course sequence will be determined by guests' preferences. Guests may order two appetizers, for example, with one being used as their main course. Others may choose to have a salad after the meal, while other guests want the salad before the main course.
- Regardless of course sequence, clear empty and soiled dishes and flatware after each course.
- Based on each guest's order, replace soiled dishes and flatware with appropriate dishes and flatware for the next course.
- If there are crumbs on the table, use a crumber to clean the table. Crumbing is done starting on the left side of the place setting, moving to the right side from guest to guest, moving clockwise.
- Separate dessert menus are usually passed out before the last course.

After-Dinner Beverages

- Take orders for tea, coffee, and other after-dinner beverages only after the table is cleared entirely and decrumbed.
- Bring appropriate cups, saucers, and utensils before serving any beverages.
- Be sure creamers are full to the top when delivered to the table and check them for refilling if guests linger.
- Be sure water for tea is boiling hot so tea will steep properly.
- Pour or serve all beverages from the right.

Presenting the Check

- Tally the check only after asking guests if they desire anything more.
- When guests are ready for the check, deliver it in the way specified by the restaurant. Many restaurants have a special folder for this, with a clear pocket inside to accommodate a credit card.
- Always include a pen when returning the check with a credit card form.

Parting Company

- Service staff should make a point of thanking guests and offering a warm good-bye such as, "Thank you for coming, we hope we'll see you again soon."
- Servers should take care not to make guests feel rushed to leave by anything that is said or done, directly or indirectly.
- However, there are times when the front of the house needs to seat guests who have been waiting for a table and seated parties have long since finished their meal or when tables linger long after it is time for the service staff to go home. Notifying guests that have finished their meal that the restaurant is backed up is a delicate matter that is usually best left to the maître d'. Restaurant policy differs, depending on the type of establishment and what the customers are paying for a meal.

BASIC CULINARY SKILLS

Service Sequence for Maître d' (Md), Server (S), and Runner (R)

1. Welcome guests warmly. (Md)
2. Hand out menus. (Md)
3. Greet guests cheerfully. (S)
4. Fill water glasses. (R)
5. Take beverage order. (S)
6. Enter beverage order. (S)
7. Serve water and beverages. (S)
8. Bring bread and butter or oil. (R)
9. Take food order and bring it to kitchen or order station. (S)
10. Deliver dupe to dupe board or station. (S)
11. Place flatware for first course, if it is not already on the table. (S)
12. Serve first course. (S)
13. Check to see if guests need anything else or have any requests. (S)
14. Clear first course. (R)
15. Reset tableware for next course. (R)
16. Deliver next course. (S)
17. Check to see if guests need anything else or have any requests. (S)
18. Clear second course. (R)
19. Crumb, and remove salt and pepper. (R)
20. Present dessert menus. (S)
21. Take order for dessert and after-dinner beverages. (S)
22. Enter dessert order. (S)
23. Reset tableware for dessert. (R)
24. Serve after-dinner beverages. (S)
25. Serve desserts. (S)
26. Refill hot beverages. (S)
27. Print check. (S)
28. Clear desserts. (R)
29. Present check. (S)
30. Pick up payment from table and process payment. (S)
31. Return receipt or change to table. (S)
32. Thank guests and show them out. (S)

FIGURE 20-13 ▶
Presenting the Check
At this restaurant, the check is delivered in a leather folder with complimentary chocolates.
Predicting *What are the effects of bringing a check too soon or making guests wait too long for it?*

Regular customers may become offended by being asked to leave, no matter how long they have lingered. More casual restaurants that depend on volume for profit are less likely to allow guests to linger if others are waiting to be seated.

 **Reading Checkpoint**

Why should service staff be careful not to give the impression to guests that other customers are waiting for a table?

20.3 ASSESSMENT

Reviewing Concepts

1. Describe four common American service styles.
2. Why should service staff be careful not to give the impression to guests that other customers are waiting for a table?

Critical Thinking

3. **Predicting** What would happen if service staff waited until asked by guests to refill water glasses or bread baskets?
4. **Comparing/Contrast** What is a dupe?
5. **Applying Concepts** Which should come first, taking the order or serving water?
6. **Applying Concepts** From which side should you pass the menu?
7. **Applying Concepts** Unless a guest volunteers an order, in what sequence should you typically take orders?

Test Kitchen

Working in teams of three, make a simple hot dish. When it is prepared, one team member acts as a runner, carrying the dish to a stand that is at least 100 feet away. Another team member acts as the server, serving the dish to a third team member, who acts as the customer. Evaluate the correctness of the service.

SOCIAL STUDIES

Descriptive Writing

Research the order in which courses are served in three traditions: Indian, Chinese, and French. Write a description of the way the meal is brought to the table. Compare the traditions.

Handling Complaints & Problems

READING PREVIEW

Key Concepts

- Handling customer complaints
- Handling problems

Vocabulary

- accident report
- walkout

> **❝I**f you can communicate with your guests and take steps to nip problems in the bud, you can turn a potentially bad situation into something positive. **❞**
>
> **– Jennifer Purcell**
> Apple Pie Bakery Café,
> The Culinary Institute
> of America

Handling Customer Complaints

Handling problems in a restaurant almost always involves communicating in an appropriate way. It doesn't matter if the customer has a problem with the restaurant or the restaurant has a problem with the customer—the way to handle the problem is by communicating appropriately.

Customer complaints are inevitable in any service business, but the restaurant business is probably the ultimate service business. Not only does a food-service establishment concern itself with providing tasty and nourishing food, it also promises to deliver it from kitchen to table with efficiency and style. There are two important steps in handling any potential customer complaints:

- Anticipating problems
- Addressing complaints quickly

Anticipating Problems The best way to avoid complaints that may arise is to prevent them before they happen. Just as a good driver practices defensive behavior behind the wheel to prevent accidents, so the server practices good professional habits to assure customer satisfaction. Here are some techniques the professional service should keep in mind:

- Keep water glasses and bread baskets full.
- Communicate with guests. Ask if they need anything more after the food is delivered and then retreat to a place that is inconspicuous but from which you can still observe activity in the dining room.
- Keep an eye on your tables even after they have been served. Watch for any signs that your tables are having problems.
- If a guest gestures to speak with you, go to the table immediately. If you are not able to help them immediately, ask another server to go in your place or say that you will return quickly (and then do so).

Figure 20-14
Keep an Eye on Your Tables
Communicate with your guests and be aware of their needs.
Inferring *What kinds of problems can be avoided by being attentive to the needs of guests?*

Addressing Complaints Quickly When something goes wrong, a professional server does two things:

- Acknowledges the problem and apologizes
- Resolves the problem as quickly as possible

Guests in a restaurant are entitled to satisfactory food and good service. Customers often don't feel comfortable complaining about unsatisfactory food, beverages, or service. They often remain silent and dissatisfied, but silent guests will usually not return to the restaurant. Again, communication is the key.

When guests do complain, apologize for their inconvenience or discomfort and show that you are genuinely interested in seeing to it that the situation is remedied. By communicating in this way, you have a much better chance that the guest will ultimately be satisfied and consider returning.

Here are some common complaints that may arise, and the ways in which a professional server is expected to remedy them. Of course, remedies are always carried out based on the restaurant's policy, but restaurants are in business to please customers. Most restaurants would rather appease guests than risk losing customers.

- **Miscooked Food.** Undercooked, overcooked, or improperly cooked food should be returned to the kitchen to be cooked further or replaced with properly cooked food. Depending on the restaurant's policies, the server may ask if the guest would prefer to select a different dish from the menu.

- **Foreign Object in the Food.** Incidents such as a fly or a hair in the food are not pleasant, but they sometimes happen despite routine precautions. In such a case, the server should apologize at once and offer to bring a new or different dish without drawing attention to the table.

- **Food Temperature.** Food that is served at the wrong temperature should be redone or replaced.

- **Dining Room Temperature.** If guests feel the room temperature is too hot, too cold, or too drafty, ask management if an adjustment can be made. If this is not possible, ask the guests if they would prefer moving to a table in a different part of the room where they might be more comfortable.

- **Lighting.** Lighting is an important part of the design plan of any restaurant because the quality and amount of light affects the mood of customers. Sometimes the lighting in restaurants is not sufficient to enable customers to read menus or see their food properly. In such a case, table lamps or candlesticks should be provided.

Figure 20-15
Potential Problem
A customer might have trouble reading the menu in a dimly lit restaurant.
Solving Problems *What do you do if a customer complains about the lighting or décor in a restaurant?*

Handling Problems

Cleaning Spills Any spills at the table should be cleaned up immediately. Minor spills should be absorbed with a clean cloth and covered with a clean table napkin. Large spills may require replacing the soiled tablecloth with a fresh one. In this case, the server should get help from other service staff to get the table back to order as quickly as possible.

To replace a tablecloth after a large spill, transfer all the objects that were on the soiled part of the tablecloth to the other side. Roll up the soiled half of the tablecloth and then place half of the fresh one in its place. Move all the objects on the table to the new tablecloth and remove the soiled tablecloth completely. Then finish spreading out the clean tablecloth. Finally, replace all the china, glassware, and flatware to their proper places.

A server responsible for spills on a customer's clothing should offer a sincere apology immediately and offer to pay for dry cleaning costs. The maître d' should discuss details for the dry cleaning.

FIGURE 20-16 ▶
Handling Spills
Replace a tablecloth after a large spill.
Predicting *How would it make guests feel if you quickly and professionally replaced the tablecloth after one of the guest spilled something?*

Emergencies The maître d' should be trained to calmly and competently handle a serious health problem or physical injury to a customer. The most important thing is to attend to the immediate needs of the guest, calling for emergency help if necessary. You may need to file an **accident report**, which is a written description of what took place, including the names of the guest, any server involved, the date, and the time.

"The show must go on" is an expression from show business. In many ways the restaurant business is like show business. The kitchen is the equivalent to backstage and the performance takes place in the dining room.

Natural events can cause electricity failure, or the sickness of a chef or other critical kitchen personnel can create chaos in the smooth running of business. Many personnel depend on the restaurant for their livelihood, so it isn't appropriate to close the restaurant unless absolutely necessary. In addition, closing the restaurant very often can cause a restaurant to lose customers permanently. Restaurants should try to construct contingency plans for such events, unlikely as they may be, so they will be prepared if an emergency happens.

Noisy Guests A restaurant is a naturally convivial place where people gather to enjoy themselves. It is also a place where people go to relax and, sometimes, to have privacy. But what if some guests want to have a noisy party while others want peace and quiet? Sometimes guests become so loud that others can't enjoy themselves.

If customers complain about the behavior of other guests, service professionals should be prepared to handle the situation without making either party angry. Thoughtless guests who disturb others should be tactfully asked to quiet down. If they continue to be loud, they should be calmly—but firmly—asked to leave before the situation gets out of hand.

Children and babies can raise the sound level in an otherwise quiet restaurant. Children's toys that beep and buzz can also be a distraction to other guests. The front desk should be stocked with coloring books and crayons or other such playthings for children that will keep them occupied quietly.

FIGURE 20-17
Quiet Children
Coloring books and crayons are a good distraction for children until the food arrives.
Applying Concepts *Are certain types of restaurants better options for families with children?*

Cell Phones, Pagers, and Electronic Devices Today many people carry cell phones or pagers. The public is accustomed to hearing them, but in a restaurant setting, they can be disturbing to other guests. However, doctors, emergency workers, and certain other professionals must answer their devices.

If an electronic device rings, the service staff should tactfully ask the customer to take their calls in the lobby or some other part of the restaurant where it will not disturb others. Only after repeated requests, when a guest persists in violating other customers' rights to tranquility, should the maitre d' ask the guest to leave.

Nonpayment Problems Wait staff is responsible for recording orders, tallying checks properly, and making sure check gets paid. If a customer has had a problem with the food and refuses to pay, the maître d' should handle the situation, not the server.

Cash or Credit Card Problems What happens if the server brings the check to the table only to learn that the guest is not able to pay it? A restaurant has a similar problem if a customer's credit card is declined. These are difficult situations for restaurants. Wait staff should notify the maître d' immediately. Restaurants typically have policies in place about such problems and the maître d' will resolve the issue accordingly.

Walkouts Customers have been known to leave their tables without paying their bills. If a restaurant is very hectic, an unpaid bill at an abandoned table may go unnoticed until it is too late. In the restaurant business, this unfortunate occurrence is called a **walkout**. This problem can be prevented. The dining room staff needs to be alert to this potential problem at all times. If someone starts to walk out without paying, wait staff should not try to approach the guest alone to avoid an unpleasant or even dangerous reaction by the guest. The maître d' should be notified and any decision to call the police should be made by management.

Customer Theft Thefts of flatware, china, and other objects is a problem with which most restaurants struggle. Guests who are seen pocketing or otherwise stealing restaurant property should be reported to the maître d, who will make the decision to confront the perpetrator.

Robbery No establishment can anticipate a robbery. In such an event, it is crucial to remain calm and to avoid eye contact with the perpetrator. Do not make any heroic attempts to intervene. If such an attempt backfired, it could endanger the lives of guests and restaurant personnel. Do your best to remember any details about the robbers and the robbery that can later help police in solving the crime. Restaurants typically protect themselves from crime losses by taking out insurance.

 **Reading Checkpoint** What is a walkout?

20.4 ASSESSMENT

Reviewing Concepts

1. What are the two things a professional server should do when something goes wrong?
2. What is a walkout?

Critical Thinking

3. **Drawing Conclusions** Why should a server avoid drawing attention to a table that has found a foreign object in the food?
4. **Applying Concepts** What should a server do if a diner says that the food she received was improperly cooked?
5. **Predicting** What could happen if service staff tried to take charge and protect restaurant patrons during a robbery?
6. **Drawing Conclusions** Why is it necessary to apologize for a complaint, even if you have acknowledged it?
7. **Solving Problems** What should you do if a guest asks you to resolve a problem in a way that is contrary to the restaurant's policies?

Test Kitchen

Divide into teams of 4. Each team member will pick a role: chef, server, maître d', and customer. The chef will select and cook a dish that is served by the server to the customer. The customer will find a reason to complain. The server will bring in the maître d' to resolve the issue. The server will return the dish to the chef, who will make the correction. The server will then present the dish to the customer again and the maître d' will check that everything is acceptable to the customer. Evaluate the interaction.

SOCIAL STUDIES

Restaurant Etiquette

Use the Internet to research sites about restaurant etiquette. Describe some of the most common mistakes people make and explain how to correctly respond to the situation.

Review and Assessment

Reviewing Content

Choose the letter that best answers the question or completes the statement.

1. The maître d' is the person responsible for
   a. explaining the menu to guests and taking orders
   b. running the restaurant
   c. running the back of the house
   d. running the front of the house

2. The captain is the person responsible for
   a. explaining the menu to guests and taking orders
   b. running the restaurant
   c. running the back of the house
   d. running the front of the house

3. The front waiter
   a. is another name for the bus person
   b. is another name for the runner
   c. is another name for the server
   d. assists the maître d' in answering the telephone

4. A sous-chef
   a. runs the back of the house
   b. is the executive's principal assistant
   c. runs the front of the house
   d. is responsible for sautéed dishes

5. A fixed seating plan
   a. has no more than six chairs per table
   b. requires customers to pay for their meal prior to being seated
   c. allows customers to be seated at any time
   d. has set meal times (such as at 6 p.m., 8 p.m., and 10 p.m.)

6. In the restaurant business, a cover is
   a. a complete place setting for one person
   b. an extra bus person
   c. an extra chef
   d. an extra server

7. A walkout is
   a. another name for a bus person
   b. another name for a server
   c. a customer who leaves without paying
   d. the person who greets guests at the door of a restaurant

Understanding Concepts

8. When something goes wrong, what should a professional server do?

9. From which direction should a server typically serve guests?

10. In most American restaurants, moving from left to right, how would you set the following silverware: knife, regular fork, salad fork, and spoon?

11. In the restaurant trade, what is the front of the house?

12. In the restaurant trade, what does it mean when you say a restaurant has a reservation policy?

Critical Thinking

13. **Recognizing Patterns** What is the rule for arranging flatware for a cover where, for example, there would be multiple types of forks?

14. **Comparing/Contrasting** What is the difference between a roundsman and a sous-chef?

Culinary Math

15. **Applying Concepts** You estimate that a fixed seating plan, with three seatings, averages 48 covers in an average night, with an average cover costing $42. You estimate that a continuous seating plan will average about 60 covers a night, with an average cost of $30. Which seating plan produces higher sales?

On the Job

16. **Communicating** What would you say to a group of noisy guests in your first discussion with them about their noise?

17. **Applying Concepts** You see that your customers are upset at the length of time it has taken to receive their check and are preparing to walk out without paying. What should you do?

Project 20: Restaurant Role Play

Answer these questions when your class works through Project 20.

- Which front-of-the-house role did you enjoy most?
- How did you feel when an irate customer complained to you?
- How important is teamwork in the front of the house?
- Which back-of-the-house role did you enjoy most?
- How did you feel when a dish was brought back because a customer had problems with it?
- How important is teamwork in the back of the house?
- How did the front of the house relate to the back of the house?

TEST PRACTICE

Choose the letter that best answers the question or completes the statement.

1. The chef de cuisine is the
   A   executive chef
   B   sous-chef
   C   second chef
   D   prep chef

2. The expediter
   A   greets customers
   B   takes customers' complaints
   C   accepts dining room orders and communicates them to the station chefs
   D   fills in for absent chefs or assists chefs in other stations

3. A roundsman
   A   greets customers
   B   takes customers' complaints
   C   accepts dining room orders and communicates them to the station chefs
   D   fills in for absent chefs or assists chefs in other stations

4. The poissonier
   A   prepares roasted meats
   B   prepares pastry
   C   prepares and cooks fish
   D   prepares grilled items

5. A dupe is
   A   a copy of an order used for passing orders to different stations in the kitchen
   B   an extra chef who fills in for other chefs
   C   an extra bus person who assists the server with a large order
   D   a customer who doesn't pay the check

6. The width of a cover should be about
   A   36 inches wide
   B   26 inches wide
   C   18 inches wide
   D   8 inches wide

7. How far from the edge of the table should you place the plate, napkin, and flatware?
   A   10 inches
   B   6 inches
   C   3 inches
   D   1 inch

8. How are spoons placed in American place settings?
   A   right side of knife, facing up
   B   right side of knife, facing down
   C   right side of fork, facing up
   D   left side of fork, facing down

9. Where should the cup and saucer be placed?
   A   centered above plate
   B   left side of plate, above flatware
   C   right side of plate, above flatware
   D   left side of plate, left of flatware

10. Where should the butter plate be placed?
    A   centered above plate
    B   left side of plate, above flatware
    C   left of plate and flatware, 1 inch from the edge of the table
    D   left of plate and flatware, 3 inches from the edge of the table

21.1 Planning the Menu

READING PREVIEW

Key Concepts

- Understand the purpose of a menu
- Identifying types of menus
- Planning the menu
- Organizing and designing a menu

Vocabulary

- à la carte menu
- California menu
- cyclical menu
- du jour menu
- entrée
- fixed menu
- limited menu
- market research
- menu
- mission statement
- modified à la carte menu
- prix fixe menu
- table d'hôte menu
- table tent menus

> **"A** menu is a powerful tool. It is a marketing and merchandising vehicle and assists the chef in organizing the day's work. **"**
>
> **– Tom Peer**
> The Culinary Institute of America

Purpose of a Menu

A **menu** is a list of food and drink choices available in a restaurant. A menu does much more than tell customers that steaks are flame-broiled or the chocolate cake is homemade. Menus are actually tools with two primary functions: planning and communication.

In most food-service operations, management plans the menu. However, in a hotel, the executive chef typically works with management to plan the menu. For chain restaurants, central management plans the menu. Generally, it is only in individual restaurants that are not part of a chain where a chef has the opportunity to plan a menu.

Menus as Planning Tools A menu is an important planning tool for a food-service operation because it affects every aspect of the operation's business. Typically, seven factors influence the choice of foods on a menu:

- **Customers' Needs and Expectations.** A menu should reflect the market for which it is intended. For example, a coffee shop in a neighborhood of office buildings will have a menu that offers sandwiches for people with little time for lunch. The menu for a restaurant at a beach resort will feature fresh seafood for tourists who expect seafood on the menu. The same idea of meeting a customer's needs applies to cafeterias. A hospital cafeteria will offer simple yet nutritious choices that appeal to the staff as well as the patients.

- **Prices.** Customers expect to pay according to the type of food and service they receive. Office workers who stop at a coffee shop usually want filling food and quick service without spending too much money. On the other hand, tourists on a vacation expect to splurge on a memorable meal, and they pay the check willingly.

- **Mission Statement.** A **mission statement** is a statement of an organization's goal. The mission statement of a restaurant or other food-service establishment must be clear before menu planning can begin. The mission statement must reflect customers' needs and expectations, as well as the price they would be willing to pay for their food. The mission of a Mexican restaurant might be to offer authentic foods of a particular region, while the mission of the snack bar at a health spa might be to offer only low-fat, healthy choices.

- **Type of Food Served.** The type of food on a menu is a direct reflection of the mission statement.

- **Service Style.** Fancy dishes or dishes that require special preparation at the table require a much different level of service than simpler food. Items on the menu determine what style of service will be required. In a cafeteria, for example, which requires minimal service, either the food is on display for easy self-service or it is plated by a minimal number of employees. Contrast that with an expensive restaurant, where several waiters sometimes work together on just one table.

- **Workers' Skills.** The food on a menu determines how many workers will be needed to

FIGURE 21-1
Lunch Counter
Looking at menu choices for a quick lunch.
Communicating *What would be an appropriate mission statement for this food-service establishment?*

prepare and serve the food. A French restaurant may require French chefs (or chefs who have trained in French cooking) and a wait staff who speaks French. A fast-food restaurant will require minimal training for staff.

- **Required Equipment.** The food on a menu determines what sort of equipment is required in the kitchen. A high-end steak restaurant may need an open-flame grill capable of using hickory wood, while a health spa snack bar might only need a couple of blenders to make shakes. When menus are modified, you also need to take the availability of equipment into consideration.

- **Competitors.** Before planning a menu, it is important to visit competing food-service operations that have the same mission as your business. You need to see what they are doing because you will inevitably be compared to them.

Menus as Communication Tools The menu is like a letter written directly to customers. It often provides such information as the location of your food establishment, the prices for food, the hours of operation, and sometimes even a history of the establishment. Menus offer an opportunity to go into detail about a new food item or a special cooking technique. Menus come in all sizes, but in terms of advertising, even the smallest menu can be as effective as a billboard for telling the public what you want them to know. Menus are essentially tools for communicating. A well-designed menu communicates in the following ways:

- **Informing Customers about Food Choices.** On its most basic level, a menu lists the food your establishment offers.

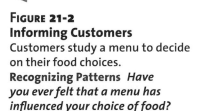

CHEF'S TIP

QUIET TIME

Take your time when creating a menu. Work in a quiet place where you can focus without interruptions. Test your concepts by asking for feedback from coworkers.

FOCUS ON NUTRITION

Healthy Eating

People have recently become interested in eating healthier meals. Keep this in mind when planning a menu. Include more fruits, vegetables, and whole grains. Focus on ways to reduce calories and fats. Try new cooking methods. It's all good for business—and good for your customers.

◄

FIGURE 21-2
Informing Customers
Customers study a menu to decide on their food choices.
Recognizing Patterns *Have you ever felt that a menu has influenced your choice of food?*

Customers want to know exactly what kind of food to expect. In a high-end restaurant with unusual ingredients or cooking methods, this might require a great deal of detail for each specific item. In a different sort of restaurant, you might not need to be very descriptive at all—just the name of the item will do. Not all descriptions need to be written. You could use a symbol to indicate a dish's degree of spiciness or whether a dish is vegetarian. It's helpful to think of your mission statement when describing individual food choices. You can even take some space on the menu to describe your mission in terms the customer will understand and appreciate.

- **Influencing Customer Choices.** A menu can influence customer choices in many ways. You can use the menu descriptions to tell customers about your establishment's most popular items. You can use the menu to list the day's special or featured items. Some restaurants use the menu to tell customers that a dish is recommended by the chef. Some menus use symbols, such as four stars, to indicate particularly popular dishes. Overall, the menu is a valuable selling tool when used effectively. It acts as not only a communication tool but also as a marketing tool. A menu influences what items customers choose, and ultimately affects their dining experience (as well as their decision to return or become a regular customer).

- **Creating an Impression.** First impressions matter. The menu is your chance to project an image for the restaurant. Decisions about the cover, the quality of paper, the use of artwork, and how the menu items are positioned all communicate a message to the customer. For example, a leather menu cover identifies a restaurant that wishes to be perceived as a higher-end, more formal, location. A menu that is printed on a paper placemat indicates that the dining experience will be more casual and probably much less expensive. A handwritten menu on a chalkboard with balloons attached indicates an informal setting where families might feel welcome, as does an oversized, plastic-covered menu with playfully named dishes.

 **Reading Checkpoint** *What are the two primary functions of a menu?*

Types of Menus

The type of menu chosen for a food establishment is based on a number of factors, including pricing considerations, location, type of customer, and hours of operation. There are many styles of menus. Some of the most popular types of menu are:

- À la carte and modified à la carte menus
- California menus
- Du jour menus
- Table d'hôte and prix fixe menus
- Fixed menus
- Cyclical menus
- Limited menus

À la Carte and Modified à la Carte Menus

An **à la carte menu** (AH LA CART) is a menu on which each food item or beverage is priced and served separately. Typically, an à la carte menu is for a specific meal, such as lunch or dinner. This type of menu is popular because customers can choose exactly what they want as main courses, side dishes, appetizers, salads, or desserts. The à la carte menu offers the freedom to mix and match according to individual taste. A customer may choose two appetizers and a salad rather than choosing a main course, for example. Hotels and upscale restaurants often use à la carte menus.

On a **modified à la carte menu**, appetizers and desserts are usually priced and served separately. Often the main course will include a soup or salad as well as a starch, vegetable, and possibly a beverage. This type of menu is often found in family-style restaurants.

California Menu

A **California menu** is a single menu listing breakfast, lunch, and dinner foods. It offers customers the freedom to choose any item at any time of day. California menus are especially popular with food-service establishments that are open 24 hours. They are also used for hotel room service.

Du Jour Menu

A **du jour menu** (DOO ZHOOR) lists food that is served only on that particular day. The next day, a different du jour menu will be offered. The words "du jour" are French for "of the day." Sometimes a restaurant has only one or two daily specials that are made just for that day. A soup du jour, for example, is a soup made just for that day. These restaurants will have a du jour menu in addition to their standard à la carte menu.

FIGURE 21-3
Du Jour Menu
A restaurant's specials of the day.
Drawing Conclusions *What is the best way to present a du jour menu, from both the restaurant's and the customer's point of view?*

❧ Today's Specials ❧
Friday, June 7

Appetizers

Louisiana Duck & Okra Gumbo	7.00
Oven-Roasted Shrimp with Rosemary White Beans	8.00

Entrees

Grilled Filet Mignon Medallions with Mushroom Sauce served with Roasted Garlic Mashed Potatoes	21.50
Seared Wild Salmon with Crispy Polenta, Goat Cheese and Glazed Baby Carrots	18.00

Desserts

Glazed Baked Apple on Puff Pastry with Vanilla Ice Cream	6.50
Hot Molten Chocolate Cake with Cherry Compote	7.00

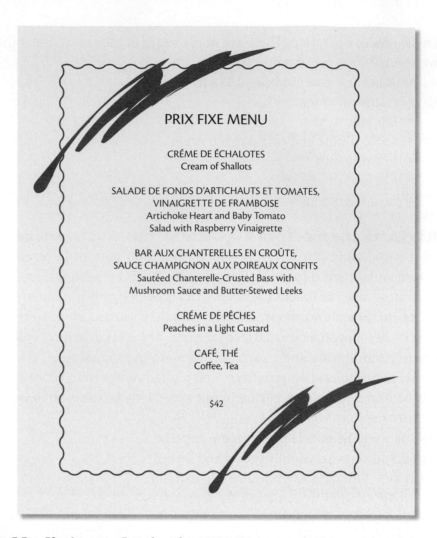

Prix fixe menu ▶

PRIX FIXE MENU

CRÉME DE ÉCHALOTES
Cream of Shallots

SALADE DE FONDS D'ARTICHAUTS ET TOMATES,
VINAIGRETTE DE FRAMBOISE
Artichoke Heart and Baby Tomato
Salad with Raspberry Vinaigrette

BAR AUX CHANTERELLES EN CROÛTE,
SAUCE CHAMPIGNON AUX POIREAUX CONFITS
Sautéed Chanterelle-Crusted Bass with
Mushroom Sauce and Butter-Stewed Leeks

CRÉME DE PÊCHES
Peaches in a Light Custard

CAFÉ, THÉ
Coffee, Tea

$42

Table d'Hôte and Prix Fixe Menus A **table d'hôte** (TAH-blah DOHT) **menu** offers a complete meal—from an appetizer to a dessert and often including a beverage—for a set price. Banquets often feature a table d'hôte menu. For example, diners might choose in advance from four meals: beef, chicken, fish, or vegetarian. Each meal would include an appetizer, a salad, rolls, a main course, a dessert, and coffee or tea. Individual meals might be priced separately.

A **prix fixe** (PREE FEEKS) **menu** is similar to the table d'hôte menu. A prix fixe menu typically offers a complete meal, often including a beverage, for a set price. Sometimes diners are offered a choice for one or more of the courses, and sometimes diners can choose, for a supplemental charge, a luxury item such as lobster or caviar. Most of the time the price of a prix fixe menu is relatively low because it reduces production costs by allowing the kitchen to operate at a set pace and flow. If the same dishes were ordered à la carte, the bill would be much higher. Both casual restaurants and upscale restaurants use prix fixe menus.

Fixed Menu A **fixed menu** offers the same items every day. Some customers like fixed menus because they continue to return to a restaurant for a favorite dish and would be disappointed if the dish weren't offered. For this reason, many neighborhood and ethnic restaurants use a fixed menu, although they often supplement the menu with du jour offerings.

Cyclical Menu A **cyclical menu** (SICK-li-cal) is written for a certain period of time and then it repeats itself. For example, a cyclical menu (also called a cycle menu) might repeat after three weeks, although the time between cycles may vary based on seasonal availability of ingredients and other factors. Some cyclical menus change four times a year, according to the seasons. Some change every week, so the same food is offered every Monday, different food is offered every Tuesday, and so on. Longer-term cyclical menus are particularly suited for institutions such as hospitals, schools, and cafeterias where the same people are being served each day. Weekly cyclical menus are particularly suited to family, casual, and neighborhood restaurants.

Limited A **limited menu** offers a limited range of choices to the customer. For example, a restaurant might offer a limited menu of four sandwiches, two soups, and a salad for lunch. A fast-food menu is an example of a limited menu. Limited menus make it easy to keep track of costs because there are typically fewer ingredients.

What are seven common types of menus?

CHEF'S TIP
COLLECT YOUR THOUGHTS
Whenever you have a menu idea, write it down and keep it in a file folder for future reference. Put any copies of menus that inspire you in the same file.

▲
FIGURE 21-4
Cyclical Menu
Colleges and institutions often have menus that are cyclical.
Drawing Conclusions *What period of time would you use as a cycle in your school cafeteria?*

Planning a Menu

When you write a menu, the goal is to please the customer as well as the owner. It is possible, with careful planning, to do both. Keep these four important considerations in mind when planning a menu:
- Type of place and customers
- Facility, staff, and equipment limitations
- Balance and variety
- Truthfulness

Type of Place and Customers It's important to understand your customers in relation to your type of food-service establishment. You need to include specific menu items that are appropriate for both your type of place and your type of customer. For example, if you have a family seafood restaurant, consider that some non-seafood items will make the menu more interesting and will offer an alternative for family members or other guests who may not want seafood. Likewise, if you are running the food service for a senior center, consider that they might welcome something entirely new on the menu. Seniors may not have an opportunity to eat anywhere else, and variations on the menu will add variety to their lives. A menu with a theme has specific characteristics. You could introduce a Mexican or other themed meal as a special surprise from time to time.

Understanding your place and your customer involves four additional factors:

- **Geography and Culture.** People have food preferences. Preferences are often connected to geography and culture. In an area of Minnesota populated by people with a Swedish heritage, hearty soups with root vegetables might be a winter preference. The same item in Florida might be unappealing.

- **Economics.** People need to feel they are getting their money's worth when they go out to eat. The price on a menu should reflect the value expected. If an expensive restaurant delivers a sense that exotic ingredients were used, the customer will be satisfied. If a budget meal is advertised at another place, the price needs to match the customers' expectations.

- **Population Density.** The number of people living in an area determines the potential number of customers. If you are in a remote rural area, it would be unrealistic to plan a menu with several pages of choices, because much of your food would be wasted. If, however, you are in the heart of a large city, such a menu would be appropriate.

- **Age.** Special menus or sections within a menu may be required for certain age groups. A family restaurant may require a special children's menu with limited offerings in smaller portions at lower prices. Senior citizens also provide a special menu situation. Elderly people tend to eat less

FIGURE 21-5
Influences on the Menu
This restaurant has a special children's menu.
Drawing Conclusions *Why might a restaurant have a children's menu?*

▼

- Kids' Corner -

For children 12 and under.

Funny Face
A big chocolate chip pancake with a whipped topping smile. Buttermilk version available upon request 2.79
Panqueque Cara Graciosa

★**Silver Five**
Five silver dollar-sized buttermilk pancakes with an egg and bacon 2.99
Cinco de Plata

Egg Sandwich
One egg, one strip of bacon and cheese on a toasted English muffin. Served with hash browns 2.79
Sandwich de Huevo

★**Rooty Jr.®**
Kid-sized version of our famous Rooty Tooty. One egg, one bacon strip, one pork sausage link and a fruit-topped buttermilk pancake 2.99

Cheese Omelette
With two buttermilk pancakes 3.99
Tortilla de Huevos con Queso

French Toast
Two triangles of French toast with two bacon strips 2.79
Torrija

Pigs in Blankets
Two pork sausage links rolled in buttermilk pancakes and served with hash browns 2.79
Salchichas Enrolladas en Panqueques

Chicken Strips
With French fries 3.99
Tiras de Pollo

Hamburger
Served with fries in a basket 2.99
With cheese 2.99
Hamburguesa

Grilled Cheese Sandwich
Served with French fries 2.99
Sandwich de Queso a la Plancha

Drinks
Soft Drinks, Milk, Chocolate Milk, Hot Chocolate .99
Bebidas

Dessert
Ice Cream Sundae 1.39
Postres

and often have flexibility in their schedules to dine outside the regular hours. They may also need food choices that are easy to chew.

Facility, Staff, and Equipment Limitations How many people a dining facility can serve is influenced by its menu and the service it requires. If a room is used as a cafeteria or for buffet-style dining, it can serve more people than if it is used for a menu with many different courses served at a leisurely pace. If space becomes a problem, a menu change could help accommodate more people.

Every business needs to make money to stay in operation. As you plan a menu, you also need to keep in mind the limits of your equipment and your staff. For example, you may want to feature French Onion Soup on your menu, but if you don't have individual ovenproof bowls or the extra staff required to apply the finishing touches, it could be too costly for your restaurant.

The cost of labor is one of the biggest expenses in the food business. The best way to maximize labor is to know the existing skills of all your workers and write a menu that uses those skills well. You could teach workers new skills to suit a new menu, but training costs time and money. On the other hand, under-using workers' time and skills is inefficient for business. The workers feel under-challenged, which leads to boredom, dissatisfaction, and job turnover.

Balance and Variety The specific items on your menu need to be appropriate for your type of place, your customers, your staff, and your equipment. They also need to be balanced and have variety. Typically, a balanced menu is one that has been written with the following considerations in mind:

- **Variety.** People appreciate variety. It makes dining more interesting and encourages return visits to a restaurant. You can add variety to a menu in a number of ways. You can use different cooking methods. For example, offer some fried, baked, or sautéed dishes and serve them with side dishes that are also prepared in a variety of different ways, such as pureed, steamed, or stir-fried. You can use different tastes and textures. Vary taste by varying spices. Make some food crunchy and others soft. Finally, use color. Remember the saying, "We eat with our eyes."

▲

**FIGURE 21-6
Equipment Limitations**
A small kitchen cannot easily increase space or equipment.
Predicting *If you were a chef in a small kitchen, would you focus on dishes that are easy to prepare and don't use many pans?*

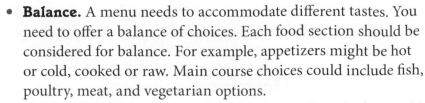

CHEF'S TIP

INVENTORY CONTROL

To increase your number of menu offerings, choose recipes that use the same cut of meat, poultry, or seafood so you will have better control of your inventory.

- **Balance.** A menu needs to accommodate different tastes. You need to offer a balance of choices. Each food section should be considered for balance. For example, appetizers might be hot or cold, cooked or raw. Main course choices could include fish, poultry, meat, and vegetarian options.
- **Special Needs.** Some customers have special needs that could be addressed on the menu. You could indicate a dish's suitability for diabetics, vegetarians, or someone with food allergies. You might also indicate that a dish could be adjusted to make it more appropriate for someone with special needs. For example, you could adjust a dish to make it suitable for someone with low-fat or low-calorie requirements.
- **Religion.** Many religious faiths have dietary restrictions. For example, some people have a tradition of sacrificing desserts or not eating meat at certain times of the year. Other people do not eat pork. Sensitivity to these considerations broadens the appeal of a menu.

- **Regional Cuisine.** People are proud of the region where they live and the food specialties found there. Maine is known for steamed lobster, and Texas has a reputation for barbecued meat. People enjoy seeing these things on a menu when they visit those regions and are more likely to patronize a restaurant that offers them.
- **Trends.** Collecting information to find out what customers like or dislike is called **market research**. Questionnaires, phone interviews, and observations are all studied to spot trends. Use these reports to find out what your potential customers favor so you can include those items as menu choices.
- **Various Price Levels.** You will need to have some dishes that are at the high end of your customers' affordability scale and other dishes that are less expensive. All your prices need to be within your customers' range.
- **Product Availability.** Before listing anything on the menu, be certain that you can get a sufficient supply of it. If you want to avoid reprinting the menu, you can put "in season" for items that may have limited availability, such as summer fruit or seasonal fish. The quality of most food depends on

FIGURE 21-7
Regional Cuisine
Different regions have different cuisines.
Applying Concepts *Why would a restaurant want to serve regional specialties?*

the seasons. Food that is in season will be at the peak of its flavor, texture, and color. For example, peaches are better in the summer, but cranberries are freshest in the fall and winter.

Truthfulness Many laws are designed to protect consumers from fraudulent claims related to foods and menus. Collectively, these laws are called the Truth in Menu laws. They are administered by dozens of agencies, but all focus on the accurate labeling of food. The laws are constantly being revised, so it is important in planning a menu to be honest—both in regard to the price that is charged and the food that is served.

▲ *Peach pie*

Truth-in-Menu Laws

Claim	Description
Quantity	Amounts and weights must be accurate. For example, if the weight shown is before the item is cooked, the menu must say so.
Quality	The stated quality must be accurate. "Prime" meat must actually be "Prime." It cannot be "Choice."
Price	The price must be accurate and not misleading. If six oysters are sold at a specific price, then six oysters should be delivered on the plate.
Brand Names	Brand names, such as Tabasco Sauce® or Godiva Chocolates®, must be represented accurately.
Product Identification	The product listed in the menu must be the product in the dish. If lobster was supposed to be included in a chowder, you cannot substitute monkfish.
Point of Origin	The location of ingredients must be accurate. Vermont maple syrup actually has to be from Vermont.
Merchandising Terms	Terms used to encourage customers to purchase menu items must be completely accurate. If the menu says that salad comes with the main course, be sure a salad comes with all main courses.
Means of Preservation	The method by which food on the menu was preserved must be accurate. This means, for example, that frozen fish can't be used if the menu says the fish is fresh.
Methods of Preparation	The method of preparation must be accurate. If the menu says the cod was broiled, it cannot be baked.
Verbal and Visual Presentation	Pictures and descriptions of food on the menu must be accurate in every detail.
Dietary and Nutritional Information	It is critically important that any dietary or nutritional information be completely correct. All dietary and nutritional data must be supported with statistical data.

 **Reading Checkpoint**

What are four important considerations to keep in mind when planning a menu?

Organizing and Designing a Menu

Three important aspects of creating a menu are organizing the menu, designing the actual menu that will be put in your customers' hands, and writing the menu descriptions.

Organizing a Menu Food is organized into categories on a menu. Usually the categories are listed in the sequence in which they are to be eaten. For example, on a lunch or dinner menu, appetizers are usually the first category and hot beverages are the last. Menus are also organized within each of these categories. For example, if the main course category has two poultry dishes and three beef dishes, the poultry would typically be listed together, as would the beef.

You should have a balanced number of categories and within those categories a balanced number of choices. A lunch menu might offer fewer choices in each category than a dinner menu. If eight main courses are listed, there might be two beef, two poultry, one fish, two vegetables, and one pasta option. Within the categories, there should also be a variety of cooking styles, such as grilling, frying, baking, and roasting.

Ethnic menus may have a unique organization and there are many variations even among relatively similar restaurants. However, as a general guideline, for non-ethnic restaurants, menu categories are typically shown on a menu in the following sequence:

- **Hors d'oeuvres.** You would list hors d'oeuvres on a menu only in a formal situation or perhaps at a banquet.
- **Appetizers.** Appetizers (also called starters) might be further broken down as cold and hot appetizers. Soups are sometimes included in the Appetizers category.
- **Soups.** Soups may be further broken down as cold or hot soups. Soups may also be included in the Appetizers category.
- **Salads.** American-style restaurants would tend to place salads before the main course. European-style restaurants might place the salad after the main course.
- **Sandwiches.** On a lunch menu or a casual dinner menu, you might find sandwiches listed as a separate category. Sandwiches might be further broken down as hot or cold sandwiches.
- **Main Courses.** The main course is usually broken down as hot or cold and then further broken down by type of meat or other similar feature. A main course is also referred to as an **entrée** (AHN-tray) in the United States.

❧ ST. ANDREW'S CAFÉ ❧
Lunch Menu

Soups

Cuban Style Black Bean Soup 4.
with Smoked Jalapeño Peppers and Croutons

Curried Apple and Roasted Butternut Squash Soup 4.
with Cilantro and Toasted Coconut

St. Andrew's Café Soup Sampler 5.

Starters and Salads

Warm Risotto Cake with Fresh Mozzarella 8.
with Shaved Prosciutto and Grilled Vegetables

Grilled Jumbo Shrimp with Pesto 9.
with Couscous and Arugula Salad

St. Andrew's Caesar Salad 6.
with Parmesan Croutons

Autumn Pear and Roquefort Garden Salad 6.
with Grapes, Hazelnuts and Verjus Vinaigrette

Warm Spinach Salad 7.
with Smoked Bacon Dressing and Pickled Red Onions

Wood-Fired Pizzas

Thai-Style Barbecue Chicken Pizza 10.
Aged Jack Cheese and Tomatillo Salsa on top

Pizza Margherita 10.
Tomatoes, Basil and Mozzarella

Indicates a Vegetarian Selection

Entrées & Specialty Sandwiches

Grilled Steak Caesar Entrée Salad 15.
with Parmesan Croutons

Japanese Udon Noodles and Jumbo Shrimp and Scallops 16.
Served with Vegetables, Mushrooms and Ponzu Sauce

Sautéed Pork Loin 14.
*Served with Prune Chutney, Herbed Spaetzle
and Braised Cabbage*

Vegetable Pita Sandwich 8.
*Grilled Vegetables, Basil and Sun Dried Tomatoes
Served on Warm Pita with Taboulleh Salad*

Smoked Ham & Fresh Mozzarella Panini Sandwich 10.
with Tomatoes and Basil

Desserts

St. Andrew's Dessert Sampler 6.
A special sampling of our Pastry Chef's delicacies of the day

Seasonal Fruit Crisp 5.
*A variety of Assorted Fresh Berries with Dark Chocolate
Served with Oatmeal-Walnut Crisp Topping and Ice Cream*

Sorbet of the Day 5.
Made daily with fresh fruit

White Chocolate and Honey Cheesecake 6.
with Strawberries

Indicates Nuts in Selection

- **Side Dishes.** Vegetables and starches that accompany the main course are usually listed as side dishes.
- **Desserts.** Sometimes restaurants that want to emphasize their dessert offerings will provide a separate dessert menu.
- **Hot Beverages.** Hot beverages that are served with dessert are usually listed last on the menu. Cold beverages, including alcoholic drinks, are often listed on a separate menu or list. If both cold and hot beverages are listed on the menu, they will typically be broken down as hot or cold.

Designing a Menu Because the menu is a communication tool between you and the customer, you need to be concerned about just what you communicate with your menu.

The three most common menu formats are:
- **Printed Menu.** The printed menu is presented to customers to look at. This is the most common type of menu. It often has a cover and back, with the actual menu printed inside on heavy paper. These are permanent menus.

▲
FIGURE 21-8
Lunch Menu
Notice that salads and starters have been combined under one category.
Analyzing Information *Why do you think this menu has a separate category for wood-fired pizzas?*

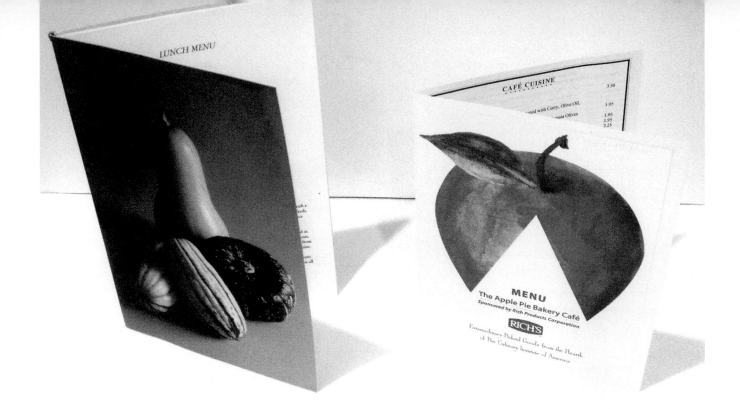

FIGURE 21-9
Menu Design
Two contrasting menu covers.
Comparing/Contrasting *What message do these menus communicate?*

▲ *Mexican restaurant menu*

When specials are offered, an insert or clip-on is attached to the menu. Some establishments place folded cards, known as **table tent menus**, directly on the tables to tell customers about specials.

- **Spoken Menu.** Some restaurants have their servers memorize the menu and then repeat it to the customers.

  This is called a spoken menu. It usually has a limited number of choices. The spoken menu creates a more intimate feeling in a restaurant, but some people find it demanding because they can't linger over the menu and study the choices.

- **Menu Board.** The menu board is on display, usually on the wall or an easel, for everyone to see. Menu items are either handwritten or printed. The menu board is associated with casual dining.

On written menus, design details such as materials, colors, and images communicate your message just as strongly as words do. Your pictures, colors, words, and materials set a tone. They tell your customers what to expect in their dining experience. You need to make the menu send a clear written and visual message about your place of business and the food being served.

Follow these guidelines in designing a printed menu:

- Make sure the menu contains your restaurant's vitals (name, address, and phone, at least).
- Design the shape and size of the menu so it is in keeping with your restaurant's concept.
- Avoid photos inside the menu.

- Emphasize the items on the menu, not their prices.
- Use graphics sparingly.
- Use print, not a hard-to-read script.
- Use numbers for the prices; do not spell them out.

Writing a Menu When writing the descriptions of your menu items, keep these guidelines in mind:
- Keep your descriptions free from misspellings and grammatical errors.
- Make sure the language reflects the restaurant's concept and style.
- Make the food sound attractive.
- Eliminate all unnecessary words.
- Do not use restaurant jargon.
- Provide customers with a road map for their dining experience, one for which they will not require further directions.
- Make sure the menu is easy to read.
- Use words that are in keeping with current food and restaurant trends.
- Be positive.

 **Reading Checkpoint** *What is the typical order of menu categories for a non-ethnic restaurant?*

21.1 ASSESSMENT

Reviewing Concepts

1. What are the two primary functions of a menu?
2. What are seven common types of menus?
3. What are four important considerations to keep in mind when planning a menu?
4. What is the typical order of menu categories for a non-ethnic restaurant?

Critical Thinking

5. **Drawing Conclusions** Equipment availability is important to remember when planning a menu. How could too many soup choices on the menu create a problem?
6. **Applying Concepts** A vegetarian diet book tops the best-seller list for two months in a row. How could that affect the choices of foods on your menu?
7. **Analyzing Information** Every entrée on a menu is deep-fried and all the sides are white. What is wrong with the menu balance and how could you correct it?

Test Kitchen

Divide into four teams. Each team will develop a semi à la carte dinner menu for a restaurant. Before writing the menu, each team will develop a mission statement for the restaurant. Each team will then produce one item, their signature item, from their Appetizer category and one from their Main Course category. Evaluate each team's results.

LANGUAGE ARTS

Descriptive Writing

Write descriptions for three du jour menu items. Tempt the customers by appealing to their sense of taste, touch, smell, and sight.

READING PREVIEW

Key Concepts

- Identifying factors that influence menu prices
- Understanding menu-pricing methods
- Making a menu-pricing decision

Vocabulary

- actual cost method
- base price method
- copycat method
- factor method
- forced food method
- gross profit method
- pricing factor
- pricing system comparison chart
- prime cost
- prime cost method
- psychological factors
- raw food cost

"There are many ways to set the prices on a menu. There's more to it than just numbers, but without good numbers, it's nothing more than a guess. **"**

– Craig Goldstein
The Culinary Institute
of America

Factors Influencing Menu Prices

You understand the purpose of your menu. You've decided on the type of menu you will be using. You have planned a balanced menu that would seem to be perfect for your restaurant. You have organized the menu, designed it, and written truthful and attractive descriptions of your menu items. One thing still remains, however. You now must assign prices to the menu items, prices that will appeal to customers while being profitable for you.

The following six factors will influence your decision about menu prices:

- **Type of Restaurant.** Your mission statement determines the type of restaurant, and the type of restaurant determines, in part, the amount you can charge for your menu items. For example, a hamburger in a fast-food restaurant will probably be less expensive than one in a family dining restaurant,

WELCOME TO
LITTLE ITALY PIZZA

REG. SLICE	1.95
SICILIAN SLICE	2.00
CHICAGO SLICE	2.00
SLICE 1 TOPPING	2.50
SLICE 2 TOPPINGS	3.25
SLICE 3 TOPPINGS OR MORE	3.75

which will be less expensive than a hamburger in a high-end restaurant.

- **Meal Occasion.** The time of day that customers eat determines, in part, what they are willing to pay for the food they are consuming. For example, customers typically expect to pay more for dinner than for breakfast.
- **Style and Elaborateness of Service.** Because of the increased labor costs, the more elaborate the service, the more expensive the items on the menu will need to be.
- **Competition.** Your restaurant cannot charge more for a menu item than your competitors unless there is a significant reason for the increased price. If your family-style restaurant charges $2.00 more for an item than another family-style restaurant in your area, customers will tend to go to your competitor's restaurant. Competitor pricing is extremely important in determining menu prices.
- **Customer Mix.** Your customer mix involves many factors, including the male-to-female ratio, the number of business people eating in the restaurant, the number of families with children, and the ages of your customers.

◄

FIGURE 21-10
Customer Mix
A restaurant's customer mix involves many factors.
Communicating *How would you describe this restaurant's customer mix?*

- **Profit Objective.** You may decide that your most popular menu items can be priced slightly higher, increasing your profit on those items. Or you may decide that you can decrease your profit on an item because you will make up for the decreased profit per item by increasing the volume.

 **Reading Checkpoint** *What are six factors influencing menu prices?*

Menu-Pricing Methods

There are actually many ways to price menu items. Only the restaurant owner or manager can actually decide which method is best for a particular restaurant. The best method is often an adaptation or combination of the following seven methods.

Copycat Method The simplest way to determine your prices is to go to a nearby restaurant that has the same menu items and copy their prices. This is the **copycat method** of menu pricing (also called the nonstructured method). Although simple, this is not a very wise method of determining your prices. Every restaurant's situation is different. For example, your competitor might own the building in which her restaurant is located, so she does not need to pay rent. You may need to take your rent into account when pricing items. Although checking competitor's pricing is important, it should not be used as the sole basis for making menu-pricing decisions.

Factor Method The **factor method** is one of the oldest, and simplest, methods for pricing menu items. To determine the price of a menu item, you multiply the **raw food cost** (that is, the cost of all the ingredients that went into a single serving of the dish) by an established **pricing factor**. This means that you mark up every item on your menu by the same amount.

To use the factor method, you first have to establish the raw food cost you would like to have. For example, many restaurants try to keep their raw food cost at 37% of the menu price. This means that 63% of the cost of the menu item is for overhead (all non-food costs associated with the restaurant except for labor), labor, and profit.

- **Determine the Pricing Factor.** Divide 100 by the raw food cost. In our example, that means you divide 100 by 37 to get a pricing factor of 2.7.
- **Determine the Price for a Menu Item.** Multiply the raw food cost by the pricing factor. For example, if the raw food cost for a hamburger is $1.70, the menu price for that hamburger will be $4.59.

Prime Cost Method The **prime cost method** was developed for use in cafeteria operations. It is very similar to the factor method but also

Raw Food Cost

To calculate the raw food cost based on a standardized menu:

1. Determine the cost of each of the ingredients that went into the dish. For example, if the dish requires a breast of chicken, you have to determine how much a breast of chicken costs.

2. Add the cost of all the ingredients in the dish.

3. Divide by the number of portions the recipe yields.

Calculate

Calculate the raw food cost for a dish with which you are familiar. Calculate the menu price by using a pricing factor of 2.7. In a restaurant, would you order this menu item at the price you calculated?

calculates the cost of preparing the menu item. With the prime cost method, you start with the raw food cost, just as you did in the factor method. Let's use the raw food cost of $1.70 for a hamburger again. The next step is to figure out the cost of the labor that went directly into producing that menu item. This would include all mise en place associated with the preparation of the item, but wouldn't include work such as cleaning the dishes or serving customers.

- **Determine Direct Labor Cost.** There are many ways to determine the cost of the labor that is directly involved in making a dish. Perhaps the easiest way is to record the time involved in making the dish, multiply by the hourly wage of the chefs making the dish, and divide by the number of portions in the recipe. Figured in this way, the chef making a hamburger might spend only a couple of minutes actually making a hamburger. If a chef makes approximately $0.50 a minute and spends only 4 minutes actually cooking the hamburger (assuming that the chef is doing other things while the hamburger is actually on the grill), you would add $2.00 (4 minutes × .50 per minute) to the raw food cost to arrive at the prime cost of $3.70 ($2.00 + $1.70 = $3.70).

- **Add Direct Labor to the Raw Food Price.** Based on their experience, many restaurants use 9% as their direct labor cost. They add 9% to the 37% raw food cost to calculate an amount that includes the cost of all ingredients plus the cost of the labor involved in making a portion of the dish. This amount is referred to as the **prime cost**. In our example, this is 46%.

- **Determine the Prime Cost Factor.** Divide 100 by the prime cost. In our example, you divide 100 by 46 to get a pricing factor of 2.17.

- **Determine the Price for a Menu Item.** Multiply the prime cost by the prime cost factor. For example, if the prime cost for a hamburger is $3.70, the menu price for that hamburger will be $8.03.

▲
FIGURE 21-12
Cost of Labor
The prime cost method includes the price of labor.
Drawing Conclusions *When might a prime cost method be more useful than a factor method of determining menu price?*

Example Base Price Method

Customer's Expected Meal Cost	$10.00	100%
Profit	1.00	10%
Overhead	2.70	27%
Labor	2.60	26%
Raw Food Cost	$3.70	37%

Actual Cost Method In the **actual cost method**, the actual cost for the raw food, labor, other expenses, and profit are all added together to determine a menu price. The raw food cost and labor are calculated in actual dollars. However, they are also calculated as a percentage of the menu price. This allows a restaurant to use percentages (based on the restaurant's total sales) for other expenses and profits.

For example, if the raw food cost and labor for a dish equals $2.00 and the restaurant calculates that this is 40% of the menu price, the menu price will be $5.00. If the actual percentage for profit is 10%, the amount of profit on this item will be $0.50.

Gross Profit Method The **gross profit method** is designed to determine a specific amount of profit that should be made from each customer who comes into the restaurant. It is a method that is used primarily in well-established restaurants, because it requires analysis of past financial statements, counts of customers over a specific amount of time (often one year), and analysis of what each customer ordered.

This method of calculating the cost of menu items guarantees the owner or manager that a predetermined amount of profit will be made on every customer. It tends to benefit the customer choosing from the more expensive items and penalize the customer ordering less expensive items. This is because the restaurant expects to make the same amount of profit from each of them, no matter what they order. It is often used in banquets or catered events when there are a known amount of customers at a specific event.

Base Price Method The **base price method** starts by analyzing what customers want to spend per meal. It works backward from there to come up with menu items, their prices, and a built-in level of profit. Similar to the gross profit method, the base price method requires data about customers' eating habits in the restaurant over a long period. Without such data, a new restaurant would be forced to make assumptions about the spending patterns of their customers. A new restaurant's mission statement would need to be very clear and the restaurant would need to be very certain of its market.

In the example, you know that your customers are comfortable spending $10.00 per meal, and you know that you want a profit of 10%, your overhead is 27%, and your total labor is 26%, accounting for a total of 63%. This means that so long as you spend less than 37% ($3.70) on a menu item priced at $10.00, you will cover your actual costs and receive a 10% profit.

Forced Food Method The **forced food method** is determined by the market—that is, by the choices your customers actually make in your restaurant. It takes into account loss and spoilage and assumes that food that is at a high risk of loss or spoilage should have a higher price. It also includes volume in the calculation. The lower the volume, the higher the price (and vice versa). Every item on the menu is analyzed in terms of its volume and price.

Each type of menu item is then given a specific profit margin based on its volume/risk category. Taking the basic volume/risk category and the type of menu item into consideration, you then calculate menu prices, using the restaurant's overhead cost, labor cost, and a predetermined profit—all as a percentage of the total cost. Subtracting this as a percentage gives you a percentage for the raw food cost. So, for example, if your total overhead, labor, and profit equal 68%, you know that your raw food cost should be 32% (100 − 68 = 32) of the menu price. If your actual raw food price for a hamburger is $2.70 and that is 32% of the menu price, the menu price will be $8.43 (calculated as (2.70 × 100)/32).

 **Reading Checkpoint** *What are the seven menu-pricing methods?*

Low Volume & High Cost	High Volume & High Cost
Low Volume & Low Cost	High Volume & Low Cost

▲ *Four basic volume/risk categories*

Appetizers	20–50%
Salads	10–40%
Main Courses	10–25%
Vegetables	25–50%
Beverages and Bread	10–20%
Desserts	15–35%

▲ *Typical profit margins*

Deciding on Menu Prices

Once you have decided on a menu-pricing option and have done all your calculations, you are ready to decide on your menu prices. However, there are a few additional considerations.

Comparison Charts A **pricing system comparison chart** is a valuable aid in making pricing decisions. It shows a comparison of the prices from various pricing methods (the example shows the factor method, the gross profit method, and the forced food cost method).

CULINARY MATH

The Q Quotient

Have you ever wondered how restaurants account for the cost of seasonings such as salt and pepper? Some restaurants add the cost of salt, pepper, condiments, bread, rolls, butter, and oil that are served at the table to the selling price of an item, typically the main course item.

This is referred to as the Q quotient. Restaurants might add the following to the cost of each main-course menu item:

Calculating the Q Quotient	
Salt & Pepper	$0.02
Bread & Rolls	$0.10
Butter & Oil	$0.08
Condiments	$0.05
Total Q Quotient	$0.25

Research

Contact 10 restaurants to see how they deal with Q-quotient items. How do the restaurants add this cost to the menu items?

Figure 21-13
Pricing System Comparison Chart
Use a pricing system comparison chart to arrive at your final menu prices.
Communicating *What kind of remarks would go in the value judgments column?*

Menu Item	Factor	Gross Profit	Forced Food Cost	Competitor A	Competitor B	Final Menu Price	Value Judgment

It also shows two competitors' prices along with your final decision for the menu price, as well as your value judgments—basically any nonscientific judgment you make concerning the price you have assigned.

Psychological Factors After you have determined the menu price by using one of the menu-pricing methods, you may need to take **psychological factors** into account. Psychological factors take into account how a customer perceives specific menu items. For example, customers might associate high-end menu items, such as lobster, caviar, or truffles, with a higher price. They may also associate specific ingredients with a higher or lower price. For example, customers who are willing to pay $6.00 for a normal hamburger may be willing to pay $9.00 for a hamburger if you add blue cheese.

CULINARY SCIENCE

5 and 9 Magic Numbers?

Did you ever wonder why prices on menus often end with a 9 or a 5? Scientific evidence has proven that certain prices—those ending in a 9 or a 5—are more enticing to customers than other numbers. These numbers are sometimes referred to as magic numbers and the type of pricing is referred to as "odd cents" pricing. No matter what it is called, this pricing seems to have some sort of special appeal to consumers. Odd cents pricing has been used for years by the food-service industry to affect customers psychologically and maximize profits. Scientists have tried to explain odd cents pricing as creating an illusion of a discount that thereby reduces customers' resistance to purchasing.

Research

Gather menus from 20 local restaurants and look for odd cents pricing. If possible, talk to the owners about the odd cents pricing strategy to see if they have any actual evidence that it works.

Price Increases Most of the time, restaurant owners wait too long to raise their prices. Once a menu price is decided on, managers tend to leave it at that price. In many cases, this can be a problem for the restaurant because it fails to take into account rising prices.

When a price increase is necessary, make it as bearable as possible. You could, for example, slightly reduce the size of the portions so you make up the difference in the profit margin. Or, you could add something to the plate to create a new dish for which a higher price is appropriate.

Avoid rapid increases over a short period of time. Timing is critical in increasing prices. It is important to make sure that you maintain quality standards when you raise prices. Otherwise, customers will sense that both value and quality have declined. Above all, avoid across-the-board increases of menu prices.

Reading Checkpoint *What is a pricing system comparison chart?*

CHEF'S TIP

WHEN TO RAISE

The best time to increase (or decrease) prices is when the government announces the current cost-of-living figures or changes the gross national product.

21.2 ASSESSMENT

Reviewing Concepts

1. What are six factors influencing menu prices?
2. What are the seven menu-pricing methods?
3. What is a pricing system comparison chart?

Critical Thinking

4. **Applying Concepts** Why is competition such an important factor influencing menu prices?
5. **Analyzing Information** Describe a situation in which using the copycat method of menu pricing could lead to problems.
6. **Compare/Contrast** Compare the factor method and the prime cost method of pricing in terms of their ease of use on a day-to-day basis.
7. **Inferring** Describe a situation, either imaginary or from your experience, in which a local restaurant may have used psychological factors to increase the price of a menu item.

Test Kitchen

Choose a recipe for a dish that is commonly offered by restaurants in your area. Divide into four teams. Each team will decide on a menu price for the dish. Team 1 will use the copycat method based on two local restaurants. Team 2 will use the factor method. Team 3 will use the prime cost method. Team 4 will use the base price method. Teams 2, 3, and 4 will calculate the raw food price and use percentages shown in the text.

CULINARY MATH

Prime Cost Method

The raw food cost for a main course is $3.25. Using a pricing factor of 2.7, what is the menu price for the factor method? Using a prime pricing factor of 2.3, what is the menu price for the prime cost method?

Review and Assessment

Reviewing Content

Choose the letter that best answers the question or completes the statement.

1. The mission statement is a statement of
   a. a bill
   b. a financial report
   c. an organization's goal
   d. job assignments

2. An à la carte menu
   a. offers each food or beverage priced and served separately
   b. offers a main course that includes soup or salad, a vegetable, and a starch
   c. offers breakfast, lunch, and dinner anytime
   d. offers a complete meal for a set price

3. A table d'hôte menu
   a. offers each food or beverage priced and served separately
   b. offers a main course that includes soup or salad, a vegetable, and a starch
   c. offers breakfast, lunch, and dinner anytime
   d. offers a complete meal for a set price

4. A California menu
   a. offers each food or beverage priced and served separately
   b. offers a main course that includes soup or salad, a vegetable, and a starch
   c. offers breakfast, lunch, and dinner anytime
   d. offers a complete meal for a set price

5. The raw food cost is
   a. the cost of a salad
   b. the cost of all the ingredients that went into a single portion of a dish
   c. the cost of all the ingredients that are used by a restaurant in one day's dinners
   d. the cost of ingredients used in a salad bar

6. In the factor method
   a. the direct labor cost and the raw food cost are multiplied by a factor
   b. the raw food price is multiplied by a factor
   c. the menu price is determined by how much a customer spends per meal
   d. the menu price is determined by how much the customer wants to spend

Understanding Concepts

7. What is the difference between a table d'hôte menu and a prix fixe menu?

8. What is the difference between the raw food cost and the prime cost?

9. How would you determine a menu price by using the actual cost method?

10. Using the forced food method of menu pricing, by which two factors would you analyze each item on the menu?

11. What is the difference between a fixed menu and a limited menu?

Critical Thinking

12. **Applying Concepts** You write truthfully in your menu that one of your dishes is your most popular dish. In what way are you using the menu as a communication tool?

13. **Comparing/Contrasting** Compare the gross profit method and the base price method of pricing menu items.

Culinary Math

14. **Solving Problems** The raw food cost of a dish is $2.37. You are using the factor method for pricing menu items and want the raw food price to be 34% of the menu price. What is the price of this dish?

15. **Applying Concepts** Your customers expect to spend $24.00 for a meal at your restaurant. Using the base price method of menu pricing, you calculate that your raw food cost should be no more than 34% of what your customer expects to spend for a meal. What is your maximum raw food price per customer?

On the Job

16. **Applying Concepts** Your menu says that a chocolate cake is "homemade" but you actually buy it from a bakery. Do you think this represents a truth-in-menu problem?

LAB ACTIVITY

Project 21: Raw Food Cost and Psychological Factors

Answer these questions when your class works through Project 21.

- What is your raw food cost?

- What would the menu price be by using the factor method? The prime cost method? The base price method?

- Based on copycat pricing, what would you expect the menu price to be?

- What psychological factors might you use to increase the price of the menu item?

- If you were running a restaurant, what would your price for the item be?

TEST PRACTICE

Choose the letter that best answers the question or completes the statement.

1. The copycat method of menu pricing is also called the
   A me-too method
   B competitor-adjusted method
   C nonstructured method
   D comparison method

2. A fast-food restaurant menu is typically an example of a
   A prix fixe menu
   B limited menu
   C du jour menu
   D table d'hôte menu

3. A du jour menu
   A offers breakfast lunch, dinner, and snacks at the same time
   B offers each food or beverage priced and served separately
   C offers food that is served only on that particular day
   D offers a complete meal for a set price

4. A table d'hôte menu
   A offers breakfast lunch, dinner, and snacks at the same time
   B offers each food or beverage priced and served separately
   C offers food that is served only on that particular day
   D offers a complete meal for a set price

5. Table tent menus are
   A outdoor menus
   B menu boards used in a tent
   C folded cards placed on tables
   D menu boards brought to each table individually

6. A menu should
   A use many photos
   B use many colorful graphics
   C spell out prices
   D none of the above

7. The prime cost method of menu pricing
   A focuses on the cost of the direct labor plus the raw food cost
   B focuses on the raw food cost only
   C focuses on profit only
   D focuses on the amount a customer wants to spend

8. Many restaurants try to keep their raw food cost at about
   A 7%
   B 17%
   C 27%
   D 37%

NUTRITION

Nutrition Basics

READING PREVIEW

Key Concepts

- Understanding the importance of nutrition
- Learning the language of nutrition
- Understanding nutrition information

Vocabulary

- amino acids
- antioxidants
- calories
- carbohydrates
- cholesterol
- complex carbohydrates
- daily values
- Dietary Guidelines
- fat-soluble vitamins
- fatty acids
- Food Guide Pyramid
- glucose
- hydrogenation
- insoluble fiber
- monounsaturated fats
- mutual supplementation
- nutrients
- obesity
- omega-3 fatty acids
- polyunsaturated fats
- protein
- saturated fats
- simple carbohydrates
- soluble fiber
- trans fats
- water-soluble vitamins

"When chefs and nutritionists learn to speak each other's language, they can get down to what matters most—great food that's good for you. **"**

– Marjorie Livingston
The Culinary Institute
of America

The Importance of Nutrition

Nutrition is a field of study that is concerned with the foods we eat and the way those foods affect our bodies and our health. Nutritionists are trying to find out which foods are the most likely to keep us healthy by learning more about how **nutrients**, the parts of food our bodies use, can help or hurt us.

The science of nutrition is still uncovering new information. Many of us have difficulty making sense of this information. Yet with so many people interested in eating a healthy diet, it is the chef's job to learn the basics of nutrition. Once you've learned these basics, you can incorporate nutrition into your cooking.

Poor Nutrition At different times in history, getting enough food was a serious everyday concern. Lack of food is still a major concern in many parts of the world. People who don't get enough to eat are not just hungry. They don't have enough energy to function well. Their appearance may change, and they are usually not able to fight off disease easily because they aren't getting certain nutrients.

Good Nutrition Good nutrition means not only getting enough food to eat but also getting enough of the right foods. When nutritionists talk about a good diet or a healthy diet, they are talking about diets that include a variety of foods and appropriate portions. A healthy diet is sometimes referred to as a balanced diet.

Even people who get enough food to eat can suffer from poor nutrition. They may gain weight if they eat too much. Gaining weight can have some serious health consequences, including diabetes, heart disease, and even cancer. People who aren't eating the right foods needed for a good supply of nutrients could develop certain diseases as well.

 **Reading Checkpoint** *What does "good nutrition" mean?*

The Language of Nutrition

Food is one of the basic requirements for life. Some people compare food to the gasoline we put in a car: it is the fuel that keeps our bodies running. Choosing the right foods makes it easier for your body to function properly.

When we talk about nutrition and food, we are talking about the following basic nutrients—proteins, carbohydrates, fats, vitamins, minerals, and water. In addition to providing us with the nutrients we need, foods also provide us with the fuel, or energy, we need to stay warm, walk, talk, and do our work. This energy is measured in units known as **calories**.

Proteins **Protein** is a nutrient our bodies need so they can grow, replace worn out tissues and cells, and help us recover from injuries and illnesses.

The basic building blocks of protein are known as **amino** (ah-MEEN-oh) **acids**. The proteins found in the cells of our skin, hair, teeth, bones, fingernails, muscles, and tendons are made up of 22 amino acids. Our bodies produce some of these amino acids on their own. However, there are nine amino acids adult humans cannot produce. They are known as essential amino acids because we must eat foods that contain them.

A food that provides all the essential amino acids is known as a complete protein. Meats, poultry, fish, and other animal products (including eggs and cheese) are complete proteins.

Grains, dried legumes, and nuts are also rich in protein; however, these foods may not contain all the essential amino acids, or they may have only small amounts of some of the essential amino acids. This does not mean that the protein they do provide is not of good quality. It simply means you need to eat other foods as a supplement to the amino acids in that food. This is sometimes referred to as **mutual supplementation**. Some traditional dishes that combine beans and grains, such as the red beans and rice served in New Orleans or the Italian soup pasta e fagioli made from pasta and beans, provide all of the essential amino acids.

If your body is growing or if it has been injured in some way (for example, a cut, a burn, or a broken bone), getting enough protein-rich foods in your diet is very important. In most developed countries, getting enough protein is not a big concern. Instead, we are more likely to be eating more protein-rich foods than our bodies need.

An excess of protein can lead to such conditions as osteoporosis (a condition where bones become brittle or porous), kidney failure, and gout (a condition characterized by painful joint inflammation, especially in the hands and feet).

FIGURE 22-1
Animal and Vegetable
Protein is found in both animal foods and vegetable foods.
Inferring *Which foods would you choose for a vegetarian entree?*

Carbohydrates Carbohydrates are an important source of energy for our bodies. Just as proteins are made up of smaller units, carbohydrates are also made up of smaller units, known as sugars. When we eat carbohydrate-rich foods, our bodies turn them into a specific type of sugar known as **glucose** (GLOO-kohs). This is the fuel our bodies need to keep us warm and keep our muscles, brains, and nervous systems working properly. There are two types of carbohydrates:

- **Simple carbohydrates** contain one or two sugars. They are found in fruit, milk, and the refined sugars used in the kitchen or bakeshop: white sugar, brown sugar, molasses, and honey. Simple carbohydrates are digested and absorbed quickly. They provide a short burst of energy.
- **Complex carbohydrates** contain long chains that include many sugars. They are found in plant-based foods such as grains, legumes, and vegetables. Before we can use the nutrients in complex carbohydrates, our bodies have to break them down into simple sugars. Complex carbohydrates are sometimes referred to as "starches." They provide a long-lasting source of energy.

CHEF'S TIP

A SWEET TASTE

You can usually tell if a food contains simple carbohydrates simply by tasting it. Simple carbohydrates taste sweet.

FIGURE 22-2
Whole Fruit or Juice
Whole oranges and orange juice.
Applying Concepts *Which of these foods contains more fiber?*

FOCUS ON NUTRITION

Health Risk
Saturated fats and products made from hydrogenated or partially hydrogenated oils (which contain trans fats) have been linked to some forms of cancer, increased cholesterol levels, and heart disease. Avoid consuming too many foods that are rich in saturated and trans fats.

Carbohydrate-rich foods such as fruit, vegetables, grains, and legumes can provide us with something else we need for good health—fiber. There are two types of fiber:

- **Soluble fiber** dissolves in water. When we eat foods that contain soluble fiber, we feel full for a longer time. Soluble fiber also slows down the release of sugar into the blood and helps lower cholesterol levels in the blood. Good sources of soluble fiber include beans, fruit, vegetables, and whole grains such as oats and barley.

- **Insoluble fiber** does not dissolve in water. It was once referred to as roughage. It acts like a stiff broom to clean and scrub the digestive tract so we can eliminate wastes from our systems more easily. Good sources include most fruit and vegetables, wheat bran, nuts, and whole grain flours.

Sometimes, fiber is removed from foods before we eat it. Carbohydrate-rich foods such as wheat or barley are sometimes processed to remove the fiber. White flour, fruit juices, and table sugar are all examples of refined and processed foods that contain very little if any fiber.

Fats and Cholesterol Fats such as butter, cream, and oils play an important part in making foods taste good or giving them a specific texture. In our bodies, fats are important for other reasons. They provide energy and fulfill several important roles in keeping our bodies functioning. Fat also slows digestion, giving our bodies time to absorb the nutrients contained in the foods we eat. By slowing digestion, fats help send a signal to our brains so we stop eating before we overeat. However, too much fat in the diet can increase the risk of heart disease, certain cancers, and **obesity** (oh-BEE-city). Being obese means being dangerously overweight and prone to many health risks.

A fat such as olive oil or butter is actually a chain made up of many smaller units known as **fatty acids**. These fatty acids are made from atoms of carbon, hydrogen, and oxygen linked together. Fatty acids are grouped into three main categories according to their structure: saturated, polyunsaturated, and monounsaturated.

- **Saturated fats** are usually solid at room temperature. They come from animal sources, with the exception of coconut oil and palm oil, which come from plants.

- **Polyunsaturated fats** come from plants and are liquid at room temperature. They sometimes undergo the process of **hydrogenation**, which changes a liquid polyunsaturated fat, such as corn oil, into a solid fat, such as margarine.

Saturated Fats

Butter, cheese, cream, lard, coconut oil, palm oil, margarine, and fatty meat are high in saturated fat.

Monounsaturated Fats

Olives, olive oil, avocados, most nuts and nut oils, canola oil, and peanut oil are foods high in monounsaturated fat.

Omega-3 Fatty Acids

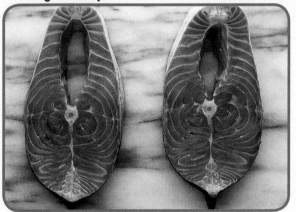

Food rich in omega-3 fatty acids include salmon, mackerel, dark-green leafy vegetables, walnuts, and canola oil.

Polyunsaturated Fats

Corn, sesame seeds and sesame oil, walnuts and walnut oil are high in polyunsaturated fat.

Cholesterol

Sources of cholesterol include eggs, organ meats, and other meats, which are also high in saturated fats.

Trans Fats

Trans fats are found in processed foods made with hydrogenated or partially hydrogenated vegetable oils.

Hydrogenation creates **trans fats** (also called trans fatty acids), a potentially harmful type of fat that has been linked to heart disease.

- **Monounsaturated fats** are considered the healthier fats, they come from plants and are liquid at room temperature. They help balance cholesterol levels in the blood, reducing the risk of heart disease.

Omega-3 fatty acids are a type of polyunsaturated fat that is linked to reducing the risk of stroke and heart attack and improving brain growth and development. They are found in some plants and in all fish.

Cholesterol (koh-LESS-ter-all) is a fatty substance that the body needs to perform various functions. The body makes its own supply of cholesterol. Cholesterol in foods is known as dietary cholesterol, which occurs only in animal foods, never in plant foods. Cholesterol in the body is known as serum cholesterol. When doctors check a person's cholesterol levels, they are trying to determine how much serum cholesterol is found in that person's blood.

The blood test for cholesterol looks at the levels of two types of protein in the blood: low-density lipoproteins (LDL) and high-density lipoproteins (HDL). Too much LDL, or "bad" cholesterol, is a health risk. It could indicate a build-up of cholesterol on the walls of arteries, reducing blood flow to the heart. The doctor will suggest changes in diet, exercise, or even medication to help reduce LDL levels. Having high levels of HDL is good news. HDL clears cholesterol out of the circulatory system.

Vitamins Vitamins are similar to the major nutrients because we need them in our diets every day to keep our bodies healthy. They differ from the major nutrients in that they do not contain any calories. They are sometimes referred to as noncaloric nutrients. Vitamins may be water-soluble or fat-soluble.

- **Water-Soluble Vitamins.** The B vitamins and vitamin C are water-soluble. They dissolve in water and are easily transported throughout the body in the bloodstream. We can store a small amount of these vitamins in our lean tissue, such as muscles and organs, but not enough to last more than a day or two. If we get more of these vitamins than our bodies can use, the excess is flushed from our bodies.
- **Fat-Soluble Vitamins.** Vitamins A, D, E, and K are fat-soluble, which means they dissolve in fat. Fat-soluble vitamins are stored in our body fat. Any excess that we consume cannot be easily flushed from the body once ingested. If we take in too much of a particular vitamin or mineral, the level can become so high that it is toxic to our bodies.

◄ Vitamin A

The form of vitamin A found in animal foods is known as retinol. Vitamin A itself is not found in plant foods, but a substance known as beta-carotene, which the body uses to produce vitamin A, is contained in orange, deep yellow, and dark-green leafy vegetables. Vitamin A is an antioxidant.

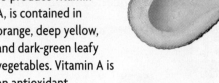

◄ B Vitamins

Meats are a good source of B vitamins, as are whole and enriched grains, legumes, leafy greens, avocados, yogurt, and fish such as tuna and salmon. The B-complex vitamins, which include thiamin (THY-uh-mihn), riboflavin (RYE-bo-flay-vihn), niacin (NYE-uh-cihn), folic (FO-lihk) acid, biotin (BY-oh-tihn), pantothenic (PANT-uh-THEN-ik) acid, B-6, and B-12) are water-soluble. They are critical to proper digestion of various nutrients and are part of nearly every cell in the body.

Vitamin C ►

Vitamin C, found in fruit (such as citrus, papaya, and strawberries) and vegetables (such as parsley, peppers, and broccoli), helps the body absorb iron and promotes the production of the proteins necessary to maintain, grow, and repair connective tissues. It is an antioxidant that boosts the immune system and may help reduce serum cholesterol levels.

◄ Vitamin D

Vitamin D is responsible in part for the proper formation of bones. A lack of vitamin D results in the disease called rickets, in which bones grow abnormally. People with limited exposure to sunlight, which is needed to produce vitamin D, may need to eat foods fortified with vitamin D: milk and cereals.

◄ Vitamin E

Vitamin E, like vitamin C, is an antioxidant that may have cancer-fighting potential. It is found in a variety of foods and is not difficult to obtain from dietary sources. Vegetable oils, sunflower seeds, wheat germ, and green leafy vegetables contain significant amounts of vitamin E.

◄ Vitamin K

Vitamin K is essential for normal blood-clotting. It is produced by bacteria found in the intestines. A person eating a varied and healthy diet also obtains vitamin K from foods, particularly dark green vegetables such as spinach, broccoli, and kale.

Several vitamins act as **antioxidants**—substances that prevent tissue damage in the body that can lead to premature aging, heart disease, or cancer.

Minerals Minerals play an important role, along with vitamins, in regulating our bodies and keeping our teeth and bones strong. Our nervous system depends on minerals to function properly as well. Some minerals, such as calcium, magnesium, and phosphorus, are needed in large amounts. Other minerals, such as iodine, iron, selenium, and zinc, are needed in very small amounts.

Mineral-Rich Foods

▲ Calcium
Calcium is the body's most abundant mineral. Ninety-nine percent of the calcium needed by the body is used in the development of bones and teeth. A calcium deficiency results in stunted growth and loss of bone density. Good sources of calcium include dairy products such as yogurt and milk, broccoli, leafy greens, and beans.

◀ Iodine
Iodine is essential for the normal functioning of the thyroid gland and also helps regulate energy metabolism, cellular oxidation, and growth. Iodine deficiency was common in the early 1900s but has since been corrected by adding iodine to table salt (iodized salt). Other sources of iodine include sea vegetables, yogurt, milk, eggs, and strawberries.

Iron ▶
Iron is a critical component of hemoglobin (HE-mo-glo-bin), the part of the red blood cell that carries oxygen from the lungs and distributes it throughout the body. People suffering from iron deficiency are considered anemic (a-NEE-mik). They may appear pale, feel weak, and have impaired immune systems. Good sources of iron are liver and other red meat, but iron is also found in beans, fish, leafy green vegetables, whole grains, and dried fruit such as raisins.

▲ Magnesium
Magnesium (mag-NEE-zee-uhm) plays an important part in the structure and function of the body, including bones, muscle contraction, nerve transmission, and bowel function. A lack of magnesium can cause possible growth failure, headaches, depression, muscle spasms, and weakness. Good food sources of magnesium include nuts, legumes, whole grains, and leafy green vegetables, such as Swiss chard.

Water Water contains no calories, but humans need it to live. It is in all our cells, blood, bones, teeth, hair, and skin. We must replenish water daily by drinking fluids and eating foods that contain water.

Water is critical to the body's chemical reactions. It dissolves minerals and other compounds so they can travel through the bloodstream. It removes impurities from the bloodstream and the body.

Water cushions joints, organs, and sensitive tissues, such as the spinal cord. Water maintains pressure on the optic nerves so we can see properly. It also stabilizes blood pressure and helps regulate body temperature.

◀ Potassium

Potassium (puh-TA-see-uhm) is essential for the body's growth and maintenance. It helps maintain the body's normal fluid balance and plays a part in nerve and muscle functions. Symptoms of potassium deficiency include muscle weakness, confusion, irritability, and fatigue. The richest sources of potassium are fruit and vegetables.

Phosphorous ▲

Phosphorus (FAHS-fuh-ruhs) plays a role in releasing energy from foods for the body to use. It also works in conjunction with calcium to maintain bone and tooth structure. A deficiency of phosphorus is rare because it is found in most foods, including meats, fish, dairy products, nuts, cereals, and legumes.

◀ Selenium

Selenium (sih-LEE-nee-uhm) is essential in very small amounts. It functions as an antioxidant that works with vitamin E. It also supports thyroid function. Lack of selenium has been associated with a type of heart disease called Keshan disease. Sources of selenium include nuts, particularly Brazil nuts, meats, whole grains, fish, and shellfish.

◀ Sodium

Salt is the major source of sodium in our diet. Although sodium helps regulate body functions, many people get far more sodium than they need, which can cause high blood pressure and other health problems. Sodium levels can be quite high in processed foods, such as soups, salad dressings, smoked fish and meats, pickled foods, and snack foods. Many people make a point of avoiding high-sodium foods.

Zinc ▲

Zinc supports the immune system, as well as our senses (sight, taste, and smell) and memory. Lack of zinc can result in loss of taste or smell, depression, lack of appetite, growth failure in children, and frequent colds and infections. Oysters, red meat, poultry, eggs, legumes, whole grains, nuts, pumpkin seeds, and sunflower seeds are all sources of zinc.

When our bodies get too hot, because we exert ourselves or our environment is hot, the water in our bodies turns to sweat to cool us off. The human body generally loses about a quart of water daily through the cleansing and cooling processes. It's a good idea to replace at least this amount of lost water throughout the day. Some sources recommend drinking double this amount—eight 8 oz glasses a day. You might need more or less, depending on how active you are and how many other fluids you consume as part of your regular diet.

Calories Eating foods unlocks nutrients so we can use them for growth, regeneration, and repair in the body. Energy from foods fuels our daily activities. No matter how little we exercise, we still need energy for basic functions such as breathing and keeping our hearts beating. We measure a food's energy value in calories.

Calories come from four sources: carbohydrates, proteins, fats, and alcohol. Not all foods that contain calories contain good amounts of other nutrients. In fact, high-calorie foods such as a soft drink or a candy bar or an alcoholic beverage may contain very few nutrients, if any. These foods are said to have empty calories. Foods that contain a lot of nutrients in relation to the number of calories they contain are described as nutrient-dense.

The number of calories that is right for an individual depends on:
- **Weight.** The more you weigh, the more calories you need to maintain your body at its current weight.
- **Activity Level.** The more active you are, the more calories you need. The less active you are, the fewer calories you need.
- **Age/Life Cycle.** Anyone who is still growing or who is in a developmental stage in the life cycle needs more calories. This includes infants and children, adolescents, and pregnant or nursing women. As people age, they require fewer calories.
- **Gender.** Men tend to require more calories than women because they typically have leaner body mass than women do.

The number of calories people consume each day plays an important role in determining whether their weight stays the same, increases, or decreases. When the calories you eat match the calories you use, your current weight is maintained. When you eat more calories than you use, you gain weight. When you eat fewer calories than you use, you lose weight.

 **Reading Checkpoint** *How do the calories in your diet affect your weight?*

Nutrition Information

Nutrition information is designed to tell us how much of a certain nutrient a food or a dish contains in a single serving, and the number of calories in the serving. We get nutrition information from a variety of sources. One of these sources is the U.S. government, which provides dietary guidelines and recommendations for healthy eating, whether you need to plan a menu for yourself or for someone else.

Nutrition Labels and Information Sheets Food manufacturers have included nutrition information on their labels since 1973. As cooks, we use nutrition labels to choose foods that give us the best nutritional value possible.

Foods that don't come with a nutrition label on the package, such as fresh produce, seafood, or meats, still have nutrition information. You can get this information from many sources, including the large database of nutrition information prepared and managed by the U.S. Food and Drug Administration (FDA).

Serving Size Read the information about serving size carefully. The nutrition information on the label is true for the serving size the label indicates.

The serving size is usually listed as a weight (grams or ounces); it may also give a volume measure (½ cup, for instance). Doubling the size of a serving doubles the calories in that serving, along with the saturated fat, cholesterol, sodium, and other nutrients.

Calorie Content The calories in foods come from protein, fats, carbohydrates, or alcohol. If you know how much of each of these nutrients is in the food by weight (gram is the most common unit), you can convert the grams into calories. Then you can add up the calories from each nutrient to get the total calories for a serving.

Calorie content is one of the most basic pieces of information nutrition labels or nutrition software can provide. You can use these numbers to help make wise choices that keep both calories and fats within the suggested limits, such as substituting a food that is lower in saturated fats, cutting back on the salt or sugar you add to a dish, or making portion sizes slightly smaller or larger.

Sources of Calories

Nutrient	Calories
Protein	4 calories per gram
Fat	9 calories per gram
Carbohydrates	4 calories per gram
Alcohol	7 calories per gram

Percent of Daily Value The FDA has established the amount of carbohydrates, fiber, vitamin C, sodium, calcium, and other nutrients your body needs each day. These amounts, known as **daily values**, are listed on nutrition labels as a metric weight (in milligrams or grams) and also as a percent value, shown as "% of daily value" or "%DV."

FIGURE 22-3
Cereal Nutrition Label
The daily values are shown as percentages.
Analyzing Information *How do the daily values change when the cereal is served with milk?*

Nutrition Facts

Serving Size 2/3 cup (55g)
Servings Per Container about 8

Amount Per Serving	Oats & Honey Granola	with 1/2 cup skim milk
Calories	230	270
Calories from Fat	50	50
	% Daily Value**	
Total Fat 6g*	**9%**	**9%**
Saturated Fat 1g	**4%**	**5%**
Trans Fat 0g		
Polyunsaturated Fat 0.5g		
Monounsaturated Fat 3.5g		
Cholesterol 0mg	**0%**	**1%**
Sodium 110mg	**5%**	**7%**
Potassium 140mg	**4%**	**10%**
Total Carbohydrate 42g	**14%**	**16%**
Dietary Fiber 3g	**12%**	**12%**
Sugars 14g		
Other Carbohydrate 25g		
Protein 5g		
Vitamin A	0%	4%
Vitamin C	0%	2%
Calcium	2%	15%
Iron	8%	8%
Thiamin	4%	8%
Riboflavin	2%	15%
Niacin	2%	2%
Vitamin B6	2%	4%
Phosphorus	15%	25%
Magnesium	10%	15%
Zinc	6%	10%

*Amount in cereal. A serving of cereal plus skim milk provides 6g total fat, less than 5mg cholesterol, 170mg sodium, 340mg potassium, 48g total carbohydrate (20g sugars) and 9g protein.
** Percent Daily Values are based on a 2,000 calorie diet. Your daily values may be higher or lower depending on your calorie needs:

	Calories	2,000	2,500
Total Fat	Less than	65g	80g
Saturated Fat	Less than	20g	25g
Cholesterol	Less than	300mg	300mg
Sodium	Less than	2,400mg	2,400mg
Potassium		3,500mg	3,500mg
Total Carbohydrate		300g	375g
Dietary Fiber		25g	30g

FIGURE 22-4 ▶
Food Guide Pyramid
The vertical stripes represent the five food groups.
Inferring *Why aren't sweets represented in the pyramid?*

The % of daily value shows what percentage of the daily requirement for that nutrient you are getting in a single serving, based on a 2000-calorie diet. Even if you eat more or less than 2000 calories each day, this information can show you which foods are good choices to meet your requirements. Anything that has a value of 20% or more is considered a good source of that nutrient.

The Food Guide Pyramid The U.S. Department of Agriculture (USDA) has developed the **Food Guide Pyramid** to help Americans make healthy food choices. Called "MyPyramid," it is a personalized system that guides you in finding a balance between food and physical activity. The pyramid is based on choosing foods from five basic food groups. The number of servings you need from each of the five groups is based on your age, sex, and activity level. If you go to the website MyPyramid.gov you can find out exactly what is recommended for your individual needs.

The five basic food groups are:
- **Grains.** Symbolized by the orange band on the pyramid. Recommended servings are 6 oz of grains a day, making half of them whole wheat.
- **Vegetables.** Shown as the green band. Recommended servings are 2½ cups a day, with a focus on dark greens (such as broccoli and spinach) and orange vegetables (carrots and sweet potatoes).
- **Fruit.** Shown as the red band. Recommended servings are 2 cups of fruit a day, choosing a variety of fruit and going easy on fruit juices.
- **Milk Products.** Shown as the blue band. Recommended servings are 3 cups a day of milk, yogurt, or other milk products, with an emphasis on low-fat or fat-free products.
- **Meat, Fish, Eggs, Beans, and Nuts.** Shown as the narrow purple band. It is recommended that we eat less from this food group than the other food groups. Servings are 5½ ounces a day. Meats and poultry should be low-fat or lean. The narrow yellow band on the pyramid represents oils. The recommendation is to get the oils your body needs from food sources such as fish, nuts, and vegetable oils, but to limit the amount of oil/fat you consume to balance your total calorie intake.

Enriched with Essential Vitamins and Minerals

This phrase has been a common sight on packages of cold cereals for so long that many of us do not think twice about how enriched foods first came about. The story of their origin begins in 1936, when a survey revealed that a growing number of people were suffering from deficiency diseases. These diseases were understood to be the direct result of diets that were lacking important nutrients.

Until that time, whole wheat bread was far more common than white bread. Bread made with whole grain flour supplied the majority of daily requirements of iron, thiamin, niacin, riboflavin, magnesium, zinc, vitamin B6, folacin, and dietary fiber.

But as milling machinery improved, it was easier to make a whiter, smoother flour that produced a softer white bread. This highly refined white bread became cheap, readily available, and far more popular than the coarser, peasant-style whole grain breads. As soon as the demand for whole grain breads dropped, nutritional deficiency diseases increased.

It became obvious that something needed to be done to boost people's nutrient supplies.

The Enrichment Act of 1942, still in effect, required manufacturers to enrich all grain products sold across state lines, including cereals, pastas, and breads. Iron, thiamin, niacin, and riboflavin levels have to be close to what they had been in the whole-grain versions.

In 1998, an amendment to the law also required that folic acid, a B vitamin shown to prevent birth defects, must also be added. Other nutrients are typically added as part of the enrichment process, but they don't have to match the original nutritional value of the grain before it was refined. And there is no requirement for replacing dietary fiber.

Enriched products are certainly a better nutritional bargain than unenriched, bleached, and refined ones. However, they are no match for whole grains. Replacing some nutrients doesn't make the product nutritionally complete, even if the label claims that a cereal offers 100 percent of eight or ten essential nutrients. The body's ability to fully absorb and process these enriched foods is still being researched as scientists uncover more about the special roles played by the nearly 50 known essential nutrients.

Research

Locate labels for three different refined, enriched products: for example, white bread, sweetened cereal, and pasta. Try to find whole grain versions of each of these products and compare the nutritional values to those of the refined products.

Dietary Guidelines Another tool developed to help people create a healthy and well-balanced diet is the Dietary Guidelines for Americans. With an emphasis on reducing risk for major diseases through diet and physical activity, the **Dietary Guidelines** are revised every five years and published by the U.S. Department of Health and Human Services and the USDA.

The Dietary Guidelines, like the Food Guide Pyramid, focus on the five basic food groups. The following recommendations are in the Dietary Guidelines.

- Get adequate nutrients without consuming too many calories. Avoid or limit foods that contain saturated fats, trans fats, and cholesterol. Avoid or limit foods with refined sugar, such as fruit drinks sweetened with corn syrup, candies, and ice cream. They contain too many empty calories and promote tooth decay.
- Choose a variety of fiber-rich fruit, vegetables, whole grains. Try not to add refined sugar, flour, oil, or fats to these foods. Choose potassium-rich vegetables whenever possible.
- Choose low-fat or nonfat dairy foods, lean meats, and low-fat or fat-free beans, nuts, and seeds.
- Keep the total amount of fat in your diet between 20% and 35% of the day's calories, and choose polyunsaturated and monounsaturated fats from foods such as fish, nuts, and vegetable oils.
- Keep your sodium intake, including the salt found in prepared and processed foods, to no more than 1 teaspoon per day (about 2,300mg).

The Dietary Guidelines also offer specific guidance concerning physical activity, alcoholic beverages, and food safety.

 **Reading Checkpoint** *What are the five basic food groups?*

22.1 ASSESSMENT

Reviewing Concepts

1. What does eating a "balanced diet" mean?
2. What are amino acids?
3. What do carbohydrates supply to our bodies?
4. What four factors determine the number of calories a person needs?
5. What are the five basic food groups?

Critical Thinking

6. **Predicting** How can a small amount of fat in a meal prevent you from overeating?
7. **Comparing/Contrasting** Why is it safer to consume excess B vitamins than excess vitamin A?
8. **Classifying** Which mineral and foods are important for anyone in a growth cycle?

Test Kitchen

Go to the kitchen pantry. Look for foods that show on their nutritional labels that they contain saturated fats, trans fats, and high levels of sodium. Knowing that these ingredients are a potential health risk, how do you feel about consuming these foods or serving them to others? How might you limit their use or use other foods as substitutes?

SCIENCE

Dietary Fiber

Research the health benefits of fiber. Describe its role in promoting health and reducing the risk of disease. Make a list of foods that are rich in soluble fiber, and make another list of foods that are rich in insoluble fiber.

22.2 Making Menus More Nutritious

READING PREVIEW

Key Concepts

- Planning healthy menus
- Using healthy food preparation techniques
- Using portioning and presentation techniques

Vocabulary

- batch cooking
- nutritional balance
- ovo-lacto vegetarian
- portion control
- vegan
- vegetarian

"**H**ealthy cooking isn't about taking things out of food. It's about adding more—more flavor, more color, more texture, and of course, more nutrition. "

– Robert Briggs

Planning Healthy Menus

Healthy menus have **nutritional balance**, which means they provide enough calories to meet energy needs and enough specific nutrients to promote health.

Some menus are planned to meet certain objectives, such as controlling weight, blood pressure, or diabetes. For specialized diets, medical professionals such as doctors or nutritionists often make recommendations about foods to eat or avoid, appropriate calorie intake, and daily values for a given vitamin, mineral, or other nutrient.

Menus are more than just a list of foods, dishes, and serving sizes, however. The challenge to the chef is planning menus that meet both nutritional and culinary objectives. In other words, a balanced and healthy menu that isn't interesting, attractive, and delicious may not get eaten. If no one eats the food, then no one gets the benefit of its nutritional value.

Robert Briggs
The Culinary Institute of America

▲ Whole wheat pizza

Choosing Healthy Ingredients The ingredients you choose play a significant role in creating healthy menus. Dietary recommendations and healthy eating plans suggest adding more fresh fruit, vegetables, and whole grains to a diet and keeping refined carbohydrates and sugars at a minimum.

- **Seasonal Produce.** Foods that are in season and locally available have several advantages for healthy cooking. They have the best flavor and texture, so they will appeal to your guests. Produce that doesn't undergo a great deal of handling or processing offers the best nutritional value.
- **Whole Grains.** Nutritionists recommend whole grains as a healthy source of carbohydrate in a balanced diet. Whole grains are minimally processed. That means that some or all of the outer layers that contain many important oils, vitamins, minerals, and fiber were not removed, even if the grain has been ground into a meal or flour. Choose whole grains whenever you can. For instance, choose brown rice instead of white rice to make a pilaf. Replace some or all of the white flour in baked goods with whole wheat flour. If you aren't sure whether a product contains whole grains, read the ingredients on the label to find out.
- **Lean Meat and Poultry.** To keep fat, calories, and cholesterol under control, choose meats that are naturally lean, especially the tenderloin and some parts of the leg or shoulder. Trim surface fat away either before you start to cook the food or before you serve it. For instance, you might want to leave the skin on a chicken while you roast it to protect the meat, but it is easy to remove before you carve the bird and serve it to your guest.
- **Fish.** Like poultry, fish is much lower in saturated fats than meats such as beef, veal, lamb, and pork. Fish has the added

FIGURE 22-5 ▶
Using Lean Meat
Trimming the fat from a beef tenderloin.
Relating Concepts *What are the problems associated with saturated fat?*

advantage of being a source of omega-3 fatty acids. Seafood is low in saturated fats, too, although some varieties may still contain enough cholesterol to be of concern for certain individuals.

- **Reduced Salt.** Consider the total amount of salt in a dish when you choose ingredients. If your recipe calls for ingredients such as soy sauce, capers, olives, anchovies, or cheeses that are already high in sodium, remember to cut back on the amount of salt you add to the dish while it cooks. Foods that are packed in a brine can be rinsed in cool water to remove some of the sodium without removing all their flavor. Substitute other ingredients for salt, such as spices, herbs, plain and flavored vinegars, and chiles. Lemon and lime juice can also add flavor without adding salt.

- **Reduced Sugar.** Adding sugar to a dish makes it taste sweet. It also adds calories, without adding any additional nutrients. Adding fresh or dried fruit to a dish also makes it taste sweet. An important advantage to using dried fruit as sweeteners is that you also add more nutritional value to the dish. You may also add color and texture. Adding fruit to a dish means you can sometimes cut back on the amount of sugar you need to add.

Food Allergies Certain ingredients, although considered healthy by most people, pose problems for people with specific food allergies. Foods such as shellfish, milk, eggs, wheat, soy, peanuts, and other nuts have been known to cause allergic reactions. Menu descriptions should list any of these ingredients in a dish, and service staff should be able to describe menu items upon request. A dish with a peanut sauce, for example, could then be avoided by a person with an allergy to peanuts. A food-service establishment should consider substitutions when planning a dish with ingredients that can cause allergic reactions. The establishment should also be careful about cross-contaminating foods with potentially allergenic foods.

Vegetarian Options Entire food groups are off limits for people who do not eat meat or other animal products. A **vegetarian** is a person who, for religious, ethical, economic, or nutritional reasons, does not eat meat, poultry, and fish. There are several types of vegetarians in the world today. An **ovo-lacto vegetarian** does not eat meat, poultry, and fish but does eat eggs and dairy products. A **vegan** eats no animal products whatsoever and consumes only plant-based foods—vegetables, fruits, grains, legumes, nuts, and seeds. A "semi-vegetarian" might eat no red meat but include poultry and fish in the diet.

CHEF'S TIP

VISIBLE AND INVISIBLE FATS

You can see fat in such foods as sausage and steak. Foods such as nuts and avocados "hide" the fat they contain. Consider not only the amount of fat in a food but the type of fat it contains.

FOCUS ON SAFETY

Food Allergy Precautions

Even a tiny amount of a food can set off an allergic reaction in a person suffering from a food allergy. That means that if a customer is allergic to walnuts, simply scraping off a walnut garnish is not enough to prevent an allergic reaction. Food for allergy sufferers should be prepared without any contact with the problem food. This also applies to the prep table and utensils used to prepare the food.

Greece

Greek cooking features intense flavors: lemon, mint, rosemary, oregano, and lamb. Olives and olive oil from the trees that grow throughout the country are woven into nearly every dish. The country is mountainous and best suited for herding sheep and goats. The Greeks make many delicious yogurt and cheeses from the milk of sheep and goats.

No part of Greece is more than 85 miles from the sea, and nearly 15% of the country is small islands, so it isn't surprising that fish and seafood are an important part of Greek cuisine.

Greece has a mild climate, so vegetables can grow year-round. Eggplant, tomatoes, lettuces, and spinach are just some of the ingredients you'll find in many famous Greek dishes. Fruit, especially melons, peaches, grapes, and cherries are also available fresh year-round.

An important study, done between 1958 and 1975 by Dr. Ansel Keyes, found that men living on the Greek island of Crete had diets that included 43% fat, a rate much higher than is typically suggested as healthy. However, they had extremely low rates of heart attacks. It was discovered that the type of fat they ate most—the monounsaturated fat found in olive oil—has important nutritional benefits.

The health-giving properties of the Greek diet are numerous: olive oil, fresh milk products, fresh fish and seafood, and locally grown produce. Meats are served less often than in the United States and in smaller portions. Dishes that feature whole grains, beans, lentils, and nuts are an important source of protein in the Greek diet.

There is one more aspect of the Greek diet that has important health benefits. A meal in Greece is often an opportunity for family and friends to gather together. No one is in a hurry to get away from the table. The social aspect of Greek dining and its relaxed pace is as beneficial as the diet itself.

Research

Locate Crete on a map of Greece. Describe the geography and climate. Research the typical diet of a person living on Crete in the 1950s. What meals did they eat? What would be a typical menu for each meal? Research Greek olives and olive oil. How many different varieties are there? How are they graded?

◄ *Olives and olive oil*

A growing number of people dining out today are seeking balanced and nutritious vegetarian meals. Dishes that offer complete protein are important menu items. To create such dishes, simply use one of these basic food group combinations:

- Grains and legumes
- Grains and dairy products
- Legumes and seeds/nuts
- Legumes and dairy products
- Seeds/nuts and dairy products

Examples include: peanut butter sandwich, baked beans on toast, peas and rice, refried beans and tortillas, split pea soup and crackers, minestrone soup, hummus on pita bread, pasta and cheese, rice pudding.

Most food-service establishments provide vegetarian options for those who have made vegetarianism their lifestyle and for those who simply want a healthy menu choice.

▲ *Minestrone (grains and legumes)*

 **Reading Checkpoint** *Most healthy eating plans recommend that you eat more of which foods?*

Using Healthy Food Preparation Techniques

When we cook foods, we change their nutritional value. Sometimes the change is minor but sometimes it is quite significant. Healthy menus call for techniques that keep as many nutrients as possible and don't add too many calories or too much fat, sodium, or cholesterol to the dish. The way a dish looks when you serve it to your guest plays a big part in the success of a healthy menu.

Techniques to Emphasize If the start of a healthy dish is choosing and handling ingredients carefully, the next step is the way you choose to cook it. Grilling, broiling, roasting, and baking are all examples of dry heat methods that have the advantage of not calling for adding fats. Moist heat methods are also almost always appropriate: steaming, poaching, simmering, boiling, stewing, and braising.

Foods that are prepared ahead of time and held for a long time in a steam table may lose most of their nutrients, especially water-soluble vitamins B and C. Similarly, if vegetables soak in water for very long before or after cooking, the vitamins dissolve into the water. A general guideline is to try not to leave vegetables in water for longer than necessary and to cook foods as close as possible to the time you want to serve them. There are situations in a food-service setting where foods have to be made in advance, but you can take steps to minimize any loss of flavor and nutrition.

FIGURE 22-6
Grilled Vegetables
Grilling helps retain nutrients and color in vegetables.
Relating Concepts *How can you add flavor to grilled foods without adding salt?*
▼

SAUCES

Choose vegetable sauces or stews such as marinara sauce, salsas, or ratatouille to replace sauces that call for lots of butter or cream. They add flavor, color, texture, and fiber to a dish.

You can prepare foods in larger amounts such as vegetables, pasta, rice, soups, stocks, and sauce. Once you have cooked or parcooked them, you can cool them down safely to below 41°F and keep them in the refrigerator.

When you need to get the food ready to serve, you can prepare just the amount you need—in other words, a small batch. **Batch cooking** is the process of reheating or finishing a small batch of food, as needed, or preparing a small amount of food several times during a service period so a fresh supply of cooked items is always available. This process improves the nutritional value, flavor, color, and texture of the food.

Techniques to Limit Any cooking technique that calls for large amounts of oil, butter, or shortening is one that you will want to limit on a healthy menu. Frying is an obvious example, but other cooking techniques might also encourage adding too many calories, fat, or sodium to a dish.

Thickeners such as roux (made from flour and butter) and liaison (made from heavy cream and egg yolks) give dishes a good texture but may not be appropriate as healthy menu offerings.

Saucing techniques vary, depending on how you want the dish to taste as well as how you want the dish to look. If a sauce gets the majority of its shine or body from heavy cream or butter, you may need to serve the sauce in a slightly different way so you can offer a smaller portion, or you may want to simply find a different sauce to replace sauces that are too high in calories or fat.

Substituting or Modifying Techniques One of the reasons we like fried foods is their crunchy crust. Fried foods are often heavily salted, another reason we enjoy them so much. But they add too many calories, fat, and sodium to most diets. Eating many fried foods, which

BASIC CULINARY SKILLS

Batch Cooking for Vegetables

1. **Rinse, trim, and peel** vegetables properly.
2. **Cut** vegetables into even pieces, as directed in your recipe.
3. **Blanch or parcook** vegetables by boiling or steaming them.
4. **Cool** vegetables quickly in ice water.
5. **Drain** vegetables thoroughly.
6. **Refrigerate** blanched or parcooked vegetables until you are ready to prepare a batch.
7. **Reheat** small batches of vegetables in simmering water.

◀
FIGURE 22-7
Coatings for Crunch
Add a crispy coating, and bake foods instead of frying.
Predicting *What would happen to your crunchy coating if you covered the pan while the chicken bakes?*

are not nutrient-rich, means you need to eat more calories than you should to meet your basic nutritional requirements.

Your challenge as a chef is finding ways to give foods that crisp crunch and salty savor without using a frying technique. Some options you can try include adding a coating such as breadcrumbs, crushed cornflakes, or shredded potatoes to a dish. When you bake foods coated this way, the coating gets crunchy and crisp. You can add fresh herbs, a little cheese, or chopped toasted nuts to add flavor.

FOCUS ON SAFETY

Keep Fruit and Vegetables Safe

Nutritious foods such as fruit and vegetables aren't good for you if they can make you sick. Remember to scrub all produce well and keep potentially hazardous foods refrigerated to keep them safe.

BASIC CULINARY SKILLS

Replacing Oil with Stock in Vinaigrette

1 **Measure** the stock, using the same amount of stock as you would use oil.

2 **Simmer** the stock.

3 **Blend** cornstarch or arrowroot with cold water to make a slurry.

4 **Add the slurry** to the stock, whisking constantly.

5 **Simmer** long enough to thicken the stock, usually two or three minutes.

6 **Cool** the thickened stock.

7 **Add** vinegar and seasonings to the stock and use as a salad dressing, dip, or marinade.

Fried potatoes are also easy to modify. Instead of cooking them in enough oil to cover them, you can brush or spray potatoes with a little oil and then roast them at a high temperature. Adding chopped garlic, herbs, pepper, and spices is a good way to cut back on the amount of salt you might otherwise want to add.

You can almost always use a little less oil when you sauté. Using nonstick and cast-iron pans also makes it easier to cook with less oil. When possible, substitute oils high in monounsaturated fats (olive, canola, and peanut) for oils high in polyunsaturated fats (corn, cottonseed, safflower, sesame seed, sunflower, and vegetable).

Many baked goods will turn out properly if you reduce the amount of added sugar by 20 or 30 percent, but you should always make a trial batch of any baked goods you want to modify. Sometimes sugar is used just to add a sweet flavor, but other times it is a major factor in making sure you get the right texture in baked goods.

 **Reading Checkpoint** *Which cooking techniques are the healthiest?*

Using Portioning and Presentation Techniques

Serving a variety of fresh vegetables, fruit, dry legumes, and whole grains as part of a menu item means that you can create an appealing and nutritious presentation. You can present a balanced dish that makes it a pleasure rather than a chore to get a variety of important nutrients. You can serve small portions of foods that are high in fat, sodium, cholesterol, or calories. You can use these foods more as seasonings than as a main element on the plate.

FIGURE 22-8 ▶
Portion Control
A nutritionally balanced meal of 3 oz of cooked chicken, ½ cup of cooked broccoli, ½ cup of cooked linguine, 1 slice of bread, and ½ cup of fruit salad.
Analyzing Information *Do these portions represent appropriate serving sizes?*

Portions One of the most important ways you can make a dish healthier is to use **portion control**, which means controlling the quantity of particular foods by using appropriately sized servings. The Food Guide Pyramid and other eating plans can tell you what a standard serving is for various foods. In some cases, the portion size might strike you or your guest as either very large or too small.

Learn what the accepted portion size is for foods in each of the five basic food groups. Once you know more about portion sizes and what a portion looks like, you can make adjustments to the way a portion looks on the plates, cups, and bowls you use in your establishment.

Serving Sizes

Food Group	Examples of a Single Serving
Grains	1 slice of bread ½ cup of cooked rice or pasta or hot cereal 1 tortilla 5 whole-wheat crackers or 7 saltine crackers 1 cup of cold cereal ½ bagel or English muffin or hamburger bun
Vegetables	1 cup of raw leafy green vegetables 1 cup of orange vegetables ½ cup of other raw or cooked vegetables ½ cup of vegetable juice
Fruit	1 whole medium-sized fruit (about 1 cup) ½ cup of cooked or canned fruit ¼ cup dried fruit ½ cup of fruit juice
Milk Products	1 cup of milk or yogurt ½ cup cottage cheese 2 slices cheese (1½ ounces)
Meat, Fish, Eggs, Beans, and Nuts	2 to 3 oz of cooked lean meat, poultry, or fish 1 egg ½ cup cooked dry beans 1 tablespoon peanut butter 1 ounce nuts or seeds

Presentation Techniques You can use the wonderful colors, textures, and shapes of foods to entice your guests to eat nutritional menu items.

Colors and Nutrients

When we talk about vegetables, we can describe them by their color: green, white, red, orange, or yellow. Vegetables have different colors because they contain different types of coloring compounds, known as pigments.

Choosing vegetables that have different colors is one of the ways you can make a menu healthier. In fact, the Dietary Guidelines for Americans make some very specific suggestions about how many servings of different-colored vegetables you should eat each week.

The colors in vegetables can give you a hint about the types of vitamins they contain. Choosing vegetables with bright vivid colors is a good technique.

When you cook vegetables, the color can change, because the pigments react to other ingredients. Acids such as lemon juice or vinegar turn green vegetables a dull olive color, but they help white vegetables stay white and keep red vegetables such as red cabbage from turning purple. The amount of time a vegetable spends cooking in hot water can also change its color.

When vegetables have a gray or dull appearance, it means that the pigments have been destroyed. It also may mean that certain vitamins are destroyed.

Experiment

Rinse and trim green beans. Divide the green beans into two equal-sized batches. Fill two pans with enough water to hold the green beans. Add 2 teaspoons of salt to one pan, 2 tablespoons of vinegar to another pan; bring the water to a boil. Add a batch of green beans to each pan. Cook the beans until they are tender. Do they differ in color? Do they differ in texture? Do they differ in taste?

Combining a variety of vibrant colors on a plate is more exciting and appealing than sticking to foods that are mainly beige or brown. Fruit, vegetables, and herbs are a good way to add color. Moist heat techniques can help "set" the bright vivid colors of some foods. Dry heat techniques can intensify or darken a food's color.

You can control the texture of foods by cutting or cooking them in particular ways. Moist heat techniques result in tender, soft foods. Dry heat techniques result in foods with exteriors that are firm or crunchy.

◀
FIGURE 22-9
Colorful Presentation
Broiled cod steak topped with a brightly colored tomato and pepper salsa, garnished with lemon zest, and served on green beans.
Relating Concepts *Which food from the grain food group might be a nice accompaniment to this meal?*

You can introduce whole-grain foods and dry legumes by serving them as a side dish or as an ingredient in a dish. You can also choose to feature them as the main part of the dish, leaving you free to serve smaller portions of meat, poultry, or fish or perhaps omit them entirely.

 **Reading Checkpoint** *What can you do to entice your guests to try healthy menu items?*

22.2 ASSESSMENT

Reviewing Concepts

1. Why are whole grains an important part of a healthy diet?
2. What can happen to the nutrients in foods held in a steam table for too long?
3. How can you prepare chicken so it's crunchy and crispy without frying it?

Critical Thinking

4. **Drawing Conclusions** Why is batch cooking a healthy cooking method?
5. **Compare and Contrast** Why serve a colorful healthy meal versus a mostly beige and brown healthy meal?
6. **Predicting** How would adding butter to a baked potato change it from a health standpoint?
7. **Applying Concepts** What is the healthiest way to sauté?

Test Kitchen

Divide into four teams. Each team will come up with four different healthful ways to sauté the same item. Evaluate the other teams' efforts. Compare appearance, taste, and texture. Decide which method produced the best result.

SOCIAL STUDIES

Vegetarianism

Research the history of vegetarianism. Explore some of the early beliefs that led to this diet and how they have carried over into the present. Describe some of the world cultures who follow a vegetarian diet, and list some historical figures who were vegetarians.

Review and Assessment

Reviewing Content

Choose the letter that best answers the question or completes the statement.

1. Energy from food is measured in units known as
   - a. nutrients
   - b. calories
   - c. amino acids
   - d. antioxidants

2. Which of the following is a water-soluble vitamin?
   - a. vitamin C
   - b. vitamin A
   - c. calcium
   - d. glucose

3. A meal that provides mutual supplementation is
   - a. fish and vegetables
   - b. meat and potatoes
   - c. rice and beans
   - d. rice and salad

4. Healthy eating plans generally recommend adding more of which food groups?
   - a. meat, fish, and eggs
   - b. milk products
   - c. fresh fruit, vegetables, and whole grains
   - d. dairy, meat, and other protein foods

5. A vegan is best described as someone who does not eat
   - a. meat, poultry, and fish
   - b. dairy products
   - c. red meat and eggs
   - d. any animal products

6. Which food group is not represented in the Food Guide Pyramid?
   - a. oils
   - b. sweets
   - c. oils and sweets
   - d. beans

7. Which of the following cooking methods should not be emphasized for healthy cooking?
   - a. grilling
   - b. sautéing
   - c. broiling
   - d. roasting

Understanding Concepts

8. Describe the health benefits of grilling over frying.

9. Which foods contain complete proteins?

10. What is glucose and how does it work in our bodies?

11. What type of fiber scrubs our digestive tract, and what are some sources for it?

12. What is the physical characteristic of oils that are high in saturated fat? Give two examples.

Critical Thinking

13. **Recognizing Patterns** You want to find the most healthful way to cook broccoli, using a moist heat method. Which method do you choose? Explain your answer.

14. **Predicting** Which would be a more satisfying fruit serving, one whole fresh fruit or ½ cup of fruit juice? Why?

Culinary Math

15. **Solving Problems** A one-cup serving of pasta provides 10% of the daily value of carbohydrates, based on a 2000 calories per day diet. If you eat 2500 calories per day, how much pasta would you need to achieve the same 10% of daily value?

16. **Applying Concepts** You need to create a meal plan that includes 2½ cups of fruit. One serving will be a whole apple. You want to divide the remaining amount of fruit into 4 equal servings. How large will each of those servings be?

On the Job

17. **Applying Concepts** Your 2-oz serving of fish, with a cream sauce, looks skimpy on the plate next to the ½ cup of rice. How can you use other food groups to fill out the plate and still present a balanced, healthy meal?

18. **Inferring** Why should your menu always specify if dishes are made with milk products, shellfish, or nuts?

Project 22: Reducing Calories and Fat in Brownies

Answer these questions when your class works through Project 22.

- Which variation of the brownies has the best color? Why?

- Which variation of the brownies is the most moist? Why?

- Which variation of the brownies has the best flavor? Why?

- Which brownie recipe would you be most likely to make for yourself, and which would you make for customers? Why?

TEST PRACTICE

Choose the letter that best answers the question or completes the statement.

1. The building blocks of protein are
   - A calories
   - B carbohydrates
   - C amino acids
   - D vitamins

2. Which makes a simple carbohydrate easy to distinguish from a complex carbohydrate?
   - A It tastes sweet.
   - B It tastes bland.
   - C It is starchy.
   - D It is pale in color.

3. Which of the following is a good source of roughage, or insoluble fiber?
   - A fruit juice
   - B oats
   - C canola oil
   - D wheat bran

4. Which of the following is not true about saturated fats?
   - A They come mostly from animal sources.
   - B They are heart-healthy.
   - C They are usually solid at room temperature.
   - D They can increase the risk of obesity.

5. One product of hydrogenation is
   - A margarine
   - B butter
   - C fiber
   - D canola oil

6. Which of the following is an antioxidant?
   - A vitamin D
   - B iron
   - C vitamin C
   - D sodium

7. Serum cholesterol levels can rise from eating
   - A avocados
   - B organ meats
   - C fish
   - D all of the above

8. Which foods are high in sodium?
   - A snack foods
   - B pickled foods
   - C smoked foods
   - D all of the above

9. Which of the following is not a factor for determining caloric needs?
   - A hunger level
   - B weight
   - C gender
   - D activity level

10. The Dietary Guidelines recommends limiting
    - A potassium-rich foods
    - B monounsaturated fats
    - C trans fats
    - D fiber-rich foods

23

THE BUSINESS OF A RESTAURANT

23.1 Owning Your Own Restaurant

READING PREVIEW

Key Concepts

- Creating a business plan
- Establishing a client base
- Marketing and promoting a restaurant
- Reading income statements

Vocabulary

- ambience
- assets
- bottom line
- brand
- budget
- business plan
- client base
- cost control
- earnings
- expenses
- fixed cost
- income
- income statement
- liabilities
- logo
- P&L
- profit
- profit and loss statement
- promotion
- sales
- theme
- variable cost

> **"M**aking the dream of a restaurant into a reality exercises every one of your business skills, from good planning to good communicating to creative problem-solving. **"**
>
> – John Storm
> The Culinary Institute of America

Creating a Business Plan

Owning a restaurant is a dream for many individuals in the food service industry, but there are no guarantees of success. The National Restaurant Association estimates that out of every five restaurants that open, only one will still be in operation after five years. Even if you are not ready to open up your own place, it is important that you understand how the business operates so you can contribute toward keeping the restaurant in which you work open by working in a business-like, professional manner.

Our mission is to be a respected leader in the food service and hospitality industries. We guarantee our customers quality products that provide real value, with the service they expect, in clean, pleasant surroundings. We dedicate ourselves to sound management practices and effective human relations, while returning maximum earnings to our stockholders.

FIGURE 23-1
Mission Statement
A mission statement is the business plan boiled down to a few sentences.
Analyzing Information *How does a mission statement affect restaurant staff?*

FIGURE 23-2
Creating an Ambience
An upscale dining room.
Communicating *Describe the ambience of this dining room.*

Before embarking on the business journey, every good business owner comes up with a business plan. A **business plan** helps you take a few steps back from your dream and turn an objective eye on the advantages and disadvantages of opening and operating the business. A good business plan makes a clear statement about the restaurant. It typically includes a mission statement, specific goals that support the mission of the business, sample menus, preliminary operating budgets, and staffing needs.

You can go about creating a business plan in different ways. Perhaps you will begin with your menu, or perhaps you have a market or type of customer you want to attract. You may already know where you want your business to be or the hours that you expect to be in operation.

No matter where you start, you will need to make decisions about the menu, staff, location, hours of operation, and prices. Although you can certainly open up a business without a written business plan, many people need to borrow money to start. To get a loan or other type of assistance, as well as to get the necessary permits to open a business, a written business plan is often necessary, or at least extremely helpful. It becomes a way for you to explain to potential lenders, partners, or governmental agencies how your business will be run.

Theme and Style A restaurant's **theme** is very important. The theme will tie everything—including the decorations, the lighting, the food, and the prices—together in one package. One aspect of the theme is the ambience (AM-bee-ance), or the feeling or mood of the restaurant. Think about any restaurant you have visited. Were there candles or fresh flowers on the table? Was the lighting bright, or was it soft and somewhat dark? All of these factors contribute to the ambience of the restaurant.

The decisions you make about the theme and ambience of the restaurant will affect how the business operates. One of the ways that you can give a potential lender or partner insight into the restaurant's feel is by including sample menus. The type of dishes you serve and the price you might charge affects the furnishings for the restaurant, the type of uniforms you might use for wait staff, and even the number of people you need to hire in the kitchen and the dining room.

Budget Each restaurant needs a **budget**, a list of planned income and expenses. Every item in the restaurant, including food items, silverware, and cleaning products, is listed in the budget. The owner tries to anticipate every expense the business might face over the course of a year to produce an annual budget. At the same time, the owner tries to anticipate the potential income the restaurant will generate.

The annual budget is used to create budgets for shorter periods of time. Budgets become an important way to measure how effectively your business is operating. They can help you determine whether the business is meeting its goals. The sooner you know that you are over-budget in an area, the sooner you can make an adjustment. For instance, if the amount you spend on salaries is too high, you can reconsider how you are scheduling your staff.

Staffing Needs Because salaries are an important part of the cost of operating a restaurant, it is important to plan the number of employees you need. Having too many people on staff means that you are spending a great deal on salaries. If you don't have enough staff, you may have difficulty providing the kind of quality food and service that will keep your customers coming back.

Salaries are a big part of the expenses in any restaurant. In addition to having a clear idea of how many people you need, you also need to decide what kind of staff you need. You may not need highly skilled individuals for some work. However, you should also understand when a skilled worker could actually help you make more money. For instance, for specialized work such as cutting meats or fish, having experienced staff can save you money.

Hours of Operation To make a good plan, you need to know when your restaurant is going to be open for service. The more hours your restaurant is open, the more staff you need and the more food you may need. After you have been open for a period of time, you can begin to see which days are busy and which days are slow.

▲
FIGURE 23-3
Dining Room Staff
A primary concern for a restaurant is the number of people needed and their skill levels.
Relating Concepts *How does the dining room staff impact a restaurant's budget?*

The Business of a Restaurant ▶ **735**

Normal hours of operation should be part of your plan, but you should also try to include additional activities. For instance, a catered event may be scheduled for a day when your restaurant is usually closed.

Reading Checkpoint *What does a business plan typically include?*

Establishing a Client Base

Your **client base** is the group of customers who come to your restaurant to dine. Your client base may be a little difficult to identify when you are planning your business or in the early stages of its operation. Before you start your restaurant and in the early stages of running it, you need to find out as much as you can about your location, your market, and your early customers' reactions to your food and service. You can use the information to make good choices when it comes to advertising and promoting your restaurant.

Location Sometimes your location determines who your client base will be. A restaurant located near a college campus is likely to count on a young clientele with limited money to spend on fancy meals. If you know that, you can tailor your business to that client base. On the other hand, if you are located near office businesses, you may have a somewhat wealthier clientele who don't have much leisure and who all want to eat at about the same time; you may have a great breakfast and lunch business but practically no one for dinner.

Market When a large company wants to introduce a new product, they do market research. They try to find out as much as they can about the market—who wants (or might want) the product, how often they might use it, and what they are willing to pay for it. To ensure your restaurant's success, you must know who your target customers are. This means you need to conduct market research to determine the likely age, income, and other related information about typical customers. Will your restaurant serve mostly families? Will it be a restaurant geared toward a younger, single crowd? An upscale restaurant has pricey menu items and the customers tend to dress up more. A

Figure 23-4
Your Client Base
Get to know your customers through opinion surveys.
Solving Problems *What might you do to attract customers who are under 30 years of age?*

casual restaurant has less expensive menu items, with customers who are casually dressed. Knowing your potential customer helps you determine what kind of restaurant you should open.

Customers' Reactions Feedback is when people give you their opinions about how things are going. Getting feedback from your customers is a great way to conduct ongoing market research in the early stages of running a restaurant. Owners can use different ways to gather information about who is visiting the restaurant and whether customers are happy. This can lead to changes in the way you do business, or it can reinforce concepts and practices that keep the customer happy.

Have you ever visited a restaurant where a person other than the waiter came up to the table and asked how the meal was? Often, a restaurant manager visits the tables and inquires about the quality of the food and the service. Have you noticed suggestion cards and questionnaires on the tables at some restaurants? This is because they want to learn what the customers think. For many restaurants, even those that have been in business for years, obtaining feedback from customers is one of the most important aspects of determining a restaurant's direction.

 Reading Checkpoint *What are three things you need to find out about early in the process of planning and running a restaurant?*

Marketing and Promoting a Restaurant

Restaurant owners have many means at their disposal to entice guests to visit their restaurant. Some obvious ways include advertisements and signs. Some less obvious ways include participating in charity events or serving on committees. Choosing the right way to market and promote your restaurant depends on your goals and your budget.

Your Brand Many people talk about a business's **brand**. What they mean is the public image of your business. It's an accumulation of all the things that come to mind when someone mentions your business, including your name, your logo, and sometimes even a slogan.

FIGURE 23-5 Brand Recognition A seafood restaurant with a lobster logo. **Classifying** *Name some restaurants that have distinctive logos.*

The Business of a Restaurant ▶ **737**

FIGURE 23-6
Outdoor Advertising
A prominent sign is another way to attract customers.
Communicating *What are the different types of outdoor advertising you have seen for restaurants?*

Your restaurant's name affects how you market your restaurant. The name gives guests a clue about your food or the kind of experience they might have. Your **logo**—a drawing, picture, or other symbol that identifies your restaurant—should be instantly recognizable.

Advertising Advertisements are the way you tell a potential customer about your business. Printed materials you might use to market or promote your restaurant run from advertisements in local papers, magazines, and entertainment guides to listings in phone directories. Some restaurants use flyers as a way to attract guests. Posting your menu outside the restaurant where walkers can read it is another example of advertising. You may also decide you need other items, such as bumper stickers or hats with your logo or name.

Newspaper and magazine articles are another way to advertise your restaurant. You may be featured in an article as an expert, someone the reporter turned to for answers to questions or for a professional opinion. You may actually write an article. Or you may prepare a press release for a magazine or newspaper about your restaurant that provides details or information about events or other happenings at your restaurant. Websites are also an effective way to give your customers information about your restaurant and a good way to advertise.

In any ad, you should include information about how to get in touch with the restaurant. You may not always have space in the ad to list the hours of operation, your menu, or directions, but you

A&W Root Beer®

One hot day in 1919 in Lodi, California, Roy Allen mixed up a batch of root beer and sold his first frosty mug for one nickel. Allen had purchased the formula for his root beer from a pharmacist in Arizona, and to this day, the blend of herbs, spices, barks, and berries remains a proprietary secret, just as closely guarded as the formula for Coca-Cola® or the "secret blend of herbs and spices" used in KFC® chicken.

▲ *An early A&W root beer stand*

By 1933, the creamy beverage was such a success that there were over 170 stands operating in the Midwest and West. In fact, A&W® may well be the United States' first official franchise. A franchise is an operation that may be independently owned by an individual but the business is still associated with a parent company. A&W Root Beer concentrate, for example, was sold to every franchise operator to ensure uniform quality.

Allen was a classic entrepreneur, someone with an idea for a business who went about his work independently. There was no corporation to guide him or veto his decisions. From that first five-cent mug of root beer, Allen followed up with a second stand in nearby Sacramento. It was there that he opened what may have been the country's first "drive-in" featuring "tray-boys" for curbside service.

Allen took on a partner, Frank Wright, in 1922. Wright was an employee from his original store in Lodi. The two partners combined their initials—"A" for Allen and "W" for Wright—and formally named their beverage A&W Root Beer. Three stands were opened in Sacramento, followed by additional stands in northern California, Texas, and Utah.

In 1950, with over 450 A&W restaurants operating nationwide, founder Roy Allen retired and sold the business to a Nebraskan named Gene Hurtz. During this time, drive-ins were becoming increasingly popular and A&W became one of the few nationally established drive-in restaurant chains. By 1960 the number of A&W restaurants had grown to over 2000.

Research

Research a franchised restaurant. What are the requirements for opening a franchise? How does the corporation work with the person buying the franchise? In your opinion, what are the advantages and disadvantages of a franchise?

need to let people know how to find out more information about your restaurant.

Word-of-mouth is a type of informal advertising. You can't really pay for it, but most restaurants depend on it. When your guests leave your operation happy with their experience, they will tell other people they know to come for a meal. Word-of-mouth advertising is not automatically positive, but it is almost always one of the most powerful types of advertising. Restaurant reviews are a type of word-of-mouth advertising.

Promoting Sometimes, you need to do more than just advertising to get people interested in your restaurant. These extra steps aimed at filling up the dining room are known as **promotion**. One example of promoting a restaurant might be to have a booth or stall at the county fair. Another way might be to include money-off coupons in your advertising. Or, you might decide to participate in a charity event. Promotional efforts can be as simple as having a special deal every Tuesday evening, such as "buy one main course and get a second one free." Promotional events can also be original and community-minded, such as having the entire kitchen staff volunteer to work at a local soup kitchen.

 **Reading Checkpoint** *What is a brand?*

Reading Income Statements

Running a business properly means keeping track of your expenses and your income. A record of your earnings (or income) and losses is known as an **income statement**, or you may hear it referred to as a profit and loss statement. A **profit and loss statement**, often referred to simply as a **P&L**, collects information about the money coming into the restaurant (its **earnings**) and the money being spent by the restaurant (its **expenses**). The P&L then calculates whether the business is making money or losing money.

You will often hear business owners refer to the **bottom line**. What they are talking about is this: the amount of money they have left after they have paid all the bills—that is, after they have subtracted the expenses from their earnings. A restaurant has many different expenses. Some of them, such as the cost of food and beverages, are obvious. Others, the cost of having garbage hauled away or having to do some repairs to the air conditioning in the dining room, for example, are not so obvious.

In a business, the **assets** are things the business owns. These include raw ingredients, of course, but also such things as chairs, large equipment, signs, carpets, appliances, and china. **Liabilities** (lie-a-BILL-i-ties) are losses that occur when the restaurant uses up assets without making a profit.

The money spent in the restaurant by the customer is referred to as the restaurant's **sales**. This is also known as the restaurant's **income**. You calculate **profit** by subtracting expenses (such as the cost of raw ingredients or labor) and losses (wasted or spoiled food, for example) from the sales (money received from customers). An income statement shows this basic equation:

> Income – Expense = Profit

If there are too many liabilities and not enough sales, the restaurant will eventually fail. A successful restaurant, on the other hand, is able to successfully minimize liabilities and maximize profits.

The food you buy to prepare is one of a restaurant's expenses. Anything you need to spend money on to run the business is an expense. Your chef might mention the kitchen's raw food cost to you. Remember from Chapter 21 that the raw food cost is the cost of all the ingredients that go into a dish. So the raw food cost for the entire restaurant is the cost of all the ingredients that go into all the dishes on the menu.

The raw food cost is a measurement of how much you are spending on food, compared to the amount of money your customers are spending in the restaurant. The raw food cost is usually expressed as a percentage. Some owners use a menu pricing method that indicates what an acceptable raw food cost percentage is. They may even include this percentage in their business plan. Most restaurant managers certainly watch this percentage and try to control it. Knowing what your raw food costs are is important if you want to make improvements in the bottom line. Dropping from a 40% raw food cost to a 35% raw food cost will improve profits.

▲ The business of a restaurant: making and selling food

Food costs are a type of expense that can vary from one day, week, month, or year to the next. They are an example of a **variable cost**. That means that the amount you spend changes from time to time. A **fixed cost** (also called a fixed expense), on the other hand, is the same from one month to the next. Your mortgage or rent payment is an example of a fixed cost.

A restaurant manager should always try to control variable costs. This means the manager will ask the staff to try to get the most they can from everything the restaurant pays for. For example, the manager will make sure that food isn't left out to spoil or that new food deliveries are put away behind the older items so you don't have to throw out food that has become too old to serve. (Remember from Chapter 1 that this is called the "First In, First Out" or "FIFO" system.) Turning ovens on when you need them rather than simply turning them on in the morning and letting them run until you turn out the lights at night is another way you can keep variable expenses in check. This is also known as **cost control**.

In addition to variable expenses, a restaurant owner or manager must keep an eye on fixed costs. For example, the owner or manager needs to account for such things as the cost of owning, renting, or leasing the property, as well as services that may be required (such as a linen service that delivers uniforms and table linens or a pest management service).

FIGURE 23-7 ▶
Catering for Added Income
A restaurant can cater parties or host special events to increase income.
Solving Problems *What types of parties or events might a restaurant cater or host?*

Just as there are fixed and variable costs at a restaurant, there are potentially other sources of income as well. Of course, the sale of food and beverages to customers typically generates the biggest income for a restaurant. However, some restaurants find other ways to add income opportunities. For example, restaurants sometimes offer catered events or special-occasion menus. These other sources of income can sometimes be good ways to add to the profit at a restaurant.

 **Reading Checkpoint** | *What basic equation does an income statement show?*

23.1 ASSESSMENT

Reviewing Concepts
1. What does a business plan typically include?
2. What are three things you need to find out about early in the process of planning and running a restaurant?
3. What is a brand?
4. What basic equation does an income statement show?

Critical Thinking
5. **Comparing/Contrasting** What is the difference between a variable cost and a fixed cost? Provide examples.
6. **Comparing/Contrasting** What is the difference between profit and sales?
7. **Applying Concepts** If your sales in a month were $150,000 and your expenses were $124,500, what would be your profit?

Test Kitchen
Divide into four teams. Each team will create a mission statement for a new restaurant and cook a signature main course that fits the mission statement. Evaluate the results as if you were a banker deciding whether to give a loan to a new restaurant business.

CULINARY MATH

Business Plans
Using the Internet, research the ready-to-use business plans that are based on such software programs as Microsoft Excel or QuickBooks. Report on two of these. If you were a small-restaurant owner, would you feel comfortable using this sort of program?

23.2 Purchasing & Inventorying

READING PREVIEW

Key Concepts

- Using basic purchasing principles
- Preparing inventories

Vocabulary

- bid
- inventory
- market quote
- order
- par-stock list
- physical inventory
- producer
- product specifications
- purveyor
- supplier
- vendor

" **T**he decisions you make about where to buy your products are as important as the decisions you make about what to buy. "

– Jay Stein
The Culinary Institute of America

Basic Purchasing Principles

Purchasing the items a restaurant needs is a big job. It is much more than simply placing an order or picking up a product at the store.

Restaurants purchase the items they need to stay in business in different ways. They can buy the same product from different places. They can buy in bulk or buy just what they need for a day or two. The challenge is determining which vendor has the quality the restaurant requires, at the best price, and who can deliver it on time.

Basic Steps of Purchasing The buyer at a restaurant needs to understand the basic steps in the purchasing process. The typical purchasing process involves five steps. After items are ordered, the vendor sends them to the restaurant, where they are formally received and stored properly.

Creating a Par-Stock List A **par-stock list** is a list of the quantity of supplies you need to have on hand in the restaurant to make every item on your menu. The quantity should be enough to last from one delivery to the next.

Usually, a small extra amount is added to the par-stock list as a type of cushion, or protection, against unexpected needs for items. The size of this extra amount depends on a number of factors: how busy the restaurant is, any special events that might change the level of business, or the time between deliveries. The more information you have about how well a dish sells and how many customers you usually have, the more accurate your par-stock lists will be.

Writing Purchase Specifications If you are the person doing the purchasing for the restaurant, you must write out an exact description of each product the restaurant needs. To let the vendor know the specific product the restaurant wants, you use **product specifications**. These specifications describe specifically such things as size, quality, grade, packaging, color, weight, or count. For instance, you may need chicken for two different dishes. The first dish might require boneless, skinless chicken breast portions to make a chicken piccata main course. The second dish might require a whole stewing chicken for your chicken soup. You might also specify that both types of chicken should be organic, free-range chickens.

Product specifications can also detail how the product is supposed to be

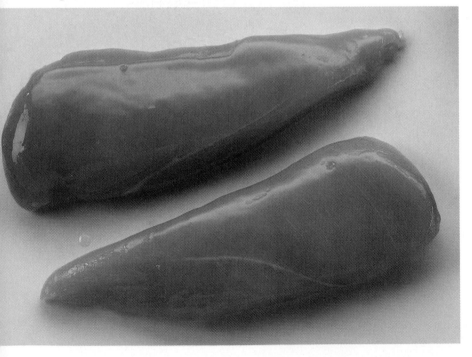

FIGURE 23-8
Purchase Specifications
Boneless, skinless chicken breasts can be the most expensive cut of chicken.
Predicting *What might happen to your food costs if you receive boneless skinless chicken breasts instead of chicken thighs?*

delivered. For example, you might specify that frozen goods must be delivered in good condition and at a temperature that maintains quality and safety.

The more detail in your product specifications, the better. Buying exactly what you need is one of the ways you can improve quality as well as profits.

Selecting Suppliers A restaurant can buy food from many sources. The person or business selling you something may be known by one of the following terms: **supplier**, **vendor**, **purveyor** (puhr-VAY-er), or **producer**. Some suppliers offer a large number of items. Others specialize in a specific type of product.

You can find suppliers for a particular product by asking other restaurant owners where they buy their goods. You can also search on the Internet. Some vendors are best for large quantities or items you want to purchase in bulk. Others are best for items that are difficult to find.

A supplier will give the restaurant a product list and a delivery schedule. Review the product lists and delivery schedules carefully. If you know that you want organic, free-range chicken, for example, and the supplier doesn't carry that sort of chicken, you will need to locate another supplier. Or, if a supplier delivers only on Mondays and your restaurant is closed that day, you may need to find someone else.

Some restaurants find it easier to deal with a small number of suppliers. They try to find suppliers that offer a wide range of products, from produce to paper goods.

Obtaining Market Quotes and Bids Once you have written your par-stock list and your purchase specifications, you can ask suppliers to give you market quotes. A **market quote** is a statement of the product's selling price and an indication of the length of time that the price will be effective. The length of time the market quote is in effect depends on the product. Some foods have prices that change a great deal from week to week. Most fresh produce, meat, and poultry fall into this category. Some products, such as canned and paper goods, have the same price week in and week out. Be sure to take note of the effective dates on the market quote.

A **bid** is essentially a proposal from the supplier, telling you the price the supplier will charge you if you accept the supplier's proposal. A bid can be affected by business factors. For example, if your restaurant buys in bulk, a supplier may give you a bid at a lower price per pound than would be charged for a smaller amount. Suppliers you have not used before might offer lower bids than usual in an attempt to persuade you to try their products.

▲
FIGURE 23-9
Units of Carrots
Carrots from this supplier come in large bags that weigh many pounds.
Drawing Conclusions *How many pounds would you guess are in these bags?*

Placing Orders An **order** is a communication between a buyer (the restaurant) and a seller (the supplier). The restaurant tells the supplier the name of the product the restaurant wants (based on the restaurant's purchase specifications and the supplier's product list) and the amount of that product that the restaurant needs.

To fill out an order properly, you need to know the unit for the product. Some foods are sold by the piece, so you may simply give a number. For example, you might order 5 legs of lamb.

Other foods are sold in cases, cartons, crates, bags, or boxes. Be sure to review the description of the packaging in the supplier's product list. Different suppliers may sell the same item in different units. A case of lettuce from one supplier may weigh 50 pounds, while a case of lettuce from another supplier may weigh 20 pounds. Both would be listed in the supplier's product list as a case, but you would need to notice that each of the individual cases have different weights.

Ordering food and other items for a restaurant can be time-consuming. In very large operations, ordering may be the job of a single individual or even a group of individuals. To be certain you do the job effectively and are following good business practices, you should have the following information to place your order:

- Par-stock
- Product specifications
- Inventory
- Suppliers and their product lists
- Suppliers' market quotes or bids

One of the ways that restaurants manage the purchasing process more efficiently is by using software and the Internet. Some software links inventory, par-stock, and menus so that parts of the work are done automatically.

 Reading Checkpoint   *What are the five basic steps in the purchasing process?*

Inventories

An **inventory** is a list of all the assets in the restaurant, usually organized by category. The par-stock list is a list of what you think you should have on hand. An inventory is an exact count of what is actually on hand. You calculate the amount of stock you need to order by subtracting the current inventory from the amount shown on the par-stock list.

Par-Stock List − Inventory = Amount to Order

Taking a **physical inventory** means actually counting up what you have. For instance, you need to count all the cans of tomato sauce, all the boxes of pasta, all the cases of paper towels, and all the 3-ounce ladles in the restaurant. This is a time-consuming but very important part of running a restaurant. Without an accurate inventory, you won't know when you are low on something or when you have so much that you are wasting space to store it.

For a small restaurant, inventory-taking usually means people with clipboards count cans, boxes, bags, and individual items. A larger restaurant's inventory may be managed completely on a computer, especially if every product has a bar code. A very exact physical inventory is taken as often as necessary. Some restaurants may take a physical inventory on a weekly or monthly basis.

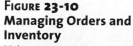
FIGURE 23-10
Managing Orders and Inventory
Using a computer program to track orders and inventory.
Drawing Conclusions *How could purchase and inventory software help improve the ordering process?*

 **Reading Checkpoint** *What is a physical inventory?*

23.2 ASSESSMENT

Reviewing Concepts

1. What are the five basic steps in the purchasing process?
2. What is a physical inventory?

Critical Thinking

3. **Compare and Contrast** What is the difference between a par-stock list and an inventory?
4. **Drawing Conclusions** Why is a par-stock list important for a restaurant?
5. **Inferring** Why would a supplier indicate the length of time for which a market quote is effective?
6. **Inferring** What type of event might require that you add a small extra amount of items to your par-stock list?
7. **Drawing Conclusions** Why would you obtain market quotes from multiple suppliers?

Test Kitchen

Divide into four teams. Each team will choose 3 main courses and 3 appetizers to put on a menu for a small restaurant. Assume that the restaurant serves only these dishes to only 30 people a night, with the dishes evenly balanced. Construct a par-stock list, assuming that there are 3 days between deliveries. Ask another team to evaluate your list.

SCIENCE

Restaurant Suppliers

Using the Internet, research three restaurant suppliers for a specific hard-to-find food . Identify what each supplier's specialty is. Check to see if they have an online product list or list of their delivery schedules.

Managing a Restaurant

READING PREVIEW

Key Concepts

- Managing facilities
- Managing people

Vocabulary

- job description
- orientation
- performance evaluation
- termination
- training
- verbal warning
- written warning

> "**F**inding, hiring, and retaining the best employees is the sign of a truly great manager. "
>
> – Marc Gleason
> Associate Dean of Business Management
> The Culinary Institute of America

Managing the Facility

The layout of a restaurant depends on factors related to safety and cleanliness. A restaurant manager starts thinking about sanitation during the design layout process. For example, there must be enough space to effectively clean each of the restaurant's areas. The materials used in the building should be easy to clean and maintain. Any equipment, such as blenders or mixers, should be easy to clean and easy to take apart for cleaning.

The health codes that affect the operation of a food service establishment are found at all levels of government, including federal and state laws as well as local and city ordinances. Restaurant owners and managers must be familiar with all the legal requirements that apply to a restaurant. The manager also has to ensure that the staff know and understand the rules as well.

Both dining and kitchen areas have to meet sanitary standards and health regulations. If the restaurant does not meet these standards, the restaurant could be fined.

Dining Room Any restaurant manager wants a dining room that will hold as many customers as possible. Having more customers typically means more profit. However, the dining room cannot be completely full of tables. Not only would that be unpleasant for diners, it is also illegal. There are capacity limits that restrict how many people a room will hold. The restaurant manager must be aware of those limits, which are usually laid out in the fire code for the building.

Aside from safety concerns, the dining room will need adequate space for the wait staff, who need to be able to navigate through the dining room with ease and with speed. If the tables are arranged too closely together, or if there is not a clear path to the kitchen, your wait staff will have difficulty performing their jobs.

Finally, all public accommodations, from seating arrangements to restrooms, must meet the standards of the Americans with Disabilities Act. This means providing adequate space and accessibility for people with special needs (for example, wheelchair-accessible restrooms). It is illegal for public establishments to deny service to customers with disabilities.

The Kitchen The kitchen usually takes up about one-third of the restaurant's entire floor space. For any commercial kitchen, there are laws about cleanliness. Any surfaces that come into contact with food must be smooth, nontoxic, nonabsorbent, free from crevices, and free from sharp corners and edges.

The floor plan of the kitchen should allow for people to move around easily between work areas. You may need areas reserved for baking and pastry work or an area where fish and meat are butchered. These areas may require special refrigeration, baking, or cooking equipment. The area should be selected with an eye to the amount of work being done and the skills of the staff.

Somewhere near the kitchen, an area is usually reserved for employees to change into uniforms or keep their personal items. There should be lockers and storage areas for cleaning products as well as for all the linens for the tables. There also has to be enough room so the kitchen staff can receive and inspect incoming products.

The waste management system is a critically important part of the kitchen. A lot of trash is created during the food preparation process.

FIGURE 23-11
Dining Rooms
Clear paths around the tables and through the dining room improve service.
Predicting *How might a restaurant's theme influence the number of tables and their positions in a dining room?*

▲
FIGURE 23-12
Managing the Facility
Properly disposing of garbage
is part of keeping the operation
running smoothly and safely.
**Cognitive Skills/
interactions** *Apart from
appearance, why should dumpsters
have lids?*

Trash containers should be leak-free, pest-proof, and easy to clean and sanitize. The trash containers should be covered when not in use and should be cleaned frequently (inside and out). Of course, you must regularly get rid of the trash, using a public or private hauler.

Other Areas The other major areas of a restaurant can include:

- An entry (common space)
- A lobby, foyer, or vestibule
- A coat room
- Customer restrooms
- An area for displays and retail sales, if needed
- A bar or lounge, if needed

Restaurants are required by law to have working hand-washing stations in both the public restrooms and the employees' restrooms. This means there must be hot and cold running water, soap, something for drying hands, and a waste container. The public restrooms must be clearly marked and be in a convenient location within the restaurant.

 **Reading Checkpoint** *Name at least three areas in a restaurant besides the kitchen and dining room.*

Managing People

One of the restaurant manager's most important jobs is managing the people who work at the restaurant. A manager must be a leader and a supervisor, and at times managers need to roll up their sleeves and work alongside the employees.

Communicating One of the most important factors in the success of a restaurant's service involves communication between the manager and the employees. A good manager knows each member of the staff and frequently communicates with each person. The manager communicates the expectations for each worker and offers the chance for each worker to check in periodically to talk about how the job is going. A manager should provide a training manual for each new hire.

Managers need to be aware not only of how they communicate with employees, but also how employees communicate with each other and with the customers. Everyone works better when they feel that they are being treated professionally and with dignity. Failure to communicate properly can also have legal implications. Using ethnic slurs, profanity, or abusive language is a serious concern. Managers need to be aware of what is appropriate and let their employees know what are considered the best practices for your restaurant.

◄

FIGURE 23-13
Communicating
The manager and chef must keep lines of communication open.
Cognitive Skills/interactions *Why is it important that the chef and manager communicate about the menu?*

Hiring and Training The manager will hire, train, and supervise most of the restaurant staff. A restaurant business typically has a high turnover rate. This means that people do not stay with the establishment for long periods of time. For this reason, the restaurant manager is frequently hiring new employees.

FIGURE 23-14
Hiring Staff
Offering an applicant the job.
Cognitive Skills/interactions *List several questions you think the employer should ask an applicant.*

▼

To locate prospective new employees, the manager can choose to place Help Wanted ads in the restaurant windows, in local newspapers, or on the Internet. The manager could also rely on word of mouth—letting current workers know that a position is available and then interviewing candidates recommended by them.

If the manager feels that a job applicant may be right for the restaurant, the manager will invite the applicant for an interview. Managers look for three basic things when making most hiring decisions:

- Is the candidate qualified for the job? Does this candidate have the right amount of experience?
- Does the candidate meet the skill standards for the position?
- Is the candidate dependable?

In the hiring process at any business, the manager must always be aware of potential discrimination. Although you do not have to hire unqualified people, you cannot discriminate on the basis of race, color, religion, sex, nationality, age, or disability. For this reason, interview questions related to these areas are strictly off-limits and should never be asked.

These sorts of questions can be used as evidence of discrimination, even if the interviewer did not intend them as such.

Each employee should know the job description for his or her position. A **job description** includes the duties to be performed and responsibilities involved, as well as the level of education and training the worker should possess. (A job description can even be used during the hiring process when the manager is seeking to fill a position at the restaurant.) These are all ways to keep the lines of communication open and to keep workers happy.

Any employee hired at a restaurant must undergo orientation and training. During **orientation**, the employee learns about the restaurant, including the menu items and the layout. This process teaches new employees about their roles in the organization and about the organization as a whole.

The **training** process allows employees time to learn the job and practice it, usually by shadowing someone who has the same or a similar position. Additionally, a good manager will have a system for ongoing training so employees can always be involved in a learning process. This lets employees grow and develop new skills and contributes to the overall success of the restaurant.

FIGURE 23-15 ▶
Training Staff
Teaching a newly hired waiter how to use the coffee maker.
Applying Concepts *What's the relationship between job training and job satisfaction?*

Periodically, the manager will sit down with each employee and conduct a **performance evaluation**. In this meeting, the manager and the employee talk about whether or not the employee has met expectations, based on the job description.

Terminating There will come a time when every manager needs to discipline an employee. This usually happens when an employee does not act according to the rules or is not performing up to expectations. Some ways of carrying out discipline on an employee include:

- **Verbal Warning.** The manager can give an employee a **verbal warning**. This means that the employee is told about the need for improvement in a particular area.
- **Written Warning.** The manager can give an employee a **written warning**. This means that the manager sits down with the employee to inform the employee of the need for improvement, and this is documented in a letter that is given to the employee and placed in the employee's file.
- **Termination.** If the employee still does not improve, the manager moves to fire the employee. This is often referred to as the **termination** of the employee.

A manager usually allows for a sequence or process of disciplinary measures. For example, an employee who breaks a rule or is not performing may receive a verbal warning for the first offense and a written warning for a second offense, before being terminated.

 **Reading Checkpoint** *What is the purpose of orientation?*

23.3 ASSESSMENT

Reviewing Concepts

1. Name at least three areas in a restaurant besides the kitchen and dining room.
2. What is the purpose of orientation?

Critical Thinking

3. **Inferring** Do you think shadowing someone in the same or similar position would be a good training method? Why?
4. **Drawing Conclusions** Why is orientation important for new employees?
5. **Drawing Conclusions** Why do you think restaurants might have a high turnover rate?
6. **Forming a Model** What kind of restaurant might have an area for displays and retail sales?
7. **Inferring** Why might using a word-of-mouth method of locating prospective new employees work well?

TEST KITCHEN

Partner with a class member. Partner 1 plays the role of an experienced employee; partner 2 plays the role of a new employee. Partner 1 will prepare an easy recipe without showing the recipe to partner 2, who will shadow partner 1, asking questions and taking notes as needed. After the dish is completed, partner 2 will describe step-by-step how to make the dish. Compare partner 2's recipe with the actual recipe.

LANGUAGE ARTS

Describing Jobs

Research restaurant employment ads in your local paper or on the Internet. Are similar jobs described in similar ways? Are some jobs made to sound more exciting than other, very similar jobs? Compare 10 ads for similar positions.

Review and Assessment

Reviewing Content

Choose the letter that best answers the question or completes the statement.

1. The ambience of a restaurant is
   a. its location
   b. its name
   c. its feeling or mood
   d. its type of food

2. Another name for an income statement is
   a. assets statement
   b. profitability statement
   c. sales statement
   d. profit and loss statement

3. The money customers spend in the restaurant is referred to as the restaurant's
   a. sales
   b. profits
   c. assets
   d. bottom line

4. A variable cost is a cost that
   a. relates only to the cost of ingredients
   b. changes over time
   c. relates only to the cost of labor
   d. does not change over time

5. A listing of the quantity of supplies you need to have on hand in the restaurant to make every item on the menu is
   a. an inventory
   b. a physical inventory
   c. a par-stock list
   d. mise en place

6. A statement of a product's selling price and an indication of the length of time that the price is effective is
   a. a market quote
   b. a par-stock list
   c. product specifications
   d. a product list

7. When restaurant owners talks about the bottom line, they are talking about
   a. sales
   b. expenses
   c. profit
   d. inventory

Understanding Concepts

8. What basic equation does an income statement show?

9. What is the difference between a variable cost and a fixed cost?

10. What does a business plan typically include?

11. What are the basic steps in the purchasing process?

12. What is the typical sequence of disciplinary measures?

Critical Thinking

13. **Comparing/Contrasting** What is the difference between profit and sales?

14. **Comparing/Contrasting** What is the difference between a par-stock list and an inventory?

Culinary Math

15. **Solving Problems** Your par-stock list indicates 280 boneless, skinless chicken breasts. Your inventory shows 30 boneless, skinless chicken breasts. You are ordering chicken today. How much chicken should you order?

16. **Applying Concepts** The monthly income for a restaurant was $124,000. The monthly expenses equaled $105,000. What was the restaurant's profit for that month? Show the profit both as a dollar amount and as a percentage of the restaurant's monthly income.

On the Job

17. **Communicating** Write a mission statement for a restaurant you would like to open.

18. **Applying Concepts** If you were planning to open a restaurant in your area, where would you locate it to achieve the highest possible sales? Why?

Project 23: Creating a Business Plan

Answer these questions when your class works through Project 23.

- What types of restaurants would members of your class open?

- Were the mission statements for the restaurants clear?

- Do you agree with the location and hours of operation?

- Were the sample menus interesting and varied?

- Were the signature appetizer and main course well prepared and appetizing? Could they be the base on which to build a new restaurant?

TEST PRACTICE

Choose the letter that best answers the question or completes the statement.

1. Assets are
   A things the business owns
   B sales
   C expenses
   D liabilities

2. Profit is equal to
   A sales + expenses
   B income – expenses
   C liabilities – sales
   D variable costs + fixed costs

3. A budget is a list of
   A planned expenses
   B variable costs
   C planned income and expenses
   D cost-control measures

4. A restaurant's profit is also known as its
   A income
   B bottom line
   C sales
   D all of the above

5. A kitchen typically takes up about what portion of a restaurant's entire floor space?
   A 50%
   B 33%
   C 25%
   D 20%

6. Food costs are
   A fixed costs
   B variable costs
   C liabilities
   D assets

7. What is usually the second step in the sequence of disciplinary measures?
   A written warning
   B termination
   C verbal warning
   D firing

8. A restaurant's client base is
   A the potential customers living within 1 mile of your restaurant
   B the potential customers living within 2 miles of your restaurant
   C the potential customers living within 3 miles of your restaurant
   D the group of customers who come to your restaurant

9. A restaurant's brand is
   A the restaurant's sign
   B the restaurant's public image
   C the restaurant's theme
   D the restaurant's ambience

10. What is typically the first step in the purchasing process?
   A writing purchase specifications
   B selecting suppliers
   C creating a par-stock list
   D obtaining price quotes

Starting Your Career in Food Service

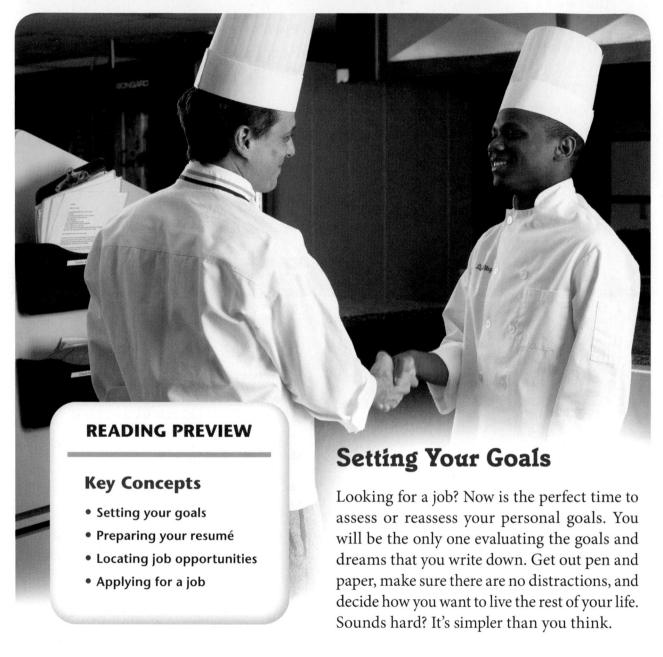

Setting Your Goals

Looking for a job? Now is the perfect time to assess or reassess your personal goals. You will be the only one evaluating the goals and dreams that you write down. Get out pen and paper, make sure there are no distractions, and decide how you want to live the rest of your life. Sounds hard? It's simpler than you think.

Organizing Your Long-Term Dreams First, record any dream or hope you have for the future. Do you want to make enough money to build your dream house? Do you want to write cookbooks? Do you want to travel the world teaching nutrition and basic cooking skills to mothers? No matter how abstract or unobtainable the goal might seem to be, write it down.

Second, put the list aside for a few days. When you're ready, pare down the list and rank the goals. For example: 1) Work my way through culinary school; 2) Make enough money to start a family; 3) Become an established chef; 4) Learn to speak Italian; 5) Write a cookbook; 6) Market own line of hot sauce.

You now have a picture of a promising future.

Developing Goals Your goals should point you toward your long-term dreams. Making this plan takes a little research. Discover schools and intern programs that offer training in your areas of interest. How long would you study? How much would it cost?

Then find out what jobs you are qualified for right now. What wages might you expect? Working in your chosen field will give you information, insight, experience, and cash.

Next, draft a timeline. In the first column, put time periods. In the second column, list what you want to be doing. Examine the Early Career Timeline below. Notice that work and study activities can overlap.

As you search for a job, and after you land one, refer to your timeline to keep yourself on track. You should change it and extend it as you go, but don't ignore it. A plan keeps you aware of what you want to do next.

REFERENCE LIST

When	What
June-July	Informational interviews, job hunt
August-December	Entry-level job in a bakery
September-December	Pastry-making course
January-June	Job as assistant pastry chef

Preparing Your Resumé

To start any job search, you need a resumé. A resumé is a summary of your job abilities. It tells prospective employers what you can do, where you have worked, and a little bit about you. The main purpose of a resumé is to get you an interview. Employers will refer to the resumé during the interview, and you can add more details then.

People with years of work experience usually prepare a chronological resumé. This is a list of their jobs (most recent first), with details of their accomplishments in each position. After you have worked for a while, look for information on the format and content of chronological resumés.

People like you, who are just starting out, usually prepare a functional resumé. A functional resumé focuses on the things you can do—your skills. It also lists education, work experience, professional activities, awards, and personal interests. The sample resumé that follows is an example of a functional resumé.

Contact Information Start your resumé with your name and contact information. Your goal is to be contacted for an interview, so you want to be sure an employer can reach you.

Objective Your objective is the job you want. If you are responding to a specific opening, describe the job they are offering as the one you want! That will help you pass the employer's first test.

You may want to send the same resumé to several employers, however, as a way of introducing yourself. In that case, you should list the related jobs you might do. The sample resumé that follows takes this approach.

Some applicants try to match their objective to the business objectives of their prospective employers. For instance, if a job ad invites you to "join our team," your objective might be "To help your restaurant succeed by becoming part of the food preparation team as a cook or assistant cook." If the slogan of an eating place is "Every Visit a Delight," your objective might be "To delight your customers by helping prepare delicious meals as a cook or cook's assistant."

Whatever approach you take, be sure the objective clearly tells employers what you can do for them.

Education List your formal training, including degrees and certificates earned. Use the same format for each item. Include the years of study or completion, the school name, and the location.

Skills List the skills you want to highlight and give examples of your performance. You'll want to use the achievements that match the needs of the job you are shooting for. If the job description lists skill qualifications, try to use those as headings. Again, you want to organize your information so employers can easily find the details they are looking for.

When describing your skills, begin with an active verb that tells what you did, such as supervised, achieved, prepared, cooked, assisted, assembled. Using the same format for each point shows you are well organized.

Work Experience People hiring for entry-level jobs want to be sure their new employees can function well in a business. Your work experience can show that you are ready to do what a job requires. It can also show a pattern of productive employment. Even if some of your jobs are not related to food service, they show that you took the initiative to get the job and did the work for the time you list. You want to list all jobs that reflect positively on you. (Don't include any jobs that started and ended on the same day!)

List your most recent job experiences first. Include the employer's name, the location, the job title, and the dates you worked. Follow the same format for each job.

Professional Involvement and Awards This heading lets you show off your contribution to the food service profession and the formal recognition you have achieved.

Use a heading that matches your accomplishments. For example, if you wrote a restaurant review or published a recipe in the school paper, you could list it under the heading "Professional Involvement and Publications." You can leave out this heading if you don't have supporting experience yet.

Personal Interests People like to work with interesting coworkers. This optional category lets the employer get a sense of you as a person. List the activities you can discuss to show your enthusiasm and your interests beyond work.

References The sample resumé ends with the notice, "References Available on Request." A reference is a person who will describe your character or job abilities.

An employer wants to be reassured that you will be productive, honest, and dependable. That means you should choose references who:
- Know you well
- Think well of you and your work
- Can verify your resumé claims
- Can impress an employer on your behalf

Former employers are ideal references. Heads of volunteer organizations and teachers also make good references.
- **Letters of Reference.** When your involvement in an organization is coming to an end, consider asking a trusted leader for a letter that you can show to future employers. Letters of reference often begin "To Whom It May Concern," and they explain how the writer knows you and his or her opinion of your work and character. Examples of accomplishments that match your resumé are also helpful. If the reference is willing to talk to future employers, be sure the letter includes the reference's contact information.
- **Reference List.** You should also prepare a reference list, so employers can quickly call the people who have agreed to speak for you. The table below shows a simple format. You will want to include three to five references.

EARLY CAREER TIMELINE

Contact Information	Best Reached	Relationship
Emma Smith (602) 555-1234 name@place.com	Business hours Weekdays	Sponsor of community emergency food service where I volunteered

Important: Be sure to ask permission *before* you list anyone as a reference. Also, let your references know when you are job hunting so they might expect calls. You can describe promising opportunities to your references so they are ready to reinforce your qualifications for the specific job.

SAMPLE FUNCTIONAL RESUMÉ

Identifying Information

Jackie Jones

Street Address
City, State Zip
E-Mail (if any)
Telephone

The Job You Want

Objective

To work as a chef, chef's assistant, or kitchen assistant.

Formal Training

Education

- Diploma, Certificate in Culinary Arts, 2006
- Mytown Vocational High School, Mytown, NH
- Environmental Sanitation in Food Service, 3 credits, 2006
  New Hampshire Community Technical College, Mytown, NH

Skills

Job Skills and Examples

Sanitation and Safety
- Supervised culinary lab cleanup including four workstations, using custom checklist
- Achieved certification in safe food-handling procedures

Cold Preparation
- Prepared mise en place for short-order restaurant
- Prepared sandwiches and salads for church soup kitchen

Hot Preparation
- Prepared grill items for private parties
- Cooked breakfast and lunch for day camp
- Assisted in soup and chili preparation for caterer

Work Experience

Plating and Presentation
- Assembled and plated meals for awards banquet
- Worked service line at soup kitchen

Work Experience

Professional Activities and Awards

- Pleasant Valley Day Camp, Mytown, NH, cook, summer 2006
- Lunchbox Café, Mytown, NH, kitchen assistant, 2005–2006
- Emergency Food Service, Mytown, NH, volunteer food preparation and line service, Sundays 2003–2005

Professional Involvement and Awards

Student Government Food Committee, Best Quiche Award, SVHS

Personal Interests

Personal Interests

Collecting kitchen tools, listening to jazz, swimming

References Available on Request

Locating Job Opportunities

There are several methods and many available resources for finding job opportunities. Be organized when conducting your job search.

Managing the Details When you begin a job search, be sure to keep records. You will be talking to many people at many businesses, and it is easy to get confused.

- **Master List.** Keep a master list like the one below, listing all your prospects. Use the "Next" and "Due" columns to organize your job searching.

MASTER LIST

Company/Person	Job	Date/Contact	Next	Due
Le Bistro Carl LaFong, Mgr. 123 Main Street Mytown, NH name@place.com (602) 555-9995	Asst. cook	8/1 – dropped off resumé and cover	phone	8/8
		8/8 – scheduled interview	interview	8/10 4PM

- **Folders.** Start a folder for each interview. Include two copies of the resumé and cover letter that you sent (one for you and one for the interviewer, who may have lost the one you sent.) Add your research notes about the company and questions you will ask. In the interview, be sure to get contact information and the correct names of all interviewers. Add any notes you have taken during the interview. Add copies of the thank you notes you sent after the interview.

Prospecting Prospecting means exploring for opportunities. You can find job openings in several ways:

- **General Mailings and Phone Calls.** Send your resumé to all businesses you want to consider. Ask about job openings in your cover letter. Try to address your inquiry to the right contact person. You can get this name from the business itself, its website, or a friend. After the resumé arrives, call your contact and ask about their needs.

- **Apply In Person.** Pounding the pavement is a legitimate job-search method in the hospitality industry. Dress professionally, have copies of your resumé, and be polite with everyone. You can offer to demonstrate your skills or to begin work "on trial."

- **Internet Advertisements.** Companies advertise openings on their websites. Go to a hotel or restaurant website and look for a Careers or Jobs link. You can try culinary websites such as escoffier.com, starchefs.com, and foodservice.com. Also try general job websites such as careerbuilder.com, myjobsearch.com, and monster.com, where you can post a resumé and get notices of jobs that fit your interests.

- **Classified Ads.** Read the hometown newspaper and check their online editions. The Want Ads often list hospitality openings. Also read trade publications such as Nation's Restaurant News. This weekly paper for the food industry has a section of employment ads in every issue.

- **Employment Agencies.** Job agencies work for employers, so you should act professionally in all your dealings with them. You should not have to pay a fee. Agencies screen applicants to save employers time, and the employer pays the agency when they hire you. Some agencies will take inexperienced applicants.

- **Networking.** The best way to find a job is through networking. Your network includes your personal contacts—and the contacts they refer you to. Write a 15- to 30-second speech about the job you want, and tell it to everyone. Find out what people do and how you might help them. Exchange contact information. Pass on leads to people you know. They will do the same for you. To expand your network, you might get involved with clubs, activities, and other professional organizations. Also, if an employer does not need anyone at the moment, ask about other places that need help.

Informational Interviewing An informational interview is a chance for you to learn about a company or a career from a professional on the inside. You are not seeking a job from this person. The professional is doing you the favor of sharing information about work.

To get an informational interview, you have to know someone. That means networking. Ask your contact for a chance to meet for a short time, and make clear the kind of information you want: how the professional developed his or her career, what is most rewarding and most challenging, what skills and traits the person wants in the people he or she hires, what it is like to work in a certain company.

- **You're the Leader.** Because this is your meeting, you have to come prepared to lead the discussion. Dress for an interview. Be ready to tell a little about yourself, and bring a resumé for the professional's information. Research the job and company before the interview, and prepare a list of questions or topics. Give a copy to the professional, and use it as an agenda. Keep the meeting short, 15 to 20 minutes. The professional's time is valuable.

- **Be Friendly and Positive.** During the interview, show interest. A little flattery never hurts. You might say, "Henry gave me your name and told me you're the best pastry chef in town. How did you get started?"

- **Get Names.** Ask for other contacts with whom you might speak. If no names are suggested, be grateful for any help provided.

- **Follow Up.** Thank the person before leaving, but don't forget to also send a letter stating your gratitude for the time given. Contact every referral you receive. Every person you speak with brings you closer to your new career. Stay in touch by phone or e-mail, and let the person know how the information helped.

Applying for a Job

After doing your research, you're ready to state your interest in a particular job.

Job Applications Most employers will ask you to complete a job application form. The information you put on the application should be consistent with your resumé. If you cannot complete this form at home, bring documents to the interview that include the details you may need: social security number, past employer addresses, list of references, and resumé.

Cover Letters and Other Introductions The purpose of the cover letter is to draw attention to your resumé. Start by identifying the job and where you learned about it. If someone recommended you, get permission to use that person's name. You can also point out your skills and experiences that match the job requirements. The prospective employer may be sorting through many resumés. A short letter that makes your qualifications clear can help get you noticed.

SAMPLE COVER LETTER

Dear _____ : [or To Whom It May Concern:]

I am applying for the position of assistant cook that I read about in Saturday's *Morning News*. My resumé is attached.

As you can see, I have the experience you need. I am trained in hot and cold preparation, plating and presentation, and health and safety procedures. I have cooked and assisted in several local establishments.

I will call to set up an interview and demonstration.

Sincerely,

Cover letters and resumés can be sent by mail or e-mail, or you can deliver one by hand with a job application.

Phone Calls If a job ad asks you to respond by phone, write a cover letter and use it as a script for your conversation. Ask for an interview, and be sure to thank the employer.

Interviewing and Demonstrating An interview is a chance for you and the employer to get to know each other. Bring your resumé and reference list, and be prepared to tell about yourself professionally. Write out a one-minute introduction and practice it. Be ready to provide positive details about every item on your resumé. Think of questions you might be asked and practice interviewing with a friend. Develop answers that are short and positive.

Generally, the interviewer will give you information about the job and the establishment. Taking notes shows your interest. Be prepared to ask a few questions about the employer's needs. "What is your greatest challenge, and how can I help with it?" "When would the job begin?" "What other information can I give you?" Before you leave, remember to find out the next step in the hiring process.

You may be asked to prepare a dish. Knowing what they want to see in advance will let you practice before the demonstration. In any case, use the opportunity to show your basic skills, including safety and sanitation.

Follow-Up Always write a thank you note immediately after an interview. It should be short and polite, thanking your hosts for showing you their establishment and taking the time to get to know you. You might say you hope you can work together.

If you call to follow up, be cheerful. Actually smile while you're on the phone—your voice will sound positive. Identify yourself and the job, and ask about the status of your application. If they hired someone else, stay positive. You might say, "Oh, too bad. You would be great people to work with! I hope you can keep my application on file. By the way, do you know of anyone else who is hiring?" By demonstrating your skills and making a personal connection, you can add to your network of culinary professionals, no matter what the outcome of a single job application.

Apprentice Programs Apprentice programs or internships are generally unpaid opportunities to gain experience in a professional kitchen. Ask your instructor or guidance counselor about companies that will train promising students. They often hire the people they successfully train!

Developing a Career Portfolio As you gather experience, you will want to assemble a portfolio, a set of exhibits of your work for future employers. Start collecting proof of your success as you develop your career:

- Diplomas and certificates
- Letters of reference
- Letters of commendation, awards, and prizes
- Written job reviews by employers

- Your special recipes
- Photos of your creations
- Reviews of restaurants where you cooked
- Restaurant reviews and recipes you published

Glossary

A

A la carte menu (AH LA CART) Menu on which each food item or beverage is priced and served separately. (21.1)

Accident report Standard form used to report accidents to OSHA; must be filed within eight hours. (2.2) Also used to describe an event related to a serious health problem or physical injury to a customer; should include the customer name, any server involved, the date, and the time it occurred. (20.4)

Actual cost method Menu-pricing method in which the actual cost for the raw food, labor, other expenses, and profit are all added together to determine a menu price. (21.2)

Aerating Adding air to food. (19.2)

Aflatoxin (aff-la-TOX-in) Toxin produced by molds, sometimes found on legumes. (13.2)

Aged (beef) Beef that undergoes a process that gives it a darker color, a more tender texture, and a fuller flavor. (16.1)

Al dente (al DEN-tay) Italian expression meaning "to the tooth;" used to describe pasta that is cooked only until it gives a slight resistance when you bite it. (13.3)

Albumen (al-BYOO-men) White part of an egg, composed of water and protein. (9.1)

All-purpose flour Blend of "soft" (low protein) and "hard" (high protein) wheat; the most common type of flour used in the bakeshop. (17.1)

Ambience Feeling or mood of the restaurant. (23.1)

American buttercream Dense and rich buttercream icing that is just buttercreamed with powdered sugar. (19.3)

American service Service style in which food is fully prepared and plated on individual serving plates in the kitchen, brought to the dining room, and served by the right hand at the right side of the guest, leaving the server's left hand free to carry other plates. (20.3)

Amino acids (ah-MEEN-oh) Basic building blocks of protein, some of which our bodies make. Others, the essential amino acids, we must get from food. (22.1)

Anadromous fish Fish that live part of their lives in saltwater and part in freshwater. (15.1)

Antioxidants Substances, such as certain vitamins, that prevent tissue damage in the body. (22.1)

Antipasto platter (an-tee-PAHS-toh) Assortment of cured meats (such as prosciutto and salami), cheeses, and pickled vegetables served on a platter. (10.4)

Appetizer Dish that is served as the first course in a meal. (11.2)

Appetizer salad Salad designed to whet the appetite before the main course. (10.2)

Aromatic (AIR-o-mat-ic) Foods with especially strong smells. (6.1)

Arson Fire that is intentionally set. (2.1)

Assembly points Meeting points at a predetermined spot at a safe distance from the building where everyone should gather after a fire. (2.1)

Assets Items a business owns, such as furnishings and appliances. (23.1)

Assignment In terms of mise en place, the food for which you will be responsible. (7.1)

Asymmetrical In terms of plate presentation, unequal numbers of items on either side of the plate. (7.3)

Automated external defibrillator (AED) Device that shocks the heart into starting again. (2.2)

Automatic systems Extinguishers, sprinklers, and alarms triggered by the heat of a fire. (2.1)

B

Baba ghanoush (BAH-bah gha-NOOSH) Vegetable-based dip made from roasted eggplant that has been pureed and seasoned with olive oil, tahini, lemon juice, and garlic. (10.1)

Back of the house In a restaurant, the kitchen area. (20.1)

Back waiter Provides overall assistance to the front waiter; may deliver food and drinks to the front waiter, clear plates, and refill bread and water. (20.1)

Bacteria Single-celled organism that can live in food or water and also on our skin or clothing; some are a potential biological hazard, capable of producing foodborne illness. (1.1)

Baguette (bag-EHT) Long, narrow French bread with a crispy, golden brown crust and light, chewy crumb dotted with holes. (17.3)

Bain marie (BANE ma-REE) Another name for a double boiler. (4.2)

Baker's chocolate Chocolate that has no sugar added. Also called *unsweetened chocolate* or *chocolate liquor.* (19.1)

Baking Dry heat method of cooking in which food is cooked by hot air trapped inside an oven. Baking typically means you are preparing smaller pieces of food than for roasting. (8.1)

Baking stones Unglazed ceramic pieces used to line an oven rack; they help develop a crisp crust on breads and pizza by holding and transferring the oven's heat evenly. (17.1)

Balance scale Scale typically used for weighing baking ingredients. Ingredients are placed on one side; weights are placed on the other side. When the sides balance, the ingredients weigh the same as the weights. (4.2)

Balsamic vinegar (bahl-SAH-mek) Vinegar that takes as long as 15 to 20 years to ferment and age. It has a mellow, sweet-sour taste and syrupy consistency and is very expensive. (10.1)

Bar cookies Cookies made from a soft batter that is spread into a pan before baking and then cut into individual cookies. (19.3)

Barley Grain that looks like a doubled grain of rice. (13.1)

Base price method Menu-pricing method that analyzes what customers want to spend per meal and then works backward to come up with menu items, their prices, and a built-in level of profit. Requires data about customers' eating habits in the restaurant over a long period. (21.2)

Batch cooking Process of preparing a small amount of food several times during a service period so that a fresh supply of cooked items is always available. (22.2)

Batonnet (bah-tow-NAY) Long, rectangular cut that is 1/4 inch wide by 1/4 thick and 2 to 2 1/2 inches long. (4.1)

Batter Coating option on foods made by blending a type of flour and a liquid. (8.1) Wet form of dough made from flour, oil or melted butter, eggs, milk or other liquids, salt, and usually baking powder. Used to create waffles, cakes, and other items. (9.2)

Battuto (bah-TOOT-oh) Aromatic combination used in Italian soups, sauces, stews, and meat dishes; consists of cooking fat, garlic, onions, parsley, carrots, and celery. (6.3)

Bavarian cream Aerated dessert similar to a mousse but without an egg foam. (19.2)

Beans Legume that is longer than it is round. (13.2)

Béchamel sauce (BAY-sha-mell) One of the grand sauces; a white sauce made by thickening milk with a white roux. (14.2)

Belly bones Fish bones found along the thinner edge of the fillet. (15.1)

Bench boxes Covered containers in which dough is bench proofed; a skin forms on the dough that holds in the carbon dioxide. (17.3)

Bench proofing Brief resting period that allows gluten to relax after dough has been pre-shaped. (17.3)

Bench scraper Tool with a rectangular steel blade, usually six inches wide, that is capped with a wooden or plastic handle. Used like a knife to cut soft ingredients such as butter or soft cheese, to lift and turn soft or wet dough, or to transfer ingredients from a work surface to a mixing bowl. (17.1)

Bid Proposal from a supplier that states the price to be charged for an item. (23.2)

Biga In baking, an Italian dough starter developed overnight or longer; can be wet or dry. (17.2)

Bi-metallic-coil thermometer Thermometer that uses a metal coil in the probe to measure temperature. Oven-safe version can stay in food while cooking and gives a reading in 1 to 2 minutes. Instant-read version is not oven-safe and gives a reading in 15 to 20 seconds. (4.2)

Biological hazards Living organisms such as bacteria, viruses, fungi, and parasites, which are a health risk. (1.1)

Biscuits Small quick breads that have little or no sugar. (18.2)

Bisque (BISK) Hearty soup made with shellfish (lobster, crayfish, or shrimp shells). (14.3)

Bittersweet chocolate Dark chocolate with less sugar than semisweet chocolate. (19.1)

Black pepper Dried, unripe berries of the pepper vine; used as a seasoning. (6.2)

Blanching Moist heat method of cooking that involves cooking in a liquid or with steam just long enough to cook the outer portion of the food. The food is immediately placed in ice water to stop *carryover cooking*. (8.2)

Blender Electrical mixing device used for combining ingredients by means of a rotating blade. (3.3)

Blending Type of mixing in which the ingredients are chopped so the overall mixture has a uniform consistency. (3.3)

Blind baked Pre-baked pie shell. (19.4)

Blinis (BLEE-nees) Very thin Russian crêpes. (10.4)

Blue-vein cheeses Cheeses in which needles are injected into the cheese to form holes in which mold spores multiply. The cheese is salted and ripened in a cave. (10.3)

Boiling Moist heat method of cooking in which food is cooked at 212°F. (8.2)

Bolster Point at the heel of a knife blade where the blade and handle come together. (4.1)

Boning knife Knife about 6 inches long with a narrow blade, used to separate meat from the bone. (4.1)

Bottom line Money left in a business after subtracting expenses from earnings. (23.1)

Bouillon (bool-YOHN) French term for broth. (14.3)

Boule (BOOL) Round loaf of white bread named for the French word for "ball." (17.3)

Bouquet garni (boo-KAY GAR-nee) Combination of fresh herbs and other aromatic ingredients used to flavor dishes. (6.3)

Box grater Hand tool that has four sides with various side holes; used for grating. (4.1)

Boxed meat Meat that is fabricated to a specific point (such as primal, subprimal, or retail cuts) and then packed, boxed, and sold to food-service establishments. (16.1)

Braising Combination cooking method in which food is first seared and then gently cooked in flavorful liquid. Braising usually indicates that the food is left whole or in large pieces. (8.2)

Braising pan Pan with medium high walls and a lid to keep moisture in. (4.2)

Bran Coating found on some kernels of grain, located just beneath the hull. (13.1)

Brand Public image of a business, including the business name, logo, and sometimes a slogan.

Bread flour Flour that contains more protein than all-purpose flour; it is used in most yeast-bread recipes. (17.1)

Brigade Group of workers, such as the staff of a restaurant, assigned a specific set of tasks. (20.1)

Brioche (BREE-ohsh) French version of sweet bread with a knotted top made in individual molds with a fluted base; it can also be made into a round loaf or rolls. (17.2)

Brochettes (BRO-shets) Small skewers containing grilled or broiled meat, fish, poultry, or vegetables. Brochettes are often served with a dipping sauce. (11.2)

Broiler Cooking unit with a radiant heat source located above the food. Some units have adjustable racks that can be raised or lowered to control cooking speed. (3.3)

Broiling Dry heat method of cooking that is similar to a grill except the heat source is above the food. (8.1

Broth Clear, thin soup made by simmering a combination of meat, fish, poultry, or vegetables in a liquid with aromatics. (14.3)

Brown rice Rice with some or all of the bran still intact. (13.1)

Brown sauce One of the grand sauces; a sauce with a rich brown color made from brown stock. (See Espagnol sauce, demi-glaçe, and jus de veau lié). (14.2)

Brown stock Type of stock made from roasted animal or poultry bones. Brown stock has a deep reddish-brown color and a roasted meat flavor. (14.1)

Brunch service Combination of a buffet-style breakfast and lunch. (20.3)

Brunoise (brewn-WHAZ) Smallest dice cut, about 1/8 inch square. Means "to brown" in French. (4.1)

Bruschetta (brew-SKEH-tahs) Type of open-faced sandwich served as an appetizer. It consists of toasted bread drizzled with olive oil and topped with tomatoes, olives, cheese, or other ingredients. See *crostini*. (11.2)

Budget List of planned income and expenses. (23.1)

Buffalo chopper Machine that holds food in a rotating bowl that passes under a hood where blades chop the food. Some units have hoppers or feed tubes and interchangeable disks for slicing and grating. (3.3)

Buffet service Serving style practical for serving a large number of people a wide variety of dishes over a period of time; servers behind the buffet table may serve guests or guests may serve themselves. (20.3)

Bulgur (BUHL-guhr) Grain cereal made from steamed, dried, and cracked wheat. (13.1)

Bus person Person responsible for clearing and cleaning tables. Also called *dining room attendant.* (20.1)

Business plan Written plan that a business owner develops to launch a new business, such as a restaurant. Includes a mission statement, goals that support the mission statement, sample menus, preliminary operating budgets, and staffing needs. (23.1)

Butler service Serving style in which the server brings a platter to the table, provides a serving spoon and fork, and guests serve themselves. (20.3)

Buttercream Icing made by aerating butter, shortening, or a combination of the two; used to decorate cakes and as a cake and pastry filling. (19.3)

Butterfat Fat content of dairy products, measured by the weight of the fat compared to the total weight of the product. Same as *milkfat.* (9.1)

Butterflied Split down the middle and then spread open, as with boneless meat. (16.1)

C

Cafeteria service Self-service where diners choose their own foods from behind a counter or barrier. Servers dish out controlled portions from the other side and diners carry their dishes on trays to their tables. (20.3)

Caffeine Chemical found in coffee, tea, chocolate, and sodas; it stimulates your body and mind. (9.2)

Cajun trinity (CAGE-uhn) Aromatic combination used in Creole and Cajun cooking; consists of onion, celery, and green pepper. (6.3)

Cake comb Triangular or rectangular piece of metal or plastic with serrated edges, used to create a decorative edge on iced cakes or to give texture to a chocolate coating. (17.1)

Cake flour Flour that has less protein than bread or all-purpose flour; it is used in most cake recipes and many cookie and muffin recipes. (17.1)

Calamari (cahl-ah-MAHR-ee) Another name for squid. (15.2)

California menu Single menu listing breakfast, lunch, and dinner foods; it offers customers the freedom to order any item at any time of day. (21.1)

Calories Measured units, derived from food, that provide energy. (22.1)

Canadian bacon Leaner than regular bacon and similar to ham; it comes in a chunk ready for slicing. (9.2)

Canapés (KAN-up-pays) Bite-sized pieces of bread or crackers with a savory topping, used as hors d'oeuvres. (11.2)

Capsaicin (cap-SAY-ih-sin) Compound that gives a chile its heat; it is most potent on the white ribs inside the pepper. (12.2)

Captain At fine dining restaurants, the person responsible for explaining the menu to guests and taking their orders; the captain is also responsible for the smooth running service in a specific group of tables. (20.1)

Caramelize Change that takes place in food that contains sugar when it is heated. The surface of the food starts to turn brown. (8.1)

Carbohydrates Energy sources for the body, made up of smaller units known as sugars. (22.1)

Carcinogenic Causing cancer, such as a toxic chemical exposure. (2.2)

Cardiopulmonary resuscitation (CPR) Technique used to restore a person's breathing and heartbeat. (2.2)

Carpaccio (car-PAH-chee-oh) Raw beef, sliced very thinly and dressed with a sauce. (11.2)

Carryover cooking Cooking that takes place in a food after it is removed from a source of heat. (8.1)

Carver Person in charge of carving and serving meats or fish and their accompaniments. Also called *trancheur.* (20.1)

Casserole Pan with medium high walls and a lid to keep moisture in. (4.2)

Caviar Type of salted fish eggs; in France and the United States, only sturgeon eggs are classified as caviar. (10.4)

Chafing (CHAYF-ing) **dish** Metal holding pan mounted above a heat source and used to keep food warm. The pan is usually contained within a larger unit that holds water. When the water is heated, the steam heats the food evenly. (3.4)

Challah (HAL-la) Sweet, airy, braided bread made with a lot of eggs; it is a Jewish bread traditionally served on the Sabbath and on holidays. (17.2)

Channel knife Tool used to cut grooves lengthwise in a vegetable such as a cucumber or carrot. A rondelle cut from the grooved vegetable has decorative edges that resemble a flower. (4.2)

Cheese board Flat platter on which cheese is served. (10.3)

Cheese cart Cart that is wheeled to the guests' table to give them an opportunity to choose cheeses of different kinds. (10.3)

Chef de cuisine (CHEF duh KWEE-zine) Head chef who commands the kitchen, designs the menu, and oversees food costs. Also called *executive chef*. (20.1)

Chef's knife All-purpose knife used for peeling, trimming, slicing, chopping, and dicing. Blade is usually 8 to 12 inches long. Also known as a French knife. (4.1)

Chef's tasting Method of presenting appetizers; it is a sampler plate with an assortment of different appetizers. The portions are often only one bite, just enough to sample the various appetizers. (11.2)

Chemical hazards Toxins such as metals, cleaning compounds, food additives, and fertilizer found in food and water. (1.1)

Chemical leavener Baking powder or baking soda, which increases the volume of a batter by the addition of air or gas. (17.1)

Chiffonade (shiff-en-ODD) Cut used for cutting herbs and leafy greens into fine shreds. (4.1)

China Dishware designed to contain food, including plates, bowls, dishes, cups, saucers, and creamers. (20.2)

Chlorine dioxide (KLOR-ene die-OX-ide) Chemical dough conditioner to facilitate handing of lean dough. (17.2)

Chocolate liquor Chocolate that has no sugar added. Also called *unsweetened chocolate* or *baker's chocolate*. (19.1)

Cholesterol (koh-LESS-ter-all) Fatty substance the body needs to perform various functions; it becomes a health risk when certain protein levels appear as elevated in the blood, indicating a possible build-up of cholesterol on the walls of arteries, reducing blood flow to the heart. (22.1)

Choux paste Versatile pastry dough made from liquid, fat, flour, and eggs; used for both sweet and savory baked goods. (19.4)

Chutney Sauce with a chunky texture, typically fruit- or vegetable-based and made with a sweet and sour flavoring. Served hot or cold. (14.2)

Clarification Mixture of ingredients including ground meat, aromatic vegetables, and an acid such as tomatoes or lemon juice used to add flavor and clear a broth to make a consommé. (14.3)

Clarified butter Butter with all water and particles removed, leaving pure fat for cooking at high temperatures. (9.1)

Cleaver Cutting tool with a large, rectangular blade; available in a range of sizes and weights. Used for many of the same applications as a chef's knife. (4.1)

Client base Group of customers who come to a restaurant. (23.1)

Clingstone Describes fruit that clings tightly to its pit, making it difficult to cut the flesh away cleanly. (12.1)

Closed sandwich Two pieces of bread with a filling between them. (11.1)

Club sandwich Double-decker closed sandwich, made with three slices of bread (or toast) and traditionally filled with chicken or turkey, bacon, lettuce, and tomato. (11.1)

Coating chocolate Chocolate made with vegetable fat instead of cocoa butter. Also called *compound chocolate*. (19.1)

Cocktail sauce Dipping sauce of ketchup, horseradish, and possibly Tabasco sauce; used with shellfish. (10.4)

Cocoa butter Cream-colored fat from cocoa beans; used in the chocolate-making process. (19.1)

Cocoa powder Unsweetened chocolate with some of the fat removed and then ground into a powder. (19.1)

Coddled eggs Eggs cooked in their shells for 30 seconds, leaving the whites warm and thickened and the yolks warm but still runny. (9.1)

Colander Large, perforated stainless-steel or aluminum bowl used to strain or drain foods. (4.2)

Cold food presentation Collection of cold foods that are presented in an artful manner, often in a buffet setting. (10.4)

Cold storage area Kitchen area where walk-in refrigerators, reach-in refrigerators, and other large refrigeration equipment is located. (3.2)

Combination steamer oven Oven powered by either gas or electricity. It can cook like a convection oven, a steamer, or both. (3.3)

Complex carbohydrates Carbohydrates that contain long chains of many sugars; found in plant-based foods such as grains, legumes, and vegetables. (22.1)

Composed salad Salad with any combination of ingredients (greens, vegetables, proteins, starches, fruits, or garnishes) that are arranged carefully and artfully on a plate or in a bowl. (10.2)

Compote Dish of fresh or dried fruit that is slow-cooked in stewing liquid. (12.1)

Compound butter Flavored butter made by blending aromatics or garnishes with softened butter, typically served with grilled meats. (14.2)

Compound chocolate Chocolate made with vegetable fat instead of cocoa butter. Also called *coating chocolate*. (19.1)

Condiments (CON-di-ments) Prepared mixtures that are used to season and flavor foods. Condiments are served on the side and added by the individual diner. (6.4)

Conditioning the pan Process of letting the pan heat up before adding any oil or food, when sautéing. (8.1)

Confectioner's sugar Sugar that has been ground into a fine, white, easily dissolvable powder. (17.1)

Conical sieve Made of very fine mesh and shaped like a cone. Also called a chinois or a bouillon strainer. Used to strain or purée foods. (4.2)

Consommé (KAHN-soh-may) Very clear broth made by simmering a broth or stock with a clarification. A consommé should be fat-free. (14.3)

Continental breakfast Light breakfast of baked goods served with coffee, tea, and juice. (9.2)

Continuous seating plan Seating plan that allows use of tables according to the flow of business. (20.1)

Convection oven Oven with fans that force hot air to circulate around the food, cooking it evenly and quickly. Some convection ovens have the capacity to introduce moisture. Special features may include infrared and/or microwave oven functions. (3.3)

Convection steamer Cooking unit that generates steam in a boiler and then pipes it to the cooking chamber, where it is vented over the food. It is continuously exhausted, so the door may be opened at any time without danger of scalding or burning. (3.3)

Converted rice Rice that is par-cooked before it is milled to shorten the cooking time. (13.1)

Conveyer belt dishwasher Large piece of dishwashing equipment that can process a high volume of dishes as a continuous flow. (4.2)

Cookware Utensils used for cooking, such as pots and pans. (4.2)

Copycat method Simple menu-pricing method that involves going to a nearby restaurant that has the same menu items and copying their prices. (21.2)

Corer Tool used to remove the core of an apple or pear in one long, round piece; can also be used to remove eyes from potatoes or the stem and core from tomatoes. (4.2)

Corn syrup Thick, sweet syrup made from cornstarch. It is available light or dark. (17.1)

Cornmeal Cereal made by grinding whole or processed kernels of corn. (13.1)

Corrective action Steps a food service establishment takes to correct a problem or situation, such as food held too long at an unsafe temperature. (1.3)

Corrosive Having the ability to irritate or even eat away other materials. (2.2)

Cost control Keeping variable expenses in check, such as avoiding waste or conserving electricity. (23.1)

Coulis (coo-LEE) Thick puréed sauce, usually made from vegetables or fruit. (14.2)

Count Number of shrimp per pound. (15.2)

Counter scale Countertop device used for weighing moderate size packages. (3.2)

Counter service Alternative to table dining; guests sit at a counter, often on stools. (20.3)

Countertop blender Blender with the motor and blades at the base and a glass, metal, or plastic container on top to hold ingredients. Also called a bar blender. (3.3)

Countertop mixer Mixer used on top of a counter in small to moderate size kitchens. It can stand about 2 feet high and weigh 100 pounds. (3.3)

Cover Complete place setting for one person; includes china, glassware, and flatware. (20.2)

Cracked grain Coarsely ground or crushed grain kernel. (13.1)

Cream soup Soup made with cream that is noticeably thick with a velvety smooth texture.

Creaming In baking, a mixing method in which fat and sugar are combined vigorously to incorporate air. (18.1)

Crème anglaise Classic dessert sauce made with the stirred custard method; often used as a base for ice cream and mousses. (19.2)

Crème fraîche (krehm fraysh) Cultured dairy product similar to sour cream but with more butterfat. French for "fresh cream." (9.1)

Crêpe (KRAYP) Thin, French-style pancake made with very thin batter in a special crêpe pan; often folded or rolled and spread with a sweet mixture or filled with savory ingredients. (9.2)

Crêpe pan Shallow skillet with very short, sloping sides; often has a nonstick coating. (4.2)

Critical control point Specific time in the process of food handling when you can prevent, eliminate, or reduce a hazard. (1.3)

Critical limits Measurements of time and temperature that indicate when a food is at risk and in need of a corrective action. (1.3)

Croissant (kwah-SAHNT) Buttery-rich crescent-shaped yeast roll. (9.2)

Cross cuts Large sections of a large drawn fish that has been cut into sections. (15.1)

Cross-contamination Contamination of food that occurs when safe food comes in contact with biological, physical, or chemical hazards while it is being prepared, cooked, or served. (1.1)

Crostini (kroh-STEE-nee) Type of open-faced sandwich served as an appetizer. It consists of toasted bread drizzled with olive oil and topped with tomatoes, olives, cheese, or other ingredients. See *bruschetta*. (11.2)

Crouton (CREW-tahn) Small cube of bread that is toasted or fried until crisp and golden brown; a popular garnish for hearty soups. (14.3)

Crown roast Roast prepared by tying a rib roast into a crown shape. (16.1)

Crudités (kroo-deh-TAYS) Vegetables that have been cut into bite-size pieces. (11.2)

Crumb topping Crumbly mixture of fat, sugar, and flour; often applied to muffins or quick breads. (18.1)

Crustaceans (crus-TAY-shuns) Shellfish that have jointed exterior shells. (15.2)

Cubano The Cuban version of a pressed sandwich. (11.1)

Cube Large dice that is 3/4 inch or greater. (4.1)

Cultured Describes dairy products such as buttermilk, sour cream, and yogurt that are made by adding a specific type of beneficial bacteria to milk or cream to achieve a desired texture, taste, and aroma. (9.1)

Cured foods Foods that are preserved by drying, salting, pickling, or smoking. Examples are ham, bacon, and salted anchovies. (6.3)

Custard cup Baking dish that is round and straight-edged; comes in various sizes. (4.2)

Custard Liquid, such as milk or cream, thickened with egg and then baked. (9.1)

Cut-out cookies Cookies made of stiff dough that is rolled flat and then cut into decorative shapes, often using cookie cutters. (19.3)

Cyclical menu Menu that is written for a certain period of time and then repeats itself. Some cyclical menus change four times a year, according to the seasons. Some change every week. (21.1)

D

Daily values Daily requirements for nutrients, as established by the FDA; amounts are listed on nutrition labels as a metric weight and also as a percent value and are based on a 2000-calorie diet. (22.1)

Dark chocolate Bittersweet or semi-sweet chocolate; it is less sweet than milk chocolate. (19.1)

Deadline In terms of the mise en place timeline, your completion time; when the dish you are preparing must be ready to serve. (7.1)

Deck ovens Ovens stacked like shelves, one above the other, like pizza ovens. Food is placed directly on the deck instead of on a wire rack. (3.3)

Deep frying Dry heat method of cooking in which foods are cooked in hot oil that completely covers the food. (8.1)

Deep poaching Moist cooking method in which food is cooked in enough liquid to completely cover it. (15.1)

Deep-fat fryer Freestanding or countertop unit that holds frying oil in a stainless-steel reservoir. A heating element, controlled by a thermostat, raises the oil to the desired temperature and maintains it. Stainless-steel wire baskets are used to lower foods into the hot oil and lift them out. (3.3)

Demi-glace (DEM-ee-glahs) Type of brown sauce; made by simmering equal amounts of Espagnol sauce and brown veal stock until the sauce is intensely flavored and thick enough to coat foods. (14.2)

Denaturing Altering the chemical structure of a protein, as with acid. (17.1)

Denominator Bottom number in a fraction. (The top number is the *numerator*). (5.2)

Depurated (DEP-yew-rate-ed) Shellfish that have been placed in tanks of fresh water to purge them of their impurities and sand. (10.4)

Derivative sauces Sauces that use a grand sauce as the main ingredient. The grand sauce is combined with other seasonings or garnishes for a specific flavor, color, or texture. (14.2)

Dessert salad Salad served as dessert often features fruits and nuts. (10.2)

Deveining Process of removing the vein in a shrimp. (15.2)

Diagonal cut Variation of a rondelle, cutting diagonally instead of straight down, to expose a greater surface area of the vegetable. (4.1)

Dice Cut that produces a cube-shaped piece of food. (4.1)

Dietary Guidelines Developed by the USDA as a method for helping people create a healthy and well-balanced diet; emphasis is on reducing risk for major diseases through diet and physical activity. (22.1)

Dining room attendant Person responsible for clearing and cleaning tables. Also called *bus person*. (20.1)

Dining room manager Person running the dining room portion of the restaurant; also responsible for training service personnel, working with the chef on the menu, arranging seating, and taking reservations. Also called *maître d'hôtel* or *maître d'*. (20.1)

Dip Sauce or condiment served with raw vegetables, crackers, bread, potato chips, or other snack food. (10.1)

Direct contamination Contamination of food caused by improperly storing, cooking, or serving food that causes the biological hazards in the food itself. (1.1)

Disjointing Cutting poultry into halves, quarters, or eighths, before or after cooking. (16.2)

Double boiler Cookware that is actually a pair of nesting pots. The bottom pot is filled with water and heated, providing steady, even heat for the top pot. (4.2)

Double-panning Using two stacked sheet pans to gently heat the bottom of cookies and avoid over-browning. (19.3)

Double-strength sanitizing solution Mixture of water and a sanitizer that contains twice the recommended amount of sanitizer suggested for normal use; used on food contact surfaces such as knives, meat slicers, and cutting boards during food preparation. (1.2)

Double-strength stock Stock that is simmered long enough to cook away half of the water. (14.1)

Dough divider Baking equipment that cuts a quantity of dough into equal pieces so they can be shaped in rolls. (17.1)

Dough sheeter Baking equipment used to roll large batches of dough out into sheets. (17.1)

Dough starter In baking, a dough mixture that starts the fermentation process before the final mixing of all the ingredients. The longer fermentation gives the dough time to develop more gluten strength and depth of flavor. Also called a *pre-ferment*. (17.2)

Drawn butter Butter that is melted to use as a sauce for shellfish. (15.2)

Drawn fish Whole fish that has the stomach removed. (15.1)

Drop cookies Cookies made from a firm dough or batter that is dropped onto a sheet pan. (19.3)

Drum sieve (SIV) Screen stretched on an aluminum or wood frame; used to sift dry ingredients or purée very soft foods. (4.2)

Dry aging Process of storing meat by hanging it in a climate-controlled area to make it more tender and flavorful. (16.1)

Dry cured Method of preserving food by rubbing it with salt and seasonings. (16.1)

Dry goods Foods such as flour, tea, sugar, rice, or pasta. (1.2)

Dry sautéing Another name for pan broiling. Dry heat method of cooking very much like sautéing except no fat is used. (8.1)

Dry storage area Kitchen area where goods such as flour, dry pasta, canned goods, and supplies are stored on shelves at room temperature. (3.2)

Du jour menu (DOO ZHOOR) Menu that lists food served only on that particular day. "Du jour" means "of the day" in French. (21.1)

Dumplings Type of pasta; made from dough that is soft enough to drop into boiling water. (13.3)

Dupes Duplicates of guest checks, passed from the dining room to the back of the house. (20.3)

Dutch processed Process used for cocoa powder to make it less acidic. (19.1)

E

Earnings Money coming into a restaurant; also known as *income* or *sales*. (23.1)

Éclair Long, straight pastry filled with cream and glazed on top. (19.4)

Effective criticism Criticism that not only points out what went wrong or where things could be better, but also indicates how you can improve. (7.2)

Egg wash Mixture of egg and water or milk; brushed onto the tops of breads and pastries to give a glossy sheen. (17.1)

Emulsifier (e-MULL-si-fy-er) Ingredient added to an emulsion that makes an emulsion permanent. (10.1)

Emulsion (e-MULL-shon) Mixture of two ingredients that would otherwise not combine; an emulsion has a uniform consistency. (10.1)

En papillote (ahn pap-ee-YOTE) Fish or shellfish baked in a wrapped package, usually made of parchment paper. Often the fish or shellfish is wrapped with aromatics and vegetables. (15.1)

Endosperm Largest part of a grain; it contains the food necessary to support a new plant and is made up almost entirely of carbohydrates, or starch. (13.1)

English service Service style for special groups or private dinners in which the table is fully preset, food is delivered on platters to the dining room, serving dishes are placed on the table or on a table nearby, and a server serves the food to the guests. (20.3)

Enriched dough Lean dough that has added butter, oil, sugar, eggs, or milk products. Also called *sweet rich dough*. (17.2)

Entrée (AHN-tray) The main course of a meal. (21.1)

Entremetier (ehn-tray-mee-tee-AY) Chef responsible for hot appetizers, pasta courses, and vegetable dishes. Also called *soup and vegetables station chef*. (20.1)

Environmental Protection Agency (EPA) Federal agency that plays a part in regulating workplace safety along with OSHA by requiring food service operations to track any chemicals that pose a risk to health. (2.2)

Espagnol sauce (ess-pan-YOLL) Type of brown sauce; made by thickening a brown veal stock with a roux. (14.2)

Essential oils Quickly evaporating oils that occur in plants and their fruit and that give the plant or fruit its characteristic odor and/or flavor.

Ethylene (EH-thih-leen) Gas that accelerates the ripening and rotting process in fruit and vegetables. (12.1)

Evacuation routes Escape routes that give everyone in the building at least two ways to get out of the building. (2.1)

Executive chef Head chef who commands the kitchen, designs the menu, and oversees food costs. Also called *chef de cuisine*. (20.1)

Expediter (ex-PED-eye-ter) Person who accepts orders from the dining room, relays them to the various station chefs, and reviews the dishes before service to make sure they are correct. (20.1)

Expenses Money being spent by a restaurant. (23.1)

Extra-virgin olive oil Finest grade of olive oil, produced by pressing olives once without using any heat. It has a fruity, grassy, or peppery taste with a pale yellow to bright green color and a very low acid content. (10.1)

Extruded Act of pushing material through an opening. Pasta machines extrude dough to make special shapes, such as elbow macaroni, spaghetti, and penne. (13.3)

F

Fabrication (of meat) Additional butchering done by a restaurant to break down a subprimal cut of meat into portion-sized cuts of meat. (16.1)

Factor method One of the oldest, simplest methods for pricing menu items; it involves multiplying the raw food cost by an established pricing factor. (21.2)

Family service Table service in which food is placed on the table in serving dishes and guests help themselves. (20.3)

Farinaceous (fare-eh-NAY-shus) Rich in starch. (13.1)

Farm-raised fish Fish raised in ponds or in penned waters. (15.1)

Fat-soluble vitamins Vitamins A, D, E, and K; they dissolve in fat; are stored in body fat, cannot be easily flushed out once ingested, and so should not be taken in excess. (22.1)

Fatty acids Small units, made of carbon, hydrogen, and oxygen atoms linked together, that are contained in a fat such as olive oil or butter. (22.1)

FDA Food Code Set of recommendations for safe food handling, provided by the Federal Department of Agriculture, that may be adopted (all or in part) by local governments as law. (1.3)

Feedback Review of one's work; it could come from a co-worker, a boss, or a customer. (7.2)

Fermentation Chemical reaction that is triggered when hydrated yeast is mixed with food; it makes dough rise until double or triple in size. (17.2)

Fermiere (FARM-ee-air) Rustic cut that produces 1/8- to 1/2-inch pieces. (4.1)

Fettuccini (feht-too-CHEE-nee) Flat, ribbon-style pasta; may be fresh or dried. (13.3)

Fillet Boneless piece of fish. (15.1)

Filleting knife Knife with flexible blade; used for filleting fish. (4.1)

Finger food Hors d' oeuvres that are served on a napkin and eaten with the fingers. (11.2)

Finger sandwich Simple, small sandwich usually made with firm, thinly sliced pullman loaves. Can be made both as closed sandwiches and as open-faced sandwiches. Also called *tea sandwich*. (11.1)

Fire detectors Devices that warn you about a fire so you can get out of a building safely; the two basic types of fire detectors are smoke detectors and heat detectors. (2.1)

Fire emergency plan Established plan of action in case of a fire. (2.1)

Fire extinguishers Handheld devices used to put out a small fire; specific types of extinguishers are designed to handle specific types of fires. (2.1)

Fish fumet (foo-MAY) Type of stock made from fish bones that are sweated until they change color and release some of their moisture. (14.1)

Fish poacher Long, narrow, metal pan with a perforated rack used to raise or lower the fish so it doesn't break apart. (4.2)

Fish station chef Chef responsible for preparing and cooking fish and seafood in a restaurant. Also called *poissonier*. (20.1)

Fixed cost Business expense that is the same from one month to the next, such as rent. (23.1)

Fixed menu Menu that offers the same items every day. (21.1)

Fixed seating plan Seating plan that uses set, staggered meal times (such as 6 p.m., 8 p.m., and 10 p.m.), enabling the kitchen to work at a steady, reliable pace. (20.1)

Flat fish Fish with both eyes on the same side of their heads. (15.1)

Flat omelet Round open-face omelet that is cooked in a pan and then often baked to produce a dense product that is cut in wedges. (9.1)

Flattop range Cooking unit with a thick solid plate of cast iron or steel set over the heat source; provides an indirect, less intense heat than an open burner. Pots and pans are set directly on a flattop, which is ideal for items that require long, slow cooking. (3.3)

Flatware Utensils used at the table or for serving; includes knives, forks, and spoons. (20.2)

Flavor Taste, aroma, texture, sound, and appearance of a food. (6.1)

Flight of cheeses Offering a number of different cheeses at the same time. (10.3)

Floor scale Device at floor level at a receiving area, used for weighing bulky and heavy packages. (3.2)

Flow of food Route food takes from the time a kitchen receives it to the time it is served to the customer. (1.2)

Fluting Giving pie crusts a decorative edge; it is done by squeezing the dough between your fingers or using a special tool. (19.4)

Foccacia (foh-KAH-chee-ah) Large, flat Italian bread, traditionally flavored with olive oil and herbs. (11.1)

Fonds de cuisine (FAHND du kwee-ZEEN) French term for stocks; translates as "foundations of cuisine." (14.1)

Food chopper Machine that holds food in a rotating bowl that passes under a hood where blades chop the food. Some units have hoppers or feed tubes and interchangeable disks for slicing and grating. Also called a *buffalo chopper*. (3.3)

Food Guide Pyramid Tool developed by the USDA to help people find a balance between food and physical activity; it is based on choosing foods from five basic food groups. (22.1)

Food mill Tool used to strain and purée at the same time. Has a flat, curving blade that is rotated over a disk by a hand-operated crank to purée foods. (4.2)

Food processor Machine used to grind, mix, blend, crush, and knead foods; it houses the motor separate from the bowl, blades, and lid. (3.3)

Foodborne illness Illness that results from eating contaminated foods. (1.1)

Food-safety audit Inspection of a food service establishment by a representative of the local health department. (1.3)

Food-safety system System of precautionary steps that take into account all the ways food can be exposed to biological, chemical, or physical hazards. (1.3)

Forced food method Menu-pricing method that is determined by the market; the choices your customers actually make in a restaurant. It takes into account loss and spoilage and assumes that food that is at a high risk of loss or spoilage should have a higher price. It also includes volume in the calculation. The lower the volume, the higher the price (and vice versa). (21.2)

Forequarter Front quarter of an animal carcass, such as beef. (16.1)

Foresaddle Front portion of the saddle of an animal carcass, such as veal. (16.1)

Forged blade Knife blade made from a single piece of heated metal; it is dropped into a mold and then the metal is cut free and hammered into the correct shape. (4.1)

Fork tender Describes foods that are fully cooked and allow a knife or fork to slide all the way into the food easily. (8.2)

Formulas Term that bakers and pastry chefs often use for recipes; it points out the importance of accuracy in all aspects of baking. (17.1)

Free-form loaf Loaf of bread that is not pressed into a mold or a pan but is shaped by hand into an oval, a round ball, or another shape. (17.3)

Freestanding mixer Mixer that sits on the floor and is typically used in commercial bakeries; it can stand about 5 feet high and weigh 3,000 pounds. (3.3)

Freestone Describes fruit that has flesh that separates easily from its pit. (12.1)

French buttercream Yellow buttercream icing made by adding sugar and butter to whipped egg yolks. (19.3)

French service Elaborate style of service based on serving a meal in three courses: the first course, or entrée, the second course, and the dessert. (20.3)

French toast Piece of bread dipped in a mixture of milk and eggs, fried until golden brown on both sides, and then served with syrup, fruit, or other toppings. (9.2)

Frenching Technique of scraping clean the bones for roasts or chops before they are cooked. (16.1)

Fresh cheeses Moist, soft cheeses that typically have not ripened or significantly aged. (10.3)

Freshwater fish Fish that live in freshwater ponds, lakes, rivers, and streams. (15.1)

Frittata (free-TAH-ta) Type of flat omelet made by pouring eggs mixed with other ingredients into a pan, cooking the mixture, and then finishing it in a hot oven. (9.1)

Fritters Small deep-fried pieces made by dipping food items, such as fruit, in a batter or other coating and then frying. (12.1)

Front of the house In a restaurant, the dining room area. (20.1)

Front waiter Person second in line of responsibility after the captain. Helps the captain take orders, makes sure tables are set properly for each course and that food is delivered properly to the correct tables. (20.1)

Frozen soufflé Frozen mousse, also called a *parfait*. (19.2)

Fully cooked Describes food that is cooked all the way through or to the doneness requested by a customer. (8.2)

Fungi Single-celled or multi-celled organisms (plural of fungus). May be beneficial; such as a mold used to produce cheese; may be a biological hazard, such as a fungus that causes a foodborne illness. (1.1)

G

Game General term for meat of wild mammals and birds. (16.1)

Ganache Emulsion made from chocolate and a liquid, typically heavy cream. (19.1)

Garde manger (GAHRD mohn-ZHAY) Person or persons responsible for cold food preparation. (10.1)

Gaufrette (go-FRET) Cut typically made by a mandoline. Means "waffle" in French. (4.1)

Gauge (GAGE) Thickness of the material of which cookware is made. (4.2)

Gelatin Protein processed from the bones, skin, and connective tissue of animals; it is used as a gelling agent to thicken and stabilize foams or liquids. (17.1)

General safety audit Review of the level of safety in an establishment. (2.2)

Germ Smallest part of a grain; the germ can produce a new plant and contains most of the grain's oils and many vitamins and minerals. (13.1)

German buttercream Rich buttercream icing made from adding butter to pastry cream. (19.3)

Giblet bag Small bag in the cavity of a whole bird; includes the liver, stomach, and neck of the bird. (16.2)

Gizzard Stomach of a bird, such as a chicken gizzard. (16.2)

Glassware Glass containers used to contain liquids, including water glasses, wine glasses, champagne goblets, cocktail or liquor glasses, beer mugs, pitchers, and carafes. (20.2)

Glaze Stock that is simmered long enough to produce an intense flavor and a very syrupy consistency. (14.1)

Glazed fish Whole fish that has been dipped in water and then frozen several times to build up a layer of ice. (15.1)

Glucose (GLOO-kohs) What our bodies turn carbohydrates into to use as fuel for warmth and for muscle, brain, and nervous system function. (22.1)

Gluten Network of long, stretchy strands that trap the carbon dioxide given off by yeast when kneading dough. (17.1)

Gluten window test Test to check the strength of the gluten in dough—pinch off a piece of dough to see if it stretches without tearing and if it is thin enough for some light to come through. (17.2)

Gnocchi (NYOH-kee) Italian dumpling. (13.3)

Goujonette (goo-zhohn-NET) Straight cut of fish, sometimes called a fish finger, usually about the width of a thumb. (15.1)

Grain (of meat) Direction that the fibers in the meat are running. (16.1)

Grains Seeds of cereal grasses. (13.1)

Grand sauces Five basic sauces. They are: brown sauce, velouté sauce, béchamel sauce, tomato sauce, and Hollandaise. Also called mother sauces and leading sauces. (14.2)

Granité Frozen dessert made from a flavored water base; it has large ice crystals, similar to shaved ice. (19.2)

Granton edge Knife edge that has a series of ovals ground along the edge of the blade to prevent moist foods from sticking to the blade while slicing. (4.1)

Granulated sugar Ordinary white sugar that is refined from sugar cane or sugar beets. (17.1)

Gratin dish Shallow baking dish made of ceramic, enameled cast iron, or enameled steel. (4.2)

Grating cheeses Solid, dry cheeses that have a grainy consistency; they are grated or shaved on food rather than cut into slices because of their crumbly texture. (10.3)

Griddle Thick cast iron or steel plate used as a cooking surface heated from below. Foods are cooked directly on this surface, which is usually designed with edges to contain foods and a drain to collect used oil and waste. (3.3)

Grill Cooking unit with a rack over a radiant heat source. Grills that burn wood or charcoal require special ventilation. Restaurant units use gas or electric heat sources. (3.3)

Grill station chef Chef responsible for all the grilled items made in a restaurant. Also called *grillardin*. (20.1)

Grillardin (gree-yar-DAHN) Chef responsible for all the grilled items made in a restaurant. Also called *grill station chef*. (20.1)

Grilled sandwich Sandwich that is assembled, the outside surface of the bread spread with butter, and then cooked directly on a heat source, usually a griddle. Also known as a griddled sandwich. (11.1)

Grilling Dry heat method of cooking that uses a grill to cook food, with the heat source below the grill. (8.1)

Grit Degree of coarseness or fineness of a sharpening stone or steel. (4.1)

Grits Type of cornmeal made from yellow or white corn. (13.1)

Gross profit method Menu-pricing method that determines a specific amount of money that should be made from each customer who comes into the restaurant. (21.2)

Grosse pièce (GROHSS pee-YES) Method of serving a main item in a presentation or buffet in which a large part of the main item is left unsliced. (10.4)

Guacamole (gwo-kah-MOH-lee) Mexican dip made from mashed avocado, seasoned with lime or lemon juice, cilantro, onions, and chiles. (10.1)

H

HACCP Hazard Analysis Critical Control Plan; a system for maintaining food safety; often pronounced "HAS-sup." (1.3)

Hanging scale Device at a receiving area, used for weighing large items that can be lifted on a hook, such as a side of beef. (3.2)

Hard cheeses Cheeses with a drier texture than semi-soft cheeses and a firmer consistency. They slice and grate easily. (10.3)

Hard dough Basic yeast dough made with the bare essentials – flour, yeast, salt, and water. Also called *lean dough*. (17.2)

Hare Type of larger rabbit; it is usually wild. (16.1)

Hash Breakfast mixture of pan-fried chopped meat (typically corned beef), potatoes, and seasonings. (9.2)

Hash browns Finely chopped or grated potatoes, pressed down in a pan or on a griddle to brown on one side and then flipped to brown on the other side. (9.2)

Haunch Hindquarters of a game animal, such as a deer, consisting of the leg and the loin. (16.1)

Hazard analysis Review of the ways foods may become unsafe during handling, preparation, and service. (1.3)

Hazard Communication Program Part of an effective safety program; it includes several important documents that can be used as evidence that reasonable care was taken if someone is injured. (2.2)

Hazard Communication Standard (HCS) Also known as Right-to-Know or HAZCOM; a health regulation that makes sure an employer tells all employees about any chemical hazards present on the job. (2.2)

Headed and gutted fish Drawn fish with the head cut off. (15.1)

Heat lamp Light with a special bulb placed directly above an area where food is held. (3.4)

Heat transfer How efficiently heat passes from cookware to the food inside it. (4.2)

Heel Widest, thickest point of a knife blade, closest to the handle; used for cutting tasks that require some force, such as cutting hard vegetables, bones, and shells. (4.1)

Heimlich maneuver Emergency procedure performed to remove an obstruction from the throat of a choking victim. (2.2)

Heirloom plant Variety of fruit or vegetable that existed many years ago, before produce was grown for mass-market consumption. Grown from heirloom seeds that have been saved by farmers. (12.2)

Herbs de Provence (AIRBS duh proVAWNS) Dried herb mixture associated with France's Provence region. Includes basil, thyme, marjoram, rosemary, sage, fennel seeds, and lavender. (10.1)

Herbs Leaves, stems, and roots of various plants; used either fresh or in a dried form to flavor dishes. (6.3)

Hero sandwich Large, closed sandwich that uses a long thin loaf of bread (often called a hero loaf). Hero sandwiches (or heroes) are known by different names in different parts of the country. Also called submarines, grinders, po' boys, or hoagies. (11.1)

High-sodium food Food that has a strong salty taste and that contains a significant amount of sodium. (6.2)

Hindquarter Rear quarter of an animal carcass. (16.1)

Hindsaddle Back portion of the saddle of an animal carcass, such as veal. (16.1)

Holding cabinet Metal container on wheels that can hold large quantities of food or plates on trays, ready to serve. (3.4)

Hollandaise sauce (HOLL-uhn-daze) One of the grand sauces; made by blending melted or clarified butter into slightly cooked egg yolks. (14.2)

Hollowware Large objects, decorative or utilitarian, including silver platters, candlesticks, large tea or coffee pots, sauceboats, fondue sets, and cake stands. (20.2)

Home fries Sliced potatoes that are pan-fried, often with chopped peppers and onions. (9.2)

Hominy (HOM-uh-nee) Kernel of corn that is processed in lime to remove the hull and make the grain easier to cook and digest. (13.1)

Hominy grits Meal made from hominy. (13.1)

Homogenized Process that evenly distributes and emulsifies the fat particles in milk. (9.1)

Honing Straightening a knife's edge on a whetstone or a steel to sharpen the knife. (4.1)

Hood systems Fire protection systems installed in the ventilation hood over ranges, griddles, broilers, and deep fat fryers; instead of water, they release chemicals, carbon dioxide, or gases that can smother and put out a fire. (2.1)

Hors d' oeuvre (or-DERV) Small, savory, flavorful dish, usually consumed in one or two bites. Means "outside the meal" in French. (11.2)

Hors d' oeuvres varies (or-DERV van-REEZ) Method of presenting hors d'oeuvres. A variety plate for one person with a combination of hors d'oeuvres on it, usually fewer than ten small offerings. (11.2)

Hot cross bun Sweet yeast bun with an icing cross drizzled on top; they originated in England and were traditionally served on Good Friday and Easter. (17.2)

Hot plate Device with an electrical heating element typically used to warm coffee and water. (3.4)

Hotel pan Stainless-steel or plastic container used for cooking, holding, and storage. Available in standard sizes that fit in steam tables and other serving equipment. (3.4)

Hull Outer layer of a grain; provides a protective coating. (13.1)

Hummus (HOOM-uhs) Popular Middle-Eastern spread made from mashed or pureed chickpeas that are seasoned and served with pita bread, chips, or raw vegetables. (13.2)

Husk Loose or firmly attached wrapper on the grain as it grows. (13.1)

Hydrogenation Process that changes a liquid polyunsaturated fat, such as corn oil, into a solid fat, such as margarine. (22.1)

I

Icebox cookies Drop cookies made from a batter that is formed into a cylinder, chilled, and then sliced and baked. (19.3)

Immersion (ih-MER-zhuhn) blender Long handheld machine that houses a motor at one end and a blade on the other end; it is placed directly in the container of the food to be blended. (3.3)

Income Money coming into a restaurant; also known as *earnings* or *sales*. (23.1)

Income statement Record of earnings (or income), losses, and profits of a business. Also called a *profit and loss statement* or a *P&L*. (23.1)

Individually quick frozen (IQF) Describes fruit that has been frozen whole or in slices or chunks, without any added sugar or syrup. (12.1)

Infrared thermometer Device for reading the surface temperature of food without touching the food by measuring invisible infrared radiation. Also used in kitchens to check holding temperatures. (3.2)

Injera (in-JEER-ah) Spongy, sourdough-tasting flatbread used as a utensil to scoop up meat and vegetables in Ethiopia. (17.3)

Insoluble fiber Fiber that does not dissolve in water. Also called roughage, it cleans our digestive tracts, assisting in waste elimination. (22.1)

Instant oats Rolled oats that have been partially cooked and then dried before being rolled again. (13.1)

Inventory List of all the assets in a restaurant, usually organized by category. (23.2)

Iodized salt Table salt to which iodine has been added. (6.2)

Italian buttercream White butter-cream icing made by adding butter to meringue. (19.3)

J

Job description Duties to be performed and responsibilities involved for a particular job, as well as the level of education and training needed for the job. (23.3)

Julienne (JU-lee-ehn) Long, rectangular cut measuring 1/8 inch wide x 1/8 inch thick and 1 to 2 inches in length. (4.1)

Jus de veau lié (JHOO duh voh lee-AY) Type of brown sauce; made by simmering brown stock with flavorings and aromatics and, in some cases, additional bones or meat trimmings. (14.2)

K

Kaiser roll (KIGH-zer) Large, round, crusty roll used for sandwiches. Also known as a hard roll or a Vienna roll. (11.1)

Keel bone Bone that joins the two halves of a breast of poultry. (16.2)

Kernel Whole seed of a grain before it is crushed or milled. (13.1)

Kitchen shears Scissors used for kitchen chores such as cutting string and butcher's twine, trimming artichoke leaves, cutting grapes into clusters, and trimming herbs. (4.2)

Knead Work dough by hand or in a mixer to distribute ingredients. (17.1)

Kosher salt (KOH-shure) Salt made without any additives; sold in coarse or fine grain styles. Typically flakier than table salt. (6.2)

Kuchen Sweet, yeast-raised cake filled with fruit or cheese; originally from Germany. (17.2)

Kugelhopf (KOO-guhl-hof) Light yeast cake, filled with candied fruit, nuts and raisins, traditionally baked in a fluted ring mold; a tradition in Austria as well as Poland, Alsace, and Germany. (17.2)

L

Ladle Tool with a bowl (1 to 16 oz. capacity) and a long handle for reaching to the bottom of a deep pot. (4.2)

Lamb Tender meat produced by young, domesticated sheep. (16.1)

Laminated yeast dough Yeast dough that has fat rolled and folded into it, creating alternating layers of fat and dough, adding flavor and flakiness to the finished product. Also called *rolled-in yeast dough.* (17.2)

Lasagna (luh-ZAHN-yuh) Layered baked pasta dish. (13.3)

Lattices Strips of pie dough laid across the top of the filling to create a cross-hatch effect. (19.4)

Lean dough Basic yeast dough made with the bare essentials – flour, yeast, salt and water. Also called *hard dough.* (17.2)

Leavener Baking ingredient that increases the volume of a dough or batter by adding air or other gas. (17.1)

Lecithin Fatty substance in egg yolk, liver, and legumes; it acts as a natural emulsifier. (9.1)

Legume (LEG-yoom) Plant that has a double-seamed pod containing a single row of seeds. Some varieties have edible seeds, some have edible seeds and pods. Seeds are often removed from the pod and dried. (13.2)

Lentils Legume shaped like a round disk. (13.2)

Liabilities Losses that occur when a restaurant business uses up assets without making a profit. (23.1)

Liaison (lee-AY-zohn) Mixture of egg yolks and cream used to lightly thicken and enrich a sauce. (14.2)

Limited menu Menu that offers a limited range of choices to the customer, such as four sandwiches, two soups, and a salad for lunch. (21.1)

Line chef Chef responsible for a particular type of food. Also called *station chef.* (20.1)

Liquid-filled thermometer Thermometer that has either a glass or metal stem filled with a colored liquid. Designed to stay in the food while cooking. Specialized versions measure high temperatures used in candy and jelly making as well as deep fat frying. (4.2)

Liquor (shellfish) Natural juices of a shellfish. (15.2)

Lo mein (low mane) Asian-style noodle, often purchased fresh. (13.3)

Loaf pans Rectangular pans used for simple cakes and quick breads. (17.1)

Logo Drawing, picture, or other symbol that identifies your restaurant. It should be instantly recognizable. (23.1)

Low boy Undercounter reach-in refrigerator unit for storing a small amount of ingredients within easy reach at a workstation. (3.2)

Lox Cured salmon. (15.1)

Lozenge (LOZ-enj) Diamond-shaped cut measuring 1/2 inch long, 1/2 inch wide, and 1/4 inch thick. (4.1)

M

Macaroni Common name used to refer to pasta in general. (13.3)

Maillard reaction Color change seen in food that contains protein when it is heated. The food turns brown. (8.1)

Main-course salad Salad that is the main course. (10.2)

Maître d' (MAY-truh DEE) Person running the dining room portion of the restaurant; also responsible for training service personnel, working with the chef on the menu, arranging seating, and taking reservations. Also called *maître d'hôtel* or *dining room manager*. (20.1)

Maître d' hotel (MAY-truh doh-TELL) Person running the dining room portion of the restaurant; also responsible for training service personnel, working with the chef on the menu, arranging seating, and taking reservations. Also called *maître d'* or *dining room manager*. (20.1)

Mandoline Tabletop device used for making slices of various thicknesses. (4.1)

Marbling Amount of fat present in lean meat. (16.1)

Marinade (MAHR-i-nahd) Combination of citrus juice, oil, aromatic ingredients, and other flavoring components. (10.2)

Market quote Statement from a supplier of a product's selling price and an indication of the length of time that the price will be effective. (23.2)

Market research Information collected to find out what customers like or dislike. (21.1)

Masa harina (MAH-sah ah-REE-nah) Cornmeal made from posole. (13.1)

Material Safety Data Sheet (MSDS) A product identification sheet, provided by a chemical manufacturer or supplier, that describes the specific hazards posed by a chemical. (2.2)

Matignon (mah-tee-YOHN) Aromatic combination of onions, carrots, celery, and ham used to flavor dishes. (6.3)

Maturation Process of reaching the full potential size and weight, as with fruit. (12.1)

Mayonnaise (MAY-oh-nayz) Thick, creamy emulsion of oil and egg yolks. (10.1)

Meal Grains that are milled into fine particles by rolling the grain between steel drums or stone wheels.

Meat grinder Freestanding machine, or an attachment for a mixer, that grinds meat dropped through a feed tube. The meat is pushed through the machine, cut by blades, and forced out. (3.3)

Meat slicer Slicing tool with a circular blade on a horizontally titled frame across which food is passed by means of a carriage. (3.3)

Medium dough Lean dough with some sugar and fat added. Pullman loaves, the soft sliced bread used for sandwich making, are made from medium dough. Also called *soft dough*. (17.2)

Melon baller Tool used to scoop smooth balls from melons, cheese, and butter. (4.2)

Menu List of food and drink choices available in a restaurant. (21.1)

Meringue Mixture of stiffly beaten egg whites and sugar. (19.2)

Mesclun (MEHS-kluhn) French-style salad mix that often includes baby red romaine, endive, mâche, radicchio, and arugala. (10.2)

Metric system Standard international system of measurements. Volume measurements are milliliter (ml) and liter (l). Metric weight measurements include the milligram (mg), gram (g), and kilogram (kg). (5.1)

Micro plane General-purpose tool used for grating food, such as grating the skin of a lemon to produce fine lemon zest. (4.2)

Milk chocolate Chocolate made with milk powder; it is sweeter than dark chocolate. (19.1)

Milkfat Fat content of dairy products, measured by the weight of the fat compared to the total weight of the product. Same as *butterfat*. (9.1)

Milling Cutting, crushing, rolling, or grinding grain; part of the processing of grain. (13.1)

Mirepoix Combination of vegetables used as an aromatic flavoring ingredient in many dishes. Common varieties are *standard, white, Cajun trinity, matignon,* and *battuto*. (6.3)

Mise en place (MEEZ uhn PLAHS) French term meaning to gather all the raw ingredients required and have all the equipment and tools necessary to carry out a culinary operation at a workstation. (3.1) (7.1)

Mission statement Statement of the goal of an organization such as a restaurant. (21.1)

Mixer Machine consisting of a bowl and mixing tool for combining ingredients, primarily for batters and doughs. (3.3)

Mixing Process of combining ingredients so they are evenly spread throughout the mixture. (3.3)

Modified à la carte menu Menu on which appetizers and desserts will be priced and served separately. Often the main course includes a soup or salad, a starch, a vegetable, and possibly a beverage. Found in family-style restaurants. (21.1)

Modified straight-dough mixing method Baking method in which ingredients are added in steps, providing better distribution for fat and sugar. Useful for enriched dough. (17.2)

Molded cookies Made with stiff dough that is shaped by hand; it can also be stamped, pressed, or piped into carved molds. (19.3)

Mollusks Shellfish that have soft bodies and no skeletons. (15.2)

Monosodium glutamate (MSG) Used in much the same way as salt. Provides the umami taste rather than the salty taste and is often associated with Chinese or Japanese food. Enhances the meaty or brothy flavor in meat, poultry, fish, and vegetables. The source of MSG is seaweed. (6.2)

Monounsaturated fats Fats that come from plants and are liquid at room temperature. Considered healthy fats, they help balance cholesterol levels in the blood. (22.1)

Mousse Aerated dessert made with a flavored base, gelatin, egg foam, and whipped cream. (19.2)

Muesli (MYOOS-lee) Swiss version of granola; a mixture of cereal (such as oats and wheat), dried fruit, nuts, bran, and sugar; eaten with milk or yogurt. (9.2)

Mutton Meat from sheep that is over 16 months old; it is tougher than lamb and has a strong, gamey taste. (16.1)

Mutual supplementation Combining foods, such as rice and beans, to create a complete protein with all the essential amino acids. (22.1)

N

Nappé (nap-AY) French term used to describe a sauce that has been properly thickened (thick enough to lightly coat foods). (14.2)

Neutral stock Another name for white beef stock; it has a very mild flavor and a light color. (14.1)

Nibs Cleaned cocoa kernels, removed from their hard outer shell. (19.1)

Nonverbal feedback Form of feedback that is not spoken. (7.2)

No-reservation policy Restaurant policy of not accepting reservations but instead serving customers on a first-come-first-served basis. (20.1)

Numerator Top number in a fraction. (The bottom number is the *denominator*). (5.2)

Nutrients Parts of food our bodies use. (22.1)

Nutritional balance Providing enough calories to meet energy needs and enough specific nutrients to promote health. (22.2)

Nutritive value All the benefits a food might have for our bodies; nutritional value. (8.1)

Nuts Dried fruit of a tree. (6.4)

O

Oat groats Whole grain of the oat, with the hull removed. (13.1)

Oatmeal Coarsely ground oats; cooked as a hot cereal or used in baking. (13.1)

Obesity (oh-BEE-city) Condition of being dangerously overweight and prone to health risks. (22.1)

Oblique (ob-LEEK) **cut** Cut for vegetables where sides are neither parallel nor perpendicular but cut on an angle, with the vegetable rolled after each cut. Used for long, cylindrical vegetables such as parsnips, carrots, and celery. (4.1)

Obstructed airway maneuver (Heimlich maneuver) Emergency procedure performed to remove the obstruction from the throat of a choking victim. (2.2)

Occupation Safety and Health Administration (OSHA) Federal agency that is charged with keeping the workplace safe. (2.2)

Offal (AH-full) Organs and other portions of an animal, including the liver, heart, kidneys, and tongue. Also known as *variety meat*. (16.1)

Omega-3 fatty acids Type of polyunsaturated fat found in some plants and in all fish; they are linked to reducing the risk of stroke and heart attack and improving brain growth and development. (22.1)

Omelet Blended eggs cooked in a sauté pan with or without other ingredients. It can be folded, rolled, or finished in an oven and served flat. (9.1)

Omelet pan Shallow skillet with very short, sloping sides; often has a nonstick coating. (4.2)

On the half shell Method of serving shellfish in which they are opened and served on one of their shells. (10.4)

One-stage cooling method Safely cooling foods to below 41°F within four hours to avoid foodborne illness. (1.2)

Opaque (o-PAKE) Indicates that light will not travel through an object. (6.1)

Open-burner range Electric or gas-fueled cooking unit with a set of adjustable open burners. Pots and pans are set directly on an electric element or on a grid over a gas flame. (3.3)

Open-faced sandwich Sandwich made with one slice of bread and topped with ingredients. (11.1)

Organic leavener Yeast, a living organism, which is used to increase the volume of dough. (17.1)

Orientation Period of time during which new employees learn about the business and their roles in it. (23.3)

Oven spring In baking, last stage of rising that determines volume; it occurs in the oven when gluten strands expand rapidly and trap steam, allowing full size to be reached. (17.3)

Over egg Fried egg cooked and then flipped once during frying. (9.1)

Ovo-lacto vegetarian Person who does not eat meat, poultry, and fish but does eat eggs and dairy products. (22.2)

P

P&L Record of earnings (or income), losses, and profits of a business. Also called a *profit and loss statement* or an *income statement*. (23.1)

Palette knife Tool with a long, flexible blade and a rounded end; used for turning cooked or grilled foods and spreading fillings or glazes. Sometimes used in baking. Also called a straight spatula. (4.2)

Pan broiling Dry heat method of cooking very much like sautéing, except no fat is used. (8.1)

Pan frying Dry heat method of cooking in which food is cooked in hot oil in a pan. (8.1)

Pan loaf Loaf of bread made by pressing dough into a mold or a pan. (17.3)

Pan proofing Allowing dough to rise one last time outside of the oven before baking. (17.3)

Pan-dressed fish Fish with the fins removed, and sometimes the head and tail cut off; usually small enough to fit easily in a pan and make a single serving. (15.1)

Panini Italian version of a pressed sandwich. (11.1)

Parasites Multi-celled organisms that can cause illness when eaten; roundworms are an example. Potential biological hazards. (1.1)

Parboiled Moist heat method of cooking in which food is cooked at 212°F. (8.2)

Parchment paper Grease-resistant, nonstick, heatproof paper; often used to line pans. (17.1)

Parcooked grain Grain that is processed by partially cooking it. (13.1)

Parcooked Stands for "partially cooked." Method of cooking in which the food is not cooked fully. (8.2)

Parfait Frozen mousse, also called a *frozen soufflé*. (19.2)

Paring knife Small knife with 2- to 4-inch blade; used mainly for trimming and peeling fruits and vegetables. (4.1)

Parisienne (pah-REE-see-ehn) **scoop** Melon baller with a scoop at each end, one larger than the other. (4.2)

Par-stock list Listing of the quantity of supplies you need to have on hand in a restaurant to make every item on the menu. (23.2)

Pasta Italian for dough; used to describe the category of starchy foods made from shaped dough that includes flour and liquid. Typically cooked in boiling or simmering water. (13.3)

Pasteurized Heated at high temperature to kill harmful bacteria. (9.1)

Pastry bag Cone-shaped bag with two open ends. Fill the bag with dough or whipped cream, apply a decorative tip to the pointed end, and then squeeze the bag to add fillings to pastries, make delicate cookies, and apply decorative finishes to cakes and pastries. (17.1)

Pastry blender Tool with a crescent-shaped loop of thin wires attached to a handle; it is used to mix fat into flour when you make a pastry dough. (17.1)

Pastry brush Brush used to apply egg wash and to butter pans and muffin tins; made of soft, flexible nylon or unbleached hog bristles. (17.1)

Pastry chef Chef responsible for making pastry and other desserts. Also called *pâtissier*. (20.1)

Pastry wheel Cutting tool with a round blade mounted on a handle; roll the blade over pastry dough to make a single, clean cut. Blade may be straight or scalloped to make a decorative edge. (17.1)

Pâté (pah-TAY) Well-seasoned ground meat, fish, poultry, or vegetables mixture that has been baked. Usually served cold. (11.2)

Pâte fermentée (pah-TAY fer-mahn-TAY) In baking, piece of dough saved from one batch and added at the end of mixing to the next batch. French term for "old dough." (17.2)

Pâté mold Oven cookware that is deep, rectangular, and made of metal, sometimes with hinged sides. (4.2)

Pathogen Disease-producing organism, such as bacteria, viruses, parasites, or fungi. (1.1)

Pâtissier (pah-tee-SYAY) Chef responsible for making pastry and other desserts. Also called *pastry chef*. (20.1)

Paupiette (pah-pee-YET) Thin fish fillet that is rolled up before it is cooked. (15.1)

Paysanne (pahy-SAHN) Rustic type of cut that produces 1/2 inch square by 1/8 inch thick pieces. Means "peasant" in French. (4.1)

Pearl barley Barley that has been polished to remove the bran. (13.1)

Pearl grain Grain that has the bran completely removed. (13.1)

Peas Legume that is round. (13.2)

Pectin Substance naturally found in certain fruits; it is used to thicken a liquid. (17.1)

Peel Large, flat wooden or metal paddle used to slide bread onto baking stones and to retrieve loaves when they are done. (17.1)

Performance evaluation Meeting at which a manager and an employee talk about whether the employee has met expectations, based on the job description. (23.3)

Perishable goods Foods, such as meats and milk, that must be properly wrapped or kept cold until they can be stored in a refrigerator or freezer. (1.2)

Pest management Approach to controlling and eliminating rodents, insects, and other pests from the kitchen by keeping the kitchen clean; maintaining the building, especially doors, windows, roof, and drains; covering garbage; and using pesticides when necessary. (1.1)

Physical hazards Object that falls into food and can cause injury or illness. (1.1)

Physical inventory Counting the actual assets in a restaurant, such as the number of cans or boxes on a shelf. (23.2)

Physical leavener Steam or air incorporated into a batter, causing it to increase in volume. (17.1)

Pickup In baking, the first stage of mixing ingredients. (17.1)

Pierogi (peer-OH-gee) Polish half-moon-shape dumplings with a sweet or savory filling. (13.3)

Pilaf (PEE-lahf) Rice dish made by cooking grain in a little oil or butter before a measured amount of liquid is added. (13.1)

Pin bones Fish bones found in the middle of the fillet. (15.1)

Piped cookies Drop cookies made of soft dough that can be piped through a pastry bag to form decorative shapes. (19.3)

Pita bread (PEE-tah) Flat round or oval Middle Eastern bread; also known as pocket bread. When cut in half, each half forms a pocket that can be filled as a sandwich. (11.1)

Pith The white, bitter, and indigestible layer that is just below the outer skin of a citrus fruit. (12.1)

Planetary mixer Mixer with a stationary bowl and a mixing tool that moves within it, like a planet orbiting the sun. Three standard attachments are a paddle, a whip, and a dough hook. (.3.3)

Plate cover Metal cover placed over a plate of food to keep the food warm on its way to the customer. (3.4)

Plate presentation The way you put food into a dish or on a plate. (7.3)

Platform scale Device on a platform of a receiving area, used for weighing bulky and heavy packages. (3.2)

Platter service Serving style typically used for banquets in which completely prepared hot food is delivered from the kitchen in large platters to a table and then served to guests without plating at a side table. Also called *Russian service*. (20.3)

Poaching Moist heat method of cooking in which food is cooked at 160°F to 170°F. (8.2)

Poissonier (pwah-sawng-YAY) Chef responsible for preparing and cooking fish and seafood in a restaurant. Also called *fish station chef*. (20.1)

Polenta (poh-LEHN-tah) Italian cornmeal porridge; also Italian cornmeal. (13.1)

Polished grain Grain with the bran completely removed.

Polyunsaturated fats Fats that come from plants; they are liquid at room temperature. (22.1)

Poolish (poo-LEESH) In baking, a wet dough starter with a consistency like pancake batter. (17.2)

Portable refrigeration cart Movable refrigerator units for temporary refrigeration or off-site catering. (3.2)

Portion control Controlling the quantity of particular foods by using appropriately sized servings. (22.2)

Portion scale Scale that measures the weight of a small amount of food or ingredient (typically a portion). Can be reset to zero to allow for the weight of a container or weigh more than one ingredient at a time. (4.2)

Portion Serving size for one person, expressed in pieces, weight, or volume. (5.1)

Portioning food Serving the correct amount of a particular food. (7.3)

Posole (poh-SOH-leh) Whole kernel of corn, with the germ and bran still intact. It is soaked in a solution of lime and water to make the hull softer and easier to digest. (13.1)

Potentially hazardous foods Foods that, because of conditions or the nature of the food itself, provide a friendly environment for the rapid growth of pathogens. (1.1)

Poultry Refers to any domesticated bird used for human consumption. (16.2)

Pre-ferment In baking, a dough mixture that starts the fermentation process before the final mixing of all the ingredients, giving the dough time to develop more gluten strength and depth of flavor. Also called a *dough starter*. (17.2)

Prep chef Chef responsible for washing and peeling vegetables and fruits, cutting meat, and preparing any other ingredients that will be used by other chefs. (20.1)

Presentation side The most attractive side of a food item. (7.3)

Pressed sandwich Sandwich that is toasted on a heavy, two-sided cooking press that compresses and grills it until it are hot and heated through on the inside. (11.1)

Pressure steamer Cooking unit that heats water under pressure in a sealed compartment, allowing it to reach temperatures above the boiling point. Cooking time is controlled by automatic timers that open the exhaust valves, releasing steam pressure so the unit can be opened safely. (3.3)

Pricing factor Factor by which a raw food cost is multiplied to arrive at the price of a menu item. (21.2)

Pricing system comparison chart Aids in making pricing decisions; it shows a comparison of the prices from various pricing methods, two competitor's prices, the final decision for the menu price, and your value judgments. (21.2)

Primal cuts Cuts made to saddles or quarters of meat that meet uniform standards for beef, veal, pork, and lamb. (16.1)

Prime cost method Used in cafeteria operations; it prices menu items and also calculates the cost of preparing the menu item. (21.2)

Prime cost Raw food cost plus the direct cost of labor involved in preparing a menu item. (21.2)

Prix fixe menu (PREE FEKS) Menu that offers a complete meal, often including a beverage, for a specific price, allowing a diner to choose one selection from each course. Similar to table d'hôte menu. (21.1)

Processed cheese Cheese made from one or more cheeses that have been finely ground, mixed together with other non-dairy ingredients, heated, and poured into a mold. (10.3)

Processed grain Grain that has been prepared to use as foods. (13.1)

Producer Person or business selling items to a restaurant. Also called *vendor, purveyor,* or *supplier.* (23.2)

Product specifications Description of a product, including its size, quality, grade, packaging, color, weight, or count. (23.2)

Profit and loss statement Record of earnings (or income), losses, and profits of a business. Also called a *P&L* or an *income statement.* (23.1)

Profit Earnings (money coming into a restaurant) minus expenses (money spent by a restaurant). (23.1)

Promotion Extra effort taken, in addition to advertising, to make a restaurant business known and get people interested in coming to it. (23.1)

Proofer Special box used in baking that holds dough as it rises. Some models have thermostats to control heat and are able to generate steam. (17.1)

Protein Nutrient our bodies need to grow and to replace worn out tissues and cells; it comes from foods such as meat, fish, eggs, milk, and legumes. (22.1)

Psychological factors Factors that take into account how a customer perceives a specific menu item. Customers may psychologically associate high-end menu items, such as lobster, caviar, or truffles, with a higher price. (21.2)

PUFI mark Mark from the United States Department of Commerce that indicates a facility has passed a Type 1 inspection. (15.1)

Pullman loaf Long loaf of bread that is baked in a rectangular pan with a lid. A slice from a Pullman loaf is square on all sides. (11.1)

Purée (pyur-AY) To process food until it has a soft, smooth consistency. (4.2) Very fine paste made by cooking a flavorful ingredient until it is very soft and then straining it or using a food processor or blender to chop it very fine. (14.2)

Purée soup Hearty soup made by simmering a starchy ingredient such as dried beans or potatoes along with additional vegetables, meats, or aromatics in a broth or other liquid and then puréeing it to the appropriate texture. (14.3)

Purveyor Person or business selling items to a restaurant. Also called *vendor, supplier,* or *producer.* (23.2)

Q

Quarter fillets Common name for the four fillets cut from a flat fish. (15.1)

Quarters (of meat) Four pieces of an animal carcass that are made by dividing two sides. (16.1)

Quiche (KEESH) Baked egg dish made by blending eggs with cream or milk and other ingredients and baking in a pie shell. (9.1)

Quick bread Type of bread that is quick to make because baking soda or baking powder, instead of yeast, is used for leavening, resulting in a ready-to-use batter rather than a dough that needs fermentation time. (18.1)

Quick-cooking oats Oats that are parcooked before they are cut and rolled into flakes. (13.1)

Quinoa (KEEN-wah) Grain originally grown in South America; it has a round kernel and becomes fluffy and light when you cook it. (13.1)

R

Radiant heat Heat transferred by rays that come from a glowing, or red hot, heat source such as burning coals, flames, or a hot electric element. (8.1)

Raft Name for a clarification that has cooked enough to form a mass and rise to the surface of a simmering consommé. (See clarification.) (14.3)

Ramekin (RAM-I-kin) Baking dish that is round and straight-edged; comes in various sizes. (4.2).

Range Similar to a stovetop on a home oven; used to heat food in pots and pans. (3.3)

Ratites (RAT-ites) Family of flightless birds, such as the ostrich, emu, and rhea. Their meat is a rich red color, lean, and low in fat. (16.2)

Ravioli (rav-ee-OH-lee) Italian for "little wraps"; made by layering a filling between two sheets of pasta and then cutting out filled squares, rounds, or rectangles. (13.3)

Raw bar Bar or counter at which raw shellfish is served. (10.4)

Raw food cost Cost of all the ingredients that went into a single serving of the dish. (21.2)

Reach-in Full-size refrigerator with a door that opens and shelves for storing food. May be a single unit or part of a bank of units. (3.2)

Receptionist In formal restaurants, the person who assists the maître d' in greeting guests and taking telephone reservations. Referred to as the host or hostess in casual restaurants. (20.1)

Recipe conversion factor (RCF) Amount you multiply a recipe's ingredients or yield to scale it up or down. (5.2)

Recipe Written record of the ingredients and preparation steps needed to make a particular dish. (5.1)

Recovery time Time it takes for a pan to heat up again after food is added. (8.1)

Refined grains Grains that have been processed to remove some or all of the bran and germ; this process removes fiber, vitamins, and minerals from the grain. (13.1)

Refined starch Starch (corn, rice, or potatoes) that has been processed enough to remove all but the starch itself; examples include cornstarch and arrowroot. (14.2)

Refrigerated drawer Small under-counter refrigerator drawer within easy reach at a workstation. (3.2)

Relish Sauce with a chunky texture, typically fruit- or vegetable-based and made with a sweet and sour flavoring. Served hot or cold. (14.2)

Reservation policy Restaurant policy of accepting reservations. (20.1)

Retail cuts Cuts made to subprimal pieces of meat to prepare smaller pieces, such as steaks, chops, roasts, stews, or ground meat. (16.1)

Retarder Refrigerated cabinet used by bakers to slow down fermentation. (17.1)

Ricer Device in which cooked food, typically potatoes, is pushed through a pierced container, resulting in rice-like pieces. (4.2)

Rind (RYND) Surface of a cheese. (10.3)

Ring-top range Cooking unit with thick concentric plates or rings of cast iron or steel set over the heat source. Removing one or more rings provides more intense direct heat. (3.3)

Ripening Process when a fruit stops maturing and begins converting starches to sugar, changes color, and becomes ready to eat. (12.1)

Risotto (rih-ZOT-toh) Creamy rice dish typically made with arborio rice, a short-grain rice. (13.1)

Rivet Piece used to attach the handle of the knife to the blade; lies flush with the surface of the handle. (4.1)

Roast station chef Chef responsible for all the roasted items cooked in a restaurant. Also called *rôtisseur*. (20.1)

Roasting Dry heat method of cooking in which food is cooked by hot air trapped inside an oven. Roasting typically means you are preparing larger pieces of food than for baking. (8.1)

Roasting pan Pan used for roasting and baking; has low sides and comes in various sizes. Roasting racks are placed inside the pan to hold foods as they cook so the bottom, sides, and top of the food all are cooked evenly. (4.2)

Rock salt Salt that is less refined than table salt; not generally consumed. (6.2)

Rolled oats Made by steaming oat groats and then rolling them into flat flakes; also called *old-fashioned oats*. (13.1)

Rolled omelet Type of omelet made by stirring the egg mixture to produce curds and then rolling it out of the pan onto a plate. (9.1)

Rolled-in yeast dough Yeast dough that has fat rolled and folded into it, creating alternating layers of fat and dough, adding flavor and flakiness to the finished product. Also called *laminated yeast dough*. (17.2)

Rolling boil Description of liquid that is rapidly boiling. (8.2)

Rondelles (rahn-DELLS) Round shapes produced by cutting through any cylindrical vegetable, such as a carrot or cucumber. Means "rounds" in French. (4.1)

Room service Delivery of food to a hotel room; the food must be delivered quickly to keep it warm and fresh. (20.3)

Rôtisseur (roh-tess-UHR) Chef responsible for all the roasted items cooked in a restaurant. Also called *roast station chef*. (20.1)

Round fish Fish with eyes on both sides of their heads. (15.1)

Roundsman Roving chef who fills in for absent chefs or assists chefs in other stations. Also called *swing chef or tournant*. (20.1)

Roux (ROO) Cooked paste of wheat flour and a fat used to thicken simmering liquids, producing a sauce. (14.2)

Rubbed-dough method In baking, process of cutting fat into chunks, chilling it, and then rubbing it into flour. This prevents the fat from fully combining with the flour and promotes flakiness. (18.2)

Rubber spatula Scraping tool with a broad, flexible rubber or plastic tip. Used to scrape food from the inside of bowls and pans and also to mix in whipped cream or egg whites. (4.2)

Russian service Serving style typically used for banquets in which completely prepared hot food is delivered from the kitchen in large platters to a table and then served to guests without plating at a side table. Also called *platter service*. (20.3)

Rye berries Whole kernel of rye. (13.1)

Rye flakes Rye kernels that have been cracked and rolled. (13.1)

S

Sabayon Egg foam made by whipping egg yolks and sugar over heat. (19.2)

Sachet d'épices Bag of fresh and dried herbs and spices tied up in a piece of cheesecloth; used to flavor a dish. (6.3)

Saddle Half of an animal carcass, such as veal; it includes the right and left sides. (16.1)

Safe foods Foods that won't make you sick or hurt you when you eat them. (1.1)

Salad Combination of raw or cooked ingredients, served cold or warm, and coated with a salad dressing. (10.2)

Salad dressing Use to flavor salads and sometimes to hold a salad together. (10.1)

Salamander Small broiler used primarily to brown or melt foods. (3.3)

Sales Money coming into a restaurant; also known as *earnings* or *income*. (23.1)

Salsa Cold sauce or dip made from a combination of vegetables, typically tomatoes, onions, chilies, peppers, and other ingredients, and often seasoned with salt, pepper, and lime juice. (10.1) (14.2)

Saltwater fish Fish that live in oceans, seas, and the water of bays and gulfs. (15.1)

Sanitizing Using either heat or chemicals to reduce the number of disease-causing organisms on a surface to a safe level. (1.1)

Saturated fats Fats that come from animal sources (except for coconut oil and palm oil); they are usually solid at room temperature. (22.1)

Saucepan Pan that has straight or slightly flared sides and a single long handle. (4.2)

Saucepot Pot that is similar in shape to a stockpot but not as large. Has straight sides and two loop-style handles to ease lifting. (4.2)

Saucier (saw-see-YAY) Chef responsible for sautéed dishes and accompanying sauces prepared in a restaurant. Also called *sauté station chef*. (20.1)

Sauté pan Shallow, general-purpose pan. (4.2)

Sauté station chef Chef responsible for sautéed dishes and accompanying sauces prepared in a restaurant. Also called *saucier*. (20.1)

Sautéing Dry heat method of cooking in which food is cooked quickly, often uncovered, in a very small amount of fat in a pan over high heat. (8.1)

Sauteuse (SAW-toose) Sauté pan that is wide and shallow with sloping sides and a single long handle. (4.2)

Sautoir (SAW-twahr) Sauté pan that has straight sides and a long handle; often referred to as a skillet. (4.2)

Savory (SAY-va-ree) Meaty or brothy flavor; the umami flavor. (6.1)

Scale To change the amount of recipe ingredients to get the yield you need. Scale up to increase the yield or scale down to decrease it. (5.2)

Scaling In baking, weighing liquid and solid ingredients to get precise measurements. (17.2)

Scimitar Knife with a long curved blade, used for portioning raw meats. (4.1)

Scone Rich biscuit that sometimes contains raisins and is served with butter, jam, or thick cream. (9.2)

Scoring Slashes cut on the top of dough to release steam that builds up during baking. (17.3)

Scotch barley Barley that retains most of its bran; also called pot barley. (13.1)

Scrambled eggs Blended eggs that are stirred as they cook in a sauté pan or double boiler over low to medium heat. (9.1)

Sea salt Salt made by evaporating sea water; not significantly refined. (6.2)

Seams (in meat) Membranes that connect muscles, in cuts of meat. (16.1)

Searing Dry heat method of cooking in which food is cooked, usually uncovered, in a small amount of fat just long enough to color the outside of the food. (8.1)

Seasonings Ingredients that enhance, balance, or cut the richness in foods without changing the flavor of the food significantly. (6.2)

Second chef Executive chef's principal assistant, responsible for scheduling personnel and temporarily replacing the executive chef or other chefs as needed. Also called *sous-chef*. (20.1)

Seed Portion of a plant capable of producing a new plant. (6.4)

Semi-soft cheeses Cheeses that are more solid than soft cheeses and retain their shape. They may be mild or strongly flavored as a result of the process used to make them. (10.3)

Semisweet chocolate Dark chocolate that has more sugar than bittersweet chocolate. (19.1)

Semolina flour (seh-muh-LEE-nuh) Pale yellow flour made from durum wheat. Semolina flour has a high protein content and makes an elastic dough; it is widely used for pasta. (13.3)

Separate-course salad Salad that refreshes the appetite and provides a break before dessert. (10.2)

Sequencing Arranging slices to overlap one another in the order they were cut. (10.4)

Serrated edge Knife edge that has a row of teeth; works well for slicing foods with a crust or firm skin. (4.1)

Service cart Cart used in a dining area to carry food and provide a work surface for carving, plating, assembling, and preparing dishes beside a table. Specialized carts are used to flame-finish (flambé) dishes, display pastry, warm food in a chafing dish, and prepare salads. (3.4)

Service style How food and drink is delivered to a guest. Also called *table service*. (20.3)

Serviceware Dishware and utensils used in the dining room, on or off the table. (20.2)

Setting priorities In terms of mise en place, deciding which tasks are most important. (7.1)

Seviche (seh-VEE-chee) Latin American dish of fish and seafood that is cooked in citrus juice and flavored with onions, chiles, and cilantro. A traditional cold appetizer or hors d'oeuvre. Also spelled ceviche. (11.2)

Shallow poaching Moist cooking method in which food is cooked in just enough liquid to create some steam in the pan. (15.1)

Sheet pan All-purpose baking pan; it is shallow and rectangular, with sides generally no higher than one inch. (4.2)

Shellfish Aquatic animals protected by some type of shell. Can be one of two types: mollusks and crustaceans. (15.2)

Shellfish stock Type of stock made by sautéing shellfish shells (lobster, shrimp, or crayfish) until bright red. (14.1)

Sherbet Frozen desert that is similar to a sorbet but has meringue incorporated to make it lighter. (19.2)

Shirred (SHURD) **eggs** Eggs topped with cream and baked in a small dish until they set. (9.1)

Shortcake Dessert made with a foundation of biscuits topped with fruit and whipped cream, such as strawberry shortcake. (18.2)

Shrimp cocktail Cold, steamed shrimp served with a spicy cocktail sauce; a traditional cold appetizer. (11.2)

Shucked shellfish Seafood that has been removed from its shell. (15.2)

Side salad Salad served on the plate to accompany the main dish. (10.2)

Sides (of meat) Two halves of an animal carcass that are made by cutting down the length of the backbone. (16.1)

Side-table service Service style in which dishes are prepared or finished off at the table on a mobile cart with a heat source. (20.3)

Sil pad Flexible pan liner made of silicone that provides a nonstick, heat-resistant surface. Can be used repeatedly. (17.1)

Silverskin Tough membrane that surrounds some cuts of meat; it is somewhat silver in color and is generally removed before cooking. (16.1)

Simmering Moist heat method of cooking in which food is cooked at 170°F to 185°F. (8.2)

Simple carbohydrates Carbohydrates that contain one sugar or two sugars. Found in fruit, milk, and refined sugars and are digested quickly. (22.1)

Simple syrup Mixture of equal amounts of sugar and water, brought to a boil to dissolve the sugar crystals. (19.3)

Single-rack dishwasher Dishwasher that processes small loads of dishes quickly. (4.2)

Skewers (SKEW-ers) Long, thin, pointed rods made of wood or metal, used to cook meat, fish, poultry, or vegetables. (11.2)

Skimmer Tool used to remove food from stocks and to skim fat from the tops of liquids; has a flat, perforated bowl and a long handle. (4.2)

Slicer Knife with a long thin blade used to make smooth slices in a single stroke. (4.1)

Smallware Hand tools, pots, and pans used for cooking. (4.2)

Smoker Used for smoking and slow-cooking foods, which are placed on racks or hooks, allowing foods to smoke evenly. Some units can be operated at either cool or hot temperatures. (3.3)

Smoothie Cold drink made by mixing fresh fruit (such as bananas and strawberries), juice, and ice in a blender until thick and smooth; can also contain milk or yogurt. (9.2)

Smothering Dry heat method of cooking that is a variation of *sweating*; food, typically vegetables, is cooked covered over a low heat in a small amount of fat until food softens and releases moisture. (8.1)

Sneeze guard See-through barrier that protects foods in a service station from cross-contamination caused by a sneeze. People can see and reach food under the guard. (3.4)

Soda bread Quick bread leavened with baking soda and an acid ingredient, usually buttermilk, and shaped into a round loaf. (18.2)

Sodium chloride Chemical name for salt. (6.2)

Soft dough Lean dough with some sugar and fat added. Pullman loaves, the soft sliced bread used for sandwich making, are made from soft dough. Also called *medium dough*. (17.2)

Soft, rind-ripened cheeses Soft cheeses that have been ripened by being exposed to a spray or dusting of "friendly" mold. (10.3)

Soluble fiber Fiber that dissolves in water; foods that contain it help us feel full and help lower cholesterol levels in the blood. (22.1)

Sommelier (suhm-uhl-YAY) Person responsible for buying and storing wines, maintaining proper wine inventory, counseling guests about wine choices, and serving wine properly at the table. Also called *wine steward*. (20.1)

Sorbet Frozen dessert made from a flavored base that is frozen and aerated in an ice cream maker. (19.2)

Soufflé (soo-FLAY) Light, puffed, baked egg dish .(9.1)

Soufflé dish Baking dish that is round and straight-edged; comes in various sizes. (4.2)

Soup and vegetables station chef Chef responsible for hot appetizers, pasta courses, and vegetable dishes. Also called *entremetier*. (20.1)

Soup station chef Chef responsible for stocks and soups. (20.1)

Sourdough In baking, a tangy, slightly sour dough starter made from wild yeast. Can be kept alive for a long time. (17.2)

Sous-chef (SU-chef) Executive chef's principal assistant, responsible for scheduling personnel and temporarily replacing the executive chef or other chefs as needed. Also called *second chef*. (20.1)

Spaetzle (SHPET-zuhl) Popular Austrian and German dumpling. (13.3)

Spice blends Combination of spices (and in some cases, herbs) used to flavor a dish. (6.3)

Spices Aromatic dried seeds, flowers, buds, bark, roots, or stems of various plants used to flavor food. (6.3)

Spine Non-cutting edge of a knife blade. (4.1)

Spiral mixer Mixer used for bread doughs in which the bowl turns instead of the mixing tool, which is a spiral-shaped hook. (3.3)

Sponge In baking, a thick, batter-like mixture created when yeast is combined with water and some flour. (17.2)

Springform pans Baking pan consisting of a hinged ring that clamps around a removable base; used for cakes that might otherwise be difficult to unmold. (17.1)

Stabilizing In mixing, the step after which the mixed ingredients reach maximum volume and the mixer is slowed down to break the large air bubbles into smaller ones, providing better texture. (19.3)

Stamped blade Knife blade made by cutting blade-shaped pieces from sheets of previously milled steel. (4.1)

Standard breading Process of coating food prior to cooking it (typically by pan frying or deep frying). Involves dusting the food with flour, dipping it in beaten eggs, and then covering it in breadcrumbs. (8.1)

Standard mirepoix Type of mirepoix consisting of 2 parts onion, 1 part carrot, and 1 part celery; used to flavor a dish. (6.3)

Standardized ingredients Ingredients that have been processed, graded, or packaged according to established standards (eggs, shrimp, and butter, for instance). (5.1)

Standardized recipe Recipe tailored to suit the needs of an individual kitchen. (5.1)

Starch slurry Mixture of a refined starch and cold water used to thicken simmering liquids, producing a sauce. (14.2)

Station chef Chef responsible for a particular type of food. Also called *line chef*. (20.1)

Steam table Large freestanding unit that keeps food hot while it is being served. It holds several inserts or hotel pans, under which is steaming hot water. Large steam tables have a thermostat to control the heating elements that maintain the desired temperature. (3.4)

Steamer Set of stacked pots or bamboo baskets with a tight-fitting lid. The upper pots or baskets have perforated bottoms so steam can gently cook or warm the contents of the pots or baskets. In a metal steamer, water is placed in the bottom pot and it is placed on the range. Bamboo steamers are generally placed over water in a wok. (4.2)

Steaming Moist heat method of cooking in which food is in a closed pot or steamer and the steam trapped in the pot or steamer circulates around the food. (8.2)

Steam-jacketed kettle Freestanding or tabletop cooking unit that circulates steam through the walls, providing even heat for cooking stocks, soups, and sauces. Units may tilt or have spigots or lids. (3.3)

Steel Tool used to maintain a knife's edge between sharpenings; it is a rod made of textured steel or ceramic. (4.1)

Stenciled cookies Delicate drop cookies made with batter that is spread very thin, sometimes onto sheet pans into stencils to make a perfect shape. They are often rolled or curled while still warm. (19.3)

Stewing Combination cooking method in which food is first seared and then gently cooked in flavorful liquid. Stewing indicates that food is cut into smaller pieces and then cooked in enough liquid to completely cover the ingredients. (8.2)

Stir frying Dry heat method of cooking that is a variation of *sweating*; food is typically cooked in a wok quickly and evenly while you constantly stir and toss it. (8.1)

Stir-ins Savory or sweet ingredients that can be chopped up and added to muffins and quick breads; examples are vegetables, fruit, nuts, cheese, and chocolate. (18.1)

Stock base Highly concentrated liquid or a dry powder that is mixed with water to make a stock. (14.1)

Stock Flavorful liquid used primarily to prepare soups, sauces, stews, and braises. Made by simmering bones, shells, or vegetables, mirepoix, herbs, and spices in a liquid (typically water). (14.1)

Stockpot Large pot that is taller than it is wide and has straight sides. Used to cook large quantities of liquid, such as stocks or soups. Some stockpots have a spigot at the base so the liquid can be drained off without lifting the heavy pot. (4.2)

Stollen (STOH-len) Sweet, loaf shaped yeast bread filled with dried fruit and topped with icing and cherries; it is the traditional Christmas bread of Germany. (17.2)

Stone Hard pit that covers a seed, such as the pit in a peach or apricot. (12.1)

Straight dough-mixing method Method most commonly used for mixing yeast dough, in which all the ingredients are mixed together at the same time. (17.2)

Strategies Skills and techniques you will use to get a job done. (7.1)

Streusel (STRU-sel) Crumbly mixture of fat, sugar, and flour that may include spices and nuts; often applied to muffins or quick breads. (18.1)

Sturgeon (STURH-jen) Large fish whose eggs are made into caviar. (10.4)

Subprimal cuts Next level of cuts made to meat after cutting primals from saddles or quarters. Subprimal cuts can be trimmed, packed, and sold to restaurants or butcher shops. (16.1)

Sugar glaze Thin liquid made by dissolving sugar in water, applied to baked goods. (18.1)

Sugar syrup Concentrated solution of sugar and water. (19.2)

Sunny-side-up egg Fried egg cooked without turning, keeping the yolk intact. (9.1)

Superfine sugar Granulated sugar that is more finely ground than ordinary sugar so it dissolves more easily. (17.1)

Supplier Person or business selling items to a restaurant. Also called *vendor, purveyor,* or *producer.* (23.2)

Suprême Boneless, skinless breast of poultry with one wing joint still attached. (16.2)

Sweating Dry heat method of cooking in which food, typically vegetables, is cooked uncovered over a low heat in a small amount of fat until food softens and releases moisture. (8.1)

Sweet rich dough Lean dough that has added butter, oil, sugar, eggs, or milk products. Also called *enriched dough*. (17.2)

Swing chef Roving chef who fills in for absent chefs or assists chefs in other stations. Also called *roundsman* or *tournant*. (20.1)

Swiss braiser Large shallow free-standing cooking unit, used to cook large quantities of meats or vegetables at one time. Most units have lids that allow the unit to function as a steamer. (3.3)

Symmetrical In terms of plate presentation, equal numbers of items on either side of the plate. (7.3)

T

Table d'hôte menu (TAH-buhl DOHT) Menu that offers a complete meal—from an appetizer to a dessert, and often including a beverage—for a set price. (21.1)

Table salt Salt that is refined to remove other minerals. (6.2)

Table service How food and drink is delivered to a guest. Also called *service style*. (20.3)

Table tent menus Folded cards placed directly on restaurant tables to tell customers about specials. (21.1)

Tableware Dishware and utensils used by customers. (20.2)

Tabling method Method of cooling melted chocolate by moving it around on a marble slab. (19.1)

Tagliatelle (tag-lee-ah-TEHL-ee) Thin, ribbon-shaped pasta. (13.3)

Tahini (ta-HEE-nee) Sesame paste. (6.4)

Take-out service Buying prepared food and taking it home or to work, as an alternative to cooking at home or eating in a restaurant. (20.3)

Tang Section of knife blade that extends into the handle. (4.1)

Tapenade (top-en-ODD) Vegetable-based dip made from black olives, capers, anchovies, garlic, herbs, lemon juice, and olive oil; originally from France's Provence region. (10.1)

Taper ground edge Knife edge in which both sides of the blade taper smoothly to a narrow V-shape. (4.1)

Tapioca Thickener made from the cassava root, a starchy tropical tuber; often used to thicken fruit pie fillings and to make pudding. (17.1)

Tare weight Weight of the container holding food on a scale. To account for the tare, reset the scale to zero while weighing the empty container. If the scale cannot be reset, subtract the tare from the total weight. (5.1)

Tart pans Baking pans made of tinned steel or ceramic, with short, often scalloped sides and usually a removable bottom. May be round, square, or rectangular. (17.1)

Tasks In terms of mise en place, smaller jobs that lead to the completion of an assignment. (7.1)

Taste One of the senses; the taste and aroma of a food. (6.1)

Tea sandwich Simple, small sandwich usually made with firm, thinly sliced pullman loaves. Can be made both as closed sandwiches and as open-faced sandwiches. Also called *finger sandwich*. (11.1)

Temperature danger zone Temperature range from 40°F to 140°F in which disease-causing organisms thrive. (1.1)

Tempering Warming a liaison (a mixture of cream and egg yolks) so the yolks will not overcook when added to a simmering sauce or other liquid. (14.2) Process of correctly crystallizing chocolate. (19.1)

Termination Firing of an employee. (23.3)

Terrine (teh-REEN). Mold for pâté. When pâté is served in its mold, it is call a terrine. (11.2)

Terrine mold Oven cookware usually made of pottery but can also be metal, enameled cast iron, or ceramic. Produced in a wide range of sizes and shapes; some have lids. (4.2)

Theme In a restaurant, the decorations, lighting, food, and prices, all of which tie the restaurant concept together. (23.1)

Thermistor (therm-IS-tor) thermometer Thermometer that uses a resistor (electronic semiconductor) to measure temperature. Gives a fast reading, can measure temperature in thin and thick foods, and is not designed to stay in food while cooking. (4.2)

Thermocouple thermometer Thermometer that uses two fine wires within the probe to measure temperature. Gives the fastest reading, can measure the temperature in thin and thick foods, and is not designed to stay in food while cooking. (4.2)

Timeline In terms of the mise en place, a schedule that tells you when certain tasks have to be completed. (7.1)

Time-temperature abused food Food that has been held in the temperature danger zone for more than two hours. (1.2)

Tomato concassé (kon-kah-SAY) Tomatoes that have been peeled, seeded, and diced. (12.2)

Tongs Tool used for picking up items such as meats, vegetables, or ice cubes. Can be spring-action or scissor-type. (4.2)

Top crust Large piece of pastry dough rolled out and placed on top of a filled shell before baking. (19.4)

Tortellini (tohr-te-LEEN-ee) Italian for "little twists"; made by cutting out circles or squares of fresh pasta, adding a filling, and then folding and twisting the dough to get a specific shape. (13.3)

Tortilla (tohr-TEE-yuh) Mexico's unleavened bread; it is round, flat, made of corn or flour. (11.1)

Tossed salad Salad in which all the ingredients are combined together with dressing. (10.2)

Tournant (toor-NAHN) Roving chef who fills in for absent chefs or assists chefs in other stations. Also called *swing chef* or *roundsman*. (20.1)

Tournée Paring knife with a curved blade. Also called a bird's beak knife. (4.1)

Training Period of time during which new employees learn the job and practice it. (23.3)

Trancheur (tran-SHUR) Person in charge of carving and serving meats or fish and their accompaniments. Also called *carver*. (20.1)

Trans fats Also called trans fatty acids, a potentially harmful type of fat created from the process of hydrogenation; has been linked to heart disease. (22.1)

Translucent (trans-LU-cent) Indicates that light will pass through an object. (6.1)

Tray stand Used by serving staff to place a tray holding multiple dishes close to the table where they will be served. (3.4)

Trueing Process of straightening a knife's edge. (4.1)

Trussing Tying or securing poultry or other food so it maintains its shape while cooking. (16.2)

Tube pans Baking pans with a center tube of metal that conducts heat through the center of the batter; they bake heavy batters evenly and quickly, without over-browning the outside of the cake. Typically made of thin metal with or without a nonstick coating. (17.1)

Tuber Fleshy portion of certain plants; usually grows underground. (12.2)

Turner Tool with a broad blade and a short handle that is bent to keep the user's hands off hot surfaces. Used to turn or lift hot foods from hot cookware, grills, broilers, and griddles. Also called an offset spatula or a flipper. (4.2)

Turntable Used to decorate cakes; you turn the cake on the turntable with one hand while the other is free to use a palette knife, pastry bag, or cake comb. (17.1)

Twice-baked cookies Cookies made of dough formed into a large log-shaped cookie and baked, and then cut into slices and baked a second time for a very crisp texture. (19.3)

Two-stage cooling method Safely cooling foods to 70°F within two hours and to below 41°F within four hours, for a total cooling time of six hours to avoid foodborne illness. (1.2)

U

Udon (oo-DOHN) Asian-style noodle, often purchased fresh. (13.3)

Umami (OO-mam-ee) Meaty or brothy flavor; also called *savory*. (6.1)

Undercounter dishwasher Dishwasher that holds portable dish or glass racks to allow for easy transfer of clean and dirty dishes. (4.2)

Undercounter reach-in Refrigerator unit under a workstation counter used for storing a small amount of ingredients within easy reach. Also called a *low boy*. (3.2)

Unsweetened chocolate Chocolate that has no sugar added. Also called *baker's chocolate* or *chocolate liquor*. (19.1)

Utility knife Smaller, lighter version of the chef's knife, with a 5- to 7-inch blade. (4.1)

V

Variable cost Business expense that can vary from one day, week, month, or year to the next, such as the cost of food. (23.1)

Variety meat Organs and other portions of an animal, including the liver, heart, kidneys, and tongue. Also known as *offal*. (16.1)

Veal Meat that comes from a young calf, generally two to three months old. It has delicate, tender flesh that is pale pink. (16.1)

Vegan Person who eats no animal products whatsoever and consumes only plant-based foods. (22.2)

Vegetable station chef Chef responsible for vegetables and starches. (20.1)

Vegetable stock Type of stock made from a combination of vegetables. (14.1)

Vegetarian Person who, for religious, ethical, economic, or nutritional reasons, does not eat meat, poultry, and fish. (22.2)

Velouté (veh-loo-TAY) One of the grand sauces; a white sauce made by thickening a poultry, fish, or shellfish stock with a blond roux. (14.2)

Vendor Person or business selling items to a restaurant. Also called *supplier, purveyor,* or *producer.* (23.2)

Venison Meat from any member of the deer family, including antelope, caribou, elk, and moose. (16.1)

Verbal feedback Form of feedback that is spoken. (7.2)

Verbal warning When a manager tells an employee about the need for improvement in a particular area. (23.3)

Vertical chopping machine (VCM) Machine used to grind, whip, blend, or crush large quantities of foods. A motor at the base is permanently attached to a bowl with blades; the hinged lid must be locked in place before the unit will operate. (3.3)

Vinaigrette (vin-eh-GRETT) Salad dressing made by combining oil and vinegar into an emulsion. (10.1)

Viruses Biological hazards that can cause illness when they invade a cell and trick the cell into making more viruses. (1.1)

Volume Measurement of the space occupied by a solid, liquid, or gas. (5.1)

W

Walk-in Large refrigeration or freezing unit that usually has shelves arranged around the walls of the unit. (3.2)

Walkout Customer who leaves the table without paying the bill. (20.4)

Warewashing station Area for rinsing, washing, and holding tools, pots and pans, and dishes. Also includes trashcans, sinks, garbage disposals, and dishwashing equipment. (4.2)

Water activity (Aw) Measurement of the amount of moisture available in a food; the scale runs from 0 to 1.0, with water at 1.0 and potentially hazardous foods at .85 or higher. (1.1)

Water bath Method of baking in which a container of food is put into a pan of water in the oven to control the heat. (8.1)

Water-soluble vitamins The B and C vitamins; they dissolve in water and are transported throughout the body in the bloodstream. They must be replenished often because they cannot be stored for very long in the body. (22.1)

Well method Quick-bread mixing method in which liquid ingredients are added to a depression in the dry ingredients and mixed minimally to avoid overmixing. (18.1)

Wet aging Process of storing meat in vacuum packaging under refrigeration to make it more tender and flavorful. (16.1)

Wheat berries Whole kernels of wheat. (13.1)

Whetstone Hard, fine-grained stone for honing tools; a general term for sharpening stones. (4.1)

Whip Hand mixing tool similar to a whisk but narrower and with thicker wires; used to blend sauces or batters without adding too much air. (4.2)

Whisk Hand mixing tool with thin wires in a sphere or an oval shape used to incorporate air for making foams. Very round whisks incorporate a large amount of air and are sometimes called balloon whisks. (4.2)

White chocolate Chocolate made from cocoa butter, sugar, and milk powder; it contains no chocolate liquor. (19.1)

White mirepoix Type of *mirepoix* consisting of onions, parsnips, celery, and, in some cases, leeks; used to flavor white stocks and soups. (6.3)

White pepper Ripe berries from the pepper vine that have been allowed to dry and have had the husks removed; used as a seasoning. (6.2)

White rice Rice with all its bran removed. (13.1)

White stock Type of stock made from unroasted bones. The bones may be blanched before simmering. (14.1)

Whole grains Grains that still have most of the nutrients found in the germ and bran, including fiber, vitamins, and minerals. (13.1)

Wild rice Seed of an aquatic grass. Not related to other rice, but cooked like them. (13.1)

Wine steward Person responsible for buying and storing wines, maintaining proper wine inventory, counseling guests about wine choices, and serving wine properly at the table. Also called *sommelier*. (20.1)

Wok Cookware for fast stovetop cooking, such as stir-frying; has tall, sloped sides. Once one ingredient cooks, you can push it up the sides, leaving the hot center free for another ingredient. (4.2)

Wontons (WAHN-tahns) Type of Chinese dumpling made with a fresh pasta wrapper; often served as an appetizer or with soup. (13.3)

Work flow Planned movement of food and kitchen staff as food is prepared. (3.1) In terms of mise en place, putting ingredients, tools, and equipment in a logical order for accomplishing your task. (7.1)

Work lines Geometric arrangements of workstation equipment and storage areas, designed to fit the available kitchen space and improve efficiency of staff. Examples include straight-line, L-shaped, U-shaped, back-to-back, and parallel. (3.1)

Work sections Combination of workstations in a kitchen. (3.1)

Work sequencing In terms of mise en place, doing the right thing at the right time. (7.1)

Work simplification In terms of mise en place, getting things done in the fewest steps, the shortest time, and with the least amount of waste. (7.1)

Worker's compensation Program run by each state that provides help for employees who are hurt or who become sick because of an accident on the job. (2.2)

Workstation Work area containing equipment and tools for accomplishing a specific set of culinary tasks. (3.1)

Wrap Sandwich that is rolled up, or otherwise enclosed in an edible wrapper, such as a tortilla. (11.1)

Wrappers Type of pasta used in Asian cooking. Sold in squares, rounds, or rectangles; can be made from wheat or rice flour. (13.3)

Written warning When a manager documents in writing to an employee that there is need for improvement in a particular area. (23.3)

Y

Yeast hydration In baking, the soaking process that activates yeast. (17.2)

Yield Measured output of a recipe, expressed in total weight, total volume, or total number of servings of a given portion. (5.1)

Z

Zest Colored outer layer of citrus fruit peel. (4.2)

Zester Tool that cuts away thin strips of citrus fruit peel, leaving the bitter pith. (4.2)

Acknowledgments

A&W® All American Food®, 739

AGE Fotostock America, Inc., 342

Aurora & Quanta Productions Inc., 474

Charlie Westerman, 206

Color-Pic, Inc., 40

Comstock Images, 735

Corbis Digital Stock, 100, 242, 295, 592, 689

CORBIS-NY, © Dave Bartruff/Corbis, 742

Corbis/Bettmann, 89, 399, 665, 671

Corbis/Bettmann, © Becky Luigart-Stayner/CORBIS, 534

Creative Eye/MIRA.com, 12, 13, 92, 316, 343, 359, 538, 580, 652, 722

Culinary Institute of America, viii, xv, xvi, xvii, xix, xx, xxi, 21, 22, 26, 27, 33, 47, 50, 57, 75, 77, 80, 82, 84, 90, 91, 93, 96, 101, 102, 103, 104, 105, 106, 107, 108, 109, 110, 111, 113, 114, 115, 117, 118, 119, 120, 122, 123, 124, 126, 129, 130, 136, 137, 149, 161, 165, 167, 170, 172, 173, 178, 179, 180, 183, 184, 191, 195, 201, 203, 204, 208, 209, 220, 221, 222, 224, 227, 228, 229, 231, 233, 234, 235, 237, 240, 241, 246, 248, 252, 253, 255, 256, 258, 260, 261, 262, 270, 271, 273, 274, 276, 277, 280, 282, 286, 287, 301, 308, 312, 319, 323, 327, 333, 334, 348, 357, 358, 371, 374, 379, 380, 381, 382, 383, 385, 386, 387, 388, 393, 395, 404, 405, 407, 409, 413, 417, 418, 419, 421, 422, 423, 428, 429, 430, 432, 433, 434, 435, 437, 438, 440, 442, 444, 445, 446, 449, 453, 454, 455, 456, 457, 458, 458, 459, 462, 464, 469, 472, 473, 474, 476, 477, 479, 480, 481, 482, 485, 487, 489, 490, 492, 494, 495, 500, 505, 506, 507, 508, 509, 510, 511, 512, 513, 514, 517, 518, 519, 521, 525, 526, 528, 535, 545, 553, 557, 558, 564, 565, 566, 582, 583, 584, 585, 590, 591, 597, 597, 598, 647, 653, 654, 659, 663, 664, 666, 668, 673, 696, 709, 712, 719, 725, 746, 751

Culinary Institute of America, Eric Jacobson, xiv, 2, 3, 136, 137, 240, 241, 532, 533, 640, 641, 756

Julia della Croce, 415

Shelley Dieterichs, 764

Richard Embery, 23

Dorling Kindersley Media Library © Dorling Kindersley, 19, 114, 129, 166, 174, 176, 180, 186, 189, 210, 251, 285, 291, 298, 300, 318, 332, 334, 335, 346, 353, 365, 368, 372, 373, 375, 378, 412, 424, 442, 465, 493, 501, 544, 551, 711, 720, 723, 734, 744

Max Alexander © Dorling Kindersley, 49

Edward Allwright © Dorling Kindersley, 528, 723

Paul Bricknell © Dorling Kindersley, 125, 129

Martin Brigdale © Dorling Kindersley, 305, 337, 486

Geoff Brightling © Dorling Kindersley, 397

Simon Brown © Dorling Kindersley, Courtesy of Simon Brown, 347

Jane Burton © Dorling Kindersley, 245

Martin Cameron © Dorling Kindersley, 179, 189, 190, 549, 550, 593

Phil Crabbe © Dorling Kindersley, 472

Andy Crawford © Dorling Kindersley, 56, 140, 146, 150, 298, 344, 353, 372

John Davis © Dorling Kindersley, 138

Peter Dennis © Dorling Kindersley, 177

Philip Dowell © Dorling Kindersley, 284, 299, 300, 345, 349, 366, 374, 378, 396, 397, 417, 419, 472, 488, 493

Julie Downing and Grahame Corbett © Dorling Kindersley, 470

Angelika Elsebach © Dorling Kindersley, 523

Neil Fletcher © Dorling Kindersley, 176, 284

Neil Fletcher and Matthew Ward © Dorling Kindersley, 122, 188, 189, 284, 318

Jo Foord © Dorling Kindersley, 366

Steve Gorton © Dorling Kindersley, 76, 164, 365, 367

Frank Greenaway © Dorling Kindersley, 473, 478

Stephen Hayward © Dorling Kindersley, 243, 287

Sian Irvine © Dorling Kindersley, 706

James Jackson © Dorling Kindersley, 399

Anthony Johnson © Dorling Kindersley, 346

Alan Keohane © Dorling Kindersley, 700

Barnabas Kindersley © Dorling Kindersley, 352

Dave King © Dorling Kindersley, 48, 105, 107, 130, 122, 123, 174, 175, 178, 179, 187, 217, 225, 249, 250, 253, 284, 285, 292, 324, 325, 347, 349, 352, 353, 360, 365, 366, 371, 374, 401, 402, 411, 492, 539, 548, 550, 566, 661, 709, 712

Dave King © Dorling Kindersley, Courtesy of The Science Museum, London, 112

Tim Knox © Dorling Kindersley, 694

Ranald MacKechnie © Dorling Kindersley, 713

Gunter Marx © Dorling Kindersley, 737

Neil Mersh © Dorling Kindersley, 261, 291, 297, 484, 555

Diana Miller © Dorling Kindersley, 272

David Murray © Dorling Kindersley, 28, 122, 123, 130, 142, 168, 176, 186, 188, 189, 190, 206, 213, 275, 279, 284, 285, 298, 300, 313, 336, 347, 349, 351, 360, 367, 368, 369, 373, 378, 396, 471, 507, 547, 689, 712

David Murray and Jules Selmes © Dorling Kindersley, 106, 107, 110, 112, 129, 150, 171, 182, 218, 219, 267, 292, 318, 335, 462, 463, 441, 483, 580

Ian O'Leary © Dorling Kindersley, 122, 148, 152, 155, 165, 166, 169, 174, 183, 281, 286, 347, 350, 353, 365, 368, 369, 373, 398, 406, 416, 447, 448, 451, 455, 463, 474, 538, 543, 560, 563, 564, 567, 574, 577, 595, 657, 713, 729

Stephen Oliver © Dorling Kindersley, 18, 285, 418

Gary Ombler © Dorling Kindersley, 317

Roger Phillips © Dorling Kindersley, 129, 130, 174, 188, 190, 247, 284, 285, 298, 299, 300, 351, 352, 353, 347, 348, 366, 367, 368, 371, 372, 396, 397, 400, 418, 471, 473, 595

Susanna Price © Dorling Kindersley, 55

Magnus Rew © Dorling Kindersley, 686

Tim Ridley © Dorling Kindersley, 130, 345

Guy Ryecart and David Jordan © The Ivy Press Limited, 178

Steve Shott © Dorling Kindersley, 373, 711

Simon Smith © Dorling Kindersley, 266, 362, 712

Clive Streeter © Dorling Kindersley, 122, 124, 125, 175, 176, 185, 250, 254, 279, 285, 290, 310, 366, 414, 425, 446, 461, 474, 485, 496, 523

Clive Streeter and Patrick McLeavy © Dorling Kindersley, 335, 372, 497, 527

Colin Walton © Dorling Kindersley, 400, 711, 713

Matthew Ward © Dorling Kindersley, 53, 352

Philip Wilkins © Dorling Kindersley, 122, 175, 336, 366, 368, 372, 463, 548

Paul Williams © Dorling Kindersley, 417

Peter Wilson © Dorling Kindersley, 695

John Woodcock © Dorling Kindersley, 162

Jerry Young © Dorling Kindersley, 212, 251

DRK Photo, © Don and Pat Valenti/DRK PHOTO, 394

DuPont & Company, 128

Envision Stock Photography, Inc., 306, 450

Epicurious.com, CondéNet, 141

Frisch's Restaurants, Inc., Reprinted by permission of Frisch's Restaurants, Inc., 734

Fundamental Photographs, NYC, 578, 713, 726

Getty Images, Getty Images, Inc., 263, 738

Stone Allstock, 38, 71, 194, 263, 264, 296, 345, 568, 586, 642, 644, 670, 698, 732, 748

Stone Allstock, Stewart Cohen/Stone/Getty Images, 309

Artville LLC, 97, 669

Digital Vision, 658, 711

Foodpix, FoodPix/Getty Images, Inc., 202, 226

Image Bank, 121, 460, 674, 743

Photodisc, 81, 87, 128, 129, 139, 144, 157, 211, 216, 265, 302, 312, 324, 328, 331, 336, 345, 348, 352, 370, 392, 410, 484, 496, 542, 549, 575, 587, 645, 646, 657, 662, 665, 672, 681, 687, 708, 713, 728, 749

Photodisc, Jessica Wedvick/Photodisc/Getty Images, 679

Taxi, 4, 51, 156, 196, 289, 447, 678, 704

Gleason Group, Pam Ross, 436, 546, 576, 692, 716

Grana Padano Cheese Consortium, 304

Images.com, 649, 705, 714, 741, 745

ImageState/International Stock Photography Ltd., 315

Index Stock Imagery, Inc., 66, 229, 322, 643, 763

Kansas Wheat Commission, Courtesy of the Kansas Wheat Commission, Wheat Foods Council/US Wheat Associates, 556, 569

Grant LeDuc, 660

Library of Congress, 59

Mary Evans Picture Library, 223

Masterfile Corporation, 762

National Oceanic & Atmospheric Administration (NOAA), U.S. Department of Commerce, 475

Omni-Photo Communications, Inc., 67, 491, 646, 707

Oneida Ltd., Silversmiths, 92

Oregon Washington California Pear Board, 348

Pacific Stock, Kyle Rothenborg/PacificStock.com, 468

Pearson Education Corporate Digital Archive, 254

Pearson Education, Inc., Cover, i, 1

Pearson Education/PH College, 13, 14, 15, 16, 17, 24, 25, 26, 29, 30, 34, 41, 43, 45, 46, 52, 74, 76, 82, 85, 94, 117, 131, 132, 175, 197, 220, 224, 233, 236, 288, 298, 300, 310, 311, 328, 329, 330, 339, 345, 346, 350, 351, 352, 364, 365, 366, 367, 368, 369, 371, 372, 374, 376, 378, 399, 471, 472, 474, 488, 506, 526, 536, 552, 554, 561, 567, 579, 581, 584, 585, 711, 720, 750, 752

Pearson Learning Photo Studio, 31, 145

Peter Arnold, Inc., 6, 20, 266, 549

Photo Researchers, Inc., 6, 7, 54, 160, 244, 366, 408, 475, 515, 537, 592

PhotoEdit, 15, 25, 460, 542, 546, 570, 650, 662, 685, 688, 736, 751, 758, 764

Phototake NYC, 11, 93

PictureArts Corporation, 463

PictureArts Corporation, © Steven Mark Needham/FoodPix, 420

Prentice Hall High School, 181, 355, 692, 711, 717

Rainbow, 44

Ross Breeders, Inc., 163

Rough Guides Dorling Kindersley, 338

Rough Guides Dorling Kindersley, Demetrio Carrasco (c) Rough Guides, 709

Silver Burdett Ginn, 129

Spencer Tucker, Photographs by Spencer Tucker, 369

Stockbyte, 106, 733

StockFood America, © Gary White Photography/Stockfood America, 365

SuperStock, Inc., 496

The Stock Connection, 39, 79, 363, 503, 554, 562, 680

U.S. Department of Agriculture, 244, 504, 716

U.S. Department of Labor/OSHA, 58, 62

Visuals Unlimited, 303, 376, 747

John Wise, 5

PDS Associates for all line art and geographic maps

Index